the battered child

the battered child

Third Edition, Revised and Expanded

Edited by
C. Henry Kempe, M.D., and
Ray E. Helfer, M.D.

The University of Chicago Press

Chicago and London

The University of Chicago Press, Chicago 60637
The University of Chicago Press, Ltd., London

© 1968, 1974, 1980 by The University of Chicago
All rights reserved
Published 1968. Second Edition 1974. Third Edition 1980
Printed in the United States of America
89 88 87 86 85   3 4 5 6

Library of Congress Cataloging in Publication Data

Main entry under title:

The Battered child.

   Editors' names in reverse order in 2d ed.
   Bibliography: p.
   Includes index.
   1. Child abuse—United States—Addresses, essays,
lectures.   2. Child abuse—United States—Prevention
—Addresses, essays, lectures.   I. Kempe, C. Henry,
1922–   II. Helfer, Ray E.   III. Helfer, Ray E.
Battered Child.   [DNLM: 1. Child abuse.   WA320
B3346]
HV741.B33   1980   362.7'1   80-14329
ISBN 0-226-43038-3

C. HENRY KEMPE, M.D., is professor of pediatrics at the
University of Colorado School of Medicine and director of the
National Center for the Prevention and Treatment of Child Abuse
and Neglect in Denver.
RAY E. HELFER, M.D., is professor in the Department of
Pediatrics and Human Development at Michigan State University.

Contents

Foreword

As much as we love and cherish our children, their violent abuse and murder by adults, often parents, is also part of the human condition and as old as recorded human history. Tragically and ironically, most of us would not want to live in a society that was able to prevent every single instance of child abuse because that could be carried out only in a totalitarian state. At the same time, all of us would like to prevent as much child abuse as possible in a relatively free, democratic society in which the values of family privacy and the pluralism of differing life-styles are protected and supported. The editors of *The Battered Child,* third edition, are recognized international leaders in this crusade.

In the United States, the famous case of Mary Ellen (1, 2) was not the first incident of child abuse to receive national attention. "Nor was it evident . . . that there were no laws to protect children from parental abuse; but because of the unusual publicity it received, it shocked many people into a greater awareness of this serious human problem, and it sparked the beginning of a massive crusade against child abuse" (3). Realizing that children should have at least as much protection as domestic animals, the New York City Society for the Prevention of Cruelty to Children was organized in December 1874. Ironically, it was the American Society for the Prevention of Cruelty to Animals which responded effectively to the previously thwarted efforts of a New York charity worker, Mrs. Etta Angell Wheeler, to remove and protect Mary Ellen from her abusive parents.

As in the 1960s and 1970s, the United States crusade against child abuse in the 1870s was dedicated to the enforcement of *existing* laws that prohibited cruelty to human beings and that were intended to protect children from assault by adults. The movement grew quickly, for the nineteenth century—though not as quickly as it grew when reborn in the 1960s. By 1905 there were four hundred societies working to prevent cruelty to children or to intervene protectively when it was discovered. "In 1908, E. Fellows Jenkins, Secretary and Superintendent of The New York Society for the Prevention of Cruelty to Children, estimated that 'almost ¾ of a *million* of children' (4, 5) had been involved in the investigations of *that society alone*" (3).

The rediscovery of the abused child was ushered in by a radiologist, Dr. John Caffey, who reported it in 1946 as a new syndrome in which subdural hematomas in infants were often associated with atypical fractures of the limb and ribs (6). However, it was not until 1962 when C. Henry Kempe referred to "the battered child syndrome" that the medical profession and the public allowed themselves to undo their denial of child abuse by treating that continuing tragic human condition as though it were a new discovery (7). Public awareness of the "battered child syndrome" has led to the passage of new laws mandating how and by whom the condition should be reported and providing protection for the reporters.

The human infant, born helpless, is able to survive and beyond that to unfold his or her own unique potential only because adults provide physical and emotional nurture, protection, and guidance. The care of their infant child provides these adults with an invitation that is also experienced as a demand to uncover and exercise their capacity for parenthood. In this way adults activate their potential to do for their child what had been done for them when they were young. Conception, pregnancy, and giving birth to the child are powerful psychological and emotional preparations for parenthood, natural derivatives of the dramatic physical experiences that characterize normative childbearing. These roots of the human family are an essential part of our biosocial heritage. When this heritage goes awry, failing to provide for continuity of affectionate nurture and protection for the child and a sense of positive fulfillment for the parents, the child is at risk of being neglected and abused.

The distinguished editors of this third edition are not satisfied with having pioneered in the rediscovery of child abuse. They have insisted that it be acknowledged for what it is by naming the victim of this inhumanity the "battered child." Recognizing that most of our current resources are concerned with reporting and identifying neglected and abused children, they have taken clear steps to get beyond what is a delayed recognition of threatening child-parent disturbances. They have selected authors and topics that provide applications of our best knowledge of the developing child and his family in order to move us toward services that can prevent the "battered child." They have emphasized the need for a wide array of available, attractive services to facilitate prevention at every level. They have turned their earlier creativity as experts in preventing and eliminating diseases caused by microorganisms into a thoughtful commitment to the prevention of what is surely one of the most shameful of all man-made disorders.

ALBERT J. SOLNIT, M.D.
1980

Sterling Professor of Pediatrics and
Psychiatry, School of Medicine,
and Director, Child Study Center,
Yale University

References

1. Coleman, S. H. 1924. *Humane Society Leaders in America*. Albany: American Humane Association.
2. Bremner, Robert, ed. 1971. *Children and Youth in America: A Documentary History,* Vol. 2, *1866–1932*, Parts 1–6. Cambridge, Mass.: Harvard University Press.
3. Hiner, N. Ray. 1979. Children's Rights, Corporal Punishment, and Child Abuse. *Bull. Menninger Clin.* 43, No. 3 (May): 233–48.
4. Jenkins, E. F. 1905. The New York Society for the Prevention of Cruelty to Children. *Ann. Am. Acad. Political and Social Sci.* 26 (November): 774–77.
5. ———. 1908. The New York Society for the Prevention of Cruelty to Children. *Ann. Am. Acad. Political and Social Sci.* 31 (March): 492–94.
6. Caffey, John. 1946. Multiple Fractures in the Long Bones of Infants Suffering from Chronic Subdural Hematoma. *Am. J. Roentgenology* 56:163–73.
7. Kempe, C. Henry; Silverman, Frederic; Steele, Brandt; Droegemueller, William; and Silver, Henry. 1962. The Battered Child Syndrome. *J. Am. Med. Assoc.* 181:17–24.

Preface to the Third Edition

Nineteen eighty marks the twentieth year since the phrase "the battered child" was coined in the attempt to bring to the attention of the country and the world the plight of abused and neglected children. This goal has clearly been achieved. Programs have been developed, laws passed, insight gained, and yet the problem persists. One and one-half percent of the children in the United States are reported annually to protective service units as victims of suspected abuse and neglect. The important word in the previous sentence is *annually*. Every year another one and one-half percent is added to the toll.

Twelve years have passed since the publication of the first edition of *The Battered Child*. Finding sufficient material to fill that edition was difficult. The opposite is true for the third edition: we found it difficult to limit the contributions.

Considerable discussion was held over the question of the title. Is it appropriate to preserve the title *The Battered Child* when the field has expanded far beyond the severely physically battered child? This book seems to be well entrenched as a primary source of current knowledge on the subject. Rather than change the title and start anew, the editors and publisher decided to maintain the title and expand the concept to include the vast array of manifestations of abuse and neglect of children. The material covered in this third edition is not, therefore, limited to physical abuse.

Part I reviews the background material, an understanding of which is necessary to put the problem of abuse and neglect into perspective. This section has been completely rewritten, and new authors have been added. Basic concepts are discussed, the historical and cross-cultural aspects reviewed, the way stress and crises (including parental alcohol and heroin addiction) affect and influence parent-child interactions is analyzed, and the devastating influences abuse has on the child's development are summarized. Dr. Steele has completely rewritten and updated his chapter on psychodynamics, a piece of work that truly is another classic.

In Part II the issues of assessment are discussed, both for the child and the family. This section contains many practical suggestions for all professionals confronted with the awesome obligation of evaluating a suspected case of child abuse. In addition to discussions of radiological assessment and pathology, six new contributions review interviewing techniques, physical findings, failure to thrive, child neglect, sexual abuse, and abuse by burning.

Part III includes seven chapters, all of which deal with current methods of intervention and treatment, both short- and long-term. Protective services, child therapy, law enforcement, and foster placement—all these difficult subjects are reviewed. Discussions of the community consortium, the roles of the lawyer, and the consequences of abuse round out this section on intervention.

Part IV is included with great hope and expectation—at last, a section on prevention. This has been a long time coming, too long indeed. Preventive programs are beginning to yield results. The future looks bright. Some states are implementing these preventive concepts as part of the routine services to new parents and their babies. We await the long overdue involvement of the school system in this endeavor. Its contribution could be most significant.

In the mid 1970s Vice-President Mondale pioneered federal legislation for the benefit of children. The results have been gratifying. How desperately do our children need a political advocate in the 1980s.

The editors are committed to improving the plight of every abused and neglected child. Our society cannot afford to do anything less. We are indebted to the contributors for their work. Together we are turning the corner and moving toward prevention.

R.E.H.   C.H.K.

Preface to the Second Edition

There are fifteen women in a house of correction just outside one of our larger cities. All of them are there for the same reason: they have been convicted of crimes against children—cruelty or manslaughter. Geraldine is one of these women. Still young, she was reared in a traumatic, motherless atmosphere, ran away from home as a teen-ager, became pregnant, married an emotionally ill college graduate, and began to have more children after placing her first child up for adoption. Her second child died in its first year of life from the effects of severe physical abuse. The third was born in prison.

The "justice" achieved by the criminal court after sentencing her to from two to four years in prison is exemplified by the sentencing judge's response to a request for early parole. No one knew who killed the baby—the mother, the father, or both—but a confession had been obtained from the mother, and so she was tried and convicted; the father, remaining at home and now on welfare, cares for the prison-born child. An attempt was made to have Geraldine released so that a program of social and psychiatric treatment could be initiated. The judge, emotional and removed from the reality of the situation, chided proponents of the therapeutic program and suggested that he would approve early parole only if the mother submitted to sterilization.

Geraldine is still in prison, but in another year she will be free and reunited with her emotionally disturbed husband and her new baby, with (no doubt) more to come; the process of criminal rehabilitation has again been flaunted. And in the same institution there are fourteen other women convicted of similar offenses.

In spite of the Geraldines, there is evidence of slow but definite progress. Since *The Battered Child* was published in 1968, understanding has deepened, many more people have become involved, some courts have improved, treatment programs are being developed all over the country, and abuse and neglect are generally recognized at a much earlier point in the child's life. For example, in 1972 almost ten thousand cases of suspected abuse and neglect were reported in New York City alone (see appendix A). This fact is encouraging to many, since the feeling is that the lid is now off and solutions must and will be found.

A second book, *Helping the Battered Child and His Family* (Lippincott, 1972), has been published; the mass media have shown increasing interest and willingness to be helpful; and a few foundations have expressed interest in funding service and research projects. The biggest lack remains the apathy of federal agencies in the field of child welfare. Time is even changing this.

In the second edition of *The Battered Child,* the editors have deleted material no longer applicable, updated other contributions, and added more recent information. A chapter on the New York experience has been added. The section on the reporting laws, pathology, and X-ray has been extensively revised. Certain discussions, covered in greater detail in *Helping the Battered Child and His Family,* have been removed and duplication avoided. The classic chapters by Steele and Pollock and by Davoren, however, have been left untouched.

Adequate demographic data which provide up-to-date evidence of the true incidence of significant child abuse in the United States are not available. Comparing current reporting of child abuse under state laws, we find that many communities are running a rate of 375 reports of suspected abuse per million population per year. No one has tried to compare the reported rate of suspected child abuse to the actual incidence—only a house-to-house, block-to-block intensive study can give us this information. Even so, such a ratio would only be valid in the community studied, because the number of reports compared to the true incidence depends on many variables, including physicians' interest and education, community attitudes, receptivity of the public agencies—especially the child-protective services—and, of course, the police and the juvenile courts.

In the absence of detailed information on incidence, it is still possible to assess the experience of a large metropolitan area such as New York City. For this reason, the appendix shows the report of the Select Committee on Child Abuse authorized by the New York State Assembly. It provides information which can be used quite readily by other metropolitan areas and is a valuable contribution to the study of a difficult problem in a major center.[1]

The editors are convinced that recognition and treatment of battered children will accelerate during the seventies. The involvement and interest of both professionals and lay workers are encouraging. Geraldine, her husband, and her family see it differently, however. They will continue to withdraw, and their children will run the risk of repeated injury until many more devoted and informed individuals proliferate into every nook and cranny of our service agencies, police, hospitals, courts, schools, and, above all, our communities.

R.E.H.   C.H.K.

1. The New York City data (see appendix C) are confusing in that the state requires the reporting of both abuse and neglect. There is no specific way of separating the N.Y.C. report into these two categories of the abnormal rearing problem. In 1972, therefore, the New York City rate for *both* entities was 1,200 per million population.

Preface to the First Edition

Tens of thousands of children were severely battered or killed in the United States in 1967. This book is written about and for these children. Who are they, where do they come from, why were they beaten, and most important—what can we do to prevent it?

Presented herein is a multidisciplinary approach to the problem. There is both agreement and controversy among the contributors, but each has one goal in mind—to provide the reader with all of the available information which can hopefully be utilized to change the fate of these children and their parents.

We would like to express our sincere appreciation to all of the contributors and their staffs for sharing with us their experiences and research in the field of child abuse. We are also greatly indebted to Miss Katherine Oettinger and Dr. Arthur Lesser and their staff at the Children's Bureau for their continued help and support. Miss Jean Rubin, a former member of the Children's Bureau, was most helpful during a critical period in our study.

Each of our patients has provided us with a unique learning experience. We would like to express our appreciation not only to these children but also to their parents, who for the most part have been cooperative and helpful in making this work possible.

R.E.H.   C.H.K.

Background

Violence has become an integral part of life for a large percentage of the families throughout the world. It erodes the very foundations upon which they are built and creeps into the next generation, unnoticed until its effects have undermined these young families as well.

The authors who have contributed to Part I discuss, in considerable detail, the dynamics of this family violence in our history, our cultures, the development of our children and future parents, and our day-to-day crises.

R.E.H. C.H.K.

Some day, maybe, there will exist a well-informed, well-considered, and yet fervent public conviction that the most deadly of all possible sins is the mutilation of a child's spirit; for such mutilation undercuts the life principle of trust, without which every human act, may it feel ever so good and seem ever so right, is prone to perversion by destructive forms of conscientiousness.

ERIK ERIKSON
J. Am. Med. Assoc. (1972)

1 Children in a World of Violence: A History of Child Abuse

Samuel X Radbill

> Moral ideas do not necessarily unfold with the flow
> of time. They have a tendency to cling to what is
> old and thereby hallowed.
> OWSEI TEMKIN, *Respect for Life*

Violence against children has been manifested in every conceivable manner: physically, emotionally, through neglect, by sexual exploitation, and by child labor. In 1895, the Society for the Prevention of Cruelty to Children summarized many of the ways London children were battered: by boots, crockery, pans, shovels, straps, ropes, thongs, pokers, fire, and boiling water. They described neglected children who were miserable, vermin infested, filthy, shivering, ragged, nigh naked, pale, puny, limp, feeble, faint, dizzy, famished, and dying. Children were put out to beggary by those responsible for their pallor, emaciation, and cough; children were held in the clutches of idle drunkards and vagrants; little girls were victims of sexual abuse. Children were little slaves of injurious employment in circuses, were displayed as monstrosities in traveling shows, and were exploited in diverse other modes (1, p. 875).

Even now abuse takes bizarre forms. One mother recently baffled seven physicians for two years while a young girl suffered repeated severe infections requiring hospitalization in at least seven hospitals. Her mother continually injected the child with fecal bacteria and then withheld the antibiotic treatment ordered, because she had a weird desire to be part of the glamor of the hospital—a sort of Munchausen syndrome by proxy (2, p. 3).

The Right to Live

In ancient times, when might was right, the infant had no rights until the right to live was ritually bestowed. Until then, the infant was a nonentity and could be disposed of with as little compunction as for an aborted fetus. The newborn had to be acknowledged by the father; what the father produced was his to do with as he wished. Proclaiming the child as his own not only assured life and welfare, but also inheritance rights (3, p. 61). Children's rights were always a prerogative of

Samuel X Radbill, M.D., is retired from the Graduate School of Medicine, University of Pennsylvania, Philadelphia.

Figure 1.1

"Gin Lane" by William Hogarth

parenthood. As head of the family the father had the ultimate authority; even the mother was subordinate.

With some, the child was not really of this world until she had partaken of some earthly nourishment. A drop of milk or honey or even water could ensure life to the newborn. An eighth-century story tells of a grandmother who, outraged by her daughter-in-law's numerous brood of daughters, ordered the next daughter to be slain. Her servants kidnapped the baby as soon as she was born, before she could be put to the mother's breast, and tried to drown her in a bucket of water. A merciful neighbor, however, rescued the infant and put a little honey in its mouth, which it promptly swallowed. The child was thus protected and the right to live assured. In British New Guinea traditionally an infant was taken to the banks of a stream and its lips moistened with water. The baby was thrown away if the water was not accepted by the baby.

To determine fitness to live, the Germans would plunge the newborn into an icy river. This was done not only to harden the child, but to test its hardiness. Some North American Indians threw the newborn into a pool of water and saved it only if it rose to the surface and cried. Elsewhere there were other ordeals for survival.

In the Society Islands, a parent could not kill with impunity a child who had survived for a day; in some places the child was safe even after a half hour of survival.

Figure 1.2

Anton Wiertz (1806–1865), a Flemish realistic artist who tended toward the gruesome in some of his work, in one of his pictures entitled ''Faime, Folie, Crime,'' depicted a crazed mother with grinning mien, swinging a knife, and holding in her lap her dead child wrapped in rags, while to her right is seen the left leg of the child stewing in a cauldron over the fire (Brussels Museum).

The child was a nonperson in some societies until it received a name. This identified the individual. The Christian child did not get heavenly recognition until he was christened, at which time a name was assigned. The soul of a child that died before baptism was believed not to go to heaven, but was condemned to everlasting limbo, and the body of such a child could not be buried in hallowed ground, but instead was disposed of in the same manner as that of a dead dog or cat (4, p. 39).

Illegitimate children have long been outlawed and especially liable to abuse. Born in sin, they were without benefit of clergy or inheritance. As William Blake lamented in the nineteenth century, ''the youthful harlot's curse blasts the new-born infant's tears.'' Earlier, in the Middle Ages, only the children of priests and bishops were permitted to marry, for money could buy a papal dispensation of legitimacy (5, p. 27). Degradation, as well as lack of family unity, led to exposure of the illegitimate and to infanticide. The church provided protective institutions that hid the mother's identity, thus hoping to encourage compromised mothers to spare their infants. Only in recent years has some alleviation from the stigma of illegitimacy been granted in the United States.

Exposure and Infanticide

Exposure and infanticide have been universal forms of lethal child abuse throughout the years. There was usually the hope that exposed children would be saved, but almost invariably exposure resulted in death. Infanticide was not only condoned, sometimes it was compulsory. A weak, premature, or deformed infant was likely to be strangled when the mother was not looking. The Greeks did not want any cripples to grow up, believing their defects would pass to their offspring, and so allowed only healthy newborns to be kept alive. Plato accepted this, and Aristotle recommended a law prohibiting crippled children to be reared. Even Soranus instructed midwives to examine each child at birth and get rid of any not fit to be raised. The image of the newborn was hardly better than that of a pet animal. This freedom for parents to kill anomalous births persisted among some European country folk into the nineteenth century (6, vol. 2, p. 173). Girls were especially at risk. They never had rights equal with their brothers and were far more likely to be killed, sold, or exposed. Under the influence of Christian missionaries, in 1654 the Chinese interdicted drowning little girls (7, p. 56). But legal punishment throughout the centuries never stamped out infanticide, exposure, or the sale of children.

The mentally retarded child also had a hard lot. The deranged instilled the fear of the devil into people. Idiots were changelings whose souls were possessed by Satan, and many a simpleton had the devil knocked out of him.

Castration, to produce eunuchs for harems, in the orient, and to preserve effeminate bodies and retain boys' good singing voices in the west, was a form of mutilation which was outlawed in the seventeenth century by China. Although the early Roman emperors frowned at gelding boys, this abuse persisted in the West until Pope Clement XIV prohibited castrates from singing in churches.

The old English coroner's records, as far back as 1194, and the Bills of Mortality, as early as 1519, provide inklings of various manners in which children were abused. Among 9,535 burials in London, the Bill of 1623 lists "seven overlaid and starved at nurse," obviously infants. The ages of those burned, scalded, or drowned were not given. In the records from 1788 to 1829, babies were listed as drowned in pits full of water, cisterns, wells, ponds, and even pans of water. These are choice contrivances for disposing of unwanted kittens, puppies, and unwanted babies. Privies were another favored disposal place (8).

Child Labor

Child labor, under the apprentice system, in workhouses, in orphanages, as well as in industry, also brutalized children. The guilds of the Middle Ages regulated

Figure 1.3

Child beating in an English woolen mill, around 1850 (Courtesy of Bettman Archive)

the work of children, not out of compassion, but to prevent competitive cheap labor. The statute of artificers in 1562 gave the government regulating control over apprentices, binding children to their masters by indenture for seven years, a system of enslavement that endured until 1815. In the seventeenth century six-year-old children toiled in the clothing industries; and the great demand for children in the factories after the industrial revolution burst forth, early in the eighteenth century, led to further excruciating exploitation.

There was no protection in the mills for children when they were mercilessly beaten and overworked, until the child labor laws initiated reforms during the nineteenth century. Children were transported to the American colonies in droves to be apprenticed until the age of twenty-four. Pauper children were sold by the almshouses into apprenticeship and treated atrociously. Colonial newspapers constantly advertised for runaway children. As late as 1866 a Massachusetts legislative report hailed child labor as a boon to society. Writing on child labor laws in 1891, Abraham Jacobi, the father of American pediatrics, cried out against the employment of mere babies in the mines and as chimney sweeps. He deplored inexpensive child labor supplied to greedy industry by the poorhouses. The working child was even more abused in the rural areas (9, p. 97).

Chimney sweeps were a particularly sad lot. William Blake called them England's disgrace, "little black things among the snow crying 'weep!' 'weep!' in notes of woe." These waifs were purposefully kept small and thin so that they could clamber up narrow, soot-clogged flues. Auenbrugger, famous in medical history for his book on thoracic percussion, wrote a libretto in 1781 for the Chimney Sweep opera in Vienna and three years later was ennobled for his humanitarian work on behalf of the poor (10).

Sexual Abuse

Concern about the battered child proceeded to an interest in sexually abused children. Historically, sexual offenses against children were common. A variety of defloration rites at puberty or in preparation for marriage could be painfully abusive; yet these rites were not just indulged, they were often publicly enforced (11, p. 347). The most enlightened, civilized human beings sometimes lapse into such rude instincts of savagery.[1]

In some cultures daughters, as well as wives, were loaned to guests as an act of hospitality. We find this in Irish heroic tales, in French medieval literature, and among the Eskimos and primitive tribes of North America. Neither was it always a disgrace to hire out girls for sexual use; the child was a marketable commodity. Physically developed, alluring youngsters of ten or twelve were apt to become prostitutes. Unemployed young girls, especially if sexually developed, frequently and willingly submitted for a reward; on occasion parents exhorted them to it. The London Society for the Protection of Young Females recorded children no older than eleven entrapped in houses of prostitution; they were not permitted to escape until they were "broken in." Very few left once they were indoctrinated. Ambroise Tardieu, in a study of sixty cases in which sex offenses were repeated on the same child, found twenty-nine girls were under eleven and all sixty remarkably well developed. Albert Moll found a child of eight copulating regularly and becoming pregnant at nine, and another child pregnant at eight. He stressed that spontaneous awakening of sexual drive in the young favored intercourse and that premature intercourse awakened sexual libido (12, p. 197).

In 1897 in one country there were 3,085 convictions for sexual offenses against children, and in 1904 there were 4,378 (12, pp. 227–28). A Parisian police commissary in 1839 devoted a full chapter of his annual report to sexual abuse of children (13).

Because boys as young as twelve or fourteen frequented the brothels, the town of Ulm in 1527 ordered brothel keepers to keep them out (14, p. 112). In France in 1848 children were legally prohibited from appearing on theater stages because of moral as well as physical iniquities.

---

1. Consider the modern-day continuance of the "rite" of circumcision, for which there is no medical need—Eds.

Pederasty

Pederasty, literally *boy loving,* refers to sexual perversion with a boy. In the early part of this century Dr. Moll was astounded to learn how many homosexuals formed affinities with schoolboys. This depravity was so common in ancient Rome that the poet Martial declaimed against the vice, applauding the emperor's law protecting children from the pander's art in one of his epigrams: "The pander seized our cradles for his prey / and forced young babies to earn a shameful pay / until Rome's great father, wrathful at the sight, / saved the poor children from their monstrous plight" (15, p. 265). In Greece pederasty inspired disgust and was punished, but the Romans continued it in spite of interdicting laws. This was particularly scandalously true during the reign of the licentious, insane emperor, Caligula (16, p. 128).

Sexual mishandling frequently led to venereal disease in children. There was a superstition that venereal disease could be cured by transference through sexual intercourse with children. The consequences are not hard to imagine. Many times sexual abuse came to light only after gonorrhea or syphilis was discovered in the child. Perverted sexual behavior among vagabond waifs and school children caused consternation when disclosed. Sometimes these children infected each other.

Masturbation

Nurses were wont to stroke an irritable child's genitals to soothe it. More often they did this to stimulate their own lust. S. A. Tissot, whose book on onanism influenced medical thought in the nineteenth century and terrified a wide public readership, warned parents about domestics who secretly instructed children in lesbianism (17, pp. 29–30). "In this kind of cultivation there are gardeners of both sexes," he warned. Men who were impotent, or feared they might be, were sometimes tempted to test their sexual prowess on children. Frequently they substituted improper contacts with girls for actual coitus. Masturbation, onanism, self-abuse, or self-pollution was considered unclean and vile and blamed for every disease imaginable.

Sexual Violence

Rape was common in the unbridled days of the past, especially during wartime. It occurs in the Bible as well as in Greek and Roman history and played a prominent part in the drama of historic violence. Hercules violated the fifty daughters of Thestius, and Helen of Troy was deflowered by Theseus at the age of seven, according to one story, and according to another at the age of twelve.

Flagellation was a common form of sexual abuse. One sadistic little girl of six abused a boy of seven, who bore his martyrdom with dull resentment, but liked his beatings because the pain gave him a thrill of bitter delight (12, p. 137). Voluptuous sensations could lead seductive youngsters to instigate beatings purposely.

In nineteenth-century newspapers appeared lurid accounts of children battered

in devious ways for the satisfaction of the sexual lust of sadists. These sex tortur-
ers placed ads in the papers to obtain children, using code words which were
understood by the initiates. German law finally put a stop to advertisements for
immoral purposes. When sexual relations with a person under fourteen became
statutory rape, complications arose if both parties were underage, willing
partners.

Incest

Incest differs from rape in that rape implies violence. The incidence of incest is
impossible to calculate, because incest always happens in secret. Figures vary
from 1 to 5,000 per million population (18). A study of 530 female college students
revealed 45 (8.5%) had experienced sexual activity with a family member, yet very
few incestuous relationships ever became known (19). The American Humane
Society in 1969 estimated between 200,000 and 300,000 female children are
molested in the United States annually, with at least 5,000 instances of father-
daughter incest (20, p. 22). Concealment was the hallmark of the endogamous
family; incest surfaced outside the family chiefly as a result of physical maltreatment, pregnancy, or venereal disease.

Anthropologically and historically sexual unions between father and daughter,
mother and son, or brother and sister were not infrequent, but it was usually
abhorred. The laws of Justinian did not require parents to nourish children conceived incestuously. Polygamous Mormons in this country practiced incestuous
marriages until it was outlawed in 1892.

Incest was especially devastating to the child because it was a taboo. The taboo
often extended to adoption, fosterage, milk-brotherhood (i.e., those who were
nursed by the same woman), and other intimate relationships similar to blood
kinship. When it extended to housemates in general, children were prudishly
separated at home and in schools. Between five and ten years of age, some
primitives terminated association of boys with their mothers and sisters. Even
where sexual freedom among children of the same household existed, illicit marriage was strictly forbidden. Father-son incest was doubly taboo.

Many reasons have been discussed by anthropologists as to why incest was
taboo. While the taboo was primarily ethical and religious, exogamy tended to
preserve family unity and to maintain better intrafamily and community relationships. A moral code imposed psychologic restraint and seemed to have
certain genetic advantages, in line with the general belief that family inbreeding
intensified hereditary traits. Because incestuous mothers were so young, there
was an increased morbidity and mortality among the offspring. Never was there a
claim that it was healthful.

Advancement of Children's Rights

Esteem for the child was slow to appear. Until the Middle Ages, childhood was
over almost as soon as the child was weaned. Among the Israelites, weaning took
place at the age of three; then the little boy could enter the house of God along

with the men; at thirteen, the age of puberty, he was counted among the men. Medieval children were sent away from home by the age of seven for upbringing; this custom eventuated in the apprentice system. The Italians thought the custom showed a lack of affection toward children by the English (4, p. 315). In the thirteenth century, children began to appear in art, portrayed with various childhood attractions. By the sixteenth century, the moral philosophy of men like Erasmus, himself a wronged illegitimate orphan, and Montaigne, raised by an indulgent father, stirred the hearts of many to adopt nonviolent methods of rearing children and wakened compassionate solicitude for the oppressed and the handicapped child. Their ethics carried over to the seventeenth century and after, influencing men like Rousseau, a libertine who had fathered at least six illegitimate children who vanished, before he turned humanitarian, preaching, "Speak less of the duties of children and more of their rights."

In the seventeenth century there was a shift from communal to family groups, and society was thrilling more deeply to the charms of children. The child gradually achieved a place of honor in the family, and the family attained an independent status (4, p. 42). Step by step, the child was increasingly idolized. In the eighteenth century, Richardson's novel, *Pamela,* spoke out against child abuse, as did Scott's *The Heart of Midlothian* in the nineteenth century. Victor Hugo's Cosette, the foster child who was abused as a household drudge in *Les Misérables,* and the many young characters in nearly all of Dickens's sentimental Victorian novels, stirred up ferment for humane treatment of children.

By 1871 the New York State Medical Society could rightly say, in a resolution supporting foundling asylums, that humanity recognized the right of every newborn to be protected and supported. This was the same year of the oft told story of Mary Ellen, the battered child for whom protective services could only be invoked through the Society for the Prevention of Cruelty to Animals (21, p. 142). By the beginning of the nineteenth century, the public conscience had been aroused on behalf of the oppressed, the neglected, and the handicapped. Schools sprang up for the blind, the deaf, and the mentally retarded, so that exceptional children were no longer jettisoned. By the end of the century, Abraham Jacobi exclaimed that the greatest improvement in public morals consisted in acknowledgment that protection of the feeble is among the inalienable rights of all such beings. Pointing at the large numbers of abandoned children devoid of the care and protection of the family circle, whose parents were either in hospitals, prisons, or were dead, he declared these all had a claim on the aid of the community (22, p. 217).

Protective Services for Children

Child welfare began in Mesopotamia 6,000 years ago, when orphans had a patron goddess to look after them (23). The *Rigveda* also mentions another deity among the ancient Hindus, who rescued the exposed child and endowed him with legal rights (24, p. 34). The gods reflected a mirror image of mankind affording a picture of what went on among the people.

The Bible commands, "Do not sin against the child." The laws of Solon, 600

B.C., required the commander of an army to protect and raise, at government expense, children of citizens killed in battle; and the wives of the Roman emperors extended child welfare. Then there was jolly old St. Nicholas Thaumaturgos, wonder worker of the third century, who was patron saint of children and protector of the feeble minded.

In the main, protective services have always consisted of placing children in institutions or under foster care. In spite of good intentions, however, children suffered physical and psychological damage under this system. Without such intervention, they were more apt to be maimed and killed.

Institutional Care

At a very early period, Athens and Rome had orphan homes; and *brephotrophia* were mentioned in 529 in the laws of Justinian. With the rise of Christianity, the church provided for foundlings and every village had a *xenodochium*, a hospice for pilgrims and the poor, which embraced children (25). By the sixth century the *brephotrophium* at Triers had a marble receptacle in which a child could be safely deposited secretly. Similar institutions throughout France in the seventh century were the antecedents of the welfare system in the nineteenth century.

The first foundling hospital was established by Datheus, the archpriest of Milan in 787. Others blossomed forth in rapid succession. In Naples, with a population of about 400,000 and 15,000 births a year in the nineteenth century, there were

Figure 1.4

"The Foundling" (1835). Reproduced from Schreiber.

Figure 1.5

New York Foundling Asylum, Randall's Island

over 2,000 foundlings in the asylum. The foundling hospital of St. Petersburg was the most magnificent in Europe. The Russians were very proud of it and endowed it munificently. Upwards of 25,000 children were enrolled regularly upon its books. About one in four died, and the foundling hospitals did not prevent exposure or infanticide (26, p. 275).

British law, which also applied to the American colonies, initiated early involvement of government in public welfare. The main reliance was on almshouses, where, to offset expense and save children from the sin of idleness, they were forced to work.

Children fared badly under the dismal routine of institutions. They suffered from deprivation and starvation, with little consideration for their recreational needs. A visitor to a foundling asylum was dejected by the sight of children sitting all day long bound to potty chairs (27, p. 188). Few survived. Those who did, were starved, overworked, cuffed, degraded, despised, and unpitied. In Paris, a street beggar could buy an infant at the Hotel Dieu for twenty sous to be maimed so that it would attract pity and more liberal alms; or a wet nurse could buy a replacement for an infant entrusted to her care that died (27, p. 198). To add to their misery, almshouses made children, as young as five or six, toil in the workhouses.

Foundling homes, orphanages, almshouses offered little surcease from death. Protestant countries were convinced that they encouraged immorality; in addition, they objected to the cost and believed foster care was cheaper. To avoid the failings of institutional life, children were farmed out to foster care as soon as possible.

Foster Care

Foster care was also mentioned in antiquity. Removal to private homes often subjected children to maltreatment and neglect, but gave them a sporting chance of survival. Even so, 80% of illegitimate children put out to nurse in London during the nineteenth century perished. As a matter of fact, some nurses had a reputation as skilled baby killers. The Germans called them "angel makers."

These harpies commanded extra fees to take charge of unwanted babies and even profited from insurance benefits on the dead infants. Foster care could be a sordid business.

A German report of 1881 stated that 31% of illegitimate children died under foster care, allegedly from natural causes, but really from freezing, starvation, or deliberate destruction. A favorite method of doing away with infants was to give them nothing but pacifiers soaked in brandy. Seldom were foster parents called to account. In spite of such gross irregularities, foundlings made out better under foster care than in foundling institutions.

When children spent their entire childhoods in a succession of foster homes, the lack of the security of a permanent home life marred their emotional development and sowed the seeds of unhappy consequences in later life. Tansilio's poem *La Balia* (The nurse) decried the eighteenth century fashion of surrogate care under some wretch of vulgar birth and frail conduct, just out of jail, or some strumpet. In England, Jonas Hanway, reporting that only one out of seventy children entrusted to parish care grew up, only to be crippled and sent out into the streets to beg, steal, or fall into prostitution, brought about parliamentary reform that required all young foster children to be registered. The *British Medical Journal,* in 1903 chided the system of baby farming and urged the licensing of foster parents and inspectors to see that the children were properly cared for (28, p. 154).

The pros and cons of institutional care versus foster care were long debated. Advanced in favor of the latter were less cost and the blessings of family life, while supporters of institutions argued the cost would be insignificant with proper economy and that surrogate parents gave little service for the pittance they received, from which they still expected to profit.

Hundreds of thousands of children and their families have been helped by the wise use of foster care. Contact with the child by one or both parents, when possible, not only aids the child's mental development, but also boosts the morale of the foster parents and their respect for the child. The Child Welfare League studied foster care in 1965, and the Columbia School of Social Work has undertaken to determine what happens to children as a result of placement under foster care. Believing that foster children are prime candidates for emotional and physical distress, a bill is before the Pennsylvania legislature to set up a panel to review the matter periodically. There is still an uneasy feeling that the thousands of children adrift in the foster care system have to be rescued (29).

Child Protective Laws

Traditionally, the father's authority, like the royal prerogative, could be asserted without question, but through the years it has been increasingly limited by statutes and changing public opinion. The father's authority was modified in Rome in 450 B.C. and again in A.D. 4. The Christian church fathers in the fourth century, in line with the Judaic commandment, "Thou shalt not kill," equated infanticide with murder. This was a landmark in the history of children's rights. A succession of imperial edicts after that guaranteed the child's right to life.

The grave injustice possible from a false accusation of sexual abuse of children created a perplexing problem for experienced physicians (30, vol. 3, pp. 878–79). According to Dr. Moll, an innocent defendent was seldom exonerated when accused by a little girl or her parents.

The church, the courts, and public opinion were often apt to be lenient toward a guilty mother in cases of infanticide. The vagaries of the law in this respect were brought out by a seventeenth-century English practitioner. One "comely, well-favored servant" the jury did not find guilty, because she was so pretty and beloved of soldiers, who "pitied her misfortune." The foreman of the jury saw "no reason why a woman should be hanged for a mistaken harsh word or two in the statutes." A less-fortunate woman who buried her child in secret in 1670 was executed. So, too, a feeble-minded girl who could not distinguish between labor pains and a bowel movement and aborted in a ditch, "though the whole bench saw she was a foole," was hanged. The penalty for disposing of a child in secret was hanging; if a mother took back her abandoned child she was exonerated (31, pp. 31–34 and 274–75).

In medieval times the church governed birth, marriage, and death, making the rules for law and medicine. A penance was set for overlaying (lying upon) a child. In the twelfth century, penance was also incurred when infants died of scalding. Refusing to nurse and death of a child by the mother's hand likewise brought church censure. The Bishop of Bamberg in the twelfth century, because killing girl babies was such a widespread sin in his domain, forbade it; but a thirteenth-century German law permitted a man distressed by poverty to exterminate or sell his children, provided he did not sell them to pagans or, in the case of girls, into prostitution.

The secular courts steadily increased their jurisdiction over infanticide. In 1224 overlaying was so prevalent that the statutes of Winchester penalized women just for keeping infants in bed with them. Church admonitions were repeated so often, eyes must have been shut to reality. The royal courts of Henry I assumed authority when a child was killed by anyone other than the parent. When Henry VIII broke off from the church of Rome, secular authorities took complete jurisdiction. The laws became more stringent, although many modifications were made through the years. Rapid urbanization made concealment more difficult, and society began to reevaluate the worth of the child (32).

In spite of shocking evidence to the contrary, numerous inquests of battered children returned a verdict of natural death. In his inimitable fashion, Dickens, in *Oliver Twist* (1839), describes the ordinary inquest:

> Occasionally, when there was some more than usually interesting inquest upon a parish child who had been overlooked in turning up a bedstead, or inadvertently scalded to death when there happened to be a washing . . . the jury would take it into their heads to ask troublesome questions, or the parishioners would rebelliously affix their signatures to a remonstrance. But, the impertinencies were speedily checked by the evidence of the surgeon, and the testimony of the beadle; the former of whom had always opened the body and found nothing inside (which was very probable indeed), and the latter of whom invariably swore whatever the Parish wished.

When young children were imported for sexual misuse, the Society for the

Prevention of Cruelty to Children became involved with the white slave question and was instrumental in passing protective laws against this kind of child abuse. The Mann Act, more recently, also particularly protects girls. The Lindbergh law against kidnapping was another step in the progress of child protective laws. The progression of child labor laws has already been touched upon.

A significant step was separation of minors from adult criminals and the institution of juvenile courts about seventy-five years ago. A juvenile court was established in Chicago at the turn of this century, and in 1907 the Los Angeles Police Department began to specialize in juvenile affairs, creating in 1910 a separate juvenile bureau. This police department in 1970 set up a desk for abused children and in 1974 established the first battered child unit to handle physical and sexual abuse of children.

Prior to 1964, there were no effectual child-abuse–reporting laws. The 1962 conference chaired by Dr. C. H. Kempe engendered the model child abuse law that, within the remarkably short space of five years, was adopted by every state. Experience and increased insight into the psychodynamics of the abusive parent led to revisions. First the laws were aimed at case finding and deterrent punishment, but soon it was apparent that the entire family was often involved in the battered child syndrome.[2]

Child Abuse as a Pedriatric Problem

Except for medical care of the injured child, the problems of the battered child in the past ordinarily were not the concern of physicians. Their mission was to heal the sick, not to deal with social problems. The cross the child had to bear was the responsibility of society. The physicians of yore were implicated, not in the course of practice, but rather in company with other compassionate citizens as a moral obligation. They did not handle social, psychological, cultural, religious, or economic afflictions, shunned politics, left morals to theologians, and scrupulously avoided any controversial police activity that might conflict with the sacred Hippocratic principle of confidentiality. They divulged privileged communications only when the public health required it, as during the plague. Child abuse, like child labor, juvenile delinquency, and similar social questions historically were ethical and moral problems, not strictly medical. Only of late have such matters been attached to pediatrics.

Nevertheless, the medical profession was not unmindful. Abraham Jacobi, when he was president of the New York State Medical Society in 1882, formed a committee to cooperate with the Society for the Prevention of Cruelty to Children in formulating legislation to improve child labor laws.

Medicine was oblivious to child abuse until concern about child abuse grew out of Dr. John Caffey's perturbation of mind about curious X-ray manifestations in the bones of some children. Radiology appeared just at the dawn of the twentieth

---

2. An extensive review of legal history relating to child abuse has been written by Brian Fraser (33)—EDS.

century. Caffey was one of the first to devote special pediatric attention to it when he took charge in 1925 of the Babies Hospital X-ray department in New York. Radiologists, like pathologists, were essentially "back-room boys" and rarely went to the bedside. Caffey, however, was trained as a pediatrician, and, even as a radiologist, he was very much involved with children, their parents, and their concerns. As an adept pediatrician he was able to relate these unexplained X-ray findings to clinical pictures. While he soon recognized that multiple fractures were due to trauma, he was unable to convince his colleagues that parents might be the instrument of this trauma. In 1946 Caffey published a paper entitled "Multiple Fractures in the Long Bones of Infants Suffering from Chronic Subdural Hematoma" (34). This attracted the attention of pediatricians to the ramifications of child abuse. This issue then smoldered for several years.

Multiple long-bone fractures had been confused with rickets, scurvy, and osteogenesis imperfecta; and even though Paré and Vesalius in the sixteenth century knew about traumatic subdural hemorrhage, Virchow in the nineteenth, decided the subdural hematomas he saw at the autopsy table were inflammatory reactions of obscure origin. Caffey and his neurosurgical colleagues were aware, as were some of his pediatrician friends, that subdural hematomas were traumatic. In 1946, he made the point in his report that trauma had to be seriously considered as a cause of long-bone fractures, since it was already recognized as the cause of subdural hematoma (35).

Dr. Frederic N. Silverman, another radiologist, extended Caffey's convictions, emphasizing in 1951 the intentional infliction of these injuries (36). Finally, when Wooley and Evans blasted the medical profession in 1955 for its reluctance to concede that the multiple injuries to children were committed willfully, the profession began to pay attention. Dr. Kempe and his staff studied all the different features of child abuse from 1951 to 1958 and linked child abuse to pediatrics. Kempe was a member of the program committee of the American Academy of Pediatrics and, when he became chairman in 1961, organized a multidisciplinary conference, with the emotive title of the "Battered-Child Syndrome" (37). This conference, and its provocative title, set ablaze an impassioned outburst on behalf of abused children. A bandwagon effect was generated. The Children's Bureau climbed aboard with generous grants for study of the subject, and the American Humane Society carried out surveys, issued pertinent publications, and convened national symposia considering many different angles. A "child abuse" heading first appeared in the *Quarterly Cumulative Index Medicus* in 1965, under which about forty published articles were listed. Centers were set up to look into the basic causes of abnormal rearing processes that generate child abuse and to initiate new methods of dealing with them.

In Great Britain a 1966 study by the National Society for the Prevention of Cruelty to Children revealed that more than half of abused children were less than a year old, battered by their own mothers. The rest were battered by fathers, stepfathers, or boyfriends of the mothers. Almost all required hospitalization, nearly half of them repeatedly. The Society set up centers with programs in corrective mothering, patterned after those set in motion by the Denver group, and named the London center "Denver House" to honor the pioneering efforts of Dr. Kempe's group.

In Sweden, child abuse was first recognized as a pediatric problem in 1957. The Swedish National Board of Health then issued regulations, offered counseling services and set up a research institute for the study of child abuse (38).

Prevention and Treatment

The approach to child protection has shifted from the punitive to the therapeutic. Slowly, but steadily, emphasis upon rescuing children and prosecuting offending parents gave way to treatment and rehabilitation. The child protective laws are now oriented toward nonpunitive protection of children, helping families in crisis, preserving good standards of parental behavior, and providing basic needs for optimum care of children in a harmonious family relationship. To cure is the voice of the past, to prevent the divine whisper of today (28, p. 155).

In the past, social problems were relegated to private benevolent societies and the law. When people were chagrined that the Society for Prevention of Cruelty to Animals founded in 1866 preceded the Society for the Prevention of Cruelty to Children, other child protective groups were organized. Their principal achievements consisted in reforming child labor and in separating abused children from further harm and finding shelter for them. The Society for the Prevention of Cruelty to Children was founded in 1874, and by the end of the nineteenth century there were such child protection agencies in England, France, Germany, Italy, the United States, and just about every other civilized country in the world.

Until Kempe issued his clarion call of the "Battered-Child Syndrome" conference, protective services comprised separation of the victim from and punishment of the evildoer. Now a new tack is taken: early recognition of children at risk and rehabilitation of troubled families, aiming to preserve the natural development of the child in his normal domestic habitat. With the acceptance of child abuse as a pediatric responsibility, new life was instilled into the campaign for children's rights.[3]

3. The modern-day history of child abuse is now being written. The third, 1980 edition of this book is now in print. Only time will determine how successful we all are in moving from our after-the-fact program into before-the-fact prevention—EDS.

References

1. Burdett, Henry C. 1895. *Burdett's Hospital and Charities Annual.* New York: Scribner.
2. *American Medical News,* 4 May 1979.
3. Harper, Robert F. 1904. *The Code of Hammurabi, King of Babylon about 2000 B.C.,* 2d ed. Chicago: University of Chicago Press.
4. Aries, Phillipe. 1962. *Centuries of Childhood: A Social History of Family Life.* New York: Knopf.

5. Tuchman, B. W. 1978. *A Distant Mirror: The Calamitous 14th Century*. New York: Knopf.

6. Ploss, H. H. 1876. *Das Kind im Brauch und Sitte der Volker*. Stuttgart. Vol. 2.

7. Payne, G. H. 1928. *The Child in Human Progress*. New York: Sears.

8. Forbes, T. R. 1978. Crowner's Quest. *Trans. Am. Philos. Soc.* 68:7.

9. Tillman, E. B. 1958. *Rights of Childhood*. Ph.D. dissertation, University of Wisconsin.

10. Willius, F. A. 1950. Historical Comments in Stroud, W. D. *Diagnosis and Treatment of Cardiovascular Disease*, 4th ed. (Philadelphia: F. A. Davis), 1:9.

11. Crawley, Ernest. 1902. *The Mystic Rose: A Study of Primitive Marriage*. New York: Macmillan.

12. Moll, Albert. 1913. *Sexual Life of the Child*, trans. by Eden Paul. New York: Macmillan.

13. Beraud, J. B. 1839. *Les filles publiques de Paris*. Paris.

14. Boesch, Hans. 1900. *Kinderleben in der deutschen Vergangenheit*.

15. Pott, J. A., and Wright, F. A. n.d. *Martial*. New York: Dutton.

16. Rosenbaum, Julius. 1839. *Die Lustseuche im Altertum*. Halle: Lippert.

17. Tissot, S. A. A. D. 1832. *Treatise on Diseases Produced by Onanism*. New York: Collins & Hanway.

18. Nakashima, I. I., and Zakas, M. S. W. 1979. Incestuous Families. *Pediatr. Ann.* 8:300.

19. Rosenfeld, A. A. 1979. Endogamous Incest. *Am. J. Dis. Child.* 133:406–10.

20. Pennsylvania Coalition Against Rape. 1979. *A Special Report: The Sexual Victimization of Children*. 12 March.

21. Riis, Jacob. 1892. Little Mary Ellen's Legacy. In *The Children of the Poor*. London: Sampson, Low, Marston.

22. Robinson, W. J. 1909. *Collectanea Jacobi*. New York: Critic & Guide. Vol. 6.

23. Radbill, S. X. 1973. Mesopotamian Pediatrics. *Episteme* 7:283.

24. Pinkham, M. W. 1941. *Woman in the Sacred Scriptures of Hinduism*. New York: Columbia University Press.

25. Radbill, S. X. 1955. History of Children's Hospitals. *Am. J. Dis. Child.* 90:3.

26. Sanger, William W. 1898. *History of Prostitution*. New York: Medical Publishing Co.

27. Peiper, Albrecht. 1965. *Chronik der Kinderheilkunde*, 4th ed. Leipzig.

28. *Br. Med. J.* 17 January 1903.

29. Editorial. *Philadelphia Inquirer*. 16 April 1979.

30. Holmes, Timothy. 1882. *System of Surgery*, edited by John H. Packard. Philadelphia. Vol. 3.

31. Willughby, Percival. 1972. *Observations in Midwifery*. Wakefield, England: S. & R. Publishers.

32. Damme, Catherine. 1978. The Worth of an Infant under Law. *Med. Hist.* 22:1–24.

33. Fraser, Brian. 1976. *Child Abuse and Neglect: The Family and the Community*, edited by R. E. Helfer and C. H. Kempe (New York: Ballinger).

34. Caffey, John. 1946. Multiple Fractures in the Long Bones of Infants Suffering

from Chronic Subdural Hematoma. *Am. J. Roentgenol.* 56:163–73.

35. Reinhart, J. B. 1979. Personal communication.
36. Silverman, Frederic. 1953. The Roentgen Manifestations of Unrecognized Skeletal Trauma. *Am. J. Roentgenol. Radium Ther. Nucl. Med.* G9:413–27.
37. Kempe, C. H., Silverman, F. N., Steele, B. F., Droegemueller, W., and Silver, H. K. 1962. The Battered-Child Syndrome. *J. Am. Med. Assoc.* 181:17–24.
38. Lagerberg, D. 1978. Child Abuse: A Literature Review. *Acta Paediatr. Scand.* 67:683–90.

2 The Cross-Cultural Context of Child Abuse and Neglect

Jill E. Korbin

One of our most cherished folk beliefs is that human nature compels parents to rear their young with solicitousness and concern, good intentions, and tender and loving care. Evidence to the contrary—the rather alarming frequency with which parents harm or fail to adequately care for their offspring—has forced the recognition that child abuse and neglect are well within the repertoire of human behavior.

Our understanding of this perplexing social problem is limited in that it is based almost entirely on studies in Western nations, the United States in particular. Western cultures, however, are rarely reflective of panhuman traits and are often on the extreme end of the cross-cultural continuum for child-rearing practices and beliefs. Our conceptualizations are thus based upon a narrow slice of humanity, and we are hampered in our abilities to untangle the web of factors contributing to child abuse and neglect.

This chapter will explore what a cross-cultural perspective can add to our understanding of the context in which child abuse and neglect occur and to our abilities to deal with the problem in a culturally appropriate fashion. To this end, we will examine cultural definitions of child abuse and neglect and what the cross-cultural record tells us about these behaviors in Western, particularly American, society.

The term *cross-cultural* refers to the perspective afforded from a consideration of widely varying groups around the world. These societies may be in such places as New Guinea, Africa, Asia, or South America, and may appear to us exotic and far removed from relevance to the problems of child abuse and neglect that we face in this country. *Cross-cultural* also encompasses groups of people that are of more readily recognizable relevance to those concerned with issues of child abuse and neglect in this country, that is, the rather remarkable cultural diversity that we find within the borders of this country, which we speak of as "subcultural" or "ethnic" diversity. There are close parallels between the kinds of knowledge and principles that can be generated by examining far-removed and seemingly exotic

Jill E. Korbin, Ph.D., is an NIMH postdoctoral fellow at the University of Southern California.

cultures and those cultures living within close proximity to one another in the United States. An ability to transcend cultural boundaries, by what may be called "cultural translation" (1) or "ethnic competence" (2), is equally important when conducting anthropological fieldwork in remote areas of Oceania as when providing 'services in ethnic communities in Los Angeles, Denver, Honolulu, or rural areas of Texas.

Culturally Appropriate Definitions of Child Abuse and Neglect

In assessing the role of culture in child abuse and neglect, the first task is to decipher cultural definitions. Conventional wisdom might lead one to believe that child abuse and neglect can be easily identified across cultural boundaries. As one begins to explore the considerable variation in child-rearing beliefs and behaviors cross-culturally, however, it becomes clear that there is not a universal standard for child rearing, nor for child abuse and neglect. This seems to present a dilemma. If we fail to allow for a cultural perspective in defining child abuse and neglect, we will be hopelessly locked into an ethnocentric position in which our own set of cultural beliefs and practices are presumed to be preferable and, indeed, superior to others. At the same time, we cannot take a stance of extreme cultural relativism in which all judgments of humane treatment of children are suspended in the name of cultural sensitivity or awareness. To reconcile this dilemma, we need to begin to structure definitional issues into a coherent framework such that child abuse and neglect can be appropriately identified within and across cultural contexts.

In this endeavor, one must be cognizant of the viewpoint of members of the cultural group in question, termed the *emic* perspective, as well as an outside, or *etic* perspective. An understanding of the *emic* perspective has been central in anthropologists' efforts to organize and explain the diversity of human behavior that has been documented cross-culturally. Thus, the anthropologist has sought to "grasp the native's point of view, his relation to life, to realize his vision of his world" (3, p. 25). At the same time, one needs an *etic* frame of reference such that behavior can be interpreted from a wider perspective. An understanding of both *emic* and *etic* perspectives is a necessity in sorting out the impact of the cultural and social context in which behavior, including child abuse and neglect, takes on meaning.

It is also helpful to distinguish between levels at which the cultural and social context come into play in defining child abuse and neglect. The first level encompasses child-rearing practices that may be viewed as acceptable by one group, but as unacceptable or even abusive and neglectful by another. It is in this realm that cultural conflict, or a disparity between *emic* and *etic* perspectives is most likely to occur in definitions of child abuse and neglect.

The second level is what more validly may be considered child abuse and neglect. That is, the idiosyncratic departure from culturally and socially acceptable standards that results in harm to a child or compromises his or her physical, emotional, cognitive, social, or cultural development. If the cultural and social context of a community is well understood from an *emic* perspective, it is likely that *etic* and *emic* agreement can be reached on such cases.

The third level, societal abuse and neglect of children, has been within the purview of those associated with the "sick society" explanation of child abuse and neglect. Social conditions such as poverty, unemployment, inadequate housing, poor health care, few educational opportunities, and so on, are seen either as contributing powerfully to the incidence of child abuse and neglect or as outweighing the proportion of child abuse and neglect that occurs at the hands of individual caretakers (4–7).

Cultural Conflict in the Definition of Child Abuse and Neglect

As cultures come into contact with one another, different child-rearing practices and beliefs create a situation ripe for cultural conflict in the definition of child abuse and neglect. Disparities between *emic* and *etic* perspectives on a given act or practice can occur both on an international level and among subcultural or ethnic groups within any one country (8–11).

Western cultures may consider, for example, the harsh initiation rites that occur in other parts of the world as abusive. During such rites, preadolescent boys, and less frequently girls, may undergo genital operations, facial scarifications, beatings, and hazings by older members of the group. Sharp reeds are used to induce bleeding of the tongue, nostrils, or urethra. The initiates are deprived of food or forced to vomit by inserting long canes down their throats (12–16). Western cultures look askance at the harsh punishments that children receive in other cultures. Children may be locked in huts for several days without food, have excrement smeared publicly on their faces, have the palms of their hands cut with knives, be given extremely hot baths, or be completely ostracized from human contact for several days (17–20).

At the same time, many of our Western child-rearing practices would be viewed as equally abusive or neglectful by these same groups. In exploring cultural aspects of child abuse and neglect, it is sobering to look at Western child rearing through the eyes of different cultures. Non-Western peoples often conclude that the anthropologists, missionaries, and other Europeans with whom they come into contact do not love their children or, at best, simply do not know how to care for them properly (21). This belief should be all the more disturbing to us in that it is based upon their observations of our normative child-rearing practices, not on instances of what we might ourselves define as child abuse or neglect. Practices such as isolating children in beds or rooms of their own at night, making children wait a given number of hours before satisfying their requests for food, forcing young children to sit all day in classrooms, or allowing children to "cry themselves out" would certainly be at odds with the child-rearing philosophies of many cultures. Such practices may seem to us benign and even enhancing of optimal child development. However, to other groups, such practices would be viewed as equally as bizarre, exotic, and damaging to child welfare as their child-rearing behaviors seem to us.

If the cultural context, or *emic* meaning, of a behavior is not well understood, ethnocentrism may dictate that the dominant culture will either tolerate the behavior or attempt to eradicate it through punishment or education. Two examples will illustrate this point.

In the first case, a woman in London cut the faces of her two young sons with a razor blade and rubbed charcoal into the lacerations. The woman was arrested and tried for child abuse. However, the woman was a member of an East African tribe that traditionally practiced facial scarification. Her actions were thus an attempt to assert the cultural identity of her children (22). Without such markings, her boys would be unable to participate as adults in their culture. A failure to assure one's children of such scarification would thus be viewed as neglectful or abusive within the cultural context of her tribe (8).

In the second case, members of a cultural group in New Guinea were appalled that the American anthropologists living in their midst allowed their newborn infant to cry without immediately picking him up. As American parents, the anthropologists were adhering to their folk belief that picking up a baby each time it cries will ''spoil'' the child. At the same time, the folk belief of the group in New Guinea was that it is dangerous for a child to be allowed to cry unattended. In addition to being detrimental to the child's immediate well-being and comfort, this group believed that if a baby cries and squalls too long, its spirit will escape through the open fontanel. The child will then die. Unable to tolerate this danger to a child, the villagers picked up the baby when it cried—perhaps their form of protective custody (23).

An awareness of such cultural differences in more remote or exotic cultures can alert us to principles that are applicable in identifying child abuse and neglect in diverse cultures within this country. This can be seen both in misinterpretations of physical trauma and in differences in child-rearing styles that can be perceived as neglect.

Misinterpretation of physical trauma has arisen repeatedly among subcultural groups. For example, the Vietnamese practice of *cao gio* (coin rubbing), in which heated metal coins are pressed forcefully on the child's body, leaves bruises that were at first interpreted by Western observers as indications of inflicted trauma. The practice, however, is a traditional Vietnamese curing technique that is believed to reduce fever, chills, and headaches (24). While bruises were indeed inflicted, in this context one would be hard pressed to define the practice as child abuse.

Similar issues arise with respect to the treatment for listlessness, diarrhea, and vomiting in Mexican-American communities. This condition is attributed to a *mollera caida,* a fallen fontanel. Traditional curing practices involve holding the child upside down, often with the top of the head in water, and shaking the child to return the fontanel to its proper position (25). However, the remedy, designed to cure, may result in retinal hemorrhages reminiscent of inflicted physical abuse (26, 27). While physical trauma may result from a too vigorous application of this treatment, it is firmly based in traditional healing practices and as such must be differentiated from idiosyncratically inflicted child abuse.

Along these same lines, colicky infants and small children might arouse among Hawaiian-Americans suspicion of child abuse. The tossing or jiggling up and down of babies and small children, within the context of Hawaiian culture, is believed to cause a condition known as *opu hule* (turned stomach or displaced stomach), with symptoms of indigestion, fussiness, and general discomfort. Since *haoles* (literally meaning "outsider," but used to refer to whites in general) do not subscribe to this medical belief, in the eyes of Hawaiians they take undue risks with the health and well-being of their children by tossing them or jiggling them to entertain them or quiet their crying (28).

Differences in child-rearing styles can similarly contribute to misinterpretations of neglect or inadequate parenting. Middle-class Americans tend to believe that each child should have his or her own bed, if not his or her own room. Hawaiian-American women, on the other hand, are incredulous that *haole* parents put their infants and young children in a separate bed and, further, in a separate room (28). While this might seem like a benign example, to a culture that believes that such a practice is detrimental to child development, and potentially dangerous, this is a serious matter. Just as protective-service workers are frequently alarmed at several children per bed, Hawaiians would be similarly alarmed by a young child sleeping in a bed alone. Hawaiians are not unique in this belief. In Japanese culture, for example, sharing a bed with a family member is preferable. This reflects the high value placed on interdependence among family members (29). The example of sleeping patterns can be instructive in illustrating the importance of the cultural context in determining whether a child is being provided with an adequate environment. In a study of several cultural groups in Texas, the same sleeping arrangements were found to have different origins and meanings in two Anglo groups. Among Mormons, infants slept with their parents, because of a belief that this is good for children. For another nearby group of Texans, however, the same sleeping arrangement reflected over-crowding and poverty, rather than cultural values (30). The assessment of an adequate environment in these two groups must therefore take differences in the cultural context into consideration.

Sibling caretaking may similarly be subject to misinterpretation of neglect among cultural groups (31). In middle-class American families, sibling caretaking is often precluded by a sibling constellation of two children separated by only a few years (32). Additionally, in the United States, the notion of a child of eight, ten, or eleven caring for an even younger child has come to be regarded as abusive or neglectful (33). The older child is seen as deprived of his or her "age of childhood" or "world of play," while the younger child is seen as deprived of the adult caretaking, usually the mother's, that our folk wisdom deems so important. Nevertheless, children of seven or eight years of age perform much of the infant and small child care tasks cross-culturally (34). In many subcultural or ethnic groups in this country, among Mexican-American, black, and Pacific peoples, for example, sibling caretaking carries a positive rather than a negative connotation. Among groups in which child care is valued, sibling caretaking is a preparation for future roles as parents, as well as a means for generating a sense of self-esteem by performing an integral function in the household. This argument is buttressed by cross-cultural studies that indicate that children who participate in child caretaking are more nurturing and altruistic, exhibit more positive social behaviors, and develop a greater sense of self-worth (35–37).

In differentiating abusive or neglectful sibling caretaking tasks from child-care assignment that can in fact be beneficial to the child, the context is again the crucial factor. Is child care a valued activity or an undesirable task imposed upon unwilling but powerless children? In a study in a rural Hawaiian-American community, children between five and eight years of age overreported the extent of sibling caretaking they performed, because of the strong cultural value placed on child-care tasks for individuals of all ages (38). Is the child supervising younger children in isolation, or, as is usually the case in culturally accepted sibling caretaking, is there someone to call upon in the event of an emergency. The young child left to care for numerous siblings in the absence of a support network certainly must be differentiated from the child who cares for his or her charge within a larger network of children performing similar tasks with adults nearby to assist if necessary. It should also be cautioned that traditionally acceptable patterns of sibling caretaking, when transposed to a new environment, may become problematical. Conditions of unsafe urban housing, for example, may cause sibling caretaking, which was adaptive in one environment, to become dangerous for all the children involved (31).

Idiosyncratic Child Abuse and Neglect

Once we acknowledge cultural variability in child-rearing practices and in definitions of child abuse and neglect, how do we assess what is abusive and what is a culturally accepted practice? An ability to make such distinctions is a frequent concern of child-protective workers. One must avoid the fallacy of equating cultural acceptance of child-rearing practices or beliefs with explanations obtained in clinical experience with identified abusive parents. As a point for discussion, we can consider discipline by the use of belts in some cultural groups. Is our position to be that belts may not be used or that damage may not be done to children through their use? From a child-rearing strategy based on positive reinforcement, we may want to say that children should not be hit with belts, hands, or any object, and that further, the acceptance of this kind of violence against children contributes to child abuse. Nevertheless, a cultural group may believe that without a very tangible threat of physical discipline, children will not grow up properly. Samoans, for example, who make considerable use of physical discipline, look askance at the white children whom they see talking back to adults in public places or running about seemingly uncontrolled and causing a disturbance to adult activities. Samoans would be unwilling to relinquish those techniques of child training that they feel produce well-behaved children for the techniques that the white middle-class advocates, but that, in the mind of Samoans, produce such bad results (39).

Difficulties in differentiating culturally acceptable child-rearing practices are exacerbated by the nature of the service delivery system. In general, service providers do not tend to come into contact with a community-wide acceptance of the use of belts, to continue with our example. Thus, workers often do not develop an understanding of the continuum of acceptable and unacceptable instances of physical punishment. Service providers tend not to see the countless times that belts are picked up in a threat or the times that a child is hit, but not harmed, in a consensus by parent, child, and community that the action is warranted and within acceptable bounds. Rather, the cases in which belts are used and children are left with buckle marks, excessive bruises or welts, and other injuries are the cases more commonly seen by those professionals concerned with child abuse and neglect. And the refrain, "this is how we do things in our culture or community," deceptively resonates to the refrain from identified abusive parents that "this is how my parents raised me, and this is how I will raise my children."

If we are to gain the support of varying cultural groups for the prevention and treatment of child abuse, it would be more fruitful to capitalize on the value in virtually all cultures that children may not be damaged, rather than attempting to eradicate deep-seated cultural practices that, further, have not been demonstrated conclusively to be harmful. An understanding of the spectrum and meaning that physical discipline has within the entire cultural context, its *emic* meaning to child and adult, is a necessity. The words of a black woman, concerned with the rise in juvenile delinquency, illustrate this:

> Children is not like they was. You never had no juvenile, nothin' like that. You never seed no police had nobody's child . . . And there's a law you can't whup your children, and if you can't whup your children, you look for all this to happen. Everybody should know how to whup 'em without beatin' 'em and bruisin' 'em up. (40)

Thus, is it the parents who maintain the right to "whup" their children or the parents who beat and bruise them that are of concern? If a parent claims that the injury he or she has inflicted is culturally acceptable, we need to know the *emic* rules concerning permissible physical punishment. While a culture may sanction parental rights to physically discipline their children, cultures do not and cannot compromise the development and survival of their immature members by permitting disciplinary measures to become harmful to the child. Discipline must be administered under prescribed cultural rules, considering such factors as the child's age, the seriousness of the misbehavior, and the appropriateness of the parents' response. Additionally, discipline in most cultures is administered within the context of a larger community. Informal intervention is likely to occur well before the child is injured or the parent labeled a child abuser (9, 10, 41). In most non-Western cultures, relatives and neighbors rarely "need any invitation to come over and intervene in the case of an unreasonably severe spanking" (42).

In summary, one must pay careful attention to the levels at which cultural analysis is relevant to the assessment of child abuse and neglect. At the first level, a behavior may be acceptable in one culture, but interpreted as abusive or neglectful by another. The cultural context of a behavior, however, must be viewed holistically. No single element of a cultural pattern can be removed from its context and examined in isolation from other integrated aspects of that culture

(43). As Erikson has noted, "[a] system of child care can be said to be a factor making for trust, even when certain items of that tradition taken singly may seem unnecessarily cruel" (44).

In this light, it is difficult to compare diverse practices taken out of their cultural contexts. How would we explain to the East African culture in the example cited earlier that their practice of scarification is abusive, while orthodontic work, for example, in our own culture is not only acceptable but often desirable. When removed from their cultural contexts, both practices would have an *etic* connotation of pain inflicted on a child. However, viewed within their contexts, both are practices that are aimed at benefiting the child by making him or her physically acceptable to other members of the culture. Additionally, for the East African group, scarification is not only cosmetic, but a prerequisite to acceptance as an adult member of the culture (8).

While culturally appropriate formulations are necessary for identifying child abuse and neglect in diverse groups, a stance of absolute cultural relativism is counterproductive. Descriptions of extreme practices, such as a religious cult that drowned all of its children in the ocean, occasionally come to light. In another group that is on the brink of extinction, children of three years of age are turned out of their parental homes to forage food and find shelter as members of small bands of children (45). These extreme instances are more properly discussed under the issue of cultural relativism (46). Nevertheless, it is important not to be misled into a philosophy of acceptance of any behavior adhered to by a large enough aggregate of individuals, such that we are deterred from recognizing legitimate cultural variability.

At the second level, until the cultural context from an *emic* perspective is understood, it will be difficult to distinguish the individual who appears to be abusing a child, but who is in reality adhering to culturally acceptable practices, from the individual who is idiosyncratically abusing his or her own child out of the bounds of cultural acceptability. Idiosyncratic departure from one's culture's continuum of acceptable behaviors is a crucial issue in reconciling *emic* and *etic* assessments of child abuse and neglect. This is so for the most indulgent, as well as the most punitive, of cultural groups. In one Polynesian society, for example, children may be pinched lightly on the mouth for misbehavior. In administering this punishment, one man left a slight scratch on the lip of his grandchild. From our *etic* perspective, this would not constitute serious harm to the child. However, the deviation from culturally accepted practices led the grandfather to be soundly berated by his cultural peers for the abuse, by -*emic* standards, of the child (47).

It is a manageable task to identify idiosyncratic child abuse across culturally diverse groups. Once misinterpretation of cultural practices has been ruled out and the continuum of culturally acceptable behaviors identified by a careful consideration of the specific cultural context, existing principles that distinguish abusive situations can legitimately be employed. For instance, research has indicated that certain children are more likely to be abused (48, 49). Thus, if a parent explains his or her behavior as part of a cultural pattern, but that pattern is applied differently to children in the family, suspicion of abuse or neglect may be justified.

However, again taking into account cultural differences, it is worthwhile to re-member that cultural beliefs can involve differential treatment of children by sex or birth order (18, 50, 51). Moreover, while children in general may be highly valued by a culture, certain children may be less valued than others and more vulnerable to abuse (10). Twins in some Native American cultures, for example, arouse ambivalence such that they may be more vulnerable to abuse or neglect (52).

With respect to the third level, there is a confounding of cultural- and societal-level abuse. Because of the nature of the clientele of social welfare agencies in this country, ethnicity and socioeconomic status are often hopelessly entangled. There can be no doubt that child abuse and neglect occur in all segments of the popula-tion. What remains problematical is whether child abuse and neglect occur with greater frequency among given cultural groups or socioeconomic classes who are subject to increased stress and also to increased scrutiny by public agencies (4–7, 53). Those statistics that exist according to culture, ethnicity, or social class present conflicting evidence about the prevalence of child abuse and neglect in any one group (54–57). Reporting biases and differential patterns of service utilization and availability cause considerable difficulties in assessment. Richard Light's re-analysis of David Gil's data is instructive in this regard (5, 58). Light compared four northern and four southern states according to the incidence of child abuse and neglect among blacks and whites. In the northern states, whites accounted for 27.3% of child abuse and neglect cases, while in the southern states whites ac-counted for 72.9% of the cases. Such differences were not attributable to the proportion of whites and blacks in these states. Rather, at the time the data were gathered, in 1967, services and facilities for black children in the South were scarce. Child abuse and neglect in the black population tended to be dealt with in "informal ways," without being reported to public agencies. In the North, how-ever, most reported cases consisted of poor and minority group families who utilized public welfare services. Since breakdowns by ethnicity and social class often have far-reaching implications for resource allocation, as well as in etiologi-cal formulations, this deserves more careful delimitation.

Western Culture as Conducive to Child Abuse and Neglect

Given this cultural variability in the definition of child abuse and neglect, what can we say about its occurrence cross-culturally? While child abuse and neglect occur with different frequencies or in different forms, all cultures have definitions of abusive or neglectful behavior and contain individuals who deviate from their culture's range of acceptable behaviors. Nevertheless, it appears that the idiosyn-cratic child abuse and neglect that we see in the United States and other Western cultures is relatively rare in small-scale, non-Western cultures (10).

We can conceptualize child-rearing practices around the world as a continuum. Western cultures, the United States in particular, tend to fall on the extreme end of the cross-cultural continuum, with respect to child-rearing practices and be-liefs. Compared to other cultures, parents in Western nations tend to be low in infant indulgence, to initiate child-training practices at an earlier developmental stage, and to be harsher in their expectations of compliance from young children (59, 60). For example, American parents toilet-train children earlier than most cultural groups and are harsher in their enforcement of toilet-training regimes. Many, if not most, non-Western cultures would have difficulty in perceiving the process by which a child learns to urinate and defecate in appropriate areas as "training," rather than as a simple and quite natural process of maturation. It should be of interest that soiling is often a precipitating incident in child abuse in this country.

In addition, Western cultures, again the United States in particular, are often on the extreme end of the cross-cultural continuum in terms of the context in which children are reared. Children are raised more often in isolated nuclear (or now single parent) households. A mother is more often isolated in her role as the exclusive caretaker. Other adults, such as grandmothers or more experienced kinswomen, are less often regular participants in child rearing. And there is less often an accepted folk wisdom or cultural blueprint for child-rearing strategies (59–62). Child rearing has moved more toward the exclusive domain of the biological parents rather than the larger community (9, 10).

It may be that Western child-rearing practices and beliefs, and the circumstances under which we rear children, make us an "at risk" population for child abuse and neglect. If we are already at the far end of the panhuman continuum, then deviations from our norms in an outward direction can be more troublesome. This is particularly so in the absence of the support networks and community embeddedness seen in most other cultures that has been importantly linked to the occurrence of child abuse and neglect (63, 64). If Western cultures believe that children should be toilet-trained at an earlier age than most cultures subscribe to, then individual parents who display age-inappropriate expectations, for example, are operating within a milieu that may be more conducive to the occurrence of child abuse and neglect than would be the case in another cultural context.

This argument is buttressed by the seeming increase in idiosyncratic child abuse with socioeconomic change. For instance, an examination of the ethnographic literature would lead one to postulate that child abuse was extremely rare in traditional Polynesia. Now, however, not only has child abuse increased among Polynesians living in urban areas of New Zealand or Hawaii, but Maori and Polynesians account for a disproportionate number of the reported child abuse and neglect cases (31). While Maori children in New Zealand constituted only 12% of the population in 1972, they accounted for 51% of the neglect cases, 41% of the detrimental environment complaints, 54% of reports of children not being under proper supervision, and 46% of all children committed to the care of the state (65). While this was in part a misinterpretation of Polynesian child-rearing styles (31), the official report concluded that "the present day Maori family is in a state of transition and consequent disruption" (65). Social disorganization, breakdown of traditional support systems, rapidly changing circumstances, and confusion about conflicting models available for child rearing contribute to an increase in child abuse in non-Western cultures (10). But beyond this, there is a rather troubling connection between this change and a movement toward Western child-rearing practices and beliefs. The attractiveness of technology and Western-oriented child-rearing practices can be seen in the tragedies brought about by the use of prepared formulas and bottle feeding in many less-developed nations. The attractiveness of bottle and formula feeding as more "modern" leads parents in some Third World nations to abandon breast feeding, even though their infants suffer from malnutrition because of problems in securing enough formula and sterilizing bottles. Thus, as other cultures emulate the earlier and more severe child-training practices of Western groups, idiosyncratic child abuse and neglect seem to increase. With the awareness that Western child-rearing styles are at the far end of the cross-cultural continuum, a movement toward these practices, in combination with social disorganization, creates a situation ripe for child abuse and one that requires further examination.

Concluding Remarks

A cross-cultural consideration affords us a perspective on child abuse and neglect in our own society and suggests directions to be taken toward culturally appropriate identification and intervention in child abuse and neglect. In this chapter we have explored the manner in which child abuse and neglect are subject to misunderstanding without a careful consideration of the cultural context in which the behavior is embedded. One must be cognizant of *emic* and *etic* perspectives and their potential for both agreement and conflict. This will enhance our abilities to distinguish idiosyncratic child abuse and neglect from cultural differences in child-rearing practices and from societal conditions that are detrimental to children and families.

Acknowledgment

The author is grateful to Hershel K. Swinger and Shelley Brazier for their helpful comments on this article.

References

1. Spradley, James P. 1979. *The Ethnographic Interview.* New York: Holt, Rinehart & Winston.
2. Green, James, and Tong, Collin. 1978. *Cultural Awareness in the Human Services.* Seattle: Center for Social Welfare Research, University of Washington.
3. Malinowski, Bronislaw. 1922. *Argonauts of the Western Pacific.* New York: Dutton.
4. Gelles, Richard. 1973. Child Abuse as Psychopathology: A Sociological Critique and Reformulation. *Am. J. Orthopsychiatry* 43:611–21.
5. Gil, David. 1970. *Violence against Children: Physical Child Abuse in the*

United States. Cambridge: Harvard University Press.

 6. Giovannoni, Jeanne. 1971. Parental Mistreatment: Perpetrators and Victims. *J. Marriage and the Family* 32:649–57.

 7. Pelton, Leroy. 1978. Child Abuse and Neglect: The Myth of Classlessness. *Am. J. Orthopsychiatry* 48:608–17.

 8. Korbin, Jill. 1976. Anthropological Contributions to the Study of Child Abuse. *Child Abuse and Neglect: The International Journal* 1:7–24.

 9. ———. 1979. A Cross-Cultural Perspective on the Role of the Community in Child Abuse and Neglect. *Child Abuse and Neglect: The International Journal* 3:9–18.

10. ———, ed. 1981. *Child Abuse and Neglect: A Cross-Cultural Perspective.* To be published.

11. Swinger, Hershel K. 1979. Black Perspectives on Child Abuse and Neglect. Paper read at the Ninth Annual Child Abuse and Neglect Symposium, Keystone, Colorado.

12. Langness, L. L. 1974. Ritual, Power and Male Dominance in the New Guinea Highlands. *Ethos* 2:189–212.

13. LeVine, Robert A., and LeVine, Barbara B. 1966. *Nyansongo: A Gusii Community in Africa.* New York: Wiley.

14. Hogbin, Ian. 1971. *The Island of Menstruating Men.* San Francisco: Chandler.

15. Barth, Fredrik. 1975. *Ritual and Knowledge among the Baktaman of New Guinea.* New Haven: Yale University Press.

16. Bateson, Gregory. 1958. *Naven.* Stanford: Stanford University Press.

17. Eggan, Dorothy. 1970. Instruction and Affect in Hopi Cultural Continuity. In *From Child to Adult: Studies in the Anthropology of Education,* edited by John Middleton. Garden City, New York: Natural History Press.

18. Johnson, Orna. 1981. The Socio-Economic Context of Child Abuse and Neglect in Native South America. In *Child Abuse and Neglect: A Cross-Cultural Perspective,* edited by Jill Korbin. To be published.

19. Meggitt, Mervin J. 1965. *The Lineage System of the Mae-Enga of Papua New Guinea.* Edinburgh: Oliver and Boyd.

20. Raum, Otto. 1970. Some Aspects of Indigenous Education Among the Chagga. In *From Child to Adult: Studies in the Anthropology of Education,* edited by John Middleton. Garden City, New York: Natural History Press.

21. Benedict, Ruth. 1938. Continuities and Discontinuities in Cultural Conditioning. *Psychiatry* 1:161–67.

22. Royal Anthropological Institute. 1974. The Case of Mrs. Adesanya. *Royal Anthropological Institute News* 4:2.

23. Langness, L. L. 1979. Personal communication.

24. Yeatman, G. W., Shaw, C., Barlow, M. J., and Bartlett, G. 1976. Pseudobattering in Vietnamese Children. *Pediatrics* 58:616.

25. Clark, Margaret. 1959. *Health in the Mexican-American Culture.* Berkeley: University of California Press.

26. Guarnaschelli, J., Lee, J., and Pitts, F. W. 1972. "Fallen Fontanelle" (Caida

de Mollera): A Variant of the Battered Child Syndrome. *J. Am. Med. Assoc.* 222:1545.

27. Sandler, Alan P., and Haynes, Vincent. 1978. Nonaccidental Trauma and Medical Folk Belief: A Case of Cupping. *Pediatrics* 61:921–22.
28. Korbin, Jill. 1975. Field notes.
29. Caudill, William, and Plath, David W. 1966. Who Sleeps by Whom? Parent-Child Involvement in Urban Japanese Families. *Psychiatry* 29:344–66.
30. Whiting, John W. M., Chasdi, Eleanor H., Antonovsky, Helen F., and Ayres, Barbara C. 1966. The Learning of Values. In *People of Rimrock: A Study of Values in Five Cultures,* edited by Evon Z. Vogt and Ethel M. Albert. Cambridge: Harvard University Press.
31. Ritchie, James, and Ritchie, Jane. 1981. Child Rearing and Child Abuse: The Polynesian Context. In *Child Abuse and Neglect: A Cross-Cultural Perspective,* edited by Jill Korbin. To be published.
32. Whiting, Beatrice B. 1972. Work and the Family. Cross-Cultural Perspectives. In *Proceedings of the Conference on Women: Resource for a Changing World.* Cambridge.
33. Hot Line Cools Child Abuse, Neglect Tragedy. *Los Angeles Times,* 19 August 1976.
34. Rogoff, Barbara, Sellers, Martha J., Pirrotta, Sergio, Fox, Nathan, and White, Sheldon H. 1975. Age of Assignment of Roles and Responsibilities to Children. A Cross-Cultural Survey. *Hum. Dev.* 18:353–69.
35. Whiting, John W. M., and Whiting, Beatrice B. 1971. Altruistic and Egoistic Behavior in Six Cultures. In *Cultural Illness and Health,* edited by Laura Nader and Thomas Maretzki. Washington: American Anthropological Association.
36. Whiting, Beatrice B., and Whiting, John W. M. 1975. *Children of Six Cultures: A Psycho-Cultural Analysis.* Cambridge: Harvard University Press.
37. Ember, Carol R. 1973. Feminine Task Assignment and the Social Behavior of Boys. *Ethos* 1:424–39.
38. Korbin, Jill. 1978. Caretaking Patterns in a Rural Hawaiian Community: Congruence of Child and Observer Reports. Ph.D. dissertation, University of California, Los Angeles.
39. Bond, John. 1977. The Samoans. *P.S.R.I. Report* 2:3–4.
40. Snow, Loudell. 1977. Popular Medicine in a Black Neighborhood. In *Ethnic Medicine in the Southwest,* edited by Edward H. Spicer. Tucson: University of Arizona Press.
41. Korbin, Jill. 1981. Very Few Cases: Child Abuse and Neglect in the People's Republic of China. In *Child Abuse and Neglect: A Cross-Cultural Perspective,* edited by Jill Korbin. To be published.
42. Olson, Emelie. 1981. Socio-Economic and Socio-Cultural Contexts of Child Abuse and Neglect in Turkey. In *Child Abuse and Neglect: A Cross-Cultural Perspective,* edited by Jill Korbin. To be published.
43. Parke, Ross D., and Collmer, Candace Whitmer. 1975. *Child Abuse: An Inter-*

disciplinary Analysis. Chicago: University of Chicago Press.

44. Erikson, Erik H. 1963. *Childhood and Society.* 2d ed. New York: Norton.
45. Turnbull, Colin M. 1972. *The Mountain People.* New York: Simon and Schuster.
46. Herskovits, Melville J. 1972. *Cultural Relativism: Perspectives in Cultural Pluralism.* New York: Random House.
47. Firth, Raymond. 1970. Education in Tikopia. In *From Child to Adult: Studies in the Anthropology of Education,* edited by John Middleton. Garden City, New York: Natural History Press.
48. Martin, Harold P. 1976. *The Abused Child: A Multidisciplinary Approach to Developmental Issues and Treatment.* Cambridge: Ballinger.
49. Lynch, Margaret. 1976. Risk Factors in the Child: A Study of Abused Children and Their Siblings. In *The Abused Child: A Multidisciplinary Approach to Developmental Issues and Treatment,* edited by Harold P. Martin. Cambridge: Ballinger.
50. LeVine, Sarah, and LeVine, Robert. 1981. Child Abuse and Neglect in Sub-Saharan Africa. In *Child Abuse and Neglect: A Cross-Cultural Perspective,* edited by Jill Korbin. To be published.
51. Poffenberger, Thomas. 1981. Child Rearing and Social Structure in Rural India: Toward a Cross-Cultural Definition of Child Abuse and Neglect. In *Child Abuse and Neglect: A Cross-Cultural Perspective,* edited by Jill Korbin. To be published.
52. Levy, Jerrold. 1964. The Fate of Navajo Twins. *Am. Anthropol.* 66:883–87.
53. Fontana, Vincent J. 1973. *Somewhere a Child Is Crying: Maltreatment—Causes and Prevention.* New York: MacMillan.
54. Lauer, Brian, Ten Broeck, Elsa, and Grossman, Moses. 1974. Battered Child Syndrome: Review of 130 Patients with Controls. *Pediatrics* 54:67–70.
55. Ebbin, J. A., Gollub, M. H., Stein, A. M., and Wilson, M. G. 1969. Battered Child Syndrome at Los Angeles General Hospital. *Am. J. Dis. Child.* 118:660.
56. Altmeier, William A., III, Vietze, Peter M., Sherrod, Kathryn B., Sandler, Howard M., Falsey, Susan, and O'Connor, Susan. 1979. Prediction of Child Maltreatment during Pregnancy. *J. Child Psychiatry* 18:205–18.
57. Department of Health, Education, and Welfare. *Child Abuse and Neglect: The Problem and Its Management. An Overview of the Problem.* Washington: Government Printing Office.
58. Light, Richard J. 1973. Abused and Neglected Children in America: A Study of Alternative Policies. *Harvard Educational Rev.* 43:556–98.
59. Whiting, John W. M., and Child, Irvin L. 1953. *Child Training and Personality.* New Haven: Yale University Press.
60. Minturn, Leigh, and Lambert, William. 1964. *Mothers of Six Cultures: Antecedents of Child Rearing.* New York: Wiley.
61. Whiting, Beatrice B. 1971. Folk Wisdom and Childrearing. Paper read at American Association for the Advancement of Science Symposium on Sources of Knowledge for Child Rearing.

62. Mead, Margaret. 1970. *Culture and Commitment: A Study of the Generation Gap*. Garden City, New York: Natural History Press.

63. Garbarino, James. 1978. Defining the Community Context for Parent-Child Relations: The Categories of Child Maltreatment. *Child Dev*. 49:604–16.

64. Green, James W. 1978. The Role of Cultural Anthropology in the Education of Social Service Personnel. *J. Sociology and Social Welfare* 5:214–29.

65. Fergusson, D. M., Fleming, J., and O'Neill, D. P. 1972. *Child Abuse in New Zealand*. Wellington, New Zealand: Government Printer.

3 Developmental Deficits Which Limit Interpersonal Skills

Ray E. Helfer

The development of any strategy to assist children and young adults caught up in the cycle of child abuse and neglect will be facilitated by an understanding of the basic developmental deficiencies these young people are experiencing. These deficiencies stem directly from inappropriate experiences during the critical developmental years of early childhood.

The purpose of this chapter is to review these basic developmental deficiencies, as well as the mechanisms by which they occurred. Intervention strategies based on these concepts are presented in Chapter 24. Both this chapter and Chapter 24 summarize material presented in detail in Part I of *Childhood Comes First: A Crash Course in Childhood for Adults* (1). The hope is that the reader will be encouraged to explore these concepts in more detail, modifying them appropriately to fit the individual need. These modifications will help us become more sophisticated in our attempts to assist those caught up in the cycle of abuse and neglect.

The Developmental Process

One should perceive an individual, as he proceeds from infancy through adolescence and into adulthood, as moving through dynamic and ever-changing periods. What happens during this day-to-day process has a most critical effect on functioning capabilities later in life. Many things are *supposed* to happen during childhood which permit a child to formulate and practice the skills necessary to function as a young adult. Those who interact with the child during these critical years have a great impact on a significant portion of this process. While certain skills a child learns seem to be rather "automatic," being influenced, for the most part, solely by time and growth, other developmental achievements must be carefully nurtured and modeled throughout the childhood years, for the child to become a reasonably functional young adult. An example of the more automatic compo-

Ray E. Helfer, M.D., is with the Department of Pediatrics and Human Development, College of Human Medicine, Michigan State University.

nents of development are motor functions, such as walking, running, and toilet training, whereas the latter developmental capabilities include interpersonal skills, i.e., the ability to get along with others and to function in an acceptable and constructive manner during the interpersonal process.

Imagine that the developmental process of a child moving from infancy through adolescence is like a missile and its payload moving through a trajectory from the launching pad to its celestial goal. The launching pad is birth, and the celestial goal is adulthood. Anything that happens to modify the trajectory will have an influence on the ultimate landing site of the payload. Those who guide the path of the missile toward the celestial body must be readily available and well trained to modify any unexpected and serious deviations in the process. To complete this analogy, the actual trajectory is child development, and the parents, family members, teachers, and others who interact with the child during these critical years are those who have the responsibility for the guidance system.

Consider, for example, an infant who is separated temporarily from her mother immediately after birth because of the illness of the mother. This is a serious developmental insult in the child's life, and every means must be made use of to correct the negative effect, if a permanent "scarring" of the developmental process is to be prevented. Consider also a three-year-old child who, because of serious illness, is placed in a hospital and undergoes surgery and a variety of other painful and difficult procedures, during which time she may well be separated from those who have the most impact on her "developmental guidance." If this insult continues for a period of three or four weeks, there may be a slowing down of growth, and there certainly will be negative effects upon the developmental process occurring during this critical period. In most situations in which the child has experienced a normal childhood prior to entering the hospital and lives in an environment where modifications can be made in order to overcome the insult to her "developmental trajectory," the effects of these insults may not be permanent. On the other hand, a child with an environment that is little more than one insult after another to this developmental process (for example, a child reared in an environment of never-ending violence as the solution to interpersonal problems) may well have her developmental process further scarred by the hospital experience.

In the discussion that follows, emphasis will be given to those developmental traits which seem to be most deficient in young adults reared in the abusive and neglectful environment. Additional emphasis is also given to those developmental deficiencies which affect interaction between child and parents. These, of course, are the developmental skills which demonstrate the most serious deficiencies in those reared in an abusive environment.

The Developmental Deficits: Growing Up to Be "Out of Control"

The Senses

Understanding the importance of serious developmental deficiencies of the senses, experienced by those who have been reared in an abusive environment, requires knowledge of the normal development of the senses (see Dr. Ann Wilson's review of the subject in Chapter 25). Dr. Wilson points out that an infant has a highly sophisticated system of touch, taste, smell, vision, and hearing. She also reviews importance of the new baby's vestibular system. There are six senses, rather than five, if one considers the significance of the sense of movement. One must not lose sight of the fact that the newborn infant is not only very capable in these six sensory areas, but also very dependent upon them for the establishment of a communication system with the world about him (1).

Now consider the environment which supresses the development of this sensory system. An infant or young child is supposed to learn that use of the senses results in positive feedback, a nice feeling. Crying brings someone to hold, rock, and comfort the infant; looking into mother's eyes makes the child feel loved and wanted; being touched is nice, most of the time; the smells of mother's house remind the child of positive feelings, and so on. On balance, the senses should be conditioned positively. Only on occasion is it necessary to have negative reactions to certain tastes, smells, etc. (2, 3).

Consider what happens when touching hurts, *most of the time:* smells about the house bring on very negative feelings, *most of the time;* mom's eyes show the threat of a swat; when the child listens to mom and dad talk, he becomes afraid, since the messages he hears are threats, screams, and anger. Over and over, day after day, the child is bombarded with negative sensory messages, messages that truly force the senses to "shut down" (see Dr. Wilson's discussion on habituation, p. 415). The child learns that it is far safer not to listen, not to look, and not to be touched, for when these senses are used, he hurts much more often than he feels good.

As a result, the child's senses become "muted," used only when absolutely necessary. This does not mean that if an individual reared in this manner were to have his hearing or vision tested, the results would indicate abnormalities. What is meant is that those reared to mute their senses have learned, very early in childhood, that their lives are less confused and hurt less when people do not look them in the eye, listen to what they say, touch them, or get too close.

The significance of these deficiencies in the senses is great. The ability to communicate with those about you and with the environment in general is severely limited. Holding loved ones very close and looking into their eyes carries messages that few can express with words. When one enters the home in which one was reared, the overall reaction to the unique smells and visual and auditory stimuli should be positive and comforting, rather than "my God, this hurts!"

Children and adults reared in abuse have had their senses trained in such a way that to use them for receiving or transmitting positive messages is not part of their communication systems. While this makes it difficult for these young people to communicate with their peers, think of the results when someone with muted senses tries to establish a communication system with a newborn infant. Recall that new babies are *dependent* upon their six senses for communication (4). Little wonder young adults, reared in abuse, find interaction with their new babies so difficult. The result is a mother-baby or father-baby interaction that breaks down all too early in their relationship.

The World of Abnormal Rearing (W.A.R.)

The senses are not the only tools for learning how to interact with our environment or those about us. Many other skills must be learned in childhood, skills which enhance the young adult's ability to interact and feel that "I'm a very special person."

A few years ago the concept of the "World of Abnormal Rearing" (W.A.R.) was proposed (5). This was devised in order to better understand what occurs when one's childhood does not provide a very favorable environment in which to learn basic interpersonal skills. Adults who are victims of the W.A.R. truly have "missed out on childhood," that is, missed learning many of those basic skills necessary to interact with others. Being aware of the W.A.R. cycle and the implications it has for the developing child and the adult will help prepare for the relearning phase (see Chapter 24). Understanding, and then overcoming, many of these basic developmental deficits requires a knowledge of their origin.

A very special note must be made at this point. Referring to W.A.R. children or adults from the W.A.R., does *not* imply that all, or even most, were physically beaten. For every adult who was actually beaten as a child, there are probably scores who look back at their childhoods and say, "I wasn't beaten, but it was really a bad experience." Some W.A.R. children are beaten, some are sexually molested, others are ignored, some are belittled, some find themselves so controlled that they cannot function outside of their own homes, and so on. This W.A.R. is hell, no matter how it manifests itself. Specific intervention programs are intended to help those adults who are trying to break loose from its tentacles, break out of the cycle.

Before discussing the relearning aspect of treatment, which will help in breaking loose from the holds that the W.A.R. has on those who lived through it, the various segments of this cycle must be reviewed. Understanding these concepts is essential to learning ways of breaking out. This W.A.R. is a never-ending cycle, passing from one generation to another. Unless a gallant effort to escape is made, and escape is possible for most, the future will most likely be a copy of the past. The "World of Abnormal Rearing" is diagrammed in figure 3.1.

Needs Met and Delayed Gratification

One of the most important skills that a child must learn, during the brief years of childhood, is how to get his or her needs met in an acceptable manner and when the most appropriate time is to seek this fulfillment. What behaviors or actions are acceptable at home, at school, or in the play yard with friends? All people have needs, and we all must fall back on the foundations laid in childhood as we develop ways to have these needs met.

An infant is hungry, cold, and wet—his needs are very specific. He cries and hopes the cries bring a soft mother or father with food, a warm body, and dry clothes. As life progresses, crying is reserved for more extreme needs which often

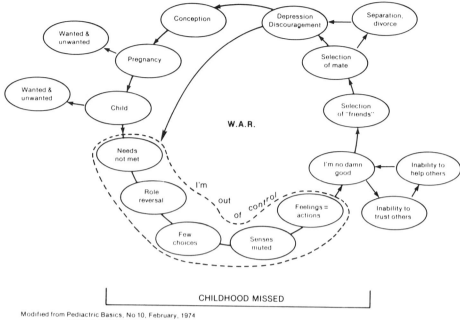

Figure 3.1

World-of-abnormal-rearing cycle

are stimulated by pain or fear. A two-year-old may not cry to get the desired ice cream; rather, he may resort to a temper tantrum. Many parents find this an undesirable behavior and work hard to teach the child to substitute for the hollering and kicking a "please" and "thank you."

A young mother said to me, as she reflected about a recent disagreement she had had with her boyfriend, "Isn't it interesting that my boyfriend beats me just like my husband used to?" Yes, I admitted that I found that interesting. I needed to hear more; so I said, "You find that interesting? Tell me, when was the last time your boyfriend beat you?"

"Oh, last weekend. We went out, and he got mad at me for flirting with another guy. When we got home, he beat me."

"Didn't it hurt?" I asked.

"Yeah, a bit. Not too much, though. Anyway, I know he likes me," she added.

Now, that raised my interest; so I replied with, "How do you know that he likes you?"

"Why would he get jealous and beat me if he didn't like me?" she responded with great logic.

That statement troubled me. It certainly made sense, but I could not muster the strength to follow through just then. A pediatrician has a built in escape from such stressful moments. He can always say, "Well, I must get on to examining your child." This ploy is used by some at the outset of the visit to avoid even the slightest chance of discussing these touchy issues. The visit ended, and I found myself writing in big letters on the child's record a reminder to delve further into this issue on the next visit.

    Later, as this matter was discussed further with this woman, I learned more about the beatings her husband had given her and how she had interpreted them. Then I asked the key question, "How was it when you were little?"

    "Oh, not bad with mom," she commented.

    "How about your dad?"

    "Well, he was pretty quiet and didn't pay much attention to me."

    "Didn't that bother you?" I asked.

    "Yes, and I used to bug him a lot."

    "What did he do when you bugged him?" I continued.

    "He'd hit me a lot," she said.

    "Why, then, did you bug him?"

    She lifted her head, looked directly at me, and for the first time our eyes met as she said very slowly, "Gettin' hit is better than being left alone."

This young woman learned very early in life that when she had a need for a man's attention she had to "bug" him so much that he would eventually show her that he was aware of her presence by beating her. She was willing to put up with the hurt to have her needs met.

All children struggle with this critical component of development. If a child's environment is reasonably stable and secure and the parents have a good understanding of what the child's needs are and what the child must do and learn to have these needs met, then the outcome will be a child who learns acceptable skills for meeting these needs and when the best time is to use them.

The development of the ability and willingness to delay one's gratification is a slow, but steady, process which progresses throughout the child-developmental "trajectory." If you ask a three-year-old if he wants a stick of gum now or a whole pack on Sunday, he'll more than likely take the stick now. Postponing the need until Sunday requires considerably more developmental skills than are present in most three-year-old children. He first must know what Sunday is, that Sunday will happen, that a pack of gum is bigger than a stick, and that he can trust you enough to be around on Sunday and to follow through with your promise. Eventually the child learns these concepts and, depending on his needs and the nature of the immediate offer, the satisfying of this need may, indeed, be postponed. Delaying gratification is a very high-level skill, one which requires considerable training and modeling during childhood to learn.

Children who are abused are not so fortunate. "Why wait? Tomorrow is never better than today." For them tomorrow never comes; it is always today!

These children find themselves in a world of unrealistic expectations. Their parents have little understanding of childhood and make demands that are far in excess of a child's capabilities. Babies shouldn't cry much, should eat well, smile early, and remind mom or dad of someone the parent likes; two-year-olds should shape up, not explore the cupboards and pull out the pots, not spill anything, and eat well. "Look after *me*," the child is told by the parent. "To hell with your needs," he hears in a variety of ways. One of the greatest struggles of the W.A.R. is the constant striving to meet the parents' *unrealistic* expectations, which they have set for the child. From success at school, to caring for mom and dad, the demands are *extreme*.

A child who struggles with these issues day after day learns, as the years of childhood wear on, that his needs are not being met; even worse, he is not learning the necessary skills to get these needs met. He is much too busy looking after the needs of his parents and other adults around him. If this weren't bad enough, the behaviors that are learned to meet the bare, essential needs are often extreme, inappropriate, and maladaptive.

Role Reversal and Responsibility

A child must learn, during the brief years of childhood, that *he* or *she* is responsible for his or her own actions. This is a concept that is acquired very gradually. It is tested by reality during adolescence, as the parents must accept less and less responsibility for a child's behavior and the adolescent begins to accept more and more. This can be an exciting and frustrating time. As the teenage years move on, one can see this maturing occur. For example, "It's your responsibility to decide," is constantly heard around our house these days. Our ten-year-old daughter wanted to watch a "special" on television on a school night. Thus began the checklist: homework done, pajamas on, teeth brushed, reading done? "Yes" was the reply to all. "OK, sounds like a good special to watch," I commented. The responsibility she took for getting ready to watch the "special" could now be rewarded. "I don't want to get up and peddle my papers;" "I don't want to mow the neighbor's lawn;" "I don't want to take grandmother to church;" yet all were commitments which had been made previously. Responsibility and follow-through are very difficult parts of childhood.

Children reared in the W.A.R. find themselves, in late adolescence, ill prepared to accept the responsibility for their own actions. There seem to be two extremes—either they aren't required to accept any responsibility for what they have done, having been protected and/or "bailed out" all their lives, or they are forced to accept the responsibility for the inadequacies of their parents. This latter is so common, and so confusing, that it requires further explanation.

Some call this turnabout "role reversal." The child accepts the role of parent, and the parent takes on the role of the child. Role reversal is easy to understand when one sees a little three-year-old soothing her crying mother, and later the same mother ignoring her crying child. The constant need to reverse roles, which often ends in failure and frustration, may well result in "learned helplessness" for this child (6).

All children, at varying ages of their development, want to please and care for "mommy" or "daddy." This is especially true in times of stress or crisis. "Thank God for children when the chips are down," for they really come through and help out. However, the extreme, the constant, the unrealistic expectations are most devastating to the developing child. Children have needs of their own that also must be met.

This aspect of role reversal, which is demonstrated by the child taking care of the parent, is relatively easy to understand. More subtle and more difficult to comprehend is when this role reversal requires and trains the child to assume the responsibility for his or her parents' errors. This feeling is embedded into the child's mind from a very early age in a variety of ways, encouraged by remarks such as these:

"If it weren't for you . . . "

"If you hadn't spilled that, I wouldn't have gotten mad."

"I hit you because you were bad."

"Your father would still be around if you . . . "

"I could have gone back to work if you hadn't . . . "

And so on and on. This child slowly begins "the guilt trip" which accompanies true role reversal. He becomes convinced that he is to blame for the parents' inability to handle crises, finances, etc. This guilt lasts into adulthood and manifests itself in a variety of ways. The ability to separate one's own responsibility from that of another is a learned function that develops in all children who are reared more normally.

This is a very gradually learned concept. A three-year-old finds the separation of his wishes from what happens very difficult, in fact almost impossible. "My mommy is mean; she won't buy me the ice cream. I wish mommy would go away forever." Ten minutes later the mother rushes out to a movie, leaves the child with a sitter, and the child believes his wish came true.

Our eleven-year-old daughter was pouring milk from a gallon jug into a glass one day. There was great shaking and grunting, but she finally succeeded. Her fifteen-year-old brother picked up the jug and mimicked his sister's every action, making fun of her. I made it very clear that I didn't find his behavior at all humorous, indicating my displeasure over what he did. Ten minutes later, the eleven-year-old said, "I got John in trouble."

"No, Betty, " I replied, "John got John in trouble."

"But if I hadn't of shook, he wouldn't have gotten into trouble."

"John got into trouble for what *he* did, not what you did," I replied—a very difficult concept to comprehend, but one of major importance. Learning that one is responsible for one's own actions and not the actions of another is *not* built into the abusive environment. In fact, it teaches the opposite.

Decision Making and Problem Solving

A child must learn the skill of making decisions during the protected years of childhood, when a "goof up" or bad decision won't be all that harmful. Options must be identified and weighed, priorities set, and a plan or solution agreed upon. One of our teenagers lamented the other day, "Decisions are too tough; you decide for me." Our seven-year-old is constantly asking, "What do you think I should do?" Sometimes we fall into the trap of making the decision for them. It often is much quicker and less painful. But a trap it is.

A young seventeen-year-old mother once called me and said, "I must see you; I'm going crazy."

When she arrived sixty minutes later, I asked, "Why do you think you are going crazy?"

"I have all these things in my head, and I don't know what to do."

"What things?" I asked. I thought she was going to tell me about some delusion or psychotic fantasy. Nothing of the sort occurred.

"Well," she said, "I'm bleeding, and my aunt is trying to get my baby; my boyfriend calls me collect, I can't say no; my rent is due; I don't know what to do with my check; my food is gone . . ." and on and on.

"Betty," I said, "stop! Tell me the last time you made a decision."

She thought for a full two or three minutes and finally said, "I don't think I ever made one." Later she did recall she made the decision to stop her birth control pills at sixteen so that she could become pregnant. She also had decided who the father was going to be.

Children must learn, at two and four and eight and sixteen, how to make decisions. Choices, choices! This is the key. "Do you want vanilla or chocolate ice cream?" "Do you want a cookie or a piece of cake?" "Do you want to go to bed *with* or *without* a treat?" "I don't want to go to bed," is the reply. "The choice is the treat, not the bed," the parent responds.

For years I used to struggle with two- or three-year-old children each time I wanted to look in their ears. The problem was clear. I used to say, "Can I look in your ears?"

"No!" he replied.

"Hold him down," I'd say to the mother, as I proceeded to look in the ears. The child screamed and hollered, vomited and peed all over me.

Now I say, "Which ear should I look in first?" With this I give him a choice. As the little hand moves toward one ear, I say, "That's going to be the one, isn't it?" His head nods slowly, and I exclaim with great excitement, "How did you know that was the ear I wanted to look in first?" Now I go home with little vomit and pee on my clothes and feel much less exhausted.

Choices lead to priority setting and decision making. But one ought not to give children choices when there are none.

"Do you want to shovel the driveway?" I ask my son.

"No," he says.

"Shovel the driveway," I command.

"Why did you ask me if I didn't have a choice?"

"Good point," I respond, "I'll figure out the answer while you're shoveling the driveway."

A clear "goof" on my part.

Children who find themselves trapped in the W.A.R. rarely are given choices and rarely are allowed to make decisions. They are just told what to do or given no directions whatsoever. Even worse, they are often encouraged to decide and then are told what a stupid decision they made.

Day after day, young adults demonstrate how ill prepared they are in decision making. What are their options and how can the priorities be established? Without the early experiences, with trials and errors in childhood, these decisions become very major obstacles.

One young seventeen-year-old mother related her story to me. "At nine, the sex started; by twelve I was enjoying it; by sixteen I hated it, and finally I hated myself." Then she added, "Do you know what one of the worse parts was; he never asked me if I wanted it?" This woman not only had the insult of incest, but lost all control over her life. She had no choice.

Trusting Others

As development continues, it enters the realm of interrelating with others. Children must learn, during their early childhood, and have it reinforced throughout adolescence, that there are some people who truly can be trusted and others who cannot. A two-year-old falls off his tricycle and hurts his knee; he runs, crying, to his mother or father, is picked up and consoled. "That really hurts," he hears. Two minutes later his knee is a bit better, and he returns to his play, having learned that knees get better and people are helpful, especially moms and dads.

Today I stayed home to work on this book. Everything was arranged for the house to be empty all day. Just as I was making progress, noontime arrived, and my seven-year-old barged in and said, "What's for lunch?"

"You were supposed to stay at school for lunch today," I said.

"I was?" he replied. As I found the cheese to make us both a grilled sandwich, the boy said, "Who goofed, you or me?"

"I guess I did," I replied; "I forgot to remind you to stay at school." After the sandwiches were eaten and we had chatted a bit, I said, "I'm glad you came home to keep me company when I ate my lunch."

"You are?" he exclaimed with obvious delight.

Look at these two incidents. What did the two-year-old and the seven-year-old learn? "It is rather nice being around people who like you. When I am in trouble and hurt or just when I want to chat, there usually is someone around." Suppose the two-year-old had heard, as his knee was hurting, "You clumsy kid, you fell off your trike again. If it weren't for you I could have some peace around here." Suppose the seven-year-old had heard, as he rushed in from school, "Oh God, are you home? You knew you were supposed to stay at school today. How do you expect me to get anything done with you around here?"

Trust is learned very gradually, as a child moves from infancy through adolescence. Trust is built. Children not only learn whom to trust, but what these people can and cannot be expected to do. By the time an adolescent wants the car, a firm foundation of trust and realistic expectations should already have been laid.

W.A.R. children find themselves without such a foundation, or a very weak one at best. Instead of learning, as a young child, that people can be trusted, they learn that people hurt or disappoint:

"Don't come to me with your problems. I have enough of my own."

"You dumb idiot, you screwed up again."

"I brought you five-hundred miles to play tennis in this tournament and you really blew it."

Over and over the W.A.R. child learns that when you go to others and seek help, you usually end up wishing you hadn't asked. This is especially devastating when the other person is mom or dad. If you cannot trust them at five or ten or fifteen years old, whom can you trust?

I asked an eight-year-old girl, reared in wealth, but also abused, "What do you do when you have a problem?"

Her immediate reply was, "It's best if I deal with those myself." She had learned, in her brief eight years, that asking others for help led to trouble.

One of the basic bail-out methods which adults have when crises arise or a problem develops is to ask someone whom they can depend upon for assistance. When one's childhood fails to teach the basic skills of how and whom to trust, this bail-out process, so critical to adults and children, is in serious jeopardy. The result—retreat, withdraw, be alone!

"Isn't it tough to be alone all the time," I asked an attractive, young, divorced mother of two children.

"Not really," she responded.

I said nothing for a full minute, and then she continued in a very soft voice directed at the floor, "No man can hurt me when I'm alone." She knew, from some very bitter experiences as a child and young adult, that being alone with a man was very risky and often led to pain. Her solution, to isolate herself from the world, was safer.

The true defense when one does not trust others is to keep people out of one's life. Keep in mind the discussion above about touching and looking. "If I don't look at you, maybe you cannot hurt me so much." If all this weren't hard enough, many have the added burden of the never-ending guilt of role reversal: "If I don't take care of mom or dad, I feel awful."

One young, seventeen-year-old mother demonstrated her concept of trust this way. When I realized that she was having problems telling her social worker some of her personal concerns, I asked why. She said, "'Cause if I tell the social worker about these things, then I have to tell my boyfriend."

"Tell your boyfriend," I added.

"Sure, that way he knows he can trust me."

Telling all was her way of gaining trust. The exact opposite is true of healthier, trusting relationships: "I trust you so much that you don't have to tell me everything." Child abuse and neglect truly distort the concept of trust.

Feelings and Actions

A child must learn, on his developmental "trajectory" toward adulthood, that how he feels and what he does are separate, but related, issues. This is such a critical point for an adult to understand that it must be emphasized over and over. Some will pick up this concept immediately; others will be most confused. The following examples may help explain.

Two of our sons, when aged ten and twelve, were playing hockey on opposite teams. The younger boy skated better than the older one and rather regularly passed him by as the scores piled up. On one of these passes, the older became furious, couldn't handle his anger any longer and tripped his younger brother. The younger of the two got mad and hit his bigger brother with his hockey stick. They both came home angry and crying. Finally the story came out—a golden opportunity to separate feelings from actions. After they both had settled down and I had a chance to plan a course of action, I said to the older boy, "I don't blame you for getting mad at your brother for skating around you all the time. I'd get mad too. *But* that doesn't give you the right to trip him."

"I don't blame you," I said as I turned to the smaller boy, "for getting mad at your brother for tripping you, but that doesn't give you the right to hit him with your stick."

Had I imposed a penalty of no hockey playing the next day, without separating how they felt from what they did, they might have thought that they were being penalized for their feelings, as well as their actions. The message they should hear is, "How you felt is understandable. What you did about it was inappropriate. For the *doing* you're being penalized."

Throughout childhood, this message must be delivered over and over:

"You *like* Susie, give her a *call*."

"You're *mad* at Jimmy, *tell* him how you feel."

"You feel *sad, crying* may help."

"You are *excited* about the game, *tell* me about it."

As these children grow into adolescents, they gradually begin to learn that they have *control* over what they *do;* they can *control* their actions. Even though feelings are hard to control, some satisfaction comes from knowing that what you do about them is your decision, your responsibility, under your control.

Adults who have been brought up in an abusive environment find this concept very difficult to understand. One mother said, "I get so mad that I scream and holler and say awful things to my kids, and then I feel awful too." Another said, "I got angry at my baby and hit her."

To both of their comments I replied, "Do you realize you are talking about two things?" Their faces revealed confusion, and both replies were almost identical: "What do you mean, two things?"

This inability to separate feelings from actions manifests itself in many ways. W.A.R. children and W.A.R. adults frequently find themselves in serious difficulty because of this deficit. Anger leads to lashing out, for some, and complete withdrawal and guilt, for others. The extremes of actions are often used.

"How can I tell my boyfriend I like him?" one young woman asked me.

"What do you do to show a man you like him?" I replied.

"Go to bed with him," she said.

"Right away?" I asked.

"What else can I do?"

This young girl found that she had no trouble finding a man to go to bed with her, but somehow it always turned our poorly. She had missed, in her childhood, learning the little inuendos of expressing her feelings. She didn't know how to touch his hand, look into his eyes, say "I like you," or smile at the right time. She replaced all of this with only one action for her feeling of liking—sex.

The major message is that how one feels and what one does are separate, but related, issues. One can control much of one's actions. A child must learn he or she has this degree of control. When abused children and adults are taught that feeling and action are the same, they are misled to believe that they have little, if any, control over their lives.

A constant source of confusion relates to feelings of guilt. "Is that an OK feeling?'' is a frequent question. ''Certainly,'' I respond, ''but you have to decide how to handle, act on, that feeling.'' This concept is rarely appreciated by those reared in the W.A.R.

And On and On It Goes

The abused child continues, around and around, learning fewer and fewer skills of interaction. He is ''out of touch'' with the world about him; control over his life is lost, actually never gained. What better way to train a child to become a nonentity, functioning in the extremes, than to:

Mute his senses.
Fail to teach him how to get his needs met.
Teach him he is responsible for the action of others.
Give him little practice in problem solving.
Convince him he cannot trust others.
Show him, day after day, that feelings and actions are one and the same.

The results! The results are contained in this book. The W.A.R. has convinced its victims that they are ''no damn good,'' unable to help others, have minimal skills for finding and keeping real, close friends, much less a suitable mate, and are easily discouraged and depressed (see fig. 3.1).

At that point in their young adult lives, they may enter the ''I think I'll have a family'' route as a solution to their loneliness. Some bypass this option and go on to work or school, trying to cope as best possible, using what few skills they learned in their childhood. Some make it, many do not.

Considerable work can be done to facilitate the breaking out of this cycle (see Chapter 24). Even more can be achieved if the cycle is interrupted before its damage has been too severe. Both of these issues are examined in this book.

References

1. Helfer, Ray E. 1978. *Childhood Comes First: A Crash Course in Childhood for Adults.* East Lansing, Mich.: privately printed.
2. Stern, Daniel. 1971. Mother and Infant at Play: The Dyadic Interaction Involving Facial, Vocal and Gaze Behaviors. In *The Effect of the Infant on Its Caregiver,* edited by M. Lewis and L. Rosenblum. New York: Wiley.
3. Montague, Ashley. 1971. *Touching.* New York: Columbia University Press.
4. The film *The Amazing Newborn* (distributed by Ross Company, Columbus, Ohio) demonstrates this capacity extremely well.
5. Helfer, Ray E. 1973. Presidential Address, Ambulatory Pediatrics Association (*Pediatrics Basics,* No. 10, February 1974, pp. 4–7).
6. See the article on role reversal in *Children Today,* November–December 1977.

4 Psychodynamic Factors in Child Abuse

Brandt Steele

Since our previous reports (1, 2, 3) of abusive parents, we have continued to study the behaviors, life histories, and psychological functioning of those parents and other persons who abuse the infants and children for whom they are providing care. Although our original work began in relation to the seriously injured children described under the title "the battered-child syndrome," we soon began including children who were less severely physically injured, those who were diagnosed as failing to thrive as a result of maternal deprivation, or those suffering from other forms of neglect. We have also seen those who were primarily suffering from emotional abuse, and particularly during the last few years, children, often older, who have been sexually abused; and we have evaluated and treated their caretakers. Thus, over the past two decades, we have covered a wide range of forms of maltreatment of children and studied a great variety of those parents or other caretakers who carry out their tasks in less than desirable or adequate ways.

The term *child abuse* will be used in this chapter to cover this whole spectrum of maltreatment of children. It is an extremely complex group of human behaviors characterized by maladaptive interactions between infants and children of all ages and their caretakers. We speak of it as maladaptive in the directly biological sense. After ensuring his or her own survival, the prime task of any individual is to take part in the production of the next generation of individuals in a condition most likely to ensure survival of the species. Child abuse is, therefore, maladaptive in the sense that, to a greater or lesser degree, it damages immature members of our species in such a way as to interfere with their optimum development and to impair their adaptive survival abilities. Abuse involves children of all ages, from infancy through adolescence, and caretakers of both sexes, all ages, and with various kinds of relationships to the child. The caretakers who abuse are most often biological parents, but they may also be stepparents, adoptive parents, foster parents, grandparents, siblings, other relatives, babysitters, parental

Brandt Steele, M.D., is with the Department of Psychiatry, University of Colorado Medical Center, Denver.

paramours, or other nonrelated persons such as teachers, either in or out of the household, who are involved in the child-caring tasks. Exceptions to this usual pattern of the caretakers being the abusers are the cases of infanticide and of serious injuries inflicted upon children by psychotic or seriously mentally disturbed strangers and the sexual abuse of children perpetrated by strangers, often with the use of force.

In the face of such a variety of interactions and participants, it would seem difficult to find any common factors in abusive behavior. Yet it is possible, through careful study of the life histories and behaviors of the many kinds of abusers, to discern common themes and recurrent patterns of psychic function. In our work with abusive caretakers over the past two decades, we have never seen two who were exactly alike. Despite all their differences, however, they share a number of characteristics which they exhibit in varying degrees. These characteristics will be discussed in some detail below.

Child abuse is an extremely complex problem and, in addition to the impact it has on both its victims and perpetrators, it has many ramifications in the fields of medicine, sociology, law, psychology, child development, psychiatry, and cultural anthropology. All of these disciplines have something valuable to contribute to the elucidation and comprehension of child abuse phenomena. Our own personal bias is to understand the problem within the framework of human psychology and, more specifically, according to psychoanalytic concepts of human development and mental functioning. While we thus follow what is essentially a psychiatric approach to the problem of child abuse, we do not mean to imply by this that the child abuse syndrome is a mental illness in the usual sense of that term, nor can it be easily subsumed under any of the commonly accepted psychiatric nosological entities. Some caretakers who abuse children may also show characteristic symptoms of schizophrenia or depression or any of the various kinds of neuroses and character disorders. These occur with approximately the same frequency as they do in the general population, and the abuse is not necessarily a part of such psychic states. Many abusers have emotional problems which are also commonly seen in what are called "narcissistic character disorders" or "borderline states." Yet, child abuse is not necessarily associated with either of these two entities. In general, it seems to be useful to consider child abusive behavior as a group of abnormal patterns of caretaker-child interactions related to psychological characteristics which can exist concurrently, but quite independently, of any psychiatric disorder or even in otherwise relatively healthy personalities. Abusive, neglecting behavior is not considered to be purely haphazard or impulsive, but rather to be understood as a particular constellation of emotional states and specific adaptive responses which have their roots in the earliest months of life.

By describing the intrapsychic state as the most necessary and basic matrix of abusive behavior, we do not mean to disregard the importance of other factors. Depending upon what particular population of abusers is studied or sampled, it can be shown with statistical significance that abusive, neglecting behavior can be precipitated or escalated by such things as poverty, bad housing, unemployment, marital strife, alcoholism, drug abuse, difficult pregnancies and deliveries, lack of education, lack of knowledge of child development, prematurity and illness of infants, deaths in the family, and a host of other things. Any of these can become a critical stress, precipitating a crisis, ending in abuse or neglect. An excellent review of social factors in abuse is that by Straus (4). In every case, such factors warrant our most intense concern and all our efforts toward alleviation. At the same time, we must realize that awareness of the importance of such social factors in situations of abuse does not answer what we consider more basic questions: Why, under circumstances of stress, do some persons respond with abusive behaviors, while others do not? Why do the majority of people in a low-socioeconomic group treat their offspring with adequate kindness, consideration, and love without abuse, even in critical times? And, conversely, why do some people with adequate housing and wealth seriously harm their infants? We feel, in our efforts to answer these and similar questions, that it is necessary to turn to a deeper, more subtle psychological understanding of these individuals. As noted above, no two abusers are exactly alike, but we commonly find among them a certain constellation of emotional states and patterns of reaction which we consider to be essential, basic ingredients in the usual syndromes of abuse and neglect. As reported in previous studies (1, 2, 3), it is common for abusive or neglectful caretakers to give a history of having experienced some significant degree of neglect, with or without accompanying physical abuse. In our experience it is quite rare to see an abuser who does not relate this history if questioned appropriately. This finding has been confirmed by other investigators (5, 6, 7, 8, 9), but has also been questioned by other workers who have not obtained the history of early life neglect or abuse with as much frequency as we did. We have noted some things which may account for at least a certain number of those who do not claim a history of physical abuse in early life. We have seen several persons who, during evaluation for maltreatment of their children, stoutly denied having been mistreated themselves as children. Upon further questioning as to who did the disciplining in the family and what disciplinary measures were used, they freely described being whipped or beaten to the point of lacerations or bruising, but in no way did they consider this abuse, because the discipline was "appropriate punishment for misbehavior." Others will, for some time, maintain a denial of having been abused because of a persistent fear that, even though they are now adults, their parents might again attack them if they complain or criticize parental actions. Others hesitate to give a true history, lest the family be brought into some sort of difficulty or be disgraced in the community. More rarely, there is a genuine amnesia for the unpleasant events of childhood as a result of unusually strong repression. For example:

Jack S., aged twenty-five, freely admitted bruising and breaking the arm of his two-year-old daughter during a hassle over an error in toilet training. Although he recalled his father whipping him once when he was an early teenager for joyriding on an illegally "borrowed" motorcycle, he firmly denied any possibility of abuse early in life. Later, he reported talking to his sister about his "crazy psychiatrist," who kept wondering if he had been abused as a child and seemed to doubt his denials. His sister responded by saying, "Jack, do you mean to tell me you've forgotten how father used to take you down to the coal bin in the basement and whip you until you were black and blue and mother was afraid he would kill you?'' (Note that the mother, although concerned, was not described as intervening.) Following this revelation, Jack's amnesia gradually lifted, and he recalled many other events of his early life.

There are others who, although they actually remember maltreatment, find it too painful to deal with and comfort themselves by maintaining a fantasy that their parents really were good to them. Such fantasies, of course, can gain a good deal of support from the fact that the parents were, in reality, ''good enough,'' at least part of the time, and the uncomfortable side of the ambivalence can be disregarded.

We have often found it more difficult to establish evidence of neglect in early life than to uncover the history of physical abuse, because it is much harder for people to describe how much love and care were not there than to recall how often they were hit. The common expressions we hear from abusive parents, both men and women, are variations on such themes as ''I never felt my mother ever really loved me or cared about me,'' or ''My parents never listened to me or paid any attention to what I felt or what was important to me,'' or ''I was the black sheep of the family, always left out,'' or very commonly, ''I never in my life felt close to either mother or father,'' or ''It was never safe to ask for anything; I just did what I was told or what was wanted of me, but nobody ever really appreciated what I did or thought it was good enough.'' Another common source of feeling uncared for was the failure of one parent to interfere or protect the child while he was being beaten by the other parent. The child felt that neither one really cared about him. Similarly, girls, when trying to complain to their mothers about being sexually abused by males in the family, were often told they were lying or else ''making it up'' to cause trouble, or that it was all their fault anyway. And their mothers did nothing about the problem. This left the girls feeling hopeless and uncared for. Other, more obvious deprivations are often glossed over as just some of the ''misfortunes of life,'' without recognition of the serious emotional impact which such things have on the growing child. We ascribe such events to a profound depression in the mother, an absence of the mother as a result of sickness or death, placements of the child with unsympathetic relatives or in unloving foster homes, absence of a father, leaving an overburdened mother without enough time for any of her children, or multiple sicknesses without hospitalization in infancy and childhood. These, and other similar experiences in early life, can leave very long-lasting feelings of deprivation and loneliness, even though they may be intellectually understood and accepted.

The history of neglect and abuse in the early years of the life of the abusive caretaker has been stressed because we believe that therein lies the source of the caretaker's later inability to provide empathic care for infants and children. By empathy we mean a caretaker's sensitive awareness of a child's state and needs and the ability to instigate appropriate responses thereto. Abuse and neglect are the outward behavioral evidences of a caretaker's inadequate empathy for the child. We believe such inadequate empathy is the tragic deficit present in the caretaker in all situations of abuse and neglect. Excessive punitive discharge of aggression or neglectful disregard of a child's basic needs could not occur if normal, adequate empathy existed in the caretaker. As a corollary to this lack of empathic awareness of the child and appropriate responses to it, we find that in times of stress or crisis, the caretaker gives priority to his or her own needs and ideas, while the child's needs are given only secondary consideration or are completely disregarded. This phenomenon is seen with striking clarity in cases of sexual abuse of small children. The child is exploited by being drawn into sexual activity which is primarily oriented toward the satisfaction of the adult caretaker, while, at the same time, little or no attention is paid to the child's age-appropriate needs and abilities. The child's obedient, submissive cooperation with the adult in the sexual activity and the pleasure which some children seem to derive from it have led many observers to minimize or disregard this nonempathic exploitation of the child.

It is quite common in situations of abuse and neglect to find the caretakers expecting their infants and small children to behave and perform tasks with unusual efficiency much too early in the child's life, while, at the same time, disregarding the child's own feelings and wants. This phenomenon has been well described by Morris and Gould (10) as *role reversal*. The child is treated as if he were an adult while the caretaker expects satisfactions of his or her own desires to be cared for.

An example is Mrs. G., a young woman whose one-year-old baby girl had been severely burned by scalding water in the bathtub. She also had a boy 2½ years old, and when asked about him she responded, "Oh, Buddy is very active. He's on the go all the time. He acts older than he is. He cleans the house, cleans my room, sweeps the floor in his room. He wants to help cook, but I think he's too young for that. Sometimes he's too helpful. He's never been with kids his own age, but it is helpful with him like that. It's not boring. Other kids his age just sit in the corner. He does watch kiddy shows, but he's up 'til two or three in the morning often helping me, and then he's up again at seven-thirty or eight. He only takes a nap once every two or three days. If I tell him to do something, he will do it. He makes his bed if I tell him to do it. If he doesn't, I bribe him. I'll send him to his room if he has a fit." When asked if Buddy was considerate of her moods, she replied "Yeah, if I'm on the couch he gets a blanket and pillow, and brings me some water. He thinks that he made me sick and says 'I sorry.' He even helps others, too." When asked if he helped her take care of the baby, she said "Oh, yeah, he bathes her, puts powder on her. He hunts for a bottle when she cries. Once there was no bottle. He took a whole half-gallon of milk out of the refrigerator and took it to her. He pushes her in her swing. He's very protective of her. He tells other kids that she's sleeping because he's afraid that they might hurt her, and he slaps kids if he thinks they will. He brings me clean diapers and throws the old ones out. He changed her once, but he did a goofy job of it. He wants to drive a car, now." This mother also spoke of how she thought her stepparents were rather cruel to Buddy and said that, as a result, she found it hard to "holler at him." However, she added, "I did give a licking last night. He knows by the tone of my voice if I'm mad. All I have to do is show him a belt lying around and he shapes up immediately." She claimed that while she was gone to a neighbor's, leaving Buddy to bathe himself, he got out of the tub and put his baby sister in water which was too hot.

It is obvious in this brief vignette that this mother gained satisfaction from the precocious pursuit of adult behavior she expected from her 2½-year-old boy. It is obvious that she was critical and punitive toward him if he did not meet expectations, that his own needs to live like a normal 2½-year-old boy were not considered. It is also significant to note how energetically this small boy devoted all his efforts toward trying to please his mother. Despite the fact that she loved her children and, in general, took very good care of them, this mother demonstrates a pervasive lack of empathy. She showed no real spontaneous, intuitive, sensitive feelings toward her infants. In talking about her boy, she uses no warm, loving words, and says essentially nothing about what kind of human being he really is. She describes only what he does that is related to his usefulness to her and the household. Leaving her one-year-old daughter in the precarious care of the 2½-year-old brother, while she goes visiting, indicates a very disturbing lack of awareness of her children's needs and behavior and their need for guidance and protection.

It is very common for physical abuse to occur as a "justified" action or "appropriate disciplinary punishment" when children fail to meet excessively high caretaker expectations. It is also possible to see significant neglect occur as a result of a child's failure to perform well enough to satisfy caretaker expectations. An infant who fails to respond to mother's inept or inappropriately timed feedings or other caretaking procedures is perceived as being defective, negativistic, generally unfit or no good and is then deemed not worth caring for, resulting in "failure to thrive" or other forms of neglect. Thus, although both abusive and neglectful parents have the same pattern of high expectations of the child, their responses to the child's failure to meet expectations are quite different. In the one case, the child is perceived as failing to follow through to his full capabilities and, therefore, is punished to make him "shape up" and do better. In the other case, the child is seen as incapable of proper response, is worthless and, therefore, is given only cursory, inadequate care or almost totally disregarded.

Another young mother, Holly, was similar to Mrs. G., but showed even more significant misperceptions of her children. She had a 22-month-old boy, whom she described as a great help around the household, although not so efficient as Buddy. While in the office with me, she frequently slapped little Sammy on his rear and would alternately tell him "Stop doing that, come here," and "Stop bothering me, go away." In the midst of this, he emptied my ashtray, wiped it with Kleenex, and replaced it on the desk. When I remarked on this behavior, mother was obviously pleased and proud of his accomplishments. However, she had not allowed him to have any pleasure or freedom during this visit. She also had a 5½-month-old boy in the hospital with a fractured skull and fractured pelvis inflicted during punishment for being stubborn and lazy. She told of how he had been a very good baby at first, but had gradually become very unsatisfactory. He would "do nothing for himself," would get sick deliberately to frustrate her, and would look at her with great anger in his eyes. This intelligent young woman was not completely unaware of normal child development, but this did not counteract her misperceptions. The punishment had occurred when she was under more than average stress due to marital difficulties and feeling very much alone and uncared for and, therefore, especially needy of compliant, helpful behavior from her two boys. Some understanding of her behavior could be gained from her statement, "My mother never cared about me, never listened to me or what I wanted. I was never anything but a servant in her house." Her inadequate empathy was documented on another occasion when she described how important it was not to spoil children by giving into them too much or by picking them up when they cried. But she added, "But I know children need to be loved, too, so I've always made it a practice to pick my little babies up and hold them for ten minutes twice a day." She at other times also alluded to rather severe physical punishment during her early years.

It is obvious that Holly is severely deficient in empathy for her two children and, also, that her behavior as a parent has been profoundly influenced by her own early life experience, especially by her relationship to her mother.

Not all abusive parents show the high expectations, lack of empathy, and punitive attitude toward failure with the unusual clarity demonstrated in the two cases above. But, they do expect simple, obedient, correct, appreciative responses from their infants and small children during the ordinary tasks of feeding, bathing, toilet training, diapering, and taking naps, all according to parental desires of the moment, and they have other misperceptions of the child's abilities and intentions. The child's failure to please or obey is met by physical attack or verbal criticism or subsequent neglect. Indications of this disordered pattern of parental behavior can be observed at the time of the birth of the baby or in the immediate postpartum period. Gray *et al.* (11), have clearly demonstrated that a most reliable sign of possible future difficulty in parenting is the evidence of poor attachment seen in the perinatal period. It is seen especially clearly in the mother's behavior toward her newborn baby immediately after delivery and during the first few feedings. It is possible to observe poor attachment by the father as well. Poor attachment is soon evidenced by the unempathic manner in which the parent performs the caretaking tasks. Caretaking is done mechanically, largely according to the caretaker's convenience and without any warm, sensitive interaction oriented toward satisfying the infant's needs and without proper responses according to the infant's state. In some ways, the abusive syndrome can be considered a disorder of attachment with all its subsequent repercussions. The work in recent years of Bowlby (13), Klaus and Kennell (15, 16), Brazelton, Kozlowski, and Main (14), Ainsworth (12), Ounsted, Oppenheimer, and Lindsay (18), and Lynch and Roberts (17), and others has amply illustrated the importance of mother-infant attachment in parent-child bonding and its effect on subsequent parent-child interactions and child development. Two processes are involved. One is the attachment of the infant to the caretaker, and the other is that of the caretaker to the infant. Disturbances can occur in either part of the process, and the factors which interfere with the infant's ability to attach well to the caretaker will be discussed below under the heading "The Role of the Child in Abuse and Neglect." It is our strong belief, however, that it is the impairment of parent-to-child attachment that is most important in situations of abuse and neglect.

The propensity and ability of humans to attach to infants is not uniform or simple. In its most uncomplicated form, it has been best understood as the more or less automatic or instinctual response of a mother to her newborn infant during the first hour after delivery, during the infant's quiet-alert state, and in the subsequent interactions between them during feeding and general care. This is true as far as it goes and is undoubtedly the most characteristic, biologically appropriate time for a mother and infant to establish a bond of relationship between them. However. this paradigm of attachment in no way accounts for the equally strong, although subtly different, attachments that occur with those who have not been involved with the actual processes of pregnancy and delivery. We refer here to the strong attachment that can occur between father and infants, between adoptive parents and infants, as well as others. It is our firm conviction that those persons who have had a good early childhood experience themselves have the empathic ability to attach well to their infants in later years and that those who have suffered from abuse and neglect in early years have poor empathy and are unable to attach well. We thus see some of the dynamics which are so basic in the abuse and neglect cycle: caretakers who have been subject to unempathic care in their earliest years cannot attach well or be empathic to their own offspring and, hence, do not attach well and do not provide empathic care, thus providing the basic matrix for the next generation of abuse and neglect (2, 19). Obviously, this cannot be a completely rigid, inescapably determined process of repetition. Other factors can and do come in to enhance or diminish the likelihood and severity of the cyclic recurrence. It is characteristic of human development that good and bad experiences in later childhood and after can influence, for better or for worse, psychological and behavioral trends established in the earliest years.

It is of interest to understand the mode of transmission and ramifications of the poor attachment and lack of empathy which we consider to be the basic core of the maladaptive, abusive, neglectful behavior of caretakers. Inasmuch as we see abusive caretakers repeating in their parental behavior the ways in which they, themselves, were treated as children, plus the fact that we see poor attachment immediately after the birth of the infant, indicates that the basic rudiments of the behavior are acquired at the very beginning of life. Benedek (20) has described how the experience of becoming a parent activates two sets of memories which are largely unconscious. One is the memory of how one was parented and the other are memories of what it was like to be a small child. These two deeply embedded psychic representations provide the templates to guide caretaking behavior. The caretaker is identified with his own parents, and the new baby is endowed, through reverse identification, with the attributes of the caretaker himself as a small child. These very early, primitive identifications are intensified by the day-to-day interactions between caretaker and infant during the ensuing months and early years. We feel that the basic pattern which can appear later in the adult as abusive, neglectful behavior is firmly established by the third year, although it can also be further modified by ensuing experiences of the child with the same or other caretakers. This acquisition of behavioral patterns by the child, which are similar to those of his caretaker, can also be appropriately understood in the frameworks of social learning theory and role modeling. Yet, we believe the more basic determinants of caretaking behavior are established during the affect-laden identification experience of the first few months before the development of more truly cognitive learning can exert an influence. This process is, in itself, not deviant. It is a normal mode of establishing the basic ingredients of caretaking behavior for all persons. Those who have had a very good experience in the first months of being cared for empathically are quite likely to attach well and to have adequate empathy in their own, later, caretaking activities. Those who have not had such a good experience of positive attachment and empathic care in their beginning lives are severely hampered in their later caretaking ability because of the identification resulting from poor attachment and deficient empathy. This early origin of the adult's ability to be empathic with children has also been noted by Olden (21, 22), Josselyn (23), and others. It accounts for the fact that sensitive, empathic mothering is not something confined to biological mothers, but can exist in persons of both sexes, of all ages, as a behavioral expression determined by their own early life experience, by either biological parents or other caretakers.

Deficits in the empathic care which all infants need for optimal growth and development are followed by specific psychological effects. In the normal, healthy, caretaker-infant dyad, there is a mutually rewarding, symbiotic relationship in which the caretaker sensitively becomes aware of appropriate responses to the infant's state and needs. As a result, the growing infant develops a feeling of what Benedek called "confidence" and Erikson described as "basic trust," a sense that the world and the people in it will be adequately good to one. In situations where there is lack of empathic care and experience of abuse and neglect, the symbiotic phase is highly distorted. Care is oriented much more toward the whims and convenience of the caretakers, with less appropriate response to the child. In this situation, it is impossible for the child to develop any sense that the world or the people in it in any way reliably respond to his own needs. Hence, he cannot develop basic trust, but, on the other hand, will view the world with some degree of doubt and suspicion. Later, facing impossible expectations from caretakers with inevitable failure followed by punishment, criticism, and disregard, he will have learned to pay little attention to his own inner feelings, because they are of diminished value in his dealings with surroundings. Constantly under primary control of the caretaker and plagued with the necessity to deny the self and adapt to caretakers, there will be marked difficulty in the separation and individuation phases of development. It is not surprising, therefore, that as a result of these experiences in childhood, we see adults who are somewhat socially isolated and have a great deal of difficulty in reaching out to others for help and assistance. They have no basic trust and have some fear that the very people to whom they will look for help will be the ones most likely to attack. They also feel their own deepest needs have never been and never will be fully satisfied. There is a low sense of self-esteem and some degree of chronic, low-grade, depressive feeling. Under these circumstances, it is not surprising that we find very commonly in descriptions of adult, abusive, neglectful caretakers characterizations of these people as dependent, immature, and having a poor sense of identity, low self-esteem, a pseudoparanoid attitude of fear of being attacked, a reluctance to form lifelines or seek help in family and community, and having a very suspicious attitude toward authority and a wish to avoid it. These characteristics of maltreating caretakers are all direct residuals of the childhood experiences and are transferences in the present-day milieu of feelings and attitudes which were appropriate toward the original caretakers of early years. It is important to understand the early origin and development of many of these characteristics, because it will help us understand the abusive, neglectful behavior of the caretakers and what strategies of management or therapy would be the most useful in helping them improve their child-caring abilities. It also points a way toward the use of helpful interventions in the perinatal period as a most effective time to help a family and prevent the recurrence of abuse and neglect and the transmission of the pattern to still another generation.

Circumstances of Attack

Physical abuse is usually not a constant or daily occurrence. There are often many days, weeks, or even months between attacks. To be sure, there may be almost daily emotional abuse in the form of yelling and verbal castigation, belittlement and criticism, as well as disregard and lack of attention. But it is the physical attacks occurring intermittently in discrete episodes which give us the clearest picture of the abusive phenomenon. There are four conditions which seem necessary for abuse to occur:

1. A caretaker who has the predisposition for abuse related to the psychological residues of neglect or abuse in his or her own early life
2. A crisis of some sort placing extra stress on the caretaker
3. Lack of lifelines or sources of help for the caretaker, either because he or she is unable to reach out or the facilities are not available
4. A child who is perceived as being in some way unsatisfactory

These four factors interact in a mutually reinforcing way. Abusive parents live in a state of precarious balance between emotional supply and demand. They are more needy because of their low self-esteem, but less able to reach out for pleasure and support, and so turn with increased need to those who are least able to provide full satisfaction, their infants. Any crisis, even a small one such as a broken washing machine, becomes unmanageable because of the parent's poor coping techniques and inability or reluctance to seek help. Financial and housing crises are very upsetting, but most devastating are emotional crises related to loss or abandonment by important persons or the emotional desertion of a spouse after marital conflict. It is the infant's disturbing behavior during ordinary caretaking, excessive crying, or his errors during toilet training which are the common stimuli to parental turmoil that culminates in the abusive act. The following discussion drawn from our previous study (2) presents our understanding of the circumstances of abusive attacks.

The parent approaches each task of infant care with three incongruous attitudes: first, a healthy desire to do something good for the infant; second, a deep, hidden yearning for the infant to respond in such a way as to fill the emptiness in the patient's life and bolster his low self-esteem; and third, a harsh, authoritative demand for the infant's correct response, supported by a sense of parental rightness. If the caring task goes reasonably well and the infant's response is reasonably adequate, no attack occurs and no harm is done except for the stimulation of aggression and accompanying strict superego development in the infant. But, if anything interferes with the success of the parental care or enhances the parent's feelings of being unloved and inferior, the harsh, authoritative attitude surges up, and attack is likely to occur. The infant's part in this disturbance is accomplished by persistent, unassuaged crying, by failing to respond physically or emotionally in accordance with parental needs, or by actively interfering through obstructive physical activity. At times the parent may be feeling especially inferior, unloved, needy, and angry, and, therefore, unusually vulnerable because some important figure such as the spouse or a relative has just criticized or deserted him or her or because some other facet of life has become unmanageable.

On a deeper psychological level, the events begin with the parent's identification of the cared for infant as a need-gratifying object equivalent to a parent who will replace the lacks in the abusive parent's own being-parented experience. Since the parent's past tells him that those to whom he looked for love were also the ones who attacked him, the infant is also perceived as a critical parental figure. Quite often abusing parents tell us, "When the baby cries like that it sounds just like mother (or father) yelling at me, and I can't stand it." The perception of being criticized stirs up the parent's feelings of being inferior. It also increases the frustration of his need for love, and anger mounts. At this time there seems to be a strong sense of guilt, a feeling of helplessness and panic becomes overwhelming, and the haziness is most marked. Suddenly a shift in identifications occurs. The superego identification with the parent's own punitive parent takes over. The infant is perceived as the parent's own bad childhood itself. The built-up aggression is redirected outward, and the infant is hit with full superego approval.

This sudden shift in identifications is admittedly difficult to document. Our patients cannot clearly describe all that happened in the midst of such intense emotional turmoil. We interpret it as regression under severe stress to an early period of superego development when identification with the agressor established a strict, punitive superego with more effective strength than the gentler ego ideal. In such a regressive state the stronger, punitive superego inevitably comes to the fore.

Following the attack, some parents may maintain a strict, righteous attitude, express no sense of guilt about the aggression, insist they have done nothing wrong, and may be very resentful toward anyone who tries to interfere with their affairs. On the other hand, some parents are filled with remorse, weep, and quickly seek medical help if the child has been seriously hurt.

It has not been possible in all patients to obtain a clear story of what they actually did to the child at the time a serious injury occurred, even though abuse is admitted. They insist they did nothing differently than usual. In some cases this may be a defensive forgetting. In others we think it is probably a true statement. They have been hitting or yanking the child routinely and are not aware of the extra force used at the time of fracture.

The following condensed case histories, when added to the fragments already quoted, will illustrate the mainstreams of the patients' lives related to the ultimate abusive behavior.

Amy, twenty-six, is the wife of a successful junior executive engineer. She requested help for feelings of depression, fear she was ruining her marriage, and worry over being angry and unloving with her baby boy. She was born and raised in a well-to-do family in a large city on the west coast. Her parents were brilliant, active intellectuals who apparently had minimal involvement in the earliest years of their children's lives. She and her younger sister and brother were cared for by governesses, about whom Amy has vague, fragmentary memories. One was very warm, kind, and loving. She recalls another who was demanding, stern, and mean and who roughly washed Amy's long hair as a punishment and held her nose to make her eat. We suspect, without adequate documentation, that the governesses raised the infants as much to meet the high behavior standards of the parents as to meet the variable needs and whims of their charges.

As a child Amy had more interaction with her mother, but she could not feel close or really understood by either parent. Both parents had compulsive traits of wanting everything in perfect order and tasks done "at once." Her father was quite aloof, uninterested in children because they could not talk to him on any worthwhile level. When Amy was about thirteen, both mother and father had psychotherapy. Since then, her father has been warmer and has some liking for small children, but he still maintains a pattern of wanting to be the center of the stage and have people pay attention primarily to him, not only in the family, but in all social situations. In recent years Amy has felt closer to her mother and has felt that they could talk more frankly and openly with each other. During her childhood, Amy felt inept, awkward, ugly, unable to be liked by other people, and somewhat dull intellectually. Even though she made good grades in school, they never seemed good enough to gain approval. (Her I.Q. is in the upper normal range.)

Although not physically punished or overtly severely criticized, Amy felt great lack of approval and developed a deep sense of inferiority, inability to please, and worthlessness; she thought of herself as almost "retarded." In college she was capable, but not outstanding, and after graduation she worked for a while, gaining a significant amount of self-respect and self-assurance. She had become a quite attractive, adequately popular girl and had made a good marriage. She and her husband are well-liked, active members of their social set.

Of her first-born child, Lisa, now age 2½ and doing well, Amy says, "I did not like her too well at first and didn't feel close to her until she was several months old and more responsive." By the time Lisa was a year old, with much maternal encouragement, she was walking and beginning to talk and Amy began to think much more highly of her, and for the most part, they get along well with each other. However, if Lisa has tantrums or does not behave well, whines or cries too much, Amy occasionally still shakes her and spanks her rather violently. Their second child, Billy, was born not quite a year and half after Lisa. He was delivered by caesarean section, one month premature. He did not suck well at first and feeding was a problem. Also, Amy was sick for a while after delivery. She never felt warm or close or really loved him and had even less patience with him than with Lisa. His "whining" drove her "crazy" and made her hate him. Because of his crying and lack of adequate response, she would grow impatient with him and leave him or punish him roughly. She spent little time cuddling or playing with him, and he became, as a result, somewhat less responsive and did not thrive as well as he might have. When he was seven months old, during a routine checkup, the pediatrician unfortunately said to Amy, "Maybe you have a retarded child here." Amy immediately felt intense aversion to Billy, hated the sight of him, couldn't pick him up or feed him easily, and began more serious physical abuse that evening. She felt depressed, angry, and irritable. Billy also seemed to stop progressing. However, when checked by another pediatrician, he was said to be quite normal. Amy felt reassured, but not convinced. She became aware that Billy was responsive and alert if she felt all right and loving toward him, but he acted "stupid" if she were depressed or angry at him. This awareness of her influence on him served only to enhance her feelings of worthlessness and guilt. At times when he was unresponsive or seemed to be behaving in a "retarded" way, and especially if he cried too much or whined, she roughed him up, shook him, spanked him very severely, and choked him violently. No bones had been broken, but there were bruises. Amy described alternating between feelings of anger at Billy because he was "retarded" and feeling very guilty because she had "squashed him" by her own attitudes and behavior.

Amy described being inadequately prepared for and overwhelmed by the tasks of motherhood. This was enhanced by her feeling that she was trying to accomplish the mothering tasks without the help that her mother had had in bringing up her children. Further difficulty arose because her husband, although overtly quite sympathetic with her difficulties and expressing wishes of helping her, would also withdraw from her in times of crisis and imply a good deal of criticism of the way she dealt with the children. She also felt that there had been no one to whom she could really turn to air her troubles and get comfort and help without too much admonition and criticism. Further, Amy had a cousin who was retarded, and she felt devastated by fantasies of the burden of bringing up a retarded child.

This case shows the identification of the abusive parent with her own parents' attitudes toward children, the premature, high expectation and need of responsive performance on the part of the infant, and the inability to cope with lack of good response. Most clearly, it shows the parental misperception of the infant as the embodiment of those bad behavioral traits (being "retarded") for which the parent herself was criticized as a young child. During treatment Amy's depressive feelings and sense of worthlessness were ameliorated. She began to interact more happily with her children, and they responded well to her change in behavior. Billy, particularly, began to thrive, grew rapidly, and became a happier, more rewarding baby. Amy and her husband began to communicate a little more effectively, and her aggressive behavior toward her children almost completely disappeared. After six months, treatment had to be terminated because of her husband's transfer to another city. We had the good fortune to see her and the children four years later. Amy was doing very well and the two children were active, happy, bright youngsters. Wisely, we believe, they have had no more children. The improvement that occurred in this situation is partly due to our therapeutic intervention, but we would guess that it is also due to the passage of time which enabled the children to grow up and inevitably become more behaviorally and conversationally rewarding to their mother.

Larry, age twenty-seven, is a quiet, shy, unassuming, little man who works as a welder's assistant. Since childhood, he has been plagued by a deep sense of inferiority, unworthiness, and unsureness of himself in his work and in all human relations. There is also a deep resentment, usually very restrained, against a world which he feels is unfair.

He was brought up on a dairy farm, the third of five children. The oldest, a sister, is ten years his senior. He has never been able to find out the truth about her from his parents or other relatives but thinks all the evidence indicates she is a half-sister and an illegitimate child of his mother's before her marriage. Some resentment against his mother is based on this situation. His two younger sisters he felt were bothersome and annoying during their childhood. His brother, two years older, took advantage of him, and his parents always took the brother's side, allowing him to do many things for which Larry was criticized or punished. This brother was quite wild, and while on leave from the navy, he was in a serious auto accident. Larry said, ''Too bad he wasn't killed,'' but then found his brother had been killed. Overwhelmed by guilt and grief, Larry took leave from the army to take his brother's body home for burial.

Larry's parents were deeply religious. He imagined his mother became fanatically so following her illegitimate pregnancy. She was against cigarettes, alcohol, coffee, tea, and most of the usual forms of amusement. Even after his marriage, his mother told his wife not to make coffee for him. Larry felt she was always much more strict with him than with his siblings. She forced him to attend Sunday school and frequent church services, much against his will. She berated him for minor misdeeds and constantly nagged and criticized him to the point where he felt everything he did was wrong and that he could never do right in her eyes. He occasionally rebelled by smoking or drinking. Larry's father drank moderately but became a teetotaler after his son's death. He often had outbursts of temper and once beat Larry with a piece of two-by-four lumber for a minor misdeed. Larry does not recall either mother or father spanking as a routine, but there were constant verbal attacks and criticism. He felt that neither of his parents, particularly his mother, really listened to him or understood his unhappiness and his need for comfort and consideration.

While he was in the army, Larry and Becky planned to marry. She was to come to where he was stationed, and they were to be married at Christmas time. He waited all day at the bus station, but she never appeared. Sad and hopeless, he got drunk. Months later, a buddy told him she had married somebody else the first of January. He saw her again a year later when home on leave. She had been divorced; so they made up and got married. She had a child, Jimmy, by her first marriage.

Larry has been dependent on Becky and feared losing her. Seeing Jimmy reminds him of her previous desertion. He feels she favors Jimmy; he is critical of Jimmy and occasionally spanks him. Becky has threatened to leave Larry over his aversion to Jimmy. During their five years of marriage they have been in financial straits, and at such times Becky and Larry have gone to their respective family homes for help until he could find a new job. Becky resented these episodes and criticized Larry for being an inadequately capable and providing husband.

They have had three more children of their own. Mary, age four, is liked very much by both parents, although Larry is more irritated by her than by their next child, David, age 2½. David is ''a very fine, active, alert, well-mannered little boy.'' He is quite responsive, and both parents like him and are good with him. Maggie, 4½ months old, was thought by both parents to be ''a bit different'' from birth. She seemed to look bluer and cried less strongly than their other babies and was also rather fussy. Becky is fond of Maggie and gives her good mothering. Larry is irritated by her, much as he is by Mary, and more than by David, but he does not dislike her as much as he does Jimmy.

Maggie was admitted to the hospital with symptoms and signs of bilateral subdural hematoma. She had been alone with her father when he noticed a sudden limpness, unconsciousness, and lack of breathing. He gave mouth-to-mouth respiration, and she was brought to the hospital by ambulance. There was a history of a similar episode a month before when Maggie was 3½ months old; when alone with her father she had become limp, followed by vomiting. Medical care was not sought until a week later. Following this, there was a question of increasing head size. No fractures of skull or long bones were revealed by X-ray. Two craniotomies were done for the relief of Maggie's subdural hematomas. During the month she was in hospital, we had frequent interviews with the parents. We were impressed by Becky's warmth, responsiveness, and concern over Maggie's welfare. Larry, however, maintained a more uneasy, aloof, evasive attitude, although he was superficially cooperative. What had happened to Maggie was not clearly established, but it seemed obvious she was the victim of trauma. We thought Larry was likely to have been the abuser, despite his maintenance of silence and innocence. We felt we had adequate, although meager, rapport with Larry and Becky and allowed them to take Maggie home with the adamant provision that she never be left alone with Larry.

A week later Larry called urgently for an appointment. Filled with shame, guilt, and anxiety he poured out his story. President Kennedy had been assassinated two days before. Larry was shocked, then flooded with feelings of sympathy for Kennedy and his family, anger at the assassin, grief over the unfair, unnecessary loss of an admired figure, and a sense of communal guilt. In this emotional turmoil he had a few beers at a tavern, went home and confessed to Becky what he had done to Maggie, and then phoned us. The circumstances of the attack were as follows: Larry's boss told him that his job was over. The construction contract had been suddenly canceled and there was no more work. Feeling discouraged, hopeless, and ignored, Larry went home, shamefacedly told Becky he had lost his job, and asked her if she wanted to go with the children to her family. Saying nothing, Becky walked out of the house leaving Larry alone with Maggie. The baby began to cry. Larry tried to comfort her, but she kept on crying; so he looked for her bottle. He could not find the bottle anywhere; the persistent crying and his feelings of frustration, helplessness, and ineffectuality became overwhelming. In a semiconfused "blurry" state he shook Maggie severely and then hit her on the head. Suddenly aware of what he had done, he started mouth-to-mouth resuscitation; then Becky came home and Maggie was brought to the hospital.

Recurrent in Larry's life are the themes of feeling disregarded and deserted and of being helplessly ineffectual in his attempts to meet expectations. These concepts of himself as worthless and incapable express the incorporation into his superego of the attitudes of his parents toward him during childhood; they have been enhanced by his later reality experiences of failure. He has further strong identifications with the aggressive parental attitudes of criticizing and attacking the weak, the helpless, and the maimed.

The attack on Maggie occurred when several of Larry's vulnerabilities were activated at the same time. He had experienced a lack of being considered and a feeling of failure in losing his job, his wife "deserted" him again with implications of criticism, he felt helpless to cope with the crying demands of the baby, and his own deep yearnings for love and care could not be spoken. Frustration and anger mounted, and the baby was struck. Larry said that in the "blurry" state he had a fleeting, queer feeling that he had hit himself.

Later we found similar circumstances were present when Maggie had been less severely injured a month before. Becky had started working evenings to supplement Larry's inadequate income. She would depart soon after he came home from his job, leaving him alone to fix supper, wash the dishes, and put the children to bed. He found the tasks difficult and was upset by the children's crying, particularly Maggie's. One evening, feeling overwhelmed, helpless, and unable to seek help, he attacked.

Larry's relationship to Becky was highly influenced by his unconscious tendency to identify her with his mother. This transference was facilitated by the reality facts that Becky had a child by a previous liaison, urged Larry to be more involved with the church, took Jimmy's side while disregarding Larry, frequently criticized Larry for failure to meet her expectations, and had several times deserted him, both emotionally and physically. Most basic and potent was Larry's urgent, dependent need to find in Becky the motherliness he had never known.

Constantly, despite disappointments, he yearningly looked to her to satisfy the unmet needs of all his yesterdays. When she failed him, there were only the children to look to for responses which would make him feel better.

The preceding case material depicts the four cardinal features of abuse—the psychological set of the parent, the presence of a crisis, the misperception of a child, and the unavailability of help. It also illustrates another factor. Even in cases where one parent is the sole abuser, the spouse is invariably, albeit often unconsciously, instigating, approving, condoning, or passively not interfering with the abuse. This connivance is not surprising, as it is a common observation that persons who have the potential for abuse tend to marry those with similar backgrounds and potential, a process of assortative mating. Young parents have told us they grew tired of following pediatric advice which was spoiling the baby and had decided to "bring it up the way we were brought up," following which the baby was punished and injured. Such marriages seem held together more by desperate, dependent neediness than by shared respect and love. Both partners have low self-esteem which leads them to believe they could never find anything better and they must cling to whatever they have. We believe in marriages where only one partner has the abusive potential that there is little likelihood of abuse or that it will be promptly discovered and treated.

Failure to Thrive

Among all the forms of child neglect, including failure to provide cleanliness, medical care, clothing, and emotional stimulation, the most clearcut clinical syndrome is that of the "failure to thrive due to maternal deprivation." (See Chapter 10 for a full discussion of this condition.) The term "maternal deprivation" should not be understood as applying only to biological mothers, but rather as a descriptive term referring to the lack of empathic, sensitive awareness and response to an infant by its primary caretaker, whether it be mother, father, nurse, or other person (24). In some ways, the condition is quite similar to "hospitalism," described by Spitz (25, 26), and it also resembles the state of infants in institutions reported by Provence and Lipton (27). The parents of infants who fail to thrive are essentially not much different from parents who abuse their offspring. Although it is mothers who are predominantly involved with the infant, fathers tend to be indifferent to the child's condition and are either uninterested or unable to intervene on the child's behalf. The mothers show the characteristics noted before in abusive mothers and, in fact, may often abuse the child physically, concurrently with neglectful behavior producing failure to thrive, or abuse the child at other times, when the other needs of the child are being met. Koel has reported on failure to thrive and fatal injury as a continuum (28), and we, too, have seen many children with evidences of both malnutrition and physical injuries.

We have found no consistent, significant, across-the-board, qualitative, difference between mothers whose infants are injured and those who fail to thrive. There is a tendency, however, for failure-to-thrive mothers to show a higher degree of depression, a lower self-esteem, and poorer coping ability in general.

Not rarely do they take very poor care of themselves physically and neglect their personal appearance. They also seem to have more suppressed anger, which is not so righteously directed against the environment, as it is in many cases of physical abuse, but rather is internalized with much self-depreciation an enhancement of a sense of worthlessness. This sense of worthlessness and ineptitude is deep and has been embedded in the character structure since early years. It seems to have been instigated by the recurring criticisms for failure to meet excessive parental demands and has been many times reinforced by the real failures of adult life which are inevitable because of the person's diminished ability to cope, to learn from experience and to ask for help. Each failure has led to more unsureness, depression, and apathy, thereby paving the way for even more failures in the future. These mothers tend to see the child more negatively, as being somehow defective, inefficient, recalcitrant, or somehow subtly deviant. Even in organically handicapped infants, they seem to exaggerate the deficits and cope with them poorly. Curiously, they may at the same time fail to see or respond to the obvious facts that the infant is significantly underweight, pale, wan, and apathetic. Their response to the infant is that the situation is hopeless, that the baby is not really worth caring for and is, therefore, significantly neglected and underfed. This misperception of the infant is related unconsciously to the mother's own perception of herself as a worthless human being. These behavioral patterns and characterological states, as well as the almost universal history of emotional deprivation or physical abuse in early childhood, have been reported by others (29–33).

It has sometimes been assumed that lack of knowledge of child development and inexperience in child care can account for cases of failure to thrive. While this may be true in some very young mothers and some culturally deprived persons, it is certainly not routine and is belied by the fact that many mothers of failure-to-thrive children have been able to take care of other babies without difficulty and that many such mothers are quite intelligent and well educated and competent in other areas of their lives. The problem lies in the mother's lack of empathic ability rather than in a cognitive deficit. We believe the programs for enhancing parental skills which can be quite successful are so largely because of the emotional support and approval provided rather than solely because of the technical knowledge gained. For instance, a young mother who was a physician and has had some experience in pediatrics, delivered a normal infant which she breast-fed and of which she was happily quite proud. However, after six weeks, it was evident the baby had gained practically no weight and began to look seriously malnourished and apathetic. She seemed oblivious of her baby's poor condition, and her husband hesitated to intervene lest she would feel criticized. On further investigation, it became evident she was unconsciously extremely unsure of her ability to be a mother, a concept related to her own poor experience of being mothered as a small child, and she was fearful of being discovered as ineffectual. It was surprising and gratifying to her and to the staff that she responded quickly to support from her pediatrician and to loving encouragement from husband and friends. Soon the baby was plump, happy, and developing normally.

In failure-to-thrive cases, more often than in physical abuse, there is a history of the mother having had difficulties during pregnancy or delivery, or there is some abnormality of the baby or prematurity. These extra stresses in prenatal and perinatal period, added to the already existing poor psychological set of the mother and her much diminished ability to cope, make it difficult for the mother to attach and to be adequately motherly, and failure to thrive can easily ensue. The following case report illustrates the complex interaction of residuals of childhood deprivation, depression, current emotional difficulties, problems in pregnancy and misperceptions of the infant.

A very well-educated, generally capable young woman consulted us because of depression, embarrassment over her failure to take good care of her baby, and anxiety over punitive behavior toward the child. She had never had a close empathic relationship with her own mother and had a lifelong feeling of being uncared for. After marriage, she lived in another city, and her pregnancy went well until the last few weeks when she returned to the city where her mother lived. She then became anxious and depressed; her relations with her husband were cold (he was absent, working on a new job), and her mother was either unconcerned or intrusive and inconsiderate. She developed mild preeclampsia and had a cesarean section. The baby was slightly small for gestational age and had mild, temporary, respiratory difficulty. Because of the baby's slight abnormalities, but more because of her own medical problems, the mother had little contact with her new infant and did not establish a good attachment. In the ensuing weeks, she did not regain full physical health, remained depressed, had difficulty feeding her baby, and would often lose patience with him, sometimes shaking and choking him with the production of minor bruises. She saw her baby as somehow inadequate, vaguely defective, and as stubbornly refusing to cooperate with her efforts to care for him. On a home visit, we observed the interaction during feeding. Mother very nicely picked up her baby boy, cuddled him in her arms, and put a spoonful of cereal in his mouth, which he eagerly accepted. However, before he had a chance to really mouth his food and swallow it, she had another spoonful of cereal, trying to push it between his closed lips. He turned his head away and refused the proffered food. Mother looked at him angrily, got up, and said, "See, he won't eat," and threw him angrily down in his crib. It is not surprising that this baby looked wan, apathetic, significantly underweight, and was behind in his development. Fortunately, the mother responded quite well to treatment. The baby quickly improved. She later had another child under better circumstances, attached well, and was a very good mother.

As noted above, failure-to-thrive parents, particularly mothers, have a very poor self-image and are particularly dubious about their abilities to be good parents. This sense of being inadequate or ineffectual can be greatly enhanced by delivering a baby with some abnormality or having a child who is sickly or unresponsive. Glaser and Bentovim (34) have reported that handicapped or chronically ill infants are more likely to be maltreated in the form of omission of care and that within this group, the neglect was worse with increase of social and emotional disturbance of the caretakers and family. They also found that nonhandicapped children were more likely to be physically abused. These observations seem to be in agreement with our idea that defective or ill children are perceived as more worthless and less deserving of care, while physically normal children are assumed to be able to perform well and deserve punishment if they do not do so.

Role of the Child in Abuse and Neglect

High-Risk Children

A great deal of information has been gained in recent years concerning the different kinds of infants and children who are at risk or who are most likely to be abused and neglected (18, 35–38). Included are essentially normal infants who are the product of a difficult pregnancy or delivery, born at an inconvenient time from an unplanned pregnancy, are illegitimate, of the wrong sex, too active, too passive, or the child of an unloved father, or born during a period of severe family stress and crisis. Other infants at risk are those who for some reason are more or less "abnormal." Included are infants born with significant prematurity, are small for gestational age, have various congenital deficiencies, abnormalities, perinatal illnesses, particularly those which require hospitalization, and those who have later chronic or recurrent illness, again, especially if there is hospitalization. There is a third group of children who can be either essentially normal physically or show very mild deficits, but who are described as being "difficult," or "different." They are hyperactive, fussy, difficult to feed, hard to cuddle, have abnormal sleep patterns, or cry excessively and are seen as generally being inadequately responsive to caretaking efforts. Adopted children seem to be at some risk, as there is a higher incidence of adoptive children in the population of abused and neglected infants than is warranted by their incidence in the general population. Finally, there are children, usually somewhat older, described as deliberately provoking or "asking for abuse" when in foster care, just as they did in their own homes.

It is true that all the children enumerated above are at high risk for abuse and neglect. Valid statistics indicate that they are overrepresented in the observed populations of abused and neglected children, but it must also be noted that only a minor percentage of all the premature, congenitally defective, sickly, and difficult children are abused or neglected and, also, that only a small proportion of the total population of abused and neglected children come from this group of excessively high-risk infants. It is our experience that a majority of abused and neglected children had originally been quite normal and that many of the emotional difficulties, evidences of retardation, and behavioral problems are the results of previous abuse and neglect rather than "causes" of it.

It has been distressing to note that some investigators have subtly implied that the observed abuse and neglect of these high-risk infants cannot only be understood, but almost forgiven, inasmuch as the infant's fault explains the parental action. We are quite aware that some of these children are extremely difficult and place an enormous burden on their caretakers. Sometimes the experienced nurses on our wards who are accustomed to and expert in taking care of extremely difficult cases find that some of these children try their patience to the breaking point. But abuse and neglect can never be considered a permissible or appropriate response in such situations. To us, it is obvious that punishment or neglect of an infant can never, in any circumstance, be considered correct response to a fussy, premature baby or to the feeding problems resulting from a cleft palate. All of these high-risk circumstances are ones which call for much more attention and careful monitoring of the parent-infant dyad and the provision of extra services to the caretakers who are faced with coping with enormous extra burdens.

How then can we account for the fact that some caretakers abuse some infants who, through no fault of their own, have "conditions which place them at high risk"? One of the basic tenets of the abusive parent is the conviction or belief that a child's primary role is to behave and respond in such a way as to please and satisfy parents. Thus, we see the very early and excessive expectation of performance which was noted above. It is also the parental belief that children who fail to perform adequately well are therefore unsatisfactory and are either worthless or need to be punished to make them "shape up." Added to this is the significantly increased amount of care and special attention which they require. For the abusive caretaker, who is plagued with lifelong feelings of being unloved and ineffectual, this creates an unbearable situation and maltreatment is more likely to occur. In our estimation this is no different than other cases of abuse and neglect, except that there are more real reasons for considering the child to be unsatisfactory and, therefore, more stressful to the vulnerable parent who might, in other less serious circumstances, with a more rewarding baby, not be so abusive.

While it is perfectly true that some children are extremely difficult and, by their behavior, push their caretakers beyond their ability to cope, we deplore any tendency to accent the provocative behavior of the child at the expense of disregarding the parents' own deficiencies in caretaking abilities. It is quite similar to the frequently noted tendency of maltreating parents themselves to blame everything on the child. This is not a new phenomenon, as indicated by the following story which has been handed down from the fifth century, B.C., in China (39).

> Tseng Tzu was one of the most famous disciples of Confucius. He was extremely dutiful toward his parents and became one of the twenty-four celebrated examples of filial piety. A story about him tells that once when he was hoeing melons for his father, he accidentally cut the root of one, and his father, becoming enraged, beat him so severely that he lost consciousness. Tseng Tzu submitted to this beating without complaint and upon reviving played his lute and sang as usual. It is said that when Confucius heard of this he told his disciples that it would have been filial for Tseng Tzu to have submitted to a light thrashing, but he should have avoided such a severe beating because, by not doing so, he was involving his father in an unrighteous act which does not become a filial son.

Attachment

The infants and children described above are not at risk simply because of immaturity, physical defects, or emotional aberrancy, etc. There is also a marked diminution or complete lack of parental attachment to such infants. These difficulties in attachment are most likely to occur with parents who have had difficult childhoods themselves and are hence already deficient in empathy. Such predispositions for poor attachment are markedly increased, especially in mothers, by troubles during pregnancy, complicated deliveries, prematurity; cesarean sections, or illness of the infant or mother, necessitating separation of the mother and child for a significant time in the postnatal period. It can be extremely difficult for even the best-prepared parents to attach to a child if, in the postnatal period, they cannot, because of medical conditions, pick up, hold, feed, or otherwise care for the new baby. In this latter case, however, it is possible for such parents to develop fully normal attachments when the medical crisis is over and they assume the normal tasks of parenting.

Attachment behavior is also profoundly influenced by the kind of fantasies had by parents during the pregnancy. This is to some extent true of fathers, but is especially true of mothers, because the fetus is inside her and part of her, as well as a separate entity. Normally such fantasies are of having a fine baby, possibly with some preference for sex, which will be a pleasurable addition to the family. Such essentially pleasant fantasies are not counteracted by the common anxieties concerning whether or not the baby will be normal and everything else all right. Parents at high risk for poor attachment and caretaking difficulties are, because of their own past lives, likely to have much more distressing fantasies during the prenatal period. One young mother described this clearly when she said early in pregnancy, "If it's a girl, it will be a mess. She will hate me as I hated my mother, and I will hate her like mother hated me." Another young mother, who could not be relieved of her anxiety that her baby might be born without arms or legs or might have defects in his back or head, delivered a normal baby, but had seriously injured it several times before it was a year old. Often, fantasies are of the baby *in utero* developing into the same kind of child which the mother was. And this, of course, is a bad omen if the mother remembers herself as an extremely difficult, bad child, who often had to be punished. More seriously psychologically disturbed mothers may have fantasies of the fetus being some kind of parasitic invader who is destructively eating her up from the inside. If carried to term, such a baby, even though apparently normal, is likely to be maltreated and thought of as some kind of "monster." It must be remembered that not only can various organic difficulties during pregnancy give rise to negative fantasies on the part of the mother, but also that negative daydreams, fantasies, and night dreams can be evidence of psychological states which can, in turn, have profoundly disturbing effects on the pregnancy itself. Unrealistic expectations of the baby can be expressed in prenatal fantasy also. One young mother expressed the conviction that she would have a beautiful little girl who would help her overcome her emotional difficulties in life, and she looked forward with happy anticipation to birth. She delivered a boy, to whom she did not attach, as it was the wrong sex, and she could not mother him well. Other parents, including fathers, may have fantasies of the child growing up to be a disruptive influence in the family, making trouble between the parents, and causing serious conflicts with siblings. Such prenatal fantasies bear a very direct relationship to the parent's own childhood and certainly do not bode well either for full attachment or subsequent attitudes toward the infant by the caretaker.

The attachment of parents or other caretakers to their new infants is thus seen, not as a simple, automatic process, but one that is highly influenced for better or worse by many other factors, particularly those which have their roots in the parents' own earliest childhood experiences and how well they were lovingly, sensitively cared for with adequate empathy. Probably, nearly all parents have, to some degree, the expectation that having a child will somehow be a rewarding, fulfilling experience which will make their lives happier and more complete. And this is true for the majority of parents, and the rewards of parenthood outweigh the trials and tribulations thereof. But it is likely that if caretakers have problems and discontents of any significant degree, having a child will not solve such problems, but probably make them worse. We believe this is one factor which leads to the somewhat higher instance of maltreatment of adopted children. The adoptive procedure itself, in almost all instances, is undertaken to solve a parental problem, particularly the deficit of infertility, and the inability to have natural children. Fortunately, most adoptive parents have inner strength and past experience and empathy enough to manage their caretaking skills quite well. A number of them, however, seem to have problems in low self-esteem, incompetence, and a sense of being defective that are too deep to be solved by the adoption of a child. Hence, the adopted child is unconsciously seen as failing to solve the parental problem, is therefore an unsatisfactory child, and is at high risk for maltreatment. The fact that so many adoptive mothers attach so effectively to their infants and become perfectly adequate mothers indicates attachment is not a purely biological phenomenon which has to be accomplished in a critical period during the first few hours postpartum, although that period when the infant is in a quiet-alert state and the mother awake is possibly the most ideal time for attachment (40).

This discussion of attachment has primarily concerned the presence or absence of attachment, but there has also been the implication that in some instances there is not only a lack of postiive attachment, but what might be called a negative feeling of antagonism or antipathy toward the infant which is quite the opposite of positive attachment. Such "negative attachments" are often related to mis-perceptions of the child associated with fantasies of abnormality occurring during the prenatal period, or with excessive identifications of the child with the parent's own, bad, childhood self. They may also be related to the baby being unwanted, because it is a product of rape, incest, or, more commonly, the child of a now discarded lover or a deserting, divorced spouse. The baby may also be unwanted because of being unplanned or coming at a time of extreme inconvenience to the family, because of financial problems, geographic moves, or family tragedies. If such replacement of attachment by negative attitudes is not paid attention to, serious difficulties in the caretaker-infant relationship resulting in maltreatment may well occur. We have often seen children seriously injured, neglected, even killed by parents who loathed their child, wanted to get rid of the child and give him or her up for adoption, but who were cajoled or shamed into keeping the child by relatives or health professionals. Negative attachments need special care. While it is sometimes true, in cases where mothers and fathers are unhappy about a child, that they will "learn to love it in time," such loving is far from automatic, and the negative feelings warrant serious attention if tragedy is to be avoided.

Atypical Abuse and Infanticide

There are some abusers, nearly all of them men in our experience, who repeatedly and cruelly injure the children with whom they are involved. They maltreat their charges much like other abusers, but do not confine themselves to the usual patterns of attacking a child because of some specific error or unacceptable behavior. They also indiscriminately attack for no more apparent reason than that the child is there as a handy object upon whom to release aggression. They may pinch, slap, or punch a baby each time they see it or go by its crib, extinguish cigarettes by stubbing them out on a child's foot or arm, or routinely kick a child playing on the floor. They have been described as "torturing" their offspring. Often, they also abuse their wives or mistresses, get into fights, pass bad checks, and have frequent brushes with the law because of numerous traffic offenses and minor crimes. They may also be clever liars and manipulative "con men." Abuse of alcohol and drugs is common. Their personal relationships are shallow and exploitative. Such persons, who constitute possibly some five to ten percent of the abusive population, can best be described as sociopaths. They are characterized by their free, unconflicted discharge of aggression, their self-centered, narcissistic demands, and especially by their extreme lack of empathic caring for other human beings and disregard of others' welfare. In childhood, they had very little love, warmth, or consistency from their caretakers and were exposed to excessive and frequent violence in their homes. They are quite similar in these respects to men who murder without apparent motive, described by Satten *et al.* (41).

Not rarely, a child will die as a result of such persistent maltreatment by its sociopathic caretaker. Typically, the abuser shows little or no guilt or remorse, denies any possibility that his own actions might have contributed to the death, blames the death on his wife or other people, even including emergency room personnel, or assumes that the child had some previously unrecognized illness or defect. We consider it important to recognize such individuals as early as possible, since we have found it extremely difficult, if not impossible, to rehabilitate them to the point of being safe caretakers. Their abuse is repetitive and is easily transferred to other children in the family.

Mental illness may significantly interfere with parental abilities, either through disregard of the child or misperceptions of him. Severe depressive or schizophrenic psychosis may seriously compromise a caretaker's ability to perceive a child's needs and respond appropriately to them. Preoccupation with obsessive thoughts, delusions, and hallucinations or withdrawal into hopeless immobility results in profound neglect of the child, leading to delayed development, starvation, illness, and, sometimes, death. In other instances, the child is woven into the caretaker's delusional system and becomes a target of paranoid attacks. This is not unrelated to the severe beatings, sometimes fatal, administered by fanatic religious groups in order to "drive the devil out" of infants perceived as "evil." Toxic psychoses and delirious states induced by various halluciongenic drugs such as LSD or by alcohol, by also lead to severe neglect, abuse, and occasionally killing of infants; in such cases there is usually a history of significant preexisting emotional disturbance or mental illness.

The direct murder of children is predominantly the act of a psychotic or seriously mentally disturbed member of the family or stranger (42). But infanticide, in general, which has existed throughout history and is still present all over the world, has much in common with the other forms of maltreatment (43, 44). It is essentially a human behavior which disregards the life and welfare of an infant and satisfies the needs and purposes of adults. The child is sacrificed for religious, military, or political purposes or for population control because of superstitions, parental convenience, or avoidance of shame and ostracism. Although legally considered as infanticide, there is a somewhat different kind of infant death which is the result of maltreatment (45) and death from prolonged failure to thrive. In the latter, there is less of an open, direct wish or attempt to kill the child, than of a pervasive indifference and disregard for the child and subsequent failure to provide life maintenance. In the more frequent cases of death resulting from repeated physical abuse, parents, as a rule, do not intend to kill the child, but on the contrary have an investment in a living child who must be punished to become more obedient and satisfying. Death is an unexpected, undesired, incidental result of the abuse. The abuser may be quite frightened by what has happened, may or may not seek immediate help, and may not understand that he has done something which would kill the child. He subsequently tends to feel guilt and great remorse, being quite opposite in this respect from the sociopath described above. There are also deaths which occur in children who are only mildly occasionally abused which are, in a sense, "quite accidental." For example, a small child may be forcefully hit on the back, causing him to stumble against a sharp corner of a coffee table, resulting in abdominal injury with ruptured liver and later death. The parent in such a case is likely to feel extremely guilty and be overwhelmed with grief, finding it quite difficult to understand why he is put in jail and treated like a common murderer.

Sexual Abuse

Although sexual abuse of children has been recognized for as long as any other form of maltreatment, it has been more concealed, less reported, and has attracted relatively little concern. Most attention has been directed toward statutory rape and toward the less serious problems of exhibitionism and pedophilia. A taboo of dealing with the common phenomenon of incest seems to have been as strong or stronger than the taboo of incest itself. However, with increasing public awareness and concern over the enormous number of cases of physical abuse and neglect and the courage given by the women's rights movement, sexual abuse, too, has become a matter of public concern. Cases, especially of incest of all varieties, are now increasingly reported in numbers approaching those of other kinds of abuse (46–51).

In view of the great variety of forms of sexual abuse—heterosexual, homosexual, children of all ages, sexual acts of all kinds—it is impossible to give a simple description which covers all cases. There are significant, different, psychodynamic factors in, for instance, those men who abuse only very young girls, those men who confine their acts to early adolescent boys, and women who selectively seduce either sons or daughters. Such specific preferential sexual behaviors can be best understood in terms of the distortions of psychosexual development commonly seen in cases of perversion and neurosis and are well described in the psychiatric literature. But the basic abusive pattern is not dissimilar from that seen in other kinds of maltreatment, physical abuse, neglect and failure to thrive, and emotional abuse. Physical and sexual abuse often coexist; a caretaker may sometimes physically abuse and, at other times, sexually abuse the same child. Or the sexual abuse itself may be accompanied by physical violence and trauma. In very young children, especially, sexual abuse is often belatedly discovered only during investigation or treatment of the more obvious physical abuse which has been reported and which called attention to the case. Older children, from latency to adolescence, are more likely to be sexually abused by their caretakers without accompanying physical abuse, although there may have been physical abuse in earlier years.

Sexual abuse of children of all ages is not an isolated phenomenon occurring in an otherwise healthy life situation. It is the obvious, overt, symptomatic expression of seriously disturbed family relationships and has always been preceded by more or less emotional neglect or mistreatment. Parents or other caretakers involved in sexual abuse are, in most ways, quite similar to those who are only physically abusive and neglectful and, as noted above, may at different times express any of these destructive behaviors. They suffer from the same severe lack of self esteem, have a poorly integrated sense of identity, tend to be somewhat socially isolated, and have a history of emotional deprivation, physical abuse, and often very chaotic family lives in their early years. As in physical abuse there is often a history of generational repetition of sexual abuse, especially incest in various forms. Langsley, Schwartz, and Fairbairn (52) report a case of father-son incest in which the father was repeating his seduction by adult males experienced in his own childhood. Raybin (53) reported homosexual incest involving three generations, and Raphling, Carpenter, and Davis (54) described multiple incestuous relationships existing in a family of over three generations. Gebhard *et al.* (55) noted that men imprisoned for sexually molesting children had often been the subjects of sexual molestation themselves as children. Lukianowicz (46) and Yorokoglu and Kemph (56) also report sexual mistreatment of children by persons who had been sexually abused themselves. In addition to the obvious learning from role-modeling which must occur in such family settings, there is also a deeper and compelling identification with the sexually abusive adults known in early childhood. This often gives incest a sort of moral approval in the subculture of some families and is clearly evident when we see some fathers say with some degree of righteous indignation, "My father had sex with all my sisters, so why should I not sleep with my daughters?" Mothers also, in identification with their own mothers, seem unable to protect daughters from sexual abuse and, in many instances, condone or actually promote the incestuous relationship between husband and daughter. Both fathers and mothers may righteously justify their incestuous activities by the rationalization that it is best for the child to learn about sex from a loving family member than from "no-good" peers.

The family backgrounds of those caretakers involved in sexual abuse of children are similar, in many respects, to the backgrounds of parents and others who have been involved in physical maltreatment and neglect. Several authors have accented the role of poverty (55, 57–59). There are also descriptions of the early absence of reliable parental figures in early life, particularly fathers, and often the child was moved from one foster placement to another, either in or out of the family. The caretakers of early life are also described as punitive or uncaring (59–63). Some sexual abusers describe extremely chaotic living conditions during their earliest years, with multiple changes of caretaking figures and exposure to extremely atypical, flamboyant sexual activities. For instance, one man described, "My father was a drunk and my mother was a whore. There were always other men and women coming into the house, and very free sexual activity of all kinds, both heterosexual and homosexual." We have, on the other hand, known sexual abusers who were brought up in extremely rigid, highly religious, but emotionally cold families, in which sex was a forbidden subject, even for education, and the children would become involved in aberrant sexual activity through seeking knowledge elsewhere. The common denominator in all these situations seems to be the absence of warm, loving, sexual relationships as a model for the child to emulate, lack of appropriate sexual education, and, most importantly for all, lack of empathic, sensitive care during the early impressionable, developmental years. Although we have no firm data, it is our impression that the more chaotic has been the sexual abuser's life in early childhood, the more likely he is to be sexually abusive to younger children, more aggressive in his abuse, and show more perverse behavior and much less consideration for the victim. The more nearly the early life experience approached "normal," the more likely the abuser was to become involved with much older children and do so only under periods of unusual stress or when drunk. Substance abuse, including alcohol, is certainly a fairly common precipitating factor to acts of sexual abuse of children. There seems to be a difference, however, between the chronic alcoholic who has been a frequent sexual abuser and the person who has indulged in sexual acts with children, either within or outside the family, only on very rare occasions when drinking as part of his futile attempts to solve the anxiety and loneliness resulting from marital conflict or the stress of other problems.

As in other forms of abuse, in sexual abuse, too, the child victim is often considered to be the one at fault or at least guilty of "contributory negligence," particularly if she gives any evidence of having had any pleasure in the activity. In cases of incest, the daughter is often said to have been quite seductive and not only willing to participate, but ready to instigate the incestuous behavior with her father. Such concepts are given further support by the observations of girls as young as three and four who have been placed in foster care because of sexual abuse in their homes, but who continue to approach all males very seductively and attempt to play with their genitals. There is no question about the accuracy of such observations. The question is how to interpret them. We believe, with very rare exceptions, that it is impossible for a young child to have such strong sexual drives and such seductive abilities that he or she can overcome a healthy adult's concepts of what is appropriate interaction between a caretaker and a child. It must also be kept in mind that little girls are often encouraged to be cute and seductive and are admired for it. For a "normal," healthy adult to be unable to resist erotic advances of a child is patently ridiculous. The essential ingredient for sexually abusive behavior is the lack of empathic consideration by the adult for the child's stage of development and abilities, plus the adult's placing the satisfaction of his own needs above those of the child. In this, we see the essence of sexual abuse of children, the exploitation of the child for the purpose of satisfying the adult. It is the recognition of having been exploited and uncared for as an individual human being that leads to the long-lasting residual damages of sexual abuse in development, rather than the actual physical sexual act itself. As in physical abuse, it is not the bodily damage or hurt itself that is most traumatic, but the fact that one was uncared for and misused by the ones to whom one must look for comfort, care, and protection. The resulting ambivalence, lack of trust, and difficulty in human relationships is inevitable and severe.

Although relationships between fathers and daughters and stepfathers and stepdaughters are by far the most commonly reported forms of incest, it is quite likely that sexual activities between brothers and sisters are even more common, ranging from simple visual inspection of each other to intercourse. It would seem useful to describe two different patterns of brother-sister interactions. The first is the fairly common effort of children to find out something about themselves and their functions by comparing themselves with the opposite sex and understanding the differences. This can happen either within the family with siblings or with other children and may progress to various attempts to explore and to imitate the sexual behavior of adults, about which they have either heard or seen examples. Such exploratory "educational" activities between brothers and sisters are usually engaged in by mutual consent and are mutually rewarding, and, even though they may, in some instances, progress to actual intercourse in older children, they are of short duration and provide channels for expanding relationships into other heterosexual contacts with peers and are not ordinarily productive of long-lasting, psychosexual difficulties. Although children involved in such activities may have some awareness that they are being "naughty," they do not develop a serious sense of guilt or disturbance of their sexual relationships unless the disapproval and punishment by authorities who discover the activity is unusually severe. There is another group of brother-sister relationships which, although superficially like the preceding, are not only motivated by normal sexual curiosity and search for identity but, in addition, a search for love, care, and acceptance from somebody. This seems to occur most frequently with siblings who, for one reason or another, feel emotionally deprived, neglected, or misunderstood by both parents and who do not feel free in any way to discuss their problems of any kind, including sexual, with the caretaking figures. Such relationships between brother and sister, expressed in the sexual sphere, become endowed with very intense needs for love and affection and are then extremely vulnerable to betrayal and exploitation, as well as abandonment. In such instances, the incestuous behavior can become traumatic and a source of much later difficulty.

Homosexual incest, like father-daughter incest, is often related to the emotional, sexual, or geographical absence, or death of the mother. The father (or stepfather), preferring out of his own insecurity to keep his sexual activity within the family, turns to the son to satisfy his sexual urges; the son submits to the sexual advances hoping to find some of the love and acceptance he has not had sufficiently from the mother, along with the satisfaction of some sexual needs. We believe the boy's gender identity has usually been at least partially compromised before the homosexual seduction occurs, because of long-lasting disturbances in family relationships. Certainly the father's homosexual tendencies existed in either open or covert form for many years.

The rarest type of incest is between mother and son; it seems to arouse more horror in people and has been the object of the most stringent taboo. In some ways it is similar to other forms of incest occurring in families with preexisting problems of many kinds, including disturbed sexual relations of the parents. The father may be emotionally or physically absent, and the mother turns to the son for love and attention, while the father is indifferent or turns to a daughter. After a father's death a teenage son may be told he is "now the man of the house and must take his father's place," and the advice is followed literally by both mother and son. Yet it seems doubtful if such social pseudoapproval would be followed if there were not preexisting excessively intimate interactions between them. In the half-dozen mother-son incest cases with which we have been involved (none of which proceeded to full intercourse) and in most of the few cases reported in the literature, there is evidence of significant neurosis, intermittent psychosis, or a severe borderline state in the mother (46, 54, 64). She has had previous difficulty in allowing separation and individuation to occur and has in other ways exploited the mother-son relationship.

We have been accenting the role of object relationships in the genesis of sexual abuse of children, and we believe this is the most important element in such behavior. It is also useful to consider the psychodynamic consequences of the Oedipus complex experienced by the victims of abuse. In the first place, it seems unlikely in view of the great extent of pregenital difficulty that there was ever the development of the fully, erotically tinged, oedipal complex as it is classically understood. At the oedipal period, these boys and girls were still too involved with the yearning for basic, empathic love, care, and consideration, and in the struggle to develop individual identity to be able to look to the parent of the opposite sex with strong, erotic yearning and a sense of concern over the reaction of the parent of the same sex. Most of them were still looking for basic care and protection in a nutritive framework. Both boys and girls turned to fathers or male figures for basic love and empathy, which they had not received in adequate quantities from their mothers. Boys thus tended to have homosexual tendencies, and girls turned toward their fathers, yearning for love and prematurely placing it in a heterosexual erotic context. The turning of girls to their fathers was not complicated by fears of loss of mother's love, because mother's love had not been there to lose. Boys could not turn to their mothers with strong erotic feelings, because they were still looking for the basic love and acceptance which was not there. Instead, they were afraid of their mothers; she was felt to be an engulfing, castrating figure, and we believe this accounts in some degree for the relative rarity of mother-son incest compared to the great frequency of father-daughter incest.

In some families, the oedipal configuration may have definite bearing on the later pattern of abuse, although not be a complete determinant of it. For instance, a young man who sexually and physically abused his two-year-old stepdaughter had grown up in a family in which he was severely physically abused by his father and mildly so by his mother. The father favored an older sister for whom he bought more clothes than he did for the mother and with whom he had an incestuous relationship. He also beat up this girl when, as an unmarried teenager, she became pregnant. The son repressed his anger at his mother for not protecting and caring enough for him and became much closer to her, with her encouragement. He also competed with his father by buying nightgowns and robes for his mother and trying in other ways to please and gain her favor. Later he became involved with women who were critical of his inability to satisfy their needs, materially or sexually, and once severely abused his wife who indicated she might be pregnant by another man. The abuse of the stepdaughter occurred under the influence of alcohol when the mother complained about the ineffectiveness of his efforts to care for her. It seemed to be a revengeful discharge of anger at females who would not be satisfied or let him love them—mother, wife, and baby. It was also a discharge of aggression in identification with the father who was incestuous and aggressive toward females, with whom he was competitive in his distorted oedipal struggles.

In most cases of sexual abuse of children the problem is an extremely complex one, and no simple etiology will explain any one case. There is nearly always a clear history of deficient "mothering" or other neglect in early years, plus the added factors of distorted sexual behavior in the family, leading to the inability to be empathic with children and to the sexual exploitation of them.

The Clinical Picture

The following condensed case history pictures with unusual clarity many of the commonly seen elements of physical and sexual abuse.

> Laura G. was an attractive young woman, age twenty-six, poised, friendly, and verbal. She was the wife of a noncommissioned career officer in the armed forces. Her reasons for coming to us were anxiety over marital problems, depression, and worry over abuse of her elder son.
>
> Laura was the elder of two children of parents living in very marginal economic circumstances on the outskirts of a small, rural town. Her father was mildly alcoholic; her mother more severely so. Her parents frequently argued and occasionally fought rather violently. Laura had never felt her mother was interested in her and had seemed far away and inattentive when Laura tried to talk to her. She recalled that even as a little child she worked very hard to do things to please her mother, but never seemed able to

do so and was often the subject of much criticism. She felt deprived, rejected, and hopeless. The younger brother, Joe, was her mother's favorite, the one to whom she gave all her love. Laura's relationship to Joe was always ambivalent—some love and companionship mixed with envy and hatred.

Laura was deeply attached to her father from her earliest years. She felt very close to him and believed he returned her warmth, cared for her, and listened to her. Father, however, was not always kind. He often beat her with his hands or a belt until she was black and blue, and his favorite saying was "I'll knock you through the wall." Sometimes he made her hold two bare electric wires in her hands while he turned on a current to give her a shock (he was an electrician by trade). He explained to her that he gave her these shocks to remind her that he was the boss and she must obey him. Despite such abuse, she felt close to him and liked to be around him and do things which pleased him. He would often praise her and give her credit for things she did well when she tried to help him. She spent much more time with him than she did with her mother, and by age four father had begun to extend his affectionate cuddling into some degree of genital fondling. She remembers him asking, "You want me to make it feel good down there?" and her answering, "Yes." By age seven, the father was having regular sex play with Laura, and this soon progressed to intercourse which continued for several years. Laura enjoyed the closeness and pleasure of the sexual activity, but also felt it was somehow wrong, because her father admonished her not to tell other people. She was puzzled about just what was "wrong," as father seemed to gain pleasure from the activity and had asked her to do it, and she had always been taught to obey him. In addition, her mother did not seem to disapprove, even though she was aware of what was happening between Laura and her husband.

The mother and father were rarely affectionate with each other and were often in open conflict. The mother rejected the father sexually and repeatedly told him to leave her alone. They usually slept in different rooms. There was no doubt that mother was aware of the incest, because sometimes after an argument with the father, she would encourage Laura to go and sleep with him. Sometimes she had asked Laura to get money from the father after she slept with him and bring it back to her so that she could buy a bottle of liquor.

When Laura was thirteen, her father became depressed, as far as she knew, because of his endless difficulties in trying to make a living. He committed suicide in the bedroom of their home using a shotgun to blow off part of his face and the top of his head, while Laura was helping her mother to cook dinner. She was utterly devastated as well as shocked. Three days later, after the funeral, on a cold, gray, rainy day, Laura and her mother came back home and went into the bedroom. It smelled badly, and she opened the shutters and the windows to let in light and air, and she recalls, "I looked around the room, and there I saw bits of flesh and hair on the wall and the ceiling, all that was left of my father. He was the only one I ever loved, and the only person who ever loved me."

The next year, when she was fourteen, Laura acquired a steady boyfriend. He was friendly and affectionate to her and spoke in a way when they were alone that made her feel very beautiful and fine. She began having intercourse with him frequently and enjoyed it. In public, however, he fought with her and treated her as "something to wipe his feet on." She could not stand the mistreatment and broke up with him. Years later, she still dreamed about him and fantasized about him, even though she realized life with him would not have been good.

At fifteen, she began dating cadets at an air force base. She loved being treated "like a lady" by these somewhat older young men. Frequently, the relationships became sexual affairs, but they did not seem meaningful to her and did not last very long. She became more promiscuous, and between ages eighteen and twenty-one she describes having affairs with thirty-two different men and had, at times, "carried on" with as many as three men in one day. She then met and married at twenty-two, a man who was very kind, patient, and considerate of her. He listened to her, tried to do things to please her and to make her happy. In spite of what seemed to her an ideal marriage, she continued periodically to have affairs and, at times, found her husband physically repulsive. By the time we knew her, she felt, by her behavior, that she had "ruined" him and changed him from a kindly person to an angry, punitive one. She avoided sex with him and was often very critical of him, despite all his efforts. Although it was not really necessary, Laura often worked part-time in order to "get money to help the family finances," thus reducing the financial burden on her husband, and also to get away from the house. At these jobs she often met the men with whom she would become involved.

Toward Jimmy, the older of her two sons, Laura had been extremely ambivalent. At times she had felt love for him and, in general, had taken good physical care of him. Yet, she was more likely to be filled with feelings of disgust and hatred, and had often wished that she could get rid of him or that he would die. She expected him to be quite capable and obedient, and for various misbehaviors she would beat him with her fists or whip him with a belt or board. She seemed to be aware that fundamentally Jimmy was a rather normal little boy, but she said, "He has all my faults, and I have tried to beat all his phobias and other problems out of him. I know it's not sensible, but I can't control myself. I think he must be me, and I'm a combination of my mother and my father. My mother would never pay any attention to me, and my father would beat me. I say to Jimmy, 'I'll knock you through the wall,' just like daddy used to say to me." Laura had a curious mixture of feeling guilty over her mistreatment of the boy, and yet, at the same time, feeling justifiably angry at him because of his deficits and failures. She also considered that she had brainwashed her husband into following her pattern of screaming and yelling at this boy, to whom he had previously been very good. Laura felt she had ruined both her husband and her son, but her guilty responsibility could not eliminate her anger. She would say, "I want to get rid of them both. I want them both to die. But I've thought of suicide myself because I've been ruining them." Although Laura did not drink regularly or excessively, after a social evening with a few drinks she was more likely to get into quarrels with her husband and have more trouble with Jimmy, with likelihood of abuse.

With her younger son, Benny, Laura had a completely different relationship. She loved him dearly and had for him a warmth and affection she had not previously known she was capable of feeling. She surmised that he was like her younger brogher, Joe, to whom her mother had given all her love and affection, and she was imitating her own mother in this. Laura was bewildered by these very intense and yet discrepant feelings. She was quite puzzled about her own identity, which she expressed at various times in such thoughts as "I think Jimmy must be me, and I'm a combination of my mother and father. When I would talk to my mother, she would be far away and not answer. I do the same thing with Jimmy. It was father who used to beat me; now it seems Jimmy is me, and I'm beating him the way father beat me. Little Benny is my brother, Joe. Mother gave all her love and protection to Joe, and I am very kind and loving to him." Another time she said, "I don't know yet who I really am. I am beginning to think I am somebody and I know a little bit about who I am, but I'm having trouble becoming it and being something. I don't know whether I am my father or my brother, Joe, or a combination of all of them or whether I am my children."

After her marriage, Laura periodically made an attempt to establish some sort of friendly relationship with her mother, and there were occasional visits. But they never did reach any true emotional rapport nor could they discuss the events of Laura's earlier life. With her brother Joe she had a distant, hostile relationship. While there was no evidence of overt incestuous activity between Joe and his mother, she seemed to have exploitatively tried to keep him close to her and had hampered his separation and individuation. He eventually became seriously disturbed, and once, when he threatened to kill their mother, Laura offered her sanctuary and protection. At that time there was some feeling of closeness which was soon ruptured by her mother's inconsiderate disregard of her daughter's feelings and criticisms of her behavior.

Superficially, Laura appeared to be a popular, attractive, young married woman with two children, similar to many other young women who lived with their armed-service–career husbands around a military base. Yet, she was seriously troubled, behaviorally and psychologically, both in her marriage and in her child-caring functions. In this tragic history are the themes of economic difficulty, alcoholism, social isolation, parental conflict, maternal deprivation, sibling rivalry, physical abuse, incest, and father-loss by suicide. As an adult, she shows many of the characteristics commonly met with in parents who maltreat children. She has a mild, chronic depression, very low self-esteem, inability to have pleasure or find satisfaction for her long-lasting emptiness and need for love and attention, lack of a coherent, consistent sense of identity, and misperceptions of her children. The striking split between good and bad objects, uncoordinated ego functions and unintegrated components of identity are similar to those described as characteristic of "borderline states." These psychological difficulties seem to be clearly related to the experiences she had with the caretakers of her early life and the necessity for her to adapt somehow to them. She has identified with the several parts of the inconsistent caretaking behaviors of both mother and father and also maintains a self-concept closely related to herself as a child. She transfers and attributes, to adults in her present environment and to her own children, attitudes and feelings she had toward the important figures of her early life. Her sexual behavior seems to be a frantic, desperate, compulsive search for a man to love and be loved by and is at least partly due to unresolved grief over the death of her father by suicide. She overidealized her father, clinging especially to the loving side of her ambivalence toward him, has never fully relinquished her attachment to him, and has been unable to find an adequate replacement for the warm closeness she had with him, including the incest. Her promiscuity is undoubtedly related to the sexualization of this early love relationship with the father. Yet, the desperateness of her search also suggests it has deep roots in an effort to find a substitute for the lack of basic, empathic love from the mother of her early life. Her inability to gain full satisfaction or pleasure from sexual activity stems partly from the fact that in itself sexual activity cannot replace this lack of a deep, early sense of being empathically loved and cared for. It is also partly due to residual guilt in relationship to the father, which is not so much a feeling of having done something wrong sexually with him, but rather that she had not been able, even in her most warm and loving sexual surrender to him, to make him happy enough to prevent the suicide. Laura was aware that her sexual behavior was not really acceptable in society. Yet this was not totally a feeling of guilt over sexuality, but more a sense that she was ineffectual and never good enough for other people. It was not a strong, inner sense of having done something wrong for which she deserved punishment, nor did she give evidence of guilt over sexual behavior in relation to having displaced her mother in her father's affections. In fact, her earliest, powerful, superego identifications are with the mother who encouraged the sexual relationship with the father and with a father who instigated and appreciated the sexual relationship. Because she is still unconsciously fixated to the loving, sexual father of her childhood, who was also abusive, she has had the recurrent tendency to attach herself to men who not only love her, but who are also cruel to her, fight with her, or attack her physically. By criticizing and frustrating her husband who was originally quite affectionate and considerate to her, she managed to change him into a person who is mean to her and maltreats their child, thus recreating the father of her childhood.

Laura relives another part of the childhood drama in her ambivalent behavior toward her older son, Jimmy, whom she misperceives as almost a reincarnation of her own childhood self. In identification with her father, she loves Jimmy at times, but she also abuses him, hitting him, using a belt on him, and repeating to him the same words her father used, "I'll knock you through the wall." At other times, she repeats the behavior of her mother toward herself and is unresponsive, inattentive, and unempathic toward Jimmy. With her younger son, Benny, she repeats the kind, preferential care which her mother gave to her younger brother, Joe, and she also lavishes on Benny the love which she wishes she had had as a little girl, gaining some vicarious pleasure from this. In view of Laura's disturbing experiences in early life and the multiple, inconsistent identifications with her parents, it is not surprising that she is significantly hampered in her child-caring activities and has become what we call an abusive parent. Her tendency to repeat the past and get herself involved in unhappy experiences is an example of moral masochism in the sense described by Berliner as "self-defeating or destructive behavior," due to attachment to a sadistic love object. Difficulties in having pleasure or enjoying life generally, as well as constantly recurring patterns of getting into difficulty, are characteristic of most of the maltreating caretakers we have known. This masochistic tendency makes such persons increasingly vulnerable and unable to cope with the troublesome crises and difficulties that inevitably occur in all people's lives, especially in the care of children.

The process of responding to the parents of earliest years, the identification with them, and the persistence of these identifications into adult life is not in any way abnormal. It is a normal part of the psychic development of all children. As noted before, the problem lies in the kind of parent available to the identification process. Laura identified with both the punitive and loving aspects of her father and with the aloof, rejecting, uncaring aspects of her mother, as well as with her mother's loving care of a boy. In her social interactions, Laura maintained superficially close sexualized relationships with men and more distant, often antagonistic, relations with women. In therapy she established positive relationships with three successive male therapists whom she felt "understood" her, but remained suspicious and cool toward female clinic personnel.

Summary

Parents and others who maltreat the infants and children under their care are not haphazardly discharging destructive impulses in the form of abuse and neglect.

They are following understandable and predictable patterns of parent-child inter-actions which have been basically determined by the way they themselves were cared for in infancy. Beginning with poor attachment in the perinatal period, followed in ensuing months and years by unempathic care, unrealistic demands, and excessive criticism, and punishment for failure, they developed poor self-esteem, poor basic trust, and fragmented identities. Deeply embedded identifica-tions with their parents and their behaviors, which will surface most strongly in times of stress, lead to repetitions of the patterns in their own child-care behav-iors. During the earliest, most impressionable period of life, while under the exclusive care of its own family before contact is made with the wider culture, the patterns are transmitted from caretaker to child, and the potentials for physical abuse, neglect, and sexual exploitation are recreated for yet another generation.

References

1. Kempe, C. H., Silverman, F. N., Steele, B. F., Droegemueller, W., and Silver, H. K. 1962. The Battered-Child Syndrome. *J. Am. Med. Assoc.* 181:17–24.
2. Steele, B., and Pollock, C. 1968. A Psychiatric Study of Parents Who Abuse Infants and Small Children. In *The Battered Child,* edited by R. Helfer and C. H. Kempe. Chicago: University of Chicago Press.
3. Steele, B. F. 1970. Parental Abuse of Infants and Small Children. In *Parenthood: Its Psychology and Psychopathology,* edited by E. J. Anthony and T. Benedek. Boston: Little, Brown & Co.
4. Straus, M. A. 1979. Family Patterns and Child Abuse in a Nationally Representative Sample. *Child Abuse and Neglect* 3:213–25.
5. Curtis, G. 1963. Violence Breeds Violence—Perhaps? *Am. J. Psychiatry* 120:386–87.
6. Oliver, J. E., and Taylor, Audrey. 1971. Five Generations of Ill-treated Children in One Family Pedigree. *Br. J. Psychiatry* 119:552.
7. Silver, L. B., Dublin, C. C., and Lourie, R. S. 1969. Does Violence Breed Violence? Contributions from a Study of the Child Abuse Syndrome. *Am. J. Psychiatry* 126:404–07.
8. Spinetta, J. J., and Rigler, D. 1972. The Child-Abusing Parent: A Psychological Review. *Psychol. Bull.* 77:296–304.
9. Fontana, V., and Besharov, D. 1977. *The Maltreated Child.* Springfield, Ill.: Charles C. Thomas.
10. Morris, M. G., and Gould, R. W. 1963. Role Reversal: A Concept in Dealing with the Neglected/Battered Child Syndrome. In *The Neglected-Battered Child Syndrome.* New York: Child Welfare League of America.
11. Gray, J. D., Cutler, C. A., Dean, J, G., and Kempe, C. H. 1977. Prediction and Prevention of Child Abuse and Neglect. *Child Abuse and Neglect* 1:45–58.
12. Ainsworth, M. 1973. Development of Infant-Mother Attachment. In *Child*

Development and Social Policy. Review of Child Development Research, vol. 3, edited by B. Caldwell and H. N. Ricciuti. Chicago: University of Chicago Press.

13. Bowlby, J. 1969. *Attachment.* New York: Basic Books.
14. Brazelton, T. B., Kozlowski, B., and Main, M. 1974. The Origins of Reciprocity: The Early Mother-Infant Interaction. In *The Effect of the Infant on Its Caregiver,* edited by M. Lewis and L. Rosenblum. New York: Wiley.
15. Klaus, M., and Kennell, J. 1976. *Maternal-Infant Bonding.* St. Louis: C. V. Mosby.
16. Kennell, J. H., *et al.* 1972. Maternal Behavior One Year After Early and Extended Post-Partum Contact. *Dev. Med. Child Neurol.* 16:172–79.
17. Lynch, M., and Roberts J. 1977. Predicting Child Abuse: Signs of Bonding Failure in the Maternity Hospital. *Br. Med. J.* 1:624–26.
18. Ounsted, C., Oppenheimer, R., and Lindsay, J. 1974. Aspects of Bonding Failure: The Psychopathology and Psychotherapeutic Treatment of Families of Battered Children. *Dev. Med. Child Neurol.* 16:447–52.
19. Melnick, B., and Hurley, J. R. 1969. Distinctive Personality Attributes of Child Abusing Mothers. *J. Consult. Clin. Psychol.* 33:746–49.
20. Benedek, T. 1959. Parenthood as a Developmental Phase: A Contribution to the Libido Theory. *J. Am. Psychoanal. Assoc.* 7:389–417.
21. Olden, C. 1953. On Adult Empathy with Children. *Psychoanal. Study Child* 8:111–26.
22. ———. 1958. Notes on the Development of Empathy. *Psychoanal. Study Child* 13:505–18.
23. Josselyn, I. 1956. Cultural Forces, Motherliness and Fatherliness. *Am. J. Orthopsychiatry* 26:264–71.
24. Bullard, D., Glaser, H., Heagarty, M., and Pivchik, E. 1967. Failure to Thrive in the Neglected Child. *Am. J. Orthopsychiatry* 37:680–90.
25. Spitz, R. 1945. Hospitalism. *Psychoanal. Study Child* 1:53–74.
26. ———. 1946. Hospitalism: a Follow-up Report. *Psychoanal. Study Child* 2:113–17.
27. Provence, S., and Lipton, R. 1962. *Infants in Institutions.* New York: International Universities Press.
28. Koel, B. S. 1969. Failure to Thrive and Fatal Injury as a Continuum. *Am. J. Diseases Child.* 118:565–67.
29. Barbero, G., Morris, M., and Reford, M. 1963. Malidentification of Mother-Baby-Father Relationships Expressed in Infant Failure to Thrive. *Child Welfare* 42:13.
30. Barbero, G., and Shaheen, E. 1967. Environmental Failure to Thrive. *J. Pediatr.* 71:639.
31. Elmer, E. 1960. Failure to Thrive: Role of the Mother. *Pediatrics* 25:717.
32. Fischoff, J., Whitten, C., and Pettit, M. 1971. A Psychiatric Study of Mothers of Infants with Growth Failure, Secondary to Maternal Deprivation. *J. Pediatr.* 79:209–15.
33. Leonard, M. F., Rhymes, J. P., and Solnit, A. J., 1966. Failure to Thrive in

Infants. *Am. J. Diseases Child.* 111:600–612.

34. Glaser, D., and Bentovim, A. 1979. Abuse and Risk to Handicapped and Chronically Ill Children. *Child Abuse and Neglect* 3:565–75.

35. Johnson, B., and Morse, H. A. 1968. Injured Children and Their Parents. *Children* 15:147–52.

36. Milowe, J. D., and Lourie, R. S. 1964. The Child's Role in the Battered Child Syndrome. *J. Pediatr.* 65:1079–81.

37. Friedrich, W. N., and Boriskin, J. A. 1976. The Role of the Child in Abuse: A Review of the Literature. *Am. J. Orthopsychiatry* 46:58–590.

38. deLissovoy, Vladimer. 1979. Toward the Definition of "Abuse Provoking Child." *Child Abuse and Neglect* 3:341–50.

39. H. G. Creel, ed. 1948. *Literary Chinese by the Inductive Method.* Chicago: University of Chicago Press.

40. deChateau, P., and Wiberg, B. 1977. Long-term Effect on Mother-Infant Behavior of Extra Contact during the First Hour Post-partum. *Acta Pediatr. Scand.* 66:137–51.

41. Satten, J., Menninger, K., Rosen, I., and Mayman, M. 1960. Murder without Apparent Motive: A Study in Personality Disorganization. *Am. J. Psychiatry* 117:48–53.

42. Adelson, L. 1961. Slaughter of.the Innocents. *New Engl. J. Med.* 264:1345–49.

43. Piers, M. W. 1978. *Infanticide: Past and Present.* New York: Norton.

44. Resnick, P. J. 1969. Child Murder by Parents: A Psychiatric Review of Filicide. *Am. J. Psychiatry* 126:325–34.

45. Steele, B. 1978. Psychology of Infanticide Resulting from Maltreatment. In *Infanticide and the Value of Life,* edited by M. Kohl. Buffalo: Prometheus Books.

46. Lukianowicz, N. 1972. Incest. *Br. J. Psychiatry* 120:301–13.

47. Nakashima, I., and Zakus, G. 1977. Incest: Review and Clinical Experience. *Pediatrics* 60:696–700.

48. Summit, R., and Kryso, J. 1978. Sexual Abuse of Children: A Clinical Spectrum. *Am. J. Orthopsychiatry* 48:237–51.

49. Westermeyer, J. 1978. Incest in Psychiatric Practice: A Description of Patients and Incestuous Relationships. *J. Clin. Psychiatry* 39:643–48.

50. Meiselman, Karin C. 1978. *Incest: A Psychological Study of Causes and Effects with Treatment Recommendations.* San Francisco: Jossey-Bass.

51. Greenberg, N. H. 1979. The Epidemiology of Childhood Sexual Abuse. *Pediatr. Ann.* 8:289–99.

52. Langsley, D. G., Schwartz, M. N., and Fairbairn, R. H. 1968. Father-Son Incest. *Comprehensive Psychiatry* 9:218–26.

53. Raybin, J. B. 1969. Homosexual Incest. *J. Nerv. Ment. Dis.* 148:105–10.

54. Raphling, D. L., Carpenter, B. L., and Davis, A. 1967. Incest: A Genealogical Study. *Arch. Gen. Psychiatry* 16:505–11.

55. Gebhard, P. H., *et al.* 1965. *Sex Offenders: An Analysis of Types.* New York: Harper and Row.

56. Yorokoglu, A., and Kemph, J. P. 1966. Children Not Severely Damaged by

Incest with Parent. *J. Am. Acad. Child Psychiatry* 51:111–24.

57. Kaufman, I., Peck, A. L., and Tagiuri, C. K. 1954. Family Constellation and Overt Incestuous Relations between Father and Daughter. *Am. J. Orthopsychiatry* 24:266–77.

58. Weiss, J., *et al.* 1955. A Study of Girl Sex Victims. *Psychiat. Q.* 29:1–27.

59. Reimer, S. 1940. A Research Note on Incest. *Am. J. Sociology* 45:566–75.

60. Lustig, N., *et al.* 1966. Incest: A Family Group Survival Pattern. *Arch. Gen. Psychiatry* 14:31–40.

61. Weiner, I. B. 1962. Father-Daughter Incest: A Clinical Report. *Psychiat. Q.* 36:607–32.

62. Winer, I. B. 1964. On Incest: A Survey. *Excerpt. Criminol.* 4:137–55.

63. Hartogs, R. 1951–1952. Discipline in the Early Life of Sex-Delinquents and Sex-Criminals. *The Nervous Child* 9:167–73.

64. Wahl, C. W. 1960. The Psychodynamics of Consummated Maternal Incest. *Arch. Gen. Psychiatry* 3:188–93.

5 Stress and Child Abuse

Murray A. Straus

Life is full of paradoxes, and perhaps even more so in the family than elsewhere. Two of these ironic or paradoxical aspects of the family concern the high level of stress and the high level of violence that is characteristic of American family life.

In the case of violence, the paradox is that the family is, at one and the same time, the most physically violent group or institution that a typical citizen is likely to encounter (22, 24, 25, 30, 31) and also the group to which most people look for love, support, and gentleness. So the hallmarks of family life are both love and violence.

Much of the work of the Family Violence Research Program at the University of New Hampshire has been designed to unravel that paradox. We are a long way from a full explanation. However, some progress has been made. This chapter examines one of the several factors which go into that explanation: the link between stress and violence.

Another irony of family life is the fact that although the family is a place where one can find respite from the tensions of the world, the family is at the same time a group with its own inherently high level of conflict and stress. The theoretical case for this view is detailed elsewhere (4, 7). In this chapter we will illustrate but two stress producing aspects of the family.

One source of family stress is the fact that, in addition to the normal differences and conflicts between two or more people, the family has built into its basic structure the so-called battle of the sexes and the generation gap. A second source of stress is inherent in what is expected of families. For example, families are expected to provide adequate food, clothing, and shelter in a society which does not always give families the resources necessary to do this. Another example is the expectation that families bring up healthy, well-adjusted, law-abiding, and intelligent children who can "get ahead in the world." The stress occurs because these traits, and the opportunity to "get ahead," are all factors which are to a greater or lesser extent beyond the control of any given family.

Murray A. Straus, Ph.D., is professor of sociology at the University of New Hampshire.

The basic argument of the chapter is probably clear by what has just been said: that a major cause of the high rate of child abuse is the stress and conflict which tends to characterize families. Of course, this is only a plausible argument. Brenner (2), for example, has shown a clear relationship between stress as indexed by the unemployment rate and the rate of assault and homicide in the United States, Canada, and Great Britain. But is it that people are assaulted or murdered by unemployed members of their own families? This needs to be demonstrated with empirical data. Consequently, a major part of this chapter is devoted to such an empirical study.

The Theoretical Model

Although the empirical findings will start with the relationship between the level of stress in families and the level of child abuse, it is not argued that stress *directly* causes child abuse. Violence is only one of many possible responses to stress. Among the alternatives are passivity, resignation, or just leaving. University departments, for example, are also stressful environments, but the rate of physical violence within such departments is close to zero.

The absence of any necessary link between stress and violence is shown in Brenner's data on the correlates of unemployment (2). Unemployment is highly correlated not only with assault and homicide, but also with annual rates of hypertension, deaths from heart attacks, mental hospital admissions, and alcoholism. Similarly, Brown and Harris (3) studied a random sample of women in London, using highly reliable and valid data on life stresses. The interesting point is that they demonstrated a clear tendency for these women to respond to stress by *depression* rather than violence.

Mediating Variables

The above suggests that other factors must be present for stress to result in violence. The central box in figure 5.1 illustrates some of the other variables. For example, people are unlikely to respond to stress by violence unless this is part of the socially scripted method of dealing with stress and frustration—as it is in our society. So, an important part of the model is the existence of norms or images of behavior which depict striking out at others when under stress as part of human nature.

However, these are very general behavioral scripts. They cannot explain *family* violence, because they are part of the society's image of basic nature in *all* types of situations. They may be part of the explanation, but they are not sufficient. To find the additional variables which will lead to a sufficient explanation, one has to look at the nature of the family itself.

Normative Legitimacy of Family Violence

One very simple, but nonetheless important, factor is that the family has different rules about violence than other groups. In an office or a factory, the basic rule is that no one can hit anyone else, no matter what they do wrong. A person can be

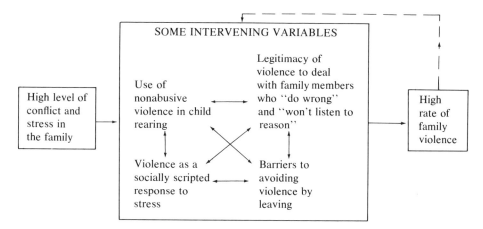

Figure 5.1

Partial model of relationship between stress and family violence. This diagram is labeled as a "partial" model for two main reasons: first, the most obvious reason is that it includes only a sampling of the intervening variables which could be included in the center box. Second, the model omits negative feedback loops (i.e., deviation dampening processes) which must be present. Without them the violence would escalate to the point where the system would self-destruct—as it sometimes, but not typically, does. See Straus (22) for a systems model of family violence which includes negative feedback processes and other elements of a cybernetic system.

a pest, an intolerable bore, negligent, incompetent, selfish, or unwilling to listen to reason. But that still does not give anyone the right to hit such a person. In the family the situation is different. There, the basic rule is that if someone does wrong and "won't listen to reason," violence is permissible, and sometimes even required.

This is clearly the case in respect to the rights and obligations of parents, but it also applies to spouses. As one husband said about an incident in which his wife threw a coffee pot at him, "I was running around with other women—I deserved it." Statements like that are made by many husbands and wives. In fact, the evidence suggests that a marriage license is also a hitting license (24, 28). Still, that does not explain why or how such a norm arose or why it persists. Here again there are a number of factors, one of which is shown in figure 5.1: the "nonabusive" use of violence in child rearing, that is, physical punishment.

Family Socialization in Violence

Physical punishment provides the society's basic training in violence, but, of course, training which applies most directly to behavior in the family. At least some use of physical punishment is just about universal in American society, typically beginning in infancy (20). What are the reasons for saying that learning about violence starts with physical punishment?

When physical punishment is used, several things can be expected to occur. Most obviously, the infant or child learns to do or not to do whatever the punishment is intended to teach, for example, not to pick up things from the ground and put them in his or her mouth. Less obvious, but equally or more important, are four other lessons which are so deeply learned that they become an integral part of one's personality and world view.

The first of these unintended consequences is the association of love with violence. Mommy and daddy are the first, and usually the only ones, to hit an infant. For most children this continues throughout childhood (21). The child therefore learns that the primary love objects are also those who hit.

Second, since physical punishment is used to train the child or to teach about dangerous things to be avoided, it establishes the moral rightness of hitting other family members.

The third unintended consequence is the "Johnny I've told you ten times" principle—that when something is really important, it justifies the use of physical force.

Fourth is the idea that when one is under stress, is tense, or angry, hitting— although wrong—is understandable, i.e., to a certain extent legitimate.

Involuntary Nature of Family Membership

The last of the mediating variables we will discuss is the simple fact that the family is only a semi-voluntary institution. This is most obvious in the case of children. They cannot leave, nor can parents throw them out until a legally set age. So leaving—which is probably the most widely used and effective method of avoiding violence—is not available as an alternative in the parent-child relationship.

A number of other factors should be included in figure 5.1 and in this discussion. Those which have been discussed, however, should be sufficient to illustrate the theory which guided the analysis in this chapter.

By way of summary, the theory underlying this chapter rejects the idea that humans have an innate drive toward aggression or an innate tendency to respond to stress by aggression. Rather, a link between stress and aggression occurs only (a) if the individual has learned an "aggressive" response to stress, (b) if such a response is a culturally recognized script for behavior under stress, and (c) if the situation seems to be one which will produce rewards for aggression.

Sample

The data used to examine this theory were obtained in January and February of 1976. Interviews were conducted with a national-area probability sample of 1,146 persons with at least one child age three through seventeen living at home. Each respondent had to be between eighteen and seventy years of age and living with a member of the opposite sex as a couple. However, the couple did not have to be formally married. A random half of the respondents were female and half were male. Interviews lasted approximately one hour, were completely anonymous, and interviewers were of the racial or language group which was predominant in the sampling area for which they were responsible (30).

Definition and Measures of Stress

There has been considerable debate about the concept of stress (12–15, 18, 19). Is the stress caused by illness, unemployment, family conflict, getting married or being promoted to a new job a property of the situation? For some people, a new set of job responsibilities is experienced as stress, whereas for others, *lack* of such new responsibility is a stress.

The definition used here treats stress as a function of the interaction of the subjectively defined demands of a situation and the capacity of an individual or group to respond to these demands. Stress exists when the subjectively experienced demands are inconsistent with response capabilities. This can be demands in excess of capabilities or a low level of demand relative to response capabilities. A more adequate formulation of the concept of stress includes a number of other elements. For example, Farrington (4) has identified six components which need to be taken into account in research on stress: the stressor stimulus, objective demands, subjective demands, response capabilities, choice of response, and stress level. Important as are these six components, they will be ignored in this chapter because there is no way to investigate them with the data available.

There is a gap between the definition of stress given above and data I will actually report. This is because the methodology of this chapter *assumes* (*a*) that some *life event,* such as moving or the illness of a child, produces a certain, but unknown, degree of demand on parents, (*b*) that on the average this is subjectively experienced as a demand, (*c*) that the capabilities of parents to respond to these demands will not always be sufficient, and (*d*) that the result is a certain level of stress. On the basis of these assumptions, it is then possible to investigate the relationship between such stressful life events and the level of violence in the family. Obviously, that leaves a large agenda for other investigators to develop a more adequate measure of stress.

As indicated above, the aspect of stress which is measured in this study is limited to what are called *stressor stimuli.* These data were obtained by a modified version of the Holmes and Rahe stressful life events scale (10). Because of limited interview time, the scale used here was restricted to the eighteen items listed in table 5.1.[1] The scores on this scale ranged from 0 to 13, with a mean of 2.4 and a standard deviation of 2.0.

1. The stress index used in this study actually departs in other ways than length from the Holmes and Rahe scale. (*a*) One of the criteria used to select items from the larger original set was to eliminate stresses which have a *positive cathexis.* This was done on the basis of methodological studies which show that it is the *negative* items which account for most of the relationship between scores on the stress index and other variables (8, 17). (*b*) We modified some items and added some which are not in the Holmes and Rahe scale to secure a set of stressors which seemed best for the purpose of this research. (*c*) The Holmes and Rahe weights were not used in computing the index score for each respondent. This was based on research which found that weighting makes little difference in the validity of scales of this type (32) and of the Holmes and Rahe scale specifically (11).

An important limitation which this stress index shares with the Holmes and Rahe index is that one does not know the time distribution of the stressful events. At one extreme, a person who experienced four of the stressors during the year could have had them spread out over the year, or at the other extreme, all four could have occurred at roughly the same time.

TABLE 5.1   **Percentage Experiencing Life Stresses during Previous Year**

Stressful Event	Male (N=519)	Female (N=616)	Total (N=1135)
1. Troubles with the boss	28.3	9.6	18.2
2. Troubles with other people at work	35.6	9.4	21.4
3. Layoff or job loss	9.8	5.9	7.7
4. Arrest or conviction for serious crime	1.9	0.5	1.2
5. Death of someone close	39.8	34.7	37.0
6. Foreclosure of a mortgage or loan	1.5	1.5	1.5
7. Pregnancy or birth of a child	8.4	15.1	12.0
8. Serious sickness or injury	15.0	15.8	15.4
9. Serious problem with health or behavior of a family member	19.6	29.6	25.0
10. Sexual difficulties	9.8	12.5	11.3
11. In-law troubles	12.7	13.7	13.2
12. New, serious financial problems	15.2	12.5	13.7
13. Separation or divorce	3.3	2.3	2.9
14. Big increase in arguments with spouse/partner	8.5	11.1	9.9
15. Big increase in hours worked or job responsibilities	33.3	17.8	24.9
16. Move to different neighborhood or town	15.8	13.6	14.6
17. Suspension or expulsion of child from school	2.3	2.6	2.5
18. Apprehension of child in illegal act	3.9	4.4	4.2

Sex Differences

The 519 fathers in this sample experienced a somewhat higher number of stressors during the year (2.7) than did the 616 mothers (2.1). Despite this fact, table 5.1 shows that for the most part the experiences reported by the fathers and mothers are quite similar. The exceptions are events to which men and women have different exposure. Thus, fewer women have paid employment, so it is not surprising that two to four times as many men as women experienced an occupationally related stress, such as trouble with a boss or job loss.[2]

There are a few other interesting sex differences. First, item 4 (table 5.1) shows that four times as many men were arrested or convicted of a serious crime. An interesting sidelight is that there is such a high rate of arrest or conviction (2 per 100 men).

The only other item with a nontrivial difference is item 7 (table 5.1) (experiencing a pregnancy or having a child). This difference is probably due to men misunderstanding the question. It was meant to apply to the men, as well as the women, in the sample, whose wives became pregnant or had a child in the last year.

2. See Straus (28) for a discussion of the reasons for the higher rate of child abuse by mothers. In respect to the difference in the relationship between stress and child abuse for mothers and fathers, it is interesting that this reverses when the dependent variable is spouse abuse. When the dependent variable is violence against a spouse (either ordinary violence or severe assaults), it is violence by *wives* which is most closely correlated with stress (see Straus 26 and p. 94).

Frequency of Different Stressors

The most frequently occurring stress among the eighteen items on the list (table 5.1) is the death of someone close to the respondent (item 5). This happened to 37% of our respondents during the year we asked about. The next most frequent stress is closely related: item 9, a serious problem with the health or behavior of someone in the family. This occurred in the lives of 1 out of 4. For men, however, occupational stresses occurred more frequently. Item 2 shows that about ⅓ had a difficulty with their bosses, and, at the positive end, about the same percentage had a large increase in their work responsibilities (item 15).

Definition and Measure of Child Abuse

Measuring child abuse also poses many difficulties (6). The technique used in this study is known as the Conflict Tactics Scales (27). It consists of a checklist of acts of physical violence. The respondent is asked about difficulties with other family members in the past year and then is asked if, in the course of such difficulties and conflicts in the past year, he or she did any of the items on the list. The list starts with nonviolent tactics, such as talking things over, and then proceeds on to verbally aggressive tactics, and finally to physical aggression—that is, violent acts.

Child Abuse

The violent acts in turn were designed to represent a measure of the severity, as well as the frequency, of family violence. The list starts out with pushing, slapping, shoving, and throwing things. These are what can be called the "ordinary" or "normal" violence of family life. It then goes on to kicking, biting, punching, hitting with an object, beating up, and using a knife of gun. This latter group of items was used to compute a measure of "severe violence" which is the measure of child abuse in this chapter, because it consists of acts that put the child at risk of serious injury.

Incidence of Child Abuse

The rates of child abuse revealed by this method are truly astounding. Each year, 14 out of every 100 American children, age three through seventeen, experienced an assault that was serious enough to be included in our Child Abuse Index (see table 5.2). This means that of the 46 million children of this age group in the United States who live with both parents, approximately 6.5 million are abused each year.

It might be objected that this index uses too liberal a definition of child abuse, because one of the items is "hitting with an object." For some parents, that could be the traditional strap, cane, or paddle, rather than an out-of-control assault. So, we recomputed the index, leaving out the data on hitting with objects. The rates drop sharply to "only" 3 or 4 out of every 100 parents and to an estimate of 1.7 million children per year.

TABLE 5.2   **Violent Acts and Child Abuse Index Rates by Age of Child**
                        (Per Hundred Children)

Conflict Tactics and Child Abuse Index	Age				Total (N=1129)
	3–4 (N=179)	5–9 (N=347)	10–14 (N=365)	15–17 (N=238)	
Kicked, bit, punched	6.1	3.2	2.2	2.5	3.3
Hit with an object	19.6	19.7	9.6	4.2	15.4
"Beat up" child	1.1	0.9	1.1	1.7	1.2
Used a knife or gun	0.0	0.0	0.3	0.0	0.1
Child Abuse Index	19.8	20.9	10.2	5.6	14.0

The data just presented might overstate the amount of child abuse, because a family is included if even one isolated incident of abusive violence occurred during that year. On the other hand, these rates may understate the extent to which children are severely assaulted by their parents, because the figures do not take into account how often such assaults occurred. The answer to this question is that if one assault occurred, several were likely. In fact, in only 6% of the child abuse cases was there a single incident. The mean number of assaults per year was 10.5 and the median 4.5.

It is obvious that the incidence of child abuse obtained by this method is many times that estimated by the United States National Center on Child Abuse and Neglect (NCCAN). NCCAN has published figures indicating approximately a million children per year are abused. However, that includes neglect, sexual abuse, and psychological abuse. The physical abuse figure they report is approximately 250,000. What accounts for the difference between that quarter of a million and our minimum figure of almost 2 million? There are two main reasons:

1. The NCCAN figures are based on incidents which come to official attention. This leaves out the vast number of cases in which physical abuse is suspected and not reported, as well as the equally vast number of cases in which a child is nonaccidentally injured, but there is no suspicion of abuse.

2. Probably the most important reason why our rates are so much higher is that our data are based on violent acts carried out, rather than on injuries produced. Fortunately, children are resilient. Many are the children who have been thrown against walls and who simply bounced off with, at most, a bruise. Only the relatively rare instances in which immediate and obvious injury occurs stand much chance of being suspected as parental abuse.

Why These Figures Are Underestimates

For reasons described elsewhere (30), the sample did not include children in the high-risk of abuse first two years of life. This is one of several factors which make even our very high rates of child abuse an underestimate. There are several other factors which push in the same direction. The second such factor is that these are self-reports by parents to a stranger doing a survey. Not every parent who has punched or kicked a child is going to admit that in such an interview. Third, the Conflict Tactics Scale include only a limited list of all the possible abusive acts. For example, we omitted burning a child, wiping out the child's mouth with noxious substances, and sexual abuse. Fourth, we interviewed either the father or the mother and have data only on that person's abuse of the child. But most children have two parents and therefore twice the risk—or at least a higher risk—of being abused than our figures show. A fifth factor making these underestimates is that our data are based on children living with two parents. The two parents need not be the child's natural parents. However, the omission of children living in one-parent households may lead to underestimating because child abuse may be greater under the strain of trying to raise children without the aid of a partner.

Stressful Life Events and Child Abuse

The data plotted in figure 5.2 show that the higher the stress score, the higher the rate of child abuse. However, the relationship between stress and child abuse is minimal for mothers. Perhaps this is because, even under low-stress conditions, the rate of child abuse by mothers is high (see n. 2, p. 91). But for fathers, there is a clear increase in abuse as the number of stressors experienced during the year increases.

An analysis identical to that in figure 5.2 was done, except that the dependent variable was not limited to severely violent acts. That is, the measure included pushing, slapping, shoving, and throwing things. Except for the fact that the rates are much higher, the results are similar.

The importance of this similarity is that it helps establish a connection which is extremely important for understanding child abuse. Over and over in our research, we find a clear connection between the "ordinary" violence of family life, such as spanking children or pushing or slapping a spouse, and serious violence such as child abuse and wife-beating. Actually, the connection goes deeper. *Verbal* aggression is also part of this pattern of relationships. People who hurt another family member verbally are also the ones most likely to hurt them physically (23). Moreover, the same set of causal factors applies to both the milder forms of violence and to acts of violence that are serious enough to be considered child abuse or spouse abuse. The similarity of the relationship between stress and the overall violence indexes with the relationship between stress and child abuse is but one of many such examples found for this sample (30).

Factors Linking Stress and Child Abuse

Interesting as are the findings presented so far, they do not reflect the theoretical model sketched at the beginning of this chapter in figure 5.1. One might even say that the data just presented distort the situation because the graph tends to draw attention away from a very important fact: most of the parents in this sample who experienced a high degree of stress did *not* abuse a child.

A critical question is brought to light by this fact. What accounts for the fact that

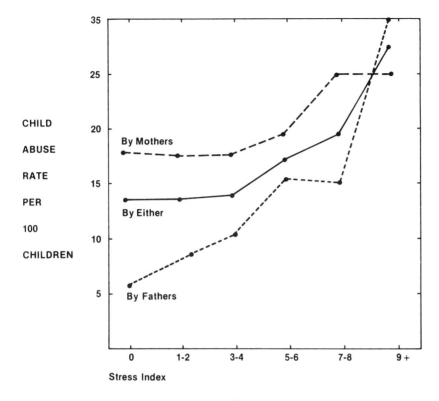

Figure 5.2

Child abuse rate by stress index score. The number of fathers and mothers on which each of the rates is based is: 0 = 73 fathers and 123 mothers; 1–2 = 198 fathers and 273 mothers; 3–4 = 147 fathers and 141 mothers; 5–6 = 59 fathers and 45 mothers; 7–8 = 19 fathers and 16 mothers; 9+ = 6 fathers and 4 mothers.

some people respond to stress by violence, whereas others do not? Part of the answer was suggested in the center box of figure 5.1 and the accompanying explanation. It will be recalled that this theory asserts that stress will result in aggressive acts (such as child abuse) only if certain mediating variables are also present. The balance of this chapter will be devoted to an empirical test of that theory.[3]

The first step in the analysis designed to take into account these mediating or intervening variables was to distinguish between parents in the sample who experienced none of the stressful events in the past year (N=196) and those in the high quarter of the stress index (N=149). These two groups were then further divided

3. Figure 5.1 is intended to illustrate the general nature of the theory, rather than to list all the variables which need to be taken into account. There are also two aspects of the model which are included simply to alert readers to their importance, but which will not figure in the empirical analysis. First, this chapter will not deal with feedback processes. Second, within the center box illustrating some of the intervening variables, the arrows show that each of these variables is related to the others. They are a mutually supportive system, and interaction effects are no doubt also present. However, in this chapter, these and other interevening variables will be dealt with one by one.

into those who were in the high quarter of each mediating variable versus those in the low quarter. This enables us to see if the mediating variable was, as specified in the theoretical model, necessary for life stresses to result in violence.

If the theory outlined in figure 5.1 is correct, the parents who had the combination of both high stress and the presence of a mediating variable will have a high rate of child abuse, whereas parents who also experienced high stress, but without the presence of a mediating variable, will not be more violent than the sample as a whole, despite the fact that they were under stress during the year.

Socialization for Violence

In the first section of table 5.3, the first line runs directly contrary to the theory being examined. It shows that parents who were physically punished the most by their *mothers* when they were teenagers were *less* abusive under stress than the parents who were not hit at this age by their mothers. On the other hand, the second line of table 5.3 shows that parents whose *fathers* hit them as teenagers have a child abuse rate which is ⅓ higher than parents who were under equally high stress that year, but who did not experience this much violence directed against them as teenagers. The difference between the effect of having been hit by one's mother versus by one's father suggests that violence by the father against a teenage child is a more influential role model for violent behavior which the child will later display under stress.

The next two lines of table 5.3 refer to violence *between the parents* of the parents in this sample. The child abuse rate by parents whose own fathers had hit their mothers was 44% higher than the rate for parents whose fathers never hit their mothers (22.7 per 100 versus 15.8). Surprisingly, there is only a small difference (and in the opposite direction) for parents who had grown up in families where their *mothers* had hit their fathers.

Legitimacy of Family Violence

The second section of table 5.3 reports *semantic differential* scores (16) in response to questions about slapping a child and slapping one's husband or wife. Each score is made up by combining the ratings for how "necessary," "normal," and "good" the respondent rated slapping.

The first line of the second section shows that parents who approved of slapping a child had a slightly greater rate of child abuse than did the parents with a score of zero on this index. When it comes to approval of slapping *a spouse*, there is a 72% difference in the predicted direction. These findings are consistent with the theoretical model asserting that the relation between stress and child abuse is a process that is mediated by social norms rather than a direct biologically determined relationship. However, since these are cross sectional data, the findings do not prove the correctness of the model. It is also quite plausible to interpret the greater child abuse rate by parents who approve of violence as an after-the-fact justification. Except for a few variables which clearly occurred at a previous time, such as the ones on violence experienced as a child, this caution applies to most of the findings to be reported.

TABLE 5.3   **Effect of Intervening Variables on Incidence of Child Abuse by Parents Experiencing High Stress**
(Per One Hundred Children)

	Child Abuse Rate	
Intervening Variable	Variable Absent	Variable Present
Childhood Experience with Violence:		
Physical punishment after age 12 by mother (0 vs. 4+ per yr.)	20.8	15.6
Physical punishment after age 12 by father (0 vs. 4+ per yr.)	14.0	18.6
Respondent's father hit mother (0 vs. 1+ per yr.)	15.8	22.7
Respondent's mother hit father (0 vs. 1+ per yr.)	17.1	15.4
Legitimacy of Family Violence:		
Approval of parents slapping a 12 yr. old (0 vs. high quarter)	15.8	17.0
Approval of slapping a spouse (0 vs. any approval)	13.5	23.2
Marital Satisfaction, Importance, and Violence:		
Marital Satisfaction Index (high vs. low quarter)	11.1	21.3
Marriage less important to husband than to wife (high=present)	15.4	22.2
Violence between the parents (none vs. any in past year)	16.7	21.6
Socioeconomic Status:		
Education (high vs. low quarter)	12.1	13.8
Husband's occupation (white collar vs. blue collar)	17.6	18.5
Income (high=>$22,500, low=<$9,000)	14.3	25.0
SES Index for family (high vs. low quarter)	10.0	20.0
Marital Power:		
Power Norm Index (present=husband should have final say)	8.3	19.6
Decision Power Index (present=husband has final say)	13.3	15.0
Social Integration:		
Organizational Participation Index (11+ vs. 0)	16.7	25.4
Religious service attendance (weekly vs. 0–1 per yr.)	12.0	27.9
Relatives living near (13+ vs. 0–2)	25.0	16.2

Note: The Ns vary because, even though the intent was for the high and low groups to be the upper and lower quarters, this was not always possible. In the case of occupational class, for example, the comparison is between a dichotomous nominal variable. In the case of continuous variables, we sometimes wanted to preserve the intrinsic meaning of a score category, such as those who with a score of 0, even though this might be more or less ¼ of the sample. Another factor causing the Ns to vary is that the division into quarters was based on the distribution for the entire sample of 2,143, rather than just the subgroup of high-stress parents analyzed in this table.

Marital Satisfaction, Importance, and Violence

The first line of the third section compares parents who were low in marital satisfaction with parents in the high quarter. The low quarter parents had an 87% higher rate of child abuse. A similar difference is shown by comparing couples in which the husband rated the marriage as a less important part of his life than the marriage played in the life of his wife. Finally, the third line of the third section shows that child abuse occurs at a 30% higher rate in families in which there was an incidence of physical violence between the parents during the year.

Of course, as noted above, these differences, like a number of others reported in this chapter, could reflect the effect of family violence rather than being a cause. Only a longitudinal study can adequately sort out this critical issue. On the basis of this study, it can only be said that the findings are not contrary to the idea that parents under stress are more likely to be violent if they do not find the marriage a rewarding and important part of their lives.

Socioeconomic Status

Four aspects of socioeconomic status (SES) are examined in the fourth section of table 5.3. The first of these, the educational level of the couple, shows findings which many will find surprising. Parents in the high quarter of education were only slightly less violent than those in the low quarter. This is inconsistent with the widely held view that less-educated people are more violent. Actually, a careful review of the available studies fails to support this widespread idea (29). A number of studies (including an analysis of this sample by Finkelhor [5]) suggest there is little or no difference in aggression and violence according to education.

The husband's occupational class also makes little difference for child abuse (second line of the fourth section). On the other hand, if the combined income of the couple was $9,000 or less, the rate of child abuse by was 75% higher than in families with a more adequate income (25.0 per 100 versus 14.3 per 100).

The last line of the fourth section attempts to take into account the several aspects of family socioeconomic status. We computed an index which combined the occupational levels, educations, and incomes of both the husband and the wife. The combination of these factors turns out to be very important. Parents in the low quartile on the SES index had a child abuse rate that is double that of parents in the top quarter of the SES distribution.

Marital Power

One of the most important factors accounting for the high rate of *marital* violence is the use of force by men as the "ultimate resource" to back up their position as "head" of their families (1, 9, 24, 25, 29). Perhaps similar processes are at work in respect to child abuse.

The first line of the fifth section of table 5.3 shows that the assault rate of parents who subscribe to the norm of male dominance in family decisions is 136% higher than it is for couples who are not committed to such male dominance norms. However, the second line suggests that in respect to the actual decision power, the difference is minimal. Perhaps the closer association between male dominance norms and child abuse than between actual male dominance in family decisions and child abuse is because many of the male dominant marriages are male dominant by mutual agreement or at least by acquiescence.

The last set of mediating factors included in this chapter explores the theory that child abuse will be higher in the absence of a network of personal ties. Such ties can provide help in dealing with the stresses of life and perhaps intervention when disputes within the family become violent.

The first line of the sixth section of table 5.3 shows that parents who belonged to no organizations (such as clubs, lodges, business or professional organizations, or unions) had a substantially higher rate of child abuse than did the parents who participated in many such organizations. The same applies to parents who attended religious services as compared to those who rarely or never did.

The third line of the sixth section, however, shows opposite results. Parents who had many relatives living within an hour's travel time had a *higher* rate of child abuse than did those with few relatives nearby. This finding is not necessarily inconsistent with social network theory. The usual formulation of that theory *assumes* that the network will be *prosocial*. Usually, that is a reasonable assumption. However, a social network can also support *antisocial* behavior. A juvenile gang is an example. That is the essence of the *differential association* theory of criminal behavior. In the present case, the assumption that the kin network will be opposed to violence is not necessarily correct. Many parents experiencing difficulty managing their children are advised by their own parents to give the child a "sound thrashing."

Summary and Conclusions

This chapter was designed to determine the extent to which stressful life experiences are associated with child abuse and to explore the reasons for such an association. The data used to answer these questions come from a nationally representative sample of 1,146 parents. Stress was measured by an instrument patterned after the Holmes and Rahe scale. It consisted of a list of eighteen stressful events which could have occurred during the year covered by the survey. Child abuse was measured by the severe violence index of the family Conflict Tactics Scales. This consists of whether during the past year the parent had punched, kicked, bit, hit the child with an object, beat up the child, or attacked the child with a knife or gun.

The findings show that parents who experienced none of the eighteen stresses in the index had the lowest rate of child abuse. As the number of stressors experienced during the year increased, so did the rate of child abuse. This was most clear in the case of the husbands.

The second part of the analysis was designed to test the theory that stress by itself does not necessarily lead to child abuse. Rather, it was assumed that other factors must also be present. Several such factors were examined by focusing on parents who were in the top quarter in stresses experienced during the year. These parents were divided into low and high groups on the basis of variables which might account for the correlation between stress and child abuse. It was assumed that, if the theory is correct, the parents who were high in the presumed intervening variable should have a high rate of child abuse, whereas the parents in the low category of these variables should not be more assaultive than the sample as a whole, despite the fact that they were under as much stress during the year as was the other high-stress subgroup of parents.

The results were generally consistent with this theory. They suggest the following conclusions: (*a*) physical punishment by the fathers of the parents in this sample and observing their own fathers hit their mothers trained parents to respond to stress by violence. (*b*) Parents who believe that physical punishment of children and slapping a spouse are appropriate behaviors have higher rates of child abuse. However, a longitudinal study is needed to establish whether this is actually the causal direction. (*c*) Parents under stress are more likely to abuse a child if marriage is not an important and rewarding part of their lives and if they engage in physical fights with each other. (*d*) Education by itself does not affect the link between stress and child abuse. However, the combination of low income, education, and occupation does. (*e*) Parents who believe that husbands should be the dominant person in a marriage, and to a lesser extent husbands who have actually achieved such a position of power, had higher child abuse rates than parents in more equalitarian marriages who were also under stress. (*f*) Parents who were socially isolated (in the sense of not participating in clubs, unions, or other organizations) had higher rates of child abuse, whereas those who were involved in supportive networks of this type, did not have higher then average rates of abuse, despite being under high stress. However, the opposite was found comparing those with many versus few relatives living nearby.

The interpretation of the data, although consistent with, was not proved by the data. Many of the findings are open to other equally plausible interpretations, particularly as to causal direction. The question of causal direction can only be adequately dealt with by a longitudinal study. In the absence of such prospective data, the following conclusions must be regarded only as what the study suggests about the etiology of child abuse.

We assume that human beings have an inherent *capacity* for violence, just as they have an inherent capacity for doing algebra. This capacity is translated into actually solving an equation, or actually abusing a child, *if* one has learned to respond to scientific or technical problems by using mathematics, or learned to respond to stress and family problems by using violence. Even with such training, violence is not an automatic response to stress, nor algebra to a scientific problem. One also has to believe that the problem is amenable to a mathematical solution or to a violent solution. The findings presented in this chapter show that violence tends to be high when these conditions are present: for example among those whose childhood experiences taught them the use of violence and whose present beliefs justify the appropriateness of hitting other family members. If conditions such as these are present, stress is related to child abuse. If these conditions are not present, the relation between stress and child abuse is absent or minimal.

Acknowledgment

This chapter is one in a series of publications of the Family Violence Research Program at the University of New Hampshire. the program is supported by the University of New Hampshire and by NIMH grants MH27557 and T32 MH15161. A program bibliography and list of available publications will be sent on request.

It is a pleasure to acknowledge the many helpful criticisms and suggestions by the members of the Family Violence Research Program seminar: Joanne Benn, Diane Coleman, Ursula Dibble, David Finkelhor, Jean Giles-Sims, Cathy Greenblat, Suzanne Smart, and Kersti Yllo, the computer analysis by Shari Hagar, and the typing of this chapter by Sieglinde Fizz.

The theoretical and methodological sections of this chapter are the same as those in a parallel paper on "Stress and Assault in a National Sample of American Families" (26), but the sample and data differ. The sample for this chapter consists of only those families with at least one child at home, and the data for this chapter focuses on child abuse rather than on assaults by the spouses on each other.

References

1. Allen, Craig, and Straus, Murray A. 1980. Resources, power, and husband-wife violence. In Murray A. Straus and Gerald T. Hotaling (eds.), *The Social Causes of Husband-Wife Violence*. Minneapolis: University of Minnesota Press, in press.
2. Brenner, Harvy M. 1976. Estimating the social costs of national economic policy: Implications for mental and physical health, and criminal aggression. Paper presented before the Joint Economic Committee, U.S. Congress 1976. Revised and printed in 1979 as, The impact of social and industrial changes on psychopathology: A view of stress from the standpoint of macrosocietal trends. In Lennard Levi (ed.), *Society, Stress, and Disease*. London: Oxford University Press, 1979.
3. Brown, George W., and Tirril, Harris. 1978. *Social Origins of Depression: A Study of Psychiatric Disorder in Women*. London: Tavistock Publications.
4. Farrington, Keith. 1980. Stress and family violence. In Murray A. Straus and Gerald T. Hotaling (eds.), *The Social Causes of Husband-Wife Violence*. Minneapolis: University of Minnesota Press, in press.
5. Finkelhor, David. 1977. Education and marital violence. Mimeographed paper.
6. Gelles, Richard J. 1975. The social construction of child abuse. *Am. J. Orthopsychiatry* 44:363–71.
7. Gelles, Richard J., and Straus, Murray A. 1979. Determinants of violence in the family: Toward a theoretical integration. In Wesley R. Burr, Rueben Hill, F. Ivan Nye, and Ira L. Reiss (eds.), *Contemporary Theories about the Family*. New York: Free Press.

8. Gersten, J. C., Langner, T. S., Eisenberg, J. G., and Orzek, L. 1974. Child behavior and life events: undesirable change or change per se. In B. S. Dohrenwend and B. P. Dohrenwend (eds.), *Stressful Life Events: Their Nature and Effects*. New York: John Wiley.

9. Goode, William J. 1971. Force and violence in the family. *J. Marriage and Family* 33:624–36.

10. Holmes, Thomas H., and Rahe, Richard H. 1967. The social readjustment rating scale. *J. Psychosom. Res.* 11:213–18.

11. Hotaling, Gerald T., Atwell, Saundra G., and Linsky, Arnold S. 1978. Adolescent life changes and illness: A comparison of three models. *J. Youth and Adolescence* 7:393–403.

12. Lazarus, Richard S. 1966. *Psychological Stress and the Coping Process*. New York: McGraw-Hill.

13. Levine, Sol, and Scotch, Norman A. 1967. Toward the development of theoretical models: II. *Milbank Mem. Fund Q.* 45:163–74.

14. McGrath, Joseph E., (ed.) 1970. A conceptual formulation for research on stress. In *Social and Psychological Factors in Stress*. New York: Holt, Rinehart & Winston.

15. Mechanic, David. 1962. *Students under Stress: A Study in the Social Psychology of Adaptation*. New York: Free Press.

16. Osood, C., Suci, G., and Tannenbaum, P. 1957. *The Measurement of Meaning*. Urbana, Ill.: University of Illinois Press.

17. Paykel, E. S. 1974. Life stress and psychiatric disorder: Applications of the clinical approach. In B. S. Dohrenwend and B. P. Dohrenwend (eds.), *Stressful Life Events: Their Nature and Effects*. New York: John Wiley.

18. Scott, Robert, and Howard, Alan. 1970. Models of stress. In Sol Levine and Norman A. Scotch (eds.), *Social Stress*. Chicago: Aldine.

19. Selye, Hans. 1966. *The Stress of Life*. New York: McGraw-Hill.

20. Steinmetz, Suzanne, K., and Straus, Murray A. (eds.) 1974. *Violence in the Family*. New York: Harper and Row.

21. Straus, Murray A. 1971. Some social antecedents of physical punishment: A linkage theory interpretation. *J. Marriage and Family* 33:658–63.

22. Straus, Murray A. 1973. A general systems theory approach to a theory of violence between family members. *Soc. Sci. Information* 12:105–25.

23. ———. 1974. Leveling, civility, and violence in the family. *J. Marriage and Family* 36:13–29 (addendum in August 1974 issue).

24. ———. 1976. Sexual inequality, cultural norms, and wife-beating. *Victimology* 1:54–76.

25. ———. 1977. Wife-beating: How common and why? *Victimology* 2:443–58.

26. ———. 1978. Stress and assault in a national sample of American families. Paper read at the Colloquium on Stress and Crime, National Institute of Law Enforcement and Criminal Justice—MITRE Corporation, 5 December 1978 at Washington, D.C.

27. ———. 1979*a*. Measuring intrafamily conflict and violence: The Conflict Tactics (CT) scales. *J. Marriage and Family* 41:1979.

28. ———. 1979*b*. Family patterns and child abuse in a nationally representative American sample. *Child Abuse and Neglect* 3:213–25.
29. ———. 1980. Socioeconomic status, aggression, and violence. Paper in preparation.
30. Straus, Murray A., Gelles, Richard J., and Steinmetz, Suzanne K. 1980. *Behind Closed Doors: Violence in the American Family*. New York: Doubleday, in press.
31. Straus, Murray A., and Hotaling, Gerald T. (eds.) 1980. *The Social Causes of Husband-Wife Violence*. Minneapolis: University of Minnesota Press, in press.
32. Straus, Murray A. and Kumagai, Fumie. 1980. An empirical comparison of eleven methods of index construction. In Murray A. Straus (ed.), *Indexing and Scaling for the Social Sciences with SPSS*, in preparation. (A mimeographed copy of this chapter is available on request from the author.)

6 Parents with Special Problems: Alcoholism and Opiate Addiction

Rebecca Black and Joseph Mayer

Over the past several years there has been increasing concern regarding the effects of parental abuse of alcohol or opiates on child care. Abuse of these substances is of particular interest because of the number of persons involved and the deleterious effects of this abuse on their lives and the lives of family members.

Treatment statistics for the United States indicate that approximately 162,500 persons received treatment for opiate addiction in 1977 (1). This figure is an underestimate, since the number of addicted persons not in treatment is unknown and statistics are not available from all treatment programs. However, if even half of these 162,500 identified opiate addicts each had one child, 81,250 children would be affected by parental opiate addiction.

The incidence of alcoholism is higher than the incidence of opiate addiction. Alcohol is the major drug of abuse in the United States. There are an estimated 9.3 to 10 million adult alcoholics in the United States with correspondingly more affected family members (2).

Alcohol and opiates are drugs which result in addiction, if abused. However, there are both similarities and differences between persons abusing these two drugs and in the consequences of this abuse.

Opiate use, without prescription, is illegal. Persons abusing opiates are young, with an average age around twenty-five. They frequently began using opiates before completing their educations and functioning as self-supporting adults. For these reasons, addiction to opiates usually results in adoption of a life-style characterized by poverty and illegal activity.

Alcohol use is legal. The life-styles of alcoholics vary widely and are typical of those of the general population. Addiction to alcohol usually develops slowly and most frequently interferes with functioning after adult independence has been achieved.

Rebecca Black, Ph.D., and Joseph Mayer, Ph.D., are with the Washington Center for Addictions, Boston.

Funded in part by the National Center on Child Abuse and Neglect, Administration on Children, Youth and Families, Office of Human Development, Department of Health, Education and Welfare.

The poverty and lack of social supports associated with some alcohol addiction and most opiate addiction and personality characteristics, such as depression, low self-esteem, impulsiveness, and dependency, attributed to both alcoholics and opiate addicts are similar to those described as associated with the occurrence of child abuse and neglect (3). Both alcohol and opiate use have been associated with damage to the fetus when used by pregnant women (4, 5). Alcohol use, in addition, has been frequently linked to interpersonal violence (6). For these reasons, a connection between abuse of these substances and child abuse and neglect has been suggested (7, 8).

Alcohol and Opiate Abuse during Pregnancy

The adequacy of child care by substance-abusing parents is first questioned during the pregnancies of addicted women. The fact that opiate and alcohol use by pregnant women may cause injury to the developing fetus has been suspected for many years. Recent documentation of these injuries has resulted in preventive intervention and raised questions concerning the rights of the unborn child (9). Whether or not damage, or potential damage, to the fetus caused as a consequence of drug use by the mother should be classified as child abuse or neglect is questionable. Several states now require the reporting to child protection agencies of infants born addicted to opiates and subsequent investigation of the adequacy of parental care. However, reporting of parents whose abuse of alcohol or other drugs also may have resulted in injury to the fetus has not been required.

Interest in the use of opiates by pregnant women was stimulated by reports linking parental use of opiates to addiction of infants at birth. The existence of infant addiction is now well documented (4). Opiate addiction, however, is a chronic problem with many remissions or periods of abstinence. Thus, children of addicted women are not always exposed to opiates during gestation. In addition, most addicts are cognizant of the fact that addiction during pregnancy may harm the fetus and many addicted women find they have the strength and peer support to abstain from drug use during pregnancy (3).

Prior to becoming pregnant, addicted women tend to neglect their physical health and nutrition. Because of poor maternal health, their pregnancies are considered at risk, even apart from drug use during pregnancy (10).

Obtaining prenatal care is particularly difficult for many addicted women. Women who are poor and not addicted often do not seek prenatal care. Lack of energy, organization, resources, and familiarity with and faith in medical care delivery systems interfere. In addition to these barriers, addicted women expect that they will be accused of harming their babies, that attempts will be made to control or eliminate their opiate use without their consent, and that the care of their infants will be taken away from them.

Treatment of opiate-addicted mothers and their infants during pregnancy, delivery, and the postnatal period has been recently summarized in a report edited by Finnegan (10). Current knowledge and experience indicate that few women addicted at the time of pregnancy succeed in withdrawing from opiates and remaining drug free. Overzealous attempts to force withdrawal from opiates may result in loss of contact with the woman, attempts to substitute other harmful drugs, or repeated episodes of withdrawal and readdiction. Since withdrawal of the mother from opiates is believed to be accomplished by simultaneous withdrawal in the fetus, repeated withdrawal is considered undesirable. Women maintained on low doses of methadone (a synthetic opiate) and helped to obtain appropriate prenatal care have been shown to have fewer medical complications during pregnancy and delivery and to deliver healthier infants than women who continue heroin use (11). Although addiction of the infant at birth is not entirely dependent on the amount of opiates used, it is less likely, if the mother is using low doses of opiates.

Infants born to opiate-addicted women may be addicted to opiates at birth. They also may have a variety of other medical problems, such as low birth weight (11). With appropriate prenatal care these problems can be greatly reduced.

Withdrawal of infants from opiates may be accompanied by: tremors, high-pitched crying, irritability, sneezing, frantic sucking, sweating, nasal stuffiness, fever, generalized convulsions, vomiting, and diarrhea (10). Severe withdrawal is very distressing to both the infant and the caretaker and makes the infant difficult to care for (12, 13).

Long-term effects of addiction at birth are currently being investigated. The few short-term studies which have been done report low birth weight and postnatal growth disturbance (14, 15). Causes, consequences, and permanence of this growth disturbance are unknown. Speculation concerning possible long-term detrimental effects of infant exposure to opiates has focused on three issues: (1) the possibility of an altered response to opiates or susceptibility to opiate addiction in later life, (2) the possibility of learning difficulties and/or difficulties in interpersonal relationships as a consequence of altered responsiveness in early life, and (3) possibilites of abuse by the parents, either as a consequence of disturbed maternal bonding or of the difficulties experienced in caring for these infants as neonates.

Damaging effects of maternal alcohol consumption on the fetus have been reported since ancient times (16). Only recently, however, have systematic investigations of this problem been undertaken. Reports of this research indicate that maternal consumption of alcohol during pregnancy is associated with a pattern of impaired fetal development designated as the fetal alcohol syndrome.

This syndrome includes various characteristic physical malformations and retarded physical and neurological growth and development (5). After review of current evidence, the National Institute on Alcohol Abuse and Alcoholism concludes that consumption of three or more ounces of alcohol (approximately six drinks) at a time presents a risk to the fetus (2). It has also been suggested that less alcohol use or any alcohol use may be damaging during, as yet, unidentified critical periods of fetal growth.

Programs for the treatment of pregnant alcohol-abusive women have only recently been established. Since the amount of alcohol which can be consumed without risk to the fetus is unknown, steps are being taken to warn all women that consumption of alcohol during pregnancy may be hazardous to the fetus.

Effects of the fetal alcohol syndrome on the child appear to be severe. While some physical malformations may be corrected through surgery, damage to the brain resulting in mental and behavioral impairment appears to be permanent (17, 18). In addition, as with the addicted infant, damage to these children may make them physically or behaviorally unacceptable to the parents and thus susceptible to abuse or neglect.

Adequacy of Child Care by Addicted Parents

One of the first studies to examine postnatal care of children by addicted parents has recently been completed at the Washingtonian Center for Addictions in Boston (19). This study was designed to investigate the adequacy of child care in families with an alcohol- or opiate-addicted parent and to determine the incidence and types of child abuse and neglect which occur in these families. In this study, 200 addicted parents, 92 alcoholics, and 108 opiate addicts, participated. All of these parents were in treatment at the time and had been caretakers for a child under the age of eighteen during the past year. Asked to participate were 75% of all parents treated at the center, and 97% of these parents consented.

Demographic and socioeconomic characteristics of the parents studied are shown in table 6.1. Although alchohol- and opiate- addicted parents participating in this study are equally likely to be unemployed, the two groups of parents differ on most other characteristics. Alcoholics are older (average age thirty-eight) and more likely to be male and Caucasian. Half of the opiate addicts are under age thirty-six, almost three-quarters are female, and more of them are black. Alcoholics have continued their education longer than opiate addicts, but are equally likely to be currently unemployed. Opiate addicts are more likely to have an illegal source of income and to have been arrested than alcoholics. Alcoholic parents are more likely to be married and have larger families than opiate-addicted parents.

Parents participating in this study were interviewed by professionals experienced in the addictions. They were asked about the care of their children and about injuries and sexual experiences of their children. Independent raters reviewed all interviews to determine for each parent whether or not a child cared for by that parent had been physically or sexually abused and/or neglected. Physical abuse was defined as: evidence of bruising or more serious injury of a child under the age of eighteen by a person responsible for the care of that child. Cases in which there was substantial evidence suggesting injury had occurred, even when no injury was reported, and situations in which injuries were reported as accidents, but explanations were inconsistent or implausible, were considered abuse. Sexual abuse was defined as: sexual activity, including fondling or attempted intercourse, with a child under the age of sixteen by an adult.

Children in all families were seen as experiencing some degree of neglect;

TABLE 6.1   **Characteristics of Alcohol- and Opiate-Addicted Parents**

Parameters	Addiction of Parent		Total (N=200)
	Alcoholic (N=92)	Opiate Addicted (N=108)	
Marital status:[a]			
Single	8.7%	21.5%	15.6%
Married	56.5	37.4	46.2
Separated	25.0	27.1	26.1
Divorced/Widowed	9.8	14.0	12.1
Number of children:[b]			
1	34.8	56.5	46.5
2–3	45.7	35.2	40.0
4+	19.6	8.3	13.5
Illegal income:[b]			
Yes	3.5	77.1	44.0
No	96.5	22.9	56.0
Number of arrests:[b]			
0	37.9	16.8	26.3
1–4	48.3	43.0	45.4
5+	13.8	40.2	28.4
Demographic and socioeconomic characteristics:			
Age:[b]			
18–25	7.6	51.9	31.5
26–35	35.9	36.1	36.0
36+	56.5	12.0	32.5
Sex:[b]			
Male	63.0	28.7	44.5
Female	36.9	71.3	55.5
Race:[c]			
Caucasian	65.2	45.4	54.5
Black	34.8	54.6	45.5
Education:[a]			
Did not complete high school	43.5	63.0	54.0
Completed high school	38.0	24.1	30.5
Continued beyond high school	18.5	13.0	15.5
Employment:			
Yes	21.7	12.0	16.5
No	78.3	88.0	83.5

[a] $p<0.05$.
[b] $p<0.005$.
[c] $p<0.01$.

however, in most families the degree of neglect was considered mild or moderate. Thus, parents were categorized either as mildly or severely neglecting their children. In determining the presence of neglect, difficulties in feeding, physical care, attention, discipline, medical care, and supervision, unusual exposure of a child to traumatic events, instability of parental care, and psychological and verbal abuse of a child were considered. Severe neglect was used to refer to multiple instances of inadequate care usually occurring in various categories.

Physical or sexual abuse of a child was determined to have occurred in 22.5% of the 200 families with an alcohol- or opiate-addicted parent. Abuse of a child occurred in 27% of the 92 families with an alcoholic parent and in 19% of the 108 families with an opiate-addicted parent.

In those families in which a child was abused, the abuse was generally repeated and, if the family included more than one child, usually involved more than one child. Of the physical abuse cases, 86% involved beatings resulting in bruises, welts, black eyes, bloody noses, swelling, black and blue marks, stitches, cuts, or scars. Injuries such as knockouts, concussions, fractures, and broken bones occurred in 5% of the physical abuse cases and burns in another 5%.

Children in all of the families with an alcohol- or opiate-addicted parent experienced some degree of neglect. In 30.5% of the 200 families, children were considered to have been seriously neglected. Serious neglect occurred in 28% of the 92 families with an alcoholic parent and in 32% of the 108 families with an opiate-addicted parent.

When information on abuse and neglect were combined, abuse and/or neglect of a child was found to have occurred in 41% of the families with an alcohol- or opiate-addicted parent. Both abuse and neglect occurred in 29% of the 82 families in which abuse or neglect occurred. There were no differences in the frequency with which child abuse or neglect occurred in families with an alcohol- or opiate-addicted parent.

Factors Associated with Difficulties in Parenting

Preparation for parenting occurs during childhood. The care received by the child serves as an emotional preparation and physical model for parenthood. Studies of the backgrounds of alcoholics and opiate addicts in treatment indicate that early separation from one or both parents and inadequate care during childhood have poorly equipped them to be parents (20, 21).

Information obtained from alcohol- and opiate-addicted parents studied at the Washingtonian Center indicates that 42% had been physically or sexually abused by their parents during childhood. Alcohol- and opiate-addicted parents were equally likely to have been abused during childhood. This high incidence of abuse is based on judgments made by independent raters using the same criteria applied to evaluations of the care of children by these parents, rather than on more subjective feelings of having been abused. Neglect was not assessed and is not included in this figure. Abuse of these parents during childhood is, in turn, associated with abuse of children by these parents.

Having never, or only briefly, experienced appropriate parenting, alcohol- and opiate-addicted parents are emotionally and experientially unprepared to be parents. Coppolillo (22) comments that "having not received mothering, they have not acquired motherliness." Since most opiate-addicted parents are young parents, they also have had little opportunity to observe and learn from more adequate parental models.

The contribution of poor preparation for parenting to difficulties in child care experienced by addicted parents is reinforced by their addiction. Parents studied at the Washingtonian Center describe addiction as directly and indirectly interfering with the time, energy, and emotional balance necessary for adequate care of children.

In families with an opiate-addicted parent, the time and effort necessary to obtain the drug and to pay for the addiction are considerable. The life-style associated with opiate addiction is highly unstructured. Addicted parents have difficulty in meeting the physical and psychological needs of children in accordance with any regular schedule. Children of addicted parents often receive little attention. In severely disrupted families, children may not be fed or physically cared for, and medical care may be neglected, even in emergencies. Inadequate supervision may result in injury or frequent absences from school. Many addicted parents report with regret that they rarely feel like playing with their children or taking them anywhere.

In families with an alcoholic parent, attention is also focused on the addiction, and parents lack time and energy for child care. In these families, inconsistency in discipline and attention are particularly marked. Periods of attention or strict discipline alternate with periods in which children receive little or no attention or little or no discipline. Role reversals occur in which children are asked to assume parental roles. In many of these families both the alcoholic and nonalcoholic parent depend on their children for comfort, as allies in conflicts with the other parent, and for care of younger brothers and sisters.

Separation of children from their parents occurs frequently in families with an alcohol- or opiate-addicted parent. Illness associated with alcoholism and opiate addiction results in repeated separations of parents and children while parents are hospitalized. Illegal activities engaged in by opiate-addicted parents also cause separation while parents are imprisoned. Many opiate-addicted parents find caring for young children impossible at times and give their children to friends or relatives for months, or even years, at a time. In the most extreme cases children are simply abandoned.

Tension and anxiety associated with repeated illnesses and financial and interpersonal problems affect both the addicted and nonaddicted parent in these families. Violence between the parents and between parents and children occurs. Eventually many of these families become single-parent families. When the single parent left caring for the children is the addicted parent, the adequacy of child care often depends on the support available to this parent.

Unusual accidental and traumatic events which occur in the lives of addicted or alcoholic parents also affect their children. Children are injured in automobile accidents by parents driving under the influence of drugs or alcohol. They witness traumatic events, such as the severe illness or arrest of a parent and deaths of parents or friends by overdose and murder. Occasionally children are given drugs inappropriately or take medication left accessible by the parents.

Many alcohol- or opiate-addicted parents, while experiencing difficulty in caring for their children, do not physically abuse or seriously neglect them. Families studied at the Washingtonian Center in which abuse or neglect of children occurred were compared with families in which child abuse or neglect did not occur. Three primary factors distinguished between these groups of families: sex of the addicted parent, occurrence of interparental violence, and degree of poverty and lack of supports.

Female alcohol- or opiate-addicted parents are more likely to abuse or neglect their children than males. This finding is supported by the results of other studies and is thought to reflect differences in roles of male and female parents, the tendency for the single parent in single-parent families to be female, and, possibly, a tendency for women to express anger primarily or more frequently within the family (23). Since the female parent is the primary caretaker, both in two-parent and in single-parent families, any interference in her functioning is likely to affect the children, especially if financial and social support is not available. Addicted women in this study are more likely to be poor and to have a spouse with a drug or alcohol problem than addicted men. Sex of the parent, therefore, is significant, for differences in resources and responsibilities which contribute to the likelihood of inadequate child care.

One of the strongest predictors of violence between parent and child in this study is violence between the parents. This finding, also supported by research on other populations (23), suggests that violence in any form within the family increases the likelihood of child abuse.

In spite of the overall low-socioeconomic status of the parents studied in the Washingtonian Center, lower financial status and poorer living conditions are associated with child abuse and neglect. Support, defined in terms of availability of spouse and relatives, is also important. If relatives live far away and/or the spouse of the addicted parent is chronically ill or has drug or alcohol problems, child abuse and neglect are more likely to occur. Financial and social supports appear to be particularly important in preventing child maltreatment in families with an alcohol- or opiate-addicted parent. When addiction of a parent occurs in an already relatively deprived family, even small differences in supports may result in, or may prevent, child abuse and neglect.

Alcohol- and opiate-addicted parents are concerned about their children and often try to protect them from the effects of the addiction. The difficulties these parents face in caring for their children, however, are serious. The high incidence of child abuse and neglect in these families emphasizes the need for increased attention to and help for these families. Although little can be done to change the childhood experiences of these parents, there is evidence that parental skills can be learned. Perhaps, in addition to parental skills, nonviolent ways of interacting with others also can be taught. Emotional problems interfering with parenting may be somewhat relieved by therapy, but provision of social and economic supports during child rearing may prove to be more effective over the relatively short time in which intervention must take effect.

Questions often asked are whether treatment of addiction or treatment of child abuse should occur first and whether treatment of addiction alone will suffice. Both need to occur simultaneously. Behavior problems resulting in personal injury cannot wait while other problems are solved. Treatment or intervention in child abuse will not remove the need for treatment of addiction. If attempts are made to treat or intervene in child abuse without corresponding attempts to attend to the addiction, it will continue to interfere, not only with the functioning of the parent, but also with the treatment attempts. Conversely, if attempts are made to treat the addiction, without intervention in the maltreatment of children, the abuse will continue.

Coordinated and simultaneous treatment of both problems is necessary. However, most addiction treatment personnel do not evaluate the care of children in the course of their work and are not familiar with signs or treatment of child abuse. Protective service workers, on the other hand, are usually unfamiliar with the treatment of addiction. Perhaps the most important goal for the immediate future is to integrate these two areas of knowledge, so that cooperative treatment programs can be developed to alleviate the abuse and neglect of children by addicted parents.

References

1. Dupont, R. L. 1978. International Challenge of Drug Abuse: A Perspective from the United States. In *The International Challenge of Drug Abuse*, edited by R. C. Petersen, pp. 3–14. National Institute on Drug Abuse Research Monograph Series no. 19.
2. U.S. Department of Health, Education and Welfare. 1978. Third Special Report to the U.S. Congress on Alcohol and Health.
3. Mayer, J., and Black, R. 1977. Child Abuse and Neglect in Families with an Alcoholic or Opiate-addicted Parent. *Child Abuse and Neglect* 1:85–98.
4. Finnegan, L. P., Connaughton, J. F., and Schut, J. 1975. Infants of Drug-dependent Women: Practical Approaches for Management. *Problems of Drug Dependence, 1975; Proceedings of the Thirty-Seventh Annual Scientific Meeting, Committee on Problems of Drug Dependence*, pp. 489–517. National Academy of Sciences.
5. Hanson, J. W., Jones, K. L., and Smith, D. W. 1976. Fetal Alcohol Syndrome: Experience with 41 Patients. *J. Am. Med. Assoc.* 235:1458–60.
6. Pernanen, K. 1976. Alcohol and Crimes of Violence. In *The Biology of Alcoholism*, vol. 4, *Social Aspects of Alcoholism*, edited by B. Kissin and H. Begleiter, pp. 351–444. New York: Plenum Press.
7. Mayer, J., and Black, R. 1977. The Relationship between Alcoholism and Child Abuse and Neglect. In *Currents in Alcoholism*, edited by F. A. Seixas, 2:429–44. New York: Grune and Stratton.
8. Black, R., Mayer, J., and Zakian, A. 1978. The Relationship between Opiate Abuse and Child Abuse and Neglect. In *Critical Concerns in the Field of Drug Abuse: Proceedings of the National Drug Abuse Conference, 1976*, edited by J. H. Lowinson, pp. 755–58. New York: Dekker.

9. Bross, D. C., and Meredyth, A. 1979. Neglect of the Unborn Child: An Analysis Based on Law in the United States. *Child Abuse and Neglect* 3:643–50.

10. Finnegan, L. P., ed. 1979. *Drug Dependence in Pregnancy: Clinical Management of Mother and Child.* National Institute on Drug Abuse Services Research Monograph Series.

11. Finnegan, L. P. 1976. Management of the Drug-dependent Pregnancy and Effects on Neonatal Outcome. In *Symposium on Comprehensive Health Care for Addicted Families and Their Children,* edited by G. Beschner and R. Brotman, pp. 59–73. National Institute on Drug Abuse Services Research Report.

12. Wilson, G. S. 1976. Management of Pediatric Medical Problems in the Addicted Household. In *Symposium on Comprehensive Health Care for Addicted Families and Their Children,* edited by G. Beschner and R. Brotman, pp. 74–78. National Institute on Drug Abuse Services Research Report.

13. Finnegan, L. P., and Macnew, B. A. 1974. Care of the Addicted Infant. *Am. J. Nursing* 74:685–93.

14. Lodge, A. 1976. Developmental Findings with Infants Born to Mothers on Methadone Maintenance: A Preliminary Report. In *Symposium on Comprehensive Health Care for Addicted Families and Their Children,* edited by G. Beschner and R. Brotman, pp. 79–85. National Institute on Drug Abuse Services Research Report.

15. Wilson, G. S. 1975. Somatic Growth Effects of Perinatal Addiction. *Addictive Diseases* 2:333–45.

16. Warner, R. H., and Rosett, H. L. 1975. Effects of Drinking on Offspring: An Historical Survey of the American and British Literature. *J. Stud. Alcohol* 36:1395–1420.

17. Streissguth, A. P. 1976. Psychologic Handicaps in Children with the Fetal Alcohol Syndrome. *Ann. N.Y. Acad. Sci.* 273:140–45.

18. Streissguth, A. P., Little, R. E., Herman, C., and Woodell, B. S. 1979. I.Q. in Children of Recovered Alcoholic Mothers Compared to Matched Controls. *Alcoholism: Clin. Exper. Res.* 3:197.

19. Black, R., and Mayer, J. 1979. An Investigation of the Relationship between Substance Abuse and Child Abuse and Neglect. Final report to the National Center on Child Abuse and Neglect, Department of Health, Education, and Welfare.

20. Aron, William S. 1975. Family Background and Personal Trauma among Drug Addicts in the United States: Implications for Treatment. *Br. J. Addict.* 70:295–305.

21. Tennant, F. S., Detels, R., and Clark, V. 1975. Some Childhood Antecedents of Drug and Alcohol Abuse. *Am. J. Epidemiology* 102:377–85.

22. Coppolillo, H. P. 1975. Drug Impediments to Mothering Behavior. *Addictive Diseases* 2:201–11.

23. Straus, M. 1978. Family Patterns and Child Abuse in a Nationally Representative American Sample. Paper read at the Second International Congress on Child Abuse and Neglect, September 1978, London, England.

Assessment

Every case of suspected child abuse and neglect must be thoroughly evaluated. With over one and one-half percent of our nation's children being reported *each year* to the children's divisions of state or local social service agencies, this becomes an enormous task. Approximately eighty to eighty-five percent of these reports can be assessed very adequately by an experienced social worker from protective service, but the remainder are so severe or complex that a thorough assessment requires the input of professionals from several different disciplines. One should keep in mind that this does not mean sitting around a table and discussing a case or family that has been seen by only one member of a team. On the contrary, these difficult families must actually be *seen* and *evaluated* by different professionals, i.e., a psychologist or psychiatrist, a pediatrician, a social worker, and possibly a nurse.

The contributors to this section have provided the necessary details for this comprehensive assessment to take place. These details should be considered with care. Reference should be made to a chapter by Friedman, Cardiff, Sandler and Friedman entitled "Coping with the Dilemma of Child Abuse and Neglect." This appears in a book edited by Judith Mearig, Ph.D., entitled, *Working for Children: Ethical Issues beyond Professional Guidelines* (San Francisco: Jossey-Bass, 1978).

C.H.K.   R.E.H.

7 Communicating in the Therapeutic Relationship: Concepts, Strategies, Skills

Mary Edna Helfer and Ray E. Helfer

Since the health provider–patient relationship is a transaction between human beings, the success of that transaction depends almost entirely on how well they understand each other, i.e., how well they communicate.

MICHELE TOLELA (1)

Communication is our most important medium for social contact and personal development. It is also our most prolific behavior; most of our daily activities involve communication. The average American spends about seventy percent of his or her active hours communicating—listening, speaking, reading, and writing (2). Communicating with others is so central to our existence that even in our attempts not to communicate, we still "say" something. Interacting with others is as vital to our survival in the social environment as the exchange of oxygen and carbon dioxide is to our physical environment.

Consider how helpless one becomes when unable to communicate. Even newborns are required to communicate from the moment of birth to maintain their very existence (see Chapter 26). Our self-identity is a product of our communication efforts (3), and our behavior is adopted and adapted in response to the communication we receive and the messages we transmit to others. Communication is the tool utilized to alter our environment. At times, one's livelihood is dependent on the ability to influence the actions of others through communication. One's basic needs and, ultimately, species survival are dependent upon mastery of an intricate set of communication rules and behaviors.

Although all persons communicate, the ability to do so skillfully and with purpose rarely occurs as a natural gift. Knowledge, practice, and experience are required to develop precise, predictable, effective, and satisfying techniques of interaction.

Communication in the Therapeutic Relationship

Communication in the therapeutic relationship can be defined as a transactional process which involves a message exchange between participants through a com-

Mary Edna Helfer, R.N., is with the Office of Educational Programs, College of Human Medicine, Michigan State University. Ray E. Helfer, M.D., is with the Department of Pediatrics and Human Development, College of Human Medicine, Michigan State University.

mon system of symbols, signs, or behaviors. The messages or signs fall into constellations of expressive behaviors (4). The three main signal systems are the lexical, kinesic, and somatic. The lexical system includes all speech activities, kinesic includes all body movements, and somatic incorporates the observable manifestations of the autonomic nervous system.

A formal language system enables us to express very complex or abstract ideas to another person. Speech is the verbal medium used by the patients to inform the health provider of symtpoms and concerns which, in turn, are used by the provider to respond to the patient's needs (5). The manner in which the content of speech is expressed provides information which is as equally important as the words themselves. The volume, rate, pitch, inflection, intensity, and continuity all convey cues to the emotional state of the patient and are sometimes referred to as *paralanguage* (6). Paralanguage may communicate a message which will cause the interviewer to question how literally he or she can accept the overt message transmitted by the spoken word alone. Active listening is required to hear both components of speech.

The unspoken dialogue, or pattern of nonverbal communication, is equally important (7). It is the medium most frequently used to communicate emotion and subtleties of meaning which could not be conveyed if we were restricted to a single mode of communication. While research in the area of nonverbal communication is still limited, some estimates indicate that as much as ninety percent of our messages concerning feelings are communicated nonverbally (8). Kinesics, derived from the Greek word for movement, is the system which includes the way patients walk, their posture, gestures, and facial expression. Birdwhistell, a primary scholar in the area of kinesics, recognizes several regions of meaningful activity: total head; face and neck; trunk and shoulders; shoulders, arms, and wrists; hands and fingers; hips, upper legs, lower legs, and ankles; and feet. These areas have the capacity of combining, resulting in an astonishing number and variety of cues. These combinations may be thought of as a "vocabulary" of the unspoken dialogue with specific meaning assigned to a constellation of cues.

The face is the most expressive part of the body (9). Ekman and Friesen conducted cross-cultural research on the recognition of facial expression, with the hypothesis that certain situations would evoke recognizable expressions of emotions among the five cultures studied. There was a high degree of similarity noted across cultures (10).

Somatic cues or signals are usually not under patients' conscious control and may be viewed as reliable signs of affect. Patients' breathing patterns, muscle tension, pupil dilatation, skin color, tearing, and body perspiration are observable somatic signs.

The triad of the lexical, kinesic, and somatic combine to give a constellation of cues with specific meaning. Sadness, for example, is mirrored in the face of a depressed patient, who presents with a downturned mouth; low, slow, monotonous voice; downcast eyes; slumped shoulders; sighing respiratory movements; and a general decrease in body movement. An angry patient may present with clenched teeth and fixed jaw, increased rate and volume of speech, increased muscle tension, flushed face, and may perspire freely.

The interviewer must avoid making judgments based on isolated signals from any given system. Communication may be very clear when all systems agree. However, as interviewers we usually must learn to actively listen and observe all three systems, determine the degree of congruence between them, and when there are discrepancies, help the patient clarify the true meaning of his or her communication.

Understanding Anger and Depression during the Interview

The potential for a productive interview will be enhanced if the interview is conducted in a professional and nurturing manner. The interviewer can give the patient or client support and a sense of being understood, as well as providing an opportunity to "tell his story." A nurturing and supportive attitude is critical, for without a sense of being understood the parent may withhold or distort information that is critical for an accurate assessment of the child's injuries. Developing appropriate treatment strategies will also be compromised by inaccurate or incomplete data.

In order for an abusive parent to feel understood, the *provider* must identify or acknowledge the emotions the parent brings to the interview. Two of the more difficult emotional states to handle are anger and depression. Anger exhibited by patients can be particularly troublesome. It frequently provokes rejection by members of the service team and sends the patient on a shopping expedition for another doctor, social worker, or another emergency room, wasting valuable time and duplication of efforts.

Anger may be expressed in a readily recognized form of direct confrontation and criticism or in a disguised indirect form. Bowden and Burstein describe several types of anger which are frequently encountered in dealing with patients (11). Parents may be characterologically angry; they may be angry as a temporary process within themselves; they may displace their anger by venting at one time feelings generated within other contexts; or they may be voicing a legitimate complaint about a given situation.

In dealing with situational anger one should listen and assess the complaint in an accepting and nonjudgmental manner. Usually the anger is temporary and, if given the opportunity for full expression, it may lead to an improvement in the openness and frankness with which the patient can talk with the physician or other provider.

Displaced anger is carried over from some preceding setting or interaction. This may be an unconscious adaptive mechanism which permits the patient to vent his/her anger, while maintaining a positive image with the service team members on whom he or she feels most dependent for care of the child. All team members need to recognize and learn to deal with displaced anger, as most of them will have opportunities to be the recipients of such anger. The quality and depth of the client's feelings should be acknowledged. This may provide some dissipation of the anger and shift the focus to the more legitimate source of anger. Displaced anger is basically transitory and if permitted open expression, may clear the way for improved communication.

Anger as a reaction to an internal process is not a reflection of the current interpersonal transactions, but a reflection of the patient assimilating the knowledge of his or her situation. It is seen in people who have suffered an acute reduction in their sense of adequacy and competence.

The characteriologically angry patient is the most difficult with whom to deal. This type of angry patient is one whose critical early childhood experiences with help givers have been such as to convince him or her in many pervasive and preverbal ways that help givers, such as physicians, teachers, and parents, are more likely to take advantage of than help him or her. They frequently present as being very rigid in their beliefs and attitudes, appear hyperalert during the interview and seem unable to accept emotional support from team members. They rely heavily on projection as an adaptive mechanism. They often give a history of growing up in a hostile, nonnurturing environment, describing their parents as persons who always overpowered or degraded them. Their past experiences have convinced them that helpers are in reality punishers and are potentially dangerous people who cannot be trusted.

Working with individuals whose basic character is built on anger is most difficult, but being very open and candid, while communicating with them, is helpful. Ambiguity is viewed as a threat. A consistent and authoritative posture may prove beneficial in working with these patients. Their anger is likely to erupt if the provider seems inconsistent or vacillates in making decisions. They despise weakness in themselves and others. Their areas of strength and competence should be maximized during interaction with them, thereby enhancing their self-esteem and reducing conflict. In extreme cases, these parents may present as paranoid or sociopaths and often require psychotherapeutic intervention. Bowden and Burstein also described a variety of depressive states and discuss some of the basic mechanisms underlying various stages of depression (11). The awareness of the several states that are frequently encountered while interacting with highly stressed patients is obligatory.

Mourning is viewed as a healthy, normal reaction to loss, whether the loss be physical or loss of self-esteem or personal failure. This usually follows a predictable series of responses as the person works through a problem and resolves the stress. The parent or caretaker of the injured child, for example, may appear very sad, as exhibited by their nonverbal behavior and crying. They may have decreased interest in their other routine activities and responsibilities. Denial may be their first psychological response. Very little emotion may be exhibited as the parent tries to block out the event by saying, ''This can't be really happening to me.'' This stage usually progresses to one of displaced anger—someone or something else is responsible for the problems.

The sense of loss, which will facilitate their moving to the grief stage, should be recognized. Grieving is a vital component, if one is to move on to reintegration and reinvolvement in trying to cope with their loss or failure. What is actually being grieved over may not be readily apparent to the interviewer, for what is important and internal for one person may have little meaning to another. On occasion, one is confronted with an individual who has every apparent reason to go through the grieving process but does not exhibit appropriate verbal or nonverbal behavior. These individuals must undergo additional assessment and possibly psychiatric care.

Secondary or reactive depression is usually exhibited in parents as a sense of worthlessness, guilt, or hopelessness about their situation and environment. Burstein describes three causes of secondary depression. A common psychological pattern appears, which may be very applicable in understanding the emotional state of many parents. There is a gap between the way the parent wants to function or feels he or she should function, and the way he or she is able to function. Burstein states:

> The childhood experiences of patients with secondary depression predispose to this reaction pattern in response to stress. Such children were often treated as inadequate and incompetent by their overly critical parents. Memories of statements such as 'you can't do anything right' are common. In addition, as children, these persons harbored much anger toward their parents but felt guilty and afraid of expressing it, and they developed the pattern of turning the anger and self-reproach inward. (11)

Guidelines for Facilitating the Interview

An important component of eliciting history from the parent is that the parent must have a cognitive understanding of why some questions are being asked. The need to understand the total environment and family dynamics pertaining to a particular child may not be obvious to the parent. Without a clear explanation the patient may not comply by providing the necessary information for a "comprehensive overview" of the current living situation, family interaction, and crisis that may have contributed to the parental neglect or abuse. The process of verbalizing their situation may act as a stimulus to have them participate in coming up with alternative solutions to help resolve the problems that contributed to the abuse.

Several specific suggestions can be made to assist in the facilitation of an interaction, especially one that has as its primary purpose the establishment of rapport as well as the gathering of certain factual information. Each of these suggestions require considerable practice to implement. The concepts will not be difficult to grasp; setting them in action will be another matter. Some find that the skill of interviewing comes very naturally; others struggle with each new (and old) interaction. Consideration of these guidelines will be helpful in both situations.

The open-ended question. Many use this technique very effectively. This can be helpful to gain the most accurate and unbiased information and determine the ability of the patient or client to organize his/her thoughts and tell his/her own story. The open-ended question can be used to gain both cognitive and affective information: "Describe the nature of your pain." "Tell me how you felt about your father's death." One must use this technique skillfully; otherwise the interview may go on uncontrolled. If the open-ended question leads to rambling, one can move to more specific, direct closed-ended questions.

The closed-ended question. Most providers are skilled in utilizing this form of questioning, in fact, so skilled, that some use nothing but closed-ended methods to gain information. "Do you have a cough?" "When did your father die?" The closed-ended question has great utility, is usually easy to answer, and usually brings forth specific information about the patient or client. When used judiciously it is most helpful. When used exclusively, it can be most destructive to the rapport-building process. Questions should proceed from open-ended to closed as the information needed becomes more specific.

Labeling. This is the most useful of all the tools in building a positive relationship with the patient/client. One skilled in the timely use of labeling can break through the most resistant barriers. In order to learn the skill of labeling one must first recognize what should be labeled. One can hardly say, "That last question must have really upset you," unless there was recognition that the person was disturbed by the last question. "It must be difficult for you to talk to me." The interviewer's feelings may also be labeled. "I'm feeling very frustrated; I keep getting mixed messages." "It is easier for me to talk to you when you smile." "I really had a bad week." *Never* say "I know how you feel," unless you really have experienced *exactly* the same situation and are willing to talk about it in some detail. A better statement is, "If that had happened to me I might have felt just like you did." The well-timed and appropriate labels can turn a difficult interview into one that is both informative and productive, for both individuals. Rapport follows. Keep in mind that labels are placed both on the patient's or client's feelings or reactions and on the interviewer's feelings and reaction. Labeling enhances a positive interaction.

Confrontation. A technique used to describe to the patient discrepancies between the verbal or logical component of his or her message and the nonverbal or kinesic cues he or she exhibits, the statement to the patient is always based on observations with no inference made regarding his/her motive. For example, "You say you had a good relationship with your mother, but you always look away from me when you talk about her." "You say things are going well at home, but you look very sad when you talk about Johnny's father." Confrontation may help the patient elaborate on these conflicting cues and help the patient get in touch with his or her feelings. Confrontation is one of the more difficult skills to acquire because it entails "listening on all channels" and is not part of our repertoire of routine social behaviors. Confrontation is more risky to the interaction and is best used after some degree of rapport has been built.

The use of silence. This skill some find most difficult to implement. The very thought of sitting, quietly waiting for the other person to say something, puts some individuals in a most uneasy situation. Even a short five to ten second pause may seem endless. This technique often is most useful in allowing one or both individuals to gather their thoughts and gain the courage to speak them. The use of silence can be self-defeating, however, if tensions rise to such a peak that one or both of the participants become so nervous that thoughts and speech vanish. Silence must be used judiciously.

Feedback gestures and synchrony. Talking with someone who does not use feedback gestures and does not "get into synch" with you is most difficult. At times we may fail to recognize synchronization has not occurred, and yet come away from the interaction feeling very strange indeed. Often this "strangeness" comes from the fact that the interviewer received no feedback, resulting in not knowing if what was being said was indeed heard. Many people get into "synch" automatically. A newborn baby can get into synchrony with his or her mother's voice, for example, if she varies the pitch sufficiently. When two adults communicate well, this synchrony is both verbal and nonverbal. The head nod, the body posture, expressions like "I see" and "Really," eye contact, and the like are all ways of enhancing synchrony. Without synchrony the interaction is sterile, cold, and short-term. Rapport does not result.

The Structure and Setting of the Interview

Careful consideration must be given to the structure and setting of the interview if one is going to get the most from any interaction with a patient or client. Doctors and social workers often pay little attention to these matters and then wonder why the interview went poorly. Sometimes psychologists and psychiatrists pay so much attention to these issues that the patient falls asleep because he or she is so comfortable. There must be a happy medium between the psychologist's over-stuffed chair and the hallway conversations between a doctor and the patient.

Comfort and privacy are critical. Both individuals should be at the same eye level. This is especially important when interacting with a child. The doctor who stands by a bedside, hovering over a patient who is passively lying in bed, does not meet the criteria for a good interactional situation. There should not be an awesome and formidable desk in between the two who are trying to establish rapport and share information. One should not be undressed and the other fully clothed with a white coat. How inappropriate for the physician to say, "Go into room two, put on the gown with the opening in the back, and I'll be right in to talk to you." Departments of Social Services are notorious for unbelievable settings in which a rather personal discussion is supposed to occur: cubicles, open-top walls, no doors, busy hallways—none of these lend themselves to data gathering and rapport building.

Equally important to the setting of the interview is the sequence of the interview. The inexperienced student is often so intent upon gathering all the data that he or she follows a rigid order of questions, regardless of the answers. One student was observed in the following sequence:

"How are things going in school?"

"Not too well," was the reply.

"Tell me about your cough."

The ability to move back and forth from one area to another is a unique skill, not easily learned. One problem resulting from being too flexible is, of course, that one may never finish obtaining the information he/she set out to gather. The skill to identify certain issues for future discussion is an important technique.

"How are things going in school?"

"Not too well."

"That sounds like something we should talk about as soon as you start feeling better."

A note is made in the record to remind them to put this on the agenda; the next question is more reasonable.

"Now tell me about your cough."

Starting the interview with an open-ended, nonthreatening question is usually best. "Tell me why you came to see me." Adding, very soon thereafter, a label or two will be most helpful. "You must have been feeling pretty lousy all week." Once the opening barriers are broken down, then a few closed-ended questions will help gather some critically important information. "Do you have any money left for food?" or "Does your cough interfere with your breathing?"

During the course of the interview the interviewer must intersperse some key techniques that help facilitate both rapport building and data gathering. Using each of the points made above will facilitate these two goals immensely. Considerable practice is required to become comfortable with each of these skills. They must become automatic, much like one's reactions when one's car hits a piece of ice and skids. These are skills, and to put skills into use takes practice. This practice is best done under observation, preferably using videotape. This enables one to obtain immediate feedback, both personally and also from another person acting as a coach or therapist.

Closure to the interview is of major importance. One must not close abruptly, say thanks, and leave. The patient's or client's final impression and feeling of satisfaction will depend, on a large part, upon how this closure is handled. If the interview is complete, with no expectations for another meeting, then summary statements and questions are in order: "Let me review what I've heard" or "Let's summarize a few major issues once again." If another meeting is anticipated, then the agenda and time table should be set: "When we meet again we need to talk about . . ." or "I want to finish up with . . ." or "That issue is pretty hard for you to talk about; we can cover this area next time." A time and place must be set for the next discussion. In either situation, final or temporary closure, the patient or client must be given the opportunity to bring up points or issues: "Is there anything else we should discuss before we close?"

Finally, no discussion on the structure and setting of an interview would be complete without mention of a few additional cues or suggestions to help achieve the goals of rapport building and data gathering.

1. Incorporate the more personal issues within less-personal matters. It is quite easy for a physician to flow from less personal to personal, e.g., in inquiring about the health of the patient's parents, asking questions about how the interaction between parents and children went when the patient was a child is very natural and nonthreatening. In inquiring about symptoms in the genitourinary system (pain, discharge, urinary frequency, etc.) seeking additional information about sexual problems and activity is an easy transition.

2. Use discretion in taking notes during an interview. Writing constantly is distracting. Not writing anything may indicate disinterest; a happy medium is necessary.
3. The concept of "tracking/Nontracking" is important to understand, for one will wish to use this technique during an interview. Some do it automatically, others find it most difficult. Tracking is following through for more details, e.g., "My mother and I look a lot alike." Your tracking response might be, "In what way?" Nontracking is to come to closure on a given issue by switching to another topic or question. Both can facilitate an interview when used skillfully.
4. One's dress and posture can "say a great deal" to the patient or client.
5. Opinion and judgmental statements present difficult issues. Giving your opinion during the interview, when done with care, can facilitate the discussion. If, however, these are felt to be judgmental, the patient may well "clam up," rapport being lost momentarily.

There are many additional cues or suggestions to improve one's interviewing techniques. The most important issue to keep in mind is that interviewing is a skill, and skills can be learned and improved with practice.

Special Consideration Relating to Child Abuse

Communicating with an abusive and/or neglectful parent presents some very special problems and requires very special skills. This is probably one of the most difficult, if not the most difficult, interpersonal relationships to establish. There are very few clinical situations which generate such strong feelings of anger, hostility, and frustration in health care providers as does dealing with parents who have abused their children. It may be a very difficult task for the emergency room nurses, physicians, or social workers to feel any empathy for the parent after caring for the child. Focusing on how the parent feels at the present time faced with the consequences of his or her own actions is helpful. One need not condone or accept the parent's behavior, but rather try to understand the parent's feelings. "I can accept how you're feeling, but not your actions." To understand these complexities fully the material covered in other chapters in this book must be understood.

One must first identify who the patient or client is. Some professionals may feel it is the child, others the mother or father, or possibly the siblings and grandparents. Approaching an interview with a predetermined notion that any one of these individuals is the patient will be most confusing. Child abuse and neglect is only the symptom seen when a family's interactional systems have broken down. The whole family must be perceived as the patients and approached and handled accordingly.

Unique, often strong, emotional ties bind the various members of this family unit together. At times, these are not easily understood, especially when a wife returns to her husband who beats her or a little girl runs to her father who sexually abuses her. These complex ties must be appreciated and considered as one is trying to establish a communication system with this family unit. Using all the skills at one's disposal, pulling all the interpersonal and interactional stops, will be necessary.

Any time a parent is being interviewed about his or her child there is a conflict of interest that must be appreciated. The parent is very emotionally tied to the child and feels responsible for what happens, or has happened, to the child. If the child has pneumonia, for example, and the doctor asks, "Did he take his medicine?" or, even worse, "Did you give him his medicine?" there is an immediate conflict set up within the parent. Consider how a parent of a suspected abused child reacts when asked, "Who hurt your child?" or, even worse, "Did *you* hit your child?"

When one knows, with a reasonable degree of certainty, that something of a very negative nature has happened to a child, the rule is, *do not ask*. Stating the problem, as you see it, is always preferable. For example, "Your child has been hurt; tell me about it" is much preferable to "who hurt your child" or even "how did your child get hurt?" The parent is much less defensive with the former approach and the conflict of interest, while still present, is less an interference.

Abusive parents have considerable difficulty using nonverbal communication skills (see Chapter 3). Even the few skills they do have are misread by most inexperienced professionals. Abusive parents often do not look at you eye to eye, may rarely cry or have other facial movements, may be slumped in a chair, and may be very aggressive or passive. Most of the skills learned in graduate or medical schools to establish rapport may be of little use, as one tries desperately to communicate with these "sensory muted" parents (see Chapter 3). Sometimes an interviewer feels as though he or she is trying to establish a communication system with a robot.

Verbal skills may be equally guarded. Since young adults who were abused as children are trained not to trust others and to believe that people hurt others, they are not likely to verbally respond to someone who says, "I'm here to help you" or "I'm here to ask you a few questions." A much more appropriate opening is the label, "You must have had a rough week" or "You look tired" or "You're probably really concerned about your child."

Abusive parents are not reared to demonstrate motivation. Why be motivated? Tomorrow is no better than today; today is tomorrow. Professionals find it very difficult to establish a communication system with someone they interpret as unmotivated. When parents do not show up, follow directions, call, say thanks, ask questions, smile, etc., we are "turned off." And yet, there *is* motivation there, shown in a variety of very subtle ways. They may peek through the window, hoping you will come back; show up late, hoping you will still be there; bring their abused child to school, hoping someone will recognize their "cry for help."

The bottom line is that abusive parents are not easy to like. Few of us were trained to communicate with someone we inherently dislike. We struggle, often very clumsily, using interactional techniques that are not helping us achieve our goals of rapport building and data gathering. There are, at best, two key factors in learning to overcome this problem: first, to understand these people, in as much depth as possible, to know them, the childhood they came from, and how they arrived where they are; second, to work hard to separate their feelings from their actions (see Chapter 3). You do not like what they are doing, or have done, to their child, but you can, in fact must, accept how they are feeling and then develop a communication system with them as people. This will not be an easy task, but when the shell is broken through one finds real, feeling people in desperate need of help, but rarely able or willing to ask for it.

Michele Tolela gave an excellent summary of the communication process in delivery of services in the abuse and neglect situations.

> Communication is a complex process—it is not a discrete phenomenon beginning with the first word spoken between two people and ending when the last word has been heard. Communication has a history in the past and pitfalls for the future. It is influenced by the assumptions, the expectations, the past experiences of the communicators; it will influence the communicator's behavior in the future. We should look at communication as a complex process that has to be learned, that can be learned. (1)

References

1. Tolela, M. Communication: A Three Part series. *Pennsylvania Medical Journal,* pp. 70–91, 1967.
2. Berlo, D. K. *The Process of Communication.* New York: Holt, Rinehart, and Winston, 1960, p. 1.
3. Miller, G., and Steinberg, M. *Between People: A New Analysis of Interpersonal Communication.* Chicago: Science Research Association, 1975.
4. Mayerson, E. W. *Putting the Ill at Ease.* New York: Harper and Row, 1976.
5. Cassell, E. J., and Skopek, L. Language as a Tool in Medicine: Methodology and Theoretical Framework. *Journal of Medical Education,* pp. 197–203, 1977.
6. Mehrabian, A., and Ferris, S. R. Inferences of Attitudes from Nonverbal Communication in Two Channels. *Journal of Consulting Psychology,* pp. 248–52, 1967.
7. Burgoon, J., and Saine, T. *The Unspoken Dialogue: An Introduction to Nonverbal Communication.* Boston: Houghton Mifflin Company, 1978.
8. Birdwhistell, R. L. *Kinesics and Context.* Philadelphia: University of Pennsylvania Press, 1970.
9. Ekman, P., Friesen, W. V., and Ellsworth, P. *Emotion in the Human Face.* New York: Pergamon Press, 1972.
10. Ekman, P., and Friesen, W. V. Constants across Cultures in the Face and Emotion. *Journal of Personality and Social Psychology,* Vol. 17, 1971.
11. Bowden, C. L., and Burstein, A. G. *Psychological Basis of Medical Practice: An Introduction to Human Behavior.* 2nd ed. Baltimore: Williams and Wilkins, 1979.

8 The Child with Nonaccidental Trauma

Barton D. Schmitt

Physical abuse or nonaccidental trauma is one of the most common types of child maltreatment seen by physicians. The incidence of injuries inflicted by caretakers is generally 510 new cases per million general population per year (1). At least 2,000 children per year die from physical abuse. Approximately 10% of children under five years of age seen by emergency room physicians for trauma have injuries that were inflicted (2). Regardless of how many specialists are trained in this field, the recognition of inflicted injuries will continue to be the responsibility of primary care physicians and nurses.

Histories Offered for Inflicted Injuries

Although many child abuse diagnoses can be based on physical findings alone, the history of how the injury occurred becomes helpful when a child presents multiple, nondescript bruises. The assessment of the plausibility of the history is always a medical judgment. Professionals from other disciplines (e.g., social work, psychiatry, law enforcement, and the law) are not trained or expected to make this decision. The following histories are diagnostic or extremely suggestive of nonaccidental trauma (see table 8.1).

Eyewitness history. When a child readily states that a particular adult hurt him, the history is almost always true. When one parent accuses the other parent of hurting a child, the story is usually accurate, if the parents are not engaged in a custody dispute. Partial confessions by a parent are not uncommon and are as diagnostic as complete confessions (e.g., a parent may admit that he caused one of the bruises, but not the others, or he may state that he felt like shaking or hitting the child prior to the injuries, but did not act on his impulse or cause any of the injuries).

Unexplained injury. Some parents deny knowing that their child had any of the bruises or burns discovered by the physician. Other parents have noticed the

Barton D. Schmitt, M.D., is with the Department of Pediatrics, University of Colorado Medical Center, Denver.

TABLE 8.1   **Histories Offered for Inflicted Injuries**

1. Eyewitness history
2. Unexplained injury
3. Implausible history
4. Alleged self-inflicted injury
   (in young baby)
5. Alleged sibling-inflicted injury
6. Delay in seeking medical care

physical findings, but can offer no explanation as to how the injury happened. They may state, "I just found him that way," or "He awoke that way." These parents would like us to believe that the injury was spontaneous. When pressed, they may become evasive or offer a vague explanation such as, "He might have fallen down." These explanations are self-incriminating. Most nonabusive parents know exactly how, where, and when their child was hurt. They also show a complete willingness to discuss the accident in detail. In these "unexplained" injuries, the exact perpetrator can often be identified by learning who was alone with the child when his discomfort and crying commenced.

Implausible history. Many parents offer an explanation for the injury, but one which is implausible and inconsistent with common sense and medical judgment. If the parents offer a blatantly phony history, the physician's job is rather easy. Occasionally, a minor accident is described, yet the injuries are major (e.g., a child reportedly has fallen onto a thick carpet, but has multiple body bruises). Another piece of strong evidence is when the behavior described which led to the accident is impossible for the child's level of development (e.g., a ten-month-old child who allegedly climbed into a tub and turned on scalding water). Some parents make their history implausible by repeatedly changing it.

Alleged self-inflicted injury. An alleged self-inflicted injury in a small baby is the most serious category. These children can be killed if they are sent home with the wrong diagnosis. In general, the child who is not crawling yet, is unable to cause an accident to himself. Fractures under this age are almost uniformly inflicted. Absurd stories such as, "The baby rolled over on his arm and broke it," or "He got his head caught in the crib and bruised it," should be considered highly unlikely and acted upon accordingly. Histories implying that the child is masochistic always should raise questions (e.g., the child who hurts himself badly during a temper tantrum, gets subdural hematomas by hitting himself with a bottle, climbs up onto a hot radiator, or burns himself up to the elbows by immersing his arm in hot water). Children rarely deliberately injure themselves.

Alleged sibling-inflicted injury. When parents have difficulty coming up with an explanation, they commonly project the blame onto rough play with a sibling. They may state that the sibling dropped a toy on the injured child or threw a bottle at him. The number and seriousness of the injuries usually contradict this explanation. In the small percentage of child abuse cases where the sibling is responsible, reporting is nonetheless mandatory to prevent recurrences.

Delay in seeking medical care. Most nonabusive parents come in immediately when their child is injured, by and large. In contrast, some abused children are not brought in for a considerable length of time, even when there is a major injury. In its extreme, they are not brought in until the child is nearly dead. One study showed that a third of abused children were not brought in until the morning after the injury. Another third came in one to four days after the injury (3). In these situations, parents are usually hoping that the event never occurred or that the injury will not require medical care. Another common behavior in the abusive situation is that the adult who was with the child at the time of the injury does not come to the hospital with the child.

Inflicted Bruises

Inflicted bruises occur at typical sites or fit recognizable patterns (e.g., human hand marks, human bite marks, strap marks, or bizarre shapes).

Typical sites. Inflicted bruises are so common at certain sites that finding them there is pathognomonic (table 8.2). Bruises that predominate on the buttocks, lower back, and lateral thighs are almost always related to punishment (i.e., paddling). Likewise, genital or inner-thigh bruises are usually inflicted for toileting mishaps (see figures 8.1 and 8.2). Injuries to the penis may include pinch marks, cuts, abrasions, a deep groove from having it tied off with a rubber band, or amputation (4). Injuries to the genital area should also raise the question of sexual abuse, especially when they are found in girls. Bruises on the cheek are usually secondary to being slapped (figure 8.3). The outline of fingers may be evident within the bruise. Accidental falls rarely cause bruises to the soft tissues of the cheek, but instead involve the skin overlying bony prominences such as the forehead or cheekbone. Bruises on the earlobe are usually due to being cuffed. Children who are pinched or pulled by the earlobe usually have a matching bruise on each surface. Occasionally a child will suffer a ruptured eardrum from a blow to the ear. Bruises of the upper lip and labial frenulum are usually caused by impatient forced feedings or by jamming a pacifier or bottle into the child's mouth. Bruises in this area cannot be self-inflicted until the baby is old enough to sit up by himself and inadvertently fall forward. Bruises inside the lip may remain hidden unless the lip is carefully everted (figure 8.4). The floor of the mouth may also be torn by similar actions (figure 8.5). Usually a history of inconsolable crying can be

TABLE 8.2	**Typical Sites for Inflicted Bruises**

1. Buttocks and lower back (paddling)
2. Genitals and inner thighs
3. Cheek (slap marks)
4. Earlobe (pinch marks)
5. Upper lip and frenulum (forced feeding)
6. Neck (choke marks)

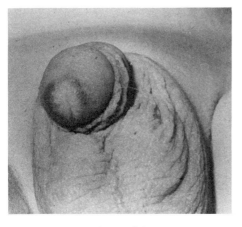

Figure 8.1

Pinch mark bruise of glans penis

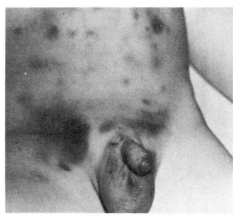

Figure 8.2

Multiple bruises and cuts of penis, scrotum, and abdomen.

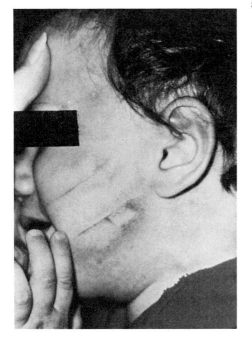

Figure 8.3

Slap mark of cheek. The outlines of three fingers are visible with a crease running through the lower one.

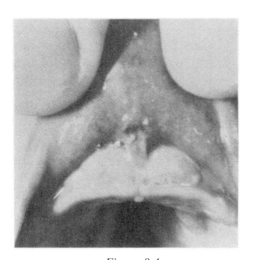

Figure 8.4

Torn upper labial frenulum in difficult-to-feed baby with cleft palate.

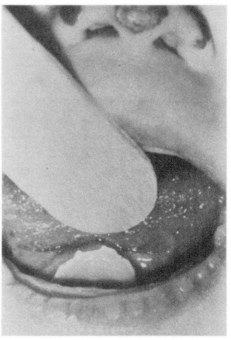

Figure 8.5

Laceration of the floor of the mouth from jamming pacifier into the baby's mouth. Note friction burn of the nose.

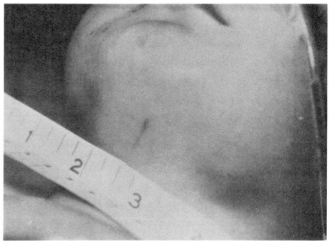

Figure 8.6

Two oval-shaped choke marks on the neck left by the human hand.

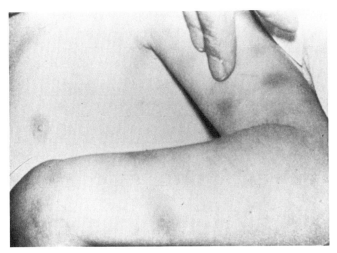

Figure 8.7

Grab marks (squeeze marks) on the upper and lower arm

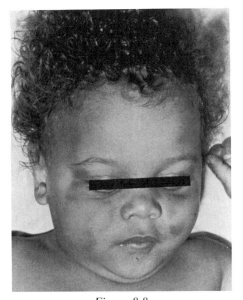

Figure 8.8

Squeeze marks on the face—one on the right cheek and two or three on the left.

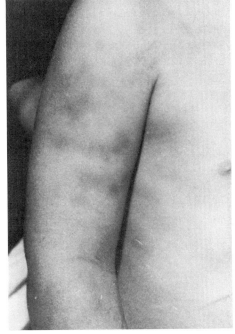

Figure 8.9

Linear finger-edge bruise on the upper arm

obtained in these cases. Bruises or cuts on the neck are almost always due to being choked or strangled by a human hand, cord, dog collar, etc. (figure 8.6). Accidents to this site are extremely rare and should be looked upon with suspicion. Choke marks may be attributed to a resuscitation attempt, when in truth they are due to lifting a child off the ground by the neck while slapping him in the face or battering him against a wall. Resuscitative attempts do not leave bruises on the face or neck.

Human hand marks. The human hand can leave various types of pressure bruises (table 8.3). The most common types are grab marks or squeeze marks, oval-shaped bruises that resemble finger prints. Grab marks are usually due to being forcibly held during violent shaking. The most common site is the upper arm, especially the forearm (figure 8.7). Grab marks of the lower extremities are also common until the child learns to walk. Grab-mark bruises can occur on the cheeks if an adult squeezes a child's face in an attempt to get food or medicine into her mouth. This action leaves a thumb-mark bruise on one cheek and two to four finger-mark bruises on the other cheek (figure 8.8). Encirclement bruises occur when a child is grabbed about the chest or abdomen. This pattern (when complete) contains as many as eight finger-mark bruises on one side of the body and two thumb bruises on the other side. The examiner's fingers can fit easily into the configuration. Linear grab marks are caused by pressure from the entire finger (figure 8.9). The outline of the entire hand print is sometimes seen on the back or at other sites. The human hand usually leaves outline bruises because mainly the capillaries at the edge of the injury are stretched enough to rupture. In slap marks to the cheek, two or three parallel linear bruises at finger-width spacing will be seen to run through a more diffuse bruise (figure 8.3). The human hand can also leave pinch marks which give two crescent-shaped bruises facing each other (figure 8.1). The shape of the bruise is primarily due to the finger nails.

Human bite marks. Human bite marks leave distinctive, paired, crescent-shaped bruises that contain individual teeth marks (figure 8.10). Sometimes the two crescents meet to form a complete ring of bruising. The most common dilemma facing the practitioner is to decide if a single bite on a child is from a playmate or from the parents. The point-to-point distance between the center of the canines (third tooth on each side) should be measured in centimeters. If the distance is greater than 3 cm., the child was bitten by an adult or someone, at least, with permanent teeth (i.e., over age eight). If the distance is less than 3 cm.,

TABLE 8.3   Human Hand Marks

---

    1. Grab marks or fingertip bruises
       (e.g., extremities or face)
    2. Trunk encirclement bruises
    3. Linear marks or finger-edge bruises
    4. Slap marks
    5. Hand print
    6. Pinch marks

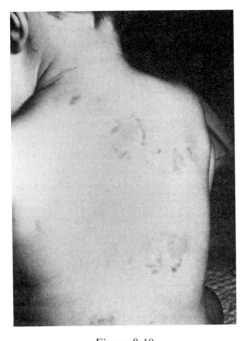

Figure 8.10

Multiple human bite marks (bitten by another child). Note the individual tooth marks.

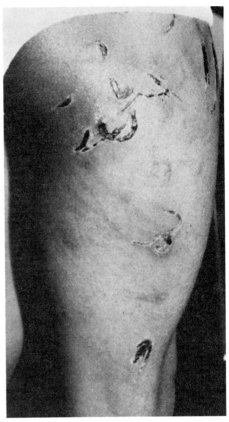

Figure 8.11

Loop mark bruises and abrasions (old and new) from beating with a doubled-over iron cord.

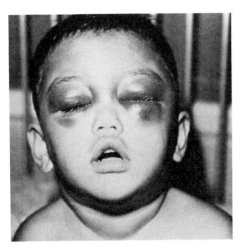

Figure 8.12

Bilateral severe swelling and bruising of the eyes from multiple blows to the upper face.

the child was bitten by another young child with primary teeth (5). In serious injuries with several suspects, the exact perpetrator can be determined by having a dentist make wax impressions of each suspect's teeth and comparing them to photographs of the bite mark (6).

Strap marks. Strap marks are one- to two-inch wide rectangular bruises of various lengths, sometimes covering a curved body surface. These are almost always caused by a belt. Sometimes the eyelets or buckle of the belt can be discerned. Lash marks are narrow, straight-edged bruises or scratches caused by a thrashing with a tree branch or switch. Loop marks are secondary to being struck with a doubled-over lamp cord, rope, or fan belt (figure 8.11). The distal end of the loop strikes with the most force, commonly breaks the skin, and may leave loop-shaped scars (7).

Bizarre marks. Bizarre-shaped bruises are always inflicted. When a blunt instrument (e.g., a toy or shoe) is used in punishment, the bruise or welt will resemble it in shape. Children have been presented with tatoos inflicted with a sharp instrument such as a pin or razor. Numerous puncture wounds may be caused by a fork. Circumferential tie marks on the ankles or wrists can be caused when a child is tied up. If a narrow rope or cord is used, the child will be left with circumferential cuts. If a strap or piece of sheeting is used to restrain a child about the wrists or ankles, a friction burn or rope burn may result, usually presenting a large blister that encircles the extremity. Rope burns have also been seen about the thighs from tying the child to a potty seat. Gag marks may be seen as abrasions that run from the corner of the mouth. Children may be gagged because of too much screaming or yelling.

Accidental Bruises

A thorough knowledge of common and unusual accidents helps the physician recognize inflicted injuries. An understanding of unusual customs or practices that leave bruises is also helpful. Finally, the physician must remember that all bluish discolorations of the skin are not bruises.

Accidental bruises. Most children periodically acquire one or two bruises during falls or rough activity. Babies in the first few months of life commonly scratch themselves on the cheek, ear, nose, or even conjunctiva. This problem is due to long fingernails and disappears if the parent cuts them regularly. The most common site for multiple easily explained bruises in children of all ages is on the knee and shin. These bruises are due to normal falling down or bumping into objects while running. Bruises on the forehead are frequent at age two when the child decides he or she is an accomplished climber. While bruises from falling usually are circular or nondescript, so are grab marks, ring marks, or blows with a fist. Accidental bruises, however, usually occur on the skin overlying bony prominences (e.g., chin, elbow, forehead, spinous process, greater trochanter, etc.). Nondescript bruises become suspect as abuse when they occur on the soft parts of the body (e.g., cheek, fleshy part of the arm, buttocks, abdominal wall, etc.). Most falls produce one bruise on a single surface. Bruises on multiple body planes are usually inflicted, unless there is a history of tumbling accidents. True tumbling accidents also give bruises and abrasions over bony prominences. "Falling down a stairway" is often offered as a last-minute explanation for unexplained bruises in a child. The child who does tumble down the stairs ends up with very few bruises. Therefore, the number of bruises and the location of the bruises speaks of an inflicted injury.

Unusual bruises. Some common practices can result in bruises that should not be confused with child abuse. The Vietnamese can induce symmetrical, linear bruises from coin rubbing (8). For symptoms of fever, chills, or headaches, the back and chest are covered with hot oil and then massaged in downward strokes with the edge of a coin, (called *Cao Gio*). Some teenagers cause multiple petechiae on their chins by sucking on a cup until they create a vacuum and then sliding the cup onto their chins (9). A passionate and prolonged kiss can lead to an area of purpura commonly known as a "hicky." Vigorous sucking on hard candy can leave an area of purpura on the soft palate. On the other hand, purpura at this site has also been reported with fellatio. Multiple petechiae of the face and neck can occur following vigorous crying, retching, or coughing. This pattern is due to a sudden increase in superior vena cava pressure. Petechiae and purpura can even be seen in the conjunctiva or mouth from this mechanism. Obviously, tourniquets can also cause petechiae, especially in children who already have an erythematous rash.

Pseudobruises. Some skin conditions have been mistaken for bruises. The most common one is a Mongolian spot. This birthmark occurs in 95% of black babies, 81% of Orientals and American Indians, 70% of Chicanos and 10% of whites (10). They are present at birth and last from two to three years. They are grayish blue, do not change color, and have clear-cut margins. Although they commonly occur on the buttocks and back, they can occur anywhere. They are a birthmark, not a bruise. Maculae cerulae are unexplained bluish spots on the skin that occur concomitantly with pubic lice. They resolve when the lice are treated. Children with allergic shiners may be referred for black eyes. Allergic shiners are due to long-standing venous congestion from allergic rhinitis and eye allergies. They are usually more brownish in color than blue, and the discoloration is mainly seen on the lower, medial eyelid. The presence of allergies and the duration of the finding points to the correct diagnosis. Hemophilus influenzae can give a bluish cellulitis of the cheek. However, these children are sick, they have a fever, and the area is quite tender.

Inflicted Eye Injuries

Ocular damage in the battered child syndrome includes acute hyphema, dislocated lens, traumatic cataract, and detached retina (11). Over half of these result in permanent impairment of vision affecting one or both eyes. Retinal hemorrhages are also a clue to subdural hematomas in children with unexplained central nervous system findings. Retinal hemorrhage can also occur without clinically important intracranial hemorrhage in children with sudden compression of their chests. This finding is called Purtscher retinopathy (12). The differential diagnosis of retinal hemorrhages is direct head trauma, shaking injuries, increased intracranial pressure, hypertension, bleeding disorders, and gymnastic twirling on a horizontal bar. Retinal hemorrhages usually last ten to fourteen days.

Inflicted black eyes are more common than serious eye injuries. Children who have been hit about the eyes with an open or closed hand present massive swelling and bruising of both eyelids (figure 8.12). Most black eyes caused by accidents only involve one side. The question that is frequently raised is whether or not a child can acquire two black eyes from a single accident, or more precisely, from striking a single object. The answer is yes. Bilateral black eyes can occur from blood seeping down from a large bruise on the forehead or from a basilar skull fracture. Blood moves with gravity. However, these children have minimal lid swelling and no lid tenderness. In addition, the onset of the black eye is delayed one or two days from the time of the injury. Therefore, these situations should not be confused with the child who has been beaten about the head and eyes.

Inflicted Head Injuries

Inflicted head injuries include subdural hematomas, subarachnoid hemorrhages, scalp bruises, traumatic alopecia, and subgaleal hematomas.

Subdural hematomas. Subdural hematoma is the most dangerous inflicted injury, often causing death or serious sequelae. These children present irritability, vomiting, a decreased level of consciousness, breathing difficulty and apneic episodes, a bulging fontanel, and/or convulsions (13). The classic case of subdural hematoma is associated with skull fractures. These fractures are secondary to a direct blow from the caretaker's hand or from being hit against a wall or door. Numerous other bruises may also be present.

Inflicted subdural hematomas can also occur without skull fractures, scalp bruises, or scalp swelling. In fact, over one-half of the cases have no fracture (14). These findings used to be called ''spontaneous subdural hematomas,'' but recent evidence points to a violent, whiplash shaking mechanism (15). Rapid acceleration and deceleration of the head as it bobs about leads to tearing of the bridging cerebral veins with bleeding into the subdural space, usually bilaterally. Proof for this etiology comes from experimental studies done on animals and also the confessions of some of the parents. Most of these cases occur in babies under one year of age, who are shaken to make them stop crying. Additional diagnostic evidence comes from the presence of retinal hemorrhages in these whiplash subdurals. X-rays of the long bones should also be obtained because they will reveal old or new fractures in 25% of the cases (14). Subarachnoid hemorrhages can result from the same mechanism and may be as common as shaking subdural hematomas. The concept of the ''spontaneous subdural hematoma'' in young infants must be discarded, lest we send a child home to be reinjured or killed. Likewise, the diagnosis of ''chronic subdural hematomas'' secondary to birth trauma must be viewed with skepticism. Subdural hematomas due to birth injury will almost always produce acute signs and symptoms within twenty-four to forty-eight hours after delivery.

Scalp bruises. Bruises of the scalp can occur with or without underlying skull fractures or brain injuries. These bruises are often difficult to see because they are deep in the scalp or they are hidden by the child's hair. Diagnosis of scalp bruises should be suspected by the finding of soft-tissue swelling on palpation or on skull films.

Traumatic alopecia and subgaleal hematomas. Some children are pulled or yanked by the hair. Sometimes the hair spirals at the broken end, probably secondary to stretching at this site prior to breakage. If the hair-pulling event is recent, the scalp may be tender and a few petechiae may be found at the hair roots. Unlike alopecia areata, there are no loose hairs at the periphery of the bald area. Unlike diseases that cause hair loss, there is no inflammation or scaling of the scalp. Violent and sudden lifting of a child by the hair can also cause a subgaleal hematoma, as evidenced by a diffuse, boggy swelling of the scalp. The aponeurosis which connects the occipital and frontalis muscles is lifted off the calvarium and the space rapidly fills with blood. This diagnosis is most likely if the child has braids at the site of the hematoma (16). Subgaleal hematoma can also be caused by shearing forces, but an unexplained one is probably inflicted.

Accidental head injuries from falls. Helfer, Slovis, and Black recently reported the outcome of 246 young children who accidentally fell out of cribs or beds (17). In 80% of the children, there were no findings whatever of an injury. The other 20% of the children had a single bruise, lump, or cut. Only 1% of the children had skull fractures and these were single and linear. Another 1% of the children had a fresh fracture at another site, usually the clavicle or humerus. Important to us, none of the children had subdural hematomas, epidural hematomas, or any serious life-threatening injury.

Inflicted Abdominal Injuries

Intraabdominal injuries are the second most common cause of death in battered children (18). Unlike the contents of the chest, the abdominal organs are not protected. Table 8.4 lists inflicted abdominal injuries in the approximate order of frequency. Most of the injuries are usually caused by a punch or kick that compresses the organ against the anterior spinal column.

The most common finding is a ruptured liver or spleen. These children present

TABLE 8.4   Inflicted Abdominal Injuries

---

1. Ruptured liver or spleen
2. Intestinal perforation
3. Intramural hematoma of duodenum
   or proximal jejunum
4. Ruptured blood vessel
5. Pancreatic injury
6. Kidney or bladder injury
7. Chylous ascites from injured lymphatic system
8. Foreign bodies (swallowed or percutaneous)

---

blood loss and shock. Second, blows to the abdomen can cause tears or rents in the small or large intestine. These children often present advanced peritonitis because of a delay in seeking medical care. An upright film of the abdomen will show free air under the diaphragm. Third, the most unique abdominal injury is an intramural hematoma of the duodenum or proximal jejunum (19). These children present projectile vomiting, (bile stained if the obstruction is distal) and other signs of gastrointestinal obstruction. With supportive management, the hematoma usually resolves without surgery. Fourth, arteries or veins can be torn and these patients present in shock. Fifth, trauma is the most common cause of acute pancreatitis in children. Again, an anterior blow to the abdomen compresses the pancreas against the vertebral column. Sometimes the pancreas is transected. Children with acute traumatic pancreatitis have symptoms of abdominal tenderness, vomiting, and fever. Their serum and urine amylase levels will be markedly elevated. If the initial injury heals, it may progress to a pseudocyst of the pancreas (20). These children have persistent abdominal pain and vomiting. Their diagnosis is finally confirmed with the discovery of an abdominal mass on physical examination and the presence of a soft tissue mass on a lateral abdominal film displacing the stomach anteriorly. Sixth, kidney injuries usually result from blows to the back and present gross hematuria. The bladder may be ruptured by a blow to the lower abdomen. Two unusual presentations of child abuse are chylous ascites and a needle perforation of the liver (21, 22).

In all of these conditions, trauma to the abdomen is usually denied (23). Bruises of the abdominal wall (when present) help to establish the correct diagnosis. Unfortunately, there are no visible bruises or marks on the abdominal wall in over half of these cases. The abdominal wall is usually relaxed at the time of the injury, and the energy from the blow is mainly absorbed by the internal organs. The physician must consider child abuse in any abdominal crisis of undetermined etiology.

Immediate Actions by the Physician

The detection of a child with suspected abuse demands some immediate actions by the physician. He must report all these cases to child protective services, hospitalize selected children, obtain a police hold on some children, and share his diagnosis and plans with the parents.

Report all suspected cases to child protective services. The physician is required to report these cases to the child protective service agency in the child's county of residence. The report should be made by phone immediately and in writing within forty-eight hours. This report should guarantee adequate evaluation, treatment, and follow-up, as well as fulfilling legal requirements.

Hospitalize any abused child needing protection during the initial evaluation period. The highest priority of initial management is to protect the child. Any child suspected of having been abused requires hospitalization until evaluations regarding the safety of the home are complete. All too often, a crying baby with a minor inflicted injury is sent home, only to return the next day with subdural hematomas or multiple fractures. The reason given to the parents for the hospitalization can be that "children with unusual injuries need to be hospitalized for a thorough evaluation." While the term "unexplained injuries" also may be used in the clinic setting, in general, the terms "inflicted injuries" or "abused child" should not. A psychosocial history or any incriminating questions usually can be delayed until the child is hospitalized. Also, discussion of the need to report the suspicious injuries to the proper authorities can be postponed. While the parents are never lied to, the best timing for telling them everything is usually after the child has been safely admitted to the ward. If the parents bring up the question of child abuse, the physician should honestly state that this is one of his concerns. If the parents refuse hospitalization, a police hold can be obtained.

In some parts of the country, child protective service workers and emergency receiving homes are available twenty-four hours a day. Unless the child's injuries require close medical observations, placement in an emergency receiving home is far less expensive than hospitalization. Approximately thirty minutes before the caseworker is expected to arrive, the physician should tell the parents that a caseworker has been called, that the caseworker is coming to the clinic to see them, and that his or her input is essential. If the delay is going to be prolonged (e.g., over one hour), less agitation is engendered if the parents initially feel they are waiting for lab results or X-ray results. Private physicians can usually be more open about these matters without running the risk that the parents will bolt from the medical facility.

Tell the parents your diagnosis. The physician (rather than someone else) should inform the parents that he has reported their child's injuries to protective services, since this report is based on medical findings. He should state that he is obligated by state law to report any unusual or unexplained injuries. He can reassure the parents that everyone involved will try to help them find better ways of dealing with their child. Maintaining a helping approach with these parents is often the hardest part of the therapy. Feeling angry with these parents is natural, but expressing this anger to the parents will jeopardize their cooperation (see Chapter 7). The physician should keep in mind that the injury may have occurred in a moment of anger, that rarely was it deliberate, and that these parents already feel inadequate and unloved. The physician should encourage hospital visits by parents and be certain that the ward personnel treat them kindly. These parents need frequent, on-going communication from the physician on their child's case or they may become unduly suspicious and angry.

The Medical Evaluation of Children with Physical Abuse

The following nine tasks represent the medical data base that must be collected in a comprehensive child abuse evaluation (see table 8.5).

1. History of injury: A complete history should be obtained as to how the injury allegedly happened, including the informant, date, time, place, sequence of events, people present, time lag before medical attention was sought, and so forth. Unlike the psychosocial interview, which can be postponed, the detailed history of the injury

TABLE 8.5   Medical Evaluation Checklist

1. History of injury
2. Physical examination of patient
3. Trauma X-ray survey on selected patients
4. Bleeding disorder screen on selected patients
5. Color photographs of selected patients
6. Physical examination of siblings
7. Official medical report in writing
8. Behavioral screening
9. Developmental screening

should be elicited immediately, before the parents have the time to change it. If possible, the parents should be interviewed separately. The parents can be pressed for exact details when necessary. No other professional should have to repeat this detailed, probing interview. The physician must talk with the parents directly so that his or her history will not be considered as hearsay evidence in court. In rare situations, obtaining the history from the parents on the phone may suffice if they cannot come in. The physician commonly forgets to interview the child, which is often helpful if the child is over age three or four. This should be done in a private setting without the parents present.

2. Physical examination of patient: All bruises should be recorded as to size, shape, position, color, and age. If they resemble strap marks, grab marks, or marks from a blunt instrument, this should be recorded. The oral cavity, eardrums, and genitals should be closely examined for signs of occult trauma. All bones should be palpated for tenderness and the joints tested for full range of motion. In addition, special attention should be paid to the retina, for hemorrhages there may point to subdural hematomas from a shaking injury. The height and weight percentiles should be plotted, and if the child is underweight, the diet history should be explored. Physicians are commonly asked to date bruises. Table 8.6 condenses data from five studies on this subject (24). In general, if the bruises are swollen and tender, they are probably less than two days old. The initial color of bruises is red, blue, or purple. As hemoglobin is broken down, bruises undergo three additional color changes, beginning at the periphery of the bruise. The first color change to green occurs at a minimum of five days. Within a few days, the color changes to yellow, and eventually it progresses to brown. The brown color may persist from four days to four weeks before the bruise completely clears.

3. Trauma X-ray survey: Every suspected victim under five years of age should receive a radiologic bone survey. These films are of great diagnostic value, since the clinical findings of fracture often disappear in six or seven days even without orthopedic care. A child with multiple fractures may still move about and play normally. For children over age five, X-ray films need to be obtained only if any bone tenderness or limited range of motion is noted on physical examination. If films of a tender site are initially normal, they should be repeated in two weeks to pick up calcification of any subperiosteal bleeding or nondisplaced epiphyseal separations that may have been present (see Chapter 13).

4. Bleeding disorder screen: A bleeding screen would include a platelet count, bleeding time, partial thromboplastin time, prothrombin time, fibrinogen level, and thrombin time (25). A normal bleeding panel strengthens the physician's court testimony that bruising could not have occurred spontaneously or as the result of a minor injury. On a practical level, bleeding tests are rarely indicated. Children with subtle bleeding tendencies demonstrate ongoing bruising in the school, office, hospital, and foster home. Screening is not needed for bruises confined to the buttocks, bruises resembling

TABLE 8.6   **Dating of Bruises**

Age	Color
0– 2 days	Swollen, tender
0– 5 days	Red, blue, purple
5– 7 days	Green
7–10 days	Yellow
10–14 days (or longer)	Brown
2– 4 weeks	Cleared

weapons, or hand-print bruises. It is also unnecessary when one parent or the child accuses a specific adult of hitting the child. The main indication for screening is nonspecific bruises, which the parent denies inflicting or for which a history of alleged "easy bruisability" is given.

5. Color photographs: Color photographs are required by law in some states (26). In most juvenile court cases, they are not essential to the primary physician's testimony. In cases where an expert witness who has not actually examined the child is to testify, they are mandatory. In cases where criminal court action is anticipated, they will usually be required and will be taken by the police photographer. Whether or not medical photography is available, the physician should carefully diagram the body-surface findings in the official medical chart and carefully date and sign the entry.

6. Physical examination of siblings: There is approximately a 20% risk that a sibling of a physically abused child has also been abused at the same time (27). Therefore, all siblings under the age of eighteen should be brought in for an inspection and palpation examination of the total body surface within twelve hours of uncovering an index case. If the parents say they cannot bring them in because of transportation problems, the protective service agency can accomplish this. If the parents refuse to have their other children seen, a court order can be obtained and the police sent out.

7. Official medical report in writing: The physician's findings should be recorded in a typed medical report. As it may be used in court, the accuracy and completeness of this report is very important. A copy of the admission work-up to the hospital or the discharge summary will not suffice, because the evidence for the diagnosis of child abuse is often difficult for nonmedical people to locate in these highly technical documents. A well-written medical report often convinces the parents' lawyer that his clients' case is in great question, and he accepts ("stipulates to") the petition before the court and agrees to therapy for his clients. Therefore, a well-written medical report may keep the physician out of court and save him or her time in the long run. The report should include: (a) a history—the alleged cause of the injury (with date, time, place, and so forth), (b) a physical exam—a detailed description of the injury using nontechnical terms whenever possible (e.g., "cheek," instead of "zygoma," "bruise," instead of "ecchymosis"), (c) results of lab tests and X-ray films, (d) a conclusion—a statement that this incident represents nonaccidental trauma, the reason behind this conclusion, a comment on the severity of the present injury (e.g., sequelae), and an estimate of the danger for serious reabuse. (A sample report is shown in the appendix.)

8. Behavioral screening: The abused child inevitably has associated behavior problems (28). Some may be primary behaviors that make the child difficult to live with and hence prone to abuse (e.g., negativism and hyperactivity). Other behaviors may be secondary to abusive treatment (e.g., fearfulness and depression). Often the abused child's individual need for therapy will be overlooked unless these symptoms are un-

covered. The child's behavior should be observed and discussed. Those children with major behavioral problems need referral for a complete assessment. The physician may provide counseling for minor problems.

9. Developmental screening: Abuse and neglect of the infant and preschool child can lead to developmental delays (29). These problems usually can be detected by routine use of the Denver Developmental Screening Test (DDST) or other developmental tests for this age group. Children with developmental problems need referral for more detailed testing. A school report may be helpful in the comprehensive assessment of the abused school-age child.

Acknowledgments

The author is deeply grateful to the following pediatricians for sharing photographs and experiences: Dr. Joan R. Hebeler provided figure 8.3; Dr. Richard D. Marble provided figures 8.6 and 8.9; Dr. George W. Starbuck provided figures 8.10 and 8.12.

Appendix

PHYSICAL ABUSE—MEDICAL REPORT

DRL
BD: 2/12/74
CGH# 123456

This four-year-old boy was seen in the Colorado General Hospital Emergency Room at 3:20 P.M. on September 5, 1978. He was accompanied by Ms. Smith, the caseworker from Denver County, and the patient's mother.

HISTORY: The patient has many bruises, and his mother states that he commonly falls down. She denies that he has any unusual bleeding. In regard to the many bruises on his body, she admits to causing the ones on his face by squeezing it vigorously with her right hand to get his attention after misbehaving. She denies causing any of the other bruises and thinks that most of them occur through accidents which she did not witness. She claims that the bruise on his forehead and right ear were caused today when she suddenly returned to the room, opened the door, and hit him with the door. However, she denies that he fell down or was pinned against the wall. She claims that the numerous bruises on his buttocks are due to falling down the concrete basement stairs. She admits to disciplining him by occasionally slapping him on the mouth and also by spanking him on the buttocks. In interviewing the boy with the mother out of the room, he says that his mother hits him both with her hand and a belt. He says the bruises on his buttocks are due to being hit with a belt and that the bruises on one of his ears, at least, were due to her slapping him. He claims that his father does not spank him or hit him.

PHYSICAL EXAM: The boy is of average height and well nourished.
1. *Face*. The boy has a fresh, tender, swollen bruise about three-quarters of an inch in diameter on the right eyebrow. He has four bruises, all of which are circular, ranging in size from one-quarter inch to one-half inch, and yellowish blue in color. There are two

on the left cheek, one on the chin, and one on the right cheek, just adjacent to the mouth. These are the bruises the mother admits to having caused.

2. *Ears.* The right earlobe is covered with large and small bruises on both surfaces. The left earlobe has approximately ten small, bleeding marks. The right eardrum has half a dozen hemorrhages on the surface. There is no bleeding apparent behind the eardrum.

3. *Scalp.* There is a one-inch-diameter tender swelling on the right parietal area. No bruise is apparent.

4. *Arms.* There are two one-half-inch circular bruises, close to each other, on the right upper arm on the outer surface. On the left mid-upper arm, there is an old, fading yellow bruise approximately one-half inch in diameter.

5. *Buttocks.* There are nine old bruises on the buttocks. These have a reddish yellow hue and are older than the mother's dating of his falling down the stairs two days ago. These range in size from two inches to one-half inch.

6. *Legs.* The right shin has three and the left shin has two old yellow red bruises, one-half inch or smaller in diameter. (These are normal.)

SKELETAL SURVEY: No bone injuries seen on X-ray.

CONCLUSION: This four-year-old boy has numerous bruises of different ages, covering many of his body surfaces. He has clearly been physically abused. The mother admits inflicting the squeeze marks on the face. The boy has obvious slap marks on both ears that could not have resulted from being hit accidentally by a door. The bruises on the buttocks are also clearly caused by spanking and substantiated by the patient himself. The bruises on the upper arms appear to be grab marks, but they are not conclusive. The bruises about the ears, the fact that the eardrum was injured on the right side, and the finding of an inflicted injury on the scalp, suggest a serious lack of restraint and the need for vigorous intervention.

JAMES L. ADAMS, M.D.

References

1. Colorado Department of Social Services. 1977. Report. Central Registry for Child Protection.

2. Holter, J. C., Friedman, S. B. 1968. Child Abuse: Early Case Finding in the Emergency Department. *Pediatrics* 42:128.

3. Smyth, S. M. 1972. Child Abuse Syndrome. *Br. Med. J.* 3:113.

4. Slosberg, E. J., Ludwig, S., Duckett, J., and Mauro, A. E. 1978. Penile Trauma as a Sign of Child Abuse. *Am. J. Diseases Child.* 132:719–20.

5. Levine, L. J. Personal communication.

6. Levine, L. J. 1973. The Solution of a Battered-Child Homicide by Dental Evidence: Report of Case. JADA 87:1,234.

7. Sussman, S. J. 1968. Skin Manifestations of the Battered-Child Syndrome. *J. Pediatr.* 72:99.

8. Yeatman, G. W., Shaw, C., Barlow, M. J., and Bartlett, G. 1976. Pseudobattering in Vietnamese Children. *Pediatrics* 58:616–18.

9. Lovejoy, F. H., Marcuse, E. K., and Landrigan, P. J. 1971. Two Examples of Purpura Factitia. *Clin. Pediatr.* 11:183–84.

10. Jacobs, A. H., and Walton, R. G. 1976. Incidence of Birthmarks in the Neonate. *Pediatrics* 58:218–22.

11. Mushin, A. S. 1971. Ocular Damage in the Battered-Child Syndrome. *Br. Med. J.* 3:402.

12. Tomasi, L. G. 1975. Purtscher Retinopathy in the Battered-Child Syndrome. *Am. J. Diseases Child.* 129:1,335.

13. Silber, D. L., Bell, W. E. 1971. The Neurologist and the Physically Abused Child. *Neurology* 21:991.

14. Guthkelch, A. N. 1971. Infantile Subdural Hematoma and Its Relationship to Whiplash Injuries. *Br. Med. J.* 2:430.

15. Caffey, J. 1974. The Whiplash Shaken-Infant Syndrome. *Pediatrics* 54:396.

16. Hamlin, H. 1968. Subgaleal Hematoma Caused by Hair-Pull. *J. Am. Med. Assoc.* 204:339.

17. Helfer, R. E., Slovis, T. L., and Black, M. 1977. Injuries Resulting When Small Children Fall out of Bed. *Pediatrics* 60:533–35.

18. Touloukian, R. J. 1968. Abdominal Visceral Injuries in Battered Children. *Pediatrics* 42:642.

19. Gornall, P., *et al.* 1972. Intra-abdominal Injuries in the Battered-Baby Syndrome. *Arch. Diseases Child.* 47:211.

20. Penna, S. D. J., Medovy, H. 1973. Child Abuse and Traumatic Pseudocyst of the Pancreas. *J. Pediatr.* 83:1,026.

21. Boysen, B. E. 1975. Chylous Ascites. *Am. J. Diseases Child.* 129:1,338.

22. Stone, R. K., Harowitz, A., San Filippo, J. A., and Gromisch, D. S. 1976. Needle Perforation of the Liver in an Abused Child.

23. O'Neill, J. A., *et al.* 1973. Patterns of Injury in the Battered-Child Syndrome. *J. Trauma* 13:332.

24. Wilson, E. F. 1977. Estimation of the Age of Cutaneous Contusions in Child Abuse. *Pediatrics* 60:751–52.

25. Hathaway, W. E. Personal communication.

26. Ford, R. J., Smistek, B. S., Glass, J. T. 1975. Photography of Suspected Child Abuse and Maltreatment. *Biomed. Commun.* 3:12.

27. Lauer, B., Ten Broeck, E., Grossman, M. 1974. Battered-Child Syndrome: Review of 130 Patients with Controls. *Pediatrics* 54:67.

28. Morse, C. W., Sahler, O. J., Friedman, S. B. 1970. A Three-Year Follow-up Study of Abused and Neglected Children. *Am. J. Diseases Child.* 120:439.

29. Martin, H. P., *et al.* 1974. The Development of Abused Children. *Advances in Pediatrics* 21:25.

9 Child Abuse by Burning

Kenneth W. Feldman

Burns are a feared, sometimes fatal injury. The pain of the wounds may be equaled by that of the treatment. Even after lengthy and successful treatment, burn victims may be disabled and disfigured. These circumstances, singly or in combination, may cause prolonged psychological disability. When viewing a burned child, a health professional's attention is drawn to the problems of the treatment and consequences of burn injury. Although the incidence, causes, characteristics and potential means of preventing burn injury may attract less attention, they often have immediate bearing on the treatment plan. The physician must assess the possibility of repeated injury, either accidental or abusive, and the probable quality of home care. Careful evaluation of the burn injury may lead to injury prevention for that child or other children.

Burns are the second most frequent cause of accidental death in children one to four years old and the third in children from five to fourteen years old (1). Child abuse has frequently been the cause of burns. Two studies found that 4% (2) and 8% (3) of hospitalized childhood burn patients were abuse victims. Abuse rates in specific burn injuries can be even higher; abuse occurred in 28% of hospitalized tap-water burn victims (4). Burns have also been found to be a frequent source of injury in child abuse. Burns have been the mode of injury in 6–17% of children in institutional studies of abuse (3, 5, 6). Gil's 1967 nationwide survey of abused children found that 10% had burns (7). Abuse should thus be a major diagnostic consideration in any case of a burned child. Most burns leave hallmarks suggesting agent, mode, direction, and time of injury. The physical findings of each burn should be studied with these questions in mind and a hypothesis of injury formulated to compare with the caretaker's history.

General Characteristics of Burn Injury

Childhood burns, and accidents in general, often result from environmental and psychiatric stress (8). In a 1974 study of burns in Edinburgh, Scotland, Wilkinson

Kenneth W. Feldman, M.D., is with the Odessa Brown Children's Clinic and the Ambulatory Division, Department of Pediatrics, University of Washington, Seattle.

noted that "bad accommodation is not so prominent a factor as the (poor) domestic habits of the family." (9). Large, poor families in crowded accommodations in which child care was absent or the responsibility of slightly older siblings seemed predisposed to burn injury. Long and Cope found a high incidence (44%) of gross emotional disturbance within the family unit in a study of nineteen children on an inpatient burn unit (10). Holter and Friedman, studying families of thirteen children with greater than 15% body-surface-area burns, found that five children, eight mothers, and five fathers had serious preexisting emotional, psychiatric, or behavioral problems (11). Only three of the marriages were stable, while seven were "unhappy and unsatisfactory" and three were emotionally unstable single-parent homes. Seven of the injuries appeared to be the direct consequences of family stress, carelessness, and poor child supervision. Three of the thirteen burns were frankly abusive. One-third of the burned children in Borland's study and another member in 29% of their families had required medical attention for accidental injury within the previous year (12). Upsetting trigger events occurred in 25% of these families just prior to the child's burn injury.

In childhood, the infant is most likely to become a burn victim. During infancy, children are physically helpless, emotionally labile, and unreasonably demanding. Their curiosity far outstrips their caution. Normal infants frequently cry immediately, but fail to withdraw, when burned. Families of injured children tend to misunderstand the developmental status of their children and the child's ability to avoid hazards in the environment (8). In addition to normal childhood immaturity, further handicaps increase a child's burn proneness by reducing the child's ability to sense or escape a burning situation and by increasing family stress. For example, meningomyelocele with paralysis and anesthesia, cerebral palsy, epilepsy, (13) and psychiatric instability predispose to injury. Seventy-two percent of the burned children reported by Borland were less than five years old (12). Waller, studying the well-defined population of a Kaiser prepaid health plan, found a burn injury rate of 29.3 per thousand per year in the first two years of life. The rate declined to a steady plateau of 3–5 cases per thousand per year from age three through childhood (14). Likewise, abusive burns are concentrated among infants and toddlers with mean ages at injury of 24.8 months (6) and 3 years (2).

Regional differences in life-style result in vastly different statistics on burn causation. In North Carolina, where open-flame gas heaters are the major mode of heating, clothing ignition burns are most common (15). In King County, Washington, where central or electric baseboard heating is the rule, scalds are the predominant form of burn injury (16). Social class may also affect the accessibility to burn hazards. Poorer southeastern United States families are more likely to have open-flame gas heaters. Superimposed on such differences in environmental hazards are social and cultural differences in the desirability and methods of child discipline. For example, Gil notes the frequent occurrence of abusive burning in Puerto Rican families as opposed to the more frequent abuse by the bare hands in white families (7).

Despite these regional and subcultural differences, 70–90% of childhood burns occur in the home (12, 16–18). Burn injuries cluster in the more stressful hours of the day: the morning when children are arising from sleep and the "poison hours" of the late afternoon when presupper hunger, tiredness, and distracting activity are at their peak (9, 12, 19). Burn injury is also most frequent in the winter months when crowding seems most oppressive and open sources of heat are in most frequent use (9, 12).

Although some studies have been biased by referral patterns to specific institutions, burn injuries seem to be overrepresented in the lower economic classes. Although only 9% of fathers in the Seattle area in 1950 were unskilled laborers, 24% of the inpatient burn victims were from this economic class (16). Most parents of burn-injured children in Missouri lack high school education, are poor, unskilled laborers, young, and have other children (12). Similarly, burns tend to occur in the English laboring classes (20). Because of inherent professional biases, actual diagnosis of abuse is more likely in the lower economic classes.

Although these comments are based on studies of burns in general, the reader should understand that abusive burns are likely to be underdiagnosed. The abusive burn is only a small, symptomatic segment of burn-prone children and their families. Nonabusive burns are frequently the result of neglectful episodes arising in families with social disruption that could have easily resulted in abuse. The high incidence of abusive burns, preexisting family stress, and psychiatric disability resulting from burn treatment and residual burn scarring has caused many burn units to routinely provide psychiatric and social work aid for burn victims. These units review all childhood burn incidents for possible abuse. Preventative intervention can then be initiated for abuse and potential abuse victims and their families.

Specific Patterns of Abusive Hot-Water Burns

Scald burns are the most frequent cause of thermal injury in children and of child abuse by burning (2, 6). Although tap water causes only a small part of all scald burns (7–17%), it is the most frequent cause of abusive scald burns (4).

In a survey of Seattle homes, 80% had water temperatures greater than 130°F and the average temperature of hot water was 142°F. This situation is largely determined by the current industry practice of presetting new electric heaters at 150°F and gas heaters at 140°F. The rapidity of scalding increases drastically above 127°F where one minute is required to cause full-thickness scalds of adult skin (figure 9.1) (21). At 130°F, such scald burns occur in thirty seconds and at 150°F in two seconds. Thus, an unsafe situation is created in most United States homes where exposure to hot tap water is likely to result in severe burns. Abused children are often held under flowing hot water or immersed in tubs of drawn hot water. As opposed to coffee and tea spills, where a thin layer of hot water cools rapidly on exposure to the air; with tap water a large reservoir of heat energy remains in direct contact with the child. This results in large, deep scalds. The mean body-surface-area receiving second- and third-degree burns in inpatient tap-water burns is 19%.

Twenty-eight percent of all inpatient tap-water scalds were found to be abusive.

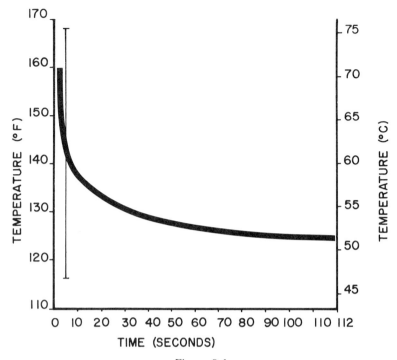

Figure 9.1

The mean ±2 standard deviations for Seattle-area home bathtub water temperatures are superimposed on the time versus temperature curve of hot water required to cause full-thickness scalds of adult skin (after Moritz and Henriques [21]).

In 60% of the cases where history indicated that an adult drew the hot water, the burn was abusive. Likewise, 48% of the time, when the history indicated that an adult was in the room at the time of injury, abuse was present. Abuse was more likely when an adult other than the caretaker at the time of injury brought the child to medical care (71%) and when care was delayed more than two hours after injury (70%). Although boys were the victims of tap-water burns only slightly more often than girls, they accounted for 69% of the abusive tap-water burns.

Abusive tap-water burns were not significantly more extensive than accidental tap-water burns, and the age of abuse and nonabuse victims was not significantly different. Although the water temperature in Seattle homes was unrelated to the family's social class, tap-water scald burns, social stress, and abusive burns were all more frequent in the laboring and unemployed classes.

As in other forms of abuse, tap-water scalds often arise when a socially and emotionally isolated and stressed caretaker reacts to what is viewed as child misbehavior. He exposes the child to hot water as punishment or as an impulsive act to end fussiness. Such episodes are often related to stool and toilet training. Abusive tap-water–flow burns will apear similar to the coffee- and tea-spill burns described later, but will involve the buttocks, perineum, and legs more frequently.

The twenty-eight-month-old daughter of an unemployed logger on welfare soiled her diapers. He rinsed her buttocks under the running hot-water tap. She sustained 12% first- and second-degree burns of the buttocks, perineum, and left thigh.

Children may also be forcibly immersed in drawn hot water. When hot water has just been drawn, the bottom of the sink or tub remains at a lower temperature than the water it contains. If an infant's body is forcibly opposed to the bottom of the container, it may be spared burning. This creates an unburned central area—the hole in the doughnut effect. If a child is firmly held in a position of flexion, intertriginous areas and opposed areas of the limbs and trunk will be spared burning. An unrestrained child in a tub of hot water may be unable to extricate himself from the water, but will usually thrash about, creating splash burns, blurring of the waterline margin, and burning of flexion crease areas. When restrained, such splashing and blurring may be minimal, and clear margins of the burn allow one to reconstruct the child's position in the water. Immersion injuries involving the buttocks and perineum only, imply that the child was held in flexion and the buttocks dipped in drawn hot water. Splash marks and burns of the hands or feet would be present if the injury was accidental. Such hallmarks of immersion injury may allow medical personnel to discount fabricated histories of accidental injury. A hypothesis of forcible restraint may be made.

A ten-month-old girl was brought to the emergency room two hours after her mother's companion was alleged to have spilled a pot of hot water on her. Forty percent full-thickness burns occurred in a pattern indicating that she had been immersed in hot water with her buttocks pressed against a cooler tub bottom. Sparing of flexion areas also implied forcible restraint. Old fractures of both radii were found on skeletal survey. Abuse was recognized because of the discrepancy between history and burn pattern (figure 9.2) (5).

Stocking and glove injuries with sharp upper margins will be seen if a child's feet or hands are held in hot water.

A three-month-old boy was being cared for by his sixteen-year-old father. The child sustained a second-degree stocking burn of his right leg. His father's history was that he had steadied the infant on top of the bathroom sink while he filled the sink, wet a wash cloth, and covered his face with it to soak a cold sore. When his father removed the wash cloth, he discovered the child's injury. The infant's mother called the child's pediatrician later in the day to express her concern about the possibility of abuse. The father had a history of emotional instability and easy frustration with the infant's fussing. After recovery, the child was discharged to the home with Children's Protective Service supervision and counseling (figure 9.3).

A child who is held in a tub of shallow water may "tripod," raise up on his hands and feet to protect his buttocks and perineum from burning. These children will present with stocking and glove burns of several limbs.

The rapidity of burning is inversely proportional to the thickness of the skin (21). Young children's thin skin is likely to burn with far less exposure time than an adult could tolerate and with cooler heat sources than an adult would expect to be damaging. When adults were surveyed to determine their awareness of hot-tap-water risk, no one knew what temperature would be hazardous. Adults will

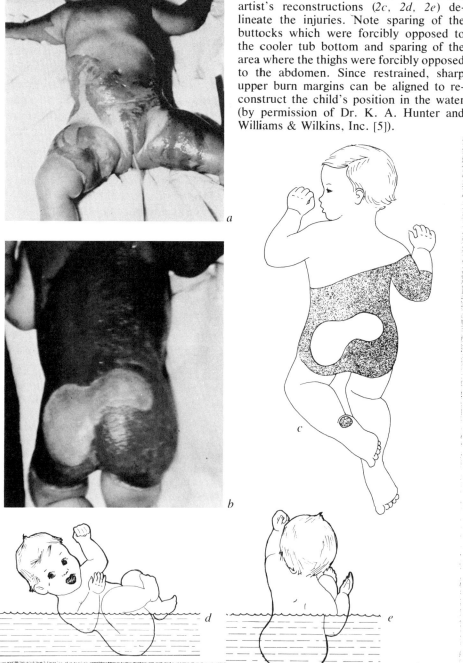

Figure 9.2

This ten-month-old girl was abusively immersed in hot water. Photos (*2a, 2b*) and artist's reconstructions (*2c, 2d, 2e*) delineate the injuries. Note sparing of the buttocks which were forcibly opposed to the cooler tub bottom and sparing of the area where the thighs were forcibly opposed to the abdomen. Since restrained, sharp upper burn margins can be aligned to reconstruct the child's position in the water (by permission of Dr. K. A. Hunter and Williams & Wilkins, Inc. [5]).

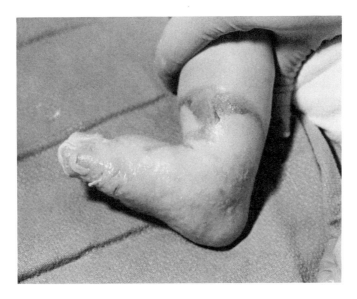

Figure 9.3

A three-month-old boy sustained a stocking burn of his right leg
in the bathroom sink. The straight, sharp upper margin of the
burn without splash burns implies restraint.

often test the temperature of an infant's bath with their thick, heat-insensitive
palmar skin. A hurried caretaker may fail to recognize the risk of hot water.

In most forms of child abuse, the instrument of injury, i.e., the hand or other
object, is ever present. As such, the only means of preventive intervention is to
recognize, treat, and support the potential abuser prior to the injury. Tap-water
scalds are unique in that it is possible to modify the agent of injury to make it less
destructive. Below 120°F, hot water is unlikely to inflict major injury. This is the
lowest hot-water temperature attainable with most current water-heater thermo-
stats. Some families will discover that their water heater cannot produce an
adequate quantity of hot water at this temperature, but most homes can successfully function with a water-heater setting of 120–130°F. The risk of scalding is
significantly greater at 130°F, but still much less than at current temperatures. The
United States Consumer Product Safety Commission has already asked plumbing
manufacturers to comply with a voluntary standard requiring mixing valves on
new tubs and showers that would limit water temperature to 120°F or less. Unfortunately, these valves are expensive to install on existing tubs, and the frequent, abusive sink burns would not be prevented. As a consequence, the commission has been petitioned to require a maximum setting of 130°F for new water
heaters. Until effective regulation is enacted nationally, individual practitioners
can recommend to their patients' families that they reset their water heaters to a
safe level. Because of the energy-saving potential, many utility companies will
reset the heater at the customer's request. In families with a recognized abuse
potential, this might be a particularly helpful preventive measure.

A smaller percentage (6%) of scalds caused by liquids other than hot tap water are the result of child abuse (4). The agents are the usual causes of scalding which one sees in practice: coffee, tea, and cooking pots from the stove. The physical hallmarks of abuse in these injuries are more subtle, so that the general characteristics of abusive families and historical clues and inconsistencies must provide a greater part of the diagnosis. The child involved in an accidental scalding usually looks up and pulls a container of hot liquid down upon himself. The resulting burn (in face, arm, and upper trunk injuries) usually involves the under side of the chin and axilla on the injured side (22). Sparing of these areas may suggest that the hot liquid was poured or thrown upon the victim. The point of initial impact of hot fluid will be burned most deeply. From there, downward gravitational flow of cooling liquid will occur. Gradually, less severely burned areas will stream down from the most deeply burned site. The presence of a flow injury and position of the victim at the time of injury can be deduced from these patterns.

A 3½-year old girl presented after having pulled a pot of hot water onto herself. She sustained 20% second- and third-degree burns. Flow patterns indicated that the burn occurred while she was upright and that the fluid came from above and behind her left shoulder. The potential discrepancy between the burn pattern and history was not noted during her hospitalization (figure 9.4).

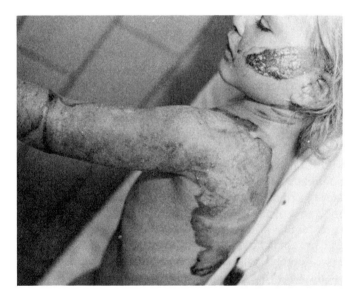

Figure 9.4

A 3½-year-old girl was said to have pulled a pot of hot water upon herself. The depth of the burn on her chest decreases in the pattern of thinning, cooling water. This downward flow pattern implies that she was upright at the time of injury. The direction of burning on her face and shoulder suggests that the water came from above and behind her left ear.

Excessive splash burns above the site of primary impact suggest that fluid was thrown at the victim. Some scalds will occur on body parts where it is virtually impossible for the injury to have been accidental. In many cases, although one may be told that "he pulled a pot of hot coffee upon himself," the burns will be compatible only with immersion, and a presumptive diagnosis of inflicted tap-water injury can be made.

Specific Patterns of Contact Burns

Contact burns are the second most frequent cause of abusive burns (2, 6). A majority involve contact with hot metal objects such as irons, stove burners, or heater grates. If such injuries occur by accident, brief, glancing contact of exposed body parts with a small portion of the hot surface is the rule. Abusive acts may result in prolonged, steady contact with a large portion of the hot surface. Symmetrical, deep imprints with crisp margins of the entire burning surface will suggest abuse, as opposed to small burn areas with slurred margins lacking a full imprint of the burning surface. Accidental contact burns are usually deeper and more intense on one edge of the burn. Burning of areas of the body where accidental brushing contact is unlikely, such as buttocks and perineum, suggests abuse (22). Multiple burned areas may also be noted.

> The father of a three-month-old child pressed his back against a heating grate to stop the infant's fussiness. Second-degree burns healed without scarring and the child was safely returned to the home after family therapy (figure 9.5).

Abusive contact burns also occur when small objects are heated and used to brand children. The top of metal cigarette lighters and knife blades are commonly used (22). Clear imprints of the burning object are often seen.

A separate group of contact burns is seen in our cigarette-smoking culture. Adults often have burning cigarettes on hand during times of frustration and may inflict deep, circular cigarette burns upon their children. These burns are often grouped and multiple, most often involving the hands and arms. Although accidental cigarette burns occur when a child brushes against a lighted cigarette that an adult is holding, these injuries are usually single, shallower, and not circular. Abuse should be suspected when cigarette burns are present on normally clothed body parts.

> Two- and three-year-old siblings were brought to the emergency room with a total of about forty cigarette burns. They had been living with their heroin-addicted mother in a home of heroin addicts. The children were removed from the home and subsequently adopted (figure 9.6).

In addition to infants, teenagers, and young adults may be the victims of inflicted burns. Some of the more violent segments of our society favor throwing caustic substances in the faces of their rivals. Fully 27% of all burns in the study of Crikelair *et al.* at the Harlem Hospital were the result of attacks (23). Fifteen of these thirty-three injuries were the result of lye or acid cocktails thrown in the face of a victim, with the intent to blind and disfigure. The remaining attacks involved

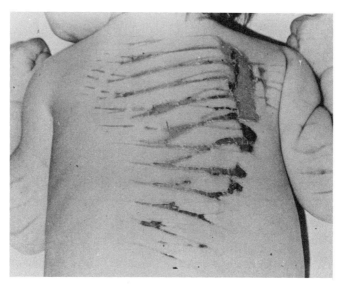

Figure 9.5

The back of this three-month-old was pressed twice against a hot wall-heating grate. The uniformity of depth of the burn, large clear imprint, and double imprint on a normally clothed body part make accidental burning unlikely. (photo courtesy of Dr. Barton Schmitt)

flames and flammable liquids (six), scalding water (eleven), and a hot knife used as a branding iron (one). Abusive clothing ignition, flammable liquid, and electrical burns will leave few physical clues of abuse, but the history and circumstances of the injury may point to the diagnosis. The victims of these injuries are often older children. Less frequently, a new parent may attempt to incinerate an unwanted infant (24).

Finally, the difference between wet burns and dry burns should be noted. The so-called wet burn, caused by a scalding liquid, has a number of characteristic features, some of which have already been mentioned. These include the splatter effect, sloughing and peeling of skin layers, varying degrees of burn in close proximity, and fewer of the signs noted in the dry burn (see below).

The burn caused by a hot, dry instrument often has the absence of the findings noted above, plus certain characteristic features. Among these are delineated margin, often branding-type, scabbing of cutaneous edges about the burn, sometimes the odor of burnt skin, and the general dry nature about the burn site.

General Patterns of Abusive Burns

Families who use burning to abuse their children exhibit many of the same characteristics of abusive families as noted elsewhere in this volume. Some

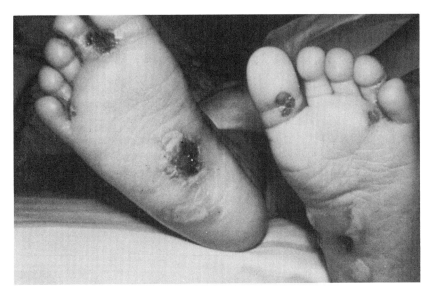

Figure 9.6

Multiple cigarette burns were present on the feet and other body parts of this two-year-old child and his three-year-old sibling. Deep and at times perfectly round burns the size of a cigarette tip are present on the sole of the foot. Multiple burns in this configuration and location rule out accidental injury. (photo courtesy of Dr. Barton Schmitt)

points, however, deserve special comment. When treating a burned child, every effort should be made to obtain parental or court permission to acquire color photographs, including appropriate patient identification within the field of the photograph. Each person interacting with the family should record as accurately as possible the history of the mode and circumstances of injury. In these cases, the nurse, intern, resident, and attending physician should take and record independent histories from all available caretakers. Skeletal X-rays should be obtained where appropriate.

Abused children may be brought to medical care inappropriately late after their injuries, when infection or other burn complications have occurred. The status of the burn may imply that it is older than alleged. They may be brought to care by someone other than the caretaker at the time of injury. Medical attendants may receive several vague and conflicting histories of how the burn occurred. They may be told the child was "found burned," strong urine or soap "burned her bottom," or simply that there was no witness to the injury. Burns may be seen in children too young to have gotten in an injury situation as alleged. A six-month-old is unlikely to climb into the bathtub and turn on the hot water. Conversely, an older child may present with a burn that he should have been able to escape. A six-year-old is unlikely to sustain a perfect glove scald. An outreach worker should visit the home to reconstruct the injury situation and measure the water temperature where appropriate. Burn victims may present with histories unlikely to explain improbable distributions.

> When a twenty-month-old boy was brought by his mother to the emergency room, she said that he had pushed a chair up to the stove, turned on the gas under the griddle, and climbed onto it. His cries woke her from her sleep, and she found him with burns of both palms and both soles only (figure 9.7). He was said to be excessively active and to misbehave in spite of twice-daily spankings.

In addition to the specific physical criteria for abuse that accompany several modes of burning, the children may have other physical signs of neglect and

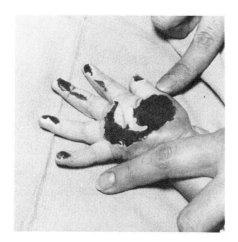
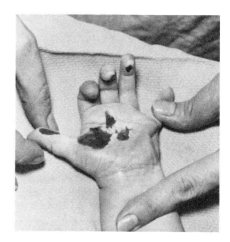
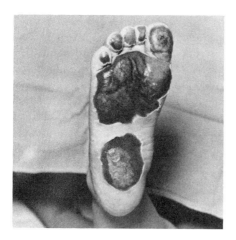
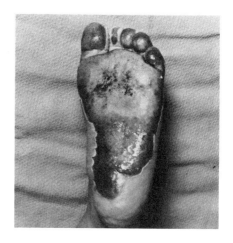

Figure 9.7

This twenty-month-old male burned only his palms and soles on a hot griddle. An injury in this pattern is unlikely to have occurred by accident.

abuse. Multiple, concurrent injuries or history or signs of repeated injury in the past may be present. Wilkinson noted that multiple episodes of burning occur in the same child or in several children in the same household (9). Keen found that twelve of sixteen burn-abused children had multiple burns, and twelve of sixteen had other evidence of recent trauma (22). Involvement of the buttocks or perineum should suggest abuse. Ninety-two percent of Stone's *et al.*'s (2) and 40% of Keen *et al.*'s (22) burn-abused children were so injured.

Although parents may describe their children as hyperactive and impulsive, burn-abuse victims may seem withdrawn, noncommunicative, and excessively fearful of the hospital staff. They may appear malnourished, ill-kempt, and developmentally retarded. After several weeks on the burn ward, although the staff have inflicted repeated painful medical procedures, the children may become more outgoing and responsive to attention. Apparent retardation may improve rapidly as the children begin to communicate and move in age-appropriate behaviors. As trust develops, older children may relate the circumstances of their injury.

Different modes of burn injury imply different degrees of intent to injure. Everyone with children is familiar with drawing the bath water, checking the temperature with one's own hand, and placing an infant in the water. The child may cry or complain bitterly that the water is too hot. People are not inherently aware of the hazard of hot tap water, and adult hands sense less heat and burn less easily than children's skin. A parent who impulsively places a child in an unchecked tub of scalding water as punishment may not expect or wish injury to result. On the other hand, stove element burns, repeated cigarette burns, or caustic assaults can hardly be without abusive intent. Whether this distinction will affect therapy of the abusive situation is problematic. A rash gesture with bath water may imply as significant a future risk of injury and is more often fatal than cigarette burns.

Pseudoabusive and Other Nonaccidental Burns

When a health professional misses the diagnosis of an abusive burn and simply treats the child for the injury, the child returns home to a high risk of future serious injury. Perhaps equally damaging for many families is an incorrect diagnosis of abuse in accidental injury cases. Many patterns of burn are not diagnostic of abuse. Misdiagnosis of abuse sets the stage for mistrust and accusation of one parent by the other and suspicion of the health care system which falsely labeled them. Schmitt *et al.* described just such situations where overdiagnosis of abusive burning resulted in increased family stress (25). Five patients sustained contact burns from sun-heated objects. Typically, on a hot summer day in a car with dark upholstery, the seat-belt buckle is heated to damaging temperatures. The child will inexplicably scream with pain when placed in the car. Only later, when the pain may be forgotten, will a circumscribed contact burn be discovered. A high index of suspicion and careful history-taking can provide the diagnosis.

Many folk-medicine treatments may result in burns. The practice of cupping (applying a heated cup to the chest to draw out congestion by cooling) may result in circular burns with central contusions (26). One Vietnamese child was treated by his family for fever by application of heated oil followed by firm rubbing with a spoon. This treatment resulted in multiple second-degree burns on his chest and upper back. This variation on the practice of *cai gio* may appear abusive unless the parent is questioned to determine the source of the burns (27). In the reported cases of *cao gio*, warm oil was placed on the chest and upper back. This area was then stroked briskly with the edge of a coin until erythema developed. When seen by physicians, linear contusions were present in the stroked region. A Saudi Arabian child had treatment for fever which resulted in superficial 4 mm burns spaced at ninety degrees around the umbilicus.

Although parents may intentionally expose their children to burning situations as a means of teaching burn hazard, subsequent burn injury may actually be more frequent in these families (8). This practice should be discouraged.

Nonaccidental burns may also be self-inflicted, usually in the context of a hysterical syndrome (28). These burns will exhibit all the physical characteristics of abusive burns, but tend to be located in easily reached areas of the body. Victims are likely to be school age. Teenagers who burn their forearms with cigarettes are probably most frequent.

Toxic epidermal necrolysis may initially appear like a widespread second-degree burn. Generalized erythema will, however, be present, and a focus of staphylococcal infection can usually be found. Treatment with staphylococcidal antibiotics is required.

Summary

Burn injury is a major cause of death and disability in childhood, often the consequence of disturbed home situations or abuse. The busy primary care or emergency room physician who is frequently faced with caring for childhood burn victims may become immersed in the technical aspects of the medical treatment, forgetting the basic question of how the injury occurred. Unless questioned specifically, the parent may not volunteer that information. Even if a history is given, it may be intended to mislead and to obscure the actual circumstances of injury. Careful clinical appraisal of the injury, combined with repeated attempts to obtain a history will allow the clinician to decide if the injury is likely to have been accidental, a reaction to situational stress, or frankly abusive. Effective treatment can only be planned with assessment of whether the child will receive good home care for his wound and if further injury is likely. In cases of severe injury or questionable social situations, hospitalization will be necessary for medical stabilization and to allow initial social service investigation and intervention. Not only the family of the abused child, but also many stressed and disorganized families of accidentally burned children, will need assistance to prevent additional injury.

Acknowledgment

Thanks to Jean Peterson for editorial comments and to Carolyn Tull and Lynda Vassar for typing.

References

1. National Safety Council. 1978. *Accident Facts*. Chicago, Ill., p. 8.
2. Stone, N. D.; Rinaldo, L.; Humphrey, C. R.; and Brown, R. H. 1970. Child Abuse by Burning. *Surg. Clin. North Am.* 50:1419–24.
3. Phillips, P. S.; Pickrell, E.; and Morse, T. S. 1974. Intentional Burning: A Severe Form of Child Abuse. *J. Am. Coll. Emerg. Phys.* 3:388–90.
4. Feldman, K. W.; Schaller, R. T.; Feldman, J. A.; and McMillon, M. 1978. Tap-Water Scald Burns in Children. *Pediatr.* 62:1–7.
5. Lenoski, E. F., and Hunter, K. A. 1977. Specific Patterns of Inflicted Burn Injuries. *J. Trauma* 17:842–46.
6. Smith, S. M., and Hanson, R. 1974. Battered Children: A Medical and Psychologic Study. *Br. Med. J.* 3:666–70.
7. Gil, D. G. 1970. *Violence against Children*. Cambridge, Mass.: Harvard University Press, pp. 119 and 122.
8. Meyer, R. L.; Roelofs, H. A.; Bluestone, J.; and Redmond, S. 1963. Accidental Injury to the Preschool Child. *J. Pediatr.* 63:95–105.
9. Wilkinson, A. W. 1944. Burns and Scalds in Children. *Br. Med. J.* 1:37–40.
10. Long, R. T., and Cope, O. 1961. Emotional Problems in Burned Children. *New Engl. J. Med.* 264:1,121–27.
11. Holter, J. C., and Friedman, S. B. 1969. Etiology and Management of Severely Burned Children. *Am. J. Dis. Child.* 118:680–86.
12. Borland, B. L. 1967. Prevention of Childhood Burns: Conclusions Drawn from an Epidemiology Study. *Clin. Pediatr.* 6:693–95.
13. Richards, E. H. 1968. Aspects of Epilepsy and Burns. *Epilepsia* 9:127–35.
14. Waller, J. A., and Manheimer, D. I. 1964. Nonfatal Burns of Children in a Well-Defined Urban Population. *J. Pediatr.* 65:863–69.
15. Bleck, E. E. 1955. Causes of Burns in Children. *J. Am. Med. Assoc.* 158:100–103.
16. Jensen, G. D. 1959. Preventive Implications of a Study of 100 Children Treated for Serious Burns. *Pediatr.* 24:623–30.
17. Colebrook, L., and Colebrook, V. 1949. The Prevention of Burns and Scalds: Review of 1,000 Cases. *Lancet* 2:181–88.
18. Moyer, C. A. 1954. The Sociologic Aspects of Trauma. *Am. J. Surg.* 87:421–30.
19. MacArthur, J. D., and Moore, F. D. 1975. Epidemiology of Burns: The Burn Prone Patient. *J. Am. Med. Assoc.* 231:259–63.
20. Tempest, M. N. 1956. Survey of Domestic Burns and Scalds in Wales during 1955. *Br. Med. J.* 1:1387–92.

21. Moritz, A. R., and Henriques, F. C. 1947. Studies of Thermal Injury: The Relative Importance of Time and Temperature in the Causation of Cutaneous Burns. *Am. J. Pathol.* 23:695–720.
22. Keen, J. H.; Lendrum, J.; and Wolman, B. 1975. Inflicted Burns and Scalds in Children. *Br. Med. J.* 4:268–69.
23. Crikelair, G. F.; Symonds, F. C.; Ollstein, R. N.; and Kirsner, A. I. 1968. Burn Causation: Its Many Sides. *J. Trauma* 8:572–81.
24. Lung, R. J.; Miller, S. H.; Davis, T. S.; and Graham, W. P., III. 1977. Recognizing Burn Injuries as Abuse. *Am. Fam. Physician* 15:134–35.
25. Schmitt, B. D.; Gray, J. D.; and Britton, H. L. 1978. Car Seat Burns in Infants: Avoiding Confusion with Inflicted Burns. *Pediatr.* 62:607–9.
26. Sandler, A. P., and Haynes, V. 1978. Nonaccidental Trauma and Medical Folk Belief: A Case of Cupping. *Pediatr.* 61:921–22.
27. Yeatman, G. W.; Shaw, C.; Barlow, M. J.; and Bartlett, G. 1976. Pseudo-battering in Vietnamese Children. *Pediatr.* 58:616–18.
28. Curran, J. P. 1973. Hysterical Dermatitis Factitia. *Am. J. Dis. Child.* 125:564–67.

10 The Infant with Failure-to-Thrive

Ruth S. Kempe, Christy Cutler, and Janet Dean

Failure-to-thrive (FTT) has emerged as one of the challenges of present-day pediatrics and one of the more important conditions to be considered in abused and neglected children. The complexities of diagnosis and the necessity for the physician to orchestrate a multidisciplinary approach to diagnosis and treatment make each case individual. The frequency with which children are admitted to the hospital, discharged with an indeterminate diagnosis, and then either readmitted with the same problem or discovered to be still malnourished years later indicates the need for a better understanding of FTT and, particularly, for more effective treatment methods.

Incidence

The incidence of FTT in the U.S. population is not well documented; figures are available primarily for cases which are legally reported or those which are formally so diagnosed in the hospital. Frequently, FTT does not appear as a hospital diagnosis; rather, the most acute problem is recorded as the diagnosis.

In its study of reported cases of physical abuse and neglect nationwide for the year 1977, the American Humane Association described 115,949 reports in which the primary character of the maltreatment was recorded (1). Of these, 1.6%, or 1,755 cases, were reported as FTT due to neglect, and an additional 1.7%, or 1,968 cases, were reported simply as cases of malnutrition.

P. C. English (2), in reviewing the charts of 9,605 children admitted to New York Hospital from 1964 to 1977, found 29 children diagnosed as nonorganic FTT. Shabeen et al. (3) studied the charts of 5,488 children admitted between July 1963 and 1964 to Children's Hospital of Philadelphia and found 287, or 5%, weighed below the third percentile on admission. Of these, 15.2% were considered nonorganic FTT.

Ruth S. Kempe, M.D., Christy Cutler, and Janet Dean are with the National Center for the Prevention and Treatment of Child Abuse and Neglect, Denver.

A review of charts at Colorado General Hospital between June 1976 and December 1978 found a total of 171 cases diagnosed as FTT. Of these, 72 cases (42%) were considered organic FTT, 51 (or 30%) nonorganic, and 48 (or 28%) as due to a combination of organic and nonorganic factors. Other recent studies (4, 5) also give a higher percentage of nonorganic etiology as the importance of family interaction is given more attention.

Definition

At the present time, FTT describes a child who has sometime during the first three years of life suffered a marked retardation or cessation of growth. This change in growth pattern can be most clearly seen on one of the standard growth charts which graph weight, height, and head circumference against age (6, 7). The chart contains the upper and lower limits of normal values for a comparable population; the cessation of growth and its timing are often dramatically shown. If a child is in the upper range of weight early in infancy, a weight loss to the fortieth or fiftieth percentile on the growth chart is a significant loss and should be evaluated. If the child was premature and of small birth weight or was small for his gestational age, these facts and their etiology must be taken into account in evaluating later size. The most frequently used criterion for FTT is the falling of weight values to the third percentile or below on the standard chart; this is a value which indicates a severe growth problem, sometimes a life-threatening one.

In addition to the inadequate weight gain, which is the more rapid indicator of nutritional state, the rate of increase in height and in head circumference may be dropping. A lag in linear growth and head circumference usually indicates growth failure of greater duration and severity and one of special concern in the first year of life, when brain growth should still be rapid. There is good evidence that severe and prolonged malnutrition during the first year of life can lead to brain damage (8–14) and perhaps permanently diminished size (15, 16).

It should be noted that the child's size at birth (if full term) is largely due to maternal factors, reflective of nutrition received through the placenta, and that following birth the influence of genetic, constitutional, and environmental factors will be important. These children may gradually shift up or down in their position on the growth curves, reflecting genetic or constitutional endowment, and then stabilize on a new growth level sometime during the first eighteen months (17).

The term FTT has been applied in many situations of differing etiologies; the dichotomy between cases due to organic illness and those due to failure of the environment to provide appropriate nurturing is the most significant division and will be indicated in this chapter by use of the terms *organic FTT* and *nonorganic FTT*. Further complexity is introduced by the fact that organic and nonorganic factors may combine to produce FTT more commonly than previously stated, particularly when the treatment of a clear organic condition does not produce the expected improvement.

The term FTT is not generally used (although often applicable) in speaking of the large population of children worldwide who suffer from malnutrition as a result of the shortage of suitable food for themselves or their breast-feeding mothers. Suskind (18) writes of roughly 100 million children under five years of age who are severely or moderately malnourished throughout the world, most of them in the underdeveloped countries where famine, war, and widespread poverty make food scarce. Yet, we know that in the United States many children also suffer from malnutrition which is undetected because of inadequate medical attention in early years or failure to diagnose it in children with another presenting illness. Even when it is not severe enough to meet the definition of FTT, it may represent effects of illness, poverty, or neglect that seriously diminish that child's potential.

FTT as a diagnosis becomes significant in the society that can presume food will be available to all its children and where knowledge of pediatric disease and normal growth and development have become sufficiently precise to define the reasons for growth failure.

Organic FTT

Simultaneously with the improved scientific understanding of infant nutrition and the development of good artificial feeding during the last fifty years, there has also been considerable increase in the knowledge of disease processes in infants, including genetic and gestational abnormalities, which has made possible the earlier detection and better treatment of early-childhood illness.

In general, the organic causes of FTT include genetically or constitutionally small stature, any chronic illness which affects growth secondarily, and those disease processes which affect food intake, absorption, or utilization.

The organic causes of growth retardation which have been identified include: central nervous system disease, such as cerebral palsy or congenital neurological anomalies; idiopathic hypercalcemia, chronic respiratory, cardiac, or kidney disease; gastrointestinal tract anomalies or malabsorption syndromes; "inborn errors of metabolism"; repeated or chronic infectious diseases, and endocrinopathies. There are "mechanical" feeding difficulties which are usually due to an undiagnosed organic condition. Poor sucking ability, which can represent delayed neurological maturation, but may be due to neurological disease and chalasia, is a common example.

This long list, which includes so many serious conditions present at birth, is only a partial summary of the causes of organic FTT. There are many subcategories and other rare conditions which may lead to growth retardation. If it were necessary to rule out each of these potential causes in the laboratory, the diagnosis of FTT would require long hospitalization, subjecting the patient to prolonged discomfort, delay of nutrition and treatment, and great expense. Fortunately, for most children, the number of laboratory tests and medical procedures need be few (5).

Nonorganic FTT

There are several causes, other than disease itself, for FTT, although undoubtedly the most important of these is a lack of nurturing care. Surprisingly, until recently, neglect was often considered last, although it is now apparent that it is probably the most common cause of FTT. Indeed, the term *FTT syndrome* is often used to describe the growth failure due to "psychosocial deprivation," or maternal deprivation.

Causes of Nonorganic FTT

Lack of knowledge about mothering can be a reason for FTT. The mother may not know how much a child needs to eat, how to prepare a formula correctly, or how to feed the baby correctly. She may not recognize the great importance of nutrition to the young infant and may be made unhappy, but not alarmed, by the thin appearance of her baby. She may not recognize the need for medical supervision or see any reason to seek advice concerning child care. In a recent study (19) Jacobs and Kent found that ten out of thirty-two families fell into this etiological group.

In our experience, such mothers account for a smaller percentage than this of nonorganic FTT cases admitted to hospital. They may represent a much larger proportion of parents of children with growth retardation seen in the clinic or the private office, who respond fairly quickly to appropriate education and advice.

Some of them are mothers of low intelligence; mental retardation in a mother can lead to dangerous neglect, because the mother may lack, not only knowledge, but also the judgment to adapt her caretaking to a changing and growing baby. Many retarded mothers do an excellent job of caring for infants, but usually they have a normal adult source of advice upon which they rely.

Sometimes a very young, immature mother, who is suddenly on her own, may have had no experience with children and may not recognize the importance of good care. Most young or inexperienced mothers, however, when faced with the necessity of caring for a young child, will seek information and advice and will learn what they need to know. When a mother remains complacent about a baby who looks emaciated to the casual observer and who acts hungry, we must begin to wonder why she herself is not anxious and what allows her to remain oblivious to her child's distress. Often one finds that the mother has received appropriate advice but has not followed it. It is important, therefore, when making the assumption that education is the primary need, to follow the family carefully, lest they revert to neglect on the basis of other reasons.

Failure-to-thrive also occurs in breast-feeding mothers who have had insufficient technical help in managing breast-feeding or inadequate support in maintaining the demanding task during the early weeks. There is, unfortunately, a lack of interest and knowledge among many physicians and nurses who are consulted about breast-feeding difficulties, and, frequently, the result is a rapid change to bottle feeding. The rapid weaning from the breast may lead to poor acceptance of the bottle by the baby, and, with both mother and infant distressed and reluctant to accept the change, feeding difficulties may result, leading to weight loss. If the mother refuses to accept the advice to bottle feed, but still has no adequate help in management of breast-feeding, the infant may fail to thrive because of an inadequate milk supply (20, 21). Referral to someone skilled in breast-feeding techniques may salvage the mother's milk supply, but monitoring and support are necessary.

Frequently, the child over five months who is entirely breast-fed has reached a size where the total caloric content of the breast-feedings are insufficient to maintain his size. These babies may remain apparently content, even as they fail to gain (23). Such a child needs supplementary food, in addition to continued breast-feeding, until his mother wishes to wean him.

There are difficulties in feeding which may become complicated by poor advice (from doctors as well as from friends) or which result from a misunderstanding of medical instructions. When an infant has an episode of diarrhea, the doctor may recommend diluted feedings for one or two days. Occasionally, a mother does not resume regular feedings in a day or two or check back with the doctor, but may continue with the diluted feedings indefinitely; or the baby who cries a lot or who vomits occasionally may be treated by the doctor over the phone, sometimes by a change in brand of formula. If the mother continues to complain that the baby is still crying and vomiting, the baby may again be treated over the phone, with manipulation of the diet for a few weeks, before the child is seen in the office or clinic, the weight loss noted, and appropriate diagnosis begun.

Dietary manipulation for *irritable colon* or possible allergies may involve actually giving a diet deficient in calories, leading to weight loss and undiagnosed FTT. In such situations, the mother may well have been concerned about the baby's discomfort, but not have recognized the child's rapidly deteriorating condition.

Difficulties in feeding may arise not only from neglect of the infant's caloric needs, but often from an overinvolvement of the mother in feeding. Some mothers are extremely anxious that the infant may not take sufficient food and interpret every cry of distress as a signal of hunger. Overfeeding can lead to gastric discomfort, crying, or vomiting, and, eventually, to resistance to feeding with anorexia. On observing a feeding, one can see the mother's lack of sensitivity to the baby's cues, her anxious, intrusive mode of caretaking, and the tension promoted by the feeding situation. If untreated, both mother and child become more tense, out of synchrony, and FTT may result.

When the child reaches six to eight months of age, his or her natural exploratory impulses lead to an attempt to participate actively in the feeding situation. At first the child's wish is primarily to explore and exploit food as a new experience. Later, toward one year of age, he or she wishes to take over some of the feeding because of the pleasure in eating and impulses toward mastery. If a mother cannot tolerate the messiness of her child's exploration of food or insists on maintaining total control of the feeding situation, there will be a battle between her wishes and her infant's developing self. Some mothers solve this impasse completely at the expense of the infant by insisting on total submission, even if physical punishment is necessary. One then sees a compliant child who eats passively, with his arms held high in surrender, or one sees a child who refuses food even to the extent of severe FTT. The mother may not recognize her part in the battle and describes only a child who will not eat, "for no reason." Treatment of these feeding battles may be slow and difficult, especially when the child resists food from all sources.

Neglect and Deprivation

Most nonorganic FTT seems to be a manifestation of difficulty in parenting. Frequently, neglect is also shown in other ways. The baby may be dirty, inadequately clothed, or suffer from diaper rash or cradle cap. The siblings may also suffer from FTT or show evidence of poor physical care. There may be lack of concern on the part of the parents about an infant who appears miserable, emaciated, weak, irritable, or hungry. By history, the child may have had little or no medical care and no immunizations.

On physical examination, the child with FTT associated with deprivation often appears emaciated, pale, weak, with little subcutaneous fat and decreased muscle mass. Most of these children appear listless, apathetic, and motionless, in spite of the fact that they may be hypervigilant. Krieger and Sargent (24) describe a characteristic infantile posture maintained for long periods and frequently associated with sensory deprivation in older infants, in which the arms are held out, flexed at the elbow with hands up, and the legs often drawn up. This hand position is like that seen in infants who are taught not to interfere with the feeding process. It must be noted that at first glance some children do not look emaciated, but on closer examination have poor muscle tone and weight gain. Bruises or burns may be signals of abuse and should be documented and followed by a trauma X-ray survey.

The children may appear retarded to variable degrees, especially in gross motor behavior and social responsiveness. They may appear miserable and depressed, or irritable and unable to be comforted or soothed. Reactions to food vary from voracious hunger to irritable or apathetic refusal. Occasionally bizarre eating habits are noted, but this is not common under two years of age. Some of these children show little evidence of bonding, reacting little to separation from parents and showing no stranger anxiety. A few children are indiscriminate, turning on a smile when approached by anyone who might give them attention.

Although improvement of nutrition will have considerable effect, the improvement in development and in social responsiveness in some children during a two-week hospital stay is sometimes remarkable. The child may suddenly begin to walk and to play and to smile when approached by a favorite staff member. These changes can be demonstrated by testing and show the child thriving in the hospital, "where no child should thrive."

In contrast, there are some children, usually older infants, who take much longer before they begin to gain weight. Sometimes they do not gain until their social behavior improves and they begin to relate better. If discharged too soon, they may remain undiagnosed and untreated.

Diagnosis

During the past few years, a simplified approach to management of FTT has been found useful. If a child has been examined very frequently in clinic or private office, he can sometimes be safely kept at home and watched while the initial steps in diagnosis and treatment are carried out. If the infant is seen for the first time with a serious weight loss from his birth weight or with a weight below the third percentile, when there has been no recent medical care, hospital admission is necessary lest the mother elect not to return. Immediate admission is also indicated if signs of dehydration, of other illness, of abuse, or other signs of neglect are present. If there is any doubt, hospitalize.

On admission, a careful medical history and complete physical and neurological examination are done. The only laboratory tests which need be done routinely are a complete blood count, sedimentation rate, urinalysis and urine culture, and stool examination. These represent baseline screening for illness (25, 26). If head circumference is minimally affected and height and weight are proportionately small, bone-age films compared to "height age" will help distinguish between constitutionally short stature (a slow growth pattern leading eventually to normal size) and genetically short stature.

If history and physical examination yield no specific indication for further laboratory tests, they should be deferred until a clinical trial of feeding has taken place in the hospital. The child is offered frequent and liberal feedings of whatever diet he received at home, in order to evaluate his true caloric intake. Calories offered should total at least 150 calories per kilogram per day or more to allow good weight gain; there may be a delay of several days before weight gain begins. A careful record of dietary intake and daily weights are recorded (using the same weighing scale each day). Even if vomiting or diarrhea were admitting complaints, they should be corroborated in the hospital before any special treatment is begun. For example, immediate treatment for chalasia by history, before vomiting is diagnosed, may lead to a false organic diagnosis. Efforts should be made to maintain caloric intake (26). As much as possible, the mother and father are encouraged to participate in the care of the child, especially in feedings. One reason for this emphasis is the child's comfort—to minimize the traumatic effects of hospitalization. The other reason is the importance of observing the caretaking situation as it occurs between parent and child.

Beyond an adequate diet, the chief emphasis should be on providing the child with a comfortable social environment and observing his behavior. It is always good pediatric practice to provide each young child with a consistent caretaker as much as personnel shortages allow, if the parents are not available. In a hospital where patients cannot be assigned a specific nurse or nurse's aide, paid volunteers, such as provided by "foster grandmother" programs, may provide some consistency in caretaking, particularly for feeding and play periods.

Most hospitals allow liberal visiting for parents. With FTT, the mother should be encouraged to spend as much time as possible with her child and to participate in his care, especially feeding. This allows for observation of mother and child in the feeding situation, in play, and in interaction under many circumstances, such as leave-taking. Any modifications in feeding techniques will need to be tried by the mother in the hospital first, rather than at home without help. The parents should be kept informed and their opinions elicited concerning the child's condition and progress. This effort to make the parents feel like allies in treatment will help in their posthospital program.

Developmental diagnosis, by doing a Brazelton (for a young infant) (27), a Bayley (28), Yale Developmental Test (29), or, at minimum, a DDST (30), should be obtained the first or second day of admission. The most marked retardation is usually noted on gross motor behaviors and on social behaviors. The early screening can then be repeated before discharge, if marked change in behavior is noted, thereby documenting the child's improvement in the hospital environment.

The behavior of the parent is observed and documented throughout the hospital stay. The feeding behavior of the child should be carefully observed as he or she is fed by mother, by staff, or is self-fed. The child's social behavior, the way in which the child relates to his or her family, nurses, other staff, and other children is described. The child's play activities, affect, and verbal ability are noted. The behavior of the parents toward the child are also important to observe.

A psychosocial evaluation of the family is begun at the time of admission; it includes the detailed history, observations of parent-child interaction, and sometimes observations of siblings and home (31).

History. The evaluation of the family includes an expanded history. In addition to the routine medical history, more detail is needed, including feeding, developmental history, special medical history, and a psychosocial history of the family. This may be done by the doctor, particularly the family medical history and detailed feeding history, or it may be done by other staff—a nurse, a social worker, psychologist, or psychiatrist. Usually the social worker assigned to the pediatric service will be the most likely person to evaluate the family, but any qualified professional especially knowledgeable with FTT may be able to do this regularly.

Feeding history. In nonorganic FTT, the history which the mother gives and which she believes to be true, may not fit the picture seen on direct observation. The mother may not recognize the serious nature of the growth failure, sometimes seems unaware of obvious emaciation, or else she may be concerned that her child is feeding poorly, but perceive the difficulty as due to vomiting, diarrhea, the wrong formula, or the child's disinterest in food, with no recognition of how her own handling of the feeding is related. On detailed questioning, the mother may say she has been giving her seven-week-old, six ounces every four hours, as directed. But when asking about other details, one finds that she makes up six bottle irregularly, perhaps only every thirty-six to forty-eight hours. Or, she may say that the baby skips all night bottles because he is not hungry, and should not be, between 10:00 P.M. and 10:00 A.M. Or, she may make up bottles individually as needed and have little idea how much the baby takes. The same bottle may be propped for the baby repeatedly until it is finished, even though he is too young to be able to take a bottle without help. Such details are usually obtained through conversation continued until the mother spontaneously reveals the details of the baby's care. Subjects to be included in a detailed feeding history are: reasons for breast-feeding or bottle feeding, reasons for change from breast to bottle, preparation of formula, total formula made in twenty-four hours and how much is left, formula changes, and doctor's feeding advice, as well as the baby's feeding pattern, schedule, appetite, length of feeding, spitting up or vomiting (with how and when), diarrhea, and constipation. Other subjects to consider are: position and place for feeding and interruption by other children or duties, bottle propping, introduction of solid foods and how they are taken, self-feeding, messiness and how it is tolerated. This history may be at variance with what is observed during feeding in the hospital.

Developmental history. (*a*) The history of pregnancy should include initial reactions to pregnancy, health and special symptoms or complications, preparations for baby, including reading or special classes, prenatal care, and use of coffee, tobacco, alcohol, and drugs during pregnancy. (*b*) The history of delivery should include length and character of labor, medications and anesthesia, and kind of delivery; condition of the baby at birth (weight, APGAR, or description); mother's initial thoughts on seeing her baby, and husband's, family's, and staff's reactions to the baby; the amount of contact in the hospital, when discharged, the situation as to help at home; and evidence of bonding. (*c*) The history should include the sex and temperament of the baby and the mother's possible identification of her baby with significant other people. (*d*) The topics touched upon should include the following: motor milestones, including eye following, social smile, activity level, vocalization, play activities, and toys; whether this baby is different from siblings and how; a typical day for mother and baby, eliciting amount and kind of attention given the baby; interactions of the baby with other family members, socially and in caretaking; and kind and frequency of babysitting and day-care arrangements.

In eliciting the developmental history, it is desirable not only to get some idea of how much time the mother spends with the baby, but also some knowledge of the quality of the interaction—which is usually evident in the mother's affect as she describes their day. Asking about the mother's other daily activities will clarify how much time is left for the baby.

Family medical history. This is, of course, part of the routine medical history, but special inquiries need to be made into the stature of maternal and paternal family members, into genetic and chronic diseases, deaths of parents and siblings, and into the health and growth of the patient's siblings. Feeding problems of siblings are also important.

Psychosocial history of family. After having discussed the baby in detail, most mothers are responsive to a tactful inquiry into their own situations. Some recognition of her concern and worry over the baby's state can lead naturally into a discussion of what it has meant to the rest of the family and of the kind of support the mother has had from husband, family, and friends. Other difficulties, such as financial and housing problems and illnesses of other family members are usually readily obtained. Discussion of whether mother and father see the baby's problems in the same way can lead to a general discussion of the parents' expectations of the children and one another, their child-rearing beliefs, and thence to the way in which both parents were brought up. This leads naturally to the mother's own childhood history—to information about abuse, neglect, or object loss in her early years and her perception of her relationship with her parents. Some history about her school and job adjustment will give additional impressions of her coping style and ability to meet stress and use help. A discussion of social activities and friendships may lead to an impression of isolation and lack of resources.

Most wives will talk about their husband's role in the family and, if questioned with empathy, will convey the prevailing emotional tone of the marriage.

In every child with FTT an evaluation of the parent's potential for physical abuse should be made; the guidelines for abusive potential may be used as a guideline in this assessment (see Chapter 8).[1]

There is an overlap of approximately one-third of cases in which abuse and neglect occur together, and later treatment may need to be modified. Even if the etiology of the FTT is organic, the psychosocial history may indicate causes for concern, and it is known that children with chronic physical abnormalities may be more prone to being abused.

The informality of a parent interview is emphasized because the establishment of an empathic relationship will make many mothers comfortable enough to speak freely. Working through one's own anger about neglect is necessary. Most mothers respond to very general or open-ended questions by bringing up many concerns, and it often takes merely an understanding comment or a small clarifying question to continue the flow of thought. Indeed, we have often found that the mother who is too preoccupied with her own problems at home to be sufficiently aware of her baby's needs is apt to become totally engrossed in this interview and may see the baby's need for attention during the time as an unwelcome interruption.

It is important, if a mother does unburden herself of many unhappy feelings, to demonstrate recognition of the difficulties for her and then to let her know that, although some of her confidences have helped much in understanding what has been happening in her family, only specific, relevant material will be shared with others involved in treatment.

Parent-child interaction. When there is no specific clue to indicate organic etiology, it is most efficient to begin the evaluation of the parent-child relationship on admission to the hospital. Ward personnel are encouraged to observe and report significant indications of parent-child interaction, both good and bad.

We have found it useful to make observations by recording an informal interview on videotape, with the parents' permission, during a feeding and play period with mother and child. The video camera is present in the room, and the procedure is both informal and comfortable. The videotape is useful in allowing for detailed review of the mother-child interaction and also can be used as a useful teaching aid with the mother, in certain circumstances. However, the major value

1. For a further discussion of long-term therapy the reader is referred to Chapter 23 of this book and Chapter 10 of *Child Abuse and Neglect: The Family and the Community,* edited by R. Helfer and C. Kempe (Cambridge, Mass.: Ballinger, 1976)—EDS.

lies in the effort to observe carefully what takes place between mother and child, and for this no special equipment is really needed.

During time spent with the mother, the observer (who may be any professional with sufficient knowledge of feeding problems, of infant development, and of the psychology of parents) may obtain information which supplements the medical history, particularly information which elucidates circumstances at the onset of the feeding difficulty.

The observation of the interaction between mother and child focuses upon the feeding and play situations. Despite the fact that the mother knows it is a diagnostic assessment, the character of the relationship is usually clear. The attachment between mother and child, their comfortable closeness, or comparative indifference to each other can be seen. The mother may be sensitive to the behavioral cues of her child and subsequently time her feeding to the infant's wishes, or she may shovel food in while the child sits motionless, hands held high. She may give the bottle to the baby while he or she is reaching out to touch her and then, as soon as the child is sucking vigorously, remove it to see how much has been taken. Each aspect of the interaction may seem insignificant, but when observed in its entirety the interaction may be found to be diagnostic. Mother and child may rarely have eye contact, never smile at each other, and the mother may speak only to utter a command ("Take your hands away from that") or a criticism ("Aren't you ever going to eat your potatoes?"). They may be unable to play with each other, the mother quickly finding an excuse for the baby not to be interested, such as, "He really likes to play alone in his crib." Yet, at the same time, the baby can be seen eagerly reaching for a toy and smiling with great pleasure at the overtures of the interviewer. At times the mother takes the toy ostensibly to show the baby how to use it and ends up playing with it herself. Parallel play may be as far as she can go in stimulating her child to play. Often the baby seems to have stopped looking to the mother for social response and watches or vocalizes to the stranger instead. The mother, too, focuses on the interviewer.

There are mothers who visit faithfully and show real concern about their babies, yet when one observes them, they rarely engage in any meaningful activity with their babies. They tend to stand around watching, and only when there is a highly structured activity do they engage well with their babies. Some of these mothers seem immobilized by depression or anxiety; the staff may recognize their concern, but not recognize how their inability to see the children's needs leads to deprivation.

Evaluation of parents. There have been many studies of parents of FTT babies, and the diagnosis may vary a great deal (32–44). Some common features do occur and can be summarized. Most parents in large-scale studies come from socioeconomic classes IV and V, and most of them suffer financial stress as well as frequent social stress. Although such statistics seem reasonable, it may well be that they overrepresent the poor patients. Nonorganic FTT may be present in the private pediatric office or private pediatric hospital service, but it is not always so diagnosed officially, and nursing or day-care help is brought in to take care of the deficient mothering. As with many studies based on statistics, the review of a problem area like FTT tends to be done on large clinic populations which are more readily available in a teaching hospital; this may give a true idea of the malignant influence of poverty, but belittle the psychiatric difficulties for these parents. In addition to financial distress, most studies describe deprivation or abuse in the childhood of parents, and social isolation, anxiety, and depression as frequently present. All of these characteristics do not necessarily distinguish the neglectful from the nurturing parents, and, indeed, thus far, there has been no definitive study on what does make the difference. The one area where there does seem to be a real difference is in the interaction between the mother and the nonthriving child, according to Egelund and Brunnquell (45).

We have been impressed in our preliminary work, which is now being subjected to a more rigorous control, that the potential for "parenting" difficulty in the mother, the significance of the particular child's behavior, and the degree of stress from the environment all play a part.

A mother who has a comparatively good interaction with her infant may have been temporarily overwhelmed by a rapid series of events which undermined her basically good capacity to be a mother, and, if given appropriate support during the crisis, she can again resume a good mothering role and respond sensitively to her child. It is our impression that such mothers can usually cope with a fairly severe amount of environmental stress, but that when it becomes overwhelming they and the baby need help, usually in the hospital, to get them "back on the track." This group might include those mothers who have suffered severe, recent loss such as the departure of a husband or death of a mother.

Another group of mothers would seem to fit into the chronically deprived, chronically depressed group described by Polansky (46, 47), among others, as neglectful. These mothers are immature and may be very impulsive in their behavior, which leads to a very poor ability to cope with the community social systems, with relationships, and with the stress of poverty and "parenting." Difficulty in coping with these issues is also found in a second, apathetic, passive group who are often described as feeling helpless.

All of these mothers have difficulty in using verbal communication effectively, which increases their interpersonal isolation and makes them feel misunderstood and uninvolved. Drugs and alcohol may play some part. All had a deprived childhood. This group of mothers are those we see who have chaotic life-styles. They may have a less serious crisis interfering with their baby's care, yet are unable to perceive and respond to the child's needs. A mother in this group is much more apt to show role-reversal and to perceive the child's care as merely another of the unwanted burdens in her life. She "loves" the baby, but the love is expected to bring her warmth and affection and does not extend to empathy for what her baby really feels or needs.

There is another group of mothers in whom the perception of the baby is much more negative—in whom the baby is not seen just as another burden, but as a bad or defective child, often one who deliberately behaves so as to cause the mother problems. In this group of parents, the life-style may be chaotic, with all the financial stresses and history of deprivation of the previous group. But here there may be strong evidence of other antisocial and aggressive behavior, difficulties with the law, fighting with others, especially with authority figures, or isolation because of marked mistrust of others. The use of alcohol may also be prominent. In this group the risk of physical abuse is especially high, and a treatment program, although difficult to implement, is very important, with particular attention given to follow-up.

Thus far, no specific study has been made of fathers in families with nonorganic FTT. The study by Green (48) of abusive fathers emphasizes their rivalry with their children for attention from the mother, a characteristic that may well be true in many fathers of children with FTT. In most studies of families with nonorganic FTT, they are described as being absent or else passive and nonhelpful. Alcohol or drugs are sometimes part of the reason they do not participate more actively. Generally, when present, the fathers are seen as sharing the same deprived background and the same difficulties in coping as their wives.

Reporting

When it is determined that a diagnosis of FTT, due to underfeeding and neglect, has been made, a report should be made to the protective services of the welfare department in the county where the family lives. The initial telephoned report is followed by a written one which briefly summarizes the facts upon which the diagnosis is made. Usually, this includes the absence of physical disease, the weight loss at home, and the large weight gain in the hospital with no special treatment except a regular diet. This report sets in motion the involvement of the child welfare agency which will then become part of the treatment program. It may be necessary to file a dependency and neglect petition to ask for court supervision and a court-mandated treatment program. In some instances, termination of parental rights may be indicated.

Treatment Plan

The marked weight gain and significant progress in social and developmental areas which occur after ten to fourteen days of hospitalization clearly demonstrate the significance of the environmental deprivation. If other possible organic causes then seem unlikely, a treatment plan can be made several days before discharge. On the basis of the mother's response to the diagnostic work with her and the child together, a decision must be made whether to send the child home or to foster care. If the child is to go home, the mother:

1. Should have demonstrated understanding of how the FTT occurred
2. Should possess a new understanding of her child's needs for both physical and emotional nurturing
3. Should be willing to receive help with home visits to improve her care of the baby
4. Should show active cooperation with specific plans for regular medical supervision
5. Should express a willingness to make some changes in her life-style, if they are necessary, i.e., no longer caring for friends' children, which gave her no time to care for her own

The child may need to go to a foster home if:

1. The mother has not visited the hospital except when absolutely necessary
2. The mother's attitude toward the infant remains negative, punitive, or indifferent
3. The mother has shown no interest in cooperating in the treatment program or understanding of her part in the child's illness
4. The mother is heavily involved in use of drugs or alcohol and may need a prolonged, intensive treatment program before she is available to care for the baby
5. The mother is suffering from a severe psychiatric illness—especially depression or psychosis which makes her unavailable to her child and which requires intensive treatment

In some cases the problems found in the parents are of such long-standing severity that there is little hope that they will respond to treatment. If the possibility of eventual termination of parental rights appears early in diagnosis, then the treatment plan should be complete and specific, practical for the parents, court ordered, and well monitored. This helps to prevent the prolongation of placement of the patient in foster care for months or years, while sporadic efforts are made to document the ability of the parents to care for their child. The parents in such cases deserve all the help social and medical services can provide; only in this way can a fair judgment be made for termination, in a time framework that allows the child some chance to grow adequately (49, 50).

Once the decision has been made that the child will go home with the family, it is important that the parents understand the reason for the FTT and be offered specific help with it. The hospital nutritionist, with a nurse or social worker, may be asked to explain a good diet and to make suggestions for cooking and feeding that will suit the patient's metabolic needs, the family's income, and culture. Recommendations need to be concrete and specific; to be sure they are understood, it is often wise to ask the mother to repeat them in her own words.

The nurse, social worker, and doctor often have a conference with the parents before discharge. To have the different disciplines talking together will reinforce, for the parents, the fact that all parts of the outpatient follow-up are important and that the doctor feels this to be true.

Treatment after Hospitalization for FTT

Early and frequent appointments to hospital clinic or private office must be made, for FTT frequently recurs when a child returns home, if sufficient change has not yet taken place in the environment. Each member of the follow-up team can reinforce the importance of the other members and communicate with one another if the situation worsens in any way.

We have found it very useful to provide a division of duties in follow-up of FTT patients. The doctor appointments and home visits by the public health nurse (PHN) are frequent, keeping close watch on the baby's weight gain by means of regular weighing, and providing advice concerning any feeding or health problems which arise.

The role of the social worker is often one of responsibility for overall monitoring and coordination of services. She (or he) makes special home visits to see that the parents are providing adequate care, to assure that the mother is being seen by the doctor and PHN at regular intervals, and to be sure the family has adequate financial and transportation resources. In addition, the social worker is often one of the few sources of support and may be the person to whom the mother turns for understanding and advice. With many of the parents there has been a long history of deprivation and sometimes abuse or severe losses in their own backgrounds, and they are themselves very much in need of someone to care about them whom they trust.

When social workers or the PHNs have the time to meet this need, they are of enormous help to the family, but frequently their time is too limited to meet such great needs. For this reason, we have incorporated, whenever possible, a home health visitor (a lay therapist or parent aide) into the treatment plan (see Chapter 22).

The health visitor works half-time with a small number of families, is paid a small salary, and acts as an interested and helpful friend to the mother. She does not confine her contacts to talking over coffee, but tries to offer help to the mother as any friend might do—where it is needed. She may help with transportation to a doctor's appointment, may accompany the mother to apply for welfare or for day care or to go food shopping. Such concrete kinds of help are more apt to overcome the mistrust of the deprived, isolated, neglectful mother than are quasi-psychiatric conversations about her problems. The discussions may well take place, but the health visitor is more apt to listen with empathy and offer the mother common sense only when it seems to be solicited and accepted well. The lay health visitor does not attempt to supervise the care of the FTT baby, although she may report to the other members of the team circumstances which she finds alarming, so that they can involve themselves and take care of the baby's interests. Thus, the lay health visitor is there for the mother's benefit, but she does not ignore danger signals. Some mothers will need more intensive help in the form of psychiatric treatment or intensive casework from a mental health facility. Group work with one or both parents involved can be very helpful. A homemaker may be needed at times if the mother cannot manage a home and her children at the same time. The other children in the family may be found in need of some kind of treatment and a referral may be made.

The very important work done in the Infant Mental Health Program under the direction of Selma Fraiberg (51, 52) is a model of treatment which few can approach at present, but teaches much about the potential for work with mothers who have FTT babies. The combination of frequent home visiting, flexibility, nurturing, and empathy begin a relationship between the skilled worker and the mother. Skillfully and carefully timed interpretations of the links between the mother's childhood experiences and her experience now with her baby help to free the mother and the baby from reliving old, unconscious conflicts and are used as a preliminary to specific recommendations for changes in child care.

Other programs are making attempts at teaching the mother in the home how to vocalize and play with her baby and understand and encourage his or her development. Such work must be done in the context of a good, supportive relationship between mother and professional (53–56). "Parenting" classes can also be helpful; they not only encourage better child care, they also provide the mother with a socially supportive group experience. Day care may be helpful in providing stimulation for the child and relief for a mother under pressure.

Treatment Failure

When the family is unable to comply with the treatment program and the child continues to lose weight at home, readmission to the hospital or foster-care placement may be needed. The diagnosis and treatment need to be reevaluated and perhaps intensified or changed in the light of better diagnosis.

Sometimes children who have earlier been hospitalized for FTT later are found to be seriously, even fatally, abused as well (57). Also, infants can be starved to death, with no evidence of any food in their gastrointestinal tract on post mortem (58). Therefore, every case of FTT must be taken seriously, the "parenting" practices well diagnosed, and effective treatment and follow-up arranged. One aspect of the treatment program deserves special mention. If the court and social services system (as represented by the hospital and protective caseworker) tell the mother initially that the child's FTT is her fault and she must take responsibility for better care, and if that social system does little or nothing to be sure the mother has enough support for herself in caring for the child, she may become abusive and/or neglectful to the child. The outcome may be disastrous for everyone.

The immaturity, neediness, and feelings of helplessness of the neglectful mother are not transformed into empathic nurturing by one or two lectures. She herself must experience from someone the empathy and nurturing she is expected to give her baby.

The Older Child with FTT

Although FTT is usually described as a problem of infants during the period of rapid growth, children between three and twelve years of age may also be found to suffer from severe growth retardation without physical disease. Often called *psychosocial dwarfism* rather than FTT, there seem to be severe emotional problems in the family which center on one child (59, 60). The child may not necessarily be deprived of food but instead have a voracious appetite, with strange eating and drinking habits, and yet fail to grow. There is a severely disturbed relationship between mother and child, in which food has come to have highly charged pathological meanings to both. An occasional child between two and three is seen for FTT in which this kind of pathological, food-centered relationship seems to be developing. Psychiatric care and often foster-home placement are needed for these families. The relationship of FTT, other feeding problems, psychosocial dwarfism, and anorexia nervosa has not yet been identified, but each represents a disordered parent-child relationship with the food-related pathology progressively more focused within the child.

Follow-up Studies of FTT

Thus far, studies of children hospitalized for FTT present a bleak picture of their later progress. Chase and Martin (8) studied nineteen children who had been hospitalized under the age of one year for FTT; at a mean time of three and one-half years later, 68% were still below the third percentile in height, 53% in weight, and 37% in head circumference. Developmental scores were also depressed, as low as 70 when the FTT was diagnosed after four months of age.

In a study of twenty-one children reviewed, a mean of six years later, Hufton and Oates (61) found five out of twenty-one children still below the tenth percentile (their original group had a milder degree of growth delay with 50% below 10%). One-half of their children were found to have personality difficulties and one-half to be functioning below average in school. Finally, this group of twenty-one had suffered subsequent physical abuse, with two deaths.

In a retrospective study of forty children hospitalized for nonorganic FTT studied by Glaser *et al.* (62), 42.5% were below the third percentile in either height or weight or both. Of the nineteen children in school, seven were experiencing school failure and several children had psychological problems. This study noted that only 20% of the families were referred to some kind of social agency for follow-up, in addition to the referrals for medical care.

A study by Elmer (63) described fifteen children at a mean time of almost five years after hospitalization for FTT due to deprivation. Of the fifteen, seven children were below the 3% in both weight and height, and these two were below in either weight or height. Over 50% of these children showed some degree of retardation intellectually. Of the seven children in school, four had a major behavioral disturbance and six were in special education.

References

1. American Humane Association. *Annual Statistical Analysis of Child Neglect and Abuse Reporting, 1977.* 1979. Englewood, Colorado.
2. English, Peter C. Failure to Thrive without Organic Reason. 1978. *Pediatr. Ann.* 7:11.
3. Shaheen, Eleanor; Alexander, Doris; Truskowsky, Marie; and Barbero, Guilio J. Failure to Thrive—a Retrospective Profile. 1968. *Clin. Pediatr.,* pp. 255–61.
4. Pollitt, Ernesto. Failure to Thrive: Socioeconomic Dietary Intake and Mother-Infant Interaction Data. 1975. *Federation Proc.* 34:1593–97.
5. Sills, Richard H. Failure to Thrive: The Role of Clinical and Laboratory Evaluation. 1978. *Am. J. Dis. Child.* 132:967–69.
6. Stuart, H. C. Standards of Physical Development for Reference in Clinical Appraisement. 1934. *J. Pediatr.* 5:194.
7. Tanner, J. M., and Whitehouse, R. H. Height and Weight Charts from Birth to 5 Years Allowing for Length of Gestation. 1973. *Arch. Dis. Child.* 48:786.

8. Chase, H. P., and Martin, H. Undernutrition and Child Development. 1970. *New Engl. J. Med.* 282:491–96.

9. Hertzig, Margaret; Birch, Herbert G.; Richardson, Stephen A.; and Tizard, Jack. Intellectual Levels of School Children Severely Malnourished during the First Two Years of Life. 1972. *Pediatr.* 49:814–24.

10. Nagera, Humberto. Social Deprivation in Infancy: Implications for Personality Development. In *Handbook of Child Psychoanalysis,* edited by Benjamin Wolman. 1970 (New York: Van Nostrand Reinhold).

11. Sandgrund, Alice; Gaines, R. W.; and Green, A. H. Child Abuse and Mental Retardation: A Problem of Cause and Effect. *Am. J. Mental Deficiency* 79:327–30.

12. Stoch, M. B., and Smythe, S. Does Undernutrition during Infancy Inhibit Brain Growth and Subsequent Intellectual Development? 1963. *Arch. Dis. Child.* 38:546–52.

13. Stoch, M. B., and Smythe, P. M.; Fifteen-Year Developmental Study on Effects of Severe Undernutrition during Infancy on Subsequent Physical Growth and Intellectual Functioning. 1976. *Arch. Dis. Child.* 51:327.

14. Birch, Herbert G. Malnutrition, Learning, and Intelligence. 1972. *Am. J. Public Health* 62:773–84.

15. Graham, George G. Effect of Infantile Malnutrition on Growth. 1976. *Federation Proc.* 26:139–43.

16. Eid, E. E. A Follow-up Study of Physical Growth Following Failure to Thrive with Special Reference to a Critical Period in the First Year of Life. 1971. *Acta Predict.* 60:39–48.

17. Smith, David W. *Growth and Its Disorders.* 1977 (Philadelphia: W. B. Saunders).

18. Suskind, Robert M. Characteristics and Causation of Protein-Calorie Malnutrition in the Infant and Preschool Child. 1977. *Malnutrition Behavior and Social Organization,* edited by E. Laurence and S. Greene (New York: Academic).

19. Jacobs, R. A., and Kent, J. T. Psychosocial Profiles of Failure-to-Thrive Infants—Preliminary Report. 1977. *Child Abuse and Neglect* 1:469–77.

20. Davies, D. P., and Evans, T. I. Failure to Thrive at the Breast (Letter). 1976. *Lancet* 2:1194–95.

21. Pfeifer, Donald R., and Ayoub, Catherine. Non-organic Failure to Thrive in the Breastfeeding Dyad. 1978. *Keeping Abreast, J. Human Nurturing* 3–4:283–86.

22. Frantz, K. B.; Fleiss, P. M.; and Lawrence, R. A. Management of the Slow-gaining Breastfed Baby. *Keeping Abreast, J. Human Nurturing* 3–4:287–307.

23. O'Connor, P. A. Failure to Thrive with Breast Feeding. 1978. *Clin. Pediatr.* 17:833–35.

24. Krieger, Ingeborg, and Sargent, D. A. A Postural Sign in the Sensory Deprivation Syndrome in Infants. 1967. *J. Pediatr.* 70:332–39.

25. Gotlin, Ronald W., and Silver, Henry K. Endocrine Disorders. In *Current Pediatric Diagnosis and Treatment,* edited by C. H. Kempe, Henry K. Silver, and Donough O'Brien. 1974 (Los Altos, Calif.: Lange Medical Publications).

26. Barbero, G. J., and Shaheen, E. Environmental Failure to Thrive: A Clinical View. 1967. *J. Pediatr.* 71:639–44.

27. Brazelton, J. B. *Neonatal Behavioral Assessment Scale*. 1974. *Clinics in Developmental Medicine, No. 50* (Philadelphia: Lippincott).

28. Bayley Scales of Infant Development. 1969 (New York: Psychological Corporation).

29. Revised Yale Developmental Schedule, Yale Child Study Center, New Haven, Conn.

30. Frankenberg, W. K., and Dodds, J. B. The Denver Developmental Screening Test. 1978. *J. Pediatr.* 71:988.

31. Schmitt, Barton D., ed. *The Child Protection Team Handbook* (1978. New York: Garland).

32. Elmer, Elizabeth. Failure to Thrive: Role of the Mother. 1960. *Pediatr.* 25:717.

33. Evans, Sue L.; Reinhart, John B.; and Succup, Ruth A. Failure to Thrive: A Study of Forty-five Children and Their Families. 1979. *J. Am. Acad. Child Psychiatry* 18:440.

34. Fishoff, Joseph; Whitter, C.; and Pettit, Mervin. A Psychiatric Study of Mothers of Infants with Growth Failure Secondary to Maternal Deprivation. 1971. *J. Pediatr.* 79:209.

35. Gaines, Richard; Sandgrund, Alice; Green, A. H.; and Power, Ernest. Etiological Factors in Child Maltreatment: A Multivariate Study of Abusing, Neglecting, and Normal Mothers. 1978. *J. Abnormal Psychol.* 87:531–40.

36. Gordon, Alan H., and Jameson, Janet Corcoran. Infant-Mother Attachment in Patients with Non-organic Failure-to-Thrive Syndrome. 1979. *J. Am. Acad. Child Psychiatry* 18:251–59.

37. Green, A. H. A Psychodynamic Approach to the Study and Treatment of Child-Abusing Parents. *J. Am. Acad. Child Psychiatry*. 1976. 15:414–29.

38. Kerr, Mary Ann D.; Bogues, Jacqueline Landman; and Kerr, Douglas S. Psychosocial Functioning of Mothers of Malnourished Children. 1978. *Pediatr.* 62:778–84.

39. Leonard, M. F.; Rhymers, J. P.; and Solnit, A. J. Failure to Thrive in Infants: A Family Problem. 1966. *Am. J. Dis. Child.* 111:600–612.

40. Melnick, Barry, and Hurley, John R. Distinctive Personality Attributes of Child-Abusing Mothers. 1969. *J. Consulting Clin. Psychol.* 33:746–49.

41. Patton, Robert G., and Gardner, L. I. Influence of Family Environment on Growth: The Syndrome of Maternal Deprivation. 1962. *Pediatr.* 30:957–62.

42. Pollitt, Ernesto; Eichler, Aviva Weisei; and Chan, Ghee-Khoon. Psychosocial Development and Behavior of Mothers of Failure to Thrive Children. 1975. *Am. J. Orthopsychiatry* 45:4.

43. Spinetta, John J. Parental Personality Factors in Child Abuse. 1978. *J. Consulting Clin. Psychol.* 46:1409–14.

44. Spinetta, John J., and Rigler, David. The Child-Abusing Parent: A Psychological Review. 1972. *Psychol. Bull.* 77:296–304.

45. Egeland, Byron, and Brunnquell, Don. An At-Risk Approach to the Study of Child Abuse. 1979. *J. Am. Acad. Child Psychiatry* 18:219.

46. Polansky, N. Childhood Level of Living Scale. 1968 (Athens, Georgia: School of Social Work University of Georgia).

47. Polansky, N.; DeSaix, C.; and Sharlin, S. *Child Neglect: Understanding and Reaching the Parent*. 1972 (New York: Child Welfare League).

48. Green, Arthur H. Child-Abusing Fathers. 1979. *J. Am. Acad. Child Psychiatry* 18:270–82.

49. Emelen, Arthur *et al*. Regional Research Institute for Human Services: Overcoming Barriers to Planning for Children in Foster Care. 1977. Department of Health, Education, and Welfare Publication No. (OHDS) 78-30138.

50. Winick, Myron; Meyer, K. K.; and Harris, Ruth. Malnutrition and Environmental Enrichment by Early Adoption. 1975. *Science* 190:1173–75.

51. Fraiberg, S.; Adelson, E.; and Shapiro, V. Ghosts in the Nursery: A Psychoanalytic Approach to the Problems of Impaired Infant-Mother Relationships. 1975. *J. Am. Acad. Child Psychiatry* 14:387–421.

52. Fraiberg, S., and Adelson, E. Infant-Parent Psychotherapy on Behalf of a Child in a Critical Nutritional State. 1976. *Psychoanal. Study Child* 31:461–91.

53. Kempe, C. Henry. Approaches to Preventing Child Abuse: The Health Visitor Concept. 1976. *Am. J. Dis. Child.* 130:941–47.

54. Barnard, Martha Undersood, and Wolfe, Lorraine. Psychosocial Failure to Thrive: Nursing Assessment and Intervention. 1973. *Nursing Clinics of NA* 8:557–65.

55. Eckels, JoAnn. Home Follow-up of Mothers and Their Failure-to-Thrive Children, Using Planned Nursing Intervention. 1968. ANA Clinical Sessions (Dallas: Appleton Century Crofts).

56. Ramey, Craig T.; Stann, R. H.; Pallas, J.; Whitten, C. F.; and Reed, V. Nutrition, Response Contingent Stimulation and the Maternal Deprivation Syndrome: Results of an Early Intervention Program. 1975. *Merrill-Palmer Quarterly* 21:45–53.

57. Koel, Bertram S. Failure to Thrive and Fatal Injury as a Continuum. 1969. *Am. J. Dis. Child.* 118:565–67.

58. Adelson, L. Homicide by Starvation: The Nutritional Variant of the "Battered Child." 1963. *J. Am. Med. Assoc.* 186:458–60.

59. Silver, H. K., and Finkelstein, M. Deprivation Dwarfism. 1967. *J. Pediatr.* 70:317–24.

60. Powell, G. F.; Brasel, J. A.; Rait, S.; and Blizzard, R. M. Emotional Deprivation and Growth Retardation Simulating Idiopathic Hypopituitarism. 1967. *New Eng. J. Med.* 276:1271–83.

61. Hufton, Ian W., and Oates, R. Kim. Nonorganic Failure to Thrive: A Long-Term Follow-up. 1977. *Pediatr.* 59:73–77.

62. Glaser, H.; Heagarty, Margaret; Bullard, Dexter M., Jr.; and Rivchik, Elizabeth C. Physical and Psychological Development of Children with Early Failure to Thrive. 1968. *J. Pediatr.* 73:690–98.

63. Elmer, Elizabeth; Gregg, Grace S.; and Ellison, Patricia. Late Results of the "Failure to Thrive" Syndrome. 1969. *Clin Pediatr.* 8:584–89.

11 Child Neglect

Hendrika B. Cantwell

Neglect complaints to child protective agencies are many in number, time-consuming in services rendered, vague in what is expected, cause difficulty in coordinating specific and diverse professional concerns, and frustrating in what can be accomplished. Statistics resulting from nationwide surveys indicate that the numbers of neglect cases are far greater than those of abuse. The American Humane Association indicates that of 99,579 substantiated cases reported recently, 58% were neglect only and 15% were abuse and neglect. Child abuse cases are often dramatic and covered by the news media. Especially if there is a death, the criminal prodeedings will be covered extensively. The public therefore has knowledge that abused children exist and that it is a serious problem as the result of which children are maimed, permanently scarred, or even killed. The public is not as aware of the serious consequences of child neglect. Sympathy for a young child who was abused is easily aroused, but sympathy for the less-dramatic tragedy of the young child who is neglected is not. Unlike abuse which can be photographed, measured, X-rayed, and diagnosed, neglect is often more difficult to document.

Any of us who have dealt with the subjects of abuse and neglect are aware that the children who are raised in a neglectful environment are very much at risk. Lack of supervision endangers them by exposure to fires, falls, poisons, medicines, and unsuitable companions, as well as risks in matters of health and education. Serious emotional disturbances are seen as the outcome of chaotic life styles which leave the child in a constant quandary as to what the environment will next visit upon him.

Parental Characteristics

In Denver last year, children dying from neglect outnumbered those dying from abuse. The incidents of neglect which lead to death usually are related to parents

Hendrika B. Cantwell, M.D., is a pediatrician for the Department of Social Services, Denver.

leaving young children alone in the home where they may drown in a bathtub, start a fire, or ingest dangerous drugs. Neglectful *parenting* can be attributed to lack of knowledge, lack of judgment, and lack of motivation.

Lack of knowledge includes such things as parents being unaware that an infant needs to be fed every three to four hours, parents being uninstructed in house-keeping skills, unable to cook a meal, or not even knowing of what a nutritional meal consists. The parent knows nothing of normal developmental milestones that children reach at certain ages and is unaware that children have stimulative needs. The lack of knowledge also expresses itself in inappropriate or absent medical care. The most serious lack of knowledge is that the parent does not recognize emotional nurturing as a need of the child. In neglectful households, emotional nurturing is often considered by the parent to be spoiling the child by giving him attention. Consistent setting of limits does not occur, because the parent has little patience. The attitude prevails that the child has been told once and should there-fore, forever afterward, remember to do or not to do something.

Lack of parental judgment is potentially dangerous to children. The child may not be perceived to be ill or, if ill, not seen as requiring medical attention. Lack of judgment also reveals itself in parents leaving young children home alone. Since neglectful parents are often immature, it is not surprising that the parent does not see a four- or five-year-old child as being different in judgment from an adult, expecting that child to be capable of looking after an infant or toddler. Serious injuries can result from lack of judgment, such as when a parent allows a one-year-old child to be burned by a hot water heater because, the parent says, "I told her it was hot. If she wanted to get hurt that was her business." Another symptom of lack of judgment is role reversal, which begins to appear as early as a one- or two-year-old child who is expected to perform parental tasks and to provide the parent with emotional satisfaction.

Motivational problems are seen in parents who refuse to make changes. Teach-ing by visiting nurses and social workers is cast aside by parents who insist they have the right to live their own life styles and to exercise their own judgments in how their children should be raised, refusing to modify gross neglect toward the children. More serious is the parent's lack of understanding of what constitutes appropriate parenting, guidance, and emotional nurturing, with no desire to learn better parenting skills. Having themselves been raised in a neglectful household, parents regard neglect as the standard of practice. There is no perception that they themselves have received poor parenting which resulted in their immature, un-nurtured, and very needy quality as adults. Unfortunately, this particular profile of the adult interferes with the ability to nurture and parent young children. As the parent is incapable of meeting the child's basic needs, the child begins to show effects of neglectful parenting.

Manifestations of Neglect

There are many opportunities for a neglected child to come to the attention of authorities. Health care providers, day-care center workers, and neighbors are often the ones to report neglected infants, toddlers, and preschoolers. It is unusual for neglect to go undetected beyond this age, but although observed, it may not be reported. Entry into school thus becomes the latest point at which the neglected child should be recognized and reported.

The first-grade teacher can pick out children who appear to have serious problems developmentally, behaviorally, supervisionally, and experientially. The school nurse can document poor hygiene, poor weight gain, and inattention to medical needs. School social workers can visit homes to document areas of neglect in the household. To wait to identify the neglected child until he is over twelve years old is unconscionable.

A neglected child may be identified by observation of his or her flattened occiput and hair rubbed off from excessive lying in the crib. The infant frequently shows poor weight gain and begins to show developmental delays at a very early age. The earliest clear sign is a baby who is unresponsive to the human face and who does not express pleasure at human interaction by a social smile, squeals, and babbles. The infant should be able to differentiate between caretakers and strangers, recognizing the face and the voice by six weeks of age. As the baby becomes older, there is evidence of the flabby musculature of a child who does not get adequate amounts of exercise, lies in the crib too much, and is delayed in holding up its head and in sitting up properly. Weight bearing is delayed.

As the child goes into the toddler stage, developmental delays become more apparent in fine motor skills, social skills, and, particularly, in the area of language. Language delays result from the parent's lack of talking to and carrying on conversation with the young child. There is such a paucity of interaction with the parent that the child does not understand even simple statements. Also noted is the lack of comprehension of specific directions such as "Give the ball to me," or "Put the pencil on the table." The lack of language interactions also prevents the child from learning the names of common objects, a knowledge expected when the child starts school.

The issue to be raised very clearly is that waiting to provide intervention until a child is a teenager exhibiting delinquent behavior is unacceptable, for children who are being neglected become recognizable by specific symptoms at an early age. If childhood records of an adolescent involved with the court system are examined, certain predictable symptoms can usually be found. Those signs, to be discussed further below, need to be heeded early in the child's life. Invervention is far more effective for a young child than for an adolescent and also less expensive.

Children need stimulation to attain age-appropriate developmental tasks. Accomplishments must be observed and documented so that in the absence of age-appropriate development of the child, parents can be given guidance to accept further evaluation of the child and to implement any needed remediation. Neglect exists when the parent cannot acknowledge or understand the need for intervention in the child's nonstimulative environment. The parents may not perceive that there is a problem, because they lack knowledge about normal child development; but parents can be expected to learn and can be expected to accept guidance, such as following through with a recommended placement of the child in a stimulating day-care environment. The child with developmental delays will continue to fall further and further behind. The parent who cannot understand that this will affect the child's schooling and adult life is in need of vigorous instruction on the subject. The absence of the parents' cooperation or their failing to recognize that the child has problems, which have been stated to them clearly by professionals, constitutes neglectful parenting. Developmental delays are not outgrown!

Multidisciplinary Aspects

Much has been said about the multidisciplinary aspects of abuse cases and how the multidisciplinary approach is put into practice. This same concept is even more important in neglect cases. If a child is found to have been abused, there are marks on the child that can be diagnosed medically or documented by a social worker or by a school nurse. In neglect cases, however, what the school nurse sees, what the social worker experiences on home visits, what the doctor has noted on the chart, and what others who are involved with the family have detailed, must be put together as a whole picture. Court intervention is possible only if the multidisciplinary aspects of child neglect are presented clearly. If a single documentation of poor school attendance is all that is available, the court may not grant intervention, such as supervision or removal of the children. However, if there is evidence of neglect in a combination of areas, such as poor medical care, developmental delays, poor school attendance, poor nutrition, and children left home alone, this total picture is well recognized by the juvenile courts as being detrimental or life threatening to the children.

Other disciplines must not relegate solely to the child protection agency the responsibility of intervention in neglect cases. Social workers are left in untenable positions vis-à-vis the family with whom they are working to correct neglectful parenting if they do not have the necessary multidisciplinary support. Many social workers are viewed by the families with whom they are working as being just "that nosy social worker and what does she know?" The parent's view is that the social worker expresses her own opinion, intervenes with her own standards, and advocates values which they do not see as having meaning in their own lives. If, however, the social worker can present standards that are recognized as those of the community regarding appropriate parenting, the community becomes the authority. Therefore, every community should have developed standards regarding the minimum parental behavior the community finds acceptable. Parents who neglect their children beget neglectful parents in the next generation. The result is that neglected children become some of the most expensive people in our society. If child neglect is taken seriously because the devastating and costly after effects are understood, then it should not be difficult for a community to encourage its early detection.

Case Assessment

The definition of neglect encompasses a number of areas. Neglect exists when inattention is given to the child by parents or caretakers in areas including medical, educational, stimulative, environmental, disciplinary, nutritional, physical, emotional, and safety needs. Neglect can be mild, moderate, or severe in any of these areas. A filing in court is clearly indicated if serious neglect exists in one or two of the areas or if moderate neglect is present in three areas or the parents' attention is not at least minimally appropriate to the children's needs in four or more areas. Community agencies, such as the Visiting Nurse Service, school personnel, health service providers, social workers, and homemakers, involved with neglectful families, should make all possible efforts to teach parents in an attempt to remediate neglect. Seeking the help of the child protective agency for evaluation and possible intervention is important, if the teaching efforts are met by the parents' inability to learn or refusal to make necessary changes.

The agencies which make the referral to the child protective agency must state concerns specifically, including exactly what efforts have been made toward remediation and what is hoped to be accomplished. If, for example, the referral is initiated by a medical facility, reporting must state the exact neglect medically, as well as any other neglect that has been observed. The referral should include specific instructions as to why and how often the child must visit the clinic, as well as the consequences if the child does not attend. A time frame in which the physician expects compliance on the part of the parent should be included.

The Academy of Pediatrics has set forth standards of optimal well-child care.[1] To deal with neglect, however, it is necessary to establish the minimal standards of well-child care. Through the input of many physicians in Denver a consensus was reached. The physicians surveyed included the Directors of Pediatric Outpatient Services in three major hospitals, physicians from the private sector, physicians from clinic settings, physicians in charge of public school health services, and physicians from two developmental evaluation clinics. By the agreement of these physicians, the minimal standard of well-child care should include two visits to the doctor before the child is six months of age, another between six to twelve months, one between 12 and 18 months, and one between 18 and 24 months, for a total of five well-child visits before twenty-four months of age. This would allow for well-child care and full immunizations to take place. Also considered necessary is one visit between ages two and five years to check for anemia, hearing, vision, growth and development, and for booster immunizations. One visit was recommended between five and eleven years of age, and one more before eighteen years of age. These latter two are less critical than the preschool visits but gain importance as more children participate in sports and as more are now seen as potential teenage parents. The consensus of the surveyed pediatricians was that the child has the civil right to grow up without major handicaps and to receive immunizations to protect him or her from seriously damaging illnesses. Religious beliefs that forbid immunization can be accommodated, but for the child's protection the risk should be carefully discussed with the parent. Parents

1. For information write the American Academy of Pediatrics, Box 1034, Evanston, Illinois 60204—EDS.

who are failing to arrange for even minimal care for their children need encouragement. Instruction and education for the parent can be accomplished with referral to a Visiting Nurse Service. If a social worker is involved, that worker may be a resource person to arrange for transportation or to remind parents to keep appointments. After two or three specific efforts have been made to instruct, educate, and appoint the parents to receive medical or preventive care for the child, depending on how real the possibility is that there may be a critical element in the medical needs of the child, the parents will be considered neglectful if they fail subsequent appointments.

Parents of children with specific handicaps should be given a very clear understanding why there is need for remediation. An example would be a child with a "lazy eye." Failure to take action to attend to the child's handicap and obtain needed care may be regarded as endangering the child's rights. If the condition has the potential to cause permanent harm to the child, then it also implies that there is danger which may be imminent danger to the child. The courts regard imminent danger or permanent harm to the child as cause for court action on behalf of the child.

The child with a chronic health problem presents a different concern. Because there is variation as to the severity of the specific medical problem, such as asthma, diabetes, or chronic urinary tract infections, the adequacy of care needs to be determined by the attending physician. If the family is not providing adequate care, a Visiting Nurse Service referral is recommended to assist in encouraging parents to keep appointments. The Visiting Nurse Service can then consult with the attending physician as to whether referral to the child protective agency is indicated.

Children who are considered to be at high rish for abuse and neglect include those previously known as failure-to-thrive children due to maternal deprivation or children who have been previously documented as having been abused or neglected. With these families, even one missed appointment is serious and should set in motion a prompt visit from the Visiting Nurse Service or child protection person. The health care provider has the responsibility to make such a referral to ascertain that the child is not injured, neglected, or in danger. If these agencies are not available, a clinic social worker or nurse in person, if possible, or by telephone should make contact with the family to determine why the appointment was failed and to urge a visit the next day. An in-person home visit is preferable because the condition of the child can be visually assessed. If there is no danger, another appointment can be made. If abuse or neglect is found, the parents should be asked to take the child to the doctor immediately. Should parents refuse such a request, the case may have to be referred to the police to take the child to a medical facility for evaluation. (In Colorado, the worker for the child protective agency does not have the right to remove a child against the wishes of the parents. There must be an order from the court or police action to remove the child to a medical facility.)

The above categories concerning children with specific handicaps, chronic health problems, or who are at high risk need to be reported to the child protective agency as constituting neglect when the physician, after consultation from allied professionals, deems the situation to be life threatening, or potentially so, or if there is a possibility of serious long-term medical consequences to the child who is not receiving proper medical care.[2] Conditions such as dirty skin, dirty clothes, lice, impetigo, scabies, insect bites, cradle cap, or a smelly child may be emotionally or educationally harmful to the child and do need to be treated; however, even though frequently reported as such, these are not always due to medical neglect.

In the prenatal and postnatal periods, child neglect may already be observed and needs to be addressed. The physicians surveyed tentatively agreed that a pregnant woman desiring to bear a child to term should preferably be seen medically by three-months gestation. It was strongly recommended that six-months gestation be the latest the first visit occurs. During the prenatal period, serious denial or rejection of the pregnancy, particularly in cases where it has been known that previous children have been abused, neglected, or removed from the home by court action should be noted carefully. Harming the viable unborn child by the mother's alcohol or drug abuse or suicide attempts constitutes neglect to the unborn child. Seriously retarded, psychotic, or mentally ill mothers, particularly where there is no family support and where there has been no planning for the arrival of the child, all constitute situations of neglect which should be reported to the child protective agency for investigation of how serious the problems are and to ascertain what can be done to assist in planning for the arrival of the infant.

Physical Findings

Perinatal Period

Conditions observed in the neonatal period which are of grave concern include the mother who physically rejects her newborn child, who threatens violence to her infant, or who makes remarks which otherwise indicate poor bonding between mother and child. Other danger signals are infants who appear to have fetal alcohol syndrome or drug withdrawal symptoms. Refusal to accept needed medical or psychological follow-up for either the mother or her newborn indicates potential for neglect. If any of the above conditions are present, the child is at risk and needs to be protected. It is recommended that a referral to the child protective agency be made. This referral may lead to court intervention. Physicians should take a role in such referrals and be concerned enough about the future of the infant to be willing to appear in court and state their concerns. These standards of minimal care, giving specific indicators for identifying neglect, are set forth in an attempt to clarify the very difficult issue of what constitutes medical neglect. These guidelines are not absolute, but are to be considered as basic principles reached by a consensus of physicians who have had experience in dealing with neglectful families. Child protective agencies will act in the role of coordinators and need the

---

2. Knowing when to send a report to protective services in cases of neglect is difficult. We prefer to develop a relationship with protective services and use them as consultants in these difficult decisions—Eds.

physician's input when the neglect case comes to court. In many instances a written report from the physician stating his concerns regarding neglect will suffice. At times, it may be necessary for the physician to appear in court. Careful record keeping of observations made concerning neglect is imperative and will make the court appearance easier, since the records clearly document the concerns.

Nutrition

Physicians are still not sufficiently conscious of the detrimental effects on the infant who does not gain weight in the early months of life. Normally, brain growth is rapid during this time, and the most serious consequence of inadequate nutrition is impaired brain development, which becomes irreversible. Nutritional neglect exists when a child does not grow or gain weight adequately in the absence of medical conditions which might impair such growth. The status of the child's health must be established. If no medical cause for poor weight gain is present, the adequacy of regular feeding must be established. This cannot be based solely on the history taken from the caretaking parent. Observations in the home by a Visiting Nurse or in the hospital may shed light on the kind of care the child receives. Most infants who fail to gain because of home conditions will show additional symptoms of maternal deprivation, such as developmental delays; failure to enjoy human interaction; a flattened, bald occiput; and generally dull affect. If there is doubt about the cause of inadequate weight gain, the child must be observed in another setting to see if weight gain is increased. This may mean a hospital admission for observation to facilitate the diagnosis of failure-to-thrive. It is neglectful of the health care provider not to make a diagnosis of the cause of failure-to-thrive in an infant. The excuse that the parents are small is not adequate, as the parents also may have been deprived.

Nutrition is also a concern for children who, as they become toddlers and preschoolers, fall away from an established growth curve. The parent may describe cooking good meals, yet a social worker or Visiting Nurse visiting the home at mealtimes can document that servings of such meals are inadequate, the food being eaten by the parents rather than the child, or that the described good meals are presented infrequently.

Even school-age children who are not gaining deserve attention, yet most of them are ignored, as physicians continue to be reluctant to intervene, often not keeping a growth chart. Nutritional neglect can and must be documented. School personnel can make observations of the child who is always hungry and eats excessively at school. The school nurse can weigh the child before and after vacations so as to compare weight gains during times he is eating at school and times he is not. This can document that the child is not receiving adequate nutrition at home. Nutritional neglect is rarely found in isolation from other neglect, and inquiry must be made about the problem. In infancy, hospitalization may establish the existence of nutritional neglect. In children of all ages, professionals such as school personnel, child protection workers, or Visiting Nurses need to be involved in evaluating and exploring basic questions such as whether the family has enough money for food, whether they qualify for financial assistance, or whether they simply need nutritional education.

Some children described in the literature as suffering from deprivational dwarfism eat adequate amounts of food and at times hoard food, yet do not gain adequate amounts of weight. Their emotional environment interferes with normal growth. This syndrome also deserves the attention of professionals, yet is too often overlooked. Multidisciplinary intervention is indicated and need not be viewed as punitive, but as helping, the family. And can be so presented to them.

Residential Placement

Legislatures in most states have become cautious in supplying large sums of money to child protective agencies to deal with abuse and neglect. One of the areas being seriously questioned is placement of children outside the home. The most expensive placements, residential treatment facilities, deal with teenagers who are out of control, poorly educated, often involved in some criminal behavior, and unable to conform within a social structure. Although there are situations where a child does benefit from such placement, it is unrealistic to expect that twelve or fourteen years of neglect in the parental home can be corrected in treatment facilities which keep the child for a much more limited time. Even the child who has improved with treatment often reverts to the old patterns of acting-out behavior when returned to the parental home because nothing in the home has changed. Can he realistically be expected to fit back into the neglectful household without reverting?

About 80% of the teenagers are placed in a treatment facility by juvenile court action. This comes about because an adolescent involved in criminal behavior has become a problem to society. Police, probation officers, and juvenile court systems insist that the child be placed somewhere, because the emphasis is on protecting society from the young person. The medical and protective services' point of view is that this is a child in need of protection and treatment. The two points of view may not always be the same on the goals of treatment.

Schooling and the School

Schooling neglect is frequently reported to the child protective agency. School personnel, including school doctors, nurses, principals, social workers, and classroom teachers in Denver were interviewed for their input as to what they consider neglectful behavior in the school setting.

Colorado law requires one-hundred and seventy-two days of school attendance per year. The public schools consider absence in excess of twenty-five days unacceptable. If the parents are unwilling or unable to ensure the child's school attendance, this should be considered educational neglect. Nonattendance in excess of twenty-five days should be viewed as symptomatic of family disorganization serious enough to warrant court intervention. In most instances, there will be found other indicators of neglect as well. The court will declare children under twelve dependent and neglected; a child over twelve would be considered a "child in need of supervision."

A school social worker should contact a family after a child has been absent for three days and should continue to make every effort to improve attendance. If there is a medical reason why the child is not attending school, it will be expected that the parent take the child to a physician for examination and treatment. The physician can then document the need for absence from school. Psychological reasons, as well as medical reasons, should be considered for a child's absence. A school social worker can assist the parents in having the child evaluated and, when appropriate, refer the child to a counseling service for treatment of the absenteeism.

At times, a child needs an examination to assist the school in providing adequate placement in the school setting. This need for psychological evaluation should be explained to the parents and their cooperation encouraged. It should be explained to the parents and their cooperation encouraged. It should be explained to them clearly that such examination would provide information which the school needs to assist the child in a proper learning experience. Neglect exists only if the school feels that without such examination the child might suffer educational or emotional damage and the parents, knowing this, refuse to have the child evaluated.

Any classroom can have a dirty or smelly child who is ostracized because of poor hygiene. The school should act by requesting that the parent send clean clothing to school if the child is incontinent. The school should also instruct parents to wash the child before he comes to school. It is considered neglectful if the parent cannot or will not follow through with recommendations to practice better hygiene, as the child may suffer emotional damage because of the condition.

There are children who come to school hungry, who complain to the teacher that they have not eaten, and who do not appear to have adequate nutrition. The school has the privilege of weighing a child if poor nutrition is a concern. (Refer to the preceding section on nutritional neglect for details.)

The teacher of home-bound children has intimate exposure to the household and may observe areas needing intervention, such as the child left alone who is unable to care for himself or who is out of control. The police may be called to remove the unattended child from this setting.

The child who threatens to harm himself or makes suicidal gestures in the school setting is always to be reported to the child protective agency. This overture should be taken very seriously.

Emotional Neglect

Emotional neglect[3] is the most difficult to define and arouses controversy, especially in a multidisciplinary setting. The medical and the social service professions

---

3. The concept of emotional neglect is considered here, as it is in many areas of the literature. Neglecting or abusing the emotions of a child is a difficult concept to comprehend. We prefer to consider this as developmental neglect, i.e., neglectful acts that result in developmental deficits for the child. These deficits then may well lead to emotional outbursts of behavior or withdrawal of the child—EDS.

tend to see neglect through the eyes of the child, describing the child with a set of symptoms which imply that emotional neglect has occurred. As the physician describes the symptomatology of an emotionally disturbed child, the lawyer may well ask, quite naturally, "How do you know that this was caused by the parents? What did the parent do or fail to do that caused these symptoms?"

Many elements of neglect have effects in the emotional area and, for the benefit of the lawyer, the specific behaviors or lack of behaviors on the part of the parent can be clearly related to the end result in the child, including the emotional symptomatology. In the younger child, the symptoms are more rapidly identified and the cause-effect relationship from parental neglect more easily substantiated. This leads back to the plea for early detection of neglect.

To reiterate, a child in infancy and early childhood is rarely exposed to influences other than those in the home, except in cases where the child is in a day-care setting. Day-care providers are the choice of the parents, and the parent has the responsibility to assure that the setting in which they leave their child for day care is responsive to the child. Parents' action or inaction which leads to what appear to be emotional disturbances by the infant can be described clearly. The symptomatology seen in a child is related to the behaviors of the mother or the caretaker. The baby who is not picked up and the child who is left lying in the crib with a bottle propped in her mouth can be recognized as previously described. The total picture is one of lack of affect and lack of responsiveness. This is significant and must be noted with great care.

Parents who are totally undemonstrative in a giving, loving, touching manner toward their children will produce predictable symtomatology in their children. The parent does not look at the child, does not talk to the child, does not show interest in the child, and, when engaged in a conversation with another adult, quickly forgets that the child is anywhere around. This results in the child's easy attachment and interest in other adults, reaching out immediately to strangers when he should, at that age, be demonstrating a clear resistance to strangers. These children will reach out to any adult to be loved, hugged, held, cared for, and to get attention. These young children may also be observed giving attention to the parents because they have learned they must satisfy the parents' emotional needs.

Predictable emotional symptoms may appear in children related to inconsistent limit setting by the parent. Children need attention and quickly learn what behavior will get attention from the parent. Even negative attention is better than none; so if the child only gets attention when he does something that does not suit the parent, he becomes accustomed to behaving inappropriately to receive attention. This is frequently referred to as negative attention-getting. Such symptomatology in the child can clearly be seen as a direct result of the parents' behavior. It can be documented with careful behavioral observations of the parent-child interaction.

In the older child, emotional symptoms appear because of a negative self-image. The parent deprecates the child, calling him "bad" or "stupid," and gives him little attention except to infer that he is troublesome. The parent gives messages as to expected misdeeds and projects the outcome such as "You'll wind up in jail" or "become a whore." The school experience then reinforces the experience at home. These children, who, because of parental neglect, cannot listen, cannot share, and cannot behave, feel that they are no good. They develop serious emotional difficulties which can be directly traced to the parents' failure to provide the child with a sufficiently positive stimulative environment to allow him to grow and be ready for school. Specific negative expressions on the part of the parent toward the child are what create the child's sense of inferiority and lack of self-worth. Both the emotional sense of lack of self-worth and the lack of stimulative behavior which allows for proper cognitive growth leave the child with a very poor self-image. Children left alone do not see themselves as valued. Since no one cares if they come home or not, they may not come home. This allows the child to be available to influences of older children experimenting with drugs or to adults dealing in pornography or prostitution. Emotional neglect by the parents causes the child to seek attention elsewhere, probably with inappropriate people.

One primary charge of the Children's Code is to keep children united with their biological family. This causes a conflict for professionals who work with children, because even though they see neglect they feel there is little that can be done with parents who do not comply with suggestions from agencies in the community such as the school, medical facility, or protective service agencies. Another problem is that many physicians, teachers, and other professionals may be hesitant to report neglect because they question whether what they see is "serious enough" to report. The multidisciplinary approach to dealing with neglect requires all concerned to keep careful records of any neglect observed. Exact instructions that were given to the parents along with dates of those instructions must be noted. Precise follow-up to determine the compliance of the family must be documented. Such records can then be used when it is necessary to institute intervention by the court on behalf of the child.

Protective Service Referrals and the Court

Child protection agencies get referrals from professionals indicating "something should be done." Often the only way anything can be done is through court action. With consistent notation of neglectful behavior of the parent and with careful documentation of the symptomatology in the child, then enough supporting evidence can be put together in such a manner that a court action can be brought. Multidisciplinary preparation is important and appropriate, for, with a paucity of information, usually little can be accomplished. Unfortunately, the child protective agency is often blamed for the fact that nothing was done.

A misunderstanding common to many professionals reporting child neglect is that the report means that the child will be removed from the family. All efforts are made to help the family to provide more adequate parenting and to keep the child in the home. The court may be asked to order supervision of a family. Essentially, court-ordered supervision means a specific list of needs and instructions arrived at with multidisciplinary input along with time limits for compliance. For example, the court may order the parents to allow the social worker to visit weekly to observe the children in the home and to counsel with the parents, may order the children to attend school regularly, and may order needed medical care to be obtained by monthly clinic visits. If, in three months, some improvement is seen in the family's functioning, then another three months may bring more positive changes. At about six months, if it can be shown that the parents are complying and enough improvement has been made, the case may then be closed. If improvement is not forthcoming within six months, a decision must be made whether court-ordered supervision should continue or whether the situation has deteriorated sufficiently that a request should be made to the court to remove the children from the home. Only when all efforts to remediate inadequate parenting have failed should court action for removal of the child be requested.

At times, court action can be therapeutic for families who are not following through with medical care or appropriate school attencance. They may do better if they hear clear orders issued from a judge in a courtroom. Occasionally, simply the threat of court action will cause the family to comply with needed care for children.

Documentation of neglect must be presented to the court in a clear manner, concisely stated so that it becomes apparent that there is pervasive multilevel neglect. Only after adjudication of the case, meaning that the court finds that neglect has taken place, is a treatment plan ordered by the court. Implementation of that treatment plan must be documented to show whether the family is complying. After such a treatment program ordered by the court has been established, there will be review hearings which will determine if the children are to remain with, be removed from, or returned to their families.

In Colorado, children can be removed from the home for a particular incidence of severe life-threatening neglect prior to the first court hearing. Examples of conditions when children would be removed are: young children locked inside the house alone; school-age children six to eleven years of age, who, on repeated occasions have been left alone; children over twelve years of age who are left in charge of younger children for long periods of time where children are out of control, without food, or generally not capable of managing the household; and handicapped children up to the age of eighteen who are left alone and cannot care for themselves.

When parents or caretakers are found passed out on alcohol or on drugs, or parents are frankly psychotic with symptoms such that they might harm the children, or are unable to provide the children's needs efforts will be made to find another appropriate caretaker such as a relative or someone in the neighborhood who is willing to take care of the children until other arrangements can be made. If such a caretaker cannot be found, the children may have to be removed to a shelter facility.

When children are found who need immediate medical care, efforts must be made by the police or social worker to have the parent bring the child to a medical facility. If the caretaker refuses and the need for care is urgent, the child will be brought to a medical facility by the police and placed in protective custody. The younger the child, the greater the urgency for indicated medical care.

Custody disputes among family members can necessitate removal of a child from a household because the quarreling parties accuse each other of violence and threats of violence.

Under the general heading of neglect, "dirty house" cases are common. Before considering immediate removal of the children, the first evaluation of a dirty house must be to determine if the parent-child relationship is good. If children appear to be healthy, happy, and relating well and warmly to the parents, the dirty house itself is not a reason for immediate removal of the children unless the house contains dangerous substances, such as drugs, broken glass, or needs major repairs before the house is safe for the children. Dirty-house cases may be chronic or acute. It is advisable that the parents be given a specific time frame, such as forty-eight hours, in which a revisitation will occur, to ascertain that the parents have cleaned up the house, removed the broken glass, have made repairs that are absolutely necessary, have removed dangerous substances, and are providing a home that is more appropriate for the children. If the house is inadequate, having no heat in cold weather, inoperative plumbing, or is otherwise severely damaged, it is advisable to offer the whole family unit temporary housing rather than to separate the children from their parents. Only if the parent refuses to accept poor housing as a problem might the children have to be removed.

The household in which there is no food and inadequate clothing for the children needs first to be evaluated to determine if the family needs financial assistance. The family may be put in touch with an appropriate helping agency and arrangements can be made for emergency food and/or clothing. Serious concern and potential for removal occurs when parents do not perceive these problems or refuse to accept assistance in finding better housing or accepting adequate food and clothing.

At times, it is the child's behavior that appears to be self-destructive and beyond the control of the parent. If evaluation by child protective agencies or a police officer supports that the child is in danger, removal to a safe environment is indicated.

Summary

In summary, child neglect is a pervasive problem in America largely because it is ignored by the public, which is unaware of the personal pain caused its victims and the tremendous expense it is to the taxpayers. Professionals, too, lack information about child neglect, its significance, and consequences. Many feel there is nothing that can be done. A primary principle is that neglect occurs as a continuum rather than as an isolated incident, and for that reason a neglected child comes into contact with professionals from a variety of disciplines. Only if all these people work in concert to document the several areas of neglect for a child can enough evidence be obtained to justify court intervention.

Early detection is vital, for, in the infant and toddler, neglect is most easily documented and most clearly linked to parental behavior as the cause. Intervention at this point is also more immediately effective and considerably less expensive financially, as well as developmentally, for the child.

All professionals are urged to make a personal commitment to being more aware of neglect and documenting what they see. Through these efforts of individuals a mutual, joint, and therefore effective impact can be made in solving the problem of child neglect.

Acknowledgment

The author is indebted to Bonnie Pobst for her assistance.

Editors' Note

For additional reading the reader is referred to N. Polansky, C. DeSaix, and S. Sharlin, *Child Neglect* (Child Welfare League of America, 1972), N. Polansky and D. Polansky, *Profile of Neglect* (Department of Health, Education, and Welfare, 1976), and "Standards of Neglect," in *Selected Reading in Child Neglect* (Department of Health, Education, and Welfare, Office of Human Development, 1980).

12 Incest and Other Forms of Sexual Abuse

C. Henry Kempe

Sexual abuse is defined as the involvement of dependent, developmentally immature children and adolescents in sexual activities that they do not fully comprehend, to which they are unable to give informed consent, or that violate the social taboos of family roles.

Sexual abuse includes pedophilia (an adult's preference for or addiction to sexual contact with children), all forms of incest, and rape. Sexual exploitation is another term frequently used. Indeed, these children are "exploited," because sexual abuse robs the children and adolescents of their developmentally determined control over their own bodies. They are further robbed of their own preference, with increasing maturity, for sexual partners on an equal basis. This is so whether the child has to deal with a single overt, and perhaps violent, act, often committed by a stranger, or with incestuous acts often continued over many years. These latter may be carried out under actual or threatened violence or may be nonviolent or even tender, insidious, collusive, and secretive.

Scientific studies of incidence are even more rare in the field of sexual abuse than in the field of physical abuse. Data collection has been impaired by what has been euphemistically referred to as a "family affair." In discovered acts of pedophilia, such as occur in fondling or exhibitionism, the child complains to his parents, the police are involved, and an incidence report is made. The same holds true of child rape. In these situations, incidence data are at least minimally correct. As far as the child is concerned, family and professional support for the victim are strong, and criminal conviction rates are relatively high. Physicians are often informed early, and they participate in the diagnosis and even the early treatment of victims. In instances of nonviolent pedophilia, particularly a single act involving a stranger, simple reassurance of the child and more massive reassurance of the parents is often all that is required. Forcible sexual abuse and

C. Henry Kempe, M.D., is with the Department of Pediatrics, University of Colorado School of Medicine, Denver.

child rape involving strangers, aside from the management of the sexual injuries, often call for long-term supportive therapy to each member of the family.

The discovery of incest, on the other hand, finds the family and the community reacting in a rather different way. If reports are made by the victim, they rarely result in family support, nor do they often result in successful criminal prosecution. Moreover, children who are regularly cared for by their physicians may be involved in incest for many years without their doctors having known it. Incest makes physicians and everyone else very uncomfortable.

Some doctors, including many psychiatrists, routinely ascribe specific complaints of incest, and even incestuous pregnancy, to adolescent fantasy. Often physicians will not even think of the diagnosis of incest in making an assessment of an emotionally disturbed child or adolescent of either sex. Histories of incest so very commonly come to the attention of psychiatrists, marriage counselors, mental health clinics, the police, and the courts ten or fifteen years after the events that the failure to consider the diagnosis earlier is somewhat surprising. Most of the youngsters we now see are under the care of a physician in private practice or a clinic setting. They represent the children of professionals, white- and blue-collar workers, as well as of the poor, in a way that reflects a cross section of our community. The same is true for racial distribution. Contrary to published reports from welfare departments and the police, there is no race, in Denver, over-represented in sexual abuse, provided one considers all levels of society who come to our attention.

Underreporting is massive. There is, in incest, often long-standing active or passive family collusion and support. Disruption of the ongoing sex relationships are generally resisted, understandably so. Disclosure may well result in public retribution with the firm expectation of total family disruption, unemployment, and economic disaster, loss of family and friends for the victim, and likely incarceration for the perpetrator, at least until bail is posted. There is also the public shame of failure for each person involved in their own roles as father, mother, and child, with resulting further loss of self-esteem by all.

Cases of sexual abuse for the United States are now estimated to be 100,000 per year. Only a small fraction of instances of sexual abuse are reported at the time of occurrence, as opposed to coming to light ten or more years later. In seven months, the Denver General Hospital alone saw eighty-nine cases. We are increasingly seeing younger and younger children who require urgent care. The group of children up to five years old has increased in recent years, from five to twenty-five percent of the total, while the incidence during the latency age period, from five to ten, has remained stable at twenty-five percent. Between 1967 and 1972, the number of sexually abused children rose ten-fold in our hospital.

Incest is usually hidden for years and only comes to public attention around a dramatic change in the family situation, such as adolescent rebellion or delinquent acts, pregnancy, venereal disease, a variety of psychiatric illnesses, or something as trivial as a sudden family quarrel. One-half of our adolescent runaway girls were involved in sexual abuse, and many of them experienced physical abuse as well.

The Management of Patients Who Have Been Sexually Assaulted

Assessment and management can be divided into three areas: first, the treatment of physical and psychological trauma; second, the collection and processing of evidence; and third, the prevention of pregnancy and venereal disease. These three areas are interrelated and the problems will probably be managed best if the professional or team has been trained to deal with these patients. If the examining physician generates a good written record, collects appropriate evidence, and ensures that the chain of evidence cannot be challenged in courts, he may help convict a criminal.

Definitions

1. *Rape:* sexual intercourse without consent of the victim
2. *Statutory rape:* sexual intercourse under the age of consent (in Colorado, age 16)—consent is irrelevant
3. *Molestation:* noncoital sexual contact with a child under the age of consent

Initial Evaluation

The patient may be brought in by a member of a local law enforcement jurisdiction, may come in of his or her own volition, or may be brought in by a parent. If the alleged attack has not been reported, the patient, parent, or physician should report it to the appropriate authority.

Evaluation should be both supportive and documentary. Important as it is to obtain a clear account of the circumstances of the alleged assault, it is equally important to traumatize patients no further by forcing them to relive the experience immediately. If it is very painful for them to do so, detailed history-taking can often be deferred.

The same philosophy applies to the physical examination, although here it is mandatory, for legal and medical reasons, to obtain certain data and provide specified treatment.

The Treatment of Physical and Psychological Trauma

The initial professional evaluation should best be done by the individual who will be responsible for the entire care of the patient. Ideally, the same individual should do the general evaluation, as well as assess the pelvic findings. A female physician or a male physician-female nurse team are best when the patient is female. In the case of a child, the presence of a supportive relative should be routine. If the patient describes symptoms that could be related to sexual abuse, the story must sometimes be drawn out by a question such as, "I have a feeling that maybe somebody has done something to your body that has frightened you. Why don't you tell me about it?" In addition to facts regarding date, time, place, and person, the physician must document sites of sexual abuse (e.g., mouth, breasts, genitals, anus). Also, information on menstrual history, whether or not force was involved, the patient's concept of intercourse, and whether or not ejaculation took place should be sought and recorded. In children under age six, this information will usually have to come from the mother. Older children can be encouraged to tell their own story in a private setting. The patient should not be disrobed until after being seen by the professional evaluator. The patient's emotional status should be evaluated and noted in the medical record. A general evaluation of the patient is then carried out, and any signs of trauma should be noted in the record. Serious consideration must be given to involving the psychiatric service in caring for the patient. Any victim of an assault has some emotional trauma which may require both acute and chronic follow-up care. In cases of rape, the female patient should be advised that a volunteer rape counselor is available to assist her and will be called if she wishes.

The Collection of Evidence

If a crime has been committed (that is not for the medical team to determine), the ability of the prosecutor to make a charge and obtain a conviction may depend upon the evidence collected and whether or not it is admissible in court.

Processing of Evidence

A search should be made of the patient's clothing for any material that may be needed as evidence. The clothing may also be considered evidence. Follow instructions in the "Rape Kit" on the type of evidence to be collected and the method of collecting evidence.

The "Rape Kit" consists of a sealed manila envelope with the necessary material for collecting evidence. The envelope should have the name of the examiner, date, and statement of time the seal was broken. All specimens should be collected, labeled with the initials of the examiner, and placed in the manila envelope. The examiner's name or initials should be retained as part of the evidence. Individual pieces of clothing should be placed in clean paper bags, sealed, and initialed by the examiner. All evidence should be placed in a cardboard box and sealed with tape. The name or initials of the examiner should be written over the seal. The box shouls be given to the investigating police officer.

The following data should be recorded, lab tests obtained, and treatment initiated, if the pelvic examination is completed:

1. Record evidence of torn clothing, bruises, blood, or semen stains on body or undergarments, and evidence of vaginal or anal penetration
2. Save any garments which are torn or stained, label such with name of patient and date, and give to on-call hospital administrator or the police officer for secure storage in cases of criminal prosecution of alleged rapists
3. Depending on history, obtain specimens of vagina, rectum, and pharynx for:
   a. cultures for gonorrhea (to be obtained by examining physician)
   b. wet prep to examine for motile sperm (to be performed by examining physician) from vagina and/or rectum
4. Obtain a serological test for syphillis (VDRL) and urine for pregnancy test in pubertal females

Prevention of Venereal Disease

After appropriate cultures and VDRL are obtained, the patient should be treated with the following:

1. Procaine penicillin, 100,000 u/kg IM (child); 4.8 mu IM (adolescent), in two sites
2. Probenecid 20 mg/kg by mouth (child) or 1 g by mouth (adolescent)
3. If patient is an adolescent *and allergic to penicillin,* give spectinomycin 2 gm IM for an adolescent male and 4 g IM for an adolescent female
4. If the patient is a child, as defined by a chronological age of less than thirteen years, and without evidence of pubertal changes (Tanner 1), *and allergic to penicillin,* use tetracycline 50 mg/kg x 10 days p.o. Under age eight this drug causes bone and teeth effects. Use spectinomycin 0.5 gm IM once for younger children.

The Prevention of Pregnancy

While it is extremely unlikely that the victim of an assault will become pregnant (there were no pregnancies in over 3,000 raped patients in a Minnesota study), it is accepted practice to use diethylstilbestrol (DES), 25 mgm bid x 5 d, for pubertal females whose menarche has occurred.[1]

1. Do not give DES to a girl who has become pregnant prior to the rape. A history of sexual activity and birth control since the last menstrual period is necessary before giving DES. If there is a possibility of an ongoing pregnancy, DES should not be given. A pregnancy test may be required.
2. DES should not be given to a girl who has been raped during a time of active menstrual flow.

Hospitalization is most desirable for a brief stay (see below).

Contact should be initiated with protective services if historical circumstances warrant it. This would include any patient under the age of eighteen years who has been sexually assaulted and/or raped by a family or household member. A minor attacked by a stranger does not require a protective service report.

Evaluation of a Suspect

Occasionally a suspect may be brought in by the same police authority bringing in the alleged victim, with the request that evidence be collected. *An examination and collection of evidence should be done only if a telephone court order is given.* Clothing, hair (pubic and head), and blood for typing should be collected in the same manner as from the alleged victim. The evidence should be processed in the same manner as for the alleged victim. A separate encounter form should be prepared for the suspect.

Male Victims of Sexual Assault

Male victims who have been sexually assaulted most frequently have been subject to fellatio (oral genital contact) or sodomy (anal genital contact). While physical injuries are uncommon, the victim may have resisted and may require emergency care for trauma. The experience is, of course, a most frightening one, especially to children and young adults, since it is generally totally unexpected and often accompanied by serious threats. In following the procedures outlined

---

1. If DES is used, a pregnancy test must be performed in six weeks. If the victim is pregnant, an abortion, post-DES treatment, must be considered. This recommendation is based upon the possible long-term complications of DES therapy to the unborn female fetus.

above, attention should be paid to culturing the pharynx and rectum, depending on history, and initiating preventive treatment for gonorrhea. Contrary to public opinion, sexual assault of males is generally perpetrated by heterosexual, rather than by homosexual, offenders. Many of the victims have concerns that the aggressive act will somehow make them follow homosexual practices in the future, and they require reassurance. Certain victims do not want to have their parents know of the event, and the doctor must exercise utmost discretion, providing needed physical and psychological care in a confidential manner. It is, however, far preferable to involve the parents and the police to facilitate a stop to any continuing assault, so often feared by the victim. Rarely is this kind of assault an isolated event for the offender, and there may be literally hundreds of victims in a metropolitan area from a single perpetrator.

Hospital Admission

Hospitalization has four purposes:

1. to distance the patient both physically and interpersonally from the scene of the rape
2. to provide him/her temporarily with a protective, nurturing surrounding
3. to enable an evaluation of the patient's ability to cope with the effects of the trauma
4. to enable the patient to establish relationships with individuals who will provide follow-up care

The physician is responsible, during the admission, for providing immediate support and for being sure that the patient leaves the hospital with a supportive social network, including a follow-up appointment. Also, the physician must be sure that the sexual assault chart (see appendix) is completed and accompanies patient's chart.

Young children may be handled by a suitable alternative follow-up mechanism. An example would be follow-up by one physician, psychiatrist, or social worker skilled in such therapy.

Nature of Sexual Abuse

Pedophilia

Pedophilia often involves nonviolent sexual contact by an adult with a child. It may consist of genital fondling, orogenital contact, or genital viewing.

Mister T. A brilliant young lawyer, father of two, on several occasions engaged in genital fondling of six- to eight-year-old girls, friends of his daughter, while they were in his house for social visits to his children. The neighbors contacted us with a view to stopping this behavior, while at the same time wanting to prevent the ruin of this attractive family and wanting to get psychiatric help for the patient. Much of this compassionate and nonpunitive view was the result of their affection for the patient's young wife, whom they greatly liked. They insisted, however, that the family promptly leave the neighborhood. The patient moved to a distant city where he entered psychotherapy and has had a long-term cure of his addictive pedophilia. His professional and family life has remained stable.

Doctor A. A fifty-three-year-old physician was accused of fondling the genitalia of his preadolescent boy patients. A hearing before the Medical Board confirmed that he regularly measured the penis of all his boy patients, much as he would examine their weight. His defense was that measurements like these are part of comprehensive care, but the Board held that the procedure was not routine anywhere, except when the specific medical problem concerned the size of the penis, as is the case in some hormonal disorders. He voluntarily resigned his license to practice, but refused offers to help.

Violent Molestation and Rape

While all sexual exploitation of minors is illegal, society is particularly concerned with retribution to prevent repetition when rape or other forcible molestation occurs. Hymenal rupture or vaginal entry need not occur to have the rape statute apply. Frequently, vaginal tears and/or sperm evidence or a type-specific gonococcal infection can be the ultimate proof. Often perineal masturbatory action leads to emission of sperm outside the vagina, on the skin or the anus. Many molestors experience premature ejaculation and many others are impotent. We find sperm less than fifty percent of the time. Orogenital molestation may leave no evidence, except the child's story. This is to be believed! Children do not fabricate stories of detailed sexual activities unless they have witnessed them. They have, indeed, been eyewitnesses to their abuse. And, it should be repeated, adult offenders against boys are almost uniformly heterosexual and not homosexual.

> *John S.* A twenty-three-year-old unemployed boyfriend of a divorced, middleclass mother was babysitting for her two daughters, aged six and fourteen. He first began to sexually assault the fourteen-year-old girl and raped her, despite her efforts to resist by screaming, hitting, and biting. While she ran for help to distant neighbors, he raped the six-year-old and fled. When captured, he told the police that he had had two beers and remembered nothing of the events. The children both required hospital care for emotional, as well as medical, reasons. The six-year-old had a one-inch vaginal tear which was repaired. The older child had a hymenal tear and bruises. Both had semen in the vagina and both required antibiotics to prevent gonorrhea with which the attacker was afflicted. Loving and supportive nursing and, later, psychiatric care was given to both victims, who seemed to view the event as "a bad accident." The mother had reason to feel guilt, since she had known of her friend's inability to handle any alcohol without becoming violent. The psychiatric diagnosis of the perpetrator had a violent sociopathic personality, not likely to change at any time. He remains in prison for an indeterminate sentence. He is a model prisoner to date and will eventually gain parole.

Incest

Father-daughter incest accounts for approximately three-fourths of cases of incest, while mother-son, father-son, mother-daughter, and brother-sister account for the remaining one-fourth. Our belief is that incest is increasing in the United States in recent years. This may be due to the great changes in family life, such as increasing divorce rates, birth control, abortion, and an increasingly more tolerant view of sexual acts between blood-related household members coming from divorced or previously separated homes. This is particularly true as it affects brother-sister incest between step-children who are living as a family but are not related. Cultural attitudes in regard to this latter group of adolescents seem to be rapidly changing to a less-concerned stance.

Father-daughter incest tends to be nonviolent, but, in the preadolescent and early adolescent, the coexisting relationship between physical abuse and sexual exploitation is often striking, though rarely discussed. Adolescent girls, who are acting out, are often suffering from both physical and sexual abuse. Men with psychopathic personalities and indiscriminate sexuality and who view children as objects are often violent. Some nonviolent incest is seen in pedophiles who seduce both their own and other children.

Most fathers involved incestuously with their daughters are introvert personalities who tend to be socially isolated and have an intrafamily orientation. Many are gradually sliding towards incestuous behavior with the extra push given, often, by a wife who either abets or arranges situations likely to make privacy between father and daughter easier. She may, for example, arrange her work schedule to take her away from home in the evenings and tell her daughter to "take care of Dad" or to "settle him down." A very loving and dependent relationship between father and daughter might result, first in acceptable degrees of caressing, and later in increasingly intimate forms of physical contact. The silent agreement between husband, wife, and daughter is a triad in which each plays a role. This relationship is generally free of marked guilt or anger unless a crisis occurs. One of these crises is public discovery. A daughter is, of course, robbed of her developmentally appropriate sexuality and is often caught in the dilemma of forcing an end to a now embarrassing affair in order to live a more usual life with her peers. In time she loses the family security which, she believes, her compliance has assured her, her mother, and her siblings. This is a terrible burden to carry for these immature women. Relief may not come until the girl leaves home and tries to build a new life apart.

Writers have, for the most part, stressed unduly the seductive nature of young girls involved sexually with fathers or brothers, as opposed to the more important participatory role played by mothers. Our experience suggests that all young girls tend to experiment in seduction a little bit, and safely, within the family. This normal behavior does not explain incest, which is not initiated by the child, but by the adult male with the mother's complicity. Stories by mothers that they "could not be more surprised" can generally be discounted. We have simply not seen an innocent mother in long-standing incest. Still, the mother escapes the punishment her husband will likely suffer.

Why do mothers play such an important role in incest between father and daughter? Often, a very dependent mother is frantic to hold her mate to the family for her needs and the financial and emotional support he provides. The sexual role of the daughter is seen as one way of providing him a younger, more attractive bond within the family than the mother can provide. This is especially true if the mother is frigid, rejected sexually, or is herself promiscuous. Rationalizations for incest abound and must be dealt with in a direct manner. The "I only wanted to show her how to do it" excuse is often talked about, but rarely encountered. The same is true for "he just needs a lot of sex." The vast majority of incestuous situations find people literally caught up in a life style from which they find no easy way out and in which discovery must, at all cost, be avoided. In order to preserve the family, even after discovery has occurred, admission is often followed by denial. The immediate family tends to condemn the victim, if she is the cause of discovery. She is then bereft of all supports and has few choices, Far more often, of course, there is no immediate discovery, and only after some time does the victim's emotional need bring about an understanding of her difficult past.

Joan. An eighteen-year-old college student with many minor physical complaints and episodes of insomnia told freely of her anger at her father who, upon her leaving for college, was having an incestuous affair with her younger sister. She maintained that she was not jealous but rather wanted him stopped; as she said, "I have given my best years to him to keep us together."

Her father, a judge, had begun to sexually stimulate her at bedtime when she was twelve and commenced regular intercourse when she was fourteen, often six times each week. Her mother knew of these acts from the start, encouraged them subtly at first and then simply would not discuss the matter. Whenever Joan threatened to leave home, she was told by her mother that she kept the family together and that her two younger siblings would be forever grateful to her for preventing a divorce. The patient had had no boy friends, and few girl friends, and was anxious until she left home to "have things stay the same." On discussion, the mother appeared scared and angry, denied that her husband, "an important man in this community," could be so ungratefully accused, asked that he not be contacted, and disowned her daughter as a chronic liar. Her father admitted, in medical confidence, that his daughter was totally correct and that he was, indeed, involved with his second daughter. He entered therapy with an experienced psychiatrist and has, over the past years, been able to desist from all incestuous relationships. His eldest daughter will not see him, and he accepts this. He blames himself fully, is puzzled by his craving for love from his daughters, and finally blames himself for his wife's frigidity. He is chronically depressed, on medication, and a borderline alcoholic, in recent years.

Leslie. A fourteen-year-old girl was seen on request by the police because her sixteen-year-old brother when arrested as a runaway had told them that his father had an incestuous relationship with his sister. The parents denied the allegation and, initially, so did the patient. But on the second interview, she began to discuss her fears about pregnancy and venereal diseases; after reassurance, she described her four-year involvement with her father, a thirty-five-year-old computer programmer with a college education. Leslie was placed in foster care but repeatedly ran away. The father lost his job when he was first arrested and, while awaiting trial, attempted suicide. Subsequently, criminal prosecution was deferred, and both parents received joint treatment around their failing marriage and their relationship with their children. Both children elected to remain in different foster homes until graduation from high school. Criminal charges were eventually dropped and employment resumed. The marriage was stabilized. Both children are in college and seem to be on friendly terms with their parents, though never remaining overnight.

Betty. A fourteen-year-old girl was seen with a history of marked weight loss and a diagnosis of anorexia nervosa. Her sixteen-year-old brother was extremely worried about her deteriorating condition and confessed to his father that he had carried on an incestuous relationship with her for four months and that he wondered if he had caused her illness. The patient recovered fairly promptly, and both youngsters received individual therapy. Each requested a therapist of their own sex. Both remained in the household and have done well.

Annette. A sixteen-year-old girl was seen because an unrelated household member, a boy of sixteen, had been treated for gonorrhea and listed her as one of his sexual contacts. She was asymptomatic, though her vaginal and rectal cultures were also positive, but for a distinctly *different* strain of the gonococcus organism. The remaining members of the large family were then cultured. Her stepfather was positive for gonorrhea with the same strain as were her fourteen-year-old and eighteen-year-old stepsisters. Throat cultures for the gonococcus were positive in her nine-year-old step-brother, as was his anal culture. Her mother was culture negative as were two cousins and another, younger stepbrother. While not admitted, the stepfather, who had a criminal record, more than likely infected, by sodomy and vaginal intercourse, Annette, who was not clinically ill and had not been infected by the boy of sixteen. The stepfather had further, through fellatio with his stepson and by sodomy infected the nine-year-old boy and caused vaginal infections in the fourteen- and eighteen-year-old girls. The Health Department administered curative doses of penicillin to all members found to be infected. The initial report of the sixteen-year-old boy was not related to the family infection. Neither did he have any part in the family's chaotic incestuous life.

Age of Those Involved

In pedophilia or child rape the age of the child tends to be between two years and early adolescence, while incestuous relationships may begin at the toddler age and continue into adult life. The median age for incestuous behavior in recent years has been between nine and ten years of age, well within the age group routinely seen by pediatricians, including those pediatricians who avoid the care of the adolescent patient.

Society tends to be more concerned with fathers sleeping with or genitally manipulating daughters or sons than mothers doing the same to sons, or very rarely, daughters. This double standard is most likely based on the belief that the sheltering mother is simply prolonging, perhaps unusually but not criminally, her previous nurturing role. Mothers who regularly sleep with, and sexually stimulate, their school-age boys, referring to them as "lovers," are very seriously mentally ill, as are their children. Intervention is very difficult because mothers are given an enormous leeway in their actions, while fathers and brothers are not.

Violent acts of sexual exploitation or rape are usually perpetrated by males under the age of thirty, while father-daughter incest tends to involve middle-aged men between thirty and fifty. Other incestuous relationships, as between siblings, can vary from mutual genital play in early childhood and school age to attempted, and sometimes successful, intercourse in adolescence. A grandson-grandmother relationship involved a boy, aged eighteen, and an exceedingly wealthy woman, aged seventy. At least three physicians dealt with the emotional problems of her delinquent grandson, but none of them was prepared to accept the diagnosis readily admitted to by both patients. Girls involved with fathers or stepfathers are often the first daughters during preadolescence or early adolescence.

Subtle Clinical Findings

Where the parents report a single episode caused either by a stranger, a babysitter, a relative, or a household member other than the parents, the diagnosis is made before the physician is ever involved. More troubling are those subtle manifestations which are not ordinarily thought to relate to the diagnosis and which call forth the pediatrician's best diagnostic acumen.

The child under six years of age. Aggressive sexual abuse, that is any forced sexual act, often results in fear states and night terrors, clinging behavior, and often some form of developmental regression. Here the pediatrician's role is to provide reassurance and, in a stable family setting, the parents, rather than the child, need repeated help. From time to time, the event will have to be worked through the child once again. This can often be done in a nursery school setting and again in adolescence, with active support from loving teachers and parents. The presence of gonorrhea in preschool children should be considered a prime indicator of possible sexual abuse. A full evaluation is required (see Sgroi 1977).

The school-age child. In the school-age child subtle clinical manifestations may include sudden onset of anxiety, fear, depression, insomina, conversion hysteria, sudden, massive weight loss or weight gain, sudden school failure, truancy, or running away.

The adolescent. Serious rebellion, particularly against the mother, is often the presenting finding. The physician who is aware of a specific estrangement between the mother and daughter should consider this diagnosis. Girls involved in incest may eventually forgive their fathers, but rarely will they forgive their mothers, who failed to protect them. Another related subtle finding is that the daughter has been assigned virtually all the functions ordinarily taken by a mother within the family group, by looking after the house and siblings. Parents have reassigned to the daughter the mother's function both in the kitchen and in bed. These youngsters must be given an opportunity to share their secret with a sympathetic person.

As children get older, we often find more serious delinquency, including massive loss of self-esteem ("I am a whore," "I am a slut"). Prostitution may accompany chronic depression, social isolation, increasing rebellion, and running away. There are, on the other hand, some very compliant and patient youngsters who carry the load of the family on their frail shoulders, at great sacrifice to their personal development and happiness.

These adolescents are in a terrible dilemma. They are in no way assured of ready help from anyone, but they risk losing their family and feeling guilty and responsible for bringing it harm if they share their secret. Youngsters may only come to the attention of the health care system or the law through pregnancy, prostitution, venereal disease, drug abuse, or antisocial behavior.

Treatment of Sexual Abuse

In certain treatable situations, there is a chance, particularly when dealing with nonviolent sexual exploitation, to use the criminal justice system to initiate treatment. Filing of criminal charges and a deferred prosecution to await evaluation and treatment is possible provided certain requirements are met:

1. Exploitation must assuredly be stopped and for good.
2. Law enforcement must be involved in planning and agreeing to the treatment plan proposed.

3. The prosecuting attorney and the court must feel that the criminal system is not being thwarted, but that rehabilitation is an acceptable course. The plan is under the supervision of the probation department or law enforcement.
4. Treatment failure, including nonparticipation in an agreed-to program should bring the criminal process back at once. While the bypass process is recognized as an option for the legal system, it is strictly limited to effecting a better outcome than can be foreseen by incarceration following conviction.

Pedophilia may never be cured, but it is often possible to bring all illegal acts under control (see patient 1, "Mister T"). There is not certain cure for the aggressive sociopath who engages in violent sexual molestation and rape. Until we know what to do for such people, we must be certain that they never have control of a child who is always defenseless in their presence. Moreover, they are often a menace to all, and, in many cases, nothing but prison is left for their management, if they are convicted, or psychiatric commitment to a secure setting, if they are judged to be legally insane and unable to stand trial.

The treatment of incest, on the other hand, is far more likely to be successful, resulting in the three desired goals:

1. Stopping of the incest
2. Providing individual and, later, group treatment to the victim and each parent
3. Healing the wounds of the victim, who may then grow up as a whole person with the ability to enjoy normal sexuality

In our experience, reuniting families has not been possible after incest has been stopped through either placing the child or removing the offender, unless two conditions have been met:

1. The mother must be willing and able to protect her children.
2. Both parents must admit to the problem, have a shared desire to remedy it, while at the same time either improving their failing marriage or divorcing.

Treatment ultimately can be judged to be successful, many years later, when the child has grown up and made a success of life.

Projective psychological tests reveal that incest victims see themselves as defenseless, worthless, guilty, at risk, and threatened from all sides, particularly from their fathers and mothers, who would be expected to be their protectors. Improvement in these projective tests is a useful aid to progress of therapy. Projective tests may well differentiate the angry, wrongful accused from the rather depressed incest victim. They are most useful in early family evaluation when the facts of incest are denied. Questions to be answered early on are: Can the child forgive the perpetrators, and can the child regain self-confidence, self-esteem and have a better self image?

In Santa Clara, California, ninety percent of the marriages were saved, ninety-five percent of the incestuous daughters returned home, and there was no recidivism in families receiving a minimum of ten hours of treatment. Regrettably, we have been far less successful! In our experience, between twenty and thirty percent of the families have not been reunited, no matter what we have attempted, and we have come to feel that they should not be. Reuniting families should not be the overriding goal. Rather, the best interests of the child should be served. Many adolescent girls do far better as emancipated minors, in group homes, or in carefully selected foster home settings. Once they have broken the bond of incest, society must not condemn these victims to an additional sentence, but rather provide loving protection, through the discovery of supportive adults who are better models than their fathers and mothers can ever hope to be. They will, of course, still have ties of affection to their family, eventually seeing them in a more mature, compassionate way. In any case, the dependency upon their family is over somewhat sooner than it would normally be.

Much less is known about the treatment of mother-son or homosexual incest between a parent and child. These general observations can be made: the gray area of incest in the preadolescent cuddly behavior is not without danger because, even quite early, children receive cues about their roles vis-à-vis each parent. Sexual models can be normal or highly distorted. After adolescence has begun, guilt, fear of discovery, low self-esteem, isolation, all extract a frightful toll. And these problems must always be faced sooner or later; later is generally very much worse.

Prognosis of Sexual Exploitation

A one-time, stranger-caused sexual molestation, particularly of a nonviolent kind, as in a pedophilic encounter, appears to cause less harm to normal children living with secure and reassuring parents. The event still needs to be talked out and explained at an age-appropriate level and all questions answered. Fierce admonishment such as "Don't let anyone touch you there" or "All men are beasts" are, at best, not helpful.

All violent molestation and rape need a great deal of care. For many reasons, joint hospital stay with mother may help for a brief time to take care of injuries, such as a vaginal tear. This will also serve to satisfy the legal requirements for gathering criminal evidence in a sympathetic and supportive setting. At examination, the presence of mother, sister, or grandmother is essential. At times, children are so afraid of anyone and in such pain that an almost equally violent form of rape occurs in our emergency rooms on the part of inexperienced and rough physicians and nurses. Far better is it to take lots of time, doing all that is needed under gentle guidance and faces, familiar and beloved by the frightened child. At times, a brief anesthetic is necessary to allow for examination and taking of samples while the child is asleep. In any event, a terrifying experience must not be made even worse. When physical examination is requested in other than violent abuse, for example to determine the status of the hymen in order to "clear things up," we have usually resisted the request.

Incest occurring and stopped *before* adolescence appears to cause less havoc than incest continuing into or throughout adolescence. The principal and very major exception to this is the not uncommon situation where a very young girl is trained to be a sexual object, giving and receiving sexual pleasures as one way of gaining approval. These little girls make each contact with any adult male an overt sexual event, with genital stimulation sought, supplied, and rewarded. They have, in short, been trained for the profession of prostitution and no other. Nothing is more pathetic and more difficult to manage. These little girls are far too knowing and provocative to be acceptable in most foster or adoptive homes. They are socially disabled until cared for, at length, by a mature and understanding couple. Fathers involved in this form of early "training incest" are not curable, in our experience. The outlook for the children also is not good, even with treatment, because of the timing and prolonged imprinting nature of this exploitation.

Incest *during* adolescence is especially traumatic because of the heightened awareness of the adolescent and the active involvement in identity formation and peer group standards. Frigidity, conversion hysteria, promiscuity, phobias, suicide attempts, and psychotic behavior are some of the chronic disabilities one sees in some women who experienced adolescent incest without receiving help. Only in retrospect are these histories obtained many years later—the affair never coming to the attention of anyone outside the family.

But boys do much worse than girls! Both mother-son (or grandmother-grandson) and father-son incest leave a boy with such severe emotional insult that normal emotional growth is blocked. They tend to be severely restricted and may be unable to handle any stress without becoming frankly psychotic. Incest, then, is ruinous for the male, while it can be overcome with or without help by many girls. In general, professionals agreed that early and humane working through of the complex emotions and distorted relationships is curative, while late discovery after serious symptoms have appeared is far less satisfactory. The focus of treatment is the family, but sometimes there really is no functional family, and the youngster must try to build an independent life with sympathetic help from others.

In contemporary society many explain the taboos against incest as having no function other than the prevention of close inbreeding, with its deleterious genetic effects. Where this explanation has been accepted as sufficient, the results have been a weakening of the sanctions that, in the past, protected the relation between adults and children, including stepchildren. Mead felt that where the more broadly based sanctioning system has broken down, the household may become the setting for cross-generational reciprocal seduction and exploitation, rather than fulfilling its historic role of protecting the immature and permitting the safe development of the strong affectional ties in a context where sexual relationships within the family are limited to spouses. Home must be a safe place!

We believe that *all* sexual exploitation is harmful and that it must be stopped.

Appendix

SEXUAL ASSAULT DATA SHEET

Name _____
Date of Birth _____
Address _____
_____
Telephone _____
Hospital No. _____

I. History
   A. Presentation to ER
      1. Date seen_____
      2. Time seen_____A.M._____P.M.
      3. Mode of entry: Police_____Friend_____Family_____Self-referral_____
         Other_____
   B. Date of assault_____
   C. Time of assault_____A.M._____P.M.
   D. Circumstances of assault _____
      _____
      _____
      _____
   E. Menarche_____
   F. Last menstrual period_____
   G. Prior sexual intercourse: Yes_____No_____ Since LMP: Yes_____No_____
   H. Method of birth control _____
   I. Patient currently taking medication: Yes_____No_____Specify_____
   J. Are there preexisting medical problems: Yes_____No_____
      Specify_____
II. Physical Examination
   A. General appearance_____
   B. T._____ P._____ B.P._____ Wt._____ Tanner Stage_____
   C. Evidence of trauma_____
      _____
      _____
   D. Description of clothing: Torn_____Blood stained_____
              Semen stained_____
              Normal _____
   E. Description of perineum: Normal_____Laceration_____
              Ecchymosis_____Bleeding _____
              Hematoma_____Rectum _____
   F. Pelvic examination: Vagina_____
              Uterus_____
              Adenexae_____

Material for this appendix has been drawn from protocols employed at the University of Colorado Health Sciences Center and Montefiore Hospital, Bronx, New York.

III. Laboratory Evaluation

	Done	Not Done	Results
A. Wet prep of vaginal fluid for motile sperm			
B. Culture of vagina for the gonococcus			
Culture of anus for the gonococcus			
Culture of pharynx for the gonococcus			
C. VDRL			
D. Pregnancy test (urine to serology lab)			

IV. Therapy
    A. Penicillin with dose
    B. Probenecid with dose
    C. Spectinomycin with dose
    D. Tetracycline with dose
    E. Diethylstilbestrol with dose
    F. Other with dose
V. Name of consultant contacted
VI. Disposition from ER: Hospital_____Home_____
VII. Reported to Children's Protective Service: Date_____Time_____
    Person contacted
VIII. Reported to police: Date_____Time_____
    Officer contacted
    Officer responded
IX. List of clothing obtained
X. Name of administrator clothing given to

      Physician signature
    Consultant signature (if any)

Suggested Readings

Barry, M. J., and Johnson, A. The Incest Barrier. *Psychoanalytic Quarterly,* 27:485–500, 1958.

Berry, G. W. Incest: Some Clinical Variations on a Classical Theme. *Journal of the American Academy of Psychoanalysis,* 3:151–61, 1975.

Brant, R., and Tankenoff, S. *Manual on Sexual Abuse and Misuse of Children* (Boston, Mass.: New England Resource Center for Protective Services).

Cormier, B. M., Kennedy, M., and Sangowicz, J. Psychodynamics of Father-Daughter Incest. *Journal of the Canadian Psychiatric Association,* 66:46–74, 1969.

Finch, S. M. Adult Seduction of the Child: Effects on the Child. *Medical Aspects of Sexuality,* 170–85, March 1973.

Gebhard, P. H., Gagnon, J. H., Pomeroy, W. B., and Christenson, C. V. *Sex Offenders: An Analysis of Types* (New York: Harper and Row, 1965).

Giarretto, H. Humanistic Treatment of Father-Daughter Incest. In *Child Abuse and Neglect: The Family and the Community,* eds. Kempe, C. H. and Helfer, R. E. (Cambridge, Mass.: Ballinger, 1976).

Kaplan, S. L., and Posnanski, E. Child Psychiatric Patients Who Share a Bed with a Parent. *Journal of the American Academy of Child Psychiatry,* 13:344–56, 1974.

Kaufman, I., Peck, A. L., and Tagiuri, C. K. The Family Constellation and Overt Incestuous Relations between Father and Daughter. *American Journal of Orthopsychiatry,* 24:266–77, 1954.

Langsley, D. G., Schwartz, M. N., and Fairbairn, R. H. Father-Son Incest, Rape in Childhood. *Journal of the American Academy of Child Psychiatry,* 8:606–19, 1969.

Meiselman, K. C. *Incest* (San Francisco: Jossey-Bass Publishers, 1978).

Mele-Sernovitz, S. Parental Sexual Abuse of Children: The Law as a Therapeutic Tool for Families. *Legal Representation of the Maltreated Child,* ed. Bross, D. C. (Denver, Colo.: National Association of Counsel for Children, 1979).

Nakashima, I., and Zakus, G. Incest, Review and Clinical Experience. *Pediatrics,* 60:696–701, 1977.

Parsons, T. The Incest Taboo in Relation to Social Structure and the Socialization of the Child. *British Journal of Sociology,* 2:101–17, 1954.

Raphling, D. L., Carpenter, B. L., and Davis, A. Incest, a Geneaological Study. *Archives of General Psychiatry,* 16:505–11, 1967.

Rasmussesn, A. The Importance of Sexual Attacks on Children Less than 14 Years of Age for the Development of Mental Disease and Character Anomalies. *Acta Psychiatric Neurology,* 9:351, 1934.

Reifen, D. Protection of Children Involved in Sexual Offenses: A New Method of Investigation in Israel. *Journal of Criminal Law, Criminology, and Political Science,* 49:222, 1958.

Rosenfeld, A. A., Nadelson, C. C., Krieger, M., and Backman, J. H. Incest and Sexual Abuse of Children. *Journal of American Academy of Pediatrics,* 16:327–39, 1977.

Schechter, M. D., and Roberg, L. Sexual Exploitation. In *Child Abuse and Neglect: The Family and the Community,* eds. Kempe, C. H. and Helfer, R. E. (Cambridge, Mass.: Ballinger, 1976).

Sgroi, S. M. Sexual Molestation of Children: The Last Frontier in Child Abuse. *Children Today,* May–June 1975.

Sgroi, Suzanne M. Kids With Clap: Gonorrhea as an Indicator of Child Sexual Assault. *Victimology,* 11:251–67, 1977.

Summit, R., and Kryso, J. Sexual Abuse of Children: A Clinical Spectrum. *American Journal of Orthopsychiatry,* 48:237–51, 1978.

13 Radiologic and Special Diagnostic Procedures

Frederic N. Silverman

A reexamination of the contributions of diagnostic radiology to the history of the concept of "the battered child" and a survey of its current role in diagnosis indicate the reliability of the features described in prior editions of this book, as well as areas where extension of conventional modalities of radiologic examination are useful. To this knowledge must be added new information derived from technics currently available which had not been tested previously. Although certain names customarily have been linked to the initial descriptions and popularization of the condition, the overwhelming support provided by scores of physicians caring for children must be acknowledged as securing the validity of roentgenographic examination in its various applications to the recognition of physical abuse of children.

The concept of "the battered child" and the developments in the elucidation of the condition are intimately related to the field of diagnostic radiology. Although the syndrome was recognized in practically all its manifestations and implications by Tardieu (1) in 1860, it was not until Caffey's radiologic observations eighty-six years later (2) that any significant impact upon medical, social, and legal activities was generated. Caffey's observations subsequently were confirmed and their significance supported by papers published primarily in radiologic journals and particularly by pediatric radiologists. The evidence of the radiologic signs of bone injury and repair provided the solid medical basis on which was built the social, legal, and psychopathologic aspects of the problem. The recognition of extraskeletal radiologic features has further emphasized the role of diagnostic radiology.

The patients described by West (3) in 1888 have been considered to represent some of the early instances of the battered child syndrome, but, because his report antedated the discovery of the X-ray in 1895, the diagnosis cannot be sustantiated. Although great advances were made in most areas of X-ray diagnosis immediately following the introduction of X-rays, the radiographic features of injuries to bones

Frederic N. Silverman, M.D., is professor emeritus of clinical radiology and clinical pediatrics, Stanford University Medical Center.

of infants and their repair were not described in any detail until almost forty years later. At that time the bizarre radiographic manifestations of recovery from epiphyseal separation during breech extraction were reported by Snedecor and his associates (4). About the same time, articles on unusual periosteal reactions in children which were primarily to be differentiated from those of congenital syphilis began to make their appearance (5–7). Caffey (2), in 1946, was the first to call attention to multiple fractures of the long bones, of unknown origin, which accompanied a significant number of cases of subdural hematoma. Accepting the view of Ingraham and Heyl (8) that the subdural hematomas were traumatic, Caffey suggested a traumatic origin for these injuries also.

Ample support for Caffey's observations on bone lesions with subdural hematomas followed quickly (9–14). Bakwin (15, 16) reported several cases of unusual traumatic reactions in bones, among which was at least one battered child. In 1953, Silverman (17), following Caffey's lead, insisted on a traumatic basis for injuries of the type now known to occur in the battered child in a presentation of three cases of the condition without subdural hematomas. Astley (18) believed that there was a primary metaphyseal fragility of bone in affected children, but this concept was discarded by Woolley and Evans in 1955 (19). These authors reviewed material seen over an eight-year period with radiographic findings suggesting injury, with or without a history of trauma. They concluded that the radiographic manifestations of injury and its repair were identical whether a history of injury was or was not obtained and that the skeletal lesions "having the appearance of fracture—regardless of history for injury or the presence or absence of intracranial bleeding—are due to undesirable vectors of force." They also emphasized that the environmental factors surrounding the infants with the radiographic changes frequently included grossly undesirable and hazardous circumstances. Numerous subsequent reports have reinforced Wooley and Evans's conclusions, which have now become generally accepted (20–30). The radiologic aspects were dealt with in detail by Caffey in 1957 (31) and by Silverman in 1972 (32). A comprehensive report has been published in French by Rabouille (33). Cameron and Rae, in 1975 (34), included a comprehensive section on radiological diagnosis in their *Atlas of the Battered Child Syndrome*. In 1978, Ellison *et al.* demonstrated computed tomography to be a useful body imaging technic in known or suspected abuse (35).

Radiologic Manifestations

Radiologic examination has two main functions in relation to the battered child. It serves as a case-finding tool, and subsequently it can be used as a guide to the management of known cases.

In many instances the diagnostic bone lesions are noted incidental to examination for conditions other than known injury; more frequently, the examination is undertaken because of a history of injury, and then lesions are found which are much more extensive than would have been anticipated from the history or which demonstrate some of the features indicating that the present episode was only one

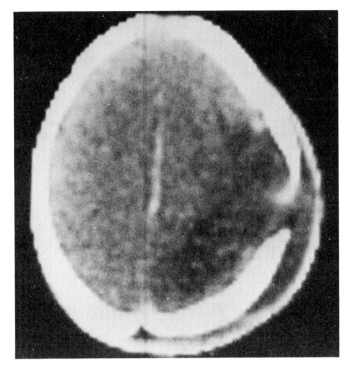

Figure 13.1

Computed tomographic image of skull of an abused child, illustrating not only the skull fracture and subgaleal fluid accumulation, but also the diminished density of a large area of the right hemisphere, presumably secondary to infarction from damage to the right middle cerebral artery. Subarachnoid bleeding adjacent to the falx is also demonstrated. (Courtesy of Dr. William H. Marshall)

of several. In instances in which the battered child syndrome is suspected, the presence of radiographic changes in the skeleton can support the diagnosis; the absence of radiologic changes does not necessarily exclude it. In well-established cases of the battered child, follow-up examinations to evaluate the nature and extent of healing are helpful just as they are in the follow-up examinations of any other type of fracture.

The radiologic signs of skeletal injury and response to it are similar whether there is a history of injury or not. Gross fractures are obvious, and their characteristics are available in standard radiologic and orthopedic texts. The outstanding features of skeletal injuries in the battered child syndrome are predilection for the metaphyses, exaggerated periosteal reaction, and multiplicity of lesions, and differing stages of healing and repair of the multiple lesions. Cameron and Rae emphasize rib injuries and particularly the combination of any common fracture with metaphyseal or rib fractures (34).

Lesions of the metaphyses are a common observation and the most typical. Their frequency is probably related to the fact that most of the injuries are incurred not so much by direct blows as by vigorous handling, as in shaking the child. The extremities are the "handles" for the mishandling. The rigidity of bone and the elasticity of ligamentous connections apparently can withstand the twisting-pulling forces of a heavy adult hand on a young extremity. In the infant under one year of age, who is the most frequent recipient of this type of maltreatment, epiphyseal separation takes place at the relatively weak cartilage-shaft junction. This may be a gross displacement, easy to recognize, a minor irregularity in the line of radiolucent cartilage between epiphyseal ossification center and shaft with slight widening (fig. 13.2) or may be so slight as to be radiologically invisible.

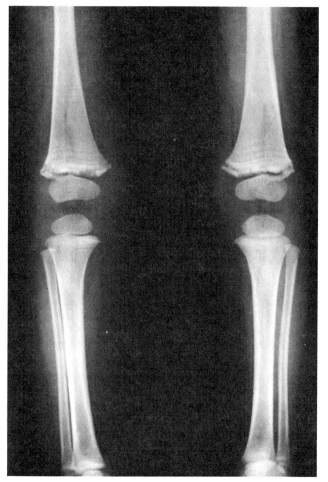

Figure 13.2

Metaphyseal fragmentation without epiphyseal displacement

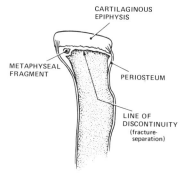

Figure 13.3

Diagram of Salter type II epiphyseal fracture (compare with fig. 13.6*b*).

The lesions correspond to what are currently known as epiphyseal fractures of the Salter types I and II (36) (see fig. 13.3). In areas where epiphyseal ossification centers are not present for their displacement to be noted, the features are initially more difficult to recognize (fig. 13.4). When a large arc of metaphyseal bone is displaced with its adjacent epiphysis, a so-called bucket-handle fracture can be observed (fig. 13.5).

In any event, the healing process of the epiphyseal separation involves a revascularization that is reflected by subepiphyseal (metaphyseal) demineralization and that can be detected radiologically approximately two weeks after an injury. If there has been no immobilization and further injury has occurred from ordinary activity, let alone further maltreatment, the destructive features are exaggerated. Rarely, epiphyseal injury is of a degree that leads to deformity and shortening.

The periosteum of young infants is relatively loosely attached to the bone in comparison with that of adults and is easily separated from it by direct physical force or by subperiosteal hemorrhage consequent to injury. In its new position, the periosteum produces new bone so that a calcified envelope (involucrum) surrounds the denuded portion of the bone (fig. 13.6). The periosteum has its strongest attachment to the epiphyseal line; as a result, most of the periosteum tends to remain attached to it even in gross epiphyseal separations. It is this

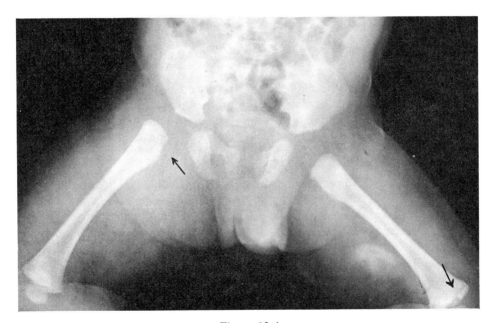

Figure 13.4

Traumatic epiphyseal separation of the right femoral head one week after vigorous pull on child's legs. Note soft tissue swelling of right thigh owing to hemorrhage. Displacement would be more obvious if ossification center for femoral head were present. Note also metaphyseal fracture at distal end of left femur.

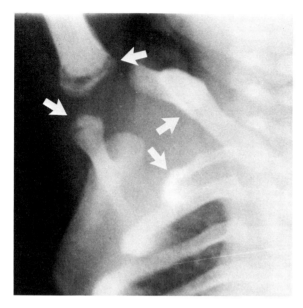

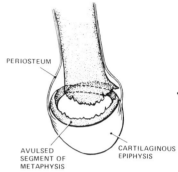

PERIOSTEUM

AVULSED
SEGMENT OF
METAPHYSIS

CARTILAGINOUS
EPIPHYSIS

Figure 13.5a

Figure 13.5b

"Bucket handle" fracture of proximal end of humerus. Same patient as in fig. 13.9. Arrows point to contemporaneous fracture of acromion process of scapula and to older, healing fractures of the clavicle and first rib.

Diagram of fracture of humerus in fig. 13.5*a*.

feature in children that permits the newly formed bone to align itself with the displaced epiphysis, and the end result of production of new bone and resorption of old bone generally is complete reconstitution. In the interval the abundant subperiosteal new bone formation may develop an appearance suggestive of osteogenic malignancy (37). Subperiosteal ossification may be delayed if there is associated infection.

The initially elevated periosteum and its underlying blood is radiolucent. Within two to three weeks following the injury, calcium is deposited on its undersurface, which becomes radiologically visible (fig. 13.7). If additional injury has taken place or if the initial injury was sufficient to tear the periosteum, calcifying callus may extend beyond the confines of the periosteum and develop gross irregular margins (fig. 13.8). Once the union of the fractured components of the bone has been accomplished, whether by fibrous or bony union, the periosteum responds to the usual stresses and strains, and the bone is remodeled to its original form; late residuals may merely present unusually thick cortices. Careful inspection of the tubular bones of children with the battered child syndrome frequently demonstrates periosteal elevations of varying degrees in different bones (see fig. 13.6). This variation is testimony to the repetitive nature of the injuries to which the child's skeleton has been subjected. An injury of considerable age may be indicated by a relatively thick, dense cortex; a slightly younger injury may have

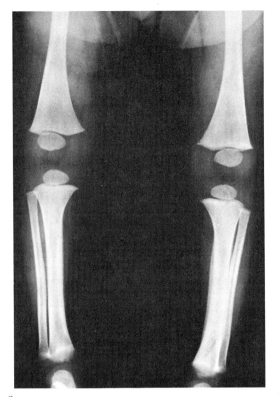

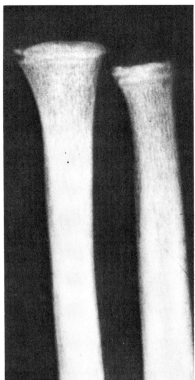

a

Figure 13.6

b

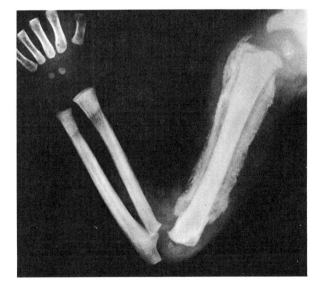

Lesions of different characters and ages attest to the repetition of injury. (*a*) The spiral
fracture in the left tibia is partially obscured by the well-
organized reparative sub-
periosteal bone production.
There is a suggestion of a recent metaphyseal fracture in
the medial aspect of the distal
metaphysis of the left femur.
(*b*) Same child, same day: recent metaphyseal injury in
radius at wrist; possible remote cortical thickening along
shaft of ulna. (*c*) Same child,
same day: recent metaphyseal
injury of radius at other wrist,
and remote fracture of distal
humerus with exaggerated
subperiosteal new bone formation. Note density of all
bones.

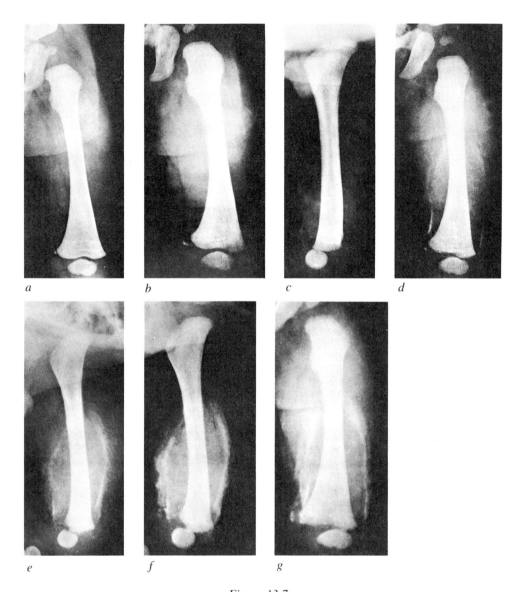

Figure 13.7

Sequence of calcification of elevated periosteum. (*a*) 4 days after unexplained swelling of knee: small chip fracture, medial end of femur at knee. (*b*) 9 days after onset, chip fracture separated from bone by subperiosteal hemorrhage. (*c*) Epiphyseal separation clearly shown by posterior displacement in later projection. (*d*) 14 days after onset: the elevated periosteum is producing new bone, and the extent of the subperiosteal hematoma becomes visible. (*e*) lateral projection, corresponding to fig. 13.7*d*. (*f*) 16 days after onset: subperiosteal ossification has increased. (*g*) the displaced epiphysis is lined up with the center of the periosteum (involucrum) rather than the shaft from which it was separated (sequestrum). (Courtesy of *J. Am. Med. Assoc.*)

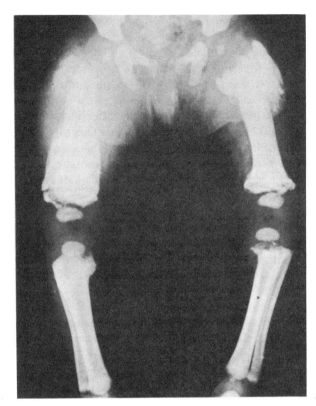

Figure 13.8

Extensive subperiosteal and metaphyseal lesions. The irregularity of the periosteal envelope suggests tears in this structure. (Courtesy of *Am. J. Roentgenol.*)

obvious subperiosteal new bone formation. More recent injuries may demonstrate massive calcium production with gross irregularities, and the most recent injury may show only soft tissue swelling without any bone production whatsoever. Periosteal new bone may occur in normal children and is said to be present in over forty percent of premature and full term babies (34), but it may be appropriate to consider the phenomenon unexplained, rather than conclusively normal.

Fractures of the shafts (diaphyses) of tubular bones do not preclude the diagnosis of child abuse even if they are less common in this context than are metaphyseal fractures. Transverse, rather than the usual oblique fractures, suggest response to a direct force, such as a blow with a hard object, if there is no predisposing local bone disease.

Although skeletal lesions predominate in the extremities, almost any bone can be affected. Rib fractures, recent or healing (fig. 13.9), are comparable to those seen after vigorous resuscitation activities. However, in combination with a more typical metaphyseal and/or periosteal lesion elsewhere, they strengthen the case for a diagnosis of battering. Cameron has called attention to fractures and their repair in the necks of the ribs (34); the features are more obvious in the posterior arcs (fig. 13.9).

Small tubular bones of the hands and feet may demonstrate reactions to repetitive beatings (38). Compression fractures of the vertebral bodies (fig. 13.10) or fractures of spinous processes may occur following forced flexion or extension injuries (39). Focal bone lesions resembling osteomyelitis or traumatic periostitis may result from medullary fat necrosis associated with pancreatitis that is secondary to child abuse (40).

It is important to emphasize that it is the healing phase of the fractures that is generally recognized radiographically. Therefore, an injury that is too recent to demonstrate reparative change (less than two weeks old) may be missed entirely. Radiographic evidence of soft tissue edema, of obliteration of deep and even superficial intermuscular fat septa, may provide a clue that the area in question should be reexamined after an appropriate interval.

The possibility of subdural hematoma must always be entertained when skeletal lesions are observed, and supportive evidence for subdural hematoma may be provided by the demonstration of separated cranial bones and widened sutures, other signs of increased intracranial pressure, or obvious fractures of the cranial bones themselves (fig. 13.11). Not infrequently, cranial fractures are not simple linear fractures, but are comminuted and resemble the multiple irregular fractures of an eggshell.

Only 3 of 246 children, aged five years or less, who had fallen out of bed at home or in hospital had identifiable skull fractures on X-ray films, and none had serious injury (41). Skull fractures, especially when multiple, invite suspicion of child abuse when an explanation on this basis is advanced.

Injuries to tissues other than bones are occasionally recognized radiographically. McCort and Vaudagna (42) reported the findings of infants with initially unexplained visceral trauma presenting as acute abdominal crisis. The most common visceral injury was rupture of the small bowel, but lacerations of the liver and a perforation of the stomach were also noted. Laceration of the lung and subpleural hemorrhage were thoracic findings. Both multiple visceral and skeletal lesions were found. The radiographic features were pneumoperitoneum (fig. 13.12), hemoperitoneum, and/or ileus. In one patient with a perforated duodenum there was considerable delay in seeking medical care and multiple peritoneal abscesses were found. Intramural hematoma of the duodenum (43, 44), well defined radiologically, occurs characteristically as a consequence of direct blows to the abdomen (fig. 13.13). Pancreatic pseudocysts also occur and can be diagnosed radiographically (45, 46). Ultrasound can be of great value in these circumstances, demonstrating the extent of the hematoma as well as its effect on contiguous structures. It is also helpful in following the course of the hematoma and to assist management (47). Other radiographically demonstrable manifesta-

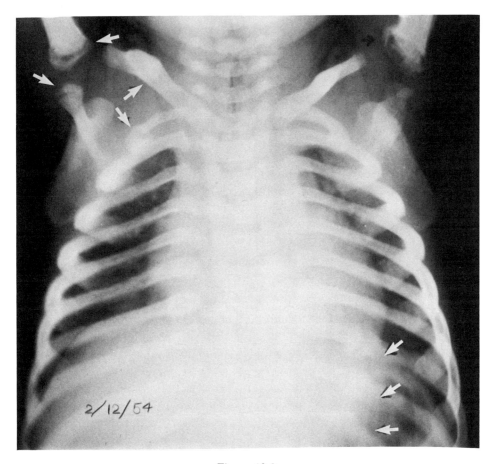

Figure 13.9a

Three month infant with recent "bucket handle" fractures of both humeri at the shoulders; old, healed fractures of the right clavicle and right first rib; and more recent healing fractures of the left 8th, 9th, and 10th ribs. Widening of the necks of several ribs (e.g., 7th right) may represent other healing fractures.

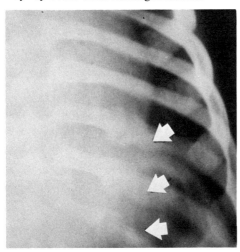

Figure 13.9b

Enlargement of the left rib fractures

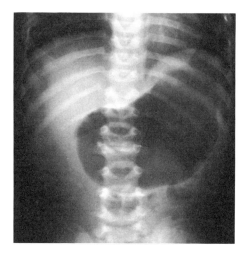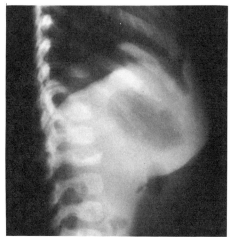

Figure 13.10

Compression fracture of vertebral body in 17-month boy with skull fracture, intramural hematoma of the duodenum, and multiple cutaneous bruises. Mother admitted punching baby in stomach.

tions have included esophageal stricture following the addition of caustic alkali to a beverage given a child (48) and bilateral dense nephrograms of long duration in children with possible renal injury as well as muscle injuries and myoglobinuria (49). Caffey (50) emphasizes the mental retardation sequels which he attributes to whiplash-shaking injuries to the brain and its vessels. Computed tomography (CT) of the head may help identify intracranial pathology in suspected cases. Signs of brain contusion have been reported with and without external evidence of head injury in children with known or suspected abuse (35). Contusions and hematomas, however, are not specific for child abuse of themselves, so that interpretations of CT scans must be very circumspect. Some have suggested that bone scanning of suspected battered children can demonstrate more abnormalities than conventional roentgenography, but further study will be necessary to establish its value and particularly its specificity (51).

Radiographic signs of retarded development and of malnutrition are commonly present in battered children, but they have no special diagnostic significance.

Differential Diagnosis

In general it can be said that the skeletal manifestations of the battered child syndrome are so characteristic as scarcely to be confused with anything else. Nevertheless, from time to time there is reluctance to accept the specificity of these lesions. It is felt that these manifestations of fracture are very uncommon in relation to the number of cases of fracture that are seen by radiologists in the course of their daily work. However, the circumstances of radiographic examina-

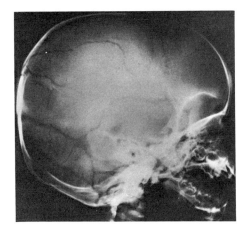

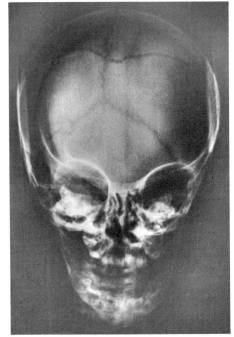

Figure 13.11

Extensive diastatic fractures of skull in child with typical extremity lesions. Subdural hematomas were present bilaterally.

tion in instances where there is known injury and those in which there is no history of injury are quite different. Given a known epiphyseal separation, the child is treated by mechanical reduction of the deformity and immobilization, usually in plaster. Films are taken initially after reduction has been accomplished and usually at a follow-up examination about six weeks after the injury, when healing is apt to be relatively complete. If, in the intervening time, another film is taken for any reason whatsoever and subperiosteal new bone formation or metaphyseal fragmentation is noted, it occasions no concern, because it is known that an injury has taken place and these are obviously the signs of repair. Such is the situation which obtains in the newborn infant (4, 52) who has been delivered by breech extraction, has an epiphyseal separation at the knee or hip, and two-and-one-half to three weeks later shows a large calcifying hematoma (fig. 13.14). The knowledge that breech extraction is an adequate explanation for skeletal trauma is generally sufficient to allay any apprehension concerning the radiographic findings. If observed incidental to examination under any other circumstances, the same findings might be alarming.

To test this interpretation, we reviewed the films of children who had had

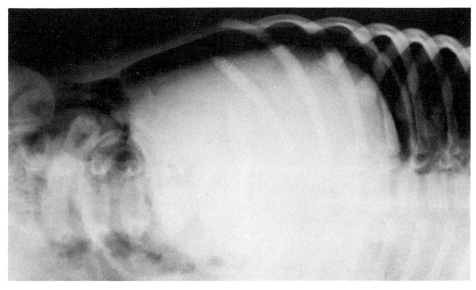

Figure 13.12a

Female, 21 months, with pneumoperitoneum shown in horizontal beam, left lateral decubitus film. Mother admitted beating on baby's body as she lay in her lap.

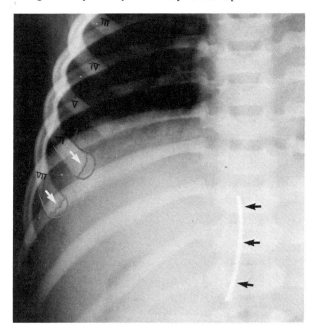

Figure 13.12b

Detail of right costochondral area and upper abdomen in antero-posterior supine film. The black arrows indicate the falciform ligament outlined by free intraperitoneal gas on both sides of the ligament. The white arrows indicate recent fractures of the anterior ends of the right 6th and 7th ribs.

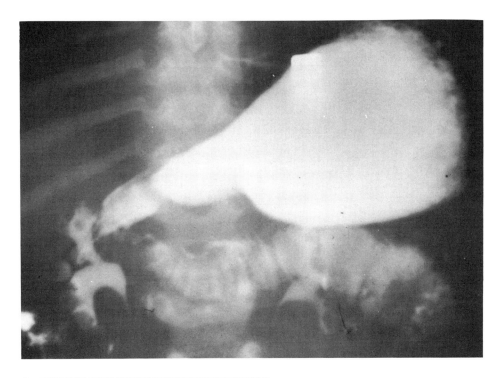

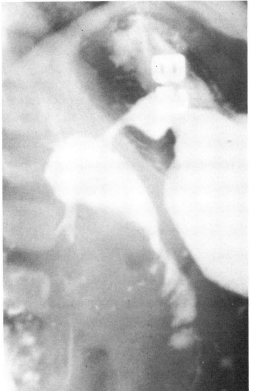

Figure 13.13

Intramural hematoma of duodenum demonstrated by barium meal in same patient as in fig. 13.10. Intravenous pyelogram had been done just before the barium examination because of microscopic hematuria. Hematoma surgically evacuated because of progressive obstruction.

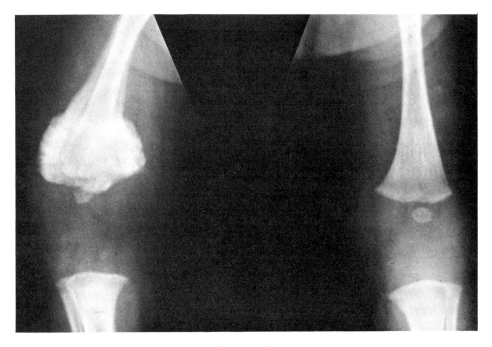

Figure 13.14

Exuberant calcified callus formation in 16-day-old infant who had unrecognized epiphyseal separation at knee as complication of breech extraction.

epiphyseal separations with known cause. Among the group there were several who had films obtained more than two and less than six weeks after the injury. Almost all of them demonstrated metaphyseal irregularities and subperiosteal new bone formation which were radiologically indistinguishable from those seen in the battered child (fig. 13.15). In addition, children with acute epiphyseal separations were brought back for reexamination between two and three weeks after the known injury. Metaphyseal rarefaction and subperiosteal new bone formation of the same nature were observed regularly (fig. 13.16), although none was so severe as occurs in the battered child who does not have the benefit of immediate and effective immobilization.

There are several conditions which occasionally are confused with the battered child syndrome:

Scurvy

Naturally, scurvy is one of the first to come to mind, particularly with older physicians who were familiar with the massive subperiosteal hematomas of healing scurvy in days gone by. None of the children with the battered child syndrome who have been studied thus far have had scurvy, although it is quite possible for the condition to develop in the environment in which some of these children grow

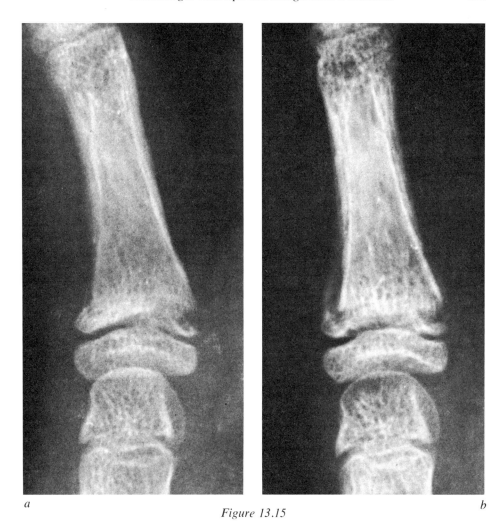

a   *b*

Figure 13.15

Epiphyseal separation in finger. (*a*) On day of injury. (*b*) 19 days later. In spite of known injury and attempt at immobilization, metaphyseal and subperiosteal reactions are present and are identical to those with unknown injury.

up. If present, scurvy would be expected to exaggerate the radiographic findings. Scurvy is a generalized disease, and although local exaggerations owing to trauma do occur, all of the bones show generalized osteoporosis. The cortices are thin, the trabecular architecture is ill defined, and the bones have a "ground glass" appearance. The epiphyseal ossification centers are sharply demarcated by the zones of provisional calcification to produce the so-called Wimberger's ring. At the ends of the shafts of all the long bones, and most prominent at the areas where growth is most rapid, there are comparable dense lines in the provisional zones of

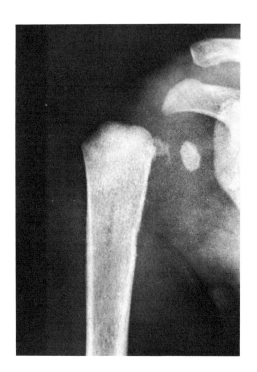

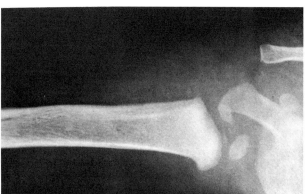

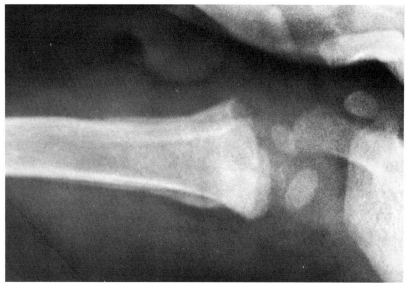

Figure 13.16

Serial films in known epiphyseal displacement. (*a*) At time of admission after motor car accident. (*b*) 24 hours later; reduction is complete in abduction. (*c*) 3 weeks after reduction, before application of new cast. The metaphysis, previously uninjured, now shows irregularity of mineralization, and a subperiosteal envelope of new bone cloaks the proximal end of the shaft. Had there been no immobilization, these reactions would have been more extensive.

calcification. The calcification of cartilage proceeds normally; the transformation to bone (ossification) is inhibited as the osteoblasts require adequate amounts of vitamin C for their function. The decreased osteoblastic activity is reflected by a low level of alkaline phosphatase in the blood. Rarefaction of bone underneath calcified cartilaginous plates and minute incomplete fractures produce the characteristic "corner sign" of active scurvy. With subperiosteal hematomas of scorbutic origin, other manifestations of the disease, such as capillary fragility and hematuria, might also be present. It is noteworthy that ecchymoses and hematuria may also occur as the result of soft tissue injuries in the battered child. It is pertinent also that scurvy is extremely rare before the age of six months, whereas many of the infants in the battered child syndrome appear with well-developed bone lesions prior to this age. In contradistinction to scurvy, exaggerated changes may be present at one end of the bone while the opposite end or the corresponding area of the uninjured bone of the opposite extremity shows no signs whatsoever of disease.

Syphilis

Syphilis in the congenital form can result in metaphyseal and periosteal lesions resembling those under discussion, especially during the first months of life. Although there is probably a traumatic factor in the distribution of the lesions of congenital syphilis, they do tend to be symmetrical, whereas those of the battered child are generally asymmetrical; and when osseous lesions as marked as those found in the battered child are produced by syphilis, other stigmata of the disease are usually present. In any questionable case serological tests for the disease are available.

Osteogenesis Imperfecta

Osteogenesis imperfecta is also a generalized disease, and signs of the disorder should be present in bones which are not involved in the immediate productive-destructive process. In the cranium, the characteristic mosaic rarefaction (multiple sutural bones) is present in the early years of life, and in children of an age to be considered as possible battered children, the fracture-like appearance of the calvarium, much more extensive than the eggshell fractures of the battered child, should be of considerable assistance in diagnosis. In osteogenesis imperfecta the fractures are more commonly of the shafts of the bones than of the metaphyses and epiphyses. Other signs of osteogenesis imperfecta are usually present in the form of blue sclerae and obvious skeletal deformities; usually, a family history of the condition can be elicited.

Infantile Cortical Hyperostosis

Infantile cortical hyperostosis is characterized by subperiosteal new bone formation, but there are no metaphyseal irregularities of defects. A healed lesion of the battered child might simulate a healing lesion of infantile cortical hyperostosis, but the clinical course can be helpful in differentiation. Involvement of the mandible occurs in approximately ninety-five percent of the children with this condition, but has been lacking thus far in the battered child in the absence of obvious mandibular fracture.

Osteoid Osteoma

Osteoid osteoma may produce swelling, pain, and periosteal reaction in a child. Metaphyseal lesions do not occur and the characteristic history of pain—worse at night, relieved by aspirin—is helpful if present. Osteoid osteoma is not a common disease in this age group. The presence of a sclerotic nidus in the center of the lesion is diagnostic.

Self-Sustained Injury

Fatigue fractures probably represent a variant of the battered child syndrome in which the child himself is responsible for the battering. More common in the metatarsal bones of adults, as in "march fractures," they do occur in the fibulas of children where they are present with pain and localized periosteal reaction (53). The remainder of the bone is normally mineralized, and there are no metaphyseal lesions.

The so-called little-league elbow (54) is another manifestation of repetitive injury where the vigorous mechanical activity of throwing a ball causes incomplete avulsions (epiphyseal separations) around the region of the elbow. The productive changes may simulate those of the battered child. The age of the patient is appreciably older than that of most battered children, the remainder of the bones is in excellent condition, and a history of trauma adequate to explain the reaction is usually elicited.

Others

Multiple fractures of bones are seen in severe rickets, hypophosphatasia, leukemia, metastatic neuroblastoma, and as sequels to osteomyelitis and septic arthritis. In general, additional signs of the primary disease and a history of prior disease adequate to explain the lesions can be elicited.

The one condition which imitates exactly the radiographic findings of the battered child is one which supports the hypothesis of a traumatic basis for the lesions—that is, neurogenic sensory deficit in relation to injury (55, 56). As has been mentioned previously, the attachment of the epiphysis to the shaft of the bone is one of the weak areas in the growing bones of the young child. If the young child also has a neurogenic sensory deficit such as that associated with paraplegia following spine injury or with meningomyelocele, seperations of epiphyses in the lower extremities as a consequence of physiotherapy, or other injury whose severity is not appreciated, can give rise to radiographic findings indistinguishable from those of the battered child (fig. 13.17).

Individuals afflicted with the so-called congenital indifference to pain (57) also fail to react normally to skeletal injuries; and metaphyseal rarefaction, excessive callus formation, and bone sclerosis develop as a consequence, just as in children with unrecognized trauma (fig. 13.18). The features of metaphyseal and physeal injuries in children with spina bifida and meningomyelocele are discussed in detail

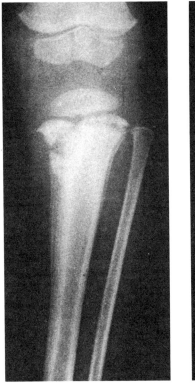 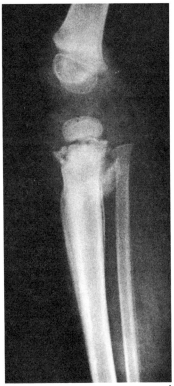

a *b*

Figure 13.17

Metaphyseal fragmentation and subperiosteal new bone formation in paraplegic child with sensory defect (meningomyelocele). Swelling noted after vigorous physiotherapy in attempt to correct contractures. (*a*) AP projection. (*b*) Lateral projection.

by Gyepes, Newburn, and Neuhauser (58). Confusion is unlikely to arise with respect to the self-mutilation lesions of the Riley-Day or the Lesch-Nyhan syndromes, but the conditions should at least enter the differential diagnosis. The question of superimposed child abuse would be difficult to resolve.

Some children who have the radiographic manifestations of the battered child and whose clinical histories support this diagnosis, have certain features in their skeletal X-rays which have led competent radiologists to ask whether there is not some underlying systemic disorder. All of the features of metaphyseal fractures, subperiosteal new bone formation, healing fractures in different stages of repair, and so on, can be found in these children, but they also demonstrate a "chalkiness" (see fig. 13.6) in the skeleton, which calls to mind the fragility of bones of children with osteopetrosis (Albers-Schönberg disease). These children do not demonstrate any of the hematologic disorders of osteopetrosis and usually lose the sclerosis of bone as they become older. None has been shown to have hypercal-

Figure 13.18

Metaphyseal irregularity, old cortical thickening, and growth disturbance in child with congenital indifference to pain. (Courtesy of *Radiology*.)

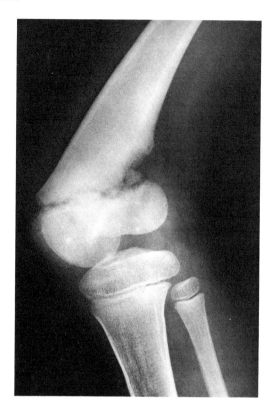

cemia, but this aspect has not been studied adequately. The sclerotic changes may merely reflect productive changes in bone owing to multiple repetitive trauma insufficient to cause obvious fractures or the usual reparative changes which are diagnostic of the battered child. This group will merit further study, but it is almost certain that, regardless of any contributing factors, they will have in common with all the other children an episode, or repetitive episodes, of physical abuse. Support for this interpretation has been expressed by DeSmet *et al.* (59).

Conclusion

The radiographic signs of the battered child are surprisingly specific. They speak for the child who is unable or unwilling to speak for himself and serve to alert the physician to a hazard of considerable magnitude which threatens the life and limbs as well as the emotional and intellectual potentialities of the child. Although they may reflect the time of the injury with considerable accuracy and permit extremely accurate deductions concerning the nature of the forces producing the injury, they provide no information whatsoever concerning the circumstances surrounding the injury or the motivation of the individuals responsible. The epiphyseal separation that results from grabbing a child by a limb to prevent a serious fall is indistinguishable from the epiphyseal separation incurred while the infant is being vigorously shaken or otherwise abused by an irate, distraught adult custodian. The recognition of the radiographic changes, however, does constitute a distinct indication to investigate the circumstances surrounding the injury. A simple survey examination has been suggested (60) which includes a single lateral skull film, antero-posterior films of the major long bones and of the hands and feet, and an antero-posterior film of the chest for ribs. Modifications of the examination are described.

References

1. Tardieu, A. 1860. Étude médico-légale sur les sévices et mauvais traitments exercés sur des enfants. *Ann. D. Hyg. Publ. et Méd. Lég.* 13:361–98.
2. Caffey, J. 1946. Multiple fractures in the long bones of infants suffering from chronic subdural hematoma. *Am. J. Roentgenol.* 56(2):163–73.
3. West, S. 1888. Acute periosteal swellings in several young infants of the same family, probably rickety in nature. *Brit. Med. J.* 1:856–57.
4. Snedecor, S. T., Knapp, R. E., and Wilson, H. B. 1935. Traumatic ossifying periostitis of the newborn. *Surg. Gynecol. Obstet.* 61:385–87.
5. Rose, C. B. 1936. Unusual periostitis in children. *Radiology* 27:131–37.
6. Caffey, J. 1939. Syphilis of the skeleton in early infancy: The nonspecificity of many of the roentgenographic changes. *Am. J. Roentgenol.* 42:637–55.
7. Epstein, B., and Klein, M. 1936. Luesähnliche Röntgenbefunde bei unspezifischen Skeletterkrankungen im Säuglingsalter. *Wien. Med. Wschr.* 86:750–53.
8. Ingraham, F. D., and Heyl, H. L. 1939. Subdural hematoma in infancy and childhood, *J. Am. Med. Assoc.* 112:198–204.
9. Lis, E. F., and Frauenberger, G. S. 1950. Multiple fractures associated with subdural hematoma in infancy. *Pediatrics* 6:890–92.
10. Smith, M. J. 1950. Subdural hematoma with multiple fractures. *Am. J. Roentgenol.* 63:342–44.
11. Meneghello, J., and Hasbun, J. 1951. Hematoma subdural y fractura de los huesos largos. *Rev. Chilena Pediat.* 22:80–83.
12. Marquezy, R.-A., Bach, Ch., and Blondeau, M. 1952. Hématome sous-dural et fractures multiples des os longs chez un nourrisson de 9 mois. *Arch. Franç. Pédiat.* 9:526–31.
13. Kugelmann, J. 1952. Uber symmetrische Spontanfrakturen unbekannter Genese beim Säugling. *Ann. Paediat. (Basel)* 178:177–81.
14. Marie, J., Apostolides, P., Salet, J., Eliachar, E., and Lyon, G. 1954.

Hématome sous-dural du nourrisson associé a des fractures des membres. *Ann. Pédiat. (Paris)* 30:1757–63.

15. Bakwin, H. 1952. Roentgenologic changes in the bones following trauma in infants. *J. Newark Beth Israel Hosp.* 3(1):17.

16. Bakwin, H. 1956. Multiple skeletal lesions in young children due to trauma. *J. Pediat.* 49:7–15.

17. Silverman, F. N. 1953. The roentgen manifestations of unrecognized skeletal trauma in infants. *Am. J. Roentgenol.* 69(3):413–26.

18. Astley, Roy. 1953. Multiple metaphyseal fractures in small children. *Brit. J. Radiol.* 26(311):577–83.

19. Woolley, P. V., Jr., and Evans, W. A., Jr. 1955. Significance of skeletal lesions in infants resembling those of traumatic origin. *J. Am Med. Assoc.* 158:539–43.

20. Jones, H. H., and Davis, J. H. 1957. Multiple traumatic lesions of the infant skeleton. *Stanford Med. Bull.* 15:259–73.

21. Weston, W. J. 1947. Metaphyseal fractures in infancy. *J. Bone Joint Surg.* 39(B):694–700.

22. Fisher, S. H. 1958. Skeletal manifestations of parent-induced trauma in infants and children. *Southern Med. J.* 51:956–60.

23. Friedman, M. S. 1958. Traumatic periostitis in infants and children. *J. Am. Med. Assoc.* 166:1840–45.

24. Marti, J., and Kaufmann, H. J. 1959. Multiple traumatische Knochenläsionen beim Säugling. *Deut. Med. Wochschr.* 84:984–88, 991, 992.

25. Miller, D. S. 1959. Fractures among children. I. Parental assault as causative agent. *Minn. Med.* 42:1209–13.

26. Altman, D. H., and Smith, R. L. 1960. Unrecognized trauma in infants and children. *J. Bone Joint Surg.* 42(A):407–13.

27. Gwinn, J. L., Lewin, K. W., and Peterson, H. G., Jr. 1961. Roentgenographic manifestations of unsuspected trauma in infancy. *J. Am. Med. Assoc.* 176:926–29.

28. Kempe, C. H., Silverman, F. N., Steele, B. F., Droegemueller, W., and Silver, H. K. 1962. The battered-child syndrome. *J. Am. Med. Assoc.* 181:17–24.

29. McHenry, T., Girdany, B. R., and Elmer, Elizabeth. 1963. Unsuspected trauma with multiple skeletal injuries during infancy and childhood. *Pediatrics* 31:903–8.

30. Teng, C. T., Singleton, E. B., and Daeschner, C. W., Jr. 1964. Inflicted skeletal injuries in young children. *Pediatrics Digest* (Sept.):53–66.

31. Caffey, J. 1957. Some traumatic lesions in growing bones other than fractures and dislocations: Clinical and radiological features. *Brit. J. Radiol.* 30:225–38.

32. Silverman, F. N. 1972. Unrecognized trauma in infants, the battered child syndrome, and the syndrome of Amboise Tardieu. Rigler Lecture. *Radiology* 104:337–53.

33. Rabouille, D. 1967. Les jeunes enfants victimes de sévices corporels. *These. Med. (Nancy).*

34. Cameron, J. M., and Rae, L. J. 1975. *Atlas of the Battered Child Syndrome* (London: Churchill Livingstone), pp. 20–50.

35. Ellison, P. H., Tsai, F. Y., and Largent, J. A. 1978. Computed tomography in child abuse and cerebral contusion. *Pediatrics* 62:151–54.

36. Salter, R. B., and Harris, W. R. 1963. Injuries involving the epiphyseal plate. *J. Bone Joint Surg.* 45(A):487–622.

37. Brailsford, J. F. 1948. Ossifying hematoma and other simple lesions mistaken for sarcomata. *Brit. J. Radiol.* 21:157–70.

38. Jaffe, A. C., and Lasser, D. H. 1977. Multiple metatarsal fractures in child abuse. *Pediatrics* 60:642–43.

39. Swischuk, L. E. 1969. Spine and spinal cord trauma in the battered child syndrome, *Radiology* 92:733–38.

40. Neuer, F., Roberts, F. F., and McCarthy, V. 1977. Osteolytic lesions following traumatic pancreatitis. *Am. J. Dis. Child.* 131:738–40.

41. Helfer, R. E., Slovis, T. L., and Black, M. 1977. Injuries resulting when small children fall out of bed. *Pediatrics* 60:533–35.

42. McCort, J., and Vaudagna, J. 1964. Visceral injuries in battered children. *Radiology* 82(3):424–28.

43. Bratu, M., Dower, J. C., Siegel, B., and Hozney, S. H. 1970. Jejunal hematoma, child abuse and Felson's sign. *Conn. Med.* 34:261–64.

44. Eisenstein, E. M., Delta, B. G., and Clifford, J. H. 1965. Jejunal hematoma: An unusual manifestation of the battered child syndrome. *Clin. Pediat.* 4:436–40.

45. Bongiovi, J. J., and Logosso, R. D. 1969. Pancreatic pseudocyst occurring in the battered child syndrome. *J. Ped. Surg.* 4:220–26.

46. Kim. T., and Jenkins, M. E. 1967. Pseudocyst of the pancreas as a manifestation of the battered-child syndrome. *Med. Ann. D. C.* 36:664–66.

47. Foley, L. C. 1979. Duodenal and pancreatic injuries following blunt trauma: Evaluation by ultrasound. Presented at Members' Miscellany, 22nd Annual Meeting, Society of Pediatric Radiology. Toronto, Canada, March.

48. Tucker, A. S., and Eloise, M. I. 1979. A spiked drink. Presented at Members' Miscellany, 22nd Annual Meeting, Society for Pediatric Radiology. Toronto, Canada, March.

49. Rosenberg, H. K. 1979. Prolonged, dense nephrograms in battered children. Presented at Members' Miscellany, Society for Pediatric Radiology. Toronto, Canada, March.

50. Caffey, J. 1972. On the theory and practice of shaking infants: Its potential residual effects of permanent brain damage and mental retardation. *Am. J. Dis. Child.* 124:161–69.

51. Fordham, E. W., and Ramachandran, P. C. 1974. Radionuclide scanning of osseous trauma. *Semin. Nucl. Med.* 4:411–29.

52. Snedecor, S. T., and Wilson, H. B. 1949. Some obstetrical injuries to the long bones. *J. Bone Joint Surg.* 31(A):378–84.

53. Griffiths, A. L. 1952. Fatigue fracture of the fibula in childhood. *Arch. Dis. Child.* 27:552–57.

54. Brogdon, B. G., and Crow, N. E. 1960. Little leaguer's elbow. *Am. J. Roentgenol.* 83:671–75.
55. Gillies, C. L., and Hartung, W. 1938. Fracture of the tibia in spina bifida vera: Report of two cases. *Radiology* 31:621–23.
56. Oehme, J. 1961. Periostale Reaktionen bei Myelomeningozele. *Fortschr. Gebiete Roentgenstrahlen Nuklearmed.* 94:82–85.
57. Gilden, J., and Silverman, F. N. 1959. Congenital insensitivity to pain: A neurologic syndrome with bizarre skeletal lesions. *Radiology* 72:176–89.
58. Gyepes, M. T., Newburn, D. H., and Neuhauser, E. B. D. 1965. Metaphyseal and physeal injuries in children with spina bifida and meningomyelocceles. *Am. J. Roentgenol.* 95:168–77.
59. DeSmet, A. A., Kuhns, L. R., Kaufman, R. A., and Holt, J. F. 1977. Bony sclerosis and the battered child. *Skeletal. Radiol.* 2:39–41.
60. Mindlin, R. L., and Palmer, W. M. 1978. When to obtain roentgenograms in suspected child abuse. Letter to the Editor. *Pediatrics* 61:330–31.

14 The Pathology of Child Abuse and Neglect

James T. Weston

Editors' Note

A book concerning the battered child would be incomplete without including the experiences of a forensic pathologist such as Dr. Weston. This material is presented for the specific purpose of assisting other pathologists and medical examiners in the recognition and handling of child abuse. We felt it important to include data dealing with neglect as well as abuse, since they are frequently interrelated.

We would advocate a consultation with a forensic pathologist in all cases of child abuse which present external lesions due to traumatic injury. His experience may prove efficacious in substantiating the extent of injury, possible etiology, and probable time at which these injuries were sustained.

Introduction

A discussion of the pathology of child abuse cannot limit itself to descriptions of the pathological findings in children who have been subjected to abuse at the hands of their parents or siblings but must be a consideration of the entire clinical pathological syndrome, including the fruits of preliminary investigation, medical examinations, and follow-up studies. It is appropriate to consider a contemporary period of a forensic pathologist's experience within several metropolitan areas such as Philadelphia and Salt Lake City and to consider in some detail all of the infant and childhood deaths which may have been the result of another person's conduct. Unfortunately, we do not have the information necessary to interpolate mortality studies of this type into morbidity statistics which accurately reflect the extent of the problem.

James T. Weston, M.D., is chief medical investigator, State of New Mexico, and professor of pathology, School of Medicine, University of New Mexico.

Procedure

Preliminary Investigation

The background of the individual conducting the preliminary investigations will vary considerably from one jurisdiction to the other. In most metropolitan areas it is the responsibility of detectives attached to the urban police force, frequently augmented by a social case worker who may have had previous contact with the family or who is regularly assigned to work with the agency responsible for the welfare of children. The pathologist himself may, on occasion, find it desirable to make an inspection of the premises and conduct much of the investigation through his own contacts. Irrespective of the background, training, and education of the individual concerned in this phase of the study, however, it is imperative that he have a thorough insight into the entire problem of childhood maltreatment. In many metropolitan areas this is accomplished by including formal presentation of the subject within the curriculum of the police academy and by annual lectures to social workers and nurses allied with any of the law enforcement agencies or health department. In addition to acquainting these persons with the ramifications of child abuse in general, any presentation should strongly emphasize the anticipated disparity between the presenting story of the parents and the circumstances as found on investigation and should endeavor to inculcate into the agency concerned a sense of responsibility for the welfare of the siblings, even in cases where only a suspicion of child maltreatment is present. This indoctrination should include specifically pointing out the social agency responsible for the welfare of the children and, specifically, how contact may be established.

If the death is reported while the body is still at the scene of demise, it is incumbent upon the investigator to immediately conduct a thorough inspection of the premises with the body in its terminal position. This examination should include a careful and objective notation of the appearance of the home, including its state of repair or disrepair, and its degree of cleanliness. This should reflect the apparent state of economic stability within the family and record the nature and quality of the furnishings, clothing, appliances, and food. Sanitary conditions should be carefully observed and similarly objectively reported. It is not sufficient in such an inspection to record a general statement such as, "The home is filthy." The report should reflect the presence or absence of trash on the floor, the state of operation of the toilet, drains, illumination, heating appliances, and the accessibility to lavatory facilities. A general description of the home should include its geographical location within the community and a general observation of the state of repair of adjoining residences, making comparison with the one in question. Evidence of insect or rodent infestation should be observed. If the home is not satisfactory for human habitation, the appropriate social agency should be notified immediately.

Careful observation of the deceased on the premises should note its location, apparent state of cleanliness, the apparent interval between death and the time originally observed by the investigator, including observation of temperature, rigor and livor mortis, and other postmortem changes. During this initial visit to the premises, the investigator should also take careful note of the condition of other siblings within the home, including their state of nutrition and general well-being. The report should reflect the apparent state of happiness of the children and the presence or absence of any indication of physical abuse. Although the initial visit is usually not the appropriate time to determine the nature of the family structure and its means of support, follow-up visits should attempt to learn the amount of support gained from public and private institutions and the manner in which these funds are expended. Investigation into the family structure should evaluate the amount of time spent in the home by members of the family, both immediate and remote. Objective evaluation of the intelligence and sincerity of the parents is also possible at the time of the initial investigation. When it seems necessary, other agencies should be involved immediately to provide for the safety and welfare of the siblings and, if necessary, the education and rehabilitation of the parents.

This initial examination of the home is much more valuable than one conducted either by surprise or appointment at a later date, since it provides an unrehearsed and unprepared representation of the home environment. It also allows the investigator and ultimately the pathologist to have first-hand acquaintance with the parents, guardians, and siblings of the deceased—all of which is sometimes of paramount importance in evaluating the pathological findings.

When the child dies after medical treatment, this inspection of the home scene should be conducted in a similar manner as soon as the appropriate authorities have been notified. Appropriate photographic documentation of all the details of the report, including the position of the body and the condition of the siblings, is desirable.

External Medical Examination

The postmortem examination should be conducted by a competent forensic pathologist who is aware of all of the implications of child abuse. The first stage of this examination should be a thorough inspection of the external appearance of the body, noting the clothing, its degree of cleanliness, and its state of repair. The description of the body of the deceased should include careful notation of all of the general external characteristics, including weight, height, the state of nutrition, and the approximate interval between death and time of examination. Special attention should be paid to the degree of preservation of the body, the degree of nutrition as reflected by the subcutaneous fatty depots, the degree of diaper rash, including the observation of secondary infection, scarring, or hypopigmentation.

This inspection should note the state of cleanliness of the body, with special attention to any obvious discrepancy between one facet of the infant's care and another—for example, severe diaper rash in conjunction with an extremely well-scrubbed, clean skin and new diaper and clean dress. Special note should be made of any evidence of insect infestation. This may consist of fresh bites or evidence of old bites with extensive scarring. External evidence of specific chronic conditions which might have precipitated the state of marasmus should be diligently searched for together with indications of specific avitaminoses or congenital malformations.

In children subjected to physical abuse, the external examination should carefully record every instance of injury, paying special attention to its size, shape, location, pattern, color, and degree of healing. Special note should be made of the more obscure portions of the body which are sometimes subjected to physical trauma with the intention of obscuring this from the other parent, physicians, or social workers. One such popular location is the soles of the feet. Incision through these areas into the underlying tissue will frequently reveal the presence of resorbing subcutaneous hemorrhage not obvious externally.

After inspection of the body as it was received, description, and appropriate photography—both before and after disrobing—the external surface should be thoroughly cleansed to allow further detailed examination in which subtle trauma may be ruled out. Such examination should note carefully any asymmetry of the head, trunk, or extremities. Following this, prior to commencement of the autopsy, roentgenographic examination of the entire skeleton should be conducted. If, on such examination, subtle changes are noted, re-X-raying following evisceration should be conducted and is often more revealing. When multiple fractures, not only of the long bones of the extremities but also of the skull and ribs, are evident, a roentgenologist may be of great assistance to the forensic pathologist in establishing the fact that there were temporally two or more distinct episodes of injury to the bony structure. An essential part of his practice is devoted to evaluation of bony repair following injury. This roentgenographic scan should not be limited to those children who expire from obvious external trauma, irrespective of the alleged cause, but should routinely be conducted on children who expire possibly as the result of neglect, with or without its obvious external manifestations. The roentgenologist's evaluation of the skeletal survey should include not only appraisal of the obvious healing of recent fractures, but should be of sufficient quality to evaluate the possibility of remote fractures wherein the healing is complete. Both the anatomic and the forensic pathologist often gain experience in evaluating their skill at aging wounds if these wounds, including the subcutaneous tissue as appropriate, are routinely biopsied, appropriately labeled, and subsequently examined microscopically to differentiate the interval between injury and death and determine whether or not there were two or more distinct episodes of trauma.

Following the initial documentation by photography of the child as it was received, with the clothing and all external injuries and matter intact, a careful search should be conducted on the exterior of the body for any type of trace evidence that may afford a clue to the actual assailant or the nature of the weapon utilized by the assailant. Such evidence should be carefully preserved, sealed, and submitted for appropriate laboratory examination in accordance with the well-established patterns for handling such trace evidence, maintaining the integrity by detailed records of the chain of possession for its handling.

Internal Medical Examination

Internal examination, as in any competent medicolegal examination, should include detailed objective observation and description of all of the injuries, paying special attention to subtle color changes and other evidences of healing which make possible the dating of traumatic lesions. This examination should also include a detailed observation, inspection, and description of all of the organ systems in the body. Competent medical photography should document all of the pathologic processes with accurate color representation without artifacts.

A detailed, complete microscopic examination should be conducted. In the neglected infants this serves to rule out underlying obscure chronic debilitating disease, which might lead to marasmus, and in the infants and children expiring as a result of injury, assists in evaluating the importance of any natural disease process. Microscopic examination of the injuries should be conducted to determine the degree of healing and to substantiate the repetitious nature of the injuries. To determine who is responsible for the injury when a child has been moved from one residence to another, the estimate of time of injury is also extremely important. Careful inspection of all of the contents of the gastrointestinal tract, with photographic documentation, is desirable.

In an effort to rule out exogenous poison as a contributing factor to the death of these children, appropriate qualitative and quantitative toxicological examinations should be conducted. A number of recent contributions to the literature point out the importance of this general toxicological examination in ruling out the introduction of exogenous poisons or overdoses of therapeutic agents as contributing factors to the death of these children. No contemporary discussion of child abuse could be considered complete without appraisal of the impact of the drug culture and illicit drug traffic upon the next group of teenagers. Children born out of legal wedlock in a transient communal domestic situation, common in the drug culture, are not only much more prone to suffer from any one of the patterns of childhood maltreatment described below but are often victims of habitual addiction or sustained overdoses of depressant drugs administered to keep the child docile and tranquilized. Several references within the literature clinically document the presence of permanent brain damage, probably as a result of transient hypoxia in the course of such administration (7). During the postmortem examination, the pathologist should carefully search for the subtle, nonspecific microscopic alterations within the central nervous system which may be the only clue to substantiate such previous injury. While these examinations are usually negative, reasonable doubt is rarely ruled out in a criminal court in large metropolitan areas without this positive documentation by the toxicologist. When infectious disease is suspected, postmortem bacteriology is equally desirable in establishing the etiologic agent causing or contributing to the death.

Follow-up

When the pathologist completes his preliminary investigation and examination, he should acquaint the investigating officer or social workers with all of the alternatives of his observations and institute a prompt and thorough follow-up investigation. This should include detailed interrogation into all of the circumstances leading up to and including the terminal episode and medical background such as the circumstances of the infant's birth, state of its maturity, the length of postpartum hospitalization, the degree of medical attendance sought, and the agencies at which this attendance was given. This should also include the nature of the family relationship, the degree of harmony within the family, and the nature of the interrelationships between the parents and other siblings.

Questioning should not be limited to the parents but should include private conferences with siblings capable of offering vocal testimony, with the understanding that, should the siblings present testimony which might be injurious to their general welfare if returned to the hands of the parents, they would be offered permanent shelter from this type of revenge. Thorough search of all social welfare agency records should be conducted to determine if there has been previous contact with the family. The neighbors should be interrogated with considered evaluation of their statements and the motives for their testimony. When the child is born out of wedlock, careful note should be made of the mother's behavior patterns, the source of income for the child's care, and the degree of responsibility of the father in providing for this care. Special attention should be paid to the temporal relationships in the physically injured children, with careful documentation of each interval of the child's terminal period of life, including detailed interrogation of the persons, including baby sitters and siblings who have been left in attendance with the children. Skilled interrogators working with law enforcement and social agencies should be employed whenever possible to gather this type of background information. Confrontation of the parents by the usual obvious disparity between the initial presenting story and the evidence as gathered by the medical investigator usually results in a slowly unfolding admission of misconduct. Repetitive interrogation of both parents may produce admissions which provoke hostility between themselves and prompt admission of further implication. Distant relatives, grandparents, and others not in the immediate family, who live within the home or are frequent visitors, may often volunteer information which will be invaluable in interrogation of the suspected assailant or assailants. An investigator thoroughly familiar with the usual reasons offered for mistreatment or abuse by the parents is in a much better position to conduct satisfactory interrogations. Any interrogation conducted by any investigator related to a law enforcement agency should be conducted after thoroughly acquainting his suspect with his legal rights and privileges in accordance with recent court decisions.

The Pathologist in Court

The pathologist, upon reaching an opinion concerning the cause and manner of death—the principal purpose for conducting exhaustive investigation and postmortem examination in harmony with the law enforcement agency—should be able to present his findings in court in such a conclusive manner as to prove his point beyond a reasonable doubt. Nonetheless, it should be remembered that these observations are merely opinions on the part of an expert witness, and he should have at his disposal all of the detailed records of observations and supporting examinations which were utilized in order to arrive at such an opinion. The rules of evidence preclude the pathologist's presenting any information except that which he derived by his own personal observations; hence, if he personally did not investigate the scene of the death, such evidence must be introduced by the investigator primarily responsible for such investigation and the gathering of this portion of the evidence.

The skilled forensic pathologist is usually the senior member of the team conducting the investigation, and, as such, he should see that all of the evidence gathered is well documented, appropriately identified, carefully kept in custody, and prepared not only for suitable presentation in court but possible examination by a designated expert for the defendant. The hospital pathologist often serves only as an adjunct to the investigating agency and, therefore, is frequently responsible only for the evidence derived from examination of the body. In either instance, however, it should be pointed out in pretrial conference and, if necessary, in the course of courtroom testimony, that neither individual, except on unusual occasions, is capable of arriving at a definitive conclusion concerning cause and manner or mode of death except by evaluation of the circumstances surrounding the death of the child in conjunction with the laboratory and pathologic findings.

When, in the course of the trial procedure, there is a determination to sequester the witnesses or restrict them from the courtroom when other witnesses are testifying, the prosecutor should take this into consideration and insure that his medical expert has all of the firsthand evidence which has been previously introduced in the course of the trial, to serve as an adjunct to his pathologic findings in establishing the mechanism of injury.

A pretrial conference sufficiently in advance of the trial should have gathered together all members of the team who have assisted in the investigation. The prosecuting attorney should thoroughly review all of his evidence at this time. When experts such as a neuropathologist or radiologist assist the forensic pathologist, their findings should be recorded independently within the body of medical evidence and these individuals should be called upon to review these findings with the prosecutor and subsequently present their testimony, if necessary. The medical expert should assist the prosecutor not only by enumerating the positive findings but by evaluating the degree of certainty of these opinions and indicating the controversial and salient negative findings from which argument in the courtroom may ensue. This type of testimony is especially important in childhood neglect cases wherein preexisting constitutional disease must be ruled out. The medical expert for the prosecution should anticipate that counsel for the defense may well request independent evaluation of all of his evidence, including photographic documentation of the external examination, radiographic examination, microscopic preparations, and other laboratory examinations to assist him in his evaluation of the opinions concluded by the state's medical expert.

It is also well for the physician to bear in mind that no matter how emotionally involved he may have been initially or during the course of his investigation, while in court it is wise not to play the role of an advocate but that of an amicus curiae.

It may be necessary to introduce photographic documentation in court to assist the physician in illustrating injuries or the general condition of the child to the jury. On occasion, such documentation may be ruled inflammatory or to be excluded from the eyes of the jury. However, increasingly, it has been the practice of the courts to allow introduction of such evidence when it is determined that word description, no matter how detailed, does not satisfactorily portray the condition of a child. All such photographs should be completely devoid of any artifact and should illustrate only those external findings present on the body prior to autopsy. When it is necessary to illustrate internal pathologic findings, this should be done with discretion and, again, without artifactual alterations produced by the pathologist. If it becomes necessary to illustrate more subtle changes such as histologic observations, these should be accompanied by appropriate illustrations of comparatively normal tissue or when dating injuries, by comparison with injuries of known duration. Numerous authoritative references are available (1).

Patterns of Maltreatment

Although the medical literature contains numerous references to patterns of child abuse written by clinicians, social workers, psychiatrists, and others in related fields, the references in the field of pathology are sparse. In classic presentations by Adelson (3, 4), the two characteristic patterns of childhood maltreatment—namely, neglect and abuse by physical injury—are well documented in a small group. Our studies in New Mexico have revealed similar findings (see Table 14.1).

TABLE 14.1   **Summary of Known and Suspected Childhood Maltreatment Deaths in New Mexico in Fiscal Years 1976–1977**

Age/Sex/Ethnic Group	Autopsy Results	Alleged Assailant (Age)	Comments
2 mo./M./Cau.	Craniocerebral inj. (fx's, contusions, intradural hemorrhage), old subdural and epidural hematomas	Unknown (sib. ?), both are natural parents	"Fell from couch" —14 mo. female sib. may have hit baby (premature—C-sect)
18 mo./M./Ind.	Separation of cranial sutures (trauma ?)	Unrelated adult male (20)	"Fell off bed"— Book fell off shelf onto child?
3 mo./F./Ind.	Malnutrition and dehydration (neglect)	Both natural parents	Parents are chronic alcoholics; acutely intoxicated at time of death— another sib. died 1 yr. before from exposure
2 yr., 10 mo./M./Cau. (Mexican nat.)	Ruptured hepatic artery and lacerated pancreas, skull fx, old fx's	Stepmother, not married to father, but with second child by him (17)	"Fell down stairs" —removed from home but returned 10 days prior to death
9 mo./M./Cau.	Bilat. subdural hematomas	Boyfriend, living with mother (38)	"Fell off bed"— 4 sibs. in foster home

Table 14.1 (continued)

Age/Sex/Ethnic Group	Autopsy Results	Alleged Assailant (Age)	Comments
			in another city for bad environment; *True Story* mag. open to article re smothering child next to body (same apt. house as previous case)
7 mo./F./Cau.	Subdural hematoma, internal chest and abdom. injuries, old brain contusions	Natural parents (21, 22)	"Fell off couch"
4 yr./M./Ind.	Cerebral injuries with bilateral sub-dural hematomata	Unrelated paramour of mother	"Fell from bed"
3 yr./M./Ind.	Lacerated mesenteric artery/old mesenteric trauma/old subdurals	Son of foster parents (approx. 18)	"Fell off tricycle" —in foster home for previous abuse
1 yr., 6 mo./M./Ind.	Duodenal perforation, bilat. subdurals, lacerations of penis, scrotum, anus (bite marks), abrasions from nails in piece of wood	Stepfather (23)	"Fell down stairs"— assailant illiterate with previous criminal record, on probation from another state, jealous of wife's attn. to child and not him
2 wk./F./Ind.	Malnutrition and dehydration (neglect)	Parents, unmarried (18, 17)	Parents alcoholics; baby being breast fed, left with friend (fed only water); term— small baby for date for baby
9 mo./F./Cau.	Consistent with suffocation	Mother's paramour (20)	"Put pillow over face to muffle crying"
4 yr., 6 mo./F./Cau.	Subdural hematoma, lacerations, liver, jejunum and rectum dilatation of anus	Stepfather (24)	Mother found child dead in A.M.; father drunk and unruly; left motel in night

Source: Reprinted from the Newsletter of the New Mexico Office of the Medical Investigator.

Childhood Neglect

A total of 24 infants, varying in age from one to thirteen months at the time of their deaths, died as a result of negligence on the part of the parent or parents responsible for providing adequate nutritional and environmental needs to the child during its helpless early months (see Table 14.2). Victims of this type of abuse represent an act of omission on the part of the parent, in contrast with those

TABLE 14.2   Age, Race, and Sex of Twenty-Four Victims of Parental Neglect

Age (months)	White		Non-White		
	Male	Female	Male	Female	Totals
0–3	1	0	5	1	7
3–6	3	2	2	1	8
6–12	1	1	5	1	8
13	0	0	1	0	1
Totals	5	3	13	3	24

suffering as the result of physical abuse or trauma. All but 1 of the infants were born with medical attendance, 16 were born at term gestation, and 8 prematurely. These premature infants were retained within the hospital for intervals of two to seven weeks to establish maturity acceptable for home care. All but 3 of the infants were dead when first seen by physicians, and with few exceptions, all presented variations of essentially the same picture.

External Examination

The appearance was one associated with gross dereliction of all of the amenities of food, clothing, and sanitation, which the helpless infant is unable to provide. Extremely soiled clothing, frequently caked or matted with vermin and feces, often had to be soaked from about the genitalia and lower extremities to avoid denudation of the skin during undressing. In two instances the clothing had obviously been changed during a period immediately prior to death or postmortem, with the underlying skin obviously having been extensively scrubbed. One of these was presented postmortem in its christening gown, beneath which the new undershirt still retained the price tag (Fig. 14.1). Infrequent changing of diapers and bedding was reflected by severe diaper rash frequently associated with complete denudation of the skin of the genitalia and perineum. In several cases this was of sufficiently long duration to result in loss of pigmentation in black infants (Fig. 14.2). In the more advanced cases, this process extended from the axilla to the soles of the feet and was associated with secondary infection and sepsis (Fig. 14.3). A tightly tied ligature around the penis, to prevent urination, resulted in early gangrene in one child.

The caked, encrusted dirt was removed only with considerable effort from the infants to reveal skin with virtually no turgor or palpable subcutaneous fat, hanging loosely over the bones of the face and extremities, while the abdomen was usually retracted and the ribs on the thorax unusually prominent. Absence of intraorbital fat resulted in marked depression of the eyes, which was associated with marked concavity of the cheeks. Infestation by insects, including ants, bees, and roaches, frequently resulted in extensive bites on the skin, many of which were secondarily infected. Many of these resulted in permanent scarring (Fig. 14.4).

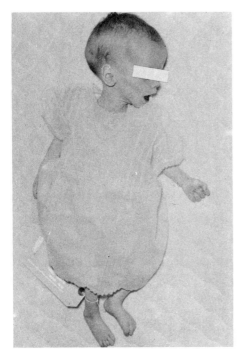

Figure 14.1

Starved infant, age five months, scrubbed and redressed in christening gown after death.

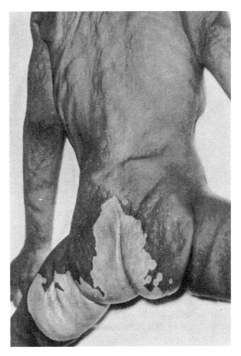

Figure 14.2

Neglected infant, age eleven months, with hypopigmentation of perineum associated with long-standing diaper rash.

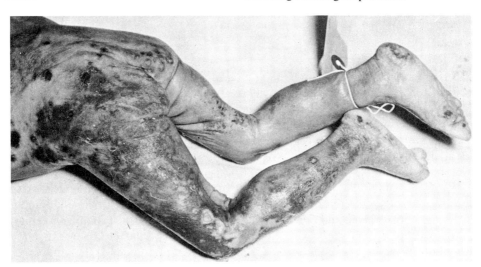

Figure 14.3

Weeping, secondarily infected diaper rash in neglected infant, age nine months

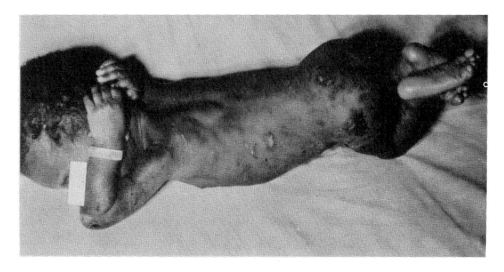

Figure 14.4

Scars resulting from infected insect bites on posterior trunk. Patient hospitalized at age eight and one-half months for marasmus and discharged after weight gain with feeding.

The infants seen during the terminal period of their lives in each instance reflected an extremely low state of metabolism, marked diminution in respiratory rate and volume, hypothermia, and vascular collapse which persisted until death in spite of the administration of parenteral fluids, oxygen, and steroids. The clinical impression in each was that of extreme malnutrition and dehydration resulting from neglect. Often this was more repugnant to the attending physician than the trauma identified in the physically battered children.

Internal Examination

Complete autopsy was conducted on all of the infants. Absence of fatty depots within the interior of the bodies was associated with the loss of subcutaneous tissue. The gastrointestinal tract in most of these infants indicated little or no evidence of food ingestion immediately prior to death. Although terminal complications were present in several of the group, examination revealed no congenital or acquired constitutional disease of sufficient severity and duration to account for the marasmus.

Bronchopneumonia was present in 3 of the infants; sepsis complicated the celluliti, associated with the diaper rash in 3 additional infants. One child had an advanced otitis media and one an acute necrotizing laryngitis. Chemical examination of each in this series revealed no indication of lead or other exogenous element. In the several infants whose weight at death approached that anticipated in an infant of their ages other obvious external manifestations of parental neglect, such as maggot infestation, prompted including them within the group. In one infant, constant sucking of the index finger in the terminal period resulted in maceration, with the skin and nail readily slipping from the underlying tissue.

Alleged and Confessed Method of Injury

Upon initial questioning, the parents repeated a monotonously uniform story of the child being in reasonably good health until one or two days before death, when it "would not take its feeding," "had a mild diarrhea," or "had a cold" as did several siblings within the family. Repeated interrogation might elaborate the story that the youngster "never did well after birth" or had always "failed to thrive." The attempted postmortem cleaning of the children and redressing reflected sufficient parental concern at the outward appearance of their offspring to warrant correction before presentation to a physician or hospital.

Table 14.2 shows the distribution of age, sex, and race of this group. Eighteen of the infants were male and 6 female; 16 were non-white and 8 white, during a period in which the ratio of non-white to white births was 16 to 25. The weights at death varied from 35 to 88% of the expected weight, averaging 65%. These were all below the third percentile, except the cases where neglect resulting in death was in an area other than food deprivation, such as complications resulting from failure to change diapers. Emphasis should again be placed upon the disparity between the presenting story of the parents and the obvious physical condition of the infants at the time examination was conducted. The degree of cachexia, dehydration, and malnutrition apparent in these youngsters was inconsistent with a history of one or two days of diarrhea, upper respiratory infection, or vomiting.

Family Background and Conditions

These children represented in each instance the last born offspring of families averaging 7 children, varying from 2 to 12 in number. The average infant within this group was five months of age at the time of his death. The parents in most cases were described uniformly by police officers, social workers, or representatives of court as being of low intellect. Slightly more than 50% of the group received all of their financial support from public assistance, while more than 80% received some public support.

An attempt was made, as by Adelson (3), to contrast the appearance of the siblings and the homes of children born legitimately with those born out of wedlock. To some degree there was a comparable parallel within this group. In general, the mother caring for families of 5 to 12 who was unable to provide proper nutrition for an offspring who died was also incapable of providing an accepted state of cleanliness or repair within her home. Exceptions within this series were limited to married couples who were usually described as considerably substandard in their intellect, whose homes were in state of extreme uncleanliness, and whose siblings were generally described as completely unkempt. Mothers of these children more often than not had offspring by more than one father and frequently housed the offspring of as many as three and four paramours, the whereabouts of whom was unknown. They were usually between eighteen and thirty years of age and were invariably held accountable for the condition of the deceased baby. They rarely lived in a residence more than six months and often shared one with another equally large family.

The most commonly encountered descriptive word characterizing the homes of these infants was "filthy," with numerous references to an odor of urine and feces permeating the residence and numerous descriptions of bedding, clothing, and floor soiled by wet and dry excreta. In more than 80% the description included reference to extensive infestation by roaches. In most of the homes, all of which were examined in the course of the investigation, careful description of the food supplies revealed only sparse quantities in refrigerators and kitchens. In three homes, with siblings numbering from 3 to 8, in which the infants were found dead, there was no provision for central heat, and in one home human excreta from 17 occupants representing two families was deposited daily by the children from a bucket into the rear yard. Invariably the descriptions included references to piles of debris and trash, not only in the yard of the residence but within the house itself. Interviews of the neighbors frequently provided evidence of disinterest of the parent for the offspring. In the group it was not unusual to have the oldest, a nine-year-old youngster, providing the complete daily and nocturnal needs of his younger siblings, ranging in age from three months on up. No provision was made for clothing the preschool children in 2 of the families.

Examination of the medical history of the children revealed that the parents had sought medical attendance in only two instances after the initial postnatal immunization. For both of these children hospitalization was considered necessary. Extensive clinical and laboratory examinations failed to reveal any condition to explain the cachexia present on admission, while striking response to feeding with resulting weight gain prompted their return to the parents in a relatively short time, only to have them expire with outright starvation several months later (Fig. 14.5; see also Fig. 14.4).

No discussion of child neglect would be complete without alluding to those conditions in which death or disease may arise out of dereliction of parental responsibility in protection and supervision of their offspring. Such deaths frequently occur upon leaving the children unattended for long periods. Acute dehydration or heat exhaustion during the summer months may contribute to the number of sudden unexplained infant deaths. Similarly, no large urban area passes through a winter without seeing at least one, and usually several, large families wiped out by fire when left unattended by competent adult supervision. This is frequently the result of mischief by one of the younger children and is often a repetitive act occurring after several admonitions by the parents on previous occasions. Death caused by a natural disease amenable to therapy requiring constant surveillance (e.g., epilepsy or diabetes mellitus) is considered by some to be due to parental neglect when it can be shown that the parents have been properly advised, provided with the medication, and have no religious objection to its use.

Physical Abuse (Single Injury)

External Examination

In most of this series (9 cases), there was obvious recent external injury to the body. In the children that were shown to have been struck by hands and fists, this was reflected by numerous poorly outlined red-blue bruises associated with swelling and predominantly distributed over the face, lateral aspect of the head, neck,

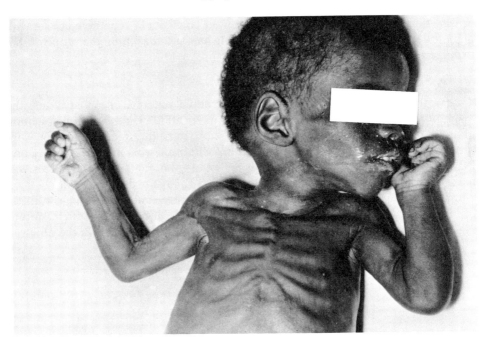

Figure 14.5

Infant in Figure 14.4 upon his death by starvation at age thirteen months

and trunk. When the soft tissues were in apposition to underlying bony structures or teeth, there was frequently denudation of the skin with abrasion or, in the more severe cases, lacerations. These were often present in the inner aspect of markedly swollen, contused lips. When a weapon, either held in the hand or thrown as a missile, was employed, a pattern injury frequently reflected its shape; for example, a linear bruise and denudation resulted from a blow by a vacuum cleaner pipe or a hairbrush (Fig. 14.6). In the one baby struck in the upper abdomen by a partially filled plastic milk bottle hurled across the room, there was only a small, semicircular, sharply outlined bruise externally, lying in apposition to a similarly sharply circumscribed, slightly semicircular laceration of the underlying liver capsule (Fig. 14.7). This infant, observed in the hospital for three-and-one-half hours, expired as a result of intra-abdominal hemorrhage, the history of trauma having been elicited only after the postmortem examination. In 3 infants in the group there was only minimal external evidence of trauma reflected by sharply outlined, superficial red-blue bruises. In 1 of the group there was no external indication of trauma, either healing or recent.

Obvious extensive second- and third-degree burns (resulting from heat) scattered over the lower trunk and extremities resulted in irreversible shock and death in the absence of other significant findings in 1 of the group. These occurred when an older sibling, pursuing his brother to punish him by partial immersion in a pan of hot water, overturned the container and spilled the water into which the deceased slipped and fell. The brother himself was a victim of repetitive abuse, with numerous old scars, and considered the punishment to be within the scope of that expected of him as a baby sitter.

Internal Examination

The internal examination of children in group 1 reflected, in most cases, the magnitude of the external trauma as well as its location. There was no indication of any old fractures within the extremities, skull, or trunk. Recent fractures were present in the skull of 2 of the children, and within the ribs in 3. The most commonly encountered pathologic finding was that of subdural hemorrhage. This was acute with no indication of any organization and in most instances was associated with a localized area of recent subarachnoid hemorrhage and underlying contusion of the cerebral cortex identified by a light pink-purple discoloration, slight softening, and sharply outlined dark red-purple petechial hemorrhages. In the children

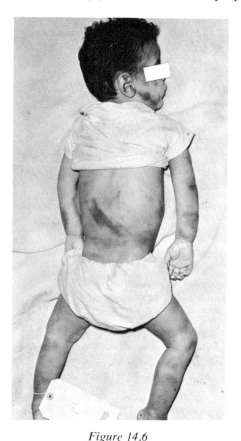

Figure 14.6

Posterior view of infant beaten in one violent episode without evidence of preexisting scars.

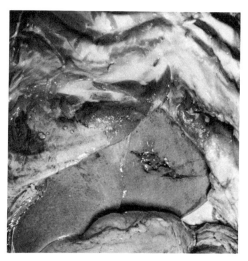

Figure 14.7

Laceration of liver produced by half-filled plastic milk bottle hurled across room.

Figure 14.8

Scalp reflected to reveal multiple galeal hemorrhages
not visualized externally.

thrown or hurled against the wall or to the floor, there was evidence, not only of a
primary contusion adjacent to the scalp lesions but also of a contrecoup injury,
reflected by contralateral subarachnoid hemorrhage and cerebral contusions.
Examination of the galea frequently revealed numerous sharply outlined hemorrhages, which often reflected the outline of the weapon employed, even in the
absence of conspicuous external bruising, abrasion, or laceration (Fig. 14.8). To
the pathologist this multiplicity of galeal hemorrhages frequently is the only clue
of discrepancy between a presenting story and the actual method of injury.

While the external examination of the anterior aspect of the thorax and abdomen may reveal only minimal, poorly outlined bruises, which may be seen only by
sectioning through the abdominal wall, the underlying viscera and fractures of the
ribs may reflect the impact of the trauma much more accurately. Within the thorax
there may be extensive hemorrhage into the thymus and anterior mediastinum,
while in the lungs and epicardium are relatively small anterior hemorrhages. In
one of the series with severe anterior contusions of the lungs, involving approximately one-third of the anterior pleural surface, there was a linear vertical laceration of the anterior wall of the right ventricle of the heart. Extensive hemorrhage
into the abdominal wall in scattered areas was encountered in several cases, again
indicating a multiplicity of blows. In the freely movable loops of bowel, sub-
peritoneal hemorrhages were small and widely scattered, although within the
more firmly attached root of the mesentery, hemorrhage was much more wide-

spread. Laceration of the splenic capsule, associated with extensive retro-peritoneal and intramesenteric hemorrhage, was seen in one case.

Alleged and Confessed Method of Injury

Follow-up investigation conducted upon completion of the medical examination elaborated a story considerably different from that alleged at the hospital. In some of the group an admission of striking the child was elicited. In the remainder either no weapon was employed except the bare hand or fist, or a readily-at-hand weapon was used, including plastic toys, a vacuum cleaner pipe, and a hairbrush. Exasperation resulting in throwing or pushing the infant accounted for injuries in 2 additional cases. Although the internal trauma was inconsistent with an accidental death in 1, no admission of injury was acknowledged and consequently the mechanism was unknown.

The assailants in most of these cases were the natural parents, the father being responsible for the trauma in 5 cases, the mother in 3, a stepfather in 1, and siblings ranging in age from fourteen to seventeen who were charged with caring for the other children in the home being responsible for an additional 3. In each instance the story elicited was quite similar, namely that of extreme exasperation at a time of parental fatigue. The exasperation was most commonly provoked by what was considered excessive crying at a time inconvenient to the parent. Soiling of pants, bed, or floor by urine and feces provoked the terminal episode in 3 additional cases. One baby, in whom the mother attempted to force mastication by placing food in its mouth and mechanically manipulating its jaws, who still would not swallow its food, provoked exasperation to the point of physical fisticuffs on its face. The episode of injury, whether it be to the head or trunk, in most of the cases was similar and described as an episode of violent outrage arising from exasperation resulting in pummeling of the most readily available part of the baby with open hands and fists. If the baby was sitting up in a highchair or carriage, the head was most frequently injured, while if the baby was in a supine position, the injury was most frequently inflicted to the anterior trunk and abdomen, although it was not necessarily limited to this portion of the body.

Although the injuries resulting in death in some of these children may have resulted from the first episode of beating in an otherwise typical battered child situation, the advanced age of some within the group, the general state of well-being of them and of their home, and the complete absence of any preexisting trauma, suggest that this group represents a clinical-pathologic entity altogether different from the typically battered children with repetitive trauma.

Physical Abuse (Repetitive Injury)

Among the 23 children who expired as a result of injuries superimposed on previous injury, 6 were white and 17 non-white. The age ranged from two months to five years, with an average of twenty-four months. All of the group were presented to the hospital or attending physician in a terminal or postmortem condition, with allegations of injury acknowledged in all but 4 who were allegedly found dead in their cribs without an intervening episode of trauma. Again, the most common explanation offered was that of a fall down the stairs or from the bed or crib.

External Examination

The external examination offered a complete range of extremes of injuries. In 4 cases there were only small, sharply circumscribed bruises associated with partially encrusted denudations, completely consistent with injury inflicted by a fall. In 19 of the group, repetitive, extensive, obvious external injury of short duration was present.

If no weapon was employed except the fist and hand, the injuries were usually limited to poorly outlined, irregular bruises similar to those noted in group 1, accompanied by lacerations when in apposition to the teeth or skull, and by moderate to marked degrees of subcutaneous swelling (Fig. 14.9). Weapons which leave a characteristic pattern were frequently encountered, the most common of which was a coiled lamp cord or rope, characteristically leaving a loop welt, simulating the arrangement of the cord (Fig. 14.10), with dark red-purple discolorations and often denudation of the skin. Older healed similar welts with varying degrees of scarring, hypopigmentation, and hyperpigmentation were frequently seen, accompanied by fresh identical patterns in which there was recent hemorrhage and superficial contusion. If a stick was employed, frequently one or both of the sharp outlines representing the borders of the weapon were present on the bruise (Fig. 14.11), often accompanied by denudation and abrasion of the skin. Bruises and abrasions resulting from weapons in these infants were not confined to the face, neck, and trunk but were also distributed over the head, genitalia, and extremities. In several within the group an unusual and characteristic pattern of abrasion or contusion remained, providing a ready means of identifying the weapon used as a file or belt buckle.

Fourteen of this series showed obvious prolonged repetitive trauma, manifested by healed scars and welts in addition to recent abrasions, contusions, and lacerations superimposed on the older injuries. The number of individual scars and marks on the children numbered from 18 to 347, with the anterior and lateral aspects of the thighs and buttocks reflecting as many as 30 individual superimposed recent linear bruises inflicted by a ruler or stick, in addition to as many as 50 healed linear welts reflected by hypopigmented and hyperpigmented scars within which there often was a slight tendency to keloid formation (Fig. 14.12, *top*). Sectioning into the buttocks and soles of the feet in several of the children revealed subcutaneous hemorrhage associated with trauma which was not obvious externally (Fig. 14.12, *bottom*).

Bony prominences frequently were the site of accumulations of subcutaneous fibrous connective tissue, presenting on the head as pseudohyperostotic frontal bossing, obviously originating from old trauma manifested by extensive scarring of the overlying skin.

In 5 children within this series, there was only minimal external healing trauma, similar in nature to that noted in the more severe cases but of lesser magnitude. In 2 of the children, although there was no external indication of any healing or

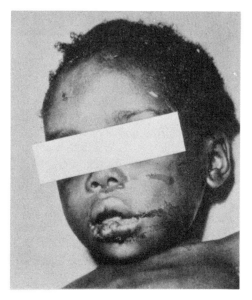

Figure 14.9

Face in typical repetitively beaten child marked by scars, abrasions, contusions, and lacerations of lip in various stages of healing.

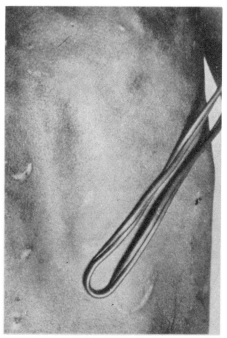

Figure 14.10

Commonly encountered lamp-cord whip with its characteristic loop pattern welt.

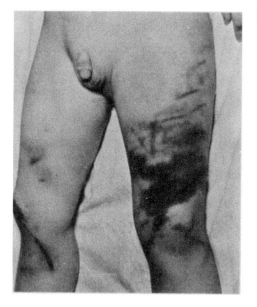

Figure 14.11

Numerous superimposed bruises of thighs resulting from repetitive blows by stick.

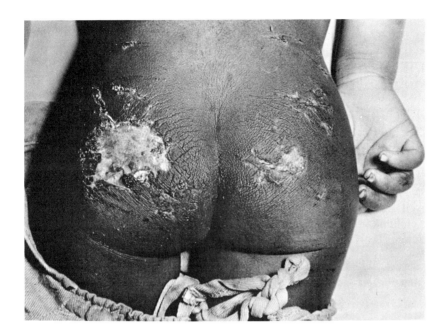

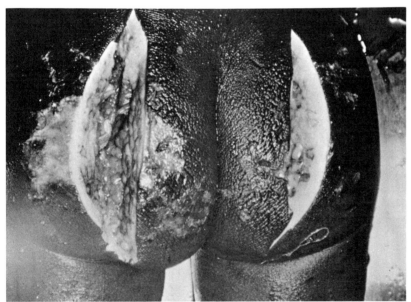

Figure 14.12

(*Top*) Healing abrasions and contusions of buttocks with scarring resulting from repetitive beating. (*Bottom*) Incision into buttocks frequently allows visualization of old hemorrhage and scarring resulting from previous trauma.

healed preexisting trauma, confession elicited a story of repetitive beating, and in 1, roentgenographic examination revealed a healing fracture. In 4 of the group roentgenographic examination revealed healing fractures, including those of the skull, humerus, femur, and ulna. Fractures with no evidence of healing were demonstrated in the skull in 5 cases, ribs in 3, and humerus in 2. In the one child alleged to have had a pint bottle of boiling water overturned upon him, there were second- and third-degree thermal burns extending from a sharply outlined transverse upper border on the posterior thorax over the entire buttocks, thighs, lower legs, and feet, including the soles. This infant was later proven to have been immersed in hot tap water and had a healed skull fracture from a previous punishment. On 1 child numerous healing and healed abrasions and contusions were superimposed on a symmetrical pattern-burn scar on the buttocks, resulting from forcing the child to sit on a hot gas plate in his basement when he soiled his diapers at an earlier age. Burns were also present on the buttocks of one child (Fig. 14.13) who was forced to sit on a hot steam radiator to dry his wet diapers.

Internal Examination

Internal examination revealed injuries essentially the same as those noted within the earlier series but of considerably greater magnitude. Subdural hemorrhage without skull fracture, associated in some instances with severe contusions of the cortex and overlying subarachnoid hemorrhage, were present in 8. Frequently this hemorrhage was revealed to be in several stages, with fresh, bright red blood bordering old, resorbed, partially organized hematomata. In 5 of the group, severe skull fractures were associated with contusions of the brain and hemorrhage in all membrane layers. Detailed neuropathologic examination of the brain may reveal tears in the white matter of the cerebral cortex which the neuropathologist by histologic examination may also be able to document as two separate episodes of trauma (11). Frequently, the multiplicity of the galeal hemorrhages, together with the indication of resorption and breakdown of blood pigment, reflected by the reddish-brown discoloration present in bruises elsewhere on the body as well, served to delineate grossly the time intervals between the various episodes of trauma. In 3 of the children, severe contusion of the brain was unaccompanied by any fracture or subdural hemorrhage. Violent trauma to the trunk and abdomen in the form of pummeling by fists was indicated in 6 of the children in whom there frequently was only minimal evidence of external trauma of the skin surface, although extensive lacerations of the liver were present in 3, in the mesentery in 2, and in the spleen in 1—all associated with extensive hemorrhage into the abdominal cavity and wall.

Alleged and Confessed Method of Injury

This group, in general, reflected the most violent treatment of any within the series. With few exceptions, most of these children came from homes of extremely low socioeconomic level, wherein the family was loosely knit, with the elder sibling serving the parental role often for several days or weeks at a time. This was reflected by the general unkempt appearance of the children. None of the

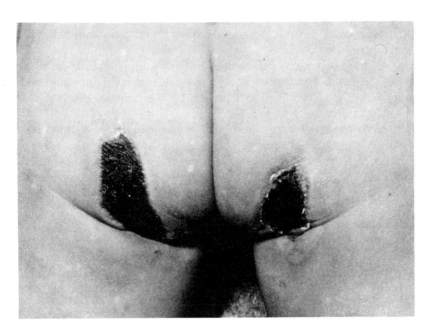

Figure 14.13

Healing burns on buttocks suffered by child forced to sit on steam radiator to dry diapers.

families within this subgroup was in a socioeconomic group consistent with upper middle class or upper class.

The reason for abuse offered by one mother in this group was constant teasing of the parents by the child. The mother interpreted this as a desire for attention by her child, who purportedly achieved satisfaction by the parental beating which ultimately resulted in death.

Parental physical abuse and burns are responsible for all of the deaths within this series. However, more unusual methods of punishment have occasionally resulted in unexpected death. Adelson (4) had reported one death following aspiration of pepper, the ingestion of which was inflicted by the parents as punishment. Death has also followed aspiration of vomitus following the ingestion of red-pepper sauce in one child and following aspiration of a soap solution used to wash out the mouth of one additional child.

The significance of trauma in the background of the parents is reflected by the fact that, in this group of 9 mothers serving as the assailants, several admitted that they had been beaten, not only during childhood but in the weeks and months immediately prior to the death of their offspring. The most violent beating within the group was that given by a twenty-four-year-old mother repetitively beaten by her husband who ultimately abandoned his home, leaving her with the resented child. The mother admitted to ritualistic orgies wherein she repetitively beat the child to a point of semiconsciousness on three occasions prior to the terminal flogging which resulted in death.

Repetitive torture (e.g., by cigarette burns) often reported by clinicians, was not proven in any of these cases nor was there any indication on the extremities of individuals in this group that they had been confined to their bed or room by restraints sufficiently tight to produce abrasion and scarring. Four of these children had been cared for by physicians and local hospitals in the year before their demises, with roentgenographic demonstration of fractures in 2, explained by family and physicians as being incident to a fall from a crib. One of these infants still had a cast on its femur upon its terminal admission to the hospital. In none of the children examined was there any indication of organic brain damage antedating the terminal episode.

Included in this group is 1 child who expired as a result of rupture of the mesentery and retroperitoneal hemorrhage, although the parents never acknowledged a beating of this magnitude. Herein lies one of the greatest problems to the forensic pathologist in arriving at a definitive conclusion concerning a manner of death. For if one is to say that every subdural hematoma, even every skull fracture, in a child who has evidence of welts and scars incident to beating on his trunk and extremities is a result of child abuse, an injustice may well be done since this type of punishment is observed clinically much more frequently than seen at postmortem, and it is impossible to preclude accidental injury superimposed on this type of abuse. In 2 infants studied in this same period, accurate, careful follow-up investigation was able to produce reliable witnesses capable of documenting accidental traumatic episodes consistent with the terminal injuries. This was superimposed on evidence of repetitive beating similar to that noted in the other children.

During this same period of study, an additional 10 children, ranging in age from one to thirty-six months, of whom 8 were non-white and 2 white, were examined and investigated. Externally on these infants, trauma was indicated to varying degrees from small, linear welts to massive single contusions of the scalp with underlying fracture of the calvarium. In 4, the explanation of a fall from the crib was offered, 2 were alleged to have been dropped inadvertently by the mother on the stairs, while 2 were alleged to have fallen down the stairs. The mechanism of injury was unknown or unexplained by the parents in 2 additional cases. Repetitive interrogation and extensive investigation failed to establish sufficient disparity between the alleged injury and pathological finding to establish proof of physical abuse. Within this group, fractures of the skull were present in 3, with subdural hematoma in 6, fractures of the humerus in 1 (resulting in fat and bone marrow emboli to the lungs), and bronchopneumonia was the terminal episode in 1. Although there was no evidence of preexisting bone disease within the skeletons of any of the infants examined within this group, several clinical observers have pointed out the importance of ruling out preexisting bone disease as a contributing factor to the fractures present. Detailed postmortem examination must rule out not only such bone disease, but other conditions such as diseases prompting hemorrhage diasthesis which may tend to aggravate or exaggerate the magnitude of injury responsible for the terminal pathologic findings.

Conclusion

This study, as do others on this and related problems in forensic medicine, demonstrates the importance of teamwork between the investigating agencies and the forensic pathologist in proving the cause and manner of death. The clinician who maintains the same degree of suspicion and objectivity while caring for the injured child and who solicits the services of highly qualified law enforcement investigators and social service workers can contribute significantly to decreasing the mortality and morbidity rates of these unfortunate children.

Acknowledgment

The author is indebted to the members of the staff of the Office of the Medical Examiner in the City of Philadelphia, in the State of Utah, and in the State of New Mexico who assisted in conducting many of the necessary investigations and examinations from which this information has been gathered.

Appendix

POSTMORTEM EXAMINATION GUIDELINES: SUSPECTED CHILD ABUSE OR NEGLECT DEATH

PROCEDURE	INTL. UPON COMPLETION

Examine exterior of body, clad, as received.
Look for any signs of cause and manner of death.

Photograph overall body as received.
These photographs will aid in the documentation of the chain of evidence and serve to refresh the memory of the investigator and examiner. They may also reveal features not noted previously to support another hypothesis for the time.

Search for and remove special items of evidence. (Individually package and label.)
Trace evidence may provide clues to identify the assailant and/or help in or rule out suspects. It may also be used to locate the scene of the crime or the location of the body after the crime.

Undress body carefully over plastic bag and air dry clothing. Seal droppings with trace evidence.
Same as immediately above.

X-ray entire body. Review with radiologist.
The radiologist is invaluable in aging bony injuries and has a large repertoire of bone and soft tissue injury described within the radiology literature, associated with specific patterns of abuse.

Examine exterior of body unclad, as received.
Look for evidence of violence.

Note and record degree, color, and distribution of livor mortis when initially examining body prior to autopsy.
It is important to know the appearance of the body at the scene to determine if rigor and livor mortis are appropriate for position of the body.

Note whether or not anus is abnormal (dilated, patulous, torn, or abraded); photograph is significant.
Anal appearance is vital to indicate recent as well as past rectal sexual intercourse and may give clues to the events leading to death. It should be described prior to swabbing.

If case appears to be sex related, remove for microscopic and/or serologic examination as follows:
1. Swab of oral cavity—smear on two glass slides, fix (with spray) and then place in sealed, labeled screw-top tube.
2. Swab of rectal cavity—prepare as in number 1 above.
3. Swab of vaginal cavity—prepare as in number 1 above.

In addition, dab liquid material into center of four-inch square of clean, new paper towel or filter paper, outline with pencil, air dry, package, and label. ———————

Sperm can be identified microscopically with the aid of special stains. Acid phosphatase determinations can be made on the swabs. The tubes and dabs must be sealed and labeled to insure the chain of evidence. Dabs can be examined for acid phosphatase or used for serological techniques.

Saliva dabs can be analyzed for secretor groups. In case of spurious results, the remainder of the vaginal contents can be evaluated as above. The dabs are of particular value in the event liquid specimens putrefy inadvertently during transmission or storage.

Describe clothing indicating general nature, defects due to violence of any type, their location, size (in centimeters), and approximate location (in inches from landmarks). ———————

Clothing defects may provide valuable clues about the cause and manner of death, as well as the events leading to death.

Photograph external unusual features of body as received with body landmarks and identifying number in photograph. ———————

These photographs will aid in the documentation of the chain of evidence and serve to refresh the memory of the investigator and examiner. They may also reveal features not noted previously to support another hypothesis for the time.

Remove control samples from body for trace evidence. Individually package as indicated. Seal and label:
a. Hair from head
b. Hair from axilla
c. Hair from pubis
d. Clippings of nails, left hand
e. Clippings of nails, right hand. ———————

Samples of the victim's hair are necessary for comparison of any hairs found on the clothing or at the scene. If the victim attempted defense, fragments of skin, blood, or other trace evidence from the assailant might be under the fingernails.

Wash body down carefully, insuring that significant external findings are not removed. ———————

Subtle evidence of injury may be seen after the body is washed, especially if the skin is dirty. Vigorous cleansing should be avoided so as not to disturb delicate evidence of injury.

Examine exterior of body after cleansing. ———————

The removal of dirt, drainage, and debris may afford better visualization of external injury. The time delay associated with these procedures may allow the development of dependent lividity, thereby affording better delineation of anterior, poorly delineated bruises.

Describe natural external features of body. ———————

This procedure is a normal part of the medicolegal autopsy and is vital for victim identification.

Describe in detail the identifying marks, scars, tattoos, etc., noting exact location, size, content, etc. Note whether tattoo is professional or nonprofessional in appearance.

In unidentified remains, more detailed information concerning marks, scars, and tattoos may later assist in establishing identity from verbal descriptions and photographs.

Describe unnatural external features of body (external evidence of injury):
1. Size, shape, color, location (either by body landmarks or above heel or buttocks)
2. Group collections of similar or contiguous injuries.
3. Note relationship of contiguous injuries to each other. Measure intervals on center.

This portion of the examination is paramount to a medicolegal autopsy, and accurate, well-performed, factual, yet concise, descriptions are priceless. Precise location of wounds in certain instances is invaluable in reconstruction of body, assailant, and scene relationships.

Photograph face of body from front with identification number in the photograph.

This photograph will establish identity in court.

Photograph unusual identifying features of body (tattoos, scars, etc.) with identifying number and landmarks in photograph.

If the identification is questioned, documentation of unusual features will aid in positive identification.

Photograph all external unusual features of body after cleansing, with body landmarks, identifying number, ruler, and if necessary, color chart in photograph.

These photographs document the descriptive report.

Conduct dissection stopping upon opening cavity to collect toxicology.

Internal evidence of injury should not be obscured by careless organ removal. The organs should be viewed in situ and traumatic findings ascertained.

Collect appropriate samples for toxicology:
a. Blood
b. Urine
c. Vitreous

Blood should be collected from the heart and a large, more peripheral artery or vein and accordingly labeled. Urine should be collected in such a way as not to contaminate the sample with blood. Vitreous humor is technically more difficult to evaluate toxicologically, but usually represents a more reliable sample in massive internal trauma cases.

Collect sample for serology:

a. Blood   _____

   Blood grouping of the victim's blood is vital information for comparison with blood stains found on the assailant or at the scene.

Describe *in situ* internal evidence of injury, in detail, then therapy (if present).   _____

   Descriptions must be thorough, accurate, and concise. Logically ordered descriptions are preferable.

Photograph internal evidence of injury or therapy, *in situ*, if present.   _____

   These photographs document the descriptive report.

Describe internal evidence of injury, then therapy (if present) after dissection of organs.   _____

   Descriptions must be thorough, accurate, and concise. Logically ordered descriptions are preferable.

Photograph internal evidence of injury or therapy on organs, dissected, if present.   _____

   These photographs document the descriptive report.

Describe internal natural findings.   _____

   Natural disease should not escape the eye of the forensic pathologist, since natural disease may often play a role in traumatic death.

Collect representative sections of unusual pathologic findings from appropriate organs and samples of all organs for histopathologic examination.   _____

   This procedure is self-explanatory, is the standard procedure for all well-conducted autopsies, and is not unique to a forensic autopsy.

References

1. Curran, W. J. 1965. *Tracy's "the doctor as a witness."* Philadelphia: W. B. Saunders.
2. Adelsen, L. 1964. Homicide by pepper. *J. Forensic Sci.* 9:391–95.
3. ———. 1964. Homicide by starvation. *JAMA* 186:458–60.
4. ———. 1961. Slaughter of the innocents. *NEJM* 264:1345–49.
5. Bowen, D. A. 1966. The role of radiology and the identification of foreign bodies at postmortem examination. *J. Forensic Sci. Soc.* 6:28–32.
6. Curphey, T. J.; Kade, H.; Noguchi, T. T.; and Moore, S. M. 1965. The battered child syndrome: Responsibilities of the pathologist. *Calif. Med.* 102:102–4.
7. Dine, M. S. 1965. Tranquilizer poisoning: An example of child abuse. *Ped.* 36:782–85.
8. Griffiths, D. L., and Moynihan, F. J. 1963. Multiple epiphysial injuries in babies (battered child syndrome). *Brit. Med. J.* 5372 1558–61.

9. Hamlin, H. Subgaleal hematoma caused by hair pulling. JAMA 204:339.

10. Koel, B. S. 1969. Failure to thrive and fatal injury as a continuum. *Am. J. Dis. Child.* 118:565–67.

11. Lindenberg, R., and Freytag, E. 1969. Morphology of brain lesions from blunt trauma in early infancy. *Arch. Path.* 87:298–305.

12. McCort, J., *et al.* 1964. Visceral injuries in battered children. *Radiology* 82:424–28.

13. Parker, G. E. 1965. The battered-child syndrome (The problem in the United States). *Med. Sci. Law* 5:160–63.

14. Palomegne, F. E., and Hairston, M. A. 1964. "Battered child" syndrome: Unusual dermatological manifestation. *Arch. Derm.* 90:326–27.

15. Swischuk, L. E. 1969. Spine and spinal cord trauma in the battered child syndrome. *Radiology* 92:733–38.

16. Woolley, P. V., and Evans, W. A. 1955. Significance of skeletal lesions in infants resembling those of traumatic origin. *JAMA* 158:534–43.

Additional Readings

Adams, P., *et al.* 1974. Kinky hair syndrome: Serial study of radiological findings with emphasis on the similarity to the battered child syndrome. *Pediatr. Radiol.* 112:401.

Anderson, W., and Hudson, R. 1976. Self-inflicted bite marks in battered child syndrome. *For. Sci.* 7:71.

Bratu, M., *et al.* 1970. Jejunal hematoma, child abuse, and Felson's sign. *Conn. Med.* 34:261.

Caffey, J. 1972. On the theory and practice of shaking infants. *Am. J. Dis. Child.* 124:161.

Curran, W. 1977. Law-medicine notes: Failure to diagnose battered-child syndrome. *Med. Intell.* 296:795.

Eisenstein, E., *et al.* 1965. Jejunal hematoma: An unusual manifestation of the battered-child syndrome. *Clin. Pediatr.* 4:436.

Garff, R. 1977. Child abuse and court procedure. *Coll. Amer. Path.*, April.

Harcourt, B., and Hopkins, D. 1973. Permanent chorio-retinal lesions in childhood of suspected traumatic origin. *Trans. Ophthal. Soc.* 93:199.

Helfer, R. 1977. Injuries resulting when small children fall out of bed. *Pediatrics* 60:533.

Jaffe, A., *et al.* 1975. Sexual abuse of children. *Am. J. Dis. Child.* 129:639.

Kim, T., and Jenkins, M. 1967. Pseudocyst of the pancreas as a manifestation of the battered-child syndrome. *Med. Ann. DC* 36:664.

Laing, S., and Buchan, A. 1976. Bilateral injuries in childhood: An altering sign? *Brit. Med. J.*, Oct.

Lansky, L. 1974. An unusual case of childhood chloral hydrate poisoning. *Am. J. Dis. Child.* 127:275.

Pickering, D. 1976. Salicylate poisoning as a manifestation of the battered child syndrome. *Am. J. Dis. Child.* 130:675.

Sims, B., and Cameron, J. 1973. Bite-marks in the "battered baby syndrome." *Med. Sci. Law* 13:207.

Slovis, T., *et al.* 1975. Pancreatitis and the battered child syndrome. *Am. J. Roent.* 125:456.

Tomasi, L., and Rosman, N. 1975. Purtscher retinopathy in the battered child syndrome. *Am. J. Dis. Child.* 129:1335.

Weston, J. T. 1976. *The medicolegal investigation of death in New Mexico.* Albuquerque: University of New Mexico Press.

PART

Intervention and Treatment

From the first call that is placed to protective services to the completion of a long-term therapeutic program, families involved in child abuse and neglect require considerable care and attention. Many very difficult decisions must be made and carried out. No one group or discipline can carry the load alone; it clearly is too heavy a burden. All of the professionals and agencies involved in a community's efforts to deal with the problem of abuse must be tied together in some type of coordinated consortium. Collectively, there is some hope for success; individually, the struggle goes on.

The authors in Part III discuss each component of the community fight against abuse, from crisis intervention to long-term therapy and the consequences of abuse on the child if our efforts fail. These consequences are not pleasant. Our efforts must not fail.

R.E.H.   C.H.K.

15 The Function of Protective Services in Child Abuse and Neglect

Claudia A. Carroll

Much of what is either effective or ineffective child abuse intervention in a community depends upon the posture taken by the local county department of social services. (Throughout this chapter the department of social services will be mentioned; however, in different localities various names are used, such as the department of public welfare, the department of human resources, the department of human services, the social welfare department, etc.) In most states, the county department of social services is the agency in the community legally responsible for the provision of child protective services. There are 3,300 such county departments of social services in the United States, most of which have either specific social workers or units to investigate, treat, and/or coordinate services to children and their parents.

The range of levels of responsiveness from social service departments to the mandate of provision of protective services is enormous. Despite formidable obstacles, many departments of social service are doing a commendable job. These departments could be characterized as having "open systems," that is, as being responsive to the needs of referred families, progressive in program planning, and open to the involvement of other agencies in the community.

The opposite of these would be what are described as "closed systems." These departments characteristically minimize the problems of child abuse and neglect in the community, provide little leadership in provision of services to families, and diligently set up barriers within their system, both to families and to other community agencies. Unfortunately, the front-line social worker often receives the brunt of the public's criticism, as it is he or she with whom it most frequently comes in contact. The public may tend to identify its frustrations over specific family situations with the social worker. In many of these situations, the social worker should be lauded for "hanging in there" when no one else will. Rather than the individual social worker, it is inevitably the administration or decision

Claudia A. Carroll, M.S.W., is with the National Center for the Prevention and Treatment of Child Abuse and Neglect, Denver.

makers of the county department who must be questioned regarding agency policies, attitudes, and stance regarding protective services to children and their families. This is not to say incompetent social work should be excused under the rubric of poor administration of an agency—they are two separate issues.

Importantly, we must not misconstrue the death of a child in a county as evidence that the county represents a poor or closed system. Even in the best of social service departments and with the best of services, children, most tragically, will die. In this field of protective services, we are making human judgments; and being human, mistakes will be made. The important factor here is to look at our mistakes and ascertain whether the child died or was injured because of a lack of responsiveness by the entire protective services system, including a "closed" social service department, or whether the death was a result of a human judgment that was incorrect. (The safest action would be to place all children referred as a result of concern for abuse and neglect in foster care. Yet, this course would be disastrous to countless numbers of children, and irreparable emotional damage would be done. Foster care is no panacea and should be used, but judiciously.)

Whether we are a part of a closed or open system of protective services must be part of the diagnosis leading to change each community faces. Enormous strides have been made in the past few years, and even though we are struggling today toward open, comprehensive protective service systems, we have not always adopted a steady course in the right direction. Considering that it was only twenty or so years ago when Drs. Kempe and Steele began their pioneer work in child abuse and neglect and that it was as recently as 1962 that the article "The Battered Child Syndrome" was published, progress has been made. This does not mean we can be complacent—far from it. The problem faced today in this work seems to be one of urgency for the children of today, the parents of tomorrow.

The field of protective services to children seems to have come full circle now as to the situations in which it will intervene. In the recent past, the most serious physical abuse cases were those in which we felt justified to intervene and protect the child. To adjudicate the court case, the pediatrician came to court fully prepared with X-rays in hand, which the court loved (1). This no longer is as necessary, as the definition of child abuse has been enlarged to include such areas as child neglect, sexual abuse, failure to thrive, and emotional abuse. Sexual abuse is new to all of us in the field, and we are learning more about and understanding this problem more each year. Emotional abuse per se is also in its infancy in terms of recognition; yet it is beginning to be recognized as just as devastating as physical abuse, or even more so in some situations. Recently, there have been court cases of emotional abuse in which termination of parental rights occurred on the basis of serious emotional abuse alone—this never would have happened even five years ago (2).

This enlarged scope of our understanding of child abuse and neglect is good, because it moves the field forward to embody a complete definition of the problem. Yet, what has happened is that an already overburdened system, the social service department, has been asked to take on even more.

In considering protective services to children we must begin by including the social service department and other community agencies in order to begin working with many resources in the community to ameliorate the problems within the family. The social service department is a major one among fifteen components of a comprehensive protective services system (3). All fifteen components are needed to do the job of protective services well. They are

Legal services
Schools
Public health services
Child protection teams
Public and private hospitals
Law enforcement
Lay and community involvement
State social services department
County social services departments
Juvenile court
Mental health private practitioners
Mental health public agencies
Private social services agencies
Parental consumer groups
Private physicians

Criteria of Good Protective Services of the Department of Social Services

As a major and central component of a comprehensive system of child protective services, the benchmarks of a good social services department, protective services division should include the following criteria:

1. There must exist a commitment to child protection services as a *priority* service of the department of social services. Families require extensive services and thus must be seen as priority by the agency administration and services staff.

2. A realistic budget must be backed by sound data collection. Inherent in this statement is the concept of long-range planning, such as a three-year plan and budget (backed by statistics collected within the department). Each social service department (with community input) should take an inventory of where they are now in terms of services and list priorities for the future. (For example, the rate of intakes this year; the anticipated rate next year, based on previous years' patterns; the treatment needs of the children; the treatment needs of parents, etc.) Budgeting must reflect both current and future needs. It can no longer be static.

3. Good working relationships with other community agencies must be maintained. Written agreements with other agencies are helpful toward this end.

4. There must be a functioning, active child protection team with a multidisciplinary and multiagency makeup.

5. A reasonable workload standard should be established for the protective services social workers. Quality service cannot be accomplished without this. Twenty-two families per social worker is the recommended maximum workload (4).

6. Consultive supervision must be provided for experienced, competent social workers, and teaching supervision for new protective service social workers. The

supervisor should be well grounded in the principles and practices of psychotherapy, as well as the realities of such stressful work vis-à-vis recent and ongoing responsibility for at least one family. Six social workers per supervisor is the maximum recommended number of supervisees per supervisor.

7. Adequate medical, psychiatric, and psychological consultation should be provided to protective services staff.

8. Guidelines should be written regarding agency policy on such important decisions as court filings, criteria for placement, criteria for return home of the child, criteria for case closures, and so on.

9. A broad variety of treatment services should be provided. (Chapter 16 discusses treatment and current treatment modalities.)

10. Skilled and trained social workers should perform protective services work by choice, not chance. Too frequently, in order to meet ever-increasing workloads, entire units originally designed for other functions are converted precipitously into protective services units. If this must be done, adequate training and education should be provided to the social workers, and anyone uninterested in doing this type of work should be relocated in the department.

11. A program of staff development should be ongoing.

12. A responsive intake system should be available seven days a week, twenty-four hours a day.

13. An active program of public awareness and community education should be geared to the problem of child abuse and neglect.

14. An adequate and responsive legal staff should be provided to the protective services units. A full-time attorney is needed per 100,000 population in the community (4, p. 302).

15. The staff should be committed to serving families with actual and *potential* situations of child abuse and neglect.

16. State and national programs and legislation on child abuse should be developed with participation of protective service professionals.

17. A positive attitude should be maintained by the department of social services toward scrutiny of the child protection system and public involvement in the system. This can be accomplished and demonstrated in enumerable ways: through an active lay involvement in the agency (i.e., volunteer programs such as Foster Grandparents, Big Brothers, Lay Therapy); establishment of communication with the news media and legislature (i.e., inviting legislators to accompany a protective services social worker on home visits one day a year); and encouragement and support of self-help groups (i.e., Parents Anonymous, Parents United, and other community groups, such as a child protection council).

A child protection council deserves some separate discussion here, as it costs nothing and can be one of the most effective groups in a community for providing community-wide education and planning regarding the problems of child abuse and neglect. A child protection council is not attached to any agency but is composed of concerned people, both lay and professional. With this approach, the traditional problems of "turfism" can be transcended so that people participate out of genuine interest. Community agencies from all fifteen components of the child protective system might participate from the professional standpoint. The list of lay groups interested in this could be quite creative, including: PTA, Junior League, Welfare Rights, League of Women Voters, Foster Parents Association, Kiwanis, Le Leche, Council of Jewish Women, and Legal Aid. Monthly general meetings can be held to serve as a forum for discussing important issues, such as child abuse legislation, new treatment programs, and problems in the system, but not cases. Such a group would exist to provide a vehicle for community involvement, not specific case planning. It is important to tap people's interest in child abuse by providing ways in which they can become involved. Thus, forming working committees becomes an important step to keeping the council alive and growing. The type of committees to consider developing include: an educational and speakers' bureau to sponsor educational workshops and foster community awareness; a legislative committee to work for improved legislation and to interpret current legislation to the public; a task force on standards to define each component of a comprehensive protective services system and the community's expectations of each; a task force with the state department of social services to help in presenting pertinent data to the legislature, as well as to provide credibility to the budget requests; a public relations committee; and a membership committee to generate more participation (5).

The Current Dilemma of Protective Services

Social service departments have received their charge from society. In general, the protective services field is struggling. Society has given social service departments a tremendous obligation to protect children at risk, while providing little help. They have been given this task in a climate of ever-increasing work loads, strikingly low budgets, and trained social workers leaving the field en masse daily because of these conditions and the inherent emotional pressures of such work. We must find better ways to keep trained social workers longer than the current average of two years.

This all speaks to the low priority given to children and children's rights in our times. Children do not vote. They, therefore, have little impact on our legislatures, and funding for the needs of children is, in general, a low priority locally and nationally.

The problem is twofold. On the one hand, children's programs are seen as unimportant by the powers that be. On the other hand, social service departments have been reluctant to request really adequate funding and have instead requested what they think the legislature will bear. The obligation of the professional is to tell society what the true needs are. Continuing to budget on a piecemeal basis will only continue our failures in protective services to children and their parents. Although politicians may not want to hear it, they need to know the true cost of good protective services programs, as well as the cost of *not* funding protective services sufficiently. For example, a brain-damaged child institutionalized as a result of child abuse costs the state $700,000 for a lifetime (6). Further, studies across the United States show a high correlation between families which reported abuse or neglect problems and subsequent delinquency in the children. If we were to look at the relationship of adult criminal offenders to their having been abused or neglected as children, that, too, would be startling. The cost to society of not adequately funding protective services is indeed great.

The Organization of Protective Services

Organizationally, county departments of social services are responsible to the state social service department and ultimately to the federal Department of Health, and Human Services. Locally, they are responsible to either the county commissioners or the city council and the local advisory board. Funding for services of county departments and protective services is in a ratio of 80% federal funding to 20% state funding.

Some of the confusion as to what a department of social services does results from its dual role of providing both financial assistance and social services. Under one roof, but in separate divisions, are housed these very different functions (see table 15.1).

TABLE 15.1   **Department of Social Services**

Assistance Payments	Social Services
Aid to dependent children	Adoption services
Aid to the needy disabled	Adolescent services
Food stamps	Child protective services
Aid to the blind	Supportive services (homemakers, day care)
Old-age assistance	Foster care division
Medicaid	Adult protective services, employment services

This distinction should be kept in mind in order to understand where protective services fit into the department of social services and how they work within the system. A large metropolitan social service department can be an amorphous, confusing system to outsiders and even to those within the agency. It could be that a family under its care would have an ADC technician who was totally un-connected with the protective services division. When wanting to make a referral or to speak with the family's social worker, it is important to clarify that the person with whom you are speaking is, in fact, from the correct division, that is, the social service division of the department.

Functions of Protective Services

Protective services can logically be divided into four services: intake or assess-ment of the referred family, provision of treatment services, case coordination with other agencies within the community, and preventive services. Philosophically, each of these services requires that we keep in mind the potential positive or potential negative impact our very presence, let alone efforts at intervention, may have on the abused child and his or her family. *At all costs, do no harm.* Intervention without long-term treatment, or treatment available only months later, can potentially do more harm than perhaps even the original incident of abuse or neglect. Whatever we do with the family, we must continually ask ourselves such things as Why are we doing this? What are the goals? To whom do we wish the child to become attached—the foster parents or the natural parents? Does the system have something better to offer the child and his parents than their current situation? For whom is this rule designed—the child, the parents, or the agency? This type of question is paramount and a necessary part of the self-awareness of the protective services social worker and the agency. We are involved in people's lives; intervention is a difficult and delicate process.

Intake

Intake is the initial phase of assessment, during which immediate responsiveness is required by the protective services division. The usual procedure is for the referral to originate from a variety of sources, i.e., school, hospital, police, private citizen, relative, or the parent. An intake social worker is assigned to pull together as much information as possible regarding the alleged incident in a defined and short time, ranging from a few hours to approximately two weeks.

The purpose of the intake investigation is to try to determine whether something happened to the child. And, if it did, What is the risk to the child? If, in a potential case, nothing has yet happened, many states' statutes also allow an investigation to take place on the basis of potential harm or circumstances which might reasonably result in child abuse or neglect.

In many respects, treatment of the abusive family begins with the first contact by the intake social worker. The tone established between the intake social worker and the family will often be carried throughout the remainder of the case. It is, therefore, essential that the intake worker be respectful, honest, and predictable with the parents.

Upon completion of the investigation, a decision is made as to whether the family requires an ongoing social worker. If so, it is usually passed to an ongoing protective services unit. This points out one of the major problems in the organization of protective services: the division of protective services often takes on cases apart from the ongoing treatment units. Thus, the continuity of involvement with the family is lost when a family must be transferred from one unit to another. The family often builds up a strong alliance with the initial worker with whom they have had contact, and it is not unusual for considerable time to be lost between the assignment of a family from one unit to another. Possible alternatives to this would include attaching an intake worker to each ongoing protective services unit. This person would function as a member of this unit, and families would then be moved expeditiously within the same unit. The same concept holds true for a foster-placement worker being attached to each ongoing protective services unit. Each placement worker would be responsible for a number of foster homes and would likely have a better sense of the type of children an individual foster family works with best. Further, this would minimize the foster family having to work with numerous foster workers.

The other alternative would be to have the child abuse/neglect intake workers rotate among all protective services units. Theoretically, it is much sounder for the family to see one social worker. The person they talk with at the point of crisis has a much better opportunity to assess and develop a treatment plan with the family before the family's defenses are again in full force. While there are a few situations in which the family is so angry at the intake worker that they are unable to work together beyond that, and it is useful to use the "black-hat" (first worker)/"white-hat" (second worker) concept, this is not necessary in most child abuse situations.

A useful model to consider for intake is the combination of a public health nurse or nurse employed by the department of social services and an intake protective services social worker. The health worker is much less threatening to the family, and she may be able to help enlist the cooperation of the family. A medical person can be very helpful in assessing the medical needs of a child and the degree of seriousness of any injuries. Also, the combination of two people assessing any serious intake situation can relieve some of the anxiety a single worker would naturally feel doing so alone.

The main task of the intake social worker is to assess the safety of the home. A full evaluation is indicated when: (*a*) the injury is inconsistent with the explanation, (*b*) the injury is the result of an unusual accident, (*c*) the parent presents with questionable psychiatric functioning, (*d*) poor parent-child interaction has been observed, and (*e*) repeated referrals to protective services have been made regarding the parents or concern for the children.

Upon completion of the intake phase, we should be able to describe these areas: (*a*) personal history of each parent, their coping and adaptive styles; (*b*) medical and developmental history of the child, including his or her current developmental and emotional functioning; perception of the child by each parent and his or her role in the family; (*d*) strengths and weaknesses of the family unit; (*e*) diagnostic impressions and an estimation of the parents' ability to use help; (*f*) past history of abuse or neglect; (*g*) support systems available to the family; and (*h*) safety of the home.

Importantly, the intake social worker should compile the data from a variety of sources. When we have made mistakes as a team at the University of Colorado Health Sciences Center, they usually stem from a lack of data or taking a shortcut, where one should not be taken, such as sending a baby home from the hospital without the trauma-series X-rays because "the parents look good." Established protocols at intake should be used and data obtained from many sources, including the parents, the child, the local child abuse registry, school and medical records, etc.

Multidisciplinary review teams have been established in many areas of the country and serve to review the action taken on new cases. In some localities the multidisciplinary team is located in the department of social services, and in others it is in another community agency. Actually, the location is of little importance as long as the county department supports the concept and is involved with the team.

Treatment

County departments of social services should be among the primary providers of treatment services to troubled families. Among the services which should be provided by the departments are the following:

1. Therapy and counseling for children and parents (individual, marital, family and group)
2. Therapeutic foster care and crisis nursery placements
3. Lay therapy
4. Volunteer programs (Big Brother, Big Sister, transportation, Foster Grandparent)
5. Day-care resources and therapeutic day-care for children with special needs
6. Homemaker services
7. Education in parenting
8. Concrete emergency assistance, such as grocery orders

Treatment is the difficult task of helping the parent grow psychologically. Treatment for the child is equally important so that he or she will not become developmentally arrested and so that the child will have the opportunity for a fulfilled, happy life. One can be optimistic about the abilities of the helping professions to work with the family successfully, given that there are a variety of treatment services from which to choose, a cooperative team approach of agencies working together, and a reasonable prognosis for the parent, indicating positive ability to change.

A good psychiatric evaluation in the early stages of a case can be instrumental in helping to sort out which cases are treatable and those few which are not. County departments of social services in the past have felt in some ways *too* responsible, that is, felt they must work with everyone beyond heroic efforts. This must be turned around so that a reasonable and fair treatment plan is set up in the beginning stages of a case, and, if after a year or so, significant progress has not been made, termination of parental rights should take place and permanent planning for the children should occur.

Treatment review teams within social service departments can be established to review the treatment plan, progress, or lack of progress, and could be an adjunct to the multidisciplinary review team, which in practice focuses mainly on intake cases. (The multidisciplinary team need not focus solely on new cases, but most existing teams have done this as a result of the sheer volume of cases.) Such treatment teams review ongoing family situations with special emphasis on treatment issues, planning regarding whether a child may safely return home, and case closures. Seemingly, some of our gravest mistakes in protective services have been made after a case has been open for a period of time and children were returned home precipitously or after an aspect of the treatment plan was decided to be changed unilaterally, by one person.

A further extension of this concept is the foster care review team, which would internally monitor those children placed in foster care, review regularly their planning for the child so he or she will not grow up in the limbo of foster care. We recently found in Colorado, for instance, that if a child was placed in foster care and remained there for two months, the likelihood was that he or she would be there for two years.

These teams—the treatment review team and the foster care review team—are staffed within the department (i.e., staff social workers, the protective service supervisors, staff psychiatric/psychological consultants) as well as externally (i.e., public health nurse, mental health center representative, etc.).

Case Coordination

In some areas of the country the protective services worker is strictly a case coordinator, that is, coordinating the services to the family which are being provided by other agencies. In other areas, the protective services worker has a mixed responsibility of doing intake evaluations, treatment, and case coordination. The latter is preferred. Transferring to other agencies all of the motivated clients, leaves the county protective services social worker dealing with just the hopeless situations. Case coordination is an important function of county protective services, yet it should not be done to the exclusion of the other two major roles—treatment and intake responsibilities.

Given the need in every child abuse/neglect situation for many agencies to be involved, someone needs to be identified as the case coordinator, so that all aspects of the family situation are viewed and so that agency representatives do not trip over each other in their efforts to help the family. We do want to help, not overwhelm. Definition of roles with the family by the involved agencies and the leadership of a good case manager can make the difference between a situation which is improving and one which is not.

One of the dilemmas which case coordinators often get into is that of becoming a passive onlooker at the family, rather than an active participant in the decision-making regarding the child and his parents. As the case coordinator, the protective services worker must be a decisive and moving influence in planning.

Prevention

When the protective services and/or child welfare staff hear someone ask what the department of social services is doing in the area of prevention, the response is usually from two very opposite ends of the continuum; intellectually they agree protective services should be involved in preventive work; emotionally they think "this person is crazy—we can't even deal with all of the current families referred to the social service department; how can prevention also be expected of this agency?"

Unfortunately, this continues to be the situation. However, there can be a role for the department of social services and that is one of attitude to accept and work with those high-risk potential cases where no physical injury has yet occurred but undoubtedly will without intervention. A newborn infant with actively psychotic parents should not, for example, have to suffer a skull fracture before something can be done. Foster care placement from the hospital and juvenile court action should be alternatives in such a potentially dangerous environment.

The other areas of prevention for which many other community agencies should carry primary responsibility are: the schools in providing parenting curriculum and experiential opportunities for youngsters to become parents, the hospitals in developing lay health visitor programs, and the health and mental health agencies in providing various parenting groups. The social service departments, through good working relationships with these other agencies, could look to them for preventive work in the community, and together they could develop new ideas for prevention (see Part IV).

Community Inventory

Having discussed the four major areas of protective services, one might wonder about developing a list of priorities of services when making the suggested community inventory. What is left, having considered this idea, is that all the services and subcategories of services are important. What is more important, perhaps, is that an inventory be made and, second, that a list of priorities be developed that is unique and applicable to a particular community. The list of seventeen suggested criteria regarding good protective services mentioned above is one model with which to begin a community inventory. This could be coupled with the list of eight types of treatment services. People sometimes become discouraged, feeling so much is necessary, and become overwhelmed not knowing where to begin. Begin with something attainable in the next year. Often we do not need a lot of resources to implement many good ideas—remember, a child protection team can be two interested, committed people. Starting with one or two things allows us to build from there. If one had to choose among all the ideas of services, the three priorities in any community should be: (1) a workload standard for protective service workers; (2) a strong lay therapy program; (3) extensive utilization of good day care.

Making Protective Service Social Work Manageable

Throughout this chapter ways in which the job of the protective services social worker might be made more manageable, and thus reduce the tremendous turnover of manpower, are discussed. Right now it is unusual for a family to have the same social worker from the beginning to the end of treatment, and the repercussions of this dilemma are many. A family may be involved unnecessarily long with community agencies; poor decisions might be made because of a lack of continuity; families may get lost, so to speak, between social workers, in terms of their needs and priorities, and so on.

Ways in which this work can be made more manageable include, but are not limited to, the following (in addition to the suggestions made above):

1. A variety of protective services experiences should be available to social workers so they do not become "burned out" in one area of responsibility. This could vary from some responsibilities for ongoing treatment with a family, to

supervision of a lay therapist, to involvement with community activities of public speaking and being a coleader of a parents group. This approach ameliorates such feelings as frustration, a sense of failure, and incompletion that result if any of these is the worker's exclusive task.

2. Agency policies should be flexible and reasonable, including compensatory time, smooth ways of obtaining concrete services for a family, etc.

3. The juvenile court system should work with the social service department and see the social workers as competent professionals.

Legal Role of Protective Services

Underlying each of the services discussed thus far (intake, treatment, case coordination, and prevention) is the legal role inherent in the department of social services. As the agency with the ultimate responsibility for protection of the rights of children, the protective services division is faced with the concomitant responsibility of initiation of civil juvenile court action in sufficiently serious cases. One wonders if it is possible to be both the provider of treatment services and initiator of court action. Skilled protective services workers are able to juggle these seemingly disparate areas if they have established a relationship with the parents that is characterized by trust and straightforwardness. While there is a small percentage of cases where these roles are not compatible, in the vast majority of protective services cases, they are.

The state statute or juvenile code provides the state definition of child abuse/neglect which indicates juvenile court action. These codes are then interpreted by the local juvenile court judges. Thus, what will be adjudicated in one county jurisdiction may not be in the next jurisdiction a few blocks away. The county department of social services must be aggressive in continuing to bring to the attention of their county court (even if they may lose these cases in court for a time) *all* those situations in which children's emotional or physical well-being is at risk. At least in bringing a case to the court's attention, the department of social services has done everything within its power. Slowly, progress will be made, but only if departments of social services have the courage to persevere in bringing all serious cases to the attention of their courts and not just the ones they think the judge will decide in their favor.

On the whole, the juvenile court's increased sophistication in understanding failure to thrive, emotional abuse, sexual abuse, and developmental lags, is impressive. If given enough data by all of us in the field, juvenile courts will indeed increasingly make decisions to protect children's rights.

As in other areas of this work, it is useful to have a checks-and-balances system to review which cases should and should not go before the court. Coupled with the professionals involved in a case, an overworked county attorney could welcome the recommendations of the multidisciplinary team in making such difficult decisions.

Conclusion

In the past two decades, we have seen a major expansion of knowledge about child abuse and neglect and an upsurge of community awareness. With this has come a concomitant upsurge in families being reported to protective services. Although services are hard pressed at this point, it seems as if there is an increased willingness of other agencies in the community to become involved in this difficult business. Child abuse is now being defined as a community problem and not as solely the concern of one agency, the department of social services. We are beginning to think of a larger protective services system encompassing the legal system, schools, health department, child protection teams, public and private hospitals, law enforcement, lay and community groups, parent-consumer groups, medical private practitioners, county and state social service departments, juvenile courts, public and private mental health resources, and private social service agencies.

Within that larger protective services system, the department of social services plays a key role, setting the stage for cooperation among agencies, and provides leadership so that together we may all be able to offer quality intervention and treatment services to abused children and their families.

References

1. Kempe, C. Henry. personal communication, 1964.
2. *The People of the State of Colorado Petitioner-Appellee, in the Interest of D. A. K., Minor Child, and Concerning J. K. S., Respondent-Appellant,* 4 June 1979 En Banc. Opinions, No. 28,363. August 1979. *The Colorado Lawyer,* pp. 1509–12.
3. Carroll, C., ed. 1979. *Standards for a Model Protective Services System* (Denver, Colo.: University of Colorado Health Sciences Center).
4. Kawamura, G., and Carroll, C. A. 1976. Managerial and financial aspects of social service programs. In *Child Abuse and Neglect: The Family and the Community,* edited by R. Helfer and C. Kempe (Cambridge, Mass.: Ballinger).
5. Carroll, C. A., and Schmitt, B. 1978. Improving community treatment services. In *The Child Protection Team Handbook* (New York: Garland Press), pp. 33–34.
6. Kempe, C. H. 1976. Approaches to preventing child abuse: The health visitor concept. *Am. J. Dis. Child.* 130:941–47.

16 Long-Term Treatment

Helen Alexander

Long-term treatment is essential to any adequate treatment program for child abuse and neglect. Many services are necessarily geared to crisis intervention, to relieve the immediate stresses for both the child and family; but without adequate ongoing care little, if any, change will occur. Problems that have been in the making for years and even generations will not be altered significantly in a brief period. Occasionally, there are important improvements that begin during a crisis, but without continuing help, they may be fleeting. If the changes are to be integrated, it is important that they be supported and that services to the family are not withdrawn at that critical point.

Long-term treatment may not mean the same thing in the context of child abuse and neglect as we might ordinarily think of it in a psychiatric or clinical practice. Actually, it is a consortium of programs which continues to make available, as needed, a variety of services geared to meeting the needs of a particular family. Psychotherapy may be a part of that network. However, it is not the only choice available in long-term treatment. Most important is an adequate diagnostic evaluation that develops an individualized treatment plan and a system that ensures periodic reevaluation with all participating services involved. The treatment may need to be altered as changes occur or as it becomes apparent that the previous plan is not working. The critical issue is that the family is not abandoned or services terminated without full consideration of what an ongoing treatment plan will be.

One of the difficulties in working together in this way is that different people within the treatment team become identified either with the child or the parent(s). Viewing the family as a whole and attempting to provide care that is balanced between parental need and child need is a difficult challenge. Those who identify with the child may become angry and frustrated over what they perceive as disregard for the child. For example, a child care worker may want to stop visits

Helen Alexander, M.S.W., is with the National Center for the Prevention and Treatment of Child Abuse and Neglect, Denver.

between parent and child because the child is visibly distressed after these visits. On the other hand, a parent's therapist may come to view the child as essential to the parent's emotional stability, fearing depression or even suicide if the child is removed from the home, without considering what effect this may have on the child's development and emotional state.

Only as regular communication and evaluation of treatment occur can this be seen and worked through to a treatment approach that is balanced and helpful to both parents and child. Rarely is an action appropriate for the child that is not in some way beneficial for the parents. At times parents may voice opposition, but they often show obvious relief when the action is taken.

> Johnnie, a young mother, whose two preschool boys had been in foster placement for some time, requested extended overnight visits with them. These were instituted, and within a month of the change Johnnie called her lay therapist the morning after a visit to report how difficult Paul, her youngest son, had been. He had been up during the night and had found medication and poisonous cleaning substances, which he had spilled all over the apartment and may have ingested. This was very atypical behavior for Paul, who was described by both his play-school teacher and foster mother as a very quiet, even lethargic boy, who rarely initiated any activity without a great deal of encouragement. Those involved were concerned that a very long time with no supervision for Paul must have passed before he could accomplish so much. Johnnie's lay therapist interpreted her call as meaning that the care of the children for these longer visits was far more than she could manage. On the basis of this, a hearing was requested to have the longer visits stopped to protect the children and also to protect Johnnie as well from having to manage a situation that was really beyond her capabilities at this point. Johnnie expressed opposition to this move, but without the usual angry tirade that was typical of her objections in other instances.
>
> When the judge returned the visiting pattern to the shorter visits, Johnnie seemed genuinely relieved and did not withdraw from her lay therapist or demonstrate any discomfort or anger over her lay therapist's reporting of the incident.

In instances where there might seem to be a conflict between the parents' needs and the child's needs, certainly the issue of the child's safety must take precedence.

Even when the parents do not agree with our decisions, it is very helpful for them to have people who deal with them openly and honestly at times of disagreement. It can lead to very real growth on the parents' part when the issues of the child's difficulties or safety are addressed openly, if judgment is not being made about them.

Only when we have an accurate picture of what is happening to the child can we understand fully what issues may yet be troubling the parents or whether treatment is having a helpful effect on the parent-child relationship. At times, parents need real help in dealing with specific behaviors the child is exhibiting or in understanding the whys of normal behavior.

Developing an appropriate treatment plan should be based on a thorough and careful evaluation. If possible, a psychiatric evaluation is most helpful, but is *required* for the small percentage of families who show symptoms of severe pathology such as psychotic behavior, serious depression, or extreme alcohol or drug dependency. These families will not respond to the kind of treatment efforts that will be useful to the majority of abusive and neglectful families. The underlying problem must be addressed through an appropriate psychiatric facility. A meaningful evaluation will help us determine what services are needed for each member of the family. For this evaluation it is beneficial to obtain as full and complete a history of each of the parent's own early lives as is possible. This is not merely to obtain information that will help us determine the "how" of the abuse or the "who did it," but also to understand how the parent or parents came to be in the situation in which we find them. As we obtain this history, it is advantageous to determine if there have been any significant relationships which the parents may have felt were warm and supportive in their early lives, such as with a loving aunt or caring teacher. Such relationships or the lack of them may be an extremely vital factor in determining whether a treatment relationship even will be possible. Experience has shown that those families who are most able to accept our help are those who have had some close relationship(s) in the past. Certainly, without any such relationship, we can expect a difficult and long process when attempting to reach someone who has not experienced this before. At best, however, these parents may long for help and care but have a deep conviction of their own inability to be aided, combined with a fear of those who offer such aid.

As well as a personal understanding of the family members, we need an accurate assessment of the parent-child relationship. Some parents personally may require and benefit from treatment, but cannot change in a reasonable span of time their relationship to the child. Others may want help in giving a child up for adoption or making permanent arrangements for his care. Always the question must be considered whether treatment can alter the situation in time for the child to have a reasonable chance. Fortunately, the courts are beginning to recognize that children cannot wait indefinitely for parents to resolve their problems.

In addition to considering the long-term outcome of the parent-child relationship, many immediate issues that will affect the treatment plan are directly related to the relationship. Questions of safety, severity of the emotional abuse that may have accompanied the physical injury, and the depth of attachment are but a few that will affect decisions regarding placement and visits, as well as the child's needs for direct therapeutic intervention.

Finally, the resources in the community must be matched with the needs of the family. It is not enough to determine that a particular service is required. If such service is not available, a reasonable substitute or arrangement must be found. In this regard, special services which have been particularly effective in working with abusive and neglectful families are the following:

1. crisis nurseries
2. lay therapists or parent aides
3. Parents Anonymous
4. day-care
5. mother-child foster care

These, along with the mandated child protection services and the usual assortment of community and mental health services, must be carefully chosen to fit the needs of a given family. However, to ensure that the plan that is developed actually is carried out, one person should be assigned the role of case manager or coordinator. This person's responsibility will be to coordinate regular treatment reviews or staffings to determine whether services are provided as planned and generally to facilitate the treatment plan. Often this role is carried out by the protective service caseworker, but could reasonably be assumed by anyone on the treatment team who is willing to carry this responsibility. It is a pivotal role in maintaining an adequate long-term treatment plan.

The characteristics that are shared by abusive parents have been well described by Steele and Pollack (1). These shared characteristics, which form a child-rearing pattern, are critical determinants in how we provide treatment and services to the family.

The first issue in any contact with these families is their underlying distrust of help. This is based on two understandable beliefs. The first is that they do not see themselves as being capable of being helped, and the second is that any source of help is dangerous. This grows out of their experience as young children with parents who could not or did not perceive their needs and responded to them with physical attacks or disregard. That they, in adult life, view the offer of help as dangerous is not an indication of paranoia or lack of motivation for help. It is, instead, a protective response, learned during a dangerous childhood. Consequently, efforts to be helpful and make a treatment alliance with these parents will require unusual efforts and sensitive responses. Considerable proof of our intentions, patience, and, most of all, true humaneness and genuine respect will be required. Frequently, concrete demonstrations of our concern, such as providing after-hours appointments, arranging child care, or acting as advocates by facilitating some necessary service, will be proof of our sincere commitment to these families. Such demonstrations may not be within the usual realm of our responsibilities, but are undertaken to comply with legitimate concerns or wishes of the parents. These "extra efforts" are useful in two ways. They illustrate our interest and caring and provide—possibly for the first time—an experience for the parents of someone truly listening to and responding to *their* concerns and needs.

Our response to the parents needs to be understood and recognized. After attempting to be as gentle and sensitive as we know how, it can be very disheartening to be verbally attacked by a hostile parent or be totally avoided. Our own anger at being discounted or unwanted can be played out in our decisions regarding further treatment or can reinforce the parents' perception of help as being hostile and dangerous. Because of the difficulties encountered in working with these families, and the countertransference issues raised, that often cannot be dealt with directly within the treatment situation, it is extremely helpful to have a staff team available for consultation. This team can assist and support the workers in their efforts with the family and provide a place for workers to sort out their feelings in relationship to the family. In this particular field, the support needed by treatment staff is considerable and becomes an important consideration in program planning to maintain personnel.

Closely related to the fear of help is a lack of basic trust, as conceived by

Erikson (2). Poor maternal attachment and nurturing which was earmarked by disregard of the infant's needs leaves a residual problem in developing close human relationships and in mild chronic depression (3). However, the emptiness and longing can often be sensed; and, once the fear of help and closeness have, in some measure, been relieved, the therapist will find an extremely needy and dependent person. This infantile level of need can be uncomfortable to tolerate for many, if not all, professionals to some degree. Professional training has often admonished against developing inappropriate dependency in clients. Such parents must be accepted as the emotionally starved infants they truly are, not in a demeaning way, but as an honest appraisal of what is necessary for them to grow to emotional adulthood and thrive. The original deprivation must be acknowledged and met to some degree before they can move on to another stage. This kind of dependency is neither inappropriate nor induced by the therapist. Finding additional sources of comfort and support can be helpful in relieving one person from the burden this can cause. Lay therapy, the provision of a long-term, trustworthy, and caring "friend," has been a very useful way of dealing with this difficult problem. It takes time, availability, and genuine concern to respond adequately. This is a critical factor in working with abusive and neglectful families. Without the support and nurturing, all other efforts to help may be futile. In some ways we are "reparenting" the parents by providing a new experience with parent surrogates. In this sense we are, as Steele suggests, "providing the facilitating environment that opens new channels of growth, development, and maturation that were blocked and distorted in their early lives . . . like reestablishing in useful form the growth of a child with two parents" (4).

Other pervasive aspects of their early deprivation are these parents' low self-esteem and poor self-concept. This may be understood as deriving from the lack of parental response to infant need in which the child does not have validation for his perceptions. On the other hand, the child quickly learns to be alert to external clues for survival. For some, the expectations were for adultlike behavior and sensitivity to parental need. Even unusual ability and response in normal terms would fall short of parental expectation.

> *Case example.* Cindy, while talking with her caseworker during a home visit, began to change her eighteen-month-old son's diaper. She laid him on the floor and removed the dirty diaper. Before replacing it with a clean one, she became engrossed in her conversation. In the interim of about fifteen minutes, the eighteen-month-old remained motionless in the position in which she had placed him—a remarkable feat for any eighteen-month-old child. When she did put the new diaper on the child, he moved in a direction she did not want him to. He was sharply reprimanded. His previous restraint by remaining quiet for such a long period of time had passed unnoticed.

Rewards for desired behavior are often withheld, while behavior that is viewed as bad or troublesome is noticed and punished. In this way, the child never develops a sense of doing anything worthwhile and expects punishment for his inherent "badness." The child becomes very keyed to the adults who care for him. As adults, they continue to have little sense of themselves as able, self-directed persons and continue to seek external reassurances for indications of how they are doing. This leads to extreme vulnerability to criticism real or imagined. Advice is often sought and sensitivity to others' expectations is well developed.

In treatment we want to help the parents begin to know what their own feelings, ideas, and perceptions are and to act on them. It can be a difficult task, especially when our sense of what is right and appropriate behavior becomes another external expectation to which they may readily comply. The authority vested in our relationship with the family must be recognized and used judiciously. To repeat a similar pattern with the parents may have temporary success in that they may perform in ways we might like them to. This does not mean, however, that the underlying pattern is altered.

The process of change begins with the experience of someone who truly listens, helps to clarify needs and concerns, and who understands and accepts the parents as they are. In such a relationship the parents can begin to idenfity what they want and begin to find ways to achieve their goals. Recognition and encouragement for every step is necessary for an extended time until the ability to trust their own perceptions and act appropriately are confidently developed. As they begin directing their own lives and experiencing some success, self-esteem will rise.

Undoubtedly there will be setbacks, particularly if these parents are criticized by their parents or spouses, as they test themselves. Even if the outcome is less than the desired one, they will need support for their efforts and encouragement for trying. Learning that others have gone through similar experiences can be comforting. It can also be reassuring to know that therapists make mistakes and are not always successful in their efforts. Sharing information or personal experiences may be a way to help the parents consider several options before making a choice. This can also demonstrate how we solve problems or make useful decisions without giving direct advice.

Community resources can be utilized in providing opportunities to try new experiences and to have real success. Education, recreation, or job training are areas that may be tapped. It is still important that the decision to make use of such resources be made by the parents themselves. Often initial attempts are dropped because undertaking a new or unknown activity may seem frightening or overwhelming. Sometimes actual participation in a new venture by a lay therapist or homemaker with the parent can ease initial apprehension.

Case example. Sally, a young, single mother, was rather obese and viewed her weight as a handicap to obtaining employment, as well as feeling ashamed and unhappy about her appearance. A home visitor from a local health department had heard Sally's frequent complaints, as well as her expressed desire to join Weight Watchers. The fee for the weight-loss group was prohibitive for her, so the home visitor arranged for a local agency to provide a "scholarship." With support of the home visitor, the public health nurse, but primarily her own desire to attend the group, she enrolled in the program, and to everyone's delight and amazement, lost a substantial amount of weight. Sally also began using some makeup and was pleased with her new appearance. She then decided to try a crafts class and subsequently was offered a position as a driver for the organization that had initially provided the scholarship for Weight Watchers. This same organization also became a source of social contacts and friendships for her. There continued to be ups and downs in her progress, but some real experiences with success and recognition of her capabilities could not be ignored.

An important outcome of this process is that it can relieve the child from being the primary source of parental hope for success. Frequently, parents have expressed their hope that at long last they will prove themselves by being good parents. Although this may be an admirable goal, it places an unrealistic hope for salvation on the child. This very need, along with the longing for love that the child is expected to meet, places the child in extreme danger of attack when it is felt she has failed. Consequently, providing nurturing for the parent along with development of self-esteem are critical in reducing risk to the child.

Crises are a way of life for most abusive families. Without confidence and faith in one's abilities, any situation is a potential crisis. Particularly stressful are situations that evoke feelings of loss or failure. Frequently initial attempts to make an alliance with the family become successful through concrete help during a crisis. In the long run, however, a real measure of the success of treatment will be the reduction of crises. Part of what leads to continual crises is the inability of parents to plan ahead or deal with anything except the immediate moment. The degree of discomfort evoked by a current situation will precipitate immediate action aimed at relieving that discomfort without consideration of possible long-range effects of a decision made in haste. Use of past experience or reflection on future possibilities are beyond their capacities in the problem-solving process. Usually these parents do not have a clear picture of what the crisis really was about or what precipitated their feelings of panic or discomfort. Helping them sort out what occasioned a particular crisis, identifying the issues that immobilized or overwhelmed them, and then contemplating alternative ways to avoid a repetition of such a situation are the bases for learning coping skills. After such examination into the problems, relief is felt, and it is then possible to use the therapist as a source of comfort or ventilation.

Case example. Joannie would become enraged when her children messed up the house. She viewed their messiness as a direct attempt to frustrate her. She was frightened by the intensity of her anger and recognized real danger in her furious attacks on them. Usually these incidents would occur after she had spent considerable time and effort in putting the house in immaculate order. Initially, she would call her therapist in great anger over some messy activity of one of the children. Attempts to understand were thwarted by a tirade about the child's impossible behavior. Finally, after her fury was spent, she could begin to reconstruct what had led up to the event. Usually some criticism from her mother or her husband's disregard for her would precipitate negative feelings about herself which she would try to bolster by cleaning the house. Being "mommy's helper," as a child had been her main way of achieving praise or recognition. First, she began to identify what caused her discomfort and then to pursue activities through which she could attain recognition and satisfaction. She became a museum guide, immensely enjoying the spotlight of this work and the genuine praise she received for a job well done. She continued to be a very conscientious homemaker, but as she found other avenues than housework for recognition, she became more relaxed about the normal, messy play of the children.

Relationships with their own parents remain important influences in these clients' lives throughout treatment. Their parents make a continuous impact on them through visits, phone calls, and correspondence. These relationships are

fraught with ambivalence and pain, usually on both sides. The pattern of parents
to expect the now grown child to respond to their needs and the continuing need
by the child for parental approval hold them together in a defeating and repetitious
cycle. At times, it appears that it would be easier if all contact would cease. We
may be tempted to encourage total separation and emancipation from contact.
However, because their own identities are rooted in their parents and rarely are
the relationships one-hundred percent "bad," it is far more useful if the parents in
therapy can rework some of the history and develop a more comfortable and
useful way of relating to their families in the present.

Often the reality of the relationship is kept a closely guarded secret. Opening up
long-closed doors and exposing the pain and fears of years past can be extremely
frightening. It is helpful to redouble our efforts to support and be available as they
begin to explore some of the nightmares of their youth. For some it comes in bits
and pieces, over a long period of time, but for others it comes in a torrent. A few
may need psychiatric evaluation and a brief hospitalization to deal with depression. Others may need extended day-care services for the children while they are
immersed in their own pain. Most, however, work this through in a slow way with
many ups and downs in the process. Ultimately, the decision about the outcome
will be in their hands, based on a clearer understanding of themselves, as well as
the realities of their experiences with their parents.

Since the relationship to the child is usually the basis for our involvement with
the family, one goal is predetermined and often reinforced by legal action. The
child must be ensured of a safe home and parents who recognize her needs and
respond adequately to her. Altering the parents' ways of interacting with the child
is usually a natural outgrowth of appropriate treatment for the parents. However,
it cannot be assumed that the situation is safe and adequate for the child without
assessing this carefully. Knowing how the parent perceives the child and how he
actually responds to the child can best be judged by some direct observation. For
some parents their own early lives were so devastating that it may not be feasible
for them ever to provide a safe and loving environment for the child. A particular
child may never be able to "make it" within her family and a "divorce"[1] between
parent and child may be necessary. Without doubt, we need to make termination
of parental rights an acceptable option and in those instances when the parents
cannot decide use the courts to make the decision. It cannot be undertaken without substantial reason and only when a reasonable effort at changing the relationship has been attempted.

Most parents do begin in treatment the process of changing most of their relationships, including their interaction with the child. As they review their own
difficult childhoods with someone who cares and understands, they may find some
empathy for their own child. As their sense of value and "goodness" increases,
they may begin to see some of this "good" self in the child.

1. The concept of divorce between parents and child has been suggested by Dr. C. Henry Kempe as
a reasonable alternative in instances of continued "incompatibility."

Case example. Kelly, after years of being viewed as dumb and inept began to see how bright she truly was as she started back to school. The work was easy and exciting, and she was able to maintain straight As. Her five-year-old was also an intelligent youngster whose capabilities she began to appreciate. She now began to see him as "smart like me."

Finally, we must address the question of how long treatment should last. Regular contact may diminish or stop, but the door needs to be left open for an indefinite period. The availability of people and resources which the family has learned to use and trust must continue. If we have provided a "facilitating environment" needed for their growth, we have in some measure become a part of their lives, just as the original family is in normal development. Termination of this never fully occurs as they carry the experience of this relationship with them. They may need to call or have periodic contact to reaffirm our interest and the importance of the experience we shared. Changes do not always occur in regular and predictable ways, so that a new stress may precipitate further involvement to rework old issues or open new areas for exploration. Frequently, a brief contact may be sufficient to allow them to sort out for themselves what they need and want to do.

Case example. Jan was referred for treatment when her son was three months old. The pediatrician was concerned because of her depression and anxiety around care of the infant. Jan recently requested help for Bobbie, now eleven years old, because of difficulties in school and with peers. In the intervening time, Jan was seen regularly, following the initial referral, for about three years which in the last year included her husband. After that time, there were periodic involvements, some brief contacts, then at times regular contacts for a longer period of several months.

Most families who make use of treatment in a significant way will maintain some contact for a very long time. None of these families, like all families, will have trouble-free lives, and the critical change will be their ability to seek help and use it when they have difficulties.

References

1. Steele, Brandt F., and Pollack, Carl B. 1968. A psychiatric study of parents who abuse infants and small children. In Helfer, R. E., and Kempe, C. H., eds. *The Battered Child* (Chicago: University of Chicago Press).
2. Erikson, Erik H. 1963. *Childhood and Society* (New York: Norton).
3. Steele, Brandt F. 1970. Parental abuse of infants and young children. In *Parenthood: Its Psychology and Psychopathology* (Boston: Little, Brown), p. 450.
4. ———. 1979. Personal communication.

17 Guidelines for Placing a Child in Foster Care

Susan L. Scheurer and Margaret M. Bailey

The decision to remove children from their home environments is among the most difficult and important issues faced by professionals who work in the area of child abuse and neglect. There is a long standing debate about the relative merits of foster care[1] versus leaving the child in the home. Legitimate concerns about foster care include the psychological trauma of separation and reattachment, selection of good foster parents, tension between natural parents and foster parents, and the frequent lack of a coordinated plan for the child. These important issues have been discussed at length by Goldstein, Freud, and Solnit (1), Martin (2), and Fanshel and Shinn (3).

In spite of the inherent problems with foster care, the reality is that many abused or neglected children are not safe in their homes and require an alternative living situation. Professionals are then forced to weigh the risks of foster care against the risks of physical or emotional injury faced by the child at home. Every community needs clear, exacting statements of the reasons for placement to guide professionals making the decisions and to evaluate whether the goals of placement were met. Unfortunately, at the present time "abuse or neglect of the child" is a frequently cited reason for foster care placement. This label does not provide specific goals or expectations for the placement, much less a timetable for their implementation.

The purpose of this chapter is to develop guidelines for foster care placement through a review of one community's cases and a comparison with other literature. While the proposed approach may not apply in all cases, we hope it will

Susan L. Scheurer, M.D., is with the Department of Pediatrics and Human Development, Michigan State University. Margaret M. Bailey, Ph.D., is with Community Mental Health, Lansing, Michigan.

1. This discussion addresses involuntary placement of children in foster care, not placements initiated by the family. The issue is temporary, not permanent, removal of children. Further, the discussion does not include placement of children in their relatives' homes. The authors believe that there are typically more problems for the child placed with a relative than with a stranger. For example, the relatives may not be able to believe that a member of their family would do what the child has alleged, placing the child in an extremely difficult situation at a time when he or she needs maximum reassurance and care.

serve as a catalyst toward other communities' development of workable guidelines.

Other Approaches

There are surprisingly few published reports regarding the decision-making process for placing children in foster care. Martin describes three major uses of foster care: protection, diagnosis, and treatment. The first is short-term placement of a child while a decision is made whether the home is safe or when it will be. The second use of placement is for diagnosis, for example, to see whether an infant who failed to thrive in her natural home will grow and develop in a foster home. The third use of placement is to provide a therapeutic experience for the child.

Schmitt (4) lists one set of guidelines for temporary, voluntary[2] foster care and another set for deciding when to take a case to court. These guidelines for temporary foster care include the symptoms of the child (severe and/or repeated abuse; unmanageable behavior), characteristics of the family (unable to protect the child; refuse intervention), and one situational category (multiple ongoing crises). Apparently, Schmitt is proposing that a portion of cases that require foster care also require court intervention. Therefore, the second set of guidelines is very similar to the first, although briefer. Schmitt's proposals correlate to some degree with Martin's goals, fitting particularly with the notion of protecting the child.

Case Review

In order to provide a clear and useful categorization, the actual practices of a community-based child protection team were examined. The evaluation provided a comparison of actual practices with ideas cited by others. A review of cases evaluated by a multidisciplinary team of professionals was conducted with particular attention paid to cases of children who were removed from their natural families.

Setting

The multidisciplinary diagnostic assessment team presently works in a community of 250,000 people, which includes a modest metropolitan area and outlying rural communities.

This group is a family-oriented assessment team which consults on cases of suspected child abuse or neglect in the community hospitals and also in an outpatient clinic. The team includes a pediatrician, child psychologist, nurse clinician, social worker, and team coordinator. The majority of referrals come from Protective Services, and on those cases, the Protective Services worker is included as a team member.[3] The team is consulted on almost all hospital cases of suspected abuse or neglect. Most of the team's outpatient cases are referrals from

2. The authors no longer utilize voluntary foster care. This issue is addressed more fully below in the Discussion section.

3. All cases in this review were open Protective Services cases.

Protective Services where the worker has screened the case and requests a team evaluation. Typical reasons for referral include the need for in-depth medical and psychological evaluations, reevaluation and redirection for families who have not responded to traditional approaches, and a consultation with the Protective Services worker, when the worker is troubled by the nature or degree of their involvement with the family.

The team's role is threefold with (1) comprehensive evaluation of cases, (2) referral to appropriate treatment agencies, and (3) follow-up of cases and coordination of care. In the cases under consideration, the assessment typically includes physical and psychological evaluations of the children, social histories, and, if necessary, psychological assessments of the parents, observations of parent-child interaction, evaluation of family styles, and development with the family of treatment plans.

The team's close link to Protective Services facilitates their involvement in the evaluation and the decision-making process. In the cases where the team felt the child should be removed, a recommendation was made to the Protective Services worker who, in turn, was responsible for petitioning the juvenile/family court for custody. The decision to petition always rested ultimately with the Protective Services worker. During the two years covered by this review, there were no cases where the team recommended removal and the worker did not concur.[4] Further, the court accepted all petitions on these cases and took the children into custody.

The recommendation to remove a child from his natural home was never the only recommendation. Treatment plans were developed with the families, and the team referred many of the children for psychotherapy or other intervention such as special education or physical therapy. Treatment recommendations for the parents might include psychotherapy, a parenting group, assignment of a parent aide, etc.

In this community, after Protective Services petitions the court, the task of case coordination moves to the caseworkers employed by the juvenile/family court or private agencies subcontracted by the court. These caseworkers assume the responsibility for reviewing cases, follow-up of the child's development, assessing the family's progress in treatment, etc. The team remains in contact with the court on a friendly, but limited, basis by supplying written reports and recommendations, testifying when necessary, and also through periodic reevaluation of the child's or family's progress in treatment.

Cases

In the two-year period reviewed (mid-1977–1979), the team saw approximately 300 children from 150 families yearly. These cases constituted 20% of open Protective Services cases. An "open" Protective Service case is one where initial investigation substantiated that abuse or neglect had occurred.

---

4. There were isolated cases where Protective Services workers recommended removal and the team did not agree. Those cases do not qualify for inclusion in this review.

During the two-year period, the team recommended placement in foster care of seventy-one children in fifty-two families. This subgroup was 17% of all families evaluated. Slightly more boys than girls were involved: forty-one boys and thirty girls. The children's ages ranged from two weeks to fourteen years, with 90% of the children under six years of age.

The records of the seventy-one children were audited to determine the key variables sufficient to account for the decision to remove the child. Identifying the significant variables was a difficult process that required several attempts at sorting and comparing cases. For example, one early attempt involved designation of cases according to the primary presenting symptoms of the children, so the categories included failure to thrive, physical abuse, neglect, etc. The problem with these distinctions was that they did not fully separate cases where foster care was recommended from those where it was not recommended. The importance of clinical judgment and familiarity with the cases became obvious during the determination of the final list of reasons for foster care. The criteria developed for foster care placement are seen as working guidelines.

Findings

Five variables accounted for the seventy-one cases in which children were assigned to foster care. The variables included two presenting characteristics of the children: desertion and serious physical abuse. The variables also included three characteristics of the parents: serious emotional disturbance, refusal or inability to guarantee the child's safety, and serious problems recurring or unresponsiveness to treatment. Definitions of the variables and examples are given below.

Child's Presentation

If present, the characteristics of the children were evident early. The injury or abandonment of a younger child, especially under five years old and certainly an infant, was considered more serious. Age alone was never the reason for recommending foster care but was an important consideration.

1. *Deserted child.* These children had been deserted in typical ways (left in a house or on a street, or at least left with no way to contact their parents). The critical factor was lack of contact by the parents or lack of suitable arrangements for the child's care.

> Case a. Sally[5] was a five month old infant brought by a Protective Service worker for evaluation of possible failure to thrive. She had been hospitalized in another county; the parents had moved and avoided a treatment plan. She had respiratory infection and developmental delays. Her parents agreed to an admission and to the development of a treatment plan. After Sally was hospitalized, the family did not call, answer their phone, or visit, for more than ten days. Protective Services chose to petition the court, as the child had been ready for discharge for several days and had no place to go.

2. *Seriously physically abused child.* In judging the seriousness of abuse to a

___
5. All child and family names are fictitious.

child, the extent of injuries and the child's age were key factors. In these cases, the child's presentation and lack of an adequate explanation for the injuries were sufficient to petition the court for custody. Although the seriousness of the injury in these cases resulted in the decision to petition the court, the extent of the injuries is not predictive of how the family will respond to treatment.

Case a. Harold was a one-month-old infant admitted with a depressed skull fracture for which there was no explanation.

Case b. Louise was a six-week-old infant hospitalized with bilateral skull fractures, which the parents attributed to a fall out of bed. The explanation was not sufficient because the child was developmentally incapable of rolling out of bed, and second, falls from a bed typically do not cause fractures and certainly not bilateral fractures.

Case c. Hester was a four-month-old infant admitted with multiple fractures in different stages of healing, which the parent said occurred while falling out of bed on one occasion. One episode of falling out of bed could not account for the injuries. Falling out of bed almost never results in fractures. This child had been injured on several different occasions.

Case d. June was a ten-month-old infant hospitalized with a second-degree iron-shaped burn on her hand, which the parents said she received by accidentally pushing against the iron. Children who casually touch a hot object do not sustain clearly delineated burns of this degree of seriousness.

Case e. Mary was a three-year-old girl admitted with a fractured femur, multiple bruises in different stages of healing, adult inflicted bite marks, and malnutrition. Her mother said she was "accident-prone."

Parents' Characteristics

In these groups of families the parents exhibited disturbed, unpredictable, and dangerous behavior, or had recurrent serious problems. These behaviors were evident early in some cases, while not clearly present for months or even years in others. While the parents usually expressed affection for their children, there was a marked difference between their intentions and their actions.

1. *Seriously emotionally disturbed.* These parents were overtly psychotic or so disturbed that their behavior with their children was unpredictable.

Case a. Mrs. H. was a thirty-four-year-old mother who hallucinated and was delusional, making statements such as "someone controls my mouth and my hands." A public health nurse recognized that Mrs. H. was very disturbed, noted that she only cared for her child intermittently, and asked for a team evaluation. At only two weeks of age, the child presented with severe diaper rash and minimal weight gain (less than one-half ounce per day).

Case b. Ms. L. was a twenty-two-year-old mother who said she loved her twin daughters but could not predict her own behavior around them. The girls, aged eighteen months, were severely beaten on the legs and back with a tree branch. Ms. L. acknowledged she was a heavy drinker and had a history of violent acts, including having stabbed another woman. This mother had long-term problems in controlling her impulses and was unpredictable.

2. *The parent who refuses or is unable to guarantee the safety of the child.* The defining characteristics of these parents were that they denied the existence of a

serious problem and refused intervention. As illustrated below, they include parents who refused to protect their children from an agressor.

> Case a. Ms. B. was the mother of a three-year-old son. She said she loved him but would not keep the child away from her boyfriend. The boyfriend repeatedly severely beat the boy, and she refused assessment or intervention.

> Case b. Mrs. R. was the mother of two boys, ages two and four. They were admitted from their babysitter's home where they had lived for over a week. The older boy had multiple bruises for which there was no explanation. The younger boy functioned at the one-year level developmentally because of chronic understimulation. Mrs. R. denied that any of these findings were problems, saying, "So what! I can do what I want with my kids." She insisted it was easier for her to leave the children with someone through the week and could not generate an alternative plan.

3. *The family with serious problems that recur and/or do not respond to treatment.* These families differed from the previous group in that they acknowledged the problems, or at least cooperated with the development of a treatment plan. With time, their lack of progress and the serious impact of the problems on the children became apparent. (See table 17.1 for a summary of the results of the chart audit.)

TABLE 17.1   Results of Chart Audit

Reason for Placement	Number of Children	Percentage of Children
A. Child's presentation:		
Deserted	4	6
Seriously physically abused	6	8
B. Parents' Characteristics:		
Seriously emotionally disturbed	17	24
Refuses or is unable to guarantee safety of child	17	24
Serious problems that recur and/or do not respond to treatment	27	38
Total	71	100

> Case a. Several agencies first became involved with Mr. and Mrs. J. and their one-year-old child, who did not have adequate medical care and was developmentally delayed. The J.'s second child, Lisa, born six months later, did not gain weight during her first month of life, at which point the family agreed voluntarily to an extensive plan, including psychotherapy for Mr. J., a parent aide for Mrs. J., and a public health nurse to assist with care of the baby. Lisa gained weight for a few months, then again failed to thrive. At nine months of age she functioned developmentally at a five-month level and showed decreased muscle strength. She was hospitalized and rapidly gained weight and improved in developmental skills. Her parents denied either child had any problems that warranted intervention. All available appropriate community agencies had attempted to help Mr. and Mrs. J., with no real success, making court involvement the only alternative.

> Case b. Protective Services asked several agencies to intervene with Mr. and Mrs. Y. and their two daughters, after a visit to the family's home. The social worker fell through

a hole in the front steps, was repelled by the odor in and around the house, found feces throughout the house, including in the beds, and dishes that had not been cleaned for several months. Many agencies attempted to assist Mr. and Mrs. Y. and were consistently unsuccessful. The children, at ages two and three years, were unsocialized, delayed in development, and usually filthy. After months of unsuccessful attempts to assist the family in getting the house clean and in caring for the children, the court was petitioned.

Case c. Maureen was a three-year-old girl first reported to Protective Services when her mother's companion beat her with a belt. Both adults agreed to seek counseling, but did not attend the sessions. One year later Maureen was hospitalized after eating a toxic cleaning powder in her mother's presence. Maureen exhibited extremely disturbed behavior patterns, including that she refused to eat almost all foods, acted and spoke like an adult, and was depressed. She reported frequent beatings, forced feedings, and having witnessed unusual sexual acts. An extensive treatment plan for both adults and Maureen was again instituted. While Maureen was hospitalized, her mother attended therapy sessions. During subsequent visits with Maureen, the mother and companion continued to abuse her, both physically and emotionally.

Case d. (In the following cases, both mothers were retarded. The cases are presented together to illustrate that both criteria, serious problems and nonresponsiveness to treatment, had to be present to warrant a petition to the court.)

Protective Services initially became involved with Mr. and Mrs. S. after reports that they failed to provide appropriate food, a clean house, or developmental stimulation for their three-year-old daughter. With initial intervention, the first two problems improved. Even with further intervention, the parents could not provide adequate stimulation but allowed the child to attend day care and undergo speech therapy. The family needed constant, comprehensive services and responded to them. There was no court involvement.

In contrast, Mrs. L. was a retarded widow, living with her eight-year-old daughter, Laurie. Protective Services became involved following allegations of lack of supervision and a very dirty house. The worker offered additional services and advice over a year's time, but the situation did not improve. Laurie missed a great deal of school, assumed most of the housework, and appeared increasingly anxious. Mrs. L. dated men who abused Laurie, including a man who gave the child daily enemas. Mrs. L. said this was wrong but did nothing to stop the abuse.

Discussion

Reflections on the Case Review

The key questions in cases of suspected child abuse or neglect are always: Do the injuries constitute abuse or neglect? Is the home safe? What must be done to make the home safe?

The reasons for foster care placement identified by the case review are guidelines for answering the second question, whether the home is safe, and also point toward what intervention may be necessary. A single reason accounted for the decision in each case, and only five reasons accounted for all the seventy-one case recommendations, simplifying the diagnostic task. While some cases met more than one criterion for foster care placement, the existence of any one of them would have been sufficient to justify removing the child. The authors suspect the prognosis is worse when more than one of the criteria are met in a single case.

In some situations, the decision about the safety of the home was made quickly because the actual injuries or the risk to the child was too great to be tolerated. These particular cases were a small portion of the total. In other, more frequent situations, the decision depended on a thorough evaluation of the causes and impact of the abuse or neglect with careful follow-up and evaluation.

The review illustrated that the most frequently cited reason for foster care was the lack of progress made by families with recurrent serious problems. The team's assessments were particularly important in these cases to document the initial findings and to assess the impact of treatment. In addition, these families often demonstrated slow, minimal gain. It was sometimes difficult, although critically important, to identify the caseworker's personal frustrations in working with these families.

In the families with recurrent or unresponding problems, there was rarely a critical incident of abuse or neglect so severe that the child definitely had to be removed. However, professionals asked themselves frequently whether the child would "do better" in another environment. The authors advocate foster care, not to provide merely a better home, but only when the natural home fails to meet the minimum standards. If the community can provide the constant supervision and intervention which may be necessary for the family to meet those standards, then the child can remain in the home.

In contrast to Schmitt, the authors do not advocate voluntary foster care in cases of abuse or neglect. When a problem is serious enough that a child cannot safely return home, then the court is needed to supervise and to decide when the child can. The basic problem with voluntary foster care is that the parents may decide when the child will return home, with no separate advocate for the child.

Schmitt's guidelines for taking a case to court are more or less comparable to the authors' guidelines for foster care placement. However, Schmitt does not include deserted children. Also, the authors' group of families with recurrent and unresponsive problems encompasses three of Schmitt's reasons for foster care, specifically, those families who reabuse children, those who accept treatment but do not improve, and those who emotionally abuse their children. Severe emotional abuse is a reason to petition the court when families do not improve with treatment.

Application of the Guidelines

There are important qualifiers to the use of guidelines or standards for foster care placement in particular communities, including age of the child, the nature and extent of community resources, and professionals' relationship with the juvenile/family court. Any abuse or neglect of infants or children under five years of age is more dangerous, because younger children are more vulnerable. These cases may require court involvement when a similar situation with an older child would not.

The nature and extent of the community's resources may also modify the use of guidelines. Communities with few resources may have to use the court more frequently, because the children are not safe at home without certain services.

Communities must come to grips with this problem and identify and attempt to provide the needed services.

Application of the guidelines also requires a close linkage with the juvenile/ family court to develop a coordinated plan for the child and family. Ideally the plan for foster care includes a statement of the reason the child is being placed, the goals for the placement, and a proposed timetable. Martin's delineation of goals for foster care (protection, diagnosis, and treatment) provides a useful framework for such statements. Protection and diagnosis are short-term goals, while a decision is made about whether and under what circumstances, the child should return home. Three months is usually enough time to complete an evaluation of the child and the family and either return the child with a treatment plan or maintain the child in foster care, also with a treatment plan and revised timetable. Treatment itself, for both child and family, may be accomplished in three months to one year, to a degree that allows reunion of the family, if such a goal is possible. If treatment will require significantly longer periods of time (any more than a total of two years), a petition for permanent wardship should be considered. Prolonged temporary removal is not fair to the child and is very damaging to all parties.

Developing a plan for a child and family requires close work and mutual trust between the court and other professionals. Two problems that inhibit an effective relationship with the court are professionals' unwillingness to give up control of a case and the court's reluctance to accept the recommendations of other professionals. When the court accepts a petition, they assume primary responsibility and control over management of the case. Unfortunately, professionals in the field often view this process as having to choose between two evils, that is, whether to continue working with a difficult family or yield control to the court.

Occasionally when professionals in the field make the difficult decision to petition, some courts deny the case for unsatisfactory reasons. This fact has led some professionals to avoid requests for custody. Avoiding the courts in this situation is intolerable; it leaves a child at great risk. When a community has developed criteria for removing a child from home and these criteria are met in a particular case, the court must be petitioned. The responsibility then lies with the court to intervene or to assume the risk for the child. While there are often problems in working with the court, in most situations a satisfactory relationship is possible, where the community and the court agree on guidelines and acknowledge each other's roles.

References

1. Goldstein, Joseph; Freud, Anna; and Solnit, Albert J. 1973. *Beyond the Best Interests of the Child*. New York: Free Press.
2. Martin, Harold P. 1976. *The Abused Child*. Cambridge, Mass.: Ballinger.
3. Fanshel, David, and Shinn, Eugene B. 1978. *Children in Foster Care*. New York: Columbia University Press.
4. Schmitt, Barton D. 1978. *The Child Protection Team Handbook*. New York: Garland.

18 The Role of Law Enforcement in the Prevention, Investigation, and Treatment of Child Abuse

Jackie N. Howell

"Few aspects in the management of child abuse generate such heat as the involvement of the police" (1). For several years the role of the police in child abuse cases has been a matter of consternation for some and a matter of concern for many others. Generally, there have been two divergent views: one that the police should not be involved at all, and the other that all child abuse cases should be reported to the police.

Physical and sexual assault are crimes in all states of the union and most countries of the world. In addition, all states have some laws specifically pertaining to the abuse of children and to the reporting of suspected child abuse to designated authorities. Viewed from the perspective of the police function within society, the issue is not whether there is a police role, but how that role is most effectively implemented and utilized.

Law enforcement agencies are charged with many and varied legal responsibilities within their communities. To be effective, an agency must continually analyze and establish priorities for responsibilities in accordance with public needs and wishes. The procedures utilized in the accomplishment of prescribed functions are also continually changing as a result of constant evaluation.

In the last decade, the management of incidents of child abuse and domestic violence has become a major concern of law enforcement. Consequently, a greater priority has been given to prompt intervention in these matters. Most police agencies have expanded their functions from investigation and prosecution of serious cases to include crime prevention, i.e., early intervention, treatment by crisis intervention, and referral services.

This chapter briefly discusses the expansion of the police role, improved training programs, improved interagency relationships, and specialized units. These issues are part of law enforcement's response to the problem of child abuse and domestic violence.

Jackie N. Howell is with the Los Angeles Police Department.

Early Intervention in Domestic Disturbances

Traditionally, law enforcement agencies assumed a conservative posture in the fields of child advocacy and domestic disturbances. The parents' right to raise and discipline children as they pleased was virtually unchallenged for many years. Police intervention was limited generally to law violations of a most serious nature, such as felonious physical or sexual assaults and homicides (2).

In recent years, however, law enforcement has become vitally concerned with the serious social issues and the repercussions of family dysfunction. There is also concern for causative factors of delinquent and criminal behavior for the purpose of crime prevention. Studies have shown there is a correlation between child abuse and later deviate behavior (3). Many of the youngsters who become involved in delinquent behavior in their teens are the same youngsters who might have been identified as children receiving neglectful or abusive family care in their younger years (4).

Many maltreated children and families involved in domestic disturbances are known to the police officer. "Although the right of parents to control and raise their own children is accepted as a fundamental right in our society, intervention is justified by a paramount social interest, protection of the child. The Fourteenth Amendment of the United States Constitution states that *everyone* has equal protection under the law. Intervention for the protection of a child may involve a broad range of possible actions including counseling and treatment, the filing of criminal charges, and/or the removal of a child from the control and custody of a parent, guardian, or other caretaker" (5).

Treatment and Referral Services

The well-trained police officer armed with crisis intervention skills and a heightened awareness to objective indications of family dysfunction provides an invaluable case-finding and screening service (6). Police are routinely requested to handle family and neighbor disputes, disturbance-of-the-peace violations, and situations involving drug or alcohol abuse. Children are frequently observed in undesirable circumstances during such routine investigations. The circumstances may not justify traditional police action. The referral of such children and families, however, to appropriate helping agencies may prevent crime and most certainly earns greater respect and trust for law enforcement within the community (7).

Police agencies should provide supportive written policies and procedures which delineate comprehensive standards regarding the alternatives available to the front-line police officer who is confronted with domestic disturbances or child maltreatment incidents. Alternatives may vary as to state laws and local ordinances as well as to the availability and reliability of referral resources (8).

Every police agency should be cognizant of available helping professionals within the community. The immediate action taken by the field officer will depend upon the availability of referral resources and interagency cooperation.

In communities where distrust and "turf" protection exists between professionals, open lines of communication must be established. Treatment professionals can take the initiative by encouraging police officers to participate in all multidisciplinary functions, including community training seminars and interagency councils. In some cities, law enforcement has taken the initiative by breaking down barriers and stressing multidisciplinary cooperation. According to Dr. Robert S. Stone, former director of the National Institute of Health, "The development of a team, as distinguished from a collection of health care professionals who happen to work in the same building, is a question of interaction between people, of each influencing the others constructively, and of each permitting himself to be influenced by the others." This same philosophy can be equally applied to community, public, and private agencies.

In addition to referral services, there are communities where alternatives to prosecution are appropriately utilized by law enforcement agencies and the justice system. Where this occurs, there is generally less reluctance by other professionals to assist and provide needed information and reports when prosecution is deemed necessary. Alternatives to prosecution may be one, or a combination, of the following:

1. A referral to a social or treatment agency or professional for the family
2. A referral to a child protection service agency
3. A release-petition request to the juvenile court asking for intervention and assistance (not for removal of the child from the home)
4. A detained petition to the juvenile court asking for intervention and assistance
5. A hearing at the local prosecutor's office, where the complaint may be held in abeyance without a court hearing
6. The criminal court setting aside or diverting a complaint for a year for purposes of ensuring treatment and rehabilitation

Law enforcement is not a treatment service and has no primary responsibilities to provide treatment. However, the early identification and referral of dysfunctioning families can be extremely helpful to the treatment process that may follow.

Special Emphasis on Investigations of Serious Cases

The recognition, evaluation, and investigation of serious child abuse and neglect is difficult, complex, and time-consuming. It is necessary for the police investigator to possess an in-depth knowledge of the symptoms of child abuse and neglect, because the victims are often too young or too frightened to comprehensively discuss what occurred. Usually there are no reliable witnesses. These investigations are similar to homicide cases, in that the court cases rely heavily upon circumstantial evidence because of the victim's inability to testify. The police investigator must have a thorough knowledge of statutes and case law and must be able to obtain, examine, and preserve the needed physical evidence, such as implements, photos, blood stains, etc. In many cases, search warrants are necessary to obtain valuable evidence.

Suspected perpetrators must be correctly advised of their constitutional rights, and each of these rights must be scrupulously safeguarded. Investigators must utilize proper interview techniques and make written or taped records of interviews of victims, perpetrators, and witnesses. Frequently, serious cases will require the temporary removal of the victim from the home for medical evaluation or treatment. Photographs of injuries or home conditions are also necessary for presentation in court. Usually, protective custody will be deemed necessary for the victims. Timeliness in the completion of these investigative tasks is a key factor for the successful presentation of the case in a court of law, juvenile or criminal.

In recent years, the juvenile or dependent-child court system has become more adversary in concept and procedures. As a result of this adversary process, allegations of abuse or neglect are becoming increasingly more difficult to sustain. This places additional burden and emphasis on the initial investigation, which must be immediate, thorough, and constitutionally correct.

An arrest of a child's caretaker and a prosecution in criminal court, even in serious cases of abuse, may be abhorrent to some treatment professionals; others are recognizing that it need not be devastating to a program of treatment and rehabilitation. Indeed, in many situations the authority of the criminal court may provide the only assurance that treatment is pursued.

Misdemeanor or felony court prosecution of parents or caretakers is necessary in many child abuse cases. Prosecutions are generally necessary in serious cases, frequently involving a caretaker/guardian other than the natural parent, a parent resistant to treatment, or untreatable parents. When this occurs, a juvenile or dependency petition should also be requested. Adequate measures for the safety and care of the victims and siblings must be assured. Additionally, it is frequently necessary in the more serious situations for relinquishment proceedings to occur.

In any case of serious physical or sexual abuse, the authority of the juvenile court should be sought to provide a treatment program for the victim and possibly the victim's siblings. Children involved in abusive situations frequently view themselves as the perpetrators of the crime rather than the victims.

Law enforcement officers and treatment professionals must remember that the police have the means to investigate and clear parents of charges, as well as to arrest them. The law is for the protection of society and not merely for punishment (9).

Physician–CPS–Police Relationships

Throughout the investigation of child abuse and neglect cases, a close partnership between the police, child protective services (CPS) workers, and the treatment professionals is essential. In serious cases this provides a more thorough and legally correct investigation, and in less serious cases it provides for a better coordination of services.

Domestic disturbances can quickly become domestic violence. Where there is any indication of violence occurring, a joint response of the police and CPS worker to a reported incident is preferable. In addition, law enforcement will frequently be requested to place a child into protective custody at a medical facility. When this occurs, the police investigator must work closely with the physician to assure that the victim is not removed prior to the completion of the investigation and/or treatment.

Varied approaches have been utilized in different areas of the country bringing about open communication and mutual cooperation between child protective services and law enforcement agencies:

Montgomery County, Maryland. Cases reported to the Department of Social Services or to the Juvenile Section of the Montgomery County Police are investigated jointly by a juvenile officer and a social worker.

San Diego, California. The Department of Social Services has a worker housed at the San Diego Police Department facility to work in conjunction with the Abused Child Unit of that department.

Honolulu, Hawaii. The Honolulu Police Department has used another approach to assure communication with the Child Protective Services Units. Communication is mandated by written policy pertaining to the "Duties and Responsibilities of the Abused Child Detail" (procedure number 321, dated August 1978).

A number of the states have mandatory reporting laws that prescribe dual reporting of suspected child abuse cases to both the department of social services and to the local law enforcement agency, with a further proviso that each agency must report to the other. This system not only provides for communication and liaison between agencies, but also provides an additional safeguard to keep a child or family from falling through the proverbial "cracks" or "getting lost" in a system. This is extremely important in large agencies in heavily populated areas.

An interagency council can also be an invaluable way to improve or maintain relationships between the police, CPS, physicians, and other service and treatment providers.

An example of a successful council in a heavily populated area is the Los Angeles County, Inter-Agency Council on Child Abuse and Neglect. The council serves as an official agent of the Los Angeles County Board of Supervisors. The primary purpose of the council is to provide overall countywide guidance for programs to prevent, identify, and treat child abuse and neglect.

Additional purposes include:

1. Providing a forum for interagency communication and coordination of services for the protection of children throughout Los Angeles County
2. Facilitating training of professionals in the identification, prevention, and treatment of child abuse and neglect
3. Developing recommendations for new and improved services to families and victims of child abuse and neglect
4. Facilitating implementation of child abuse programs throughout the county
5. Disseminating information regarding existing child abuse and neglect programs
6. Increasing public awareness of the problems of child abuse and neglect programs

Problems in Dealing with Numerous Law Enforcement Agencies

One of the problems urban treatment and social agency professionals encounter is the large number of law enforcement agencies with which they must work. The various police agencies may respond differently to child abuse and neglect allegations. In large densely populated counties, there may be as many as sixty separate police jurisdictions, each with autonomy as to policies and procedures. Within a state, there will be hundreds of police entities. The degree of awareness and sophistication will vary from agency to agency, as will the willingness to become involved in domestic disturbances or to provide intervention services in cases not involving felonious assaults or criminal neglect.

This problem was addressed in the state of California by legislation which requires a prescribed curriculum of training in the investigation, prevention, and treatment of child abuse cases for all law enforcement officers within the state. The training is a condition of receiving basic certification from the California Peace Officers Standards and Training Commission. In addition, detailed guidelines and training packages are provided to all law enforcement agencies within the state. An advanced, specialized training program and certification is available for those officers desirous of specialization. The curriculum was designed with the assistance of representatives from various public and private agencies, including educators, law enforcement, the legal and medical professions, and social service agencies (10). Similar mandated programs would be beneficial and should be encouraged in all states not already providing direction in this area.

Recently published federal standards will also assist in bringing about consistency of response in child abuse cases. The Draft of Federal Standards for Child Abuse and Neglect Prevention and Treatment Programs and Projects, developed by the National Center on Child Abuse and Neglect, of the United States Department of Health, Education, and Welfare, lists the following standards for law enforcement:

1. The law enforcement agency should develop policies, procedures, and organization models that facilitate decision-making in cases of suspected child abuse and neglect.
2. The law enforcement agency should participate in the state Child Protection Coordinating Committee and on the community Child Protection Coordinating Council.
3. The law enforcement agency should develop programs and strategies to prevent child abuse and neglect and to assist officers in identifying children and families at risk.
4. The law enforcement agency should assist officers in identifying and responding to cases of suspected child abuse and neglect.
5. The law enforcement agency should report suspected cases of child abuse and neglect as mandated by state law.
6. The law enforcement agency should emphasize the interview as a significant tool in a child abuse and neglect investigation.
7. The law enforcement agency should develop and participate in multidisciplinary approaches to preventing and treating child abuse and neglect in cooperation with the local child protective services unit.
8. The law enforcement agency should educate its personnel in the legal aspects of child abuse and neglect.
9. The law enforcement agency should participate in the development of improved and innovative approaches to preventing, identifying, and treating child abuse and neglect.

While it is recognized that there are problems with the number of separate law enforcement agencies, it is also significant that each is a recognized part of the local community it serves. "They are well known and readily identifiable. When help is needed, they can be quickly located. Other agencies such as child protective services agencies, though also charged with responsibility for child protection, may not be so well known to the average citizen seeking assistance in behalf of an endangered child. Therefore, the law enforcement agency is often the community resource citizens turn to first when child abuse and neglect is discovered" (11).

Training and Coordination

Law enforcement agencies generally are very cognizant of the necessity for comprehensive training programs.

In many parts of the country, specialized training is providing officers with the knowledge, skills, and sensitivity to work with children and families involved in domestic disturbance and/or violence. To accomplish this training, large police departments have developed detailed training guidelines and materials for multilevel training programs. Their officers study all aspects of prevention, investigation, and treatment of child abuse and neglect. Other agencies are utilizing training programs provided by universities or organizations such as the University of Southern California's Delinquency Control Institute course on child abuse.

Outstanding training materials are also provided by the International Association of Chiefs of Police, titled *The Police Perspective in Child Abuse and Neglect*. The material includes a training manual, training slides, and information pamphlets titled *Training Keys* (12).

An effective basic program generally includes information on the following: scope and definition of the problem, criteria for identification and intervention, legal aspects of child abuse, purpose of child abuse investigations, crisis intervention and interview techniques, the investigative process, police alternatives in dispositions of cases (regarding the child and the perpetrator), criminal prosecution, multi-disciplinary approach, and treatment programs and referral resources.

Police officers having specialized duties in this area are or should be receiving intensive in-service training in order to function as experts. This training is frequently accomplished by attending local or regional seminars and national conferences such as the annual National Conference on Child Abuse sponsored by the United States Department of Health, Education, and Welfare's National Center on Child Abuse and Neglect.

Cross-training between police and related agencies is also extremely effective. Not only is this informational, but it develops greater liaison and understanding between agencies and their personnel.

Many police agencies are implementing a system of centralized controls within their individual departments. A centralized control provides the functional responsibility for all matters pertaining to child abuse and domestic incidents. In small departments, this may be one officer or juvenile officer. In some large departments, a specialized investigative unit is utilized. A specialist's approach with a centralized control provides the direction and emphasis needed within the agencies, for improved coordination, training, investigation, and community liaison. A system of control and expertise is necessary to accomplish a concerted effort to combat the increasing reported incidences of child abuse.

Specialized Child Abuse Units

Police agencies have for many years utilized specializations for law enforcement responsibilities that require considerable knowledge and training. The assignment of officers to youth services bureaus or juvenile divisions is common throughout the world. These officers are generally responsible for investigations where juveniles are either the perpetrators or the victims of a crime.

The increased public concern over child abuse and neglect, coupled with the increased reported incidences, has necessitated the implementation of specialized child abuse units.

The carefully selected personnel for these plainclothes assignments are highly skilled and sensitive to the complexities of the problems they must deal with. Their duties combine social and family services functions with the traditional role of the police.

In 1974, the Los Angeles Police Department implemented the first specialized Abused Child Unit in the nation (13). The unit was funded by the city of Los Angeles at the insistence of the professional community. The unit's designated responsibilities include investigation and coordination of abuse cases, in addition to training and liaison functions. The unit is broken into male/female teams, which is of primary importance. This composition of teams provides for flexibility in the interview process, particularly in sensitive sexual abuse cases. Additionally, better rapport is established with the entire family unit.

Since the inception of this unit, numerous police agencies throughout the country have implemented similar specialized units and details.

There are many advantages to specialized units within the larger departments. Investigations can be accomplished more efficiently within the required time constraints. Training, advice, and assistance can be provided to all department officers, and a greater degree of cooperation and liaison can be established with related agencies and professionals. The most significant advantage is the ability to accomplish designated responsibilities with a minimum of stress to the victims and families.

Specialized juvenile officers or units help to counteract the perceptions of some professionals that all reported cases are handled in a strict and punitive manner. The ability of police agencies to respond sensitively to child abuse situations will favorably impress and impact the community they serve. The police must ensure that appropriate action is taken in a coordinated fashion on an individual case basis for every child.

Summary

Many improvements are needed throughout the entire criminal justice system in order to effectively deal with child abuse and domestic disturbance. Police agencies are the gatekeepers to that system. Early identification and intervention, improved training, and increased support between agencies and professionals have been discussed in this chapter. There are many such issues involving children and families that can and must be addressed by law enforcement. Effective leadership must be provided within both the justice system and the community. The police tradition is one of service to humanity. What better way of serving humanity than in providing an improved quality of skills, knowledge, and systems in the protection of children and the prevention of crime. "Children are the greatest resource that a society has; therefore, they should have the opportunity to develop and grow in a wholesome environment, free from all forms of neglect, cruelty, and exploitation" (14).

References

1. Renovoize, J. *Children in Danger: The Causes and Prevention of Baby Battering.* London, 1974.
2. Howell, J. N. The Year of the Child. *Crime Prevention Review.* Sacramento, California, October 1974.
3. Alfaro, Jose D. *Summary Report on the Relationship Between Child Abuse and Neglect and Later Socially Deviant Behavior.* Select Committee on Child Abuse, New York, N.Y., March 1978.
4. Glueck, Sheldon, and Glueck, Eleanor T. *Unraveling Juvenile Delinquency.* Harvard Law School Studies in Criminology. New York, N.Y., 1950.
5. California Department of Justice, Pamphlet 8, *Child Abuse: The Problem of the Abused and Neglected Child.* Sacramento, California, 1978.
6. Aguilira, D., Messeck, J. M., and Farrell, M. S. *Crisis Intervention Theory and Methodology.* St. Louis, 1970.
7. Bard, Morton. Training Police as Specialists in Family Crisis Intervention, in Sager, C., and Kaplan, H., *Progress in Group and Family Therapy.* New York, 1972.
8. The Metropolitan Washington Council of Governments. *Child Abuse, a Current Study.* Washington, D.C., 1977.
9. Collie, J. The Police Role, in *Concerning Child Abuse.* Edinburgh, Scotland, 1975.
10. The California Peace Officers Standards and Training Commission. *Curriculum and Guidelines, Child Abuse and Neglect.* Sacramento, California.
11. Broadhurst, Diana D., and Knoeller, James S. The Role of Law Enforcement in the Prevention and Treatment of Child Abuse and Neglect. *Draft of Federal Standards for Child Abuse and Neglect Prevention and Treatment Programs and Projects.* National Center on Child Abuse and Neglect, Department of Health, Education, and Welfare Publication No. (OHDS) 79-30193.

12. International Association of Chiefs of Police, Inc. *The Police Perspective in Child Abuse and Neglect.* Gaithersburg, Maryland, 1977.
13. Department of Health, Education, and Welfare, National Center on Child Abuse and Neglect, Children's Bureau. *Child Abuse and Neglect: The Problem and Its Management,* Vol. 2, *The Roles and Responsibilities of Professionals.* Washington, D.C. Publication No. (OHD) 75-30074.
14. Matusinka, Jean E. *Equality.* Paper presented at the Second International Congress on Child Abuse and Neglect, at London, England, 1978.

19 Liberty and Lawyers in Child Protection

Donald N. Duquette

The distinguishing feature of the juvenile or family court which sets it apart from all other elements of the child protection system is that the court acts as *arbiter of personal liberty*. When society at large, through child protective services, attempts to intervene in the private life of a family on behalf of a child, the court must assure that the rights of the parents, the rights of the child, and the rights of the society are protected and are abridged only after full and fair and objective court process. Only the court can abridge these personal rights in other than emergencies. Only the court can compel unwilling parents (or children) to submit to the authority of the state. The court, then, controls the *coercive* elements of our society and allows those coercive elements to be unleashed only after due process of law.

If the personal freedom of parents or of children stands to be limited or infringed, then the court must hear the circumstances and decide whether or not the infringement of personal freedom is warranted. Except in emergencies, personal freedom may not be taken away without the authorization and legitimization of the court.

The personal rights at stake for both parents and children in child protection have been recognized in our law as fundamentally important constitutional rights (1). The rights of parents to the care and custody of their children and the rights of children to live with their parents without government interference can be infringed only after due process of law.

The law is an essential partner with the medical, social, and mental health professionals in coping with children who may be abused or neglected. The perspective and orientation of the lawyer and judge, however, is somewhat different from that of the other professionals. Personal rights and liberties, their protection and their abrogation in certain cases, is the unique business of the court.

Lawyers act as advocates for one side or another or for one set of interests or

Donald N. Duquette, J.D., is with the University of Michigan Interdisciplinary Project on Child Abuse and Neglect.

another. Lawyers need not pursue the solution best for all concerned and need not ascertain what is best in the circumstances. The lawyer must merely determine his clients' position and advocate for that position—zealously.[1] The legal proceedings are ultimately adversarial—even in family or juvenile court, despite disclaimers to the contrary. Attorneys come from a background of reliance on the adversarial system and must adjust their thinking in juvenile court to a less-adversarial approach and greater reliance on negotiation and mediation.

On the other hand, physicians and social workers come from a reliance on trust and cooperation and find the adversarial process in court discomforting, foreign, nonproductive or counterproductive in terms of the "real problems" faced by the family. Even if lawyers successfully reduce the adversary level in juvenile court, the nonlawyers are likely to remain uncomfortable. Alternative ways to protect personal liberties of parents and children need to be explored. Greater reliance on negotiation and mediation is one such alternative to adversarial trial. Until nonadversarial alternatives are widely used, however, we all must work with the adversarial process. The advantages of the adversarial process must be appreciated and the disadvantages minimized. The following discussion is offered as a step toward interdisciplinary understanding of the court process and the legal profession's responsibilities.

The lawyer's role in criminal cases is well defined by ethical tradition and practice and needs no further elaboration here. More importantly, the criminal prosecution is a poor means of coping with child abuse and neglect. All states have cruelty-to-children or assault-and-battery statutes that make it a crime to abuse or seriously neglect a child. While criminal prosecution is nearly always possible, it is rarely done in most jurisdictions. The criminal case is difficult to prove and must be proved beyond a reasonable doubt; it takes considerable time, provides no help to the family unit, and the family unit, if successful, may break up, rather than stabilize. If unsuccessful, the accused parent may feel vindicated and justified in his previous treatment of the child. The possibility of criminal prosecution may have an affect on the parents in terms of getting them to agree to a treatment program and juvenile court jurisdiction in exchange for dismissal of the criminal charges. Generally, criminal prosecution of child abuse or neglect cases is not recommended (2).

The Danger of Overreaching

A danger exists in child protection that personal rights of parents and children will *not* be protected in our well-intentioned zeal to protect and help children and parents. Our good intentions do not alter the need to recognize and respect personal integrity and autonomy of clients. Some may advocate, "Beware of the benevolent ruler; they intend, nevertheless, to rule."

Monrad Paulsen addressed the risks of well-intentioned overreaching:

---

1. The editors would disagree with this point in civil court cases—EDS.

> The "reaching out" with Protective Services, whether by a public welfare department or a voluntary agency, presents a problem which the good motives of the agency ought not to obscure. If help is offered when it is not wanted, the offer may contain an element of coercion. There is a danger of overreaching when the agency deals with the most vulnerable members of the community who may easily be cowed by apparent authority. [What is] the extent to which the offering of protective services should be reviewed by some judicial or administrative agency[?]... The privacy of a family ought not to be upset lightly. (2, p. 158)

Child protective services is an area of state control over individuals and families rarely visible to most members of the community. Social workers and other helping professionals involved in child protection activities intend no harm to client families, but aspire instead to stabilize the family as a unit, protect the child, and impart skills of child rearing where they are lacking. In spite of the benevolent motives of child protective services, however, significant intrusions by government into personal and family life is possible without the safeguards of due process of law. The governmental intrusions, in the form of child welfare services, may not be warranted in some cases.

Children's services workers and supervisors should recognize that their clients often attribute considerably more power and authority to them than they may actually possess. The threat of court action is present in every child welfare case, whether expressed or implied. Clients may agree to protective services involvement out of fear of departmental authority or fear of court petition. Overestimating the power of the department, the family may believe that a petition to the court is tantamount to removal of their children, not understanding that they have rights in the legal process too. The exaggerated perception of protective services authority and the fear of the court process may intimidate clients so that they will acquiesce in "voluntary" plans for services or for placement of their child. Such "voluntary" and nonjudicial arrangements provide neither safeguards for the rights of the parent and the children nor checks on a possibly overzealous agency or social worker. A good part of any legal case brought on behalf of children (and against their parents, as the parents may see it) often comes from the parents' own statements and admissions. Parents are often "condemned out of their own mouths."

Add to the above the fact that child welfare clients are often poor and powerless, the risk of arbitrary social work action, of agency coercion, and of overreaching in violation of personal liberty and personal integrity looms large indeed. How should personal freedoms of parents and children be preserved in child welfare? Should procedural safeguards be established within the administrative structure of children's services to protect the privacy and personal liberties of clients? Or should we rely on individual social workers to respect personal liberties and clearly advise clients of their legal rights and the limitations of social work authority whenever involuntariness and coercion may exist?

Some civil libertarians have suggested that all child welfare clients be given a warning upon first contact that anything they say can be used against them in court and that a warrant be required prior to any protective services investigation (3).

Such warnings and warrants are not now required by law. Basic fairness and good social work practice and ethics require that clients be fully advised of the protective services role and the limits of agency authority from the very first contact.

Because child abuse and neglect cause such great societal concern and because the child protection network has been seen as benevolently motivated, society has, up to now, been willing to run the risk of occasional coerced and perhaps unwarranted invasions of family privacy in exchange for swift identification and response to child abuse and neglect and related ills. The law has not required that notice and hearing be provided before the child protective service is allowed to become involved with the family. Child welfare professionals, however, ought to be aware of the personal liberty issue and be responsive to it in every dealing with potential clients.

The Child's Attorney

Statutes in nearly all states require or permit the appointment of an attorney for the child in child protection cases (4). That lawyer is generally charged with representing the "best interests" of the child and with making an independent judgment of what the "best interests" might be. The statute in Michigan is illustrative:

> The court, in every case filed under this act in which judicial proceedings are necessary, shall appoint legal counsel to represent the child. The legal counsel, in general, shall be charged with the representation of the child's best interests. To that end, the attorney shall make further investigation as he deems necessary to ascertain the facts, interview witnesses, examine witnesses in both the adjudicatory and dispositional hearings, make recommendations to the court, and participate in the proceedings to competently represent the child. (M.C.L.A. 722.630 [Mich.])

In most settings the lawyer has a client to articulate what he or she wants, and this determines the position the lawyer will take. In a criminal case the client wants off as lightly as possible; in a civil action the client wants as large a recovery in dollars as possible. In child protection, however, the position to be taken by the lawyer is often quite unclear. The child is often too young to express a view. Even when the child is old enough, the attorney, charged with representing the child's "best interests" may be compelled to disagree with the youthful client and advocate a different position.

The anomaly deepens when one recognizes that there are two other attorneys participating in the proceedings. Child protective services and their attorney often perceive their goal as achieving the best interests of the child. The parents' attorney will argue for what his clients see as the best interests of the child, which is to be at home with his or her parents. And, of course, the judge makes the ultimate decision of what is in the best interests of the child. Many judges act as advocates in terms of assuring proper social services to the child and his or her family. Describing the role of the child's attorney as advocate for the best interests of the child does little, then, to distinguish his or her role from that of the other actors in child protection. Nor does this description give the attorney guidance as to what he or she should *do* in pursuit of the nebulous "best interests of the child."

If the lawyer for the child is to decide what is in the child's best interests, nothing in the lawyer's training has equipped him or her to assess parental conduct, to appraise the harms to a child presented by environment, to recognize strengths in the parent-child relationship, or to evalute the soundness of an intervention strategy proposed by the social agency. The child's counsel's role is complex. The counsel must synthesize the results of the protective services investigation; the child's psychological, developmental, and physical needs; the child's articulated wishes; his or her own assessment of the facts and of the treatment resources available. The ultimate decision as to the course of action to be taken by the child's attorney in any given case is basically *nonlegal* in character. The role of child's counsel imposes heavy responsibility and requires independent social judgments.

In coming to a position for the child, the attorney must ascertain the facts of the case. Many commentators have suggested that the child's attorney do a completely independent investigation including interviews with all relevant witnesses before arriving at an independent position (5). While such zeal on behalf of a child is commendable and probably necessary in some cases, it is also an expensive duplication of effort between the protective services worker and the lawyer. The lawyer can rely on the protective services investigation in most cases—interviewing family members, neighbors, and other witnesses only if warranted by the case. The lawyer should interview, or at least see, the child client in every case—even if it is only for the purpose of getting a "feel" for the child as a real person facing a serious personal dilemma. The child should be personalized to the lawyer beyond the paper work of court petitions and social work reports.

The emphasis of protective services and their attorney in the court is generally on proving the facts alleged in the petition and gaining court jurisdiction. The child's attorney's role goes beyond that, to looking at the entire proceeding—both the legal and social aspects—from the perspective of the child. The attorney must come to an independent judgment as to what course of action will be best for the child, based on his or her personal appraisal of the totality of the circumstances affecting the child.

Having come to a position on behalf of the child, the attorney should advocate vigorously for that position, both in the courtroom *and* within the social service bureaucracy. The traditional role of a *guardian-ad-litem,* still the name given to the child's attorney in some jurisdictions, is not as advocate, but is rather a technical watchdog. Traditionally, the guardian-ad-litem would examine pleadings and other material in the file and ascertain that the proceedings which affect the child are legally correct (6). In child protection proceedings children need more than a technician to ensure legal precision; they need more than a passive observer and advisor to the court; they need an *advocate* (6).

The attorney's advocacy should begin with the social agency that has filed the petition. Questions about the child's separation from his or her parents should be raised. How long has the separation lasted? What is the likely harm to the child of prolonged separation? Are regular visits, supervised if necessary, being arranged for the child? *What is the agency treatment plan for this child and this family?* The agency must be pressed to come to an intervention strategy quickly for the child and family so that the agency and court intervention does not just drift aimlessly without guidance or direction.

The child's lawyer must not agree with social work recommendations without question. He or she should question closely and extract the underlying basis for the social work position and recommendations. The child's counsel may or may not defer to the social work judgment and may or may not agree with their recommendations. The lawyer's conclusions should be reached by independent thought processes even though the protective services worker may be the person most often relied upon to supply fact.

Despite disclaimers to the contrary, child protection proceedings normally reflect most of the essential elements of an adversary proceeding. Attorney for the child, however, unlike lawyer roles in most other litigations, is not required to take an adversary position. The child's attorney is not called upon either to prosecute or defend, but rather to ensure that there is presented to the court all relevant facts necessary to adjudication and disposition, and to exert his or her efforts to secure an ultimate resolution of the case which, in his or her judgment, best serves the interests of the child.

The child's attorney may play a significant role in facilitating negotiation and mediation. Swift resolution of the legal dispute is nearly always in the child's interest. A cooperative and nonadversarial resolution which provides the needed protection and services to the child is also nearly always in the child's interest. The child's attorney should encourage negotiation and could even play the role of mediator between agency and parents in the interests of a swift and nonadversarial resolution of the dispute.

The role of the child's attorney after adjudication should remain vigorous and active. The attorney should press and persuade the responsible social agencies for services and attention which the child client (and perhaps his or her family) needs. Caseworkers are often overextended with caseloads that are too large. Advocacy within the bureaucracy may ensure that the lawyer's client gets the services and attention needed. Preferably such nudging of the social agencies can be done in a collegial, nonaccusatory manner. If, however, social workers or agencies are not fulfilling their responsibility to a particular child (or to the parents) the child's attorney should insist on a higher standard of service either by a direct request to the agency or by formally raising the issue before the court.

Methods of appointment and payment of lawyers for children must encourage vigorous advocacy, in and out of court, over the long term. Often attorneys are appointed or paid only for a single court action without a mandate to advocate before trial or to follow-up after the court has entered its orders. Vigorous advocacy over time is discouraged by short-term lawyer appointments for children. The term *guardian-ad-litem* implies a temporary appointment for the litigation only. Certain fee schedules pay a lawyer in such a way that court preparation, mediation, and independent case assessment are not encouraged. For example, a lawyer may be paid per court hearing attended or per case handled rather than by the hour spent. The fee schedule may be so low that the economics of law practice do not allow the experienced lawyer to spend the necessary time or the energy to perform the lawyer role as he or she might like. Vigorous, competent, and long-term child advocacy has a price tag. Economics significantly affects the quality of legal representation provided children.

Considering that much of the child's attorney's role is nonlegal in nature and that traditional law school education does not prepare a lawyer for this role, should lawyers be the ones representing children in such cases? Lawyers are well equipped to handle the prodecural aspects of child protection cases, but the judgment as to what is in the best interests of the child and the critical surveillance of the social service agencies may be done as well or better by nonlawyers. Perhaps para-professionals or volunteers trained in the legal and social aspects of child protection cases can perform this function economically, with lawyer consultation and service as needed. Communities experimenting with nonlawyer representatives for the child, as complements to the child's attorney, include Seattle, Washington, and Kalamazoo, Michigan (7).

Protective Services Attorney

Traditionally in child protection cases no attorney appeared in most court actions on behalf of the social agency or individual who filed the petition alleging child abuse or neglect. In the recent past, if an attorney did appear, he was likely to be a young assistant prosecutor or assistant county corporation counsel with little preparation time, limited experience in such cases, and little familiarity with juvenile court and child protection law. The child neglect attorney was often the one most recently arrived in the office. Attorneys complained about the lack of specificity with which their social worker clients presented their cases and about the "murkiness" and lack of legal standards in the juvenile court generally. Juvenile court, and especially child abuse and neglect cases, often received low priority among the bar.

In recent years, concurrent with the due process revolution in juvenile court, the role and functioning of all attorneys in juvenile court has acquired importance and greater definition. The need for competent legal advice for petitioning agencies in child protection is increasingly recognized. Proving child abuse or neglect in child protection cases is very difficult. The parents are generally represented. The child may be independently represented. A petitioning protective services worker is at a distinct disadvantage if he or she is charged with the burden of proof in an adversarial court without legal counsel.

The role requirements of the petitioner's attorney in child protection cases include conventional attorney duties, but differ from the traditional lawyer tasks in several respects. Some of the special problems faced in child protection are addressed below.

Lawyers who represent banks learn the banking business very well. Lawyers who represent labor learn labor unions and organizing from top to bottom.

Likewise, lawyers who represent child welfare agencies should know and understand social work as a profession and the child welfare system. The child welfare lawyer must understand and appreciate the emphasis on nonjudicial (yet fair) handling of child protection cases. In addition to traditional legal skills, understanding juvenile court and family law and philosophy is essential. The attorney should know and respect the functions, the capabilities, and even the limitations of social workers and other behavioral scientists. The foster care system, its limitations and its strengths, its advantages and its disadvantages, the benefits and risks to children, also must be appreciated.

What is the nature of the attorney-client relationship between the child protection agency and its lawyer? The legal agency which assumes responsibility for legal representation of the child protection petitioners in the juvenile or family court vary from state to state and sometimes even from county to county. The duties are variously assumed by the local prosecuting attorney, the state attorney general's office, the county corporation (civil) counsel, and sometimes by lawyers who are actually employees of the child protection agency. Some legal agencies representing protective services assume a quasi-judicial role so that they will initiate legal action as requested by the social agency only if in their judgment such action is warranted. The lawyer exercises a sort of prosecutorial discretion about what child protection cases are brought to court.

In contrast, a recommended position is that the legal representatives of the agency see themselves in a traditional attorney-client relationship. The child protection agency in fulfilling its responsibilities to children and to families needs assistance and authority from the court from time to time. In invoking the court system they should have access to a lawyer whom they can trust and who will act as their advocate as necessary.

Points of view and judgments about strategy may differ between the lawyer and the agency personnel, but such differences are not unusual between lawyer and client, they are rather common in both personal and corporate practice. When such disagreements occur the lawyer should rely on the traditional counselor function of the lawyer in which the matters are discussed in-house and recommendations for actions arrived at. If differences cannot be resolved in this manner the lawyer should defer to his or her social agency clients in matters within the scope of their expertise, i.e., in social judgments and assessments as to what the needs of the child and family are, while the agency should defer to the lawyer in matters of trial strategy and legal judgment. Unfortunately the legal and social spheres of expertise are often not clear and distinct in this context. Almost every judgment in child abuse and neglect cases reflects a value judgment that certain parental behavior constitutes legal neglect. Normative fact judgments are made at every step of the child protection process: by the reporting person, by the social worker, by the social work supervisor, by the lawyers, and finally, and most importantly, by the judge. What is the minimum community standard of child care to which every child is entitled? What is the threshold of child care below which the state may and should intervene, even coercively, on behalf of the child (and for the good of the family unit, or so goes the theory)? These questions, addressed in every child protection case either consciously or not, blur the distinction between legal and social spheres of expertise.

With the understanding that the spheres of competence are not always clear and distinct, the attorney and the client agency ought to arrive at in-house positions, each deferring to the other's expertise where appropriate, with the lawyer acting as advocate for the position jointly arrived at between the child protection agency and legal counsel.

The interface between the child protection agency and the court system must be explored and understood by the attorney representing the agency. The role of the court must be placed in context for the agency by their lawyer. The court acts as arbiter between the individual citizens and the social agency as to the agency's right to intervene in the privacy of the family. When the family does not voluntarily agree to the agency intervention, the court must decide whether or not the circumstances justify coercive/authoritative state intervention on behalf of the child.

Delivery of services to the dysfunctional family remains the duty of the child protection agency whether or not court action is taken. The social workers have the charge and the skills and the expertise to actually provide assistance to the children and their families. The court's role is to authorize the agency to act in cases in which parents will not voluntarily accept services. The court's authorization facilitates the agency intervention. The court itself, however, has no treatment expertise, nor should it be relied upon to develop a treatment plan. The social worker may not recognize the limited role of the court as judicial body and that the social agency bears the responsibility to develop and implement a treatment plan for the children and family. The agency lawyer must make clear to the social worker clients that the court itself can do no treatment or social planning for a family. The court's role is to prevent unwarranted interferences with their private lives.

The agency lawyer must understand the role and functioning of protective services well enough to identify the social objectives of the agency as separate and distinct from the generally shorter-term, more immediate legal objectives. If the lawyer understands the agency goals he or she can be more creative in the use of the court process. The agency lawyer should not define the client's goals only in terms of legal objectives—for instance, to acquire temporary jurisdiction, to prove probable cause, or to obtain emergency detention; with the help of the social worker, the attorney must identify the *social goals* of the agency with as much particularity as is possible. Thereafter, by creative use of the court process, the lawyer may be able to accomplish the social goal, whether or not the most apparent legal goals are attainable.

The legal process itself may contribute to the family dysfunction to which the agency is trying to respond. Sometimes the trauma of adversary litigation cannot be avoided. But often, when the social objectives of the agency are clearly in mind, an attorney can accomplish the goals of the agency without trial, through strategies of negotiation, mediation, and pacing the litigation.

The attorney should work closely with the protective services agency. In the intitial interview with the agency social worker the lawyer must ask: What do you want to result from the legal action? What are your professional (i.e., social work) goals for the client family? The lawyer should test the social work strategy in a collegial but "devil's advocate" way. Will court action facilitate the social work intervention strategy? How will it do so? Can each of the elements of the intervention plan be justified by facts presentable to the court?

The social worker, with his or her experts and team members, must be able to articulate the social objectives of court action. The lawyer may wish to attend treatment team meetings (SCAN meetings) regarding cases on which he or she is or may be active. The lawyer needs to know the behavioral science reasoning behind a particular intervention strategy and may also be able to contribute knowledge to the team as to the legal process available to facilitate the strategy. Knowing the plan and its bases, the lawyer is better able to support it in court through expert and material witnesses.

The further challenge for the lawyer is to achieve the social results in an efficient, effective, and direct way which avoids or minimizes the negative effects of the adversary process. A process of mediation or negotiation may avoid the adversary system in which family members must testify against family members and helpers, such as social workers and physicians, must testify against the parents they are trying to help. Skills and tactics in negotiation and mediation are especially important to the child protection attorney.

We have identified two separate aspects of the attorney role for the protective services agency: first, to prove and present the clients' case in the most persuasive fashion possible; second, to understand and embrace the social goals of the client agency and to further those goals by nonadversarial means if possible.

We now come to a third aspect of the agency attorney's role, that of preparing the client agency for on-going court review of a treatment plan ordered by the court. Certainly preparation of the treatment plan remains the sphere of the social worker. However, the lawyer understands the degree of specificity and prompt action required by the court for such plans, and serves the client well when the client is prompted to efficiently and clearly state what the goals of a plan are and what the specifics of a plan are. The lawyer understands the legal importance of the treatment plan and ramifications that noncompliance by the agency or the parents may have in subsequent court proceedings.

The court retains ultimate responsibility for the well-being of children under its jurisdiction. It cannot abrogate that responsibility. New legislation and several recommended model statutes contain procedures for formalizing the legal standards for review of continued intervention in a family under court authority (8).

At a review hearing the child protection agency is in a position of giving account of its stewardship. Before such a hearing, the court will have taken jurisdiction over a child and ordered certain interventions which may have included placement of the child and counseling or other treatment for the family. At a review the agency must give account to the court of what services have been provided and what progress has been made by the family. The agency attorney can aid his or her client by not letting matters drift. Correlatively, the parents must give account of themselves and show what progress they have made in correcting problems that brought their child to the attention of the court.

The agency, in essence, is asking that the court continue its authorization to intervene in the family, including perhaps continued placement or termination of parental rights. Agencies must show that a treatment plan has been in place and that the legal and social intervention is justified by correlative benefits, either realized or nearing realization, to the child and family.

If the agency cannot justify its continued involvement in the family by demonstrating good faith efforts to rehabilitate the family, the court may revoke the agency authority to act, i.e., terminate the court jurisdiction or return a child home in spite of agency requests to the contrary. Admittedly, a return home against the agency recommendation is a rare and probably risky thing for a judge to do without some expert opinion to counter the agency recommendation or without additional resources to deal with a particular family.

The agency attorney's role demands well-developed traditional legal skills. However, the role also requires that the attorney know the "business" of his or her clients very well. Ultimately, a successful intervention in a family requires close collegial cooperation between the lawyer, the child protection agency, and the psychiatric, psychological, and medical consultants to the agency.

Attorney for the Parents

The attorney for the parents is charged with representing the interests of his or her clients zealously within the bounds of the law. Advocacy for the parent usually takes the form of minimizing the effects of state intervention on the family. Advocacy for parents may include diplomatic attempts to get petitions dismissed, in-court advocacy for dismissal, insistence that the charges brought by the state be legally proven in court, and negotiation for dispositions that are most acceptable to the parents.

Representation of parents in cases of alleged child abuse and neglect requires unique skills and resources in addition to traditional lawyer advocacy. Lawyers must first deal with their negative feelings toward the client parent accused of child abuse or neglect. The feelings toward a client parent, unless dealt with properly, can sabotage a lawyer's advocacy either consciously or unconsciously. These feelings must be dealt with from the beginning. One means of dealing with personal feelings toward allegedly abusive or neglectful parents is to understand the dynamics behind child abuse and neglect. Read the rest of this book for that. Parents accused of child abuse and neglect often have difficulty trusting others, forming relationships (including relationships with their lawyers), and deferring gratification. (See Chapter 3). The lawyer must understand and cope with these and other characteristics of many parents.

Lawyers are counselors at law as well as advocates. In the agency attorney's role the lawyer may advise a client social worker to pursue nonlegal avenues in a case before taking legal action or to consult other professionals about treatment strategy before initiating court action. Similar advice may be given to parents.

The lawyer as counselor to parents must feel comfortable engaging the parent as a person, must evaluate the parents' difficulties and their legal and social situation, and then provide legal counsel as to how to accomplish their goals. The lawyer may well explore with parents whether or not personal and family problems exist with which the social agencies may assist. He or she may counsel parents to accept certain services, seeking postponement of the court process in the interim. As a result the parents may be willing to accept some limited assistance from an agency voluntarily. The parents may even be well advised to forego immediate legal advantage in order to benefit from a social intervention that is calculated to prevent recurrence of abuse or neglect.

The parents' attorney can sometimes perform valuable functions for the parents by encouraging nonjudicial resolutions of the case. A voluntary plan of treatment may avoid formal court jurisdiction and still protect the child and address the problems which may have been identified by protective services. Nonjudicial resolutions with legal representation of the parents avoids the danger of improper invasion of personal liberties without due process. A lawyer representing parents should provide an assurance that whatever agreement the parents enter into is done voluntarily and knowingly, i.e., with full awareness of possible consequences.

Where the parents are willing to accept some services under the shadow of court action, the parents' lawyer should obtain from the social worker a detailed treatment plan for the family. The social worker should also make a contract with the parents defining in concrete terms the problems that are to be worked on, the obligations of the parents and of the agency, and what is expected to be achieved by the parents prior to return of the child or termination of intervention by the agency.

The counselor's role is quite consistent with traditional lawyer functioning. It is based on trust and dealing with the client parents as important individuals. However, these nonadversarial tasks of the lawyer may be even more important in child protection than in other areas of the law. In exercising the counselor function the lawyer must be careful to establish whatever trust he or she can with the clients. When recommendations of cooperation with social agencies are made, they should be made carefully so that the clients understand that if the suggestions of the lawyer are not accepted, the lawyer will stand by them as advocate of their position in subsequent proceedings.

After exercising the counselor function, the lawyer may decide that vigorous advocacy to accomplish his or her clients' goals is necessary. This decision may be based on an appraisal that the case against the parents is weak or unfounded, or the agency response may seem unduly harsh or drastic in light of the problems identified by the agency or the parent. The decision may also be based on the clients' firm denial of the allegations in the petition and their instructions to contest the case. After fulfilling the counselor function, the lawyer must zealously advocate his or her client's position. While others may believe that a child may be at grave risk, the lawyer's duty is to advocate for his or her client, regardless of the opinion of others and regardless of his or her personal beliefs in the matter.[2]

The lawyer's advocacy should start in the agency itself. Some discussion and negotiation may lead to a resolution of the conflict between parents and agency. Lawyers must learn the important art of persuading a large bureaucracy convinced of the inherent rightness of its position to modify it. In spite of the desirability of nonjudicial resolutions of disputes between the parent and the social agency, it is often necessary to proceed to trial. Lawyers must first possess traditional skills of trial advocacy and be ready to go to trial when necessary.

Responsibility of the parent for injuries to or possible neglect of a child may be a contested issue. The lawyer has a duty to defend this client with the utmost vigor and resourcefulness. The lawyer in juvenile court, no less than in any other court, must stand as the ardent protector of his or her client's constitutional and personal rights. The lawyer must bring to the task the usual tools of the advocate— familiarity with the applicable law, the ability to logically present the pertinent facts, and the facility for forceful and persuasive exposition of his or her clients' cause. Many professionals often find the lawyer's role as zealous advocate for the parent in serious child abuse cases disquieting and difficult to understand. This issue is one raised regularly in interdisciplinary groups concerned with child abuse and neglect.

In the dispositional phase of a case, the parents' lawyer may serve several different functions. (*a*) The lawyer can ensure impartiality by acting as a counterbalance to pressures exerted on the court by the very nature of the issues. (*b*) He or she can assure that the basic elements of due process are preserved, such as the right to be heard and the right to test the facts upon which the disposition is to be made. (*c*) He or she can make certain that the disposition is based upon complete and accurate facts and that all the circumstances which shed light upon the conduct of his or her client are fully developed. (*d*) The lawyer can test expert opinion to make certain that it is not based on mistakes either arising from erroneous factual premises or limited expertise. (*e*) He or she can give the frequently inarticulate parents a voice in the proceeding by acting as their spokesman. (*f*) The attorney's relationship with the parents may even enable him or her to give the protective services or court staff new and meaningful insights into the family situation. (*g*) Finally, the parents' attorney can interpret the court and its processes to the client and thus assist the parent in genuinely accepting the actions of the court (9).

Attorneys in child protection, whether representing the child, the parents, or the state, face unique challenges for which traditional law school education has probably not prepared them. To function effectively in any of the lawyer roles, the attorney needs advice and consultation of social work and mental health professionals. Nonlawyers in child protection need to have some ideas of what to

---

2. The lawyer can ask the court to be relieved of the case if his or her withdrawal will not prejudice the interests of the client—EDS.

expect of the lawyers they meet in the court system. Interdisciplinary knowledge is as important to effective legal proceedings as it is in other aspects of state intervention on behalf of children.

References

1. See Meyer v. Nebraska, 262 U.S. 390 (1963); Pierce v. Society of Sisters, 268 U.S. 510 (1925); Griswold v. Connecticut, 381 U.S. 479 (1965); Stanley v. Illinois, 405 U.S. 645 (1972); Roe v. Wade, 410 U.S. 113 (1973); Moore v. City of East Cleveland, 431 U.S. 494 (1977); Smith v. Organization of Foster Families for Equality and Reform, 431 U.S. 816 (1977).
2. Paulsen, Monrad G. 1974. The Law and Abused Children, in Helfer, R. E. and Kempe, C. H. (Eds.) *The Battered Child, Second Edition,* Chicago: The University of Chicago Press. Delaney, James J. 1972. The Battered Child and the Law, in Kempe, C. H. and Helfer, R. E. (Eds.) *Helping the Battered Child and His Family,* Philadelphia: Lippincott.
3. Levine, R. S. 1973. Caveat Parens: A Demystification of the Child Protection System. *University of Pittsburgh Law Review* 35:1.
4. Excerpts from State Child Abuse and Neglect Laws, U.S. DHEW National Center of Child Abuse and Neglect, May 1978.
5. Fraser, B. and Martin, H. P. (Eds.) *The Abused Child,* Cambridge: Ballinger, 1976.
6. Delaney, James J. 1976. New Concepts of the Family Court, in Helfer, R. E. and Kempe, C. H. (Eds.) *Child Abuse and Neglect: The Family and the Community,* Cambridge: Ballinger.
7. Downs, S. Guardian at Litem Program in Seattle, *Case Record* Portland State University 1979; Personal communication Hon. James S. Casey, Kalamazoo Juvenile Court, June 1979.
8. IJA-ABA Juvenile Justice Standards Project. 1977. *Abuse and Neglect,* Cambridge: Ballinger.
9. Isaacs, J. L. 1972. The Role of the Lawyer in Child Abuse Cases, in Kempe, C. H. and Helfer, R. E. (Eds.) *Helping the Battered Child and His Family,* Philadelphia: Lippincott.

20 Community Council for Child Abuse Prevention

Sharon Williams Shay

Introduction

Isolation remains a common characteristic of those families in which child abuse [1] is a problem. The complexity of today's social structure, with its bureaucratic layers of services and carefully defined "turfdoms," poses an intimidating barrier to anyone seeking help. Even the most motivated become discouraged. For those persons unskilled in communicating with others, in making decisions, and in solving problems, the barriers are overwhelming. Fear and uncertainty keep them isolated while stress mounts and leads eventually to violence or apathy.

Day care staff and teachers work with children everyday; they may be the only positive adult role models in a neglected child's life. Doctors are held in high esteem by many who would trust no one else. They are in a unique position not only to identify a child in danger, but to encourage parents to seek help, offering a listening ear and linking the family to community counselors. Bankers can offer vital contacts and skills in raising dollars for needed staff, community education, and other identified needs. Journalists can enlighten the public about the problems faced by families and publicize resources so that early intervention becomes more probable.

Any one of the above people could be touched personally by child abuse. All of them are affected by the destructive ripples generated in every community, i.e., juvenile crime, drug and alcohol abuse. All have an investment in preventing child abuse, and each has a special role in achieving that goal. But to be effective in making long-lasting changes, these people must work together. A community council provides the vehicle needed for that work. A council offers a neutral focal point for involvement and action. It allows diverse interests and skills to be channeled into comprehensive community action on behalf of children and

Sharon Williams Shay, M.A., is executive director of the Council for the Prevention of Child Abuse and Neglect, Lansing, Michigan.

1. The term child abuse will be used throughout this chapter in reference to problems of both child neglect and abuse.

families. It also provides a mechanism for advocacy concerning local, state, and national policies which affect all families.

In the early 1970s, Helfer and Kempe described a center for the study of abused and neglected children, the goal of such a center being "to develop methods and gain understanding which in some way would decrease the incidence of child abuse and neglect within the specific geographic area in which the program was located" (1). Primary functions included education, demonstration, and research; staff at such a center would provide consultation relative to a variety of issues facing community workers, and serve as experts in treatment, providing service to a limited number of cases.

The community council concept, which has evolved out of this model, incorporates an additional function—coordination. Since multidisciplinary roles, within complex delivery systems, are required in order to reach the stated goal, leadership in interagency cooperation and community involvement is essential. Though well informed regarding child abuse, the expertise of a community council lies not in treatment and diagnosis, but in the field of community action and resource and program development. They are facilitators and bridge-builders for acute care, treatment, and educational needs within a given geographic area. The needed expertise in clinical diagnosis and treatment approaches comes from the membership of the council, those agencies and individuals in the community who have committed themselves to the goal of child abuse prevention and whose talents help build the network needed to support families and protect children.

This chapter will summarize basic principles for developing a community council, discuss potential problems, review needed program components, and suggest models for coordinated service delivery.

Process of Getting Started

The process of forming and the organizational structure of a council for child abuse prevention will vary from one community to another. Size and characteristics of the population to be served, existing resources, levels of general public and professional awareness about the problem, and other factors determine what methods a community selects. Further, the nature of a given council changes from year to year, as is true in any developmental process. In a growing network, goals are frequently redefined, methods reexamined, and new systems created when old ones no longer work or need revitalizing.

Given these variables, there remain certain absolutes which every community needs to recognize in developing and maintaining an interagency system for child abuse prevention.

Step 1: Gathering Together a Small, Interested Group

A small group of ten to twenty people meet periodically to talk about child abuse. Over brown-bag lunches they share ideas and frustrations about how to more effectively help troubled families. Participants may include a nurse from the county health department, a school counselor, a police officer, a pediatrician, a therapist, a protective service worker, a hospital emergency room nurse, a volunteer from the Junior League, and others with a range of interests.

In coming together, this group has taken a giant step toward community action for child abuse prevention. By regularly meeting, participants review certain facts and feelings about the nature of child abuse and its solutions. These form the foundation for future goals and action to be undertaken, actions which eventually lead to a more formal community council.

Step 2: Identifying and Discussing the Issues

The group must reach the point of accepting child abuse as a service problem which warrants their involvement and time. Predictably, every group member will interpret the problem somewhat differently. The community's view of child abuse will, therefore, be defined as a continuum of parent-child interactional problems, ranging from severe cases which demand immediate, intensive intervention by interdisciplinary teams to more common cases of confused and overwhelmed parents who need support.

Despite the wide range of manifestations, the problem of child abuse is related to the pressures within today's society which destructively impact upon the family, e.g., isolation, stress, and inadequate or inaccessible community support (2). Attacking the problem, therefore, involves building effective systems for improving each community's ability to support families and protect vulnerable children. These issues must be identified and discussed as the group gains knowledge and builds trust.

Step 3: Reviewing Available Resources

Every community possesses resources which will play a vital role in building a system to impact upon the problem. The group needs to assess available resources and determine how they function. Gaps in service or problems in delivery must also be identified in this ongoing process.

Most frequently, the major roadblocks uncovered are fragmented service delivery and resources which are inaccessible or unknown to the families that require them. The goals of a community council are accessibility of services to anyone who needs them, decreased duplication of programs, and an end to splintered services which often shatter the family and waste limited funds.

Step 4: Involving Others

At this point the group faces a complex human problem which crosses all disciplines and social definitions. People from all walks of life need to be involved. This includes professionals in public and private organizations, volunteers, neighbors, churches, civic clubs, leaders in business, labor, and government, in short, anyone who wants to see their community offer families the resources needed to be effective in carrying out the most fundamental social function of all—nurturing children to happy, healthy adulthood.

As the group becomes more diverse and talented people assume a commitment to each other and to a defined purpose, they must form a coalition. Out of this process a name will emerge which reflects the group's identity in the community—it may be called a consortium or a council or a network—whatever the choice, the name will represent an *interdisciplinary, interagency* group of concerned people actively planning and working to prevent child abuse in their community.

A procedure for identifying members of the group is needed and the meaning of group membership must be discussed: What privileges do members have? What responsibilities? Will agencies be members? Other community organizations, such as Big Brothers/Big Sisters or the Mental Health Association, can help to identify ideas and can help in finding models that are comfortable to the group. Once these issues are clarified, a membership form should be developed, with annual dues determined, and regular meetings scheduled. Dues will provide a pool of funds to cover printing and postage costs for the group's mailings. Staff time for typing and preparing mailings might be rotated among members whose organizations are willing to donate such services. The cash value of these donations should be documented by the coalition as "in-kind" support which may eventually be used as the local match for Title XX or other state and federal funding.

As the process unfolds, the critical elements needed for successful group interaction become obvious. Interestingly, these are the same basic elements needed for families, or any group, to function effectively (3). As trust develops the group will eventually become comfortable in turning toward one member for guidance. This is a critical stage of growth.

Step 5: Identifying a Leader

Though each participant will bring his or her unique leadership style and special talents, a designated person needs to assume responsibility for the group's general direction and momentum. She or he will guide the group in establishing norms for interaction and in building trust and cohesiveness.

The leader's role may be filled by a trained volunteer or, if funding is available, a paid staff member; in some cases, two people may share this responsibility. Leading such a diverse group is difficult. The person selected to assume this important function should be skilled in group dynamics, knowledgeable about the community, and have available time and energy to commit at least two years of time to the tasks.

Throughout the life of a consortium, many different people will assume strong leadership roles. In the early stages, consistent and committed leaders are important. As the coalition grows, a more formalized system for identifying and maintaining leaders must be developed; eventually, this will probably include a board of directors and a funding mechanism for paid staff.

Step 6: Setting Goals

Clearly defined goals provide the coalition with directions which serve to avoid floundering on complex issues. They clarify resources and avenues of activity which previously may not have been visible.

Goals may be formally or informally stated. Some communities choose to write bylaws with stated purposes and objectives; this document serves as the basis for incorporating and developing an identity in the community. Other coalitions simply write a statement of purpose with accompanying objectives and distribute this within and outside the group. Regardless of the choice, two guiding principles apply: first, goals must evolve from a consensus of involved group members; and second, they must be reviewed regularly and redefined. Periodic meetings and brainstorming sessions provide effective vehicles for goal setting and review of the group's direction. Table 20.1 shows examples of directions a community might consider.

Once established, goals provide a framework for determining specific objectives, tasks, timetables, and needed resources. Individual and agency roles become clearer. For example, in meeting the objective "to inform and educate the public," the health department and other participating organizations might agree to release one staff person for ten hours of work per month on the council's education and training committee, while a service club volunteer agrees to provide leadership, as chair of the committee for two years. The objective "to foster preventative services" might inspire a hospital social worker to approach the administration about rooming-in policies for newborns in the maternity wards; other council participants might agree to send letters supporting such a program change.

An annual work plan complete with specific tasks, roles, and target dates will

TABLE 20.1   Sample Objectives of Council

---

a. To inform and educate the (specify city, county, or other geographic scope) community with respect to child abuse and neglect.

b. To assist in developing educational and training services to professionals concerned about families with children in need of protection.

c. To help organize and coordinate case consultation services for community agencies concerned about families with children in need of protection.

d. To help organize and coordinate family treatment services provided by public and private community agencies concerned about families with children in need of protection.

e. To stimulate the development of community services for children in need of protection and their families.

f. To assist in the development and coordination of additional and alternative intervention resources where needed.

g. To directly operate services that fill a void in current services and/or relate to coordination with the goal of transferring the on-going operation of each new resource to another social agency, where appropriate and desirable.

h. To foster prevention services for abused and neglected children and their families.

i. To stimulate research into child abuse and neglect.

j. To assess the effectiveness of the network of programs serving abused and neglected children and their families.

k. To communicate with the legislature, state agencies, and the courts about the needs of children and families and to advocate for appropriate reforms.

---

give the group clear direction and a mechanism for evaluation. (For example see table 20.2.) The number of objectives addressed in the plan will depend on the number of people and the amount of time available. So much needs to be done, it is tempting to try to do everything at once. To avoid feelings of defeat and eventual failure, realism is necessary, focusing on quality of action rather than quantity. Careful, realistic planning will facilitate the group's progress (4).

Common Problems to Resolve

Communicating

A council's success and very existence depends upon free-flowing exchange of information. Ideas, feelings, insights, gripes, concerns, and facts which are openly

TABLE 20.2   **Sample Work Plan**

Objective	Activity	Person Date	Evaluation
1. To inform and educate	1. a. Form and hold meetings of the education and training committee	1. S. Smith, Chair a. 9/79–6/80	1. a. List of members, minutes on file
	b. Write tasks/time line for 1980, relative to: -Speaker's Bureau list -Information flyer on council -CA/N resource list and bibliography -General format for presentations to community groups -System for responding to requests for presentations	b. 12/79	b. c. d. Plan with tasks, persons responsible, needed resources, on file
	c. Identify persons responsible and resources needed for tasks	c. 12/79	
	d. Implement plan	d. 1/80–6/80	d. Monthly reports to council re progress

shared result in waves of creativity. Such exchange also prevents erosion of the group's strength by hidden streams of dissatisfaction and conflict.

Several vehicles for communication need to be established. Regular meetings offer one such mechanism; others include newsletters, educational forums, volunteer programs, committees, and task forces. In offering these activities, identified leaders must set an atmosphere which nurtures open communication. Frequent attempts to broaden the base of people reached, skillful listening, and a respect for each person's unique perspective facilitate such an atmosphere.

Conflict

Conflict, when effectively resolved, strengthens a group. The pressure released in confrontation, the search for solutions, and successfully overcoming a roadblock combine to bolster the group's cohesiveness and sense of purpose. In community councils, as in any group, conflict is a sign of healthy diversity and open expression of views.

Several pitfalls may prevent councils from resolving conflicts, hampering progress. First is the temptation to avoid problem areas in order to bypass conflict for the sake of equilibrium. Since struggles are a natural part of group process, such attempts are not only futile, but also devastating to the future of the group. On the surface, the equilibrium maintained may seem pleasant; if allowed to continue, however, hidden tensions may destroy the group's trust and cohesiveness. Leaders must promote an atmosphere which gives permission for participants to disagree; playing devil's advocate, asking for other opinions, presenting different perspectives will help set such a tone.

The second pitfall is the tendency to personalize conflict and allow individual agendas to interfere in the group's problem-solving process. Because conflict charges the group's emotional climate, members can easily fall into this trap. For example, one member, a teacher, feels strongly that education should be the coalition's priority for the 1980s, while another, a doctor, feels the formation of a multidisciplinary team is paramount. The group is not large enough to undertake both areas simultaneously. When discussing the problem, these two individuals debate endlessly about which is most effective in preventing child abuse, medical intervention or heightened public awareness. Neither budges from the conviction that his or her professional role is the most central. Meanwhile, the workplan for the group gets delayed week after week. The question has become a test of personal power: Who will win control of the group's direction? Creative problem-solving depends on flexibility and openness among members. While it is important that members feel free to assert their perspectives and convince others of their positions, care needs to be taken to assure that emotional energy is channeled toward group goals rather than the vested interests of one or two members.

Third, groups tend to hide behind issues rather than resolving them. Pat phrases are used to describe the problem, but specific concerns never seem clearly defined. The group may be struggling, for example, with the development of a procedure for reaching and treating families in which children are sexually abused. When the suggestion is made that protective services be called when a therapist learns of an incestuous relationship, "confidentiality" is raised as a barrier to this first step. The group is stymied. The therapist-client relationship must be respected. In this case, the very real problem of maintaining a positive client-therapist relationship when a child needs protection goes undefined because the word "confidentiality" stops discussion. When this occurs, council members need to stop action and focus on specifics. What are our objectives? Does this discussion help us reach them? What is the specific problem? How can we work around it?

Members must agree to disagree on those issues which do not relate to established goals. In coming together, people representing a wide range of interests have committed themselves to a purpose which requires the unique talent and role of each participant. During conflict it is especially important to recognize that the common goals which brought the group together represent a higher plane of community response than any single member can achieve.

In short, the pitfalls described can be avoided by maintaining a professional approach to problem-solving with open communication and mutual respect, while frequently recalling the group's purpose.

The Component Parts of a Community Council

Generally, the work of a community consortium will fall into the three components previously described by Helfer and Schmidt (5). These include acute care, treatment, and education (fig. 20.1). This figure modifies their model to include concrete coordinating roles of a council, models for interagency service delivery, and specific community services needed in each program area. This figure will be used as a basis for the following discussion.

Common Denominators

Webster's Third New International Dictionary defines coordination as "harmonious functioning." Facilitating alliances among people and agencies who share common goals promotes harmony; coercing cooperation does not.

In a community consortium, specific coordinating activities fall into two categories: administrative coordination, which involves keeping the council or consortium afloat and moving on course at a safe speed, and program coordination, through facilitating community action toward program development and implementation within each component. Throughout this process, whoever carries the title of coordinator needs to remember that few really want to be coordinated.

The shaded areas represent the coordinating role of the council. The membership, the interagency board of directors, and council office serve as focal points for communication, comprehensive planning, uniform program development, models for coordinated service delivery, and advocacy. A sample organizational chart for a staffed council would look something like that found in figure 20.2.

The administrative staff assists community agencies through grantsmanship, contract management, consultation, and evaluation. Program coordinators working within the shaded areas of each component in figure 20.1 identify and help

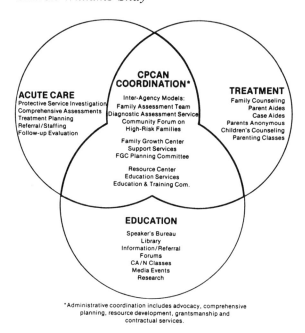

Figure 20.1

Conceptual framework: community coordination for child abuse prevention

carry out specific objectives with assistance and input from interagency advisory committees. This approach assures ongoing sharing of the expertise and resources available within the community. The structure further allows administrative accountability and sound fiscal management.

Program coordination is facilitated by the council's interagency models for service delivery. In figure 20.1, these models are defined as the multidisciplinary team (A), the Family Growth Center (B), and the Resource Center (C); a complete description of each is provided below. Such models offer visible evidence of the council's work within the community. The services listed outside the shaded areas, within each component, reflect programs facilitated by the council's advocacy and resource development, which are administered by direct service providers within the community. For example, the parent aid program grew out of council efforts to obtain Title XX funds through the department of social services for a contract with Catholic Social Services to provide supervision and training of parent aides for protective service clients. This service is now in the community because of council activities, through the cooperative efforts of the council, the department of social services and Catholic Social Services. It is administered by an agency whose main function is service to families and children.

Services provided in each component must reflect the range of family needs assumed by a continuum definition of child abuse. Programs reflect levels of services ranging from primary prevention to treatment of families in which the need for intensive specialized intervention has been determined. Some services

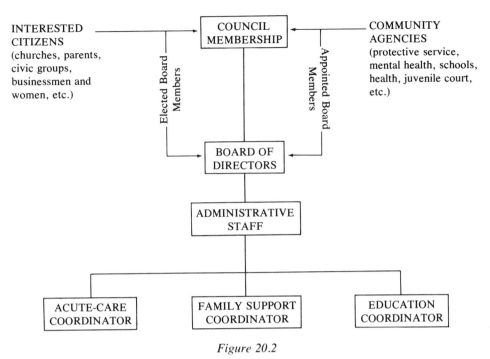

Figure 20.2

Community council sample organizational structure

will provide both. For example, drop-in child care provides prevention services to the community at large while simultaneously serving a treatment function as an alternative to foster care placement for clients referred by protective services. Finally, services outlined in one component depend upon resources available in another. For example, treatment planning and referral, performed in the acute care component, are not complete unless parents aides and counseling are available in the treatment component. Each component must be seen as equally important to the other. The council structure provides the interface which allows balanced growth and comprehensive planning. The overlapping areas of the three intersecting circles in figure 20.1 graphically illustrate this principle.

Acute Care (Component A)

A multidisciplinary team (MDT) provides a critically important backup service for the core of the community's acute care component, i.e., protective services. This team functions as the expert resource for comprehensive assessment services to families and children who are most at risk. Community characteristics and needs will determine how a team is formed and what roles are provided. In small communities, cooperative sharing of staff from medical, public health, mental health, and social service agencies allows coordinated planning and delivery of services. In metropolitan communities, specialized team roles need to be funded to assure the level of participation and expertise needed to handle large numbers of cases. Funded teams, such as the one described below, can function as a regional resource for satellite teams in surrounding communities.

Protective services provides a key role in the acute care system. As child abuse cases are referred to protective services, the worker investigates, assesses, makes treatment plans, and refers families for services. She or he weeds out the most severe or confusing cases and refers them to the MDT for comprehensive assessment, meeting with the team to help determine the most appropriate treatment for the family and attending follow-up staffings. The MDT may also receive referrals from the probate court, private physicians, police, and hospital emergency room personnel. Cases referred are reviewed and screened prior to setting appointments for the family at the out-patient diagnostic clinic. Emergency cases may require hospital admission and subsequent in-patient assessment.

Specifically, the MDT provides comprehensive medical, psychological, and developmental evaluations of referred families with particular emphasis on domestic crises and problems within the parent-child relationship. Following the assessment, the team and the referring individual prepare the family for referral to treatment services, developing a treatment plan and often bringing in service providers. One team member assumes the case-coordinating role for each family during the MDT's involvement. When the family returns for follow-up appointments, the team, referring worker, and service providers evaluate the effectiveness of the treatment plan and make necessary changes.

Core team members include a pediatrician, a child psychologist, a clinical nurse, and a social worker. The MDT is augmented, from time to time, with other professional services, such as those of an attorney, a physical therapist, an infant-mental-health specialist, etc. The interagency focus of the team is expanded by the community forum on high-risk families, which meets twice monthly. The forum, attended by workers with a wide range of community interests and roles, offers a vehicle for information exchange, development of protocol, and identification of problem areas.

The council's acute-care coordinator facilitates the forum, assists the MDT in carrying out clinical services, and provides liaison between hospitals, protective services, and others involved in acute-care services. Funds for the coordinator and core team members are obtained by the council from a variety of sources and subcontracted to appropriate service providers within the community.

Treatment (Component B)

The term *treatment* encompasses many levels of intervention ranging from supportive services such as transportation to temporary foster care placement and intensive therapy. In many communities a myriad of treatment services lies hidden in mazes of bureaucratic regulations and procedures. Families stumble hopelessly down blind alleys while caseworkers search futilely for the form which will open a secret stairway to needed services. The council holds the key: coordination and advocacy provide essential tools for tearing down mazes.

Through the council's communication channels, community services can be identified and made available to families in stress. This is facilitated to a large degree by the work of the multidisciplinary team and protective services which link families to needed services. In this process, gaps will be identified and the council's mechanism for resource and program development can be put into motion to meet the identified need. For example, as the problem of sexual abuse is documented by protective services and MDT assessments, a gap in treatment resources may become obvious. Based on the assessed need, the council staff can search for funds and coordinate a proposal for provision of treatment through a direct service provider. Simultaneously, educational programs and media impact about the problem can be addressed through the education component.

Most troubled families, however, will not require new program development but better service delivery. For example, many abusive parents are intimidated by the thought of walking through the door of a mental health agency. The treatment is there; the family is in need; but getting the two together sometimes seems impossible. Outreach counseling, in the client's home, is one option. Frequently, though, therapists find no one answers the door when they arrive for a scheduled appointment, and if they manage to get inside, the confusion of the environment prevents any real therapy from occurring.

A partial solution to this dilemma has been achieved for some through the Family Growth Center, a community-based support center for parents, children, and workers. Operating out of donated space in a downtown church, the center offers centralized support services to families and a nonthreatening environment for treatment. This makes available a developmental-oriented drop-in child-care program, parent recreation and involvement, parent-child activity sessions, transportation, and informal educational programs. The family's needs can be met while treatment occurs either at the center or elsewhere in the community. Several agencies use the center to deliver services. Recent examples include a series of group sessions for single parents sponsored by Catholic Social Services, Parents Anonymous chapter meetings held twice weekly, and group counseling for high-risk children offered by community mental health. Others refer clients to the center for support, while therapy is provided at the agency.

The council's family coordinator directs activities at the center and serves as program coordinator for the community's treatment component.[2] Funds are also obtained and administered by the council for four staff roles at the center, including a preschool teacher, an infant-toddler specialist, a resource specialist responsible for volunteer coordination and transportation, and a case aide who offers outreach and crisis support to parents. Volunteer recruitment and training is also part of the center's program, and the center is used as a laboratory for practical experience and training in child development and child care by the community college and area high schools. Approximately forty community volunteers and students help staff the center in any month.

Interagency input for the program and for treatment services occurs through the

---

2. Whether or not the council should provide any direct service to clients is debatable. If it does, the risk of becoming another bureaucratic agency also exists. Ideally, all services of the council should be directed to member agencies and *not* directly to patients—EDS.

family growth planning committee, which sets objectives for program development, recommends policies for operation, and addresses specific problem areas.
Members of the committee include representatives from the health department,
Catholic Social Services, department of social services, Parents Anonymous, and
other agencies.

Education (Component C)

Maintaining high levels of public awareness and professional expertise about
child abuse helps build bridges over the schisms of misunderstanding existing in
every community. As more people become informed, more attention is paid to the
problem; this leads to increased community involvement and investment.

Educational programs must focus both on general presentations to the public-
at-large and on specific skill training to professionals and volunteers. Because the
populations to be reached represent different disciplines, expertise is needed from
many fields of interest. This component, perhaps even more than the others,
depends on the active involvement and commitment of people from a wide variety
of agencies and community groups. The key to success in training is the ability to
accurately assess the needs of a target group and effectively design and deliver a
specialized program to that group. This is impossible without the support and
involvement of the group to be trained.

The education and training committee of the council serves as an interdisciplinary training vehicle for the community. The committee identifies populations to be trained and develops specialized programs. The resource center,
housed at the council office, provides a focal point for educational support. A
speakers bureau functions as the clearinghouse for trainers and consultants, as
well as presenters to the public at large. Other resources include a library, audio-
visuals, and publications, such as a monthly newsletter. Classes on child care can
be developed by the council and turned over to the local community college to
administer. The council holds regular community forums for members and
friends, through brown-bag lunches, seminars, and conferences. Information and
referral services are available to anyone who calls, walks in, or writes.

Ongoing contact with the media is maintained through frequent public service
announcements. Council staff, members, and volunteers plan and implement an
annual program to heighten public awareness; a press conference kicks off a range
of activities, from library exhibits to panels on local television stations.

Finding Funds

The arena of funding is a two-edged sword for the council. On one hand, funds cut
through red tape, motivating interagency cooperation, program expansion, and
improved delivery of services. Concrete signs of the consortium's existence appear. On the other, obtaining funds means carrying the burden of maintenance and
accountability. Particularly in the early stages of development, a substantial
amount of time and energy on the part of board members and hired or volunteer
administrators will be devoted to funding issuess. The degree to which the council

is ready and/or willing to assume such responsibility will determine how much and what type of funding is sought. Once the decision is made to obtain funds, several general categories of sources may be considered.

Private Donations

The membership of a council offers ongoing community-based financial support, ranging from annual membership dues to memorial bequests. A nonprofit tax-exempt status makes donations tax deductible, encouraging community investment.

The council should continuously attempt to maintain and broaden its membership, thereby increasing financial and political support for stated goals. Offering vehicles for member involvement, such as educational forums, committee work, and volunteer programs, stimulates commitment through heightened communication and activity within the consortium. Further, the energy and time of such efforts contribute countless dollars in in-kind donations. Twenty volunteers working ten hours per week for one year is equivalent to $30,000 in staff support at minimum wage. Some government programs allow use of volunteers as in-kind service for part of the local match to obtain federal dollars.

Civic groups, labor unions, churches, and professional organizations provide another source of community support. Offering educational presentations about child abuse to such groups not only heightens general public awareness but often spurs action which may take the form of financial and in-kind contributions. New members will emerge from these groups, strengthening the diversity of the coalition.

Local and state foundations provide pools of funds for community action. Personal contacts are the most essential ingredient in obtaining such support. As the network broadens and credibility increases, the likelihood of identifying contributing foundations multiplies. Several excellent guides to foundation funding are now available: some give step-by-step direction in exploring this option (6).

Fund-raising Events

Successful fund-raising events, though generally time-consuming and demanding pay off not only in raised community consciousness and group solidarity but also financially. Realistic planning is critical; too ambitious an effort may mean hard-earned dollars are lost through hidden expenses and forgotten details.

Events used for community fund-raising will range from marathons to magic shows, from sales incentives to lotteries; the possibilities are endless. Whatever the choice, committed volunteers are essential to prevent the activity from draining the consortium's energy away from the true business at hand, building systems for preventing child abuse.

Specific direction in building successful fund-raising activities is available in a concise, down-to-earth paperback called *Grass Roots Fund-raising* by Joan Flanagan (7).

An incorporated, nonprofit council may choose to apply for membership in the local United Way, thus avoiding the need to develop its own fund-raising activities. Such membership will also link the organization, in a formal way, to other human service agencies in the community, as well as to business and labor interests which support United Way campaigns.

Contractual Agreements and Government Funding

In many communities, filling gaps in acute care, treatment, and educational services means locating funds for agencies to increase staff and operating expenses. Contractual agreements offer a vehicle for formalizing the coordinating role of a consortium, as well as providing needed services. This funding option presumes staffing for the council, since a great deal of time will be needed for negotiation, administration, and maintenance of such contracts.

The interagency structure of the consortium makes it an ideal bridge between funding sources and providers. The council can comprehensively assess needed resources, locate a source of funds, identify a provider, negotiate contractual agreements, and administer funds through subcontract agreement.

For example, in a given community the most feasible way of obtaining psychological services for the multidisciplinary team may be through community mental health. However, current staffing levels and caseloads mean the mental health service is reluctant to commit staff time. Through Title XX, the department of social services has available funds to purchase services for protective service clients. These funds could allow the mental health service to hire additional staff and provide a psychologist to work with the team. The council can facilitate the arrangement, negotiating a contract with the department of social services to provide multidisciplinary assessments to protective service clients, then subcontracts with the mental health service for a team psychologist. Other needs in the community can be built in the same way, using different funding sources and providers. A spin-off of multiple funding sources is broadened eligibility for clients who receive coordinated services.

After the trusting relationship between a funding source and provider is well established, the council may facilitate *direct* contractual agreements between the source and the provider. However, some contracted services will require on-going coordination because of the involvement of multiple funding sources and service providers. In maintaining a multidisciplinary team, for example, the council serves as the resource through which funds from a variety of sources are used to pay staff from several agencies. The council carries responsibility for maintaining the team. If a funding source is in jeopardy, council staff seek alternative funds, allowing agency personnel to focus on providing services.

When dealing with a complex of bureaucracies, as exists in every community, this process reduces the chance of duplicated services or overlooked gaps, centralizes negotiations, and encourages comprehensive planning. The council staff soon develops expertise in grantsmanship and contract management, as well as program development, which can assist the community in numerous ways.

In developing and maintaining such a system, two roadblocks must be faced and overcome. First is finding the skill and time required to assure sound fiscal management and program compliance that will satisfy and an array of bureaucratic regulations. Competent staff will need to be hired to assume day-to-day administrative responsibility. Funds for coordination must therefore be added to the list of needed resources. Partial reimbursement for these expenses can be built into each contract through an administrative charge. Local government units, such as city councils and county commissions, should also be approached for supplemental funds through revenue-sharing or other federal dollars. When requesting funds from any source, emphasis must be given to the services to be provided, the number of families who will be reached, rather than coordination.

Second, as long as "soft" funds (year-to-year contracts with no long-term commitment) make up the major source of funding, the total program may collapse when one contract is threatened. Stable funding must eventually be found to assure basic administration of the consortium, thus allowing attention to be focused on new directions rather than just keeping afloat. Two categories of funding sources mentioned above provide avenues for this search. In addition, financial commitment from participating agencies should eventually be pursued. In this way, those organizations whose clients are benefiting from coordinated services will be pooling funds needed to maintain comprehensive programs.

Elements of Political Power

In deciding to be an advocate for children and families, the consortium automatically enters the field of political power. To survive, this arena must be entered, regardless of preference. Every council needs political experts among its members, those people who understand this power and who come alive when the group is challenged.

As worthwhile as the goals are, someone else will think theirs more so. Council members must be ready to interact with skill and know-how. One of the consortium's early goals must therefore be to develop a system for political advocacy.

Seeking the support and expertise of an established politician will be necessary. Many of the elements of power identified by this individual are built into the fabric of a healthy community consortium and need only be used effectively. These include many members, alliances, unity, knowledge about an issue, and support from influential persons and informed community leaders. Other elements include knowledge about the political and legislative process, relationships with people in power positions, and use of the media. Voting gives power as well and can be used as a leverage when talking to elected officials. Because children cannot vote, adults concerned about their welfare must speak loudly on their behalf.

Political experts within a given council can provide guidance to the rest of the group on when and how to demonstrate community-based power to attain goals. Generally, an ongoing attitude of cooperation and special efforts to provide information and data to elected officials create a positive relationship and build credibility for the consortium.

At times a council will need to protect the interests of the group; a funding contract may be threatened or a policy proposed which hurts families. Conversely the group may choose to support an action or legislative bill which will help attain goals. To impact either way, position statements need to be developed and strategy determined which will demonstrate power quickly and effectively.

Networking

Political advocacy on behalf of children and families requires alliances with local, state, and national organizations which share the council's goals. These relationships can be maintained by exchanging newsletters and program models, providing staff or volunteer liaison, or developing cooperative projects. If a comprehensive network for child abuse prevention is to become a reality, every local consortium needs to be affiliated with a state and national counterpart. As people from different communities come together to share ideas about common goals, visions broaden and everyone benefits—most of all our children.

References

1. Kempe, C. Henry, and Helfer, Ray E. *Helping the Battered Child and His Family*, Philadelphia: Lippincott, 1972.
2. Gil, David G. *Violence Against Children*, Cambridge: Harvard University Press, 1973.
3. Lippett, R., Benne, K., and Bradford, L. *Group Dynamics and Social Action*, New York: Anti-Defamation League of B'nai B'rith, 1950.
4. *Bylaws*, Council for the Prevention of Child Abuse and Neglect, Lansing, Michigan, and *Conceptual Framework*, CPCAN, Lansing, Michigan.
5. Helfer, R., and Schmidt, R. The Community-based Child Abuse and Neglect Program, in Helfer, R. E., and Kempe, C. H. (Eds.), *Child Abuse and Neglect: The Family and the Community*, Cambridge: Ballinger, 1976.
6. Hillman, H., and Abarbanel, K. *The Art of Winning Foundation Grants*, New York: Vanguard Press, 1975.
7. Flanagan, Joan. *The Grass Roots Fund-raising Book*, Chicago: Swallow Press, 1977.

21 The Consequences of Being Abused and Neglected: How the Child Fares

Harold P. Martin

At least one of every 100 children in the United States is significantly mistreated through physical abuse or neglect. There are considerable data accumulated which address the consequences of this form of child-rearing. Variations in sample bias and in the adequacy of comparison or control groups prohibits a statistically exacting prognosis; however, the accumulated weight of report after report with similar findings gives us a most useful clinical picture of the mistreated child. This clinical picture is a somber one, a grim identification of deviations in development, biological inadequacy, and personality problems, both serious and long-lasting. This chapter discusses treatment for these children's problems. However, intervention plans and strategies must be formulated on a clearly focused identification of the problems to be treated. This chapter, then, is intended to describe and portray the consequences of the abuse-neglect syndrome to the child. Some attention will also be given to the pathogenesis of these consequences inasmuch as the design of treatment for abused children must rest not only on a base of knowledge of the problems the child has, but be equally based upon an understanding of why the abused-neglected child has incurred such bio-psycho-developmental disturbances.

Medical Consequences

The spectrum of injuries to children is considerably wider now than when abuse and neglect were first identified a decade ago. The earliest reports included mainly children with fractures, subdural hematomas (bleeding inside the skull), and other dramatic or bizarre injuries. More recently, less-severe and less-obvious mistreatment have been identified and reported. While bruises will fade, burns will heal, and lacerations and welts will rarely lead to permanent impairment, the forms of physical mistreatment for which one must have most concern are those

Harold P. Martin, M.D., is with the John F. Kennedy Child Development Center, University of Colorado Health Sciences Center, Denver.

which have the potential to permanently affect the central nervous system. These are injuries which may leave the surviving child with some of the multiple signs of brain damage: seizures, mental retardation, sensory deficits (hearing or visual impairments), cerebral palsy, learning deficits.

Physical assault (hitting, shaking) or metabolic assault (undernutrition, water deprivation, lack of care of infections) can result in permanent damage to the brain. The damage can be a result of bleeding within the head, swelling of the traumatized brain, lack of oxygen supply to brain cells, or various metabolic derangements which affect brain cells and developing brain tissue. In addition to the risk of brain damage causing deficits in learning, thinking, attending, and perceiving, there is additional cause to believe that psychological deviations may result from biological damage to the developing brain and nervous system. The magnitude of these developmental delays and personality deviations will be amplified below in this chapter.

There are medical problems for which the mistreated child is at increased risk other than the identified signs of abuse and neglect which first lead to identification of mistreatment. Abused children have poorer medical care than other children (1). When compared to children with accidental trauma, abused children were noted to have seven times more chance of having other significant lapses in child care, e.g., lack of immunizations, inadequate hygiene, erratic treatment for illnesses, etc. A recent report (2) shows that mistreated children have a much greater incidence of presenting at hospital emergency rooms with ingestion of a variety of poisonous substances. Studies comparing abused children with their nonabused siblings found more illness in the early years of the abused subjects (3–5). A report from Australia (6) of fifty-six abused children and a control group found the former group to have more than five times the chance for significant illnesses in infancy. In sum, mistreated children are more likely to be in poor health from previous illnesses and from neglect of physical care by the caretakers.

Anemia is more common in abused children (7, 8), even in infancy. This is probably due to an inadequate supply of iron-containing foods. In infancy this phenomenon is classically seen in the "milkaholic" child who is given a bottle with milk, juice, water, or Kool-Aid when the child is fretful. These have practically no iron, and the child may rapidly become iron-deficient as calorie needs are met with iron-poor foods and there is minimal intake of meat and other iron-containing nutrients. Apathy, lassitude, decreased attention span, and poor learning ability are consequences of anemia and can be reversed through treatment of the iron-deficient state.

While there is sparse research documentation, empirical observations by this author and others suggest that mistreated children are at increased risk of having hearing deficits. Even mild hearing losses in infancy and early childhood interfere with language development and cognitive development (9–11). It is postulated that the frequency of mild to moderate conductive hearing loss in abused and neglected children is secondary to inadequately treated ear infections. The long-range effect on learning and language development is further compounded by the phenomenon of the hearing-impaired child being less responsive to parents and, thus, less able to elicit language and stimulation from his or her caretaker.

Chapter 10 discusses the child with failure-to-thrive. Redundancy must be risked in pointing out the frequency with which abused children have poor physical growth and undernutrition. From thirty to fifty percent of children at the time that physical abuse is identified show signs of growth failure and/or undernutrition (7, 12–16). Most of these children do not have classical failure-to-thrive. Yet, they have signs of poor weight gain, short stature, and inadequate protein-calorie intake. Protein-calorie deficiency can result in permanent brain damage or impaired learning and energy level (17).

In summary, the medical problems of abused and neglected children are not limited to the assaultive incident or the obvious neglect. Pervasive medical problems include inadequate nutrition, increased rate of illness, erratic medical care for previous infections, anemia, hearing loss, increased risk of poisonous ingestions, and a greater chance of having generally poor health.

Developmental Problems of Childhood

The mistreated child is at greatly increased risk of mental retardation, language delays, learning disorders, poor gross motor ability, and perceptual-motor dysfunction. The evidence for this heightened risk is overwhelmingly consistent. Clinicians have reported alarmingly high rates of such developmental delays, while researchers have shown mistreated children to have poorer developmental courses as compared to siblings or matched control groups. While an exact risk factor cannot be established, there is no doubt whatsoever that mistreated children have lower I.Q.'s, poorer language, and show less competent academic progress than children who have been well parented. A brief review of these data seems indicated.

The classical work of Elmer and Gregg documented developmental outcome in a group of fifty-two children with fractures (18, 19). They described an eighty-eight percent morbidity, using criteria of mental retardation, physical defect, speech and language inadequacy, and emotional disturbance. Fifty-seven percent of the abused children had I.Q.'s below 80 at follow-up and thirty percent had signs of brain damage. The incidence of such developmental outcomes varies considerably with subsequent reports. Clearly, one major reason for the variation in reported outcome is the nature of the abused children studied. Some authors have studied only hospitalized children. Others report only abused children with fractures, for example. Further, there are great differences in treatment programs which will alter the outcome in such studies. Comparison and control groups vary in the exactitude with which they were matched with the mistreated children. And, yet, despite all of these factors, with rare exception, investigators and clinicians consistently find developmental delays and deviations in abused children.

An early report by Denver Child Welfare (12) suggested that seventeen percent of abused children were mentally retarded, while Birrell and Birrell reported that almost thirty percent of their hospitalized sample were retarded (20). Kent's studies (21) suggest that neglected children are at greater risk of retardation than physically abused children (39% versus 24%). Martin's studies of relatively mild physical abuse, from a physiological viewpoint, still found approximately one-third of the children at follow-up to have low I.Q.'s (14, 15).

More recent reports of mistreated children find that while the averge I.Q. of abused and neglected children may fall within the normal range, their I.Q.'s are lower than nonabused siblings or control children. A study of three federally funded treatment programs for abused children reports that the children scored at or slightly below one standard deviation below the mean, indicating generally poor functioning, but not grossly serious delays (22). Similarly, a recently completed study of five- to eight-year-old abused children (23) showed that while the mean I.Q.'s were quite within the normal range, the mean I.Q. was eleven points lower than a carefully matched control group of children. The reader must beware of some methodologic problems in such studies. The investigators, often by design, deliberately exclude brain-damaged or retarded children from their programs or studies, hence artificially raising the reported I.Q.'s of mistreated children. Importantly, though, even when significantly handicapped children are excluded from such studies, the remaining mistreated children have I.Q. scores which are significantly below other children from similar socio-economic backgrounds.

Others have reported impaired cognition in abused and neglected children (16, 24–30). One investigator has even noted lower mental abilities on the Bayley Test at five months of age as compared to a control group (8).

Only one important report in the literature could be found which refutes such findings (31, 32). This enigma is yet to be satisfactorily explained, although methodologic issues in this piece of research and an unusually deviant control group may explain this discrepancy.

Developmental abilities other than those measured by intelligence tests are more likely to be delayed in mistreated children. A three-year follow-up from Australia found thirty-six percent of the abused children delayed in language compared to only eight percent of controls (6). Blager has similarly found language delays in abused and neglected children (33, 34).

A summary of federal demonstration projects by Berkley Planning Associates notes that over fifty percent of the children were one or more standard deviations below the mean in cognitive, as well as language and motor, abilities (35). A recent six-year follow-up of neglected children noted that sixty-six percent of the children had reading disabilities (25). A South African report noted lower performance of abused children in areas of reasoning, performance, hearing and speech, and personal-social skills (28).

There are less data as to the reversibility of these developmental deviations in mistreated children. Cohn's recent summary of treatment programs (22) does suggest that some improvement was evident, especially in personality traits. While most children had higher cognitive, language, and motor-skill scores on the standardized tests at follow-up, they were still at the low end of the "normal" range. Kent's follow-up, wherein there was minimal intervention for the children other than foster-home placement, notes that "despite the improvement of the affected children on the follow-up, incidence of continuing problems is alarmingly high" (21). Other programs which direct therapy to the specific needs of the child also show improvement, albeit incomplete recovery (36).

One recent report (37) suggests that the cognitive abilities of children exposed to undernutrition and deprivation can be overcome through an active program which includes nutritional, health care, and educational intervention.

In summary, mistreated children are at increased risk of developmental delays and deviations. A partial review of the literature points to the risk of retarded intelligence, learning disability, language delay, and perceptual-motor dysfunction. The reasons for these problems, i.e., the dynamics or pathogenesis of these delays, will be addressed below. Regardless of the dynamics, the professionals who work with mistreated children must be alert to these consequences of mistreatment. There is an absolute implication that child protection agencies and teams must include developmental screening or assessment as a routine part of their evaluation of suspected child abuse and neglect. With incidence rates as high as fifty to eighty percent, there should be routine assessment of developmental status of mistreated children. Treatment for these delays will only be planned if professionals are aware of the problems for which treatment is necessary. The developmental status of all mistreated children must be clarified so that pertinent intervention strategies can be found and implemented.

Psychological Consequences of Mistreatment

Numerous traits and characteristics have been noted to be overrepresented in populations of mistreated children. A listing of those traits and characteristics will be less valuable than a general understanding that children who grow up in abusive and neglectful families can rarely escape psychological wounds of clinical significance.

Consider the milieu of the mistreated child. He is born into a home where there are apt to be unrealistic expectations of him and his behavior. He grows up in a family where the parents are products, themselves, of unhappy childhoods. From earliest infancy, the child has little reason to develop a sense of trust in his parents or in his own ability to master or control his environment. Behaviors such as crying may be responded to at times with comforting behaviors, while at other times, they will be ignored. At other times he will be responded to by verbal or physical assault. His environment is unpredictable, and he has little chance to successfully control it. The family in which he lives is typically an isolated unit where there are unusual amounts of social and psychological stress. His parents are usually unhappy adults, frequently dependent and childlike, or inept and violent. His basic needs are often ignored and neglected: needs for physical care (food, warmth, medical care), needs for stimulation (play, verbal stimulation, perceptual-motor experiences), and needs for love and caring through empathic responsiveness of adult caretakers. The very people to whom the child typically turns for love and understanding are capable of unpredictable physical assault and neglect of basic needs. He is not valued as a person but only valued insofar as he meets parents' needs and expectations, which are typically excessive and un-realistic. He is regularly reinforced in feeling that he is a bad child and an un-wanted child. The question truly is: How can any child survive such a childhood without psychic scars? Indeed, the mistreated child rarely can.

A few general principles apply in regard to the psychological status of mis-treated children. The first principle is that such children's behavior is typically at one end of the spectrum or the other, with few middle-ground behaviors evident. For example, the child is apt to be excessively shy and inhibited, fearful and anxious, or is apt to be excessively aggressive and provocative. Both extremes of behavior are reported in studies of mistreated children. Some abused children tend to be noticeably neat and compulsive, while as many others are disorganized in behavior and thought.

A second point to be understood about abused children is that they are generally unhappy children. There is a diminished capacity to enjoy age-appropriate play activities. This often takes the form of a somberness and seriousness which prob-ably reflects clinical depression. It may alternately take the form of acting out behaviors at any age, including infancy. There are few smiles, rare laughter, and minimal gratifying peer relationships in any population of mistreated children.

The third most important deficit in mistreated children falls under the heading of object relations. The abused or neglected child has not learned to have healthy, gratifying, age-appropriate relationships with adults or with peers. The impaired sense of trust-mistrust most often shows itself in one of two ways. The more common is the fearfulness and suspiciousness such children show toward adults. This embryonic paranoia requires the child to be exquisitely attuned to his or her enrivonment, searching the faces and movements of adults to quickly read the mood and anticipate the behavior of adults. An alternate form of this impaired trust in others is the frequent indiscriminate affection which mistreated children show to virtual strangers. It is as if the child had no reason to believe that certain adults are more trustworthy than any other adults or any reason to invest more trust in them. There is no capacity to order the importance of different re-lationships. The adult is appreciated for his capacity to meet the needs of the child, with no special relationships carrying special affection, interest, love, or attachment.

Peer relations are similarly impaired in mistreated children, from infancy through adulthood. There has been little opportunity to learn to play with others and little modeling of normal interpersonal relationships in the families of such children. The social isolation of abusive and neglectful families precludes the child from opportunity to learn these social skills outside of the home. Further, the child's increasingly poor self-concept augurs poorly for normal interpersonal re-lations with peers. This dynamic is seen throughout life, as the potential abuser so typically chooses a mate who is similarly unhappy and inadequate. For instance, it is very common to see abusive women repeatedly find mates who are physically abusive to them. This is but one form of self-destructive behavior which starts in infancy and may continue throughout the life of the mistreated child.

Several papers by Green have focused on self-abusive behavior of mistreated children (38–40). Indeed, especially distressing was the finding that 8.3 percent of abused children with a mean age of 8.5 years had attempted suicide and 20 percent had self-mutilative behavior.

At least two authors have noted that abused children tend to be more aggressive than neglected or control children (21, 41). This should not be surprising given the frequency of abusive homes from which most aggressive or criminal adolescents and adults come (42–46).

Cohn (22) and Martin and Beezley (47) have each listed common traits in abused and neglected children. Others (48) have pointed out the behavior problems and maladjustment of abused children, as seen by their school teachers.

Even more interesting, from a developmental point of view, is the recent work with infants and toddlers with abuse and failure-to-thrive (49, 50). Disruption of attachment was noted in the failure-to-thrive infants and their parents. Gaensbauer (49) addresses distorted affective communication patterns of the child and the mother, highlighting the infant's predilection for withdrawal and the unpredictability and shallowness of emotional communication. He also notes the child's frequent negative expression of affect through anger, distress, and sadness, as well as the meager capacity for pleasure these children show as compared to a control group in similar circumstances. This suggests, then, that emotional distress and character traits have their beginnings quite early in life, as early as six months of age. In a comparison of 295 abused children and their 284 nonabused siblings, parents remembered the abused children as less enjoyable in early life, listing behavior problems, troubles in eating and sleeping, etc. (5).

There is no question that abused and neglected children are at considerably greater risk of acquiring emotional disorders and character traits which are much like the personalities of their abusive parents. The mistreated child is very likely to be an unhappy child with minimal capacity for healthy, gratifying interpersonal relationships. She has difficulty in dealing with her own anger and aggression and is likely to engage in a variety of self-defeating and self-abusive behaviors. This toll in emotional health is taken early in the life of the mistreated child and can progress throughout the various stages of childhood into adult life.

Long-Term Effects of Abusive Environment

What happens to abused and neglected children as they progress through childhood and become adults? Treatment planning and placement decisions will be influenced by the long-range prognosis of abuse and neglect. Unfortunately, there are no prospective long-term studies of mistreated children. The data which are available are largely anecdotal and retrospective. Nonetheless, there are some implications to be drawn from these data which do give a reasonable estimate of the life-long toll which is taken by the abusive environment.

The most obvious long-term effect of the abusive environment is its influence on parenting patterns in the next generation. The generational transmission of abuse and neglect was first posited by Steele and Pollock (51) as they were impressed that most abusive parents were themselves abused or neglected in childhood. This empirical observation has had documentation more recently. Hunter and colleagues (52) reported on 255 mothers who gave birth to premature or small babies. Ten of those mothers had abuse or neglect reports filed against them during the first year of their babies' lives which were subsequently confirmed. Nine of the ten abusive mothers gave a history of having been abused or neglected, while only seventeen percent of the 245 comparison mothers had such a history—a significant difference at the .0005 level. While these sorts of data confirm our belief that abusive, neglectful home environments greatly increase the risk of growing up to be an abusive parent, one must also note that seventeen percent of the control mothers (a total of forty-two mothers from the 245 nonreported group) had a history of having been abused or neglected. If one assumes that the 245 mothers in whom abuse and neglect were not reported were adequately parenting their children (an assumption of tenuous validity), one must realize that of fifty-two mothers who gave a history of abuse and neglect in their childhoods, only ten (or 19%) were identified as abusive to their babies during the first year of the babies' lives. While the numbers in this study are too small to make exacting predictions, nonetheless, the data support one's clinical impression, that is, that while many children who have been mistreated can grow up to be adequate parents, there is a tremendously increased risk they will grow up to be abusive or neglectful parents.

It might be hoped that as abuse and neglect are identified, and treatment is provided for the child, this risk could be lessened. One is unable to state, presently, why some mistreated children become abusive parents and others do not. However, the common traits and characteristics of abusive parents (53) give us some clue as to how the mistreated child has grown up and developed. A logical step, then, is to address those issues in mistreated children so that they will not develop character traits similar to their parents and repetitiously carry on a family pattern of child mistreatment (54–57).

Delinquents, criminals, school drop-outs, and teenage parents are populations assumed to have an overrepresentation of individuals with histories of abuse and neglect in childhood. Without prospective studies of mistreated children, the risk of these long-term outcomes is statistically uncertain. And, yet, there can be little doubt that these are high-risk paths which mistreated children may tred through adolescent and adult life. These long-term consequences convincingly make the point that all of society pays a price when any member mistreats a child. If you mistreat your child, my life is changed, for his or her eventual life pattern may well be one of antisocial acting out behavior which impinges on my safety and security.

Rather than explicating all of the possible outcomes of an abusive childhood, general principles of long-term sequellae might be highlighted by considering the relationship between child abuse and subsequent aggression. Several authors (43–46) have pointed to the potential for violence begetting violence. Supporting evidence for this postulation can come from noting the abusive childhoods of notorious personages such as Hitler, Stalin, or Sirhan Sirhan. Other data include interviews and histories of violent criminals wherein alarmingly high rates of childhood mistreatment are found.

The recent research of Lewis and colleagues sheds a convincing light on this issue (42). The study consisted of ninety-seven boys who had been incarcerated at a correctional school in adolescence. These boys were rated on a scale of 1 to 4 for violence. Nineteen were rated 1 or 2, which included children with no evidence of offense against a person or those with only a potential for violence. Seventy-eight of the boys were rated 3 or 4, which included those who had committed serious offenses against persons or who had demonstrated extraordinary brutality toward others. Seventy-five percent of the violent delinquents had been abused, while only thirty-three percent of the nonviolent boys reported a similar childhood history. Even more striking was the finding that seventy-nine percent of the violent delinquents had witnessed extreme violence in childhood, while only twenty percent of the nonviolent boys had a similar past history. This makes it clear that violent families raise children who are at increased risk of repeating violent assaults on strangers, spouses, and children.

This author's experience suggests that another type of long-term effect of maltreatment is a life of incompetence and failure. This is a typical pattern for abusive adults who were themselves victims of maltreatment. School failure, job failure, and marital failure are common in the histories of abusive adults. This is a natural accompaniment of a person with low self-esteem, a sense of helplessness, external locus of control, or a clinical picture of depression. Indeed, this might be predicted from the developmental failure of the infant and preschooler, the frequent learning disabilities of the latency-aged child and the school drop-out, and antisocial behavior of the mistreated adolescent. In a sense, then, the mistreated child is at increased risk of a lifetime of wasted potential, a pervasive experience of failure and incompetence. Inherent in this experience of failure and ineptness are the seeds of neediness, loneliness, and dependency which can so easily be turned into a pathological need for a child who will nurture and heal the wounds of loneliness, despair, and hopelessness. The stage is set, then, for a repetitious pattern of abuse and neglect.

An exposition on the long-term effects of childhood mistreatment would not be complete without commenting on the potential for successful resolution by the victim. In any population of highly stressed individuals there will always be a subset who adapt quite well to the stress. Unfortunately, these successful outcomes are rarely studied, precluding the opportunity to tease out the factors which may have led to successful adaptation. Clinical experience does give us some clues which would benefit from brief description:

1. In the lives of some mistreated children there are fortuitous individuals who can make up much of the difference in the child's growth and development. At times there is an older sibling, a dedicated aunt or uncle, or some other person who takes on a surrogate parenting role, albeit in a very informal manner (58, 59). In such instances the child's milieu is transformed into a life where someone other than the formal parent supplies the nurturing, empathy, responsiveness, and

stimulation the child requires. This informally assigned parent-surrogate mutes the harmful effects of abuse and neglect.

2. One would hope that the treatment strategies which child protection agencies devise for abused and neglected children may alter the outcome for the developing child. These data are not readily available.

3. There continues to be a concept of the "invulnerable child" (60). There are children who are more capable of satisfactorily adapting to loss, to neglect, to abuse, or to a whole host of malevolent socio-familial influences. Brazelton (61, 62) has certainly reinforced the knowledge that from birth some children are more resilient and adaptive to noxious stimulae than other newborns. No wonder, then, that throughout life children will vary in their capacities to successfully adapt to an abusive or neglectful home. Some credence must be given to the hypothesis that there are, from birth, variations in adaptive skill. Some babies are more able to soothe themselves in the absence of a comforting caretaker. Some babies are more able to ignore noxious stimulae. There are variations in babies' capacities to adapt to changes in routine or surrounding. There may well be differences in children's abilities to master their environments through understanding and manipulation of that environment, even from early infancy.

There are clear differences in children's abilities to cope with physiologic stress, such as hunger, infection, or illness. What is posited here is a belief that there are, analogously, variations in capacity to cope with psychological stress which may account for some of the children who seem less scathed by an abusive environment.

4. The reader must beware of overestimating the resiliency and adaptability of mistreated children. An abused child may fare well in terms of intelligence and academics and yet be a very unhappy, lonely child. Another type of child may appear quite happy and socially competent and yet be forfeiting stages of childhood for which he or she will pay a price in later life.

Our intense interest in the invulnerable child may tempt us to be so attuned to the successful adaptations of the child or adult that we ignore, in our fervor, the maladaptations which are less obvious. Edward Arlington Robinson's poem "Richard Cory" is a literary reminder of the whole spectrum of consequences and adaptations of the mistreated child.

Dynamics of the Effect of the Abusive Environment on Development

One treads on thin ice in attempting to explain behavior. This is especially true in dealing with child abuse, as there are practically no data to convincingly prove that an abused or neglected child suffers developmental consequences because of a specific causative cluster of events. There are important reasons to address this issue, however, not the least of which is that preventive efforts or treatment must be based on some rationale other than diagnosis, i.e., the treatment for a language delay will differ depending on the reason that the abused child has this delay. The following points can be helpful clinically in unravelling the dynamics and pathogenesis of the child's problems.

Biologic Damage

Some of the consequences of abuse and neglect lie in biological damage to the brain and central nervous system of the child. Most often, when this is the case, the neurological function of the child is so affected that a thorough neuro-developmental examination can lend credence to this etiology. Damage to the brain can and does affect the various ego functions of learning, memory, language, motor coordination, etc. Less well appreciated is the fact that brain damage can influence personality. Rutter, Tizard, and Whitmore's (63) survey of children in the famous Isle of Wight studies make the point convincingly. Children with brain damage, even in the face of normal mental abilities, have a risk of significant psychiatric disturbance which is five to six times the normal population and twice the rate of children with nonneurologically based chronic handicaps. The damaged nervous system may not function as capably in perceiving, learning, and processing cognitive information. It is postulated that the damaged nervous system may not function as well in psychiatric functions such as social perception, identification of one's own feelings, etc. The personality is built and developed through events and experiences which must be processed by the brain. Hence, no large leap in logic is required to assume that a damaged nervous system may function less well in a host of psychological processes. Drugs, endocrine disorders, and metabolic disturbances can affect personality function. Certainly, then, other types of biological influences on the brain can similarly affect personality.

The Psychological Milieu

There are cumulative data which suggest that for the survivors of abuse, developmental deviations are more apt to be the result of the pervasive abusive environment than a result of the isolated incidents of physical assault (15, 36). Psychiatric symptoms in a group of abused children with normal neurological examinations and with no history of head trauma were shown to correspond to the stability of the home (regardless of whether biological, foster, or adoptive), the number of moves the child had experienced, and the sense of permanence or impermanence the child perceived in his or her present family placement (47).

This rather obvious conclusion has far-reaching treatment implications. The cessation of physical assault or neglect to the child—without a change in family function and parent-child interaction—may not provide a developmentally safe home for the child. If a child's developmental delays and personality deviations are being caused by a style of parenting, and not by incidents of abuse, then that style of parenting must be changed if the child is to be able to overcome his or her developmental and psychological wounds.

Developmental Line of Mastery and Competence

A more speculative hypothesis regarding the developmental delays of abused and neglected children is related to a derailment in the child's sense of mastery and competence rather than to true inability. The infant is born with an innate drive for mastering the environment (64). This developmental line of mastery or competence fuels the drive to learn, understand, affect, and conquer the environment of objects and people. The abused or neglected child may not be reinforced for successful attempts at mastery. Such behaviors as curiosity, investigativeness, autonomy, and independence result in verbal or physical abuse. Attempts at success are not only not reinforced but are met with impatience and punishment. This smacks very much of Seligman's work (65) in learned helplessness in animals and humans which relates to the work in internal, versus external, locus of control. There is reason to believe that abused children are more apt to feel that they are not able to impact on the environment and that external forces rather than their own efforts determine the outcome of events (23).

Insofar as this dynamic is operant, there are pertinent implications for treatment (66). If, for instance, a child's delay in some area of development, such as language or reading, is not really due to biological or psychological inability but rather is a manifestation of impairment in mastery or competence, then treatment would be focused quite differently. Instead of traditional remediation in language or reading, the therapist might need to deal with the basic deficit in developing a sense of pleasure mastery. The issue may be one of fostering the child's sense of worth and competence and working on the developmental line of mastery rather than the developmental line of communication skills.

Iatrogenic Factors

Iatrogenic factors may be at the root of many of the consequences of abuse and neglect. It is essential to start from the theoretical and practical position of admitting that all therapeutic procedures carry some risk of harm. When considering the mistreated child, one is forced to acknowledge that very often our interventions provide extra psychological stress. The child may be put in the hospital, a place which is detrimental to growth and development. The child may be abruptly separated from parents whom he or she loves and to whom he or she is attached. The child may be put into a new and strange family, where there are considerable impediments to the adults truly becoming "psychological" parents to the child (67). Visiting with the biological parents may be arranged too infrequently to continue the bond of attachment. The child is often at the center of legal processes wherein the child and the child's injuries are being used to prove inadequacies in the parents. Foster care can often stretch into weeks, months, and years, with the most frequent pattern being that of repeated changes in foster home, i.e., repeated parent losses to which the child must adapt.

All of these therapeutic maneuvers take their toll on the infant or older child. An individual abused child's sense of worthlessness, isolation, loneliness, and minimal ability to truly attach and bond to significant others may be more related to the experiences of separation from parents and repeated foster home placements than to the original aberrant parenting he or she received from the biological parents.

Again, there are implications for treatment and for ways in which the harmful effects of our interventions can be prevented or muted. The most glaring example is the importance of discontinuing the practice of long-term foster care. Interminable and frequently changing foster care is detrimental to the development of these abused children and must be avoided when possible (68).

The Transactional Model

An understanding of the developmental and psychological deviations in abused children requires, in this author's opinion, an appreciation of the transactional model of parent-child as described by Sameroff (69, 70). One's understanding of the child will be quite limited if one only considers traits or characteristics of the parent or exclusively focuses on traits or characteristics of the child which make that particular child special. Both parent and child make some contribution to most instances of abuse or neglect, although one or the other may play the more promiment role in specific instances.

Other chapters in this book and years of research have established quite satisfactorily that there are specific traits and characteristics in adults which increase the proclivity to mistreat children, especially in socially or psychologically stressful situations. Equally clear are the conditions or characteristics of children which may place them at higher risk of abuse or neglect. For instance, almost all studies of mistreated children find an overrepresentation of children who had low birth weights, had significantly more illnesses in infancy, and perhaps who have more minor or major congenital anomalies. These conditions in children must be transformed into how they affect the child's behavior. Chess and Thomas first attempted this by describing temperamental differences in children (71) and later emphasized that it was not the temperament of the child which was most predictive of later parent-child problems, but rather it was the interaction between this particular type of child and this particular type of adult (72, 73). The more recent work of Gaensbauer (49) sheds even more light on this transaction between infant and parent. He observed forty-eight mistreated children as well as a cohort of 100 nonabused children from six to thirty-six months of age. He found that, compared to normal infants, the abused and neglected children showed a variety of distorted affective communications which interfered with mutual engagement and which elicited negative responses from their caretakers. So, even in infancy, a dyadic relationship has been established wherein the infant is less competent in engaging with adults and is even actively eliciting negative responses from the parent. The parent, on his/her part, has been playing a role in engendering or reinforcing these infant behaviors. The interaction between the child and parent is distorted and deviant, with each playing their part in its development and continuation.

Much of the dynamic of abuse and neglect may stem from disruptions in early attachment and bonding (74). However, it does not seem likely that that alone can explain assault on children or the massive neglect and deprivation which may follow. A more likely explanation is that in some adult-infant dyads, this inadequate early attachment is just the beginning nidus for a distorted and deviant parent-child interaction which may take slightly different forms in different dyads.

This transactional model, which stresses the role of both partners, the child and the adult, is an essential conceptualization in understanding the child's developmental consequences, as well as essential for treatment strategies. The learned behaviors of the child must be understood to maximize the chances of successful foster placement or adoption (75). The failure of so many adoptions and the remarkable turnover in foster placements is very largely due to a failure to identify and provide help in changing these learned behaviors of the child.

Alternately, when the child can remain with biologic parents, the transactions between parent and child must be diagnosed and treatment must be provided which has the goal of modifying those abnormal transactional patterns.

In Sameroff's transactional model, it is clear that the child and parent each influence and change each others' behavior; it is not just a matter of two people interacting on the basis of their character structure or temperaments, but rather the behavior of the child changes the behavior of the adult, which in turn affects the subsequent behavior of the child and so on. Further, the environment in which the two people are interacting influences their behaviors, their transactions, so that behavior varies depending upon the place and circumstances in which it occurs; it is not an immutable constant regardless of the environment or the other person's behavior.

Conclusions

There are innumerable consequences of a child being mistreated physically and emotionally. There are immediately obvious medical consequences of assault or physical neglect. There are less obvious physiological consequences which may include anemia, hearing loss, growth failure, and poor health.

Over one-half of mistreated children may be expected to have developmental problems in some line(s) of autonomous ego functioning, i.e., motor ability, learning, memory, understanding, perception, or speech and language. These may be due to biological damage to the child but are more often a consequence of the family environment which has limited opportunity, has not provided adequate modeling, stimulation, and reinforcement, and which has imbued in the child a sense of helplessness through derailing the child's sense of mastery and competence.

Children who have been abused and neglected can hardly escape some psychological effects. Adaptations which may be valuable for survival are usually self-defeating in helping the child grow up with a sense of worth, with ability to have friends, and with the capacity to enjoy and appreciate one's self and others.

The long-term effects of an abusive or neglectful environment give some urgency to the need to provide treatment of the child. Without direct treatment services to the child, the future stretches out with increased risk of being unhappy, socially and academically inept, and continuing a repetitious pattern of abuse and neglect through repeating the parenting patterns to which the child, himself, was exposed.

Knowing the statistical risk of various types of consequences to the abused and neglected child is not enough. Also required is that one appreciate the reasons why these consequences have eventuated. Intervention strategies and both primary and secondary prevention of abuse must be predicated on an understanding of the dynamics of the effects of abuse and neglect on children. The role of the child must be appreciated. The added damage that helping systems do to the child must be obviated or muted through anticipatory prevention. An understanding of the invulnerable child's escape from these consequences may give critical information which can be used in treating other less-resilient children.

The mistreated child does not fare well. An understanding of the ways in which such children do poorly, the neuro-psycho-developmental pitfalls to which they are exposed, and an understanding of the dynamics of such consequences can be used as a springboard to provision of treatment services which can greatly lessen the consequences of abuse and neglect.

References

1. Gregg, G. S., and Elmer, E. Infant Injuries: Accident or Abuse. *Pediatrics* 44:434–39, 1969.
2. Sobel, R. The Psychiatric Implications of Accidental Poisoning in Childhood. *Pediatric Clinics of North America* 17:653–85, 1970.
3. Lynch, M. Risk Factors in the Child: A Study of Abused Children and Their Siblings. In H. P. Martin (ed.), *The Abused Child: A Multidisciplinary Approach to Developmental Issues and Treatment*, Cambridge, Mass.: Ballinger, 1976, pp. 43–56.
4. ———. Ill Health and Child Abuse. *Lancet*, 2:317–19, 1975.
5. Herrenkohl, E. C., and Herrenkohl, R. C. A Comparison of Abused Children and Their Non-Abused Siblings. *Journal of American Academy of Child Psychiatry*, 18:260–69, 1979.
6. Oates, R. K., Davis, A. A., Ryan, M. G., and Stewart, L. F. Risk Factors Associated with Child Abuse. *Abstracts: Second International Congress on Child Abuse and Neglect*, London: Pergamon Press, 1978, p. 171.
7. Ebbin, A. J., Gollub, M. H., Stein, A. M., and Wilson, M. G. Battered Child Syndrome at the Los Angeles County General Hospital. *American Journal of Diseases in Children*, 118:660–67, 1969.
8. Dietrich, K. M. *The Abused Infant: Developmental Characteristics and Maternal Handling*, Masters thesis, Wayne State University, 1977.
9. Zinkus, P. W., Gottlieb, M. L., and Schapiro, M. Developmental and Psychoeducational Sequelae of Chronic Otitis Media. *American Journal of Diseases in Children*, 132:1100–1104, 1978.
10. Needleman, H. Effects of Hearing Loss from Early Recurrent Otitis Media on Speech and Language Development. In F. Jaffe (ed.), *Hearing Loss in Children*, Baltimore: University Park Press, 1977, pp. 640–48.
11. Holm, V. A., and Kunze, L. H. Effect of Chronic Otitis Media on Language and Speech Development. *Pediatrics*, 43:833–39, 1969.
12. Johnson, B., and Morse, H. *The Battered Child: A Study of Children with*

Inflicted Injuries, Denver: Denver Department of Welfare, 1968.

13. Morse, C. W., Sahler, O. J. Z., and Friedman, S. B. A Three-Year Follow-up Study of Abused and Neglected Children. *American Journal of Diseases in Children*, 120:439–46, 1970.

14. Martin, H. P. The Child and His Development. In C. H. Kempe and R. Helfer (eds.), *Helping the Battered Child and His Family*, Philadelphia: Lippincott, 1972, pp. 93–114.

15. Martin, H. P., Beezley, P., Conway, E. F., and Kempe, C. H. The Development of Abused Children–Part I: A Review of the Literature; Part II: Physical, Neurologic, and Intellectual Outcome. *Advanced Pediatrics*, 21:25–73, 1974.

16. Smith, S. M., and Hanson, R. 134 Battered Children: A Medical and Psychological Study. *British Medical Journal*, Sept. 14:666–70, 1974.

17. Martin, H. P. Nutrition: Its Relationship to Children's Physical, Mental, and Emotional Development. *American Journal of Clinical Nutrition*, 26:755–66, 1973.

18. Elmer, E. *Children in Jeopardy*, Pittsburgh: University of Pittsburgh Press, 1967.

19. Elmer, E., and Gregg, G. S. Developmental Characteristics of Abused Children. *Pediatrics*, 40:596–602, 1967.

20. Birrell, R. G., and Birrell, J. H. W. The Maltreatment Syndrome in Children: A Hospital Survey. *Medical Journal of Australia*, 2:1023–29, 1968.

21. Kent, J. T. A Follow-up Study of Abused Children. *Journal of Pediatric Psychology*, 1:25–31, 1976.

22. Cohn, A. H. An Evaluation of Three Demonstration Child Abuse and Neglect Treatment Programs. *Journal of American Academy of Child Psychiatry*, 18:283–91, 1979.

23. Barahal, R., Waterman, J., and Martin, H. P. Social-Cognitive Functioning in Abused Latency-Aged Children, submitted for publication.

24. Ryan, M. G., Davis, A. A., and Oates, R. K. 187 Cases of Child Abuse and Neglect. *Medical Journal of Australia*, 2:623–28, 1977.

25. Hufton, I. W., and Oates, R. K. Non-organic Failure to Thrive: A Long-Term Follow-up. *Pediatrics*, 59:73–77, 1977.

26. Manciaux, M., and Deschamps, J. P. L'enfant victime de mauvais traitements. *Vie medicale au Canada français*, 4:244–47, 1975.

27. Buchanan, A., and Oliver, J. F. Abuse and Neglect as a Cause of Mental Retardation. *British Journal of Psychiatry*, 131:458–67, 1977.

28. Van Staden, J. The Mental Development of Abused Children in South Africa. *Abstracts: Second International Congress on Child Abuse and Neglect*, London: Pergamon Press, 1978, p. 212.

29. Sandgrund, A., Gaines, R. W., and Green, A. H. Child Abuse and Mental Retardation: A Problem of Cause and Effect. *Journal of Mental Deficiency*, 19:327–30, 1975.

30. Goldson, E., Fitch, M. J., Wendell, T. A., and Knapp, G. Child Abuse: Its Relationship to Birthweight, Apgar Score, and Developmental Testing. *American Journal of Diseases in Children*, 132:790–93, 1978.

31. Elmer, E. A Follow-up Study of Traumatized Children. *Pediatrics,* 59:273–79, 1977.

32. ———. *Fragile Families, Troubled Children: The Aftermath of Infant Trauma,* Pittsburgh: University of Pittsburgh Press, 1977.

33. Blager, F., and Martin, H. P. Speech and Language of Abused Children in H. P. Martin (ed.), *The Abused Child: A Multidisciplinary Approach to Developmental Issues and Treatment,* Cambridge, Mass.: Ballinger, 1976, pp. 83–92.

34. Blager, F. Effect of Intervention on Speech and Language of Abused Children. *Abstracts: Second International Congress on Child Abuse and Neglect,* London: Pergamon Press, 1978, p. 21.

35. *Evaluation of Child Abuse and Neglect Demonstration Projects 1974–1977,* Vol. 6, *Child Client Impact: Final Report,* U.S. Department of Commerce, PB 278–448, December, 1977.

36. Martin, H. P. (Ed.). *The Abused Child: An Interdisciplinary Approach to Developmental Issues and Treatment,* Cambridge, Mass.: Ballinger, 1976.

37. McKay, H., Sinisterra, L., McKay, A., Gomez, H., and Lloreda, P. Improving Cognitive Ability in Chronically Deprived Children. *Science,* 200:270–78, 1978.

38. Green, A. H. Self-Destruction in Physically Abused Schizophrenic Children: Report of Cases. *Archives of General Psychiatry,* 19:171–97, 1968.

39. ———. Self-Destructive Behavior in Battered Children. *American Journal of Psychiatry,* 135:579–82, 1978.

40. ———. Psychopathology of Abused Children. *Journal of American Academy of Child Psychiatry,* 17:92–103, 1978.

41. Reidy, T. J. The Aggressive Characteristics of Abused and Neglected Children. *Journal of Clinical Psychology,* 33:1140–45, 1977.

42. Lewis, D. O., Shanok, S. S., Pincus, J. H., and Glaser, G. H. Violent Juvenile Delinquents: Psychiatric, Neurological, Psychological, and Abuse Factors. *Journal of American Academy of Child Psychiatry,* 18:307–19, 1979.

43. Duncan, G. M., Frazier, S. H., Litin, E. M., Johnson, A. M., and Barron, A. J. Etiological Factors in First-Degree Murder. *Journal of the American Medical Association,* 168:1755–58, 1958.

44. Easson, W. M., and Steinhilber, R. M. Murderous Aggression by Children and Adolescents. *Archives of General Psychiatry,* 4:27–35, 1961.

45. Curtis, G. C. Violence Breeds Violence–Perhaps? *American Journal of Psychiatry,* 120:386–87, 1963.

46. Steele, B. F. Violence in Our Society. *Pharos of Alpha Omega Alpha,* 33:42–48, 1970.

47. Martin, H. P., and Beezley, P. Behavioral Observations of Abused Children. *Developmental Medicine/Child Neurology,* 19:373–87, 1977.

48. Roberts, J., Lynch, M. A., and Duff, P. Abused Children and Their Siblings: A Teacher's View. *Therapeutic Education,* 6:25–31, 1978.

49. Gaensbauer, T. J., and Sands, K. Distorted Affective Communications in Abused and Infants and Their Potential Impact on Caretakers. *Journal of*

American Academy of Child Psychiatry, 18:236–50, 1979.

50. Gordon, A. H., and Jameson, J. C. Infant-Mother Attachment in Patients with Non-organic Failure to Thrive Syndrome. *Journal of American Academy of Child Psychiatry,* 18:251–59, 1979.

51. Steele, B. V., and Pollock, C. B. A Psychiatric Study of Parents Who Abuse Infants and Small Children. In R. Helfer and C. H. Kempe (eds.), *The Battered Child,* Chicago: University of Chicago Press, 2nd ed., 1974, pp. 89–134.

52. Hunter, R. S., Kilstrom, N., Kraybill, E. N., and Loda, F Antecedents of Child Abuse and Neglect in Premature Infants: A Prospective Study in a Newborn Intensive Care Unit. *Pediatrics,* 61:629–35, 1978.

53. Steele, B. F. *Working with Abusive Parents: From a Psychiatric Point of View,* U.S. Department of HEW, Office of Child Development, #0H075-70, 1975.

54. Straus, M. A. Family Patterns and Child Abuse in a Nationally Representative American Sample. *Abstracts: Second International Congress on Child Abuse and Neglect,* London: Pergamon Press, 1978, p. 75.

55. Burgess, R. S., and Conger, R. D. Project Interact: Patterns of Interaction in Abuse, Neglect, and Control Families. *Abstracts: Second International Congress on Child Abuse and Neglect,* London: Pergamon Press, 1978, p. 85.

56. Conger, R. D., and Burgess, R. L. Reciprocity and Coercion in Child Abuse. *Abstracts: Second International Congress on Child Abuse and Neglect,* London: Pergamon Press, 1978, p. 254.

57. Martin, H. P. A Child-Oriented Approach to Prevention of Abuse. In A. M. Franklin (ed.), *Child Abuse: Prediction, Prevention, and Folow-up,* New York: Churchill Livingstone Publishers, 1978.

58. Korbin, J. A Cross-Cultural Perspective on the Role of the Community in Child Abuse and Neglect. *Abstracts: Second International Congress on Child Abuse and Neglect,* London: Pergamon Press, 1978, p. 78.

59. Kagan, J. The Child in the Family. *Daedalus: Journal of the American Academy of Arts and Sciences,* 106:33–56, 1977.

60. Anthony, E. J. The Syndrome of the Psychologically Invulnerable Child. In E. J. Anthony and C. Koupernik (eds.), *The Child in His Family: Children at Psychiatric Risk,* New York: John Wiley & Sons, 1974, pp. 529–44.

61. Brazelton, T. B. *Neonatal Behavioral Assessment Scale: Clinics in Developmental Medicine, No. 50,* Philadelphia: J. B. Lippincott, 1973.

62. Brazelton, T. B., Koslowski, B., and Main, M. The Origins of Reciprocity: The Early Mother-Infant Interaction. In M. Lewis and L. A. Rosenblum (eds.), *The Effect of the Infant on Its Caregiver,* New York: John Wiley & Sons, 1974.

63. Rutter, M., Tizard, J., and Whitmore, K. *Education, Health, and Behavior,* New York: John Wiley & Sons, 1970.

64. White, R. W. Ego and Reality in Psychoanalytic Theory. *Psychological Issues,* 3:1–196, 1963.

65. Seligman, M. E. P. *Helplessness: On Depression, Development, and Death,* San Francisco: W. H. Freeman, 1975.

66. Martin, H. P. Child Abuse and Child Development. *International Journal of Child Abuse and Neglect,* 3(2):415–22, 1979.

67. Goldstein, J., Freud, A., and Solnit, A. J. *Beyond the Best Interests of the Child,* New York: Free Press, 1973.

68. Martin, H. P. *User Manual on Upgrading Child Abuse and Neglect Programs: Treatment of Abused and Neglected Children,* National Center on Child Abuse and Neglect, ACYF, HEW, Washington, D.C., (OHDS) 79-30199.

69. Sameroff, A. J. Early Influences on Development: Fact or Fancy? In S. Chess and H. G. Thomas (eds.), *Annual Progress in Child Psychiatry and Child Development,* New York: Brunner/Mazel, 1976, pp. 3–33.

70. Sameroff, A. J., and Chandler, M. J. Reproductive Risk and the Continuum of Caretaking Casualty. In F. D. Horowitz *et al.* (eds)., *Review of Child Development Research,* Chicago: University of Chicago Press, 1975, 4:187–244.

71. Thomas, A., Chess, S., and Birch, H. G. *Temperament and Behavior Disorders in Children,* New York: New York University Press, 1968.

72. Thomas, A., and Chess, S. *Temperament and Development,* New York: Brunner/Mazel, 1977.

73. Chess, S., and Thomas, A. Temperamental Individuality from Childhood to Adolescence. *Journal of American Academy of Child Psychiatry,* 16:218–26, 1977.

74. Klaus, M. H., and Kennell, J. H. *Maternal-Infant Bonding: The Impact of Early Separation or Loss on Family Development,* St. Louis: C. V. Mosby, 1976.

75. Fanshel, D. Status Changes of Children in Foster Care: Final Results of the Columbia University Longitudinal Study. In S. Chess and A. Thomas (eds.), *Annual Progress in Child Psychiatry and Child Development,* New York: Brunner/Mazel, 1977, pp. 625–51.

PART

Prevention

An Overview of Prevention

The goal of any individual or group working in as devastating a field as child abuse and neglect is prevention. While this goal is truly admirable, the very thought is overwhelming. Preventing a phenomenon that occurs at least a million times each year, which adversely affects children's physical growth and emotional development and eats away at the very foundation of our society, i.e., the family, is an achievable goal.

The authors in this section of the book clearly feel the task of prevention is possible, at least to a very significant degree. To understand their approach and the reasons why one particular direction has been taken in preference to another, a few comments, definitions, and a diagram are necessary.

What Is Being Prevented?

In the narrow sense, the answer to the question of what is being prevented is very clear, physical abuse. Broadening this answer only slightly would add overt severe neglect. Limiting the goal to these two manifestations makes the studies and research in this field rather simple. Expansion of the answer to include the prevention of adverse forms of parent-child interactions complicates the research picture considerably, and yet both extremes have been studied.

O'Connor demonstrated that rooming-in after the delivery of a newborn decreases risk of physical abuse, abandonment, and failure to thrive (1). Burgess demonstrated that mother-child interactions are more negative and less frequent in abusive situations than in nonabusive families (2). Both extremes of this interactional continuum can be measured and the preventive intervention assessed. Combining both extremes of this continuum into one definition is difficult, but feasible.

Child abuse: any interaction or lack of interactions between a caretaker and child, which results in nonaccidental harm to the child's physical and/or developmental state.

At Whom Are Prevention Programs Directed?

The question of the appropriate goal for preventative programs is usually resolved by inserting the word *primary* in front of prevention, thereby indicating prevention before the fact. While this should help, the fact that child abuse is a cyclical event, from one generation to another, adds complexity to this terminology. Treatment of parents after a child has been abused (see Chapter 16) would be considered secondary prevention as far as the child is concerned (preventing recurrences). Treatment of the child, on the other hand, would be primary prevention as far as the child's children are concerned (see Chapter 23). Providing a new mother, formerly abused, with special training in how to interact with her baby (see Chapter 26) is primary prevention for the baby and secondary for the mother.

Enough for semantics. The goal is to develop programs which will prevent child abuse, in whatever form, from occurring. Many programs have this potential. No one solution is likely to be the panacea. In combination, the outlook is very bright.

Figure 1 diagrams the ages of development in cyclical fashion, listed according to the inner aspects of this life cycle. Outside the circle various intervention programs are identified. These programs are lettered, with a brief discussion for each given below. Appropriate references are given where they are available. With this diagram the reader should be able to place the programs discussed in this part of the book and in the literature in some perspective. (The following discussion amplifies figure 1.)

A. *Perinatal coaching.* New parents are provided training in the interactional skills necessary to communicate with their newborn (see Chapter 26) (3, 4).

B. *Home care training.* New parents (and some young parents) are provided home visitors to assist them in resolving day-to-day issues, health problems, and increasing interpersonal communication skills with their infants (see Chapter 22) (4, 5).

C. *Expanded well-baby care.* The proposal here is that physicians and nurses must better meet the needs of young parents when they bring their new babies in for traditional well-child care. No longer is it appropriate to limit the service provided to those which demonstrate the well-child is well (4).

D. *Interpersonal cognitive problem-solving skills.* Techniques have been developed by Spivack and Shure to teach small children (ages four to ten years) how to solve everyday problems. These can be taught by preschool and primary school teachers (6, 7).

E. *Interpersonal-skills (IPS) teaching for middle (junior high) school and high school.* This program, at this time, is a fantasy, but an achievable one. Schools should be teaching "how to get along" skills—getting along with peers, teachers, parents, girls, boys, dates, mates, and one's children. They should *not* isolate one or two of these issues (e.g., sex education and parenting). The IPS curriculum should be continuous throughout this six- to eight-year period. No good study of this concept has yet been found by this author. All of the above are proposed for everyone. No preselection process (see Chapter 24) is proposed.

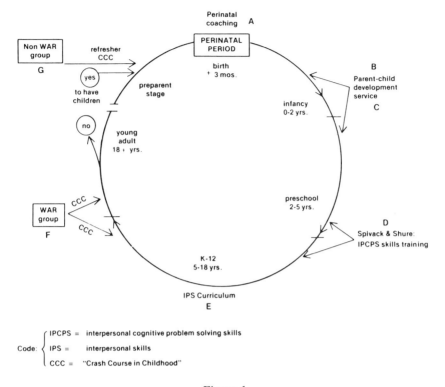

Code:
IPCPS = interpersonal cognitive problem solving skills
IPS = interpersonal skills
CCC = "Crash Course in Childhood"

Figure 1

A paradigm for prevention. See text for references.

F. Crash course in childhood for adults. Some young people have arrived at adulthood by way of a childhood which, to say the least, was less than optimal. These young adults need a second chance to learn the skills of interaction, skills which should have been learned during their childhoods. This relearning and retraining is best done before one arrives at the preparent stage of life (see Chapters 3 and 25) (8).

G. Preparent refresher. Many of the young adults, both men and women, who had a positive childhood experience and those graduates of the "Crash Course in Childhood" will decide to enter the preparent stage (getting ready for pregnancy and parenthood). Some will have placed many years of work and/or cognitive learning (college and graduate school) between their childhood and their parenthood. These soon-to-be parents need a refresher course in the concepts of interacting with children and mates (8).

R.E.H. C.H.K.

References

1. O'Connor, Susan (Department of Pediatrics, Metropolitan Nashville General Hospital, 72 Heritage Avenue, Nashville, TN 37210). Private communication, 1979.
2. Burgess, Robert (Division of Individual and Family Studies, 5-110 Human Development Building, Penn State University, University Park, PN 16802). Private communication, 1979.
3. Helfer, Ray. Preventing the Abuse and Neglect of Children: The Physician's Role. *Pediatric Basics* 23:4–7, 1979.
4. ———. *Child Abuse: A Plan for Prevention*. Chicago: National Committee for the Prevention of Child Abuse, 1978.
5. Kempe, C. H. Approaches to Preventing Child Abuse: The Health Visitor Concept. *Am. J. Diseases Child.* 130:940–47, 1976.
6. Spivach, George, and Shure, Myrna. *Social Adjustment of Young Children*. San Francisco: Jossey-Bass, 1974.
7. Spivach, George, Pratt, Jerome, and Shure, Myrna. *The Problem Solving Approach to Adjustment*. San Francisco: Jossey-Bass, 1976.
8. Helfer, Ray. *Childhood Comes First: A Crash Course in Childhood for Adults*. Lansing, Mich.: privately published, 1978.

22 The Lay Health Visitor Program: An Eighteen-Month Experience

Jane Gray and Betty Kaplan

Introduction

In the past twenty years, child abuse and neglect have been reported with increasing frequency. In the overwhelming majority of cases, the diagnosis was not made until after the child exhibited the physical and emotional characteristics of his or her environment. However, diagnosis and treatment, after the occurrence of child abuse and neglect, are crisis oriented and rarely effect significant changes in the family's functioning. Early identification of a family's underlying pathologic patterns affords the opportunity for immediate intervention. We hope this early intervention can modify the parents' child-rearing patterns and thus help prevent abnormal parenting practices. Previous data by Gray *et al.* (1) have revealed that early intervention in families can prevent serious injuries in a high-risk population.

European countries have successfully used nurses as health visitors for many years. Dr. C. Henry Kempe has proposed that a lay health visitor (LHV) program in this country could provide early intervention and be instrumental in preventing child abuse and neglect (2). In Dr. Kempe's concept, as set forth in his Armstrong lecture, the lay health visitor program would be offered to all mothers during their postpartum hospitalization. This program would provide an extensive outreach approach to the family in an attempt to reduce stress and thus prevent abnormal parenting practices, one extreme of which could be child abuse and/or neglect.

The Department of Pediatrics of Colorado General Hospital has organized an LHV program based on these principles. Operating with a staff which includes a pediatrician, a nurse coordinator, and seven half-time home visitors, the program has provided outreach services to approximately 550 families over the last eighteen months. During this eighteen-month period, all mothers who delivered their babies at Colorado General Hospital (CGH) and who also lived in Denver County were interviewed on the postpartum ward, and the services of a lay health visitor were offered to them as a routine part of pediatric health care. The advantage of

Jane Gray, M.D., and Betty Kaplan, R.N., are with the University of Colorado Health Science Center, Denver.

this approach is that it prevents the stigma of labeling families as "high risk" for child abuse and neglect. It also satisfies the moral obligation that all families, even those not at risk for parenting problems, have the opportunity to receive supportive services.

Program Development

During the initial planning stages and early implementation phase for the lay health visitor program its philosophy and scope were explained to the hospital administration and especially to the Department of Obstetrics and Pediatrics. Inservice training sessions were held with the administrators, attending physicians, house staff, and nurses. Inservice training not only explained the inpatient functions of the program and the outreach services that the LHV could provide, but was also utilized to establish mutual trust and understanding. This approach helped confront the issues of territoriality often demonstrated by some professionals. Early acknowledgment that these issues existed but could be dealt with opened communication and fostered the acceptance of the LHV program. The final consensus was that the program was a needed addition to inpatient services, i.e., interviewing the mothers and observing mother-infant interactions, and that it would be a valuable asset to have an LHV follow the family into the home and serve as a liaison with the medical and social agencies of the community.

Utilizing the same format, inservice training was given to community agencies. Most of these professionals were very accepting of the LHV and the extra services she could provide. The community agency which felt the most threatened was the Visiting Nurse Association, as they thought that the LHV duplicated many of their functions. Indeed, in most instances, some duplication did occur, but close communication between the LHV and the visiting nurse did help alleviate some of the feelings that the visiting nurse's traditional role was being threatened. As the visiting nurses became more familiar with the type of extra services the LHV could provide, they became more supportive of the LHV's role and even eager to have an LHV involved with families assigned to them. In many instances, the visiting nurses had overwhelming caseloads, and once communication and role definition had been established the nurses appreciated the extra services the LHVs provided.

Staff Qualifications and Responsibilities

The program at CGH consists of two phases: inpatient (on the postpartum ward) and an outpatient phase. The present staff includes a pediatrician, an RN (who also coordinates the program), two research associates, and seven lay health visitors (who each work half-time).

The hospital-based LHV program coordinator is a registered nurse who has experience in working with families and has knowledge of child-rearing practices, mothering, infant care and development, and community resources. Personal qualities of flexibility and empathy are necessary for working with a variety of families and for modeling nonrigid, nonjudgmental attitudes, which can then facilitate these attitudes in the lay health visitors. The coordinator's inpatient assessment of the family includes reviewing charts, interviewing the mothers and any other family members who visit the hospital, observing the mother-infant interactions, and observing any interactions between other family members.

The LHV is a woman who has been a successful mother or who has had extensive experience with mothers and young children. In addition to her background of working with young children, she must *also* possess qualities of flexibility and empathy. These personality qualities are necessary for working with needy and demanding families. An important personal attribute is that the lay health visitor possess high self-esteem. This is important because some of the families make limited progress, which can cause the LHV to feel that her efforts have been ineffective.

In the home environment, the LHV observes and assesses a family's strengths and needs. She then identifies the problem areas and refers the family to appropriate services. She provides the family with information about health care, child development, behavior, discipline, and home safety. The LHV also acts as a role model for parenting and offers emotional support in times of stress. Essentially, the LHV is a liaison between the family and the community and serves as a "lifeline" in times of crisis.

Another important function of the LHV is the provision of emotional support to the mother. The LHV is available both by home visits and by telephone contact seven days a week, twenty-four hours a day. Her ability to listen to the mother, provide her with support, and offer practical advice reassures the new parents of their parenting skills. In addition, the LHV offers friendship to those mothers who feel isolated and uncared for. This supportive relationship is the one mothers turn to in time of crisis.

There have been a total of ten lay health visitors who have worked with the program during its operation. Four of these women are still involved; two resigned to take better-paying jobs; two returned to school; one resigned because of ill health; and one resigned without giving an explanation.

The lay health visitors are paid through private funds both from the Grant Foundation and the Robert Wood Johnson Foundation. They receive a minimum wage and are not reimbursed for car expenses involved in making home visits.

Daily Program Operation

The coordinator and the pediatrician develop the initial relationship with the mother on the postpartum ward. All new mothers are approached in a nonthreatening, nonjudgmental manner. The major focus of the interview is to evaluate the mother's attitudes, perceptions, and feelings for the baby in order to assess her ability to care for the infant. The pediatrician and the coordinator contact the mothers frequently during their postpartum hospitalization to obtain as much information as possible about the family and to facilitate the home follow-up by the LHV. Another important responsibility of the coordinator and pediatrician is the communication of information to hospital staff, community agencies, and home visitors so that discharge plans and follow-up services can be arranged.

The utilization of a hospital-based pediatrician and coordinator who interview *all* mothers has several advantages. First of all, it enables the interviewer to observe a wide range of mothers, infants, and family situations. Thereby, expertise in assessing the potential for parenting problems is developed. The pediatrician and coordinator are also able to gather more information from a new mother when they can sit down and talk to the mother and do not have to perform a task (i.e., take blood pressure or temperature). In informal conversation they can gather information that is more subtle than that revealed to the hospital staff.

The pediatrician and the RN coordinator see all the mothers on a daily basis and, on occasion, some are seen more than once daily in order to build trust, answer questions, and help resolve any current problems. During their contacts with the mother, information is gathered in eight general areas:

1. the prenatal, labor, and delivery experience
2. the family's support system
3. attachment behaviors of the parents
4. the mother's relationship to significant others (her parents, husband, and older children)
5. the mother's background
6. the father's background
7. the parents' financial status and source of health care
8. the parents' expectations for the baby

After information is gathered in the categories listed above, the program is explained to the mother as a service which is offered to all mothers in order to provide extra support, answer questions about care of a newborn, and to serve as a liaison for medical care and community agencies. If the mother accepts the program (the majority do), her LHV meets her on the postpartum ward, and they arrange a home visit during the first week after hospital discharge. This affords immediate continuity of care, which is generally unavailable in other agencies.

The subsequent LHV service involves a minimum of contact of two home visits during the first month. At that point, the LHV and her supervisor (pediatrician, coordinator, or research associate) assess the family's strengths and needs and determine the focus for subsequent intervention. The intervention may take any one of many directions but is primarily geared to reducing family stresses in ways that would be beneficial for the entire family. This can mean that medical care for the family is arranged, that a public health nurse (PHN) referral is appropriate, or that any community agency (e.g., department of social services, ADC, food stamps, etc.) is necessary. The mother and the LHV work together on problem solving. This shared problem solving gives the mothers increased self-confidence and raises their self-esteem.

Training and Supervision for the LHVs

Other considerations for implementation of an LHV program relate to the training, supervision, and support for the LHVs. Prior to contact with families, an intensive three-week training period for the home visitors provides them with information about (1) interviewing techniques; (2) child-rearing practices; (3) infant care; (4) parenting skills; (5) community resources; (6) observational skills; and (7) the dynamics of child abuse and neglect. During the training, the LHV's personal values are clarified, since these may influence her interaction with the family. Supervision is provided to the individual LHV by the coordinator, the pediatrician, and research associate. This occurs weekly and is utilized to assess a family's strengths and needs as well as the LHV's role in the family.

In order to address the issue of "burn out" so common in this field, there is a weekly staff meeting for mutual support. This group process enables the lay health visitors to verbalize feelings and frustrations about families, to share information and to provide and receive support from their peers. Also, since the lay health visitor works independently, the group situation encourages interaction with the other LHVs and the hospital-based coordinator, pediatrician, and research associates. Monthly inservice education for the entire staff provides new information about common issues. Another factor which helps avoid the "burn out" issue is that the majority of families that the LHVs visit are normal, happy, healthy families. This is because the program is offered to *all* mothers.

Early impressions are that a relatively small percentage of the families have had serious problems with parent-infant interactions. These have included families who (with support and guidance from the LHV) voluntarily relinquished their babies, mothers who have called the LHVs in times of crisis when they or the father might have hurt the baby, and families in which the LHV identified that the child was not receiving appropriate physical or emotional care and the need for referral to the county department of social services was identified and accomplished.

The Refusal Population

The refusal population most frequently stated that they had enough support systems to help them readjust their lifestyles to care for the needs of the new baby. Other reasons given included that the mother had older children and felt confident with child care. Some families stated that they had no problems. In most of these cases the interviewers felt there was validity to their refusal and the reason given.

However, other families that refused the program were very concerning. Some of these refused to sign the refusal form; others signed but gave no reason for their refusal; some wanted to cope alone or did not want anyone to come into their homes. These families who generated concern were always referred to a visiting nurse and to a medical facility that could provide continuity of care. If there were extreme concerns for the immediate safety of a new infant, the county department of social services was contacted, and one of their child protective workers came to the hospital. She conferred with the hospital staff and then interviewed the parents. At this point, a decision was made as to whether the child could safely be discharged home or whether a court hearing for temporary custody was necessary. In four cases where the home was not deemed safe, the judge awarded temporary custody to the child welfare department, a plan of rehabilitation for the parents was established, and the family's progress was documented before the baby was returned to the parents' care.

Program Evaluation

Approximately 550 families received an LHV in their homes during the first eighteen months of program operation. The majority of cases could be phased out during the second or third months of intervention; however, no case was closed, and families were encouraged to recontact their LHV if new problems arose. A small percentage have reinitiated contact, usually when an unexpected crisis occurred. Of those in the program, about one-third were carried for longer than six months. These families generally were chaotic and prone to violence and clearly required continued intervention to maintain and monitor the safety of the home. As far as is known, during the first eighteen months of operation, only two children who were followed by an LHV received injuries thought to be secondary to nonaccidental trauma. The injuries were minor and will not cause any physical residual.

Formal evaluation of the program is just beginning. It will consist of comparisons between three groups: (1) those who were offered the program and received intervention, (2) those who also were offered the program, but who refused to participate, and (3) a control group from another county who delivered their babies at CGH but, because of their county of residence, were not offered the LHV program.

These three groups will first be compared as to the number of well-child visits the baby had and the number of community agencies that were involved with the family. These areas will be examined in order to see if an LHV can indeed serve as a liaison between families and medical and community agencies. Another aspect to be assessed is that of injuries—both accidental and nonaccidental. This will be accomplished by chart review and by documenting reports that appear in the central registry for child abuse and neglect. Children who failed to thrive will also be assessed through chart review and through the central registry. Assessment of these areas (injuries and failure to thrive) will hopefully help us evaluate whether a supportive person in the home during the newborn period can indeed relieve family stresses to a degree that will help prevent child abuse and neglect.

References

1. Gray, Jane D., Cutler, C., Dean, J., and Kempe, C. H. Prediction and Prevention of Child Abuse and Neglect. *Child Abuse and Neglect* 1:45, 1977.
2. Kempe, C. H. Approaches to Preventing Child Abuse: The Health Visitor Concept. *Am. J. Diseases Child.* 130:941–47, 1976.

23 Treatment of the Child

Mary McQuiston and Ruth S. Kempe

The classic works of Steele and Pollock (1) emphasize the intergenerational patterns of child abuse and neglect. One might conclude that the prevention of the continuation of the battered child cycle is possible through early intervention. The work of such leaders as Burton White and Sally Provence in the fields of early childhood education and child development points to the overwhelming importance of the first few years of life and the devastating effects that deviant parenting and lack of appropriate intervention have on future development (2–4). With the passage of Public Law 94-142, the American educational system is at long last recognizing the importance of early childhood education as critical for the physically and/or emotionally handicapped child.

Studies of mother-infant attachment by Klaus and Kennell (5) and Bowlby and Ainsworth (6–9) point to the critical periods of attachment that affect even the healthiest of families. A look at dynamics in abusive families by Gray and colleagues (10) reveals far different responses in the bonding process. Developmental problems are often seen within months after birth and can become more severe with time. As with the profoundly handicapped child, the abused child needs early intervention as part of the comprehensive treatment program for his or her family.

There can be no argument that early identification and intervention are needed for the abusive family. A young child's timetable of development cannot sustain many limitations without hampering future potential for adequate functioning. Since much of children's feelings about themselves as individuals is formed within their first five years of life, without early intervention many of the behaviors seen in older abused and/or neglected children are difficult to change or modify. The young child, if given a positive, predictable therapeutic experience, is more likely not to manifest such intensely deviant coping styles as seen in the older child who has received no treatment or who has been referred for treatment after many years of emotional problems.

Mary McQuiston and Ruth S. Kempe, M.D., are with the National Center for the Prevention and Treatment of Child Abuse and Neglect, Denver.

The description by Dr. Martin in Chapter 21 of the effect of abuse and neglect on children emphasizes the extensive deviations in personality development which result. The form deviation will take and its severity varies with the age of the child at which abuse or neglect began, the continuous or intermittent nature of the abuse as well as its specific form, and the presence of other more benign influences in the home which can prevent or help counteract some of the damage to the developing child. With very early abuse or neglect the issue of safety may be paramount; however, early foster home placement may prolong difficulties in bonding and, therefore, in object relations, especially if changes in placement from home to foster home or crisis center occur frequently.

Even when the child remains in the home continuously, the absence of attachment between mother and child leads to poor object relations; and the issues of basic trust, object constancy, and separation-individuation may never have been solved. Relationship problems will then persist, making the development of a trusting relationship a prime goal of treatment.

Other results of early abuse or neglect include poor health maintenance and perhaps growth retardation, retardation of development in gross motor and perceptual functions, and in speech as a mode of expression and as communication. Behavior extremes of withdrawal, wary and compliant behavior or aggression, and poor impulse control reflect the adaptive efforts of young children to cope with inconsistent and inappropriate expectations from their parents. This behavior also demonstrates how little they have been allowed to learn about more positive coping styles such as awareness and expression of affect, verbal communication, problem solving, negotiation, mastery, as, for example, through play. Their lack of joy or playfulness, their expectation of criticism and expectation of failure show their poor self-image and how difficult it will be for them to venture into new tasks and be available for learning. Sometimes they internalize the punitive qualities of their parents and abuse themselves.

Recommendations for treatment made after a thorough medical, psychological, and/or educational evaluation may vary according to the severity and immediacy of the child's special needs. Often medical referrals will be made to specialized clinics where organic problems can be delineated. Treatment in the form of specialized individual and/or group programs may be indicated, as may be foster care placement or residential treatment facilities. In any case, considerations for such treatment vary according to developmental lines, environmental influences, and degree of pathology in both the child and his/her family.

In all age groups, one of the most urgent problems to be solved in offering therapy to abused or neglected children is the sanction and participation of their parents (11). Even when treatment is court ordered for both parent and child, it may be difficult to get the parents involved. Parents tend to find many ways to avoid participation unless they can be convinced that treatment can be useful to them. Sometimes the use of a lay therapist in the home or a parents group may be an intermediary step by which parents develop enough trust to participate. In treatment, parents may become involved in their own problems and resent any focus on the problems of their children. If they do not receive what they desire for themselves from their own therapy, they may well sabotage the therapy of the child by preventing attendance, by forbidding communication in the therapy hours, or by criticizing and increasing the child's mistrust of treatment. They may see treatment of the child as a criticism of themselves as parents or feel threatened by fear of the loss of the child's love. They may also resist any changes in the child's behavior which, in the past, has met parents' needs. Treatment of the child, therefore, may be limited in its effectiveness by the attitudes of the parents. Indeed, the parents who are neglectful but indifferent may be less detrimental to the child's treatment than the more interested but uncooperative parent.

One might expect that family therapy could solve some of these problems (12). With younger children, however, the need for verbal communication as a primary mode in family therapy is usually not possible. Such sessions might be useful primarily for diagnostic purposes. Consequently, not only the child's readiness for treatment, but also the parents' willingness to allow the child treatment must be considered. The subsequent involvement of the parent with the treatment will change as he or she is able to make individual progress in accepting the child as an individual with his or her own needs.

Frequently, a combination of group and individual therapy is most effective for abused and neglected children, as it is for their parents. Behavior modification may be useful for some children, but, in most of these children, expressive needs and relationship problems are too urgent to make it an adequate mode by itself.

Special Considerations

Care must be taken to ensure, whenever possible, that every reasonable chance be given to keep the family intact and that foster placement be used with discretion and careful planning. It may often be a relief for the professionals involved to treat a family where the child is placed in the safety of a foster care home, but as was alarmingly pointed out in Victor Pike's Oregon Project (13), many children are placed in foster care and then receive little treatment or consistent contact with their families. It is especially critical for foster care to work to the benefit of the children placed there and that the biologic and foster parents be included in the treatment plan whenever possible. If a return home is anticipated, continuation of the parent-child relationship must be enhanced, not sabotaged. This is particularly important in the case of the infant, where bonding must be maintained. Participation in such a plan requires that foster parents receive support and gain confidence from those helping professionals involved in the permanent planning for that child. A devastating tug-of-war often occurs between biologic and foster parents for the loyalties of the child, with little gain for anyone involved, especially the child.

Therapeutic foster care programs that focus on strengthening the parent-child relationship are helpful in aiding the child's return home with a positive prognosis for future family functioning (14). If a return home is not indicated, permanent planning for the child may take the form of termination of parental rights or long-term, consistent foster placement or guardianship. With either alternative, the child's special needs and developmental timetable cannot allow for lingering indecision nor the use of inadequate foster care.

Another special consideration in planning treatment programs for abused and neglected children is assessment and educational planning in the schools. Commonly found in the evaluation process of such children is the tendency for them to perform at a lower level than that of which they are capable (15). When coupled with disturbed behaviors described previously low test scores often prompt school personnel to place these children in special education classes that do not focus on the emotional issues which so desperately need attention. Characteristics commonly used to identify learning disabilities are also often used to describe the abused and neglected child. They are frequently defined as: hyperactivity, distractibility, perseverative behaviors, behavioral problems, impulsivity, perceptual and language problems, and visual or auditory problems.

Many children who are labeled as learning disabled, behaviorally disturbed, or even mentally retarded may indeed be very capable of functioning normally, but are so emotionally restricted that their functioning in the school setting is hampered. Caution must be used when special school placements are made so as to treat the problem and not the symptoms, which are often manifested as learning/ behavior problems.

Treatment Goals and Modalities

Considerations regarding the goals and mode of treatment vary according to the child's age and level of development, role within his or her family, his or her level of social interaction and ego strengths, verbal accessibility, and physically handicapping condition. The following section focuses on intervention goals and techniques when dealing with the infant, the preschooler, school-age child, and adolescent.

Infancy

Tasks for the infant to accomplish in his or her first two and one-half years of life have to do with attachment, object relations, and separation-individuation. In order to successfully integrate these developmental processes the infant's physical and mental needs must be met by a nurturing, caretaking figure.

A major therapeutic goal, then, would be the provision of a *constant*, nurturing mother figure, who would respond appropriately to the child's needs and be aware of his or her changes with development. When such a goal must be accomplished in the home with the infant's immature, needy mother in the caretaking role, a good deal of emphasis must be placed on providing her with every support possible to nurture her, to help in her understanding the child's needs, and to help her change some of her behavior by showing her better alternatives (16). (A discussion of parent-infant skill building is found in Dr. Wilson's work in Chapter 25.) A lay therapist or health visitor, (17) homemaker, public health nurse, or protective services caseworker may provide some of this help once she has developed a relationship of trust with the mother. Parenting classes may also be of help, but they frequently change the mother's intellectual understanding of development without changing her child-care skills.

If these goals cannot be met in the home, the child may need to be placed in a day-care home or center, infant-stimulation program, or crisis nursery. Intervention techniques can be used in a variety of settings; choice of the setting will depend on the needs of the child and the child's family. Day care may be used to provide relief for the mother, safety for the child, social stimulation for the child, or special treatment for specific developmental delays. Programs that incorporate the mother into the child's program are optimum for introducing various role models for alternative parenting skills.

In placing the child in a day-care or infant-stimulation program, it is important to look at the age range, group size, and developmental levels of the children with whom the child must interact in the group. Some children may need the availability of a therapeutic program part-time. However, others may need to be placed for eight to ten hours at a time.

Staff who are sensitive to the needs of the abused and neglected child as well as to his or her parents are critical to the success of intervention. An understanding of the dynamics of abusive parents is important so that parents' behaviors are not misinterpreted.

When these goals of treatment cannot be obtained in the home, or with the help of a day-care program, foster care may be a therapeutic alternative. Again, bonding and the maintenance of contact between parent and child must be encouraged.

With the very young, developmental delays may have to be made up before the child has the skills with which to make an attachment. These children need emphasis on orienting to and differentiating stimuli that normally elicit attachment behaviors. At the same time, it is important to look at the child's ability to exhibit attachment behaviors and enhance the skills he or she already has.

As young children slowly build up a new-found relationship, it is then important for them to begin to experience influence over their environment. Consistent and appropriate responses from the caretaker will enable the children to develop a feeling of mastery and effectiveness to realize their separateness.

Once within the framework of a trusting relationship, the toddler can then be given assistance with specific problem areas. Major areas of concern might be:

1. Sensory stimulation with an emphasis on physical contact and eye contact
2. Stimulation of language skills
3. Discrimination between familiar people and strangers and the modeling of appropriate behaviors with each
4. Introduction to play and acquisition of play skills
5. Improvement of fine and gross motor skills
6. Introduction to safety issues
7. Reinforcement to build self-help skills

Without the child's acquisition of a sense of basic trust, he or she cannot maintain an attachment, nor can he or she develop a sense of self needed to separate and individuate. Children must see themselves as a part of the world and develop influence over their environment. Without these precursors, the concepts of object relations will not be fully realized and a sense of control will be undeveloped. Problems with the integrative process begin to emerge and need to be addressed as the child approaches the preschool years.

Preschool

Normally, by the time the child reaches the preschool years (ages two to five), issues of independence and autonomy are progressing toward a stage of competence and mastery. Peer relationships and socialization skills become important as children begin to see themselves as separate entities. Major tasks for the preschoolers are the acquisition of new cognitive and motor skills, the development of speech and language, and self-help skills. Sex roles emerge as the child begins the process of identification.

Often the abused and neglected preschool-age child has not yet experienced a positive attachment with one caretaking figure. Basic issues of trust have often not yet been resolved, and deviant ways of coping begin to become more solidified.

Treatment more often takes place outside the home. Daily therapeutic intervention may attempt to provide the unattached child with a relationship through a single adult or may offer to the more mature child a variety of relationships with adults and/or peers.

Often indicated for the abused and/or neglected preschool-age child is placement in a therapeutic nursery school or day-care program. Serious developmental deficits are commonly found in this age group. Behaviors observed include (see Chapter 3):

1. Extremes in behavior—angry acting out versus overly compliant, withdrawn responses
2. Poor language skills
3. Delayed gross and fine motor development
4. Pseudoadult role-reversal behavior with adults and peers
5. Hypervigilance
6. Distractibility and hyperactivity
7. Poor impulse control
8. Disturbed integrative process of thought
9. Indiscriminate affection with adults.

These precursors of learning problems can then be considered in the treatment plan which would include speech and language therapy; physical therapy; specialized medical care, as well as psychotherapy; behavior modification; or an individual educational plan (18).

Experience at the National Center for the Prevention and Treatment of Child Abuse and Neglect in Denver (19) has shown many preschool-age children in the therapeutic nursery school exhibit serious delays and disturbances in social/emotional functioning. The imposition of structure and clarity within the daily routine offers the child the opportunity to reduce anxiety and obtain aid in the integrative process. Developing impulse control which may appear to be at a very primitive level is a major focus in treatment. The teacher intervenes to help the child tolerate delay between stimulus and response by verbalizing the thought process and offering alternatives for action. Expansion of play themes and cognitive activities is encouraged by teacher modeling with an emphasis on verbalizations.

A narrative style is used to give the child words for actions and feelings (20). At the same time, one is careful to limit stimuli, introducing them according to the child's capacity for integration.

By limiting the number of children in a group to approximately twelve, one can avoid overstimulation and provide consistency and predictability. Recent Department of Health, Education, and Welfare studies of day-care programs have shown a limit of fifteen to sixteen normal preschoolers in a group to be the maximum regardless of staff-child ratio (21). Our experience has shown a one-to-three ratio as being needed when working with abused and neglected preschoolers, who need much attention, nurturing, and a one-to-one relationship experience.

As they become more comfortable with the routine, their attempts to explore the environment and try new activities begin to emerge. Often they are afraid to attempt anything new and need the reassurance of an adult to make the first step. Again, as is critical in all child treatment, the relationship between the teacher and the child is vital.

As in play therapy, children in the group setting repeat themes in their play that can be clarified and interpreted verbally for the child. Children in the preschool setting often relive an abusive incident through doll play. The teacher can provide empathy for the doll victim (child), question the mode of parenting, and, through role modeling, can teach alternative ways of parenting with the dolls. Consistent limits of allowable behavior and logical consequences help the child with reality-testing in social situations by reducing the anxiety associated with punishment.

Although most abused or neglected preschool-age children benefit considerably from the group experience in a therapeutic playschool, the therapeutic opportunities may be too fragmented or diluted by the group setting. The addition of play therapy allows the child to develop a more intense relationship in which more individual goals can be attempted (22). The continuity and structure of the play hours allow play themes and behavior patterns to be more clearly repeated, related to specific events, and interpreted verbally or in play by the therapist. As in the school, themes frequently addressed are object constancy, trust, separations, verbalizing of affect and experience so as to increase reality testing, limit-setting on behavior, and encouragement of mastery.

As previously stated, in order for the child's treatment to be more effective, the parent must receive treatment as well. A goal in such treatment is for the child to be more appealing to the parent and to receive allowance to grow and develop in the therapeutic milieu. Sabotage or competition within the child's program will be lessened if the parent, too, receives support and services (see Chapter 16).

School-Age Child

In the school-age children (ages six to twelve) referrals for psychotherapy are apt to be made only when the child has serious psychiatric symptoms (23, 24), is failing in school (25, 26), or exhibits disruptive behavior. By this time, the child's behavior is apt to be seen as intrapsychic, and its origin in a neglectful or abusive home environment may be missed. The same difficulties in involving parents may be found as with younger children. Parents are sometimes more receptive to the child's having treatment when they see the problem as the child's and when the repercussions are becoming more anxiety provoking. Their own involvement may still be marginal or even negative. Because so few of these referrals receive cooperation and follow-through by the parents, there have been experiments in incorporating psychotherapy in a special school program for some of those children who cannot function in a regular classroom (27). Some schools also provide individual or group therapy in the school setting for children with school-manifested behavior problems. Some abused and neglected children may fall into these categories. Another treatment modality which may be helpful to this age group, by itself or sometimes supplemented by individual therapy or sometimes as part of a residential program, is the activity and therapy group (28, 29).

Our own experience with such groups indicates that they may be effective with neglected or abused school-age children and also with sexually abused girls in the age group (30). Because parents are so seldom supportive, transportation may need to be provided. The group time can often be divided up into a structured activity or a talk time, followed by free play activity, and concluded by a quiet snack time which often provides the best discussion participation. Goals for such groups vary somewhat but include development of trust in the adult cotherapists, improvement of peer relations, learning to verbalize and share feelings, socialization and limit setting, and experiencing the respect of the group for oneself as a person. There may be less conflict of loyalty to parents and facilitation of expression of feelings when the child finds other group members share his or her problems. Although some children may be too disturbed for this mode and require individual treatment or special placement, there has been surprisingly good improvement, especially in school, with some of these children.

Individual psychotherapy for the latency-age child would address the same issues as with other children, but the slow development of trust in the therapist and testing of the therapist's reliability might take considerable time, particularly in the one-to-one situation. The goals in one-to-one therapy can be more individual and the pace of treatment adjusted to the child's response. The child's interpretation of the parents' behavior toward him or her can be more readily recognized and corrected. Participation of the parents in some kind of treatment modality is very important for the school-age child in individual treatment; there is more pressure on these children to reconcile their families' expectations of them with the different view taken by the outside world and their therapists. This may induce conflict not just of loyalty but of identification with parental behavior or pathology. Although mental health centers should be available as an alternative to psychiatric clinics or private psychotherapy, they rarely have trained personnel or the time to provide individual treatment for children (31).

In sexually abused school-age girls, group treatment can be very helpful in allowing the girls to feel less isolated and different, to find a healthier meeting of their needs for closeness and companionship, and to learn about more appropriate family life. Information about sex becomes part of the group goals, as most of the children have inaccurate fantasies and deviant sexual behaviors for their examples in the past. The issues of placement and separation are major for many of the children, as well as other concomitant problems of neglect or abuse. Boys of this age have rarely been referred in the past and are usually offered individual treatment. If the abuse for a boy involved a male perpetrator, the parents may become very concerned about homosexuality as an outcome of the abuse and seek treatment.

Adolescence

Treatment of adolescents is more apt to be precipitated by their behavior, particularly school failure, delinquency, and running away. During adolescence, children's efforts at becoming independent may be jeopardized by their parents' need to maintain a relationship in which they continue to meet their needs and in which they are obedient to their authority. The long years of frustration and unexpressed anger may find expression in delinquent behavior; the lack of loving family relationships may lead to gang membership or premature sexual partnerships. School failure becomes increasingly serious if the early learning difficulties were not resolved. Running away may be the only way some adolescents can deal with abuse at home, including sexual abuse. Recognizing this possibility can lead to family evaluation and treatment. Some adolescents become increasingly depressed by the long-standing neglect or the underlying message expressed over the years that they are unwanted and attempt suicide (32).

Many adolescents may become involved in juvenile court supervision, and the need for treatment becomes obvious during that referral. The family and, by now, the teenager may be resistant to the idea of treatment, making the process slow and difficult. The choice of individual, group, or residential treatment will depend upon the severity of the child's pathology and the presence or absence of support for a treatment program in the home.

For sexually abused girls, a group may be suitable in much the same way as for school-age girls. Attitudes about the parents and resentment of separation from the family, guilt for sexual activity, and disruption of the family pattern are shared in the group. Reevaluation of identification and sexual issues are major treatment goals as well. Boys involved in incest are usually found to be more disturbed and require individual and/or residential treatment. The use of foster care or residential group homes combined with individual or group psychotherapy might give the adolescent a second chance.

Summary

Clearly, the effective treatment of physically or sexually abused and neglect children is still in elementary stages. The increased reporting of maltreatment has brought to light the plight of great numbers of children who are still so young that they would not ordinarily be subject to detailed scrutiny. Evidence that many children are being subjected to stress which distorts their development, while it is disturbing, also offers the opportunity for developing treatment programs for them long before they enter school poorly equipped to cope.

Treatment for the abused and neglected child should begin whenever the diagnosis is first made. It may begin before he or she is born, if there are indications that the mother might have difficulty bonding with her coming child. It may begin with delivery and extra support to the mother. It may begin during infancy with home visiting to the mother, provision of good medical care for the infant, and stimulation or mother-child interaction intervention and parenting classes. Foster care, we hope, will not be required, but if it is, the foster parents must be trained and subsidized to promote the bond with the family for an early return. Good day care and continued support for the mother, through someone like a home health visitor, may be necessary. If the child's entry into treatment comes later, therapeutic day care or a preschool may be required. Perhaps, this may be supplemented by individual play therapy and involvement of the parents. An experimental program involving the use of lay people for play therapy has been suggested as one way of coping with the large numbers of children who could be involved. Another helpful measure is to increase the knowledge and therapeutic capabilities of day-care preschool and school personnel.[1]

By the time the child enters the school system, more established treatment programs may be available, providing his or her family can be helped to participate. These include private or clinic play therapy, psychotherapy, child analysis in rare cases, special school programs, group therapy, relationship programs through Big Brother and Big Sister programs, residential treatment, or hospitalization. The same treatment programs are also available to adolescents.

When treatment fails, the removal of the child from the family is the only alternative. The sooner this decision can be made, while safeguarding the interests of parents and children, the better the prognosis will be for the child. The list of programs may sound impressive, but considering the numbers of personnel needed to offer services to the many children involved, they are woefully inadequate.

---

1. The school personnel can have a significant role in working with these children if the teachers, coaches, counselors, and administrators are given some guidance—EDS.

References

1. Steele, B. F., and Pollock, C. B. 1974. A psychiatric study of parents who abuse infants and small children. In C. H. Kempe and R. E. Helfer (eds.), *The Battered Child,* 2nd ed. Chicago: University of Chicago Press.
2. White, Burton. 1975. *The First Three Years of Life.* Englewood Cliffs, New Jersey: Prentice-Hall, Inc.
3. Lipton, Rose, and Provence, Sally. 1962. *Infants in Institutions.* New York:

International Universities Press, Inc.

4. Coleman, Rose W., and Provence, Sally. 1957. Environmental retardation (hospitalism) in infants living in families. *Pediatrics*, 19:285–92.

5. Klaus, Marshall H., and Kennell, John H. 1976. *Maternal Infant Bonding*. St. Louis: C. V. Mosby Co.

6. Ainsworth, M. D. S., Bell, S. M., and Slayton, D. G. 1974. Infant-mother attachment and social development, socialization as a product of reciprocal responsiveness to signals. In M. P. M. Richards (ed.), *The Integration of a Child into a Social World*. London: Cambridge University Press.

7. Ainsworth, Mary. 1967. Object relations dependency and attachments: A theoretical review of the infant-mother relationship. *Child Dev.*, Vol. 40.

8. Bowlby, John. 1958. The nature of the child's tie to his mother. *Internat. J. Psychoanalysis*, 39:1–23.

9. ———. 1969. *Attachment and Loss*, vol. 1. New York: Basic Books, Inc.

10. Gray, J., Dean, J., Cutler, C., and Kempe, C. H. 1977. Prediction and prevention of child abuse. *Child Abuse and Neglect: The Internat. J.*, 1:45–58.

11. Martin, H. P., and Beezley, P. 1976. Resistances and obstacles to therapy for the child. In H. P. Martin (ed.), *The Abused Child*. Cambridge, Mass.: Ballinger Press.

12. Malone, Charles A. 1979. Child psychiatry and family therapy: An overview. *J. Am. Acad. Child Psychiatry*, 18:1.

13. Pike, Victor. 1976. Permanent planning for foster children: The Oregon project. *Children Today*.

14. McBogg, P., McQuiston, M., and Schrant, R. 1978. Foster care enrichment program. *Child Abuse and Neglect: The Internat. J.*, 3:863–68.

15. Martin, H., and Rodeheffer, M. 1976. Special problems in development assessment of abused children. In H. Martin (ed.) *The Abused Child*. Cambridge, Mass.: Ballinger Press.

16. Fraiberg, S., and Adelson, E. 1976. Infant-parent psychotherapy on behalf of a child in a critical nutritional state. *Psychoanal. Study Child*, 31:461–91.

17. Kempe, C. H. 1976. Approaches to preventing child abuse: The health visitor concept. *Am. J. Dis. Child.*, 130:941–47.

18. Council for Exceptional Children. 1978. Understanding what they are and are not. PL 94-142 and Section 504. Reston, Virginia: Council for Exceptional Children.

19. Mirandy, Joan. 1976. Preschool for abused children. In H. Martin (ed.), *The Abused Child*. Cambridge, Mass.: Ballinger Press.

20. Fishbein, Justin, and Emans, Robert. 1972. A question of competence: Language intelligence and learning to read. Chicago: Chicago Science Research Assoc. Inc.

21. Smith, Allen. 1979. Children at the center: Office of human development, U.S. Department of Health, Education, and Welfare. Cambridge, Mass.: ABT Assoc.

22. In McDermott, J. F., Jr. 1976. The treatment of child abuse. *J. Am. Acad. Child Psychiatry*, 15:430–40.

23. Green, A. H. 1978. Psychiatric treatment of abused children. *J. Child Psychiatry*, 17:356–71.
24. Beezley, Patricia, Martin, H. P., and Kempe, Ruth. 1976. Psychotherapy. In H. Martin (ed.), *The Abused Child*. Cambridge, Mass.: Ballinger Press.
25. Sandgrund, Alice, Gaines, R. W., and Green, A. H. 1974. Child abuse and mental retardation: A problem of cause and effect. *Am. J. Ment. Deficiency*, 79:327–30.
26. Wilkinson, Judith K., and Donaruma, Patricia. 1979. The incidence of abuse and neglect among children in special education vs. regular education. Unpublished copyrighted manuscript, the Family Resource Center, Boulder, Colorado 80203.
27. Graffagnino, P. N., et al. 1970. Psychotherapy for latency age children in an inner city therapeutic school. *Am. J. Psychiatry*, 127:626–34.
28. Gratton, Laurent, and Pope, Lillie. 1972. Group diagnosis and therapy for young school children. *Hospital and Community Psychiatry*, 23:40–42.
29. Rose, Sheldon D. 1974. *Treating Children in Groups*. San Francisco: Jossey-Bass Publishers.
30. Beezley, Patricia J., and Schrant, Robert. 1976. Play therapy and group therapy with abused and neglected children. Presented at Workshop on Treatment of the Abused and Neglected Child, at University of Colorado Medical Center, Denver, Colorado.
31. Cohn, Anne Harris. 1978. An evaluation of three demonstration child abuse and neglect treatment programs. *J. Am. Acad. Child Psychiatry*, 17:2.
32. Sabboth, Joseph C. 1969. The suicidal adolescent—the expendable child. *J. Am. Acad. Child Psychiatry*, 8:272–86.

24 Retraining and Relearning

Ray E. Helfer

What happens when the years of childhood do not provide a person with the opportunity to learn and practice the skills of "getting along," interacting with others?[1] Childhood is supposed to provide, under the guidance of a positive model, the practice time to "goof up" and make mistakes, time to learn. One of the nicest words in the English language is "play." We somehow have managed to keep play nonthreatening and fun. When children play they are learning how to "get along," interact with each other. They are practicing skills, both interpersonal and physical. Childhood should provide a safe time for learning, where a mistake is not a disaster.

Every young adult can look back upon his or her childhood and identify specific incidents, or a whole series of incidents, which didn't "go" very well. We all can recall times when certain skills or tasks were learned poorly and when the modeling was less than it should have been. From learning to hold a golf club or learning to solve a math problem to learning how mothers and fathers interact with each other, the child learns many skills during these very critical years. The more incidents that didn't "go so well" and the more skills that were poorly learned, the more difficult interactions become as an adult, whether it be interaction with a golf ball, a math problem, or a spouse.

The answer, then, to the question posed above, is this: when childhood hasn't provided this training, an individual becomes poorly trained in many very important skills. But the outlook need not be one of utter dismay. If these skills can be learned during childhood, why not learn them or relearn them as a young adult? The answer is that they can be learned, albeit with some difficulty. Relearning a skill that was learned poorly the first time is always more difficult, but not impossible. Children do make it look pretty easy at times, but the more we know

Ray E. Helfer, M.D., is with the Department of Pediatrics and Human Development, College of Human Medicine, Michigan State University.

1. The reader should refer to Chapter 3 prior to reading this chapter. This chapter will be more meaningful if the two are considered together—EDS.

about how they learn these interactional skills, the easier it will become for young adults to relearn them.

Emphasis is placed on the concept of skill learning because of the active nature of this word. To learn a skill implies learning how *to do* something. This is different than content or fact learning, where a knowledge base is increased. Teaching someone "to do" requires a different approach than teaching some one "to know."

This chapter will consider how one learns certain skills, providing several examples of how to teach a young adult who had a very deficient childhood the skills of interacting with another.

The Learning of Skills

Think for a moment how skills are learned. How does an individual learn *to do* something? The next time you are with a small group of colleagues ask them to make a list of the various components of skill learning. The group should *free associate,* brainstorm, as this list is constructed. It can be reordered and regrouped later. An example is often necessary, e.g., teaching the skill of serving a tennis ball or interviewing an angry client or patient. When finished some of the items on the list might be:

Content base
Practice
Demonstration
Teacher
Coach
Small components
Process
Start simple
Need to know
Motivation
Steps logical
Feedback rapid
Feedback positive
Individual/group

Many of these items overlap, some should be eliminated, and others added. After the group discusses the concept further the key components of skill learning and teaching will evolve. They are:

1. Motivation and desire—by both student and teacher
2. Factual content base
3. Small subsets of the skill
4. A simple beginning
5. Positive modeling by the teacher or coach
6. Logical, small, *progressing* steps
7. Practice, practice—over time
8. Rapid and positive feedback

If one adds to this the student who learned the skill incorrectly as a child, then there is the interfering stage of unlearning which must take place during the relearning process. If a father teaches his son the wrong way to hold a golf club and the son uses this incorrect method for fifteen years, the unlearning of the old and learning of the new takes time and practice. The same is true for skills of interaction with others. If one is taught to holler and insult when interacting with a spouse, the unlearning and relearning take time and practice.

These immediate questions might be asked: Does the golf enthusiast need to be taught by someone who is a professional golfer? Does the person wanting to improve his interviewing skills need to seek out the best interviewer in the state as the teacher? Clearly, no!

Another issue arises very frequently. Does the golf enthusiast need to analyze whether or not his father *intended* to teach him incorrectly, how he related to his father, and what he now thinks and feels about his father, in order to change or improve his golf stroke? Does the interviewer have to analyze the motivations of the teacher who taught the original and incorrect techniques? Here the answers are more complex. Certainly new skills can be learned without analyses. However, at some point in the relearning phase some understanding and feelings about the original learning process will take place.

What is very clear is that analysis *without* learning the new skills is not sufficient. One of the major deficiencies of many of the existing treatment approaches for those whose early childhoods were very negative is too much emphasis on the analysis of early life events and too little emphasis on learning new skills of interaction. This should *not* imply that the former is unimportant, just not sufficient. New skills should be taught as soon as the young adults are ready. This is usually long before they are ready to consider the true significance of their negative childhoods.

Examples of Skill Relearning

Touching

Consider the young woman who was trained to believe that touching hurts, looking leads to very negative messages, and being held brings back very negative feelings. This woman has had her senses conditioned very adversely. Her ability to communicate with the world about her has been curtailed. Now give this young woman her new baby, who is most dependent upon the senses to establish a communication system with his mother (see Chapter 25). Here we have a very sensory-dependent infant and a very sensory-deficient mother. The combination may prove most devastating.

Ideally the young woman will have been identified as abused in her own childhood (see Chapter 26) prior to having her first baby and the skills of touching, looking, etc., will be relearned *before* she establishes a negative and disruptive communication system with her baby.

The first seven tasks devised to help such patients in *Childhood Comes First* (1) teach relearning skills. They are reprinted below to serve as an example of the process used in this technique.

Task No. 1: Touching cloth and fur. Start with something that is not frightening to you. Try running your hand over the back of a chair, a fur coat, or silky cloth. Now close your eyes and feel. What do you feel? Do you like what you feel? Not especially? Do it again and again. It is not all that bad. Tell yourself how it feels—soft, rough, fluffy, hard. Make yourself touch many things everyday, and tell yourself what they feel like.

Task No. 2: Touching a cat or dog. Now you can progress to something alive. Touch a cat or a dog. Close your eyes and feel the fur. When you get good at it, you can feel the animal respond to you. This indicates real progress. Do this often—many times a week. Reach the point where you really can tell that the cat or dog likes to be touched *by you.* Write down your reactions in a notebook.

Task No. 3: Touching a child. If you have a child, move on to touching him or her. Right about now you may be saying, "That's silly; I touch my child all the time." Maybe not! You may hold, or hang on to, or grab; now *touch.* If it is too frightening at first, try it when the child is asleep. Walk into his room and sit by his bed. Look at the child and then say to yourself, "He's mine. I want to touch him." Gently place your hand on his face and describe to yourself how that feels. Is this comfortable for you? If so, try it when he's awake. If not, for awhile touch him only while he's sleeping. Then try it when he's awake. If he's little, it will be easy because you can pick him up, set him on your lap, and stroke his face. If he's big, try it anyway. Then he may say, "Whatcha doin' Mom?" At that point you say, "Practicing my touching, silly!" He will clearly be confused, but it will be fun. Do this retraining of your touching while listening to some pleasant music or when you are with someone you like a lot. *You are trying to learn how to associate this new feeling of touching with something positive, rather than with those painful memories.* Write down your feelings about this task.

Task No. 4: Touching yourself. Let's move on to something a little scarier now. Next, touch yourself. Close your eyes and feel your face and your body. Do this very gently. This may be frightening or upsetting, for when you touch yourself you may hear your mother say, "Don't touch yourself; you'll become a homosexual." If that voice is still too loud and frightening, go back to the cat for few days.

Eventually you want to arrive at a point where touching yourself makes you feel good. "*I* can please *me*. That's good, not wrong!" I am not necessarily speaking here of having sexual fantasies or even of the stimulation of the sexual organs. Just reach the point where rubbing and touching your face, legs, or body feels good and you have convinced yourself that it is OK to make yourself feel good.

Task No. 5: Touching someone else. All of the above can be done in the privacy of your own room or house. But now we must move on to the next step—touching someone else. You are trying to convince yourself that touching doesn't hurt and that to touch is a nice experience.

Now try it with your mate or a good friend. If he or she is your mate your may want to start when he or she is sleeping. The trouble here is that if your mate is a light sleeper, he or she may wake up when you touch his or her face and say, "What the devil are you doing?" You may find that your mate likes it so much that he or she will want you to continue. A little love-making at this point will be good for both of you.

I must not make light of the fear and anguish that many adults have of touching another adult or a child. A large number of children learned that touching another person, especially of the same sex, has very negative meanings. They were convinced that it might even mean that they were homosexual.

The importance of physical contact in communicating with someone you really like cannot be overemphasized. Again, I'm not necessarily connoting anything sexual here. The touch on the hand or the shoulder, the arm about the waist, the holding of an arm, the stroke of the face all say, "I like you," "I want to be near you," or "I care." When you awake in the middle of the night and move close to your mate in bed, touch his or her hand or arm; the message you convey will be clear to both of you.

Task No. 6: Being touched by someone else. Next, we must move to the most difficult part of this section of the course, being comfortable when *you* are touched. If you learned this early in childhood, great. However, there are many who find that the touching hand is most frightening. Memories of pain or fear may flash into the conscious mind as the hand nears. Your whole body may tense up, or grow weak, as the hand of another touches you. Equally as bad is when you have trained yourself not to feel the touching; it just happens and you allow it, but nothing is happening to *you*.

If any of these are true of you, or even partially true, this must and will change. Find someone you like a lot, possibly a little child. This person should be as nonthreatening as possible. Have him or her touch your hand or arm. Close your eyes and describe to yourself how it feels. Write down what you feel. Be very specific. Then tell yourself your own reactions. If it's scary, then hold off for a little while and try again. Convince yourself that feeling good when you're touched is OK. You don't have to feel guilty.

Now move to an adult. This will be hard, for you won't want to admit to any adult that you're practicing being touched. But keep at it. Finally it will come. You'll begin to find that being touched is a beautiful experience, especially when the person who touches you is someone you like very much. Convincing yourself that this magnificent form of communication is OK, and that you do not have to feel guilty about touching, may be difficult. Keep practicing. It may take you many months or years to reach a point where touching will be completely comfortable.

Gradually you will realize when touching is best used, or not used, to share your feelings and thoughts with another person. Right now your goal is to bring yourself to the point that touching is available to you to use in your interaction with others. You will find it helpful, as you work on this relearning process, to observe others making their senses work for them. They need not know they are being observed; just look around you as you move about in groups and watch and take note what is happening.

Task numbers 7–16 deal with relearning of looking, hearing, smelling, and tasting. Note that skill relearning requires motivation, factual content, small subsets, a simple beginning, positive modeling, small, progressive steps, practice, and rapid and positive feedback.

Feelings and Actions

Learning how to gain some control over one's life is a long and difficult process. The first time around, when this control should be learned, takes at least eighteen years of childhood and adolescence. Trying to relearn these skills as an adult is a struggle, but it can be done, and very well in a comparatively brief time.

The young adult reared under adverse circumstances has many developmental deficiencies. One of these is the great confusion between the difference in one's *feelings* and one's *actions*. This relearning process requires very gradual stages. Consider the following sample tasks that might be assigned a patient from *Childhood Comes First* (1):

Task No. 21: Feeling is OK. Every morning, noon, and evening say to yourself, "How I feel is OK." You must convince yourself that feelings are not bad. "I'm angry; I'm mad;

I love you; I like you; I'm sad or upset." These are OK feelings. Too often people feel guilty over how they feel. You get angry at your mother or boyfriend and suddenly there is that old guilt feeling coming back. You do not have to feel guilty over how you feel. We have enough problems handling our guilt over what we *do* and hardly need to be burdened with guilt over how we feel.

Three times a day say to yourself, "How I feel is OK." At the end of each day, *write down* the feelings that you had. These might include: "I got *mad* at my boss or the children." "I really *wanted* a piece of strawberry pie." "I saw a new coat and *felt* that I had to have it." "I got *ticked off* when Jim didn't call." "I really *liked how I felt* when the flowers arrived."

Check your list and make sure you have written down feelings, not actions. Don't mix action verbs and feeling verbs. For example, "I *hollered* at the children," "I *drove* too fast." The verbs *holler* and *drove* are what you did, not how you felt. For this task record your feelings. Now, at the bottom of the page write in big letters: "These feelings are OK!"

Task No. 22: Mad and glad feelings. When you get mad at somebody, convince yourself that you probably had every right to get mad. The way you were treated by that person warranted your getting mad. Now do the same for a good feeling. Let yourself feel very positive about someone. What he or she just did made me feel great, and then say, "How I felt was OK."

Task No. 23: Negative phrases. Now that your are convincing yourself that your feelings are OK, you must begin to remove certain phrases or expressions which give others the impression that you are very insecure, such as "That's not wrong, is it?" or "That's OK, isn't it?" or "What's wrong with that?" or "Is that dumb?" If you are seeking others' approval for your feelings, knock it off. *No one has to give you permission to feel.* Feelings are your God-given right.

Task No. 24: Label your feelings. The concept of labeling is important. It means that you should learn to express, verbally and nonverbally, how you are feeling or what is happening to you or another. Crying may represent an outward label of a feeling of sadness. Many are reared to believe that expressing how they feel is wrong. How sad. These next few tasks will help you begin this labeling process. It will take a lot of work and practice, first to be comfortable doing it, and second to begin labeling automatically. There are some rules to follow. Begin to label your feelings to others. This will be difficult, but it is very essential. If a friend does something that makes you really mad, tell him or her how you feel: "I really got upset when you hollered at me." "When you didn't drink at the party, I was very happy." "I feel good when you look at me like that." Be careful: don't be vague or generalize so much that the other person becomes very confused. For example, these statements are confusing: "It makes mommy feel good when you're a *good* boy," "I really get mad when you're *bad*." "Everytime you look at me *that way*, I feel awful." The words "good," "bad," and "that way" are too nonspecific to help the interaction. These words don't tell the other person what they did or didn't do to bring forth your feeling.

Be specific. "When you spit in public, I really get ticked."

One husband told me that he got mad when his wife hollered at their little boy. Her reaction was that she had been hollering all her life; how could she stop just like that? I listened to their interchange and finally asked was there anything *specific* that she did or said that bothered him.

"Hollering is just too general," I said. "Be specific."

He thought for a bit and commented, "Well, she always calls our boy 'a little shit' when she hollers." Now that was specific enough.

"Is that what bugs you?" the mother asked. Clearly that bothered both the father and the boy. "If I can keep hollering," she commented, "I'll stop calling him 'a little shit.' "

All agreed to this compromise, and it worked out well.

At the end of your day, write down *specific* feelings that you have labeled. Also record the reactions of the other person to this labeling. "I told Howard that I was mad, and he said he was sorry." Label your feelings more often.

Task No. 25: Label other's feelings. Now your are ready for a big task, one that is even harder than the last seven. Label the feelings of others: "You really look happy today." "My, you seem upset." "What I just said made you sad." "You really must have had a bad day."

One of the reasons that this is difficult is the fear that you might be wrong; then you feel that you are open to criticism. Not really. You are labeling the way you perceive another person. You are not attacking the other person. Say "You seem upset." If he denies it, just say, "I'm glad I was wrong. I just got the feeling that you were upset." Chances are that you were very right, as a matter of fact, and he was too uncomfortable to admit it.

The other risk one takes when labeling another's feelings is that the door is open to many additional issues and problems. If you don't want the door open, it is best not to label. Practice this type of labeling regularly and record the results in your notebook.

This concept of labeling will have to be studied in detail and practiced repeatedly. At the outset this new concept may be used incorrectly. You may label in the form of a question and/or an implied interpretation. For example: "Do you feel upset about that?" rather than "I'm getting the message that you are upset."

"When you went to see your mother, I really got mad." This implies your anger was because he went to see his mother. Unless he is very alert, he'll get the wrong message; the real one may never come to the surface, i.e., that your remark was *not* an antimother statement, but a statement of anger over the fact that he didn't get home on time. Implied interpretations can really confuse a relationship. In this example, he might reply, "So what's wrong with my mother?" (The coach must help the student label by keeping the statement open, such as, "I really got mad at you this afternoon." The discussion which follows may help identify that the anger was over not getting home on time rather than the visit to his mother.)

Task No. 26: Feelings don't equal actions. When you get upset at yourself, it should be over something that you *did* or *didn't do* rather than over how you felt. Write down three or four incidents when you were upset at yourself. Record specifically what it was you *did* or *didn't do* that upset you. Now do the same thing for a time when you really felt good about yourself. If there are feelings on this list, go back and review the tasks 21–27. There should be only actions on the list. Once the list is completed, write at the bottom in big letters "I can and will learn to control my actions."

Task No. 27: Choices for yourself. Give yourself choices and force yourself to pick one of these choices. Do this very deliberately: "Tonight I can cook meat loaf or stew for dinner. Which one do *I* want?" "Jim called and asked me to go the movie. Do *I* want to go or don't I?" "Bill wants me to go to bed with him tonight; do *I* want to or don't I?"

Don't give yourself choices when you don't have any: "Should I feed the children tonight?" "I promised Jane I'd take her to the movie. Do I really want to?" The choice was made when you agreed to take her to the movie, not three days later.

Force these choices upon yourself. You are trying to convince yourself that you indeed have options. Define them, write them down. You do have some control over your life, more than you think. There are certain responsibilities over which we don't have control; these are not choices and should not be considered as such. Write down six choices you had in the past three days and the decisions you made for each. What were the options for each? Record six things over which you had no control.

Task No. 28: Choices for others. Begin to take some control over others who influence your life by giving them choices or options. For example, insist that friends call before showing up at the door.

"He just shows up," one woman said.

"Tell him he must call first and ask if he can come over," I replied.

"Why?" was her question.

"This puts you in control. When he calls, then you must decide, do *you* want him to come over or don't you?"

This works well with children as well as adults: "Which ear can I look at first?" "Do you want a cookie or apple before going to bed?" Make a list of choices like these that you gave others this week.

Task No. 29: Choices for parents. Giving your parents choices will be most difficult. "Mom, you can come between 2:00 and 4:00 PM, but not between 4:00 and 8:00. I'm too busy with dinner and the kids then." When you arrive at this point, you know that great progress is being made; for trying this out on others is much easier than using this new skill on your parents.

Task No. 30: Say "No" without feeling guilty. When you are trying to establish a positive relationship with someone, there is a tendency to want to please that person, even to the extent of not saying "no" when "no" is appropriate.

"But that will make him think I don't like him," you say.

"Saying no at key times can strengthen a relationship," I reply.

That is a difficult concept to understand, much less believe. To say "no" often requires a high degree of self-confidence and the conviction that actions truly can be separated from feelings. Consider two examples:

"What do I do when a guy wants to go to bed with me on the first date, and I don't want to?"

"What are your options?" I asked. As she listed them, I noted, with interest, that she had not included "say no" in her list. "How about just plain no?" I inquired.

"Do you think that might work?"

"It's sure worth a try," I suggested.

"That's a good idea!"

A whole new world had opened up. This, of course, had to be offered as an option *only* after she had been convinced that she didn't *owe* him her body and she didn't have to feel guilty about saying no.

Convincing yourself that saying "no" when you really do not want to do something will not damage a firm relationship with a good friend, or potential friend, will be difficult. You even can say "no" without any lengthy explanation, just say "no," if that is how you feel. During the next week or two you will have an opportunity to practice this. When these occasions arise write them down in your notebook and discuss them with your coach at the next meeting.

Automatic Behavior

The concept of classical conditioning is familiar. A specific stimulus generates specific response. This occurs frequently in childhood and remains with the individual sometimes for life.

"That smell reminds me of home."

"The dentist's office smell means pain."

"Every time I walk into my mother's house I see and smell the kitchen, and it hurts all over again."

"I love the smell of roses; they remind me of George."

These are automatic reactions. Teaching automatic responses requires considerable effort, both on the part of the coach (teacher) and student. Practice is essential. Consider task number 34 from *Childhood Comes First* (1):

> *Task No. 34: Certain actions should be automatic.* Some things you do you will want to be automatic; then you won't have to think about them. Earlier we referred to one's reactions in driving on a patch of ice. This reaction must occur without thinking—a true, *automatic reaction.*
>
> Make a list of the five or six actions that you would like to make automatic. Some suggestions are:
>
> 1. When I'm given a compliment, say "Thank you."
> 2. When I feel really positive about something, tell someone.
> 3. When someone offers a suggestion I like, say "That's a good idea."
>
> There will be a need to include some "stop" orders on your list. The stopping of certain automatic *negative* behaviors is also important and difficult. This will often take rapid feedback from someone else. For example:
>
> 1. Have Jim tell me every time I say "shit."
> 2. When my mother makes me mad, stop clamming up.
> 3. Stop screaming at the children every time they upset me.
>
> To eliminate certain negative behaviors and to substitute positive behaviors will take considerable practice. This will also require the help of another person, someone who can give you feedback, both positive and negative.
>
> "You haven't sworn in four days; you're doing great!" or "Mom doesn't scream nearly as much as she used to."
>
> Actions you want to become automatic must be practiced, day after day. Eventually this will happen, and you will be most pleased.

Most of the deficiencies discussed throughout this book can be put into this relearning and retraining framework. The basic concepts of skill learning must be kept in mind as one undertakes this approach.[2]

Risks and Complications

Every approach to relearning any skill carries some risks. This approach is no exception. Not long ago I decided to improve my tennis game. As the coaching progressed, I got worse. I unlearned the bad habits before I learned the good ones.

One risk with this approach is that the patient (student) may "get worse" in the process of "getting better." But in reality, he may only seem as though he's getting worse. Teach him how to "label his feelings" and he may label every feeling, at any time or any place. He clearly needs to "smooth" out his approach and become a bit more tactful. One of our daughters kept her feelings to herself, and we encouraged her to tell us when she was angry. She tried out this new skill for the first time when I was entertaining a lawyer friend in our home. My daughter later commented that we never told her not to label her feelings when we had company. Fortunately the lawyer had children of his own.

Other risks must be considered. Some of these are:

2. The *Crash Course in Childhood for Adults* continues with many more tasks to improve instructional skills—EDs.

1. Knowing *what* to do usually precedes the skill of knowing *how* to do it. This is very frustrating. "I know I shouldn't belittle myself, but I just do it out of habit."
2. Seeing someone very skilled perform may be helpful, but it also may be most discouraging. "I'll never be able to do it that well."
3. If two people are working on the same skill, one invariably learns it faster than the other. If these two people are mates, the problems become very real. "I'm not going to accept Jim's drinking any longer."
4. Getting started is difficult, especially when the tasks are too simple or too complex. This takes a skilled coach or trainer. "Touching my cat is easier than touching my kids."
5. The skill-relearning process invariably brings up issues and incidents of the past which are not pleasant. Helping the student place these in perspective, not moving too rapidly, is essential. "I can label my feelings with my friends; but my mom, that's impossible."
6. Some students will try to "hide behind" the skill-relearning concept as one method of avoiding the past. As analysis is not sufficient, neither is skill relearning. A good coach or teacher will be required to balance the two processes. They need not be done by the same individual, i.e., the coach does not have to be the therapist. They can work hand in hand.
7. Whether or not these skills can be relearned in a group or must be an individual process will only be answered in time and by each student/coach pair. Likely, they will start with individual relearning and move to groups.

Summary

The concepts of skill-relearning have been reviewed. Specific components to teaching skills must be considered in every attempt to work with young adults whose early childhoods have resulted in basic developmental deficiencies. Only a few of the basic deficits have been discussed here, many others are available in *Childhood Comes First: A Crash Course in Childhood for Adults*, and many more can be generated by an enlightened teacher or coach. One *can* teach "the old dog new tricks" and have fun doing it.

Reference

1. Helfer, Ray E. *Childhood Comes First: A Crash Course in Childhood for Adults*. East Lansing, Mich.: privately published, 1978.

25 Promoting a Positive Parent-Baby Relationship

Ann L. Wilson

How do newborn babies begin to know their parents? How do new parents begin to know their new babies? No one would deny that the parent-baby relationship is vitally important for the baby's future development and the parents' sense of fulfillment as a mother and father. Yet, how does this relationship begin, and what can be done to assure that it can begin positively? These questions will be addressed in this chapter with a discussion of how time for bonding, for attachment, and for learning interactional skills plays an important role in the process of developing a positive parent-baby relationship.

As researchers have turned their attention to examine the nature of newborns' behavioral capabilities and how hospital care practices may affect parents' behavior with their new babies, there has grown a heightened sensitivity to the importance of how the parenting relationship begins. This sensitivity includes an awareness of how the early hours following birth offer a unique opportunity to help parents and babies begin the process of getting to know one another in as positive a way as possible. Findings from such studies will be reviewed with attention focused upon how help can be provided to a new family to promote their development of a positive relationship with their baby.

Time: Its Role in Bonding and Attachment

Shared time plays an essential role in the development of the relationship between newborn baby and parents. By being together, babies and their parents can become accustomed to each other's behaviors and begin to respond to one another in a reinforcing way. Without sharing such time together, getting to know someone and being able to understand another person is most difficult. With parents and new babies this is especially true.

Ann L. Wilson, Ph.D., is with the Department of Pediatrics, University of South Dakota, Sioux Falls, South Dakota.

Importance of Initial Contact between Parents and Baby for Bonding

Recently, great interest has been expressed in the phenomenon of bonding and the effect of early mother-baby contact on the future parenting interaction and the baby's development. The hypothesis has been made and tested that the early hours following birth comprise a "sensitive period" for emotional feelings of attachment to develop between parents and their new baby (1).

The significance of the timing of mother-infant contact has long been recognized in the maternal behavior of animals. In rural areas, farming families can easily define the hazards of separating a mother animal from her newborn baby. In agricultural communities where the thriving of livestock represents a family's livelihood, the importance of maintaining the maternal care of a newborn animal is a financial necessity.

Rural stories about lambing season include tales of how sheltering newly born lambs by separating them from their mothers and bringing them into a farm house during a blizzard causes the mother ewe to then reject her baby when the storm has passed and she and her baby are reunited. If the mother is able to have even a faint scent of her baby before they are separated the chances that she will accept her new baby, albeit reluctantly, are increased.

If rejection does take place, the farmer is faced with the dilemma of having a surviving lamb who is orphaned by the ewe. The farmer must then deal with the problem of persuading another ewe to care for the orphaned lamb. To do this, "tricks" are played on a ewe to make her think that an orphan is her own off-spring. Farmers report that one of the best ways to have an orphan accepted by an unsuspecting ewe is to introduce the orphan lamb to a new mother ewe in the period immediately following her delivery of a lamb. The placenta of the just-delivered lamb is rubbed over the body of an orphaned lamb. The common odor between ewe and lamb is believed to stimulate maternal behavior during the period following birth.

When a lamb is orphaned, and attempts to get a ewe to care for it fail, the lamb is often bottle-fed by the farming family. The "bottle lambs" are reported to grow up as "misfits." They can be easily spotted by their behavior as "odd balls" in a herd, and often they cannot be allowed to pasture with other sheep. Bottle lambs, even the females, are frequently the first to be sent to market. The behavior of these sheep is often not suitable for mating, and the females do not make adequate mothers for their own offspring (2).

While this is anecdotal information, it highlights how strongly the forces of nature are at work in the process of rearing offspring among animals. Clearly, the timing of an animal mother's first interaction with her new offspring plays a very important role in stimulating her protective maternal behavior. To separate a mother and baby at this time may lead to life-threatening circumstances for newly born animals and financial loss for the farmer. Farmers are very aware of this natural phenomenon, and their work must be in harmony with nature's way of providing for the continuity of life.

Animal studies conducted in laboratories have confirmed what farmers have always known. In a study with laboratory rats, Rosenblatt and Lehrman (3) have shown that when newborn rat pups were separated from their mothers immediately following birth and then reunited with their mothers five days later none were able to survive. The mother deprived of early interaction with her pups was observed to be unresponsive to these pups when she was again introduced to them, and the pups subsequently died. Interestingly, if the mother rats were separated from their babies after four days of contact with them, they were then able to resume caretaking when reunited with their babies.

In a study of maternal behavior of monkeys, Meier (4) has investigated the effects of separation of a mother and her baby monkey for two hours following birth. In this experiment, Meier used two groups of monkeys: one group of seven reared by their mothers in a natural feral environment and another group of seven monkeys reared in cages without the care of their mothers. All fourteen monkeys were delivered by cesarean section. The seven cage-reared monkeys rejected their newborns and by the third day after delivery continued to refuse to accept them. In the group of feral-reared monkeys, four of the seven mothers accepted their offspring by the end of the first day following birth, and by the second day the remaining three accepted and began to care for their babies.

These findings demonstrate that, in animals, the timing of maternal contact is crucial for the mother's acceptance of her young. Interestingly, until recently, modern medical care has ignored how the timing of initial contact between human mothers and their babies may affect the emerging mother-baby relationship. Clinical observations of mothers separated from their newborns for extended periods led to speculation about how life-sustaining medical care may possibly be damaging the future relationship between babies and parents.

Like the farmer sheltering the new lambs from bitter weather in the warmth of his home, perinatal medicine has abounded with ways of saving babies from the perils of preterm birth and from illnesses of the newly born. Studies of the interaction between mothers and sick babies have indicated that difficulties may exist for them in the establishment of a relationship under these circumstances (5, 6). Findings from these studies have captured national attention and have highlighted how human maternal behavior can be altered by events in the perinatal period.

The studies of mothers and their sick babies are often reported with data gathered from retrospective investigations of preterm newborns who experienced extended periods of separation from their mothers following birth. These retrospective data indicate that, in samples of children who are abused or who fail to thrive, there is a disproportionate number of babies who experienced separation from their mothers following birth (7–9). From the observational and retrospective studies, the hypothesis has been made and tested that when contact between a mother and her new baby is interrupted, the parenting relationship may be affected, thereby producing a negative impact upon the child's future.

Some investigators have extended findings from studies of preterm babies one step further and asked how different forms of care offered to healthy full-term babies and their mothers can affect the nature of their beginning relationship. The original study which pursued this question involved an experimental design with two treatment groups (1). One group of mothers received sixteen additional hours of contact time with their new babies during the first three postpartum days; the other study group received routine postpartum care which included contact between the mothers and babies during feeding times. Follow-up observations of these two groups have revealed differences in maternal responsiveness during the babies' first year of life (10). The major behavioral differences were noted in the mothers' linguistic style when their toddlers were two years old (11) and in the later intellectual status of the infants when they became five years of age (12). The mothers with the extended contact with their babies persisted in showing more responsive, nurturing behavior during their first year of life (1, 10). At two years of age, these mothers were noted to be providing a more-enriched linguistic environment for their children (11). When five years old, differences in intelligence were noted between the two groups of children. The preschool-aged children who had extra time with their mothers following birth scored high on IQ tests five years following birth (12).

This series of studies is often quoted to support care practices which allow early and extended contact for mothers and babies. Though there should be no doubt that allowing mothers and their newborns to be together is important and facilitative of the beginning of an affectionate relationship, questions have been raised about the interpretation of the findings of these early studies (13). The research was based on small samples with confounding variables. In at least one replicative study, the findings supporting the notion that early contact has long-range consequences have not been replicated (14). The complexity of all that transpires during the early days of life does indeed present numerous factors which are very difficult to control in research designs. While the criticisms of the bonding studies must be considered, the fact remains that research which investigates the early hours following birth has drawn to the attention of those who care for mothers and newborns the importance of how and when parents become acquainted with their new babies. Though what may be meant by the "sensitive period" hypothesis and its long-term consequences may be debated, the significance of this special time must be recognized by those caring for new mothers and babies.

The terms *bonding* and *attachment* have been used interchangeably in association with the sensitive period hypothesis (15). A distinction can be made between the meanings of the two terms which may help highlight the process involved in how the new parent-baby relationship develops. *Bonding* is the term used to describe the development of the strong affectual tie experienced by new parents toward their newborn during the hours following birth. *Attachment* represents the mutual closeness that develops as interaction between parent and baby continues. The immediate postpartum period, as just described, can provide parents with a unique opportunity to express their exhilaration following birth in claiming their baby, through watching, cuddling, and talking. Parents describe how the experience of having contact with their babies during this time enhances their positive feelings of closeness with them. By allowing a mother to have skin-to-skin contact with her baby, to feed him or her immediately following birth, and for staff to delay the admission of silver nitrate in the baby's eyes permits parents to express and experience these warm and positive feelings about their new baby and bond to him or her.

Immediately following birth, babies are also very alert and attentive to those sharing time with them (16, 17). This responsiveness can be very reinforcing to the attention they receive, further promoting the bond. The time following birth seems to be uniquely suited as an opportunity for mothers and fathers to begin to experience delight and to bond to their babies as they see and handle them for the first time. Though discussion may ensue about how early parental behavior may be affected, present knowledge and common sense should dictate allowing parents as much time as possible with their newborns following birth so that they may experience the excitement of being with their new babies and beginning to know them during these special early hours of their new lives together.

Effective Use of Time to Promote Attachment

Attachment, as opposed to bonding, is an activity which takes place over time as parents become increasingly involved with their babies and babies with their parents. Parental feelings of attachment become manifest in responsive nurturing behavior which then affects babies' selective attachment to their parents.

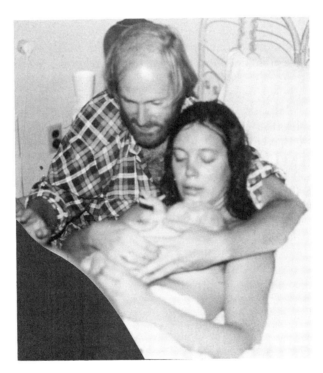

Figure 25.1

New parents enjoying the important time to bond with their new baby.

The question remains: Does bonding have to occur for the attachment process to proceed? Many families for a variety of reasons (i.e., a preterm birth, adoption) do not enjoy the opportunity to experience time with their babies during the postpartum period. They may be observed to grow closer to their babies with time but may report that "things didn't seem real at first" and that time was necessary before they could "claim him [or her] as my own." Perhaps such observations by parents indicate that an attachment can slowly take place when the opportunities for bonding are interrupted.

Ainsworth's (18, 19) studies highlight how a mother's sensitivity in interpreting her baby's behavior can enhance the selectivity and nature of the baby's attachment to her. The proposition can be made that bonding during the postpartum period can play an important role in promoting a mother's responsiveness toward her baby's behavior. A mother's heightened responsiveness and sensitivity may then positively affect how a baby will subsequently respond to and attach to her. While this contention has not been supported by data, it seems very plausible. Bonding appears to provide an optimally strong foundation for the process of attachment between a parent and a child that will serve as the basis for the child's future emotional growth. How the timing of contact between parents and baby may affect bonding has been described. The importance of how the time parents and babies experience together is spent will now be considered. Particular emphasis will be given to how to enhance the process of attachment.

Assuming that bonding optimally occurs during the early hours following birth, the beginning of the attachment process can be viewed as dovetailing with bonding as parents and their new babies begin to know one another. For the past thirty years, hospital routines have allowed mothers only limited time with their babies following birth. Many of these hospital practices were established to protect mothers and babies from infection. While these goals must not be lost, these rigid practices have outlived their original purpose. Some variations in hospital routines have been instituted, the effects of which are being documented. These interesting findings are beginning to provide evidence of how the attachment process can be affected by hospital care.

Rooming-in, the hospital practice of having new mothers take the major responsibility for their baby's care, has been used in some hospitals for many years in this country. Such an arrangement provides a mother with an opportunity to have unlimited time to spend with her baby and to begin to feel comfortable with baby care in the hospital setting where help is readily available.

This care arrangement has positively affected the development of mothers' feelings of competence and their ability to understand their babies' behavior. In 1951, McBryde (20) reported that when rooming-in became compulsory on the ward and private newborn service at Duke Hospital, there was a marked drop in the number of telephone calls made back to the hospital by mothers requesting advice on baby care following their discharge home. The implementation of rooming-in was also accompanied by an increase in breast-feeding among the mothers.

Two recent studies have contributed important information about the value of rooming-in. The first study compared fifty primiparous mothers who were randomly assigned to room-in with their newborns with fifty primiparous mothers who received customary maternity care (21). The two groups in this study were matched for background factors. One day prior to discharge the rooming-in mothers judged themselves to be more confident and competent in baby care and thought they would need less help at home with their infants when they left the hospital than did the mothers who did not receive this care. The rooming-in mothers also could attribute more to their newborns' cries than could the mothers who did not have rooming-in. These findings indicate that mothers who had additional time with their babies during the days following birth left the hospital feeling more prepared for the responsibilities of baby care and more able to interpret their babies' behavior.

A second set of findings about the effects of rooming-in comes from a large study conducted to investigate factors predictive of child abuse (22). This research was done with a sample of mothers receiving care from a large hospital/medical school clinic. The mothers were randomly assigned to either room-in with their new babies or to receive the standard nursing care, which allowed them and their babies to be together for the first time seven hours following delivery. The results of this study showed that there was only one case of major parent-infant breakdown (abuse, neglect, failure to thrive, or abandonment) reported during the first year of life among the 143 mothers who roomed-in with their newborns. Nine such cases of breakdown among the 158 infants who received the usual nursing care were cited. The babies who had rooming-in with their mothers experienced fewer parenting failures. The additional time that these mothers and their babies had together may well have affected their attachment, which positively influenced their beginning relationships.

Early contact between mother and baby and extended opportunity during a hospital stay for mothers to care for their babies appear to be helpful in increasing maternal confidence and competence in baby care. Parke (23) has hypothesized that allowing fathers optimal time with their newborns gives them, as well, an opportunity to become more involved with their babies during the early days and weeks following birth. Rooming-in is one practice which facilitates the maximization of a mother and father's time to get to know and care for their new baby.

With practices like rooming-in, hospitals can do much to facilitate the bringing together of parents with their babies to use the special time following birth for the acquaintance process to begin. More than practices, however, need to be present to assure an environment which fosters a positive beginning to a relationship. An attitude must exist among hospital personnel which reinforces the concept that their involvement with a family during and immediately after a birth affects the establishment of a parent-child relationship. If staff perceive new practices and activities on a hospital ward which have been developed to help promote this beginning relationship as merely a nuisance, then attitudes can be destructive to the best of plans. Mothers on hospital maternity wards have been reported to say:

> I wanted my baby on a demand feeding schedule. It was odd that she seemed to demand every three hours and was brought to me at the same time as the babies on a regular schedule.

> I wanted to get to know my baby but the nurses kept encouraging me to go to classes on baby care. I went to one where they used a rubber doll to teach how to bathe your baby. Why couldn't we use our own babies?

An approach to the care of the mother and newborn must be established which includes attention that is responsive to helping parents begin to interact with their newest family member. To do this all those who care for postpartum and nursery patients need to broaden their focus of care and begin to perceive how their behavior with patients can affect the beginning mother-baby relationship. This task may be simplified if staff are aware of some basic facts about the behavior of newborn babies. Two studies will be reviewed which demonstrate how newborns respond to the different kinds of care provided to them following birth. Such information highlights how hospital care can alter the pattern of a newborn's behavior to better adapt to the care he or she receives.

To investigate the effects of single versus multiple caretakers, Burns *et al.* (24) studied the behavior of infants during their first ten days of life. The infants in the study had been released by their mothers for adoption. At first, half the babies received care from a single caretaker and were on demand feeding schedules while the other half received the usual care from multiple caretakers in the nursery and were on fixed feeding schedules. The babies with multiple caretakers and the fixed schedules showed more general distress measured by the babies' amounts of grimacing, turning away from the nipple, fussing and crying, than did the babies with single caretakers. When care regimens were alternated, the infants who were switched to multiple caretakers began to show more irritability, while those who were given to a single caretaker began to show less distress in their behavior.

A second study also involved two groups of newborn babies. Six babies were cared for in the nursery and three roomed-in with their mothers. By the third day of life the rooming-in babies showed a lesser degree of restlessness than did the newborns cared for by the nursery and also cried less than did the babies in the other group. Interestingly, the rooming-in babies also began to show a shift toward more daytime wakefulness and a twenty-four-hour pattern of activity (25). The consistent care mothers were able to give to their babies by rooming-in with them may have played an important role in helping these babies adapt to extrauterine life and reintegrate their biological rhythms to a cyclical pattern.

The data from these two studies reveal that even during the earliest days of life, babies respond differentially to the nature of the care they receive. This illustrates that not only does rooming-in assist mothers in feeling more competent in caring for their babies but also that consistent care plays an important part in helping babies regulate their own behavioral rhythms to be more suited to positive patterns of interaction with caretakers. With shared time, a new baby and a primary caretaker can develop a sensitivity to each other's behavior which permits more mutually pleasing interaction that would seemingly promote positive feelings of attachment. The interesting aspect of these data is that they provide behavioral evidence of how a baby responds to care. Such information allows a view of life from the baby's perspective and reinforces the concept that time shared by new parents and their babies is important to their beginning relationship.

TABLE 25.1   **Development of a Positive Parent-Baby Relationship**

Components	What Hospitals Should Provide	Desirable Behavioral Outcome
Bonding	Time for early parent-baby contact, i.e., birthing rooms, skin-to-skin contact, nursing, delay in administering silver nitrate, fathers' involvement with labor and delivery	Parent's heightened emotional response to claiming newborn following birth
Attachment	Time for parents to be with baby and take responsibility for care, i.e., rooming-in, limited number of caretakers, family-centered nursing care	Parents' responsiveness and sensitivity to interpreting baby's behavior, baby's responsiveness to parents' caretaking
Synchrony in Interaction	Opportunities for parents to learn interactional skills, i.e., teaching about newborn capabilities and unique behavioral traits, demonstrations and reinforcement of techniques for initiating interaction and responding to baby's behavior	Mutually reinforcing interaction between parents and baby

Table 25.1 presents three essential components to the development of a positive parent-baby relationship. So far, this chapter has considered how time plays an important role in the bonding of parents to their new baby and the mutual attachment of parents and baby. For the relationship to develop positively a third component is considered essential. Along with the emotional feelings of closeness and the heightened sensitivities which develop with bonding and attachment, parents need to learn skills which assist them in interacting with their baby so that the time they spend together can be mutually reinforcing and pleasurable. This additional component, synchronous interaction, will now be discussed.

Interactional Skills: Their Role in Developing Synchrony between a Parent and Baby

What information about a new baby can be shared with and demonstrated to new parents, and how can this assist them in developing skills which can foster positive parent-baby interaction? Traditionally, maternity wards in hospitals have used the time new mothers and their babies are together to provide mothers with information about baby care. Information given to the mother usually includes instructions about how to feed, bathe, and dress the newborn. Now that the postpartum period is recognized as a sensitive period for the emerging relationship and the importance of early parent-baby contact has been identified, hospital care must be expanded to do more than teach the "how tos" of baby care. The special few days following birth should capitalize upon this very unique time to help parents develop sensitivity to the behavior of their individual baby, thereby facilitating positive interaction.

The sensitivity which can develop between parents and baby has been described as promoting interaction which is *in synchrony* between a baby and caretaker. Synchrony, the timing of interactions leading to an enmeshment of responses which are reinforcing to each partner in the interaction, helps to develop rapport in the relationship between parents and baby. To help the development of synchrony, hospitals not only need to develop ways of keeping new parents and their babies together following birth but also to provide mothers and fathers with specific techniques and skills which will help them promote positive patterns of synchronous interaction with their babies. So often, parent teaching centers around handicraft skills of physical care rather than assistance which will help them get to know their babies.

It is to be hoped that care can be given which is sensitive both to the major transition new parents are experiencing in their lives and to how the baby is adapting to his or her new life with them. To help parents sensitively respond to their babies' behavior and babies, in turn, to their behavior, information shared with parents about how their babies are perceiving the world around them is helpful. Information about a baby's behavioral capabilities and demonstrations of how they may be observed to respond to various stimuli is a starting point in facilitating parents' positive interaction with their baby.

From current knowledge about the behavior of newborns the following points can be integrated into a plan to provide this knowledge base for parents:

1. Babies have different states of consciousness which affect both their response to stimulation and the kind of stimulation they perceive.
2. Babies are sociable. They have, within their behavioral capabilities, responses which both elicit caretaker interaction and positively reinforce interaction.
3. Babies are selective in both the kind and amount of stimulation they will process.
4. Each baby is different and is born with a unique pattern of behavior which contributes to the nature of his or her interaction with the caretaker.

These four points of information can be integrated into the kind of teaching that takes place on a postpartum ward. More than teaching these facts is necessary. They must be converted into skills which can be used by the parents (see Chapter 24). This information should be taught and demonstrated to a mother and father and their attempts at practicing this demonstration reinforced to help them develop techniques to enhance positive exchanges of interaction with their baby. With assistance from a knowledgeable and understanding helper, new parents can practice observing their new baby and responding to his or her behavior in a way that will help develop an appreciation for how the infant perceives and interacts with the world.

Babies Have Different States of Consciousness

A shallow, unenlightened view of newborns includes only the perceptions that they weigh six to eight pounds and are warm babies who spend their time either sleeping, eating, or crying. Encapsulated, this description is of self-centered human beings who occupy all their time and energy satisfying their own physiological needs. Even with a tiny preterm baby such a description fails to recognize a very important part of the baby's behavioral repertoire, the infant's periods of alert attentiveness. All babies experience episodes of very alert behavior during which time they visually explore the world around them and respond to the sounds of their environment. Babies during these periods are amazingly responsive to those caring for them.

To capture these moments of wonderful attentiveness, parents need to become aware of when their baby is alert and will be most responsive to them. The different states of consciousness that can be observed in a newborn's behavior have been examined carefully (26). With an understanding of these states, parents can better perceive their babies' level of consciousness and how they will respond to the attention received.

Brazelton identifies six states of consciousness which can be easily observed in a newborn's behavior (27). They are:

1. Deep sleep—eyes closed, regular breathing, no activity except startles, no eye movement
2. Light sleep—eyes closed with rapid eye movement observed, low activity level with random movements and startles
3. Drowsy—semidozing with open or closed eyes, variable activity level
4. Alert—bright look, attention on source of stimulation, minimum motor activity
5. Active—considerable motor activity, thrusting movements of extremities, fussing may or may not be present
6. Crying—intense cry which is difficult to break through with stimulation

During the alert state, babies are best able to respond to the attention caretakers give them. When crying, babies are in need of an entirely different kind of attention. In this state, babies need stimulation that can calm them. With the appropriate amount of stimulation a crying baby can be helped to become calm so that he or she can again become alert or drift into a sleep state. By holding babies and providing them with movement and soft talking, one can often calm them. The warning is often offered by well-intended bearers of wisdom on baby care that picking up a crying baby will "spoil him." Actually the movement provided by handling a baby clearly helps to calm a crying baby (28). Tending to a crying baby during the first six months of life in the manner described will *decrease* the amount of irritability demonstrated during the second half of the first year (29).

Babies have ways of calming themselves when they are in a crying state. Crying infants when brought to caretakers' shoulders, often calmed by the movement they receive, will hold up their heads and scan the visual surroundings. By doing this, babies may well continue to calm themselves through visual stimulation. New babies are also often able to calm themselves by sucking on their fists or fingers. Both of these actions are examples of self-initiated attempts made by babies which provide them with calming self-stimulation. Parents do not have an innate understanding of these facts. They must be taught and demonstrated.

While in the two sleep states, parents can note how babies gradually awake and "come up" to the drowsy state. The drowsy state can often be mistaken as an alert state, and attempts to interact with a drowsy baby can be frustrating. A baby's response to stimulation when in this state is similar to an adult's reaction to a bright-eyed, eager individual immediately after turning off the alarm clock in the morning. Neither the adult nor the infant can be fully alert during these moments (see table 25.2).

TABLE 25.2   **Suggestions for Observation and Interaction**
                      States of Consciousness

1. Watch your baby during the day and determine when he is most often alert—following feedings? when awakening from sleep? between feedings?
2. Talk to your baby when he is in a crying state, if he does not calm, pat him, then pick him up, and walk him. Become aware of how much stimulation it takes to calm your baby from a crying to a quiet state.
3. Observe your baby when asleep. Is he in a quiet or an active sleep state? Depending on his state, does he startle to noise?

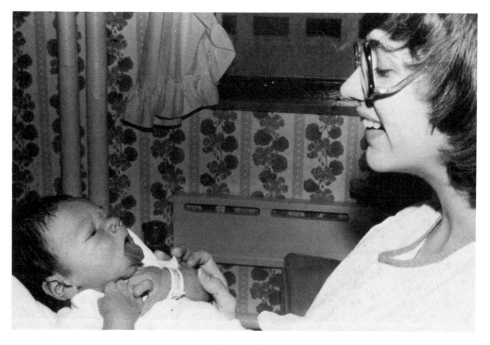

Figure 25.2

Mother and baby getting to know each other during the infant's period of alert attentiveness.

Looking at babies from the perspective of states gives parents a framework for understanding how babies' levels of consciousness are affecting the way they respond to stimuli. Helping parents gauge their interaction according to their babies' state is a first step to helping them become successful in knowing *when* their babies will be most responsive to the attention and affection they wish to share with them.

Babies Are Social

To have a positive interaction with a baby requires that the infant be approached in an alert state. The next step in this process requires that whoever is interacting with a baby be aware of what the capabilities of a baby are and what kind of responses a baby can be expected to make. When a newborn baby is carefully observed, one can easily see how amazingly equipped the infant is to enter a social relationship and respond to caretakers.

In an evolutionary sense, human newborn babies will spend a relatively long proportion of their early years dependent on others for their survival. This is a biological fact; yet newborns have innate capabilities which reinforce their caretakers' attention and contribute to the building of the relationship upon which their survival depends. This relationship serves as the foundation for the baby's future social, emotional, intellectual, and physical development. The behaviors which help bind the early relationship include the baby's visual, auditory, and olfactory sensory responses. Newborns at the time of birth can use these senses to interact with their caretakers. Within days following birth they can also use their sensory capabilities to discriminate a familiar from an unfamiliar person. These sensory capabilities not only permit mutually reinforcing interaction to occur but also reflect the babies' cognitive capabilities, which demonstrate their preferential responsiveness to interaction with familiar caretakers (see table 25.3).

Visual Responsiveness

Newborns can see immediately following birth. Interestingly, they can best

TABLE 25.3   **Suggestions for Observation and Interaction**
Social Capabilities

1. When your baby is in an alert state, hold her head in a midline (center) position. Capture her attention by gently talking with her. Without talking, move your head slowly 30° to the left then to the right. Does she follow your eyes? If she is unable to do so talk with her as you move your head from left to right.
2. Repeat suggestion 1 using a red ball rather than your face. See how far your baby will follow the ball horizontally, then vertically, and finally in a circular pattern.
3. Hold your baby at eye level in front of you. Put her sideways on her back with her head lying on one of your hands and her bottom on your other hand. Talk gently to her and watch her turn her head toward your voice. She may search with her eyes for your face and make eye contact with you.

focus upon a target as close as six to eight inches away, the usual distance between them and the person who is caring for them. A newborn baby is able to both visually fixate and follow a moving target. Though at first, visual following may be jerky and the baby may lose sight of the visual target, this capability becomes increasingly refined within a few days or weeks. By four months of age, a baby's vision is as mature as it will ever be. This area of development obviously far exceeds many other capabilities which require years to reach maturity.

Accompanying babies' innate visual skills is their obvious spontaneous desire to visually explore their environment. New babies in the alert state will persist in scanning the immediate environment until they see an object of interest, at which time they will fixate upon it. Research studies using methodology developed by Fantz (30) have investigated the visual preferences of newborns. By presenting two visual stimuli to infants and then measuring how long they look at each visual configuration, the stimuli which are best able to attract babies' attention can be discerned.

These studies demonstrate that new babies prefer patterned, over plain, stimuli and that they prefer to examine configurations which resemble the human face (31). Of particular interest to a new baby are round shapes similar to eyes. Eye-to-eye gazing seems to be a very primitive response and certainly is a very elementary, but critical, aspect of human interaction, which can be observed as a new baby responds to those who care for him or her.

Auditory Responsiveness

Along with well-developed visual capabilities, a newborn baby is able to hear well and visually locate the source of auditory stimulation. Evidence has accumulated which indicates that babies exhibit heightened sensitivity to human-like auditory stimuli (32). In particular, they prefer high-pitched sounds, especially those made by female voices. These findings provide further evidence that babies are born ready to respond to those who care for them. They are able to discriminate and preferentially respond to those sounds which have social significance for them. Knowing these facts can facilitate new parents' ability to develop an auditory communication system with their infants.

Olfactory Responsiveness

Within five days following birth, breast-fed babies can differentiate the smell of their mother's breast pads from those of another woman (33). When presented with the breast pad of another woman and one of his or her mother, a baby clearly preferred to smell his or her mother's breast pad. Mothers, too, have been reported to detect a particular scent of each of their babies. By allowing close contact between a mother and baby, they can begin to identify each other's individual odor and learn to know each other through the use of this sensory mechanism.

Babies' Selection of the Amount and Kind of Stimuli They Can Process

In 1890 William James wrote that the baby experiences life "all as one great blooming, buzzing confusion'' (34). Today, almost 100 years later, we know this to be inaccurate. How the baby's sensory capabilities provide the basis for social interaction has been discussed. Next to be considered is how babies are able to regulate the input from their environment so that it is not experienced as a great blooming, buzzing confusion. Most certainly, James's comment has been disproven as observations of newborns clearly demonstrate that babies attend to the salient features of their environment and can "tune out" stimuli to avoid disorganization in their processing of stimuli.

Habituation is the term used to describe how an individual decreases his response to repeated stimulation and can thus avoid bombardment by environmental stimuli. Newborns can clearly habituate immediately after birth and probably *in utero*. If babies used their sensory apparatus indiscriminately, their world would be perceived as one of confusion and chaos. In response to a repetitious stimulus, babies will "shut down" their response or habituate to this stimulus. This can be observed with a sleeping newborn. While the baby is in the light sleep state a bell may be rung over the infant's ear; the baby usually responds to the sound. If fifteen seconds later the bell is rung again, the baby more than likely will again respond to this auditory stimulus. With repeated presentations of the same stimulus, the infant will begin to show less and less response to it. This decrement in response is considered to indicate that the baby has habituated to the sound. Studies of visual attention demonstrate that habituation is a form of primitive learning by which a baby learns not to respond to the familiar while still being able to respond to a new or unfamiliar stimulus (35).

This principle also functions when the baby is awake and alert, socially interacting with a caretaker. When the infant's level of arousal becomes too high, the infant will attempt to avoid increased stimuli. The child may do this by averting his or her gaze, changing body position, or by altering his or her state of consciousness. When excessively stimulated, the response is often crying or irritability. The infant may then need the help of soothing care to bring his or her state to a level where he or she can again attend to the environment (36).

To interact effectively with a baby requires that a degree of sensitivity be used to help identify *how much* as well as *what kind* of stimuli a baby will be optimally responsive to. This sensitivity develops with experience. Mothers often say "he's too tired to sleep," or "the company has her too excited." These are the extreme examples of situations where the baby has become over-stimulated. When closely examining behavior while babies and caretakers are interacting, one can watch babies determine how much stimulation they will tolerate. The babies may momentarily turn away, close their eyes, stare unresponsively, or change their state in response to the stimulation. These are ways babies can control input from the environment. New parents must be shown how to gauge their interaction with the baby and the baby's level of tolerance for such stimulation. Demonstrations can be provided to new parents to assist them to observe and interpret what the baby is indicating by his or her behavior. A new mother and father can easily feel rejected by her or his baby if attempts made to play with the baby do not become pleasurable episodes of mutual exchange (see table 25.4).

TABLE 25.4   **Suggestions for Observation and Interaction**
Modulation of Stimuli

---

1. When your baby is in an alert, quiet state, watch him visually explore all that is around him. What does he seem to prefer looking at? How does he respond to sounds? Does he seem to "tune out" some sounds or visual stimuli?
2. Hold your baby out in front of you. Talk with him gently and watch him as he responds to your face and voice. Does he indicate when "he has had enough" by slightly turning away, closing his eyes, or becoming irritable? If so, wait until he seems to calm and again becomes alert. Pay attention to the message he is giving you about how he is most comfortable with the timing of his interaction with you.

Each Newborn Is Unique

The above three sections of this chapter have discussed how each newborn has behavioral capabilities which facilitate how he or she responds to and interacts with those who care for him or her. What must also be highlighted is the fact that each newborn has behavioral characteristics which represent his or her individuality and will contribute to the quality of the infant's interaction with others.

The notion that a child's temperament can be identified early in infancy and has long-lasting affects on the child's future development was carefully described by the work of Thomas and Chess (37). Three constellations of temperament were identified by the clinicians and researchers, i.e., the "easy child," the "slow-to-warm-up child," and the "difficult child." The nine behavioral characteristics which were used to form these categories are: activity level, rhythmicity, approach-withdrawal, adaptability, threshold of responsiveness, intensity of reaction, quality of mood, distractibility and attention span, and persistence. Their work, begun in the 1950s, has made an important contribution by focusing upon how innate characteristics of babies will affect how they will interact with others in the future. Progress in this area has gone beyond this early work. The original research on infant temperament began with observations and parent interviews when the babies were two to three months of age. Today studies are looking at the behavior of infants in the neonatal period to identify behavioral characteristics which will affect how they begin the interactional process with their parents.

The *Brazelton Neonatal Assessment Scale* (27) allows babies' interactive behaviors to be measured, thereby evaluating newborns' capacities to initiate and respond to the care given them. Such information can then be used to help parents view their babies' own unique characteristics. We hope that from such a perspective they can develop an appreciation for their infants' own unique characters and can begin very early to adapt their behavior to them as unique individuals.

Specifically, individual differences exist in babies' abilities to control their states of consciousness, in how they are able to respond to disturbing stimuli, and in how they respond to animate and inanimate visual and auditory stimuli. Babies also vary in how easily they are able to console themselves or be consoled by others, their cuddliness, the quality of their motor activity, and their overall degree of irritability. Even without formal Brazelton assessments, these behavioral characteristics can be observed in a nursery and the information shared with new parents in a way which begins to highlight the positive characteristics of babies and their beginning ways of interacting with their parents.

By noting each baby's observable characteristics and sharing these observations with parents, those working with new parents and babies can do much in assisting parents to become more aware of the ways their baby is able to interact with them. When special strategies for interaction are necessary, these can be discussed and demonstrated to new parents. With such help, parents can be made to feel more competent learning how to interact positively with their baby. Their baby then will be seen as already having unique characteristics which express the individual nature of his or her behavior (see table 25.5).

TABLE 25.5   **Suggestions for Observation and Interaction**
               Unique Characteristics

---

1. As you spend time with your baby do you notice ways that she likes to be held, comforted, or fed? Is she beginning to let you know her dislikes and preferences?
2. Does your baby seem to be a quiet or an active baby? Does she entertain herself by looking around and/or with body movements?
3. How long is your baby able to entertain herself? How quickly does she need you to offer different kinds of stimulation?

Summary

The goal of postpartum and nursery hospital care for any new mother, father, and baby has been to assure their well-being during the days following birth. This goal can be expanded to assure that assistance be provided to help the parent-baby relationship begin positively.

A relationship involves more than interaction; yet interaction is the beginning of a relationship. By enabling early contact to occur between parents and their new baby, the special moments following birth can be experienced by new parents. As their excitement following birth culminates in their response to being with their new baby for the first time, bonding can take place. A mutual attachment then develops as parents and baby interact with each other over time. An affectual tie becomes stronger as parents and their baby begin to more sensitively interact with each other, reinforcing the nature of their mutual relationship.

Parents must be helped to develop positive interactional patterns with their babies before they leave the hospital following birth. With both opportunities to receive assistance in observing their newborn's behavior and with guidance in responding to particular behavioral patterns, parents can practice and develop new skills during the postpartum hospital stay. What better opportunity exists for modeling, guiding, and helping parents feel more comfortable and competent as they begin to care for their new baby? What better time is available to have the most impact on a beginning relationship? The perinatal period is an ideally suited time for this kind of assistance to be given to new mothers and father. Those who are involved with the hospital care of new parents and babies must begin to perceive how the care they give following birth can help positive relationships begin and develop.

References

1. Klaus, M., Jerauld, R., and Kreger, N. 1972. Maternal attachment: importance of the first postpartum days. *New Engl. J. Med.* 286:460–63.
2. Soule, D. 1977. Personal communication of information from former South Dakota sheep farmer.
3. Rosenblatt, J. S., and Lehrman, D. 1963. *Maternal Behavior in Mammals,* edited by H. R. Rheingold. New York: John Wiley and Sons, Inc.
4. Meier, G. W. 1965. Maternal behavior of feral and laboratory-reared monkeys following the surgical delivery of their infants. *Nature* 206:492–93.
5. Klaus, M., and Kennell, J. 1970. Mothers separated from their newborn infants. *Pediatr. Clinics N. Am.* 17:1015–37.
6. Klaus, M., Kennell, M., Plumb, N., and Zuehlke, S. 1970. Human maternal behavior. *Pediatrics* 46:187–92.
7. Klein, M., and Stern, L. 1967. Low birth weight and the battered child syndrome. *Am. J. Diseases Child.* 122:15–18.
8. Shaheen, E., Alexander, D., Truskowsky, M., et al. 1968. Failure to thrive—a retrospective profile. *Clin. Pediatr.* 7:255–61.
9. Elmen, E., and Gregg, G. S. 1967. Developmental characteristics of abused children. *Pediatrics* 40:596–602.
10. Kennell, J., Jerauld, R., and Wolfe, H. 1974. Maternal behavior one year after early and extended postpartum contact. *Dev. Med. Child Neurology* 16:172–79.
11. Ringler, N. M., Kennell, J. H., and Jarvella, R. 1975. Mother to child speech at two years—effects of early postnatal contact. *J. Pediatr.* 86:141–44.
12. Ringler, N.,Trause, M., and Klaus, M. H. 1976. Mother's speech to her two-year-old—its effect on speech and language comprehension at five years. *Pediatr. Res.* 10:37.
13. Campbell, S. G., and Taylor, P. 1979. Bonding and attachment: theoretical issues. *Seminars in Perinatology* 3:3–13.
14. Ottaviano, C., Campbell, S., and Taylor, P. 1979. The effects of extra contact on infant-mother attachment at one year. *Pediatr. Res.* 13:64.
15. Klaus, M. H., and Kennell, J. H. 1976. *Maternal-Infant Bonding* St. Louis: C. V. Mosby Company.
16. Emde, R. N., Swedberg, J., and Suzecki, B. 1975. Human wakefulness and biological rhythms after birth. *Arch. Gen. Psychiatry* 32:780–83.
17. Desmond, M. M., Franklin, R., Vallbona, C., et al. 1963. The clinical behavior of the newly born. *J. Pediatr.* 62:307–25.
18. Ainsworth, M., and Bell, S. 1969. Some contemporary patterns of mother-

infant interaction in the feeding situation. In *Stimulation in Early Infancy*, edited by A. Ambrose. New York: Academic Press.

19. Ainsworth, M., and Bell, S. 1979. Attachment exploration and separation illustrated by the behavior of one-year-olds in a strange situation. *Child Dev.* 41:49–67.

20. McBryde, A. 1951. Compulsory rooming-in in the ward and private newborn service at Duke Hospital. *J. Am. Med. Assoc.* 145:625–28.

21. Greenberg, M., Rosenberg, I., and Lind, J. 1973. First mothers' rooming-in with their newborns: its impact upon the mothers. *Am. J. Orthopsychiatry* 43:783–88.

22. O'Connor, S. M., Vietz, P. M., Hopkins, J. B., et al. 1977. Postpartum extended maternal-infant contact: subsequent mother and child health. *Pediatr. Res.* (A).

23. Parke, R. 1975. Father-infant interaction. In *Maternal Attachment and Mothering Disorders: A Round Table*, edited by M. Klaus, T. Leger, and M. Trause. N.p.: Johnson & Johnson Company.

24. Burns, P., Sanders, L. W., Stechler, G., et al. 1972. Short-term effects of caregiver environment on the first ten days. *J. Am. Acad. Child Psychiatry* 11:427–39.

25. Sanders, L. W., and Julice, H. L. 1966. Continuous interactional monitoring in the neonate. *Psychosomatic Med.* 28:822–35.

26. Prectle, H., and Beintema, D. 1964. The neurological examination of the full-term newborn infant. *Clin. Dev. Med.* no. 12 (London).

27. Brazelton, T. B. 1973. Neonatal Behavioral Assessment Scale. *Clinics in Developmental Medicine*, No. 50. Philadelphia: J. B. Lippincott.

28. Korner, A., and Grobstein, R. 1966. Visual alertness as related to soothing in neonates: implications for maternal stimulation and early deprivation. *Child Dev.* 37:867–76.

29. Bell, S., and Ainsworth, M. 1972. Infant crying and maternal responsiveness. *Child Dev.* 43:1171–90.

30. Fantz, R. L. 1961. The origin of form perception. *Scientific American* 204:66–72.

31. Fantz, R., L. 1963. Pattern vision in newborn infants. *Science* 140:296–97.

32. Hutt, S. J., Hutt, C., Lenard, H. G., Bernuth, H. V., and Muntjerverff, W. J. 1968. Auditory responsivity in the human neonate. *Nature* 218:888–90.

33. MacFarlane, J. A. 1975. Parent-infant interaction. In *Ciba Foundation Symposium 33*. Amsterdam: Elsevier Publishing Company.

34. James, W. 1890. *Principles of Psychology*. New York: Holt, Rinehart, and Winston.

35. Friedman, S., Carpenter, G., and Nagy, A. 1970. Decrement and recovery of response to visual stimuli in the newborn human. *Proc. 78th Annual Convention Am. Psychological Assoc.* 5:273–74.

36. Kearsley, R. B. 1973. The newborn's response to auditory stimulation: a demonstration of orienting and defensive behavior. *Child Dev.* 44:582–90.

37. Thomas, A., and Chess, S. 1977. *Temperament and Development*. New York: Brunner Mazel.

26 Screening for the Potential to Abuse: A Review

Carol Schneider, Ray E. Helfer, and James K. Hoffmeister

The concern over the abused and neglected child has increased significantly over the past several years. Five years ago, less than 4% of the adult population was aware of the serious nature of this problem. In 1978, almost 34% of the population admitted to such an awareness. This increase in public awareness has been accompanied by an equally rapid expansion in the understanding of the nature of the abuse and neglect problem, its ever-increasing incidence, the psychodynamics of those who abuse and are abused, and new methods of therapeutic intervention (1).

Associated with an increased awareness of any problem which seriously affects a large segment of society is the desire for earlier and earlier identification, treatment, and preventive approaches. This was true for the polio epidemics of the 1940s and 1950s, for the smallpox epidemics of previous centuries, for the increasing prevalence of crime in the streets of large cities, and certainly is equally true for the problems relating to the increasing incidence of child abuse and neglect. Professionals and nonprofessionals alike are demanding earlier and better methods of screening, diagnosis, and preventive approaches to the problem.

This places upon the professional responsibility which is somewhat different than the early recognition of an already abused and/or neglected child. Earlier recognition, while difficult, is a much pleasanter and more rewarding task than waiting for a child to be abused and then submitting a report to a protective services worker. While this after-the-fact involvement is still necessary, attention can now be placed on a variety of preventive endeavors.

In reality, the fact that this new role can now be defined indicates considerable progress in the field of child abuse and neglect. Just twelve years ago the first edition of this book, *The Battered Child*, was published (in 1968) with further

Carol Schneider, Ph.D., is with the University of Colorado, Boulder. Ray E. Helfer, M.D., is with the Department of Pediatrics and Human Development, College of Human Medicine, Michigan State University. James K. Hoffmeister, Ph.D., is with the Test Analysis and Development Corporation, Boulder.

Part of this chapter is reprinted with permission from "Preventing the Abuse and Neglect of Children: The Physician's Role," *Pediatric Basics* 23 (1979): 4–7.

additions appearing only six years ago (in 1974). The purpose of this review is to discuss the current status of screening for those young adults who are likely to have difficulty interacting with their children.

Guidelines for Screening

The basic issues relating to the screening of the parent who is at high risk of having major difficulty interacting with his or her child are discussed in some detail in two recent publications by R. Helfer (2, 3). While this theoretical material need not be reviewed in detail, many will benefit from a brief review of the concepts and language which now appear in the literature. One must develop a cautious approach to reports and claims found both in the supermarket tabloids and the carefully edited professional journals. One should read the reviews of screening most carefully, keeping in mind the following points (4).

1. Screening is not a diagnostic tool. Those screened as "positive" need further assessment.
2. Facilities and personnel must be available to carry out the required further assessment.
3. If someone is identified as having a potential for a given problem, this does not necessarily mean he/she has the problem.
4. Screening is not warranted unless treatment is possible to improve upon the prognosis, if the condition being searched for is found.
5. Adequate time after screening must be provided to implement a helpful plan.
6. "The cost of screening, diagnosis, and treatment...should be outweighed by the saving in human misery and fiscal expenditure if the problem is not discovered...." (4).
7. Screening methods must be reliable, that is, show consistent results.
8. Screening methods must be valid, that is, measure what they are supposed to measure.
9. Screening and any subsequent intervention must be ethical and not label an individual in an offensive manner.
10. Screening becomes unnecessary when the prevalence of the problem in any given population is so extensive that an intervention program becomes warranted for all.
11. Research studies must be properly controlled, i.e., results compared to a population "free" of the variable being studied.
12. Group differences are not equivalent to individual differences, i.e., factors which are suitable to differentiate groups may not be suitable to differentiate individuals in those groups.

While the above precautions hold true for any screening program, there are a few unique issues in the child abuse/neglect field which must be mentioned. These are reviewed here, prior to outlining a practical role for a physician, to help the pediatrician or family physician place into perspective special complexities of the early recognition and prevention of child abuse.

Methods Used and Problems Confronted in Screening

In reviewing screening techniques, we find that in the field of child abuse and neglect, three major methods are currently being used, singly or in combination.

These are: (1) open-ended and/or closed-ended questionnaires, (2) a standardized interview, and (3) direct observations of interactions. Each has certain advantages and disadvantages. The self-administered questionnaire, while cheap and easy, requires literacy. The one-to-one interview permits direct observation and increases the interviewer's ability to follow up on cues. However, it must be standardized, is time-consuming, and expensive. Both of these methods assess the perceptions of the person answering the questions. Direct observation of interactional behavior, e.g., a mother feeding her baby or reacting to her baby in the delivery room, requires careful standardization of technique and the presence of a trained observer. The advantages, however, are evident: they observe actual behavior, rather than merely the interviewer's perceptions or attitudes.

One or more of these techniques are utilized to gather data in at least four major areas of content to produce the data upon which most current research in screening or early prediction are based. These four areas are: (1) early childhood experiences of the adult being screened; (2) the interpersonal or interactional skills of the individual; (3) perceptions of and/or interaction with children, especially the subject's own; (4) the presence or absence of crises, stresses, and family support systems.

The interviewer's use of these techniques to assess her or his perceptions and/or behavior in the above four areas presents many problems. As we review the literature in this field, these difficulties fall into one or more of the following categories.

Reliability and Validity

The matter of reliability and validity of screening instruments must be elaborated upon, for they represent critical issues which are particularly difficult to resolve in research in the field of child abuse and neglect.

First, consider the matter of reliability. For a screening test to be reliable requires obtaining the same answer or drawing the same conclusion when the test is repeated a second time, i.e., test and retest reliability. Young adults reared in a very negative, nontrusting, chaotic, inconsistent environment throughout their childhoods are taught, from infancy, to be inconsistent or unreliable. Expecting these individuals to answer questions on a questionnaire or in an interview in a consistent or reliable manner is unrealistic. On the contrary, one of the criteria for a high-risk parent may well be a high degree of inconsistency in answering questions. This problem is considered in the scoring system for questionnaires used by Hoffmeister, i.e., convergence analysis (5).

Second, consider the matter of validity. This must be divided into two areas, the sensitivity and the specificity of the screening method. The former (sensitivity) relates to correctly identifying, from a large population, those who *have the potential* to abuse or neglect. The latter (specificity) relates to correctly identifying, from the same population, those who *do not have such a potential*. This is best understood by considering the accuracy of "hits," or correct identification, as depicted in figure 26.1.

Developing a sensitive instrument to correctly identify a high-risk population

Screen Prediction of Potential		Actual Presence of Abuse: Yes	Actual Presence of Abuse: No
	Yes	"Hit" A	"Miss" C
	No	"Miss" B	"Hit" D

Figure 26.1

Sensitivity is the percentage of correct "Yes" "Hits": $A/(A + B) \times 100$. Specificity is the percentage of correct "No" "Hits": $D/(C + D) \times 100$.

requires asking the right questions and/or making the correct observations. Either, or preferably both, of these methods will single out a group of individuals, a high percentage of whom will demonstrate major breakdown in interactions with their child(ren). While most of the major breakdowns in parent-child interaction will be identified correctly (sensitivity high), many in that same group may not demonstrate the breakdown, thus lowering the specificity. To improve the specificity the interviewer must screen more tightly, resulting in fewer "misses" that incorrectly predict abusive potential (the *C* box in fig. 26.1). This, then, decreases sensitivity by increasing the "misses" that fail to predict actual abusive potential (the *B* box in fig. 26.1).

Ethical Aspects of Screening

The dilemma of sensitivity and specificity has another critically important facet, i.e., the ethical aspects of screening for abusive or neglectful potential. Frankenburg points out that it is unethical to screen for a condition that cannot be treated (4), such as the presence of high lead levels in an urban group of children. While treatment is possible, it only becomes feasible if some group comes forth with the money required for this extensive treatment. This issue certainly is equally present in the field of abuse.

Another factor which must not be overlooked is the issue of labeling (6). Striving for a high degree of sensitivity and specificity is admirable; but labeling potential child abusers had best be done correctly. Even if the label is correct, what happens if nothing is done? Or, even worse, what if that label somehow turns into a self-fulfilling prophecy? Another question must be considered: Is it fair to the child who is likely to be abused not to place such a label on the parent, assuming help will be provided? Researchers in the field find themselves between the proverbial rock and hard place.

Group Difference versus Individual Differences

The review of research in the field of prediction and screening has revealed another problem which occurs all too frequently. Some have suggested that if a characteristic is present in a group of known abusers, and significantly less common in a group of known nonabusers, this characteristic can be used for prediction or screening. For example, poverty is reported to be present as a common variable in the abuse population. Poverty should not be used as an identifying screening variable for an individual. Significant differences between groups do not necessarily mean the same variable will identify, accurately, a potentially abusive individual.

A Word about Control Groups

A control group in a research study should be made up of individuals who are similar to those in the study group in every way *except* for the characteristic being studied.

If a researcher is going to assess responses of parents known to abuse or neglect a child to a given set of questions, these responses should be compared with those of parents who are similar in every way except that they are known not to abuse or neglect their children. Randomly picking parents from an emergency room, hospital ward, or school system does not guarantee the absence of the factor being tested, i.e., abusive or neglectful behavior.

The problem of finding true control or comparison groups has plagued many researchers in this field. Even worse, failure to use adequately defined control groups may result in misinterpretation of results. For example, a ''control'' group, contaminated by high-risk parents, may make the data appear inconclusive or insignificant. The same study, done with noncontaminated controls, might well have revealed very significant differences between the two groups.

A Review of the Literature Relating to Screening

The review of literature on this subject has identified many studies which provide us with only partial answers to the search for an ideal screening instrument. What is clear is that this research has made a significant contribution to the further understanding of the dynamics involved with this complex problem of abuse and neglect.

Parent Factors

Over a twelve-year period, Helfer, Schneider, and Hoffmeister and others (7–9) have identified a parent factor they called ''emotional needs met'' which identifies the feelings of emotional or physical abuse or deprivation at present and in the childhood background of questionnaire respondents. Using a method called ''convergence analysis'' (5), approximately an 80% sensitivity and specificity in predicting known abuse and high-risk groups and known good parents and low-risk groups has been achieved.

Gordon (10) reports on potential child abuse factors in the mother in the perinatal period. This study used these predictors: single mother, young mother having a known social problem, who was mentally dull, had frequent pregnancies, and was late for prenatal care and defaulting. Sensitivity was 75%. No information regarding specificity was recorded.

Crain and Millor (11) document the problem of maltreated children of mentally retarded parents and suggest that children of mentally retarded parents must be considered at high risk. No data are provided regarding the sensitivity/specificity characteristics of this factor. However, clinical experience suggests this factor be considered in a list of parent factors.

Bavolek, Kline, and McLaughlin (12) have developed an Adolescent Parenting Inventory (API) for the purpose of identifying high-risk adolescents prior to parenthood. They are using a method by which anyone responding from one to three standard deviations below the mean preparent attitude data would be labeled high risk. Sensitivity and specificity data are difficult to obtain in this type of study, as these adolescents do not have children with whom their interactions could be observed or who could be asked about their attitudes toward them. However, this is an interesting idea, and long-term follow-ups of their risk groups ought to be done.

Child Factors

Several researchers have written about the importance of child factors in determining parent response. Brazelton *et al.* (13) have pointed out that even slight differences in physiology or temperament, which can fall within the normal range, can negatively influence parent-child interactions. Martin (14) identifies any baby who is retarded, handicapped, neurologically impaired, or who has some congenital defect as a high-risk infant. He points out that high-risk infants fail to shape or elicit positive responses from their parents. Their behaviors may be grating and nongratifying, eliciting hopeless and incompetent feelings in parents. Also, the high-risk infant may elicit fear, sadness, disappointment, and other distancing feelings and behaviors from the parent. These feelings make it less likely that either parents or child will have their emotional or even physical needs met in the interaction between them.

Carey's (15) questionnaire studies of infant temperament have yielded factors which some investigators have tried to use to identify infants at high risk (16, 17). As far as is known by these reviewers, none of the infant scales or factors have shown any real predictive validity in attempting to determine high risk.

Stress Factors

Steele (18) was among the first to point out that abuse occurs most often at crises in the family or when an overwhelming stressor is present. Gil (19) and Elmer (20) see abuse as resulting from social stress factors, and they particularly implicate poverty as a stressor. While in some families it is true that living in the environment of poverty is a severe stressor, there is no evidence that poverty is a causal agent for abuse. There is evidence from Gelles's (21) study that 25% of a predominantly middle-class sample of entering freshmen in college answered "yes" to questions describing abusive events ranging from being hit more than once with a closed fist to being shot at by a parent.

Using a model which looked at the interaction between parental stress factors and environmental stress factors, Newberger's group achieved 75% specificity and 70% sensitivity. Newberger *et al.* (22) have identified a factor they call stress in the mother's childhood which includes frequent family mobility, a broken home, and volunteered information about a personal history of violence and/or neglect. The scale "stress in the current household" was based on recent mobility and change in household composition. This latter factor appeared as the best predictor of child abuse and neglect. Newberger has called the childhood disease syndromes that stress factors predict "pediatric social illnesses."

Polansky *et al.* (23) report that families described as neglectful by agency workers tend to be more isolated than those described as not neglectful. Newberger *et al.* (22) also identified a parental social isolation factor which included the absence of a telephone and a mother's perception of her neighborhood as unfriendly.

Interactional Factors

The interaction between mother and baby has been exceedingly important to the theoreticians. Klaus and Kennell's research on bonding is well known for emphasizing this viewpoint (24). Recent primate research supports the idea that relaxation of maternal attention may be as vital as bonding in the promotion of social competence of the infant (25). Johnson states, "The competent mother's early responsiveness secures attachment, but it also enables exploration and other social experiences that gradually substitutes social bonds for maternal proximity.... The failure of a mother-infant pair to make this transition is potentially harmful." Very little has been done to predict future difficulties in humans based on this theory, although Mahler's work has extensively studied the phenomena (26).

Screening research using the model of studying family interactions has become more common in recent years. Gray's studies are a landmark in using videotaped material which assesses how the mother reacts to the baby in the delivery room (27–29). This group tries to predict high risk for abnormal parenting on the basis of these interactional observations combined with data from a standardized interview. They report 79% sensitivity in predicting risk for abnormal parenting. At seventeen months age of the infant, they had 100% specificity in predicting to low risk. These authors point out that by having good sensitivity in excluding those who do not need help, you are justified in going ahead and providing intervention to all the rest, even if they are not all high risk, that is, providing intervention is positive, helpful, nonthreatening, and that the label of the group in which one intervenes is nonjudgmental, e.g., "people in need of extra services." In recent studies, this group reports a very low incidence of major breakdown in parent-child interaction in the high groups when they provide extra services. This is a clear case in which a high-risk designation can be helpful to parent and child. In this group's earlier studies, their high-risk group had a four to five times higher incidence of abnormal parenting, including abuse, neglect, placement in foster homes, relinquishment, suspicious injury to child, parental kidnapping, severe parental negligence resulting in accident and/or leaving the awake infant alone in the house for over thirty minutes.

Burgess (30) reported a tendency for abusive and neglectful mothers to display lower rates of positive behavior and higher rates of negative and coercive behavior to their children than did control mothers.

Altemeir's (17) study used a multifactor assessment including parent-child interactions, early childhood and present-day life experiences, perceptions of children and assessment of life stresses. They report four to five times more severe parent-child interaction breakdowns in their high-risk group. Neither sensitivity or specificity is as yet known.

Disbrow *et al.* (31) also used a multifactor prediction scale using parent-child rearing attitudes and assessment of social support networks and observational data. Her sensitivity of about 80% and her specificity in matched controls of about 80% on parent-child interaction suggest the instruments have considerable potential for screening for high risk.

Wilson (32) was trying to predict good parent-child interaction four to six weeks after birth. She noted very high correlations between the desire by the mother to have rooming-in and later good mother-child interaction. Actually experiencing rooming-in was not correlated, only the mother's desire to have it.

Polansky *et al.* (33), using a revised version of the Childhood Level of Living Scale, were able to differentiate significantly between children who lived in families classified as neglectful and the control families. The rate of sensitivity was 100%; the rate of specificity was 80% (34). Two factors, which the authors labeled "physical care" and "emotional/cognitive care" accounted for much of the observed variation. These factors appear useful here, for both imply a regularity, consistency, and a sensitivity in the parent-child interaction involving eating, sleeping, and educational activities.

Besides looking at parent-child interactions, the type of parental interaction in the home is of some importance. Newberger (35) reported that the occurrence of spouse abuse in the home accounted for 40% of the variance in predicting child abuse. It seems obvious that the occurrence of other family violence would be a good predictor to study. This means sibling abuse should be added to the interactional factors in the expanded model.

Future Research in Screening

We have seen in our review that the best of the research studies (9, 27, 29, 31) have misidentified approximately 20% of their risk groups and control groups. The questions, why has this happened? and what can be done to improve the situation? seem worthwhile asking. Efforts must be made to collaborate based on an expanded model. Recently, the MSPP, the questionnaire of Helfer, Hoffmeister, and

Schneider, (36) has been expanded so that child factors, stress factors, interactional problems, and a wider array of parent factors may be identified with a single instrument. If to this the efforts of Disbrow *et al.* (31) are added in order to study the social support system and observe parent-child interaction, plus Polansky's and/or Newberger's isolation and stress or cultural type items (23, 22) that appear to describe the environment in which the child is being raised, this collaboration has a good chance of increasing sensitivity and specificity. However, considerably more research is required before this expanded model can be accepted and put to use. Clearly, the "art" of screening for the potential of child abuse is still in the hands of the researcher.

References

1. 3M Company survey. 1974 and 1978. St. Paul.
2. Helfer, R. E. Early Identification and Prevention of Unusual Child Rearing Practices. *Pediatr. Ann.* 5:106–13, 1976.
3. ———. Basic Issues Concerning Prediction. In R. Helfer and C. Kempe, eds. *Child Abuse and Neglect: The Family and the Community*. Cambridge, Mass.: Ballinger, 1976.
4. Frankenburg, W. K. Pediatric Screening. *Advances Pediatr.* 20:149, 1973.
5. Hoffmeister, J. K. *Convergence Analysis: A Clinical Approach to Quantitative Data.* Boulder, Colorado: Test Analysis and Development Corporation, 1975.
6. Brody, H., and Geiss, B. Commenting on Ethical Issues. In R. Helfer and C. Kempe, eds., *Child Abuse and Neglect: The Family and the Community*. Cambridge, Mass.: Ballinger, 1976.
7. Schneider, C., Helfer, R. E., and Pollock, C. The Predictive Questionnaire: A Preliminary Report. in C. Kempe and R. Helfer, eds., *Helping the Battered Child and His Family.* New York: Lippincott, 1972.
8. Schneider, C., Hoffmeister, J. K., and Helfer, R. E. A Predictive Screening Questionnaire for Potential Problems in Mother-Child Interaction. In R. Helfer and C. Kempe, eds., *Child Abuse and Neglect: The Family and the Community.* Cambridge, Mass.: Ballinger, 1976.
9. Helfer, R. E., Schneider, C. J., Hoffmeister, J. K., and Cloutier, A. E. Report on the Research Using the Michigan Screening Profile of Parenting (MSPP): A Twelve-Year Study to Develop and Test a Predictive Questionnaire. East Lansing, 1978.
10. Gordon, R. R. Predicting Child Abuse. Letter to the editor. In *Brit. Med. J.* 841:6064, 1977.
11. Crain, L. S., and Millor, G. K. Maltreated Children of Mentally Retarded Parents. *Pediatrics* 61:30, 1978.
12. Bavolek, Steven. Department of Special Education, University of Wisconsin, Eau Claire, Wisconsin. Unpublished.

13. Brazelton, T. B., Koslowski, B., and Main, M. The Origins of Reciprocity: The Early Mother-Infant Interaction. In M. Lewis and L. A. Rosenblum, eds., *The Effect of the Infant on Its Caregiver*. New York: John Wiley & Sons, 1974.

14. Martin, H. *The Abused Child*. Cambridge, Mass.: Ballinger, 1976.

15. Carey, W. Infant Temperament and Its Implications. Paper presented at the third Annual Child Development Symposium, at University of Massachusetts Medical School, Worcester, Maine, 1979.

16. Anderson, S. K. Ph.D. dissertation, University of Colorado, 1977.

17. Altemeir, William. Chief, Department of Pediatrics, Metropolitan Nashville General Hospital, 72 Hermitage Avenue, Nashville, Tennessee. Unpublished.

18. Steele, B. Working with Abusive Parents: From a Psychiatric Point of View. U.S. Department of HEW, Office of Child Development, OHO75-70, 1975.

19. Gil, D. G. Unraveling Child Abuse. *Am. J. Orthopsychiatry* 45:345–56, 1975.

20. Elmer, E. Child Abuse: Overview of the Problem and Avenues of Attack. Paper presented at Fifth Annual Mental Health Institute, 1966.

21. Gelles, Richard. Yale University, New Haven, Connecticut. Unpublished.

22. Newberger, E. H., Reed, R. B., Daniel, J. H., Hyde, J. N., and Kotelchuck, M. Pediatric Social Illness: Toward an Etiologic Classification. *Pediatrics* 60:178–85, 1977.

23. Polansky, N. A., Chalmers, M. A., Buttonweiser, E., and Williams, D. P. Isolation of the Neglectful Family. *Am. J. Orthopsychiatry* 49:149–52, 1979.

24. Klaus, M., *et al.* Maternal Attachment: Importance of the First Postpartum Days. *New Engl. J. Med.* 286:460–63, 1972.

25. Johnson, C. Implications for Adult Roles from Differential Styles of Mother-Infant Bonding. *J. Nerv. Ment. Dis.* 167:29–37, 1979.

26. Mahler, M. *The Psychological Birth of the Human Infant*. Chicago: University of Chicago Press, 1978.

27. Gray, J., Cutler, C., Dean, J., and Kempe, C. H. Perinatal Assessment of Mother-Baby Interaction. In R. Helfer and C. Kempe, eds., *Child Abuse and Neglect: The Family and the Community*. Cambridge, Mass.: Ballinger, 1976, pp. 377–88.

28. Gray, J. O., Cutler, C. A., Dean, J. G., and Kempe, C. H. Pediatrics and Prevention of Child Abuse. *Seminar in Perinatology*, Vol. 3, 1979.

29. ———. Prediction and Prevention of Child Abuse and Neglect. *Child Abuse and Neglect* 1:45–58, 1977.

30. Burgess, R. L. Child Abuse: A Behavioral Analysis. In B. B. Lakey and A. E. Razdin, eds., *Advances in Child Clinical Psychology*. New York: Plenum Publishing Corp., 1978.

31. Disbrow, M. A., Doerr, H., and Caulfield, C. Measures to Predict Child Abuse. Paper presented at the Society for Research in Child Development, in New Orleans, March 1977.

32. Wilson, Ann. Ph.D. dissertation, Michigan State University, 1975.

33. Polansky, N. A., Chalmers, M. A., Buttonweiser, E., and Williams, D.

Assessing Adequacy of Child Care: An urban scale. *J. Child Welfare* 47:439–49, 1978.

34. Polansky, N. A. Personal communication, 1979.

35. Newberger, Eli. Personal communication, 1979.

36. Helfer, R. E., Hoffmeister, J. K., and Schneider, C. *Manual for Use of the Michigan Screening Profile of Parenting (MSPP)*. Boulder, Colorado: Test Analysis and Development Corp., 1978.

Final Thoughts
and Future Directions

The six years that have passed since the second edition of *The Battered Child* have seen enormous progress in the study of child abuse and neglect. In every area of our society there is some understanding and involvement. The National Committee for the Prevention of Child Abuse has been formed and many states have developed chapters.[1] Awareness is increasing. Even the children in less-developed countries are being given attention, and their plight from the effects of abuse and neglect is finally being recognized.

Truly, children in many Third World countries face the eminent threat of starvation, chronic malnutrition, and death or disability from a variety of infectious diseases. Priorities in the allocation of national and world resources are such that child abuse must take a secondary role. Surprisingly, there is increasing interest and discussion even in these countries about the problems resulting from abuse and neglect. The International Society for the Prevention of Child Abuse was formed within the past six years, with some 1,000 participants attending the 1978 international meetings in London.[2] Over twenty-five countries were represented. National societies have sprung up in many of these countries since the advent of the international organization. *The Internation Journal of Child Abuse and Neglect* is now in its third year of publication.

The worldwide movement on the behalf of children has begun. The rights of children are slowly being recognized.

The future looks less bleak than it did in 1974. We hope a fourth edition of *The Battered Child* can be devoted almost entirely to the area of prevention.

C.H.K. R.E.H.

---

1. NCPCA, Chicago, Illinois.
2. ISPCA, 1205 Oneida Avenue, Denver, Colorado 80220.

Index